An Introduction to Community Psychology

An Introduction to Community Psychology

MELVIN ZAX
University of Rochester

GERALD A. SPECTER
University of Maryland

John Wiley & Sons, Inc., New York • London • Sydney • Toronto

Copyright © 1974, by John Wiley & Sons, Inc.

All rights reserved. Published simultaneously in Canada.

No part of this book may be reproduced by any means, nor
transmitted, nor translated into a machine language without the written permission of the publisher.

Library of Congress Cataloging in Publication Data:

Zax, Melvin.
　　An introduction to community psychology.

　　1. Community psychology.　I. Specter,
Gerald A., joint author.　II. Title.
[DNLM:　1. Community mental health services.
2. Pyschology, Social.　WM30 Z39i　1974]
RA790.5.Z38　　　362.2'04'2　　　73-20190
ISBN 0-471-98135-4

Printed in the United States of America

10 9 8 7 6 5 4 3 2 1

Preface

The most recent revolutionary development in psychology and the mental health fields in general involves a variety of approaches to behavioral and social problems that implicate the community both as a causative factor and as a potentially therapeutic agent. This development has been of sufficiently great magnitude to be described by Nicholas Hobbs as the "third mental health revolution." Thus he gives community psychology an importance equal to that of the humanitarian reforms in hospital care promulgated by Pinel and others in the late 18th century, and to the monumental contributions of Freud in the late 19th and early 20th centuries. Clearly, the general concept of community psychology has enjoyed wide acceptance and has stimulated the development of exciting and daring new approaches to dealing with man's mental health problems.

In the rush to develop these approaches and to make operational new new and drastically different ideas about ways of providing service, much that has been written about the field has been fragmented. Writings have referred to isolated programs or to the development of ideas associated with program building in a specific area. Many collections of these writings have been edited and set forth for the student who would like to deepen his understanding of what is occurring. These readings have been helpful but have been inevitably limited, and they have failed to provide overall scope with respect to the many areas on which community psychology is having an important impact. This mode of communicating typifies a field's earliest stages of development. Now, however, sufficient work has proliferated in community psychology so that a broad coverage of the field is needed. It is for this reason that this book has been written. Intended as an introduction to the field of community psychology, it describes the historical roots out of which the field has grown, provides a broad sampling of the types of endeavors that are seen as falling under the rubric of community psychology, and communicates an understanding of what has been accomplished in the field, what problems must be dealt with and how much is yet left to be done.

As a textbook, this work is of interest to both graduate and undergraduate students who require a broad survey of community psychology. It also is of interest to many graduate and undergraduate students who are currently involved in some type of community psychology program. One characteristic of community psychology is that it draws large numbers of relatively untrained people into various kinds of human service work on a career, on a part-time, or a temporary volunteer basis. Many college students who are in these categories are presently engaged in projects of various kinds for university credit and even in activities that are not sponsored under university auspices or credited in the usual academic fashion. The book provides these students with a sense of perspective about the kind of work that they are doing and their reasons for doing it. It also conveys a feeling for the experiences of others who are engaged in similar enterprises and the satisfactions and problems that they have encountered in this work.

We were inspired to write this book as the result of our own experiences over a period of years in developing various types of community programs, an exercise that has helped to build considerable commitment to the worth of community approaches. In these enterprises, we have been joined by a number of colleagues, all fellow students in a very exciting new venture. We extend our gratitude to all these individuals who, on reading this work, will recognize their own contributions. One who must be singled out for special mention is Emory L. Cowen, whose energetic interest in a variety of practical programs involving both of us, as well as the stimulation that he provided in thinking through with us many of the problems and issues in this field, have been of inestimable value. Our special thanks also go to James G. Kelly, Brendan A. Maher, and Charles Speilberger who read the entire manuscript, provided the encouragement we needed to push ahead with the project, and make many constructive criticisms that led to a much better manuscript than could have been produced without their help.

Finally, our typists, Mrs. Hannah Berner and Mrs. Cathleen Allen, deserve a special mention. They have borne a heavy burden with good humor and efficiency above and beyond the call of duty.

MELVIN ZAX
GERALD A. SPECTER

Contents

An Introduction to Community Psychology

1.   introduction

In a historical survey of clinical psychology, Hersch (1969) set the birth date of community psychology as May 1965. During that month a group of psychologists actively engaged in developing community mental health programs met in Boston under the joint sponsorship of Boston University and the South Shore Mental Health Center of Quincy, Massachusetts to consider the education of psychologists for work in community mental health (Bennett, Anderson, Cooper, Hassol, Klein, and Rosenblum, 1966). In discussing the role of the community psychologist, the Boston conferees were inevitably defining the area of community psychology. They characterized community psychologists as "change agents, social systems analysts, consultants in community affairs, and students generally of the whole man in relation to all his environments" (Bennett, 1965, p. 833). Many of the participants favored broadening the community psychologist's role through his going beyond consultation to be-

1

come a political activist who assumes decision-making powers. The community psychologist was further urged to use his scientific training to create knowledge and promote programs, thereby functioning as a "participant conceptualizer" (Bennett et al., 1966).

The Boston conference generated much thought about community psychology and stimulated the establishment of a division of Community Psychology within the American Psychological Association and the creation of several university training programs. However, if the Boston conference marked the birth of community psychology, several earlier discussions and statements about the role of the psychologist in the mental health field must be acknowledged as contributors to its conception.

Sanford (1958), speaking as a member of the Joint Commission on Mental Illness and Health, a presidential commission established to study the mental health needs of the nation, spoke eloquently in 1958 in favor of the psychologist's playing a fuller role in the mental health movement. He said, "I want to predict that the mental health movement, as a social and cultural phenomenon, will move in this positive direction, with emphasis on promotion of resiliency and creative living. I want to observe that psychologists, if they can devote their fertile minds to the problem, if they do not adjust too much to the clinical-medical way of life, can make an enormous social contribution to this kind of mental health movement" (p. 84). In this paper, Sanford chided psychology for being diffident with respect to important public issues and urged that the field renounce its exclusive focus on clinical problems in favor of new approaches to deal not only with the sick or troubled but also with those manifesting less obvious problems. Much of what Sanford proposed in 1958 was very similar to the views of community psychology that emerged from the Boston conference several years later.

A few years after Sanford's paper appeared, Gelfand and Kelly (1960) wrote a short endorsement of Sanford's recommendations. They added, however, that in addition to assuming new community roles outside of clinics and hospitals, psychologists needed to bring to bear their scientific expertise on the problem of developing an orientation toward health. This expertise, these authors believed, represents the truly unique contribution that psychology can bring to the emerging field of community psychology.

In describing a training program in "community clinical psychology," Jones and Levine (1963) also affirmed the need to reject an illness or disease model in favor of greater concern for promoting healthy behavior or optimal functioning. Here, again, was a view of an applied area of psychology consonant with the view of community psychology that was to emerge from the Boston conference.

Subsequent to the Boston conference, Rieff (1968) spoke passionately of a need for the community psychologist to develop a new conceptual outlook that would permit the professional to intervene in a social system on behalf of some aggregate of individuals needing assistance. He asserted that the clinical skills used to intervene in behalf of an individual labeled schizophrenic, the skills with which mental health professionals are most familiar, are of little use in the new venture in the community. Thus Rieff called for the development of a new school of psychology.

Interestingly, in these examples of statements made directly and indirectly about community psychology, there seems to be relatively little variability about the direction the field ought to take. Each example calls for a renunciation of the exclusive concern for the mentally ill. Each insists that psychology should develop a greater concern for the healthy adaptation of large masses of individuals, only a few of whom are likely to end up as mental patients. The only points on which variability or disagreements seem to arise involve the question of how far the psychologist should go in attempting to shape the healthy community. Some would stop at the point of becoming consultants to influential, power-wielding agents of society. Others would go so far as to inject themselves into the power structure where they could themselves hold the administrative reins.

Since the selection of material included in this book requires a working definition of community psychology to serve as a guide, we have extracted a common denominator running through the many conceptions used to characterize this field. Also we have made an effort to achieve a view that is broad enough to encompass the diverse service programs tending to be classified as community approaches. On this basis:

Community psychology is regarded as an approach to human behavior problems that emphasizes contributions made to their development by environmental forces as well as the potential contributions to be made toward their alleviation by the use of these forces.

Such a definition stresses a shift in thinking away from concentration on intrapsychic dynamics in considering all manner of behavior problems, including those falling within the traditional domain of the clinician, and allows for actve preventive interventions.

It would be a mistake to come away from this discussion with the impression that the elements of community psychology's approach are unique to practitioners within the field of psychology itself. Actually, community psychology has emerged within a context in which all of the mental health professions have manifested considerable concern regarding the role of environmental forces in creating behavioral problems.

This concern has found expression at the federal level in a commission established by the Mental Health Study Act of 1955, consisting of leading members of the mental health professions. This group (Joint Commission on Mental Illness and Health, 1961) was charged with conducting a thorough, objective study of the mental health needs of the nation and with recommending steps that the federal government might take to alleviate these needs. Their recommendations included the establishment of broad-scale mental health centers to be made available for each 50,000 of the general population. The functions of these centers were described to include treatment for traditional mental health disorders, particularly acute ones, care for mental patients not yet requiring hospitalization or for others who had been discharged from hospitals, and to serve as a base for consultation with various community agents capable of providing mental health services. Thus the guidelines for community mental health centers included a balance between service for manifest mental illness as well as preventive efforts. For many (Golann and Eisdorfer, 1972) the establishment of community mental health centers was viewed as an opportunity for the mental health professions to intervene in the social context within which many problems breed.

In keeping with the rising concern for community mental health, many individuals in a variety of social service fields have hoped that traditional approaches to dealing with mental health problems could be made more flexible. Furthermore, recognizing that the traditional mental health agency has badly neglected large segments of our population, particularly the poor and the educationally underprivileged, many have called for increased community participation in the management and operation of mental health centers. This, hopefully, would ensure that the services offered would be those that are badly needed by the community rather than only those that mental health professionals trained in a traditional mold and coming from a particular social class are comfortable in providing. As we discuss in chapters that follow, efforts to revise traditional structures and to innovate as a means of providing broader services have resulted in exciting new departures. Mental health agencies have reached out to school systems, lower class neighborhoods, community political and administrative structures, and a myriad of other settings that have been virtually ignored up to this time. In the process, a variety of new types of mental health workers have developed. Furthermore, many of these programs have differed in purpose from the traditional goals of the clinic. Thus community approaches represent a revolutionary departure within all the mental health fields that has been innovative and exciting from many viewpoints. These approaches have also created a variety of stresses and strains within the mental health fields. The new conceptions that these approaches have engendered concerning the way service should be delivered, who should be the recipient of such services, who should provide them, and where they can most profitably be provided has been the source of interest, excitement, upset, and threat.

To place community psychology within a context that includes other mental health professions, it is well to review a few terms that have the modifier, "community," such as *community psychiatry* and *community mental health,* as well as the term, *social psychiatry,* which has been widely used in recent years with reference to activities that sound suspiciously similar to many that characterize the community approaches.

DEFINITIONS

Community Psychiatry

At one extreme are those who view community psychiatry as having precisely the same aims as traditional psychiatry, the treatment of mental illness, but differing from it methodologically. Whereas the traditional psychiatrist focuses exclusively on the patient, the community psychiatrist grants considerably more significance to the social forces acting on the patient and focuses on them as well. This position is held by Bernard (1964) who, even more traditionally, regards community psychiatry as a psychiatric specialty, hence, one requiring medical training for all its practitioners. Bellak's (1964) definition of community psychiatry as "the resolve to view the individual's psychiatric problems within the frame of reference of the community and vice versa" (p. 5) also falls in this category. Another example of a definition that focuses on mental illness is offered by Loeb (1969, p. 235) : "Community psychiatry is the use of community resources in addition to interpersonal and intrapersonal resources to help mentally ill and emotionally disturbed people achieve greater personal and social adequacy." Other writers (Dunham, 1965; Halleck, 1969; Mechanic, 1969) , although not offering specific definitions of their own, indicate by their critiques and admonitions about the evolving community psychiatry that this new field should not go beyond the bringing to bear of a solid understanding of social forces on the problems of the traditional psychiatric patient.

At the other extreme are those who, although agreeing that a major mission of community psychiatry ought to be the treatment and rehabilitation of patients suffering the problems traditionally dealt with by the psychiatrist, consider *prevention* of the development of mental disorder as an equally significant function. Thus Hume (1964) lists consultation to educational and nonpsychiatric agencies and public information programs as services to be rendered by community psychiatry. Caplan (1965) asserts that community psychiatry deals with entire populations, all age, cultural, and socioeconomic groups whether agency cases or not. He goes even further in specifying that part of the preventive function of the community psychiatrist is to collaborate actively with a variety of civic leaders and government administrators in an effort to reshape the structure of the community to make it a psychologically healthier place in which to live. Duhl (1965) holds that the community psychiatrist must not only provide service for those suffering traditional mental illness and attempt to prevent development of such illness, but must also tackle the broader problems of human concern today—poverty, unemployment, security, and recreation. To this end he feels that community psychiatry must also be concerned with the normal growth of the general population.

From a practical as well as theoretical viewpoint these two views of community psychiatry are poles apart. One position clings to a traditional view of the problems to which mental health professions should address themselves. The other greatly expands the scope of the profession and, by doing so, brings the psychiatrist as well as other mental health workers into contact with people and roles that are entirely new to him as a professional.

Social Psychiatry

The term *social psychiatry* is also defined in various ways with major definitional differences relating to the issue of whether it refers to an applied or to an exclusively theoretical field. Leighton's definition (quoted in Goldston, 1965, p. 198) states:

"In the United States, the term usually brings to mind preventive community programs, industrial and forensic psychiatry, group therapy, the participation of psychiatry in administrative medicine, the utilization of the social milieu in treatment, and the study of social factors in the etiology and dynamics of mental illness."

This viewpoint places the major emphasis on the application of social psychiatry to a number of psychiatric problems. In this respect it overlaps considerably with virtually all definitions of community psychiatry. The same may be said for other definitions such as that offered by the World Health Organization (quoted in Goldston, 1965, p. 199) :

". . . social psychiatry refers to the preventive and creative measures which are directed towards the setting of the individual for a satisfactory and useful life in terms of his own social environment. In order to achieve this goal, the social psychiatrist attempts to provide for the mentally ill, and for those in danger of becoming so, opportunities for making contacts with forces which are favorable to the maintenance or reestablishment of social adequacy."

On the other hand, many view social psychiatry as a field of research and study that contributes useful information to the community psychiatrist but that is itself not concerned with applications. This is clearly stated by Redlich and Pepper (quoted in Goldston, 1965, p. 198) :

"Our own brief definition, influenced by Rennie, defines social psychiatry as the study of psychiatric disorders and psychiatric therapy, hopefully including prevention, within a social setting. This implies that social psychiatry is defined as an exploration of social systems and culture and their impact on psychiatric phenomena rather than as a type of psychiatric practice."

Along similar lines, Srole (1965) says in comparing social and community psychiatry:

"Social psychiatry can be marked off from community psychiatry, somewhat arbitrarily perhaps, but I think meaningfully, by its different priority orientations, timetable, methods and personnel requirements. I have just suggested that community psychiatry's research function tends to be a secondary priority, of the operational ('applied') kind needed to facilitate, assess, revise, and enlarge its service and training activities . . . Social psychiatry, on the other hand, is conceived as placing first priority on long-term research of basic variety, directed by established social scientists and psychiatrists working either jointly or separately" (p. 39).

Several others maintain a distinction between community and social psychiatry that is similar to Srole's (Kahn, 1969; Sabshin, 1969) .

In summary, when social psychiatry is viewed as having a basic applied component, it overlaps considerably with most definitions of community psychiatry. When it is regarded as primarily an area of study and research, social psychiatry maintains a separate existence as a potentially useful contributor to community psychiatry because it is devoted to understanding the effects on individual behavior of the social forces that the community psychiatrist seeks to manipulate.

Community Mental Health

As is true for the concepts that we have discussed thus far, community mental health is defined in broadly differing ways. Goldston (1965, p. 198) quotes one brief definition that states, "Community mental health refers most frequently to the administration and provision of a variety of mental health services." Likewise Bellak (1964) , in speaking of the community mental health centers that are being developed, stresses their focus on traditional diagnostic and treatment services, day and night hospital care, foster home care, and the development of mental health information programs for the general public. These viewpoints are very similar to many relatively conservative definitions of community psychiatry that have been discussed. The problems that are being addressed are those that have become traditional for the mental health fields. The only innovation involved is that a broader outlook is taken concerning etiology and treatment.

On the other hand, a number of people whose definitions differ in many respects agree in viewing community mental health much more broadly. Bernard (1964) sees community psychiatry as a component of the more inclusive field of community mental health. Hume (1964) feels that community mental health programs, unlike community psychiatry, are directed toward normals with the aim of promoting *positive* mental health. Kahn (1969, p. 187) views the community mental health function as a ". . . general coalition of people and organizations which comes together around social goals and which consists of many loosely interrelated components from several intervention systems and social institutions joined together for the purpose."

The extremely broad outlook regarding goals and involved agencies that characterizes Kahn's view typifies the outlook of many others. Lemkau (quoted in Goldston, 1965, p. 197) sees community mental health as inclusive of community psychiatry and states:

"Thus we have the concept emerging that community mental health is a communitywide responsibility, that the program is to be under professional and lay auspices, and that mental health is promoted and fostered not solely through medical treatment, but also through a variety of institutions and agencies with numerous disciplines joining in the effort."

Similarly, Howell (quoted in Goldston, 1965, p. 197) states:

"Community mental health encompasses all activities which are involved in the discovery, development, and organization of every facility in a community which effects all attempts which the community makes to promote mental health and to prevent and control mental illness."

Another such example is offered by the psychiatric staff of a prominent clinic (quoted in Goldston, 1965, p. 197):

"This (community mental health) is the broad, multidisciplined field concerned with the wide variety of forces and structures in a community which affect the emotional stability (positive growth, development, and functioning) of a significant group of its members. It is contrasted with the traditional clinical approach which focuses on the particular individual in emotional distress."

In summary, the narrowest conceptions of the term community mental health fail to distinguish it from a narrow view of community psychiatry. Broader views of the concept, which seem, incidentally, to be more prevalent, encompass all community forces affecting the psychological state of most members of the community. Its goals are not only the alleviation of suffering but the promotion of positive growth as well. Its agents are not just psychiatrists or even mental health professionals, but any community agents or agencies capable of contributing to cure, prevention, or optimal development.

Since community psychology and other current community approaches are, at least, in part, outgrowths of clinical psychology and psychiatry, the historical roots of these disciplines are to be found in the same soil. Essentially, community psychology may be viewed as a theoretical outlook and a method of practice that has evolved out of clinical psychology, in keeping with the reasonably orderly change that has taken place in thinking about mental illness over many years.

CHANGING CONCEPTIONS OF MENTAL DISORDER

To understand theories about mental or behavioral disorder, and to grasp why professionals treat this disorder as they do, one must first specify just what behavior is regarded as disordered. A careful study of the history of thought regarding this human problem reveals that conceptions of behavior considered to be disordered or abnormal have not been constant. References in ancient writings to abnormal behavior include examples such as epileptic seizures, severe depression, grandiose delusions, and severe mental deterioration. Homeric writings describe the insane Ajax as killing sheep instead of his enemies. In his attempt to appear mad, Ulysses is described as yoking a bull and horse together, plowing the sand, and sowing salt rather than seeds. Other mentally aberrant mythological figures are described as hallucinating or running through the forests bellowing like animals.

Hippocrates, the Greek physician considered to be the father of all medicine, wrote many good descriptions of what were seen as mental disorders in his time. These include what we would now call postpartum psychoses (usually a severe depression following childbirth) and the delirious states sometimes associated with high fever. He also described epilepsy, mania (extreme excitement), melancholia (severe depression), extreme intellectual deterioration and alcoholic delirium similar to what we term delirium tremens (the DTs).

Imperial Rome imported Greek medicine and produced many outstanding practitioners who also wrote of the mental disorders of their time. Thus Roman physicians described depression and delirious states as well as a condition characterized by "stupefaction of the sense of reason and other faculties of the mind." In some cases, the latter condition involved so severe a mental deterioration that "sensibility and intelligence fall into such a degree of degradation that, plunged into an absolute fatuousness, they forget themselves, pass the remainder of their lives as brute beasts, and the habits of their bodies lose all human dignity." Many will recognize in this description elements of a disorder that many centuries later came to be called schizophrenia.

The Middle Ages saw a decline in the richness of thought and observation that characterized the Greek and Roman cultures. Nonetheless, it is apparent that mental disorders which characterized earlier times were prevalent during the Middle Ages and, in addition, a few behavioral aberrations appeared that were unique to the period such as the group phenomenon involving large processions of people who, believing the world was about to end, traveled about the countryside doing public penance for their sinful behavior. These people, known as flagellants, carried banners, crosses, and candles. Their entirely black costume was marked by a red cross, and they carried heavy leather whips, often metal tipped, with which they flogged themselves until blood flowed.

Doubtless, these peculiar behavioral phenomena of the Middle Ages were induced by the stark religiosity of the time. The flagellants were, undoubtedly, frightened, guilty people with an overwhelming need to expiate their sins. For some reason, ordinary church ritual did not suffice for them.

From the end of the Middle Ages through the 19th century, man's conception of what was behaviorally abnormal continued to emphasize the types of disorders already described. Many efforts were made to classify behavioral aberrations and new terminology was introduced from time to time, but relatively few new conditions were described. Perhaps the most significant contribution of the 19th century to what was thought of as behaviorally abnormal was the concept of *dementia praecox,* out of which grew the entity known as schizophrenia. Dementia praecox, popularized by Emil Kraepelin, encompassed several disorders that had been recognized earlier but had not necessarily been associated with each other.

The salient point of this brief review of behavior considered to be abnormal up to the 20th century is that mental disorder was in the past almost exclusively associated with extreme and dramatic behavioral deviancy. To be sure, a few behavioral disorders less extreme than what are now considered psychoses were noted by some. For example, hysteria, now looked on as a psychoneurosis, was described by Hippocrates and later physicians. This condition, however, often characterized by dramatic physical symptoms (paralyses, anesthesias, blindness, etc.) which fail to respect physiological facts, must have appeared to the ancient healer as a very serious disorder.

Other disorders more subtle than hysteria were also noted in early times by particularly sensitive observers, but these did not attract the interest of the mental health professions of the day. The Roman philosopher Cicero described grossly antisocial behavior, which might now be called sociopathic, as resulting from mental disorder. Arabian physicians described the ruminations and anxiety that typify a disorder we now call obsessive-compulsive neurosis. Around A.D. 400, ·a Roman physician characterized various sexual perversions, common at the time, as the product of mental disorder. Each of these was, however, largely an isolated insight having no significant impact on thought concerning mental disorder and its treatment.

It appears that man approached the task of self-examination gingerly. For many hundreds of years he was concerned only with behavior that was so different from the ordinary that those manifesting it seemed almost other than human.

The work of Sigmund Freud, which began at the end of the 19th century, culminated in a major mental health revolution and was the impetus for several significant revolutions that followed. The revolutionary aspect of Freud's work derived in part, of course, from the content of the theories he expounded, but it also resulted from his experiences with hysterics and psychoneurotics. Freud was not trained in any of the traditional mental health professions of his time and, like many physicians, he came in contact with numerous patients whose problems seemed more psychological than physical. Not being psychotic, however, they were ignored by the psychiatrists of the day. Such individuals were usually treated by general practitioners in the best of circumstances and, otherwise, by quacks, faith healers, or charlatans. Since Freud was a neurologist, many hysterics whose overt symptoms seemed to be neurological were referred to him. One very significant effect of Freud's work with such patients was *a redefinition of the scope of the mental health field.*

The quality of Freud's work and thought, his explanations of how neuroses developed, and his apparent success in treating them by psychological means attracted wide interest among those concerned with mental disorders. To be sure, many of Freud's ideas were adapted for application to the serious psychoses with which most traditional mental health workers of the time were grappling. Still, a significant segment of the field came to accept neuroses, far less disabling than psychoses, as problems worthy of concern and effort. In so doing, the services of the mental health worker came to be called on by a much larger percentage of the population than ever before and the terms abnormal or disturbed were applied to symptoms such as severe anxiety, phobias, disabling compulsions, hysterical complaints, and the like.

In addition to encouraging the mental health professions to accept psychoneuroses as a part of their area of concern, Freud expounded a theory of personality development that prompted still further scope-broadening redefinitions of what was abnormal. His efforts at understanding diverse behavioral phenomena were guided by the essential faith that all behavior could be explained deterministically, and his theory emerged out of his experience with the patients who came to him. Psychoanalytic theory placed great stress on biological forces but it also acknowledged the importance of the interaction between biological drives and the environment in which they are expressed. Thus two people with similar urges of equivalent force might deal with these urges quite differently depending on how various behaviors are reacted to by those with whom each must live. Therefore, great stress was placed in the theory on the role of life experience in shaping personality. Furthermore, in pointing up the various ways personality problems might arise in the course of development, Freud was also describing the kind of experiences that could lead to optimal development and what he regarded as the normal personality.

Freud's theories as well as the therapeutic efforts of his followers led to several later redefinitions of what was regarded as psychologically abnormal. One such redefinition resulted in the emergence of the field of *psychosomatic medicine*. Once theories were advanced concerning the role of the psyche in causing, maintaining, or exacerbating physical illness, the scope of the mental health field was again broadened considerably. Whereas the mental health professional had focused for centuries on psychoses, within a few short years he found himself becoming concerned about psychoneuroses and a variety of physical complaints that were suspected to have essential psychological components.

A still more broadening redefinition of the mental health field was to arise with the introduction of the concept of *character disorder*. The development of this concept did not come about suddenly, nor can it be associated with the work of a single person. Perhaps the earliest suggestion of the concept of character disorder can be attributed to Wilhelm Reich (1949). In the mid-1920s, Reich, one of Freud's students, wrote a book on psychoanalytic technique. As one of the pioneer practicing analysts, Reich had believed that most of man's problems derived from troublesome inner urges that could neither be permitted free expression nor completely prevented from affecting behavior. These urges were thought to reside in an aspect of the human psyche known as the *id*. It was felt that the prime task of psychoanalysis was to bring troublesome id forces to consciousness where they could be dealt with more effectively by another psychic agency postulated by Freud, the *ego*. The ego was seen to emerge as an aspect of the id devoted to gratifying impulses in a way that accords with the demands of both outside reality and one's own conscience (part of the *superego* in Freud's scheme). While the id operated according to a pleasure principle whereby immediate gratification was its uppermost concern, the ego depended heavily in its functioning on logic, reasoning, and a grasp of the workings of the world external to the individual. Thus, it often imposed a delay of gratification when acting on the immediate aims of the id might lead to trouble.

In his book, *Character Analysis,* Reich wrote of the serious obstacles that impede the uncovering of unconscious forces. He found in his analytic practice that, although the first rule of psychoanalysis is that the patient should associate freely with whatever comes to mind to provide clues to significant unconscious elements, most patients could not comply at the outset. Thus a good deal of time in analysis was devoted to overcoming the resistances that prevented exposure of the unconscious. But these resistances were not seen to derive from the id itself. Rather, they were protective mechanisms developed by the ego. Thus the same energy that the ego devotes to restraining the id and to denying it expression or access to consciousness was seen by Reich to be used against the analyst's efforts to expose id forces. Most of Reich's book was devoted to the problem of dealing with ego resistance.

On the basis of his experience, Reich distinguished between two types of neuroses: *symptom neuroses* and *character neuroses.* The symptom neurotic suffers the classic symptoms of neurosis whereas in the character neurotic the most striking features are certain character traits. Actually, Reich felt that a neurotic character was present to some degree in all patients, even in those manifesting classic neurotic symptoms. The neurotic character was described as differing from the symptom neurotic in two important ways. First, he lacks insight into his condition. Thus, while the symptom neurotic feels his problem acutely as an uncomfortable, alien condition, the character neurotic accepts his difficulties as long-standing features of his personality. Second, the character neurotic can more readily rationalize his symptoms than the symptom neurotic. The shy person may be unhappy about his shyness, but he rarely sees it as a sign of mental disorder. Instead, he is apt to view the trait as a fundamental part of his personality, a given about which nothing can be done. The symptom neurotic, on the other hand, beset by extreme anxiety, a disabling phobia, an obsession, or a crippling hysterical symptom can hardly deny the significance of his disability.

Reich referred to these long-standing character traits as a *character armor,* and later Anna Freud (1946) wrote of them as *defense mechanisms.* Both writers saw these traits as a psychologically protective covering that people begin to wear early in life, not as a defense against outer forces, but against inner ones. Eventually these character traits, which had been regarded simply as part and parcel of the personality, came to be recognized as symptoms of a disorder, at first referred to as *character disorder* and later as *personality disorder.* By 1952, such disorders received formal recognition by their inclusion in the American Psychiatric Association's *Diagnostic and Statistical Manual: Mental Disorders* (Committee on Nomenclature and Statistics of the American Psychiatric Association, 1952). Thus, behaviors such as overdependence, schizoid withdrawal, excessive orderliness, cautious isolation from others, moodiness, and hyperactivity came to be considered as reflecting emotional disorder. In addition, this new diagnostic entity encompassed many behavior disorders such as antisocial behavior, sexual deviations, and addictions, which had long been recognized as problems but were regarded as belonging within the province of legal or religious authorities rather than of mental health professionals.

The new conception of behavioral abnormality represented by the personality disorders has caused another significant broadening of the scope of the mental health professions. The many subtle but chronic types of behavior viewed as the symptoms of personality disorder are likely to be present in a large number of people who find their lives unsatisfying because of them. Thus the process of periodically redefining and broadening the scope of what is conceived of as behavior disorder has led to a commitment on the part of the mental health field to a staggeringly high percentage of the general population—in effect, many times as many individuals as was the case when its domain extended only to psychosis, psychoneurosis, and psychosomatic disorders. This fact has created many problems and has played an important role in the recent development of community psychology as a new, and possibly more effective, way to deal with overwhelming service needs.

CHANGING CONCEPTIONS OF CAUSE AND TREATMENT OF MENTAL DISORDER

Just as man's conception of what constituted mental disorder has changed over the years, so too has there been a periodic alteration in the conception of what causes mental disorder, how it is best treated, and by whom. To some extent, changes with respect to these notions have corresponded to changes in the idea of what constituted mental disorder, but this has not always been the case.

Man's earliest theory of the cause of mental disorder, of course, invoked supernatural forces. Just as primitive man was aware that he could cause certain events to occur because he willed them, he assumed that events which were out of his control such as natural phenomena were caused by some power higher than himself who willed that these events should occur. With respect to illness in general, primitive man recognized that some disorders resulted from observable causes and could be treated directly. A wound, for example, could be cleansed and protected against further injury until healing took place. Other disorders, however, were entirely internal, affecting organs that could not be seen in ways that could be understood. For such disorders, it was assumed that a supernatural power was causing this phenomenon, and it was into this class that most behavior disorders were placed.

When one assumes that mental disorder is caused by supernatural powers, the obvious agent to treat this disorder should be someone adroit at intervening for man with the gods. In ancient times, such individuals held different titles in different societies (priests, shamans, witch doctors), but in all instances their roles were similar. They studied the ways of the gods and developed and maintained rituals thought to be useful in placating or mollifying an angry god or in maintaining the good will of a god who had not yet vented his wrath.

The first change in man's conception of the etiology of both physical and mental disorder took place during the classical period of Greek history. Up to that time the centers of healing in Greece were the Aesculapean temples where priests, thought to have inherited the secrets of healing, tried to cure illnesses with impressive religious ceremonies. Several Greek thinkers contributed to the change in approach toward understanding the development of mental disorder, but Hippocrates (460–337 B.C.) generally receives the most credit for this change. Hippocrates stubbornly held that all disorder, physical or emotional, could be explained on the basis of entirely natural causes. He completely rejected the popular notion that spiritual forces could cause behavioral disorder. For example, in speaking of epilepsy, which was popularly regarded in his time as a "sacred" disease, Hippocrates wrote: "If you cut open the head, you will find the brain humid, full of sweat, and smelling badly. And in this way, you may see that it is not a god which injures the body, but disease."

The rational approach introduced by Hippocrates and other Greek thinkers of his time resulted in the establishment of schools to train medical practitioners. To be sure, the practitioners produced by these schools operated in a culture that also accepted the healing role of priests, but Hippocrates' approach and work represented the beginnings of a scientific modern medicine that received greater and greater acceptance in Europe at that time. As Rome came to dominate the major part of the civilized world militarily and politically, Greek physicians were imported to Rome, and the Greek tradition of medicine was extended. Hippocrates' approach to medicine led to the development of a variety of theories concerning the occurrence of mental disorder and a number of different therapeutic approaches, particularly advances in various forms of physical therapy.

During the Middle Ages men turned away from rationality in favor of an emphasis on the spiritual. As a result, the religious figure as a healer and spiritual theories of the etiology of behavior disorder again became prominent. Superstitious beliefs and magical practices tended to proliferate. Unknown and powerful supernatural forces were thought to play a prominent role in the development of behavior disorder.

A return to rationality did not begin to take place in a significant way until the Renaissance, which spanned the 13th, 14th, and 15th centuries. Threatened by this turning away from orthodox religious practices, the establishment of the time rigidified its views in many ways that created serious hardships for those who were mentally disturbed. The mentally disabled who were accused of witchcraft and of having formed some type of invidious alliance with the devil were particular targets of abuse, punishment, and even physical destruction.

The 17th century brought an increase in the pace of the intellectual reawakening which had begun during the Renaissance and a resumption of rational theorizing concerning the etiology of behavior disorders. Natural causes including various psychological forces were stressed. Philosophers and literary figures played important roles in this change along with some of the healers of the time. Eventually, these changes culminated in the work of a number of 19th-century figures who sought to establish a completely physiological basis for many mental disorders as well as in the work of Freud and his followers in the late 19th and, particularly, in the early 20th century, who stressed psychological causes.

Freud's efforts have already been described as causing the first major revolution within the mental health fields through their scope-broadening effect. This effect derived from the fact that Freud was concerned primarily with psychoneurotics, a group ordinarily shunned by the mental health workers of his time. Freud also offered a theory of mental functioning and a theory of personality development that had relevance for all behavior. As a result, this theory came to be applied to a variety of disorders with which Freud had little or no experience. As a scientist, Freud himself was rooted in the strictly deterministic tradition of the biology of his time. Furthermore, he was primarily concerned with man as a biological entity. In his earliest work Freud attempted to develop a theory of hysteria based on neurophysiology. When that failed, he shifted to attempting to understand hysteria on psychological grounds. Holt (1965), a scholar of psychoanalytic theory, has questioned whether Freud actually ever did shift completely, observing that many of Freud's fundamental psychoanalytic principles are based on assumptions about man's biology that were commonly held in his day. Brenner (1955) has also observed that Freud's undying hope was that he could establish the biological basis of mental phenomena.

In much of his early writing, Freud tended to undervalue man's experiences as a social being and not uncommonly referred to external circumstances as "accidental factors." This implied that the only regularity in man's experience was what occurred within his body and that external forces were so irregular as to be unsuited for scientific study. For Freud the forces that moved man, that prompted behavior, were always internal ones. The few social regularities of which Freud's early theories took cognizance were thought to have arisen as the result of the inheritance of acquired characteristics. Thus the transmission of cultural practices was thought to have become part of man's internal genetic structure rather than being derived from external environmental factors.

Freud's thinking tended to stimulate in others considerable theorizing regarding mental functioning, and a number of theories appeared during the first half of the 20th century to explain the development of behavior disorder as well as man's personality in general. Some were advanced by students of Freud, and in many instances these theories deemphasized the biological factors stressing, instead, the significance of social forces. Theorists like Alfred Adler, Erich Fromm, and Karen Horney emphasized the regularity of certain of man's social experiences and the effect that they can have on development. The writings of these theorists culminated in the advancement of a social psychological theory by the American psychiatrist Harry Stack Sullivan that was, perhaps, as elaborate as Freud's own. In his writings Sullivan regarded man's social experiences as being the most significant forces in shaping his personality. He went so far as to insist that even physiological functions are shaped by man's interpersonal experiences in that the organism acquires socialized ways of breathing, eating, digesting, and eliminating.

Another significant modification in psychoanalytic theory resulted from the work of the group of psychoanalysts who became known as "ego psychologists." These men became well known in the 1930s through their reformulation of some of Freud's theories regarding the ego. As described earlier in this chapter, the writings of Wilhelm Reich and Anna Freud had highlighted the importance of ego functioning within psychoanalytic practice. Reich and Anna Freud, however, emphasized the ego's defensive role. Theorists like Heinz Hartmann and later Rudolf Kris, Ernst Lowenstein, David Rapaport, and Erik Erikson had much to say about the ego's positive side, its adaptive capacity.

These theorists regard the ego as an independent psychic agency with energy sources of its own and a need to develop on its own, independently of its role as a gratifier of the id. Freud's original theories assumed that the ego's existence was entirely based on the necessity for having an agency equipped to deal with outer realities to maximize gratification for the id and to minimize the development of conflict between the individual and outside forces. To further his aims this agency was seen to utilize man's cognitive and sensory apparatus. Presumably, therefore, man developed his sensory and perceptual capacities, exercised his imagination, sharpened his memory, and manifested his curiosity solely because these qualities enabled the ego to do its job for the id more effectively. It was this notion that was disputed by the ego psychologists.

Hartmann (1958) felt that the exercise of perceptual and cognitive skills was gratifying in and of itself. There is a joy in learning about the world—in developing inner potentialities of all kinds. This observation prompted Hartmann to theorize that the ego, or the potential for an ego, exists within the newborn infant and will be developed regardless of the demands of the id. Freud's relatively narrow view of the ego was thought to have developed mainly because early psychoanalytic theorists were attempting to deal with psychopathology. With the broader view that the ego functioned in conflict-free spheres, it became possible to begin a study of positive aspects of human behavior such as the process of adaptation. Hartmann emphasized the need to know how one's abilities and character related to his adaptive capacity, a largely neglected area within psychology. Other theorists, notably Erikson (1950), have attempted to describe the process by which man's ego adapts to the varying social forces which act on him from birth onward.

The work of the recent theorists who have emphasized social factors in man's development as well as that of the ego psychologists have provided a theoretical underpinning for the community psychology movement. The social theorists' work has led to a concern for the nature of the forces to which man must adapt and toward some thinking about how these forces might be altered to ease man's adjustment. The thinking of the ego psychologist has led to the idea that a personality can be strengthened as it develops, to be better able to withstand the life stresses that must inevitably be faced. Thus mental disorder can be prevented and the necessity for treatment eliminated. Turner and Cumming (1967) have pointed out that personality growth within the framework of ego psychologists, for example, Erikson, results from the resolution of developmental crises (the problems to which all are exposed in their growth through various periods of life such as childhood, adolescence, adulthood, middle age, etc). The successful resolution of a particular crisis provides the individual with a new set of skills that can be used to meet later crises. This benign cycle can build a strong personality well suited to weathering future stresses. People like Lindemann (1944) and Caplan (1964) have extended this idea and regard nonnormative crises (such as bereavement, accidents, and divorce) as opportunities for personal growth if they are dealt with successfully. Thus it is asserted that man's unhappiest and most stressful experiences can be capitalized on to enhance personality development and to render the individual less vulnerable to future stress.

The idea of capitalizing on crisis as a means of building strength, as well as of reordering social forces to render them less stressful and more growth enhancing presumes an active, intervening, "busybody" role for the mental health professional. Such a role is drastically different from the traditional one. For this reason many community psychologists question traditional roles and the service model on which these roles have been based, the so-called "medical model."

THE MEDICAL MODEL

A number of writers have referred to the medical model without defining it. Several have defined it but in different ways. Therefore, one is again confronted by a semantic morass needing ordering and clarification.

First, any model serves as an exemplar for guiding others. In the mental health field models can provide a fundamental set of assumptions with which one approaches data and which both guide observations and determine how these observations will be grouped and evaluated. Models can also define the "turf" on which people will interact and set limits on the possible operations the professional might engage in. Thus models, as guides to professional thinking and practice, have a number of characteristics and implications. To speak of a medical model without specifying how it is being defined or without describing the aspect of the model to which one is referring can only be confusing.

Brown and Long (1968) have reviewed the recent community psychology literature that refers to the "medical model" and have attempted to describe the trends they find in the various meanings applied to the term. They point out that the notion of a medical model is frequently associated with issues such as the "realities of power," "the press of manpower needs and resources," and "the pressure of increasing public demand for mental health services." These authors regard such uses of the term as a confusing composite of several "theoretical and operational issues."

Essentially Brown and Long believe that the term has been used three different ways. First, the medical model has been used to refer to the disease concept of illness that involves the idea of a host organism, invading bacteria, and the like in which disease-specific cures are possible as in the case of physical illness. Brown and Long feel that this approach has been unjustifiably contrasted with other models that emphasize psychological etiology of behavioral dysfunction. They find no reason why the two approaches cannot be viewed as complementary. Sarason and Ganzer (1968) have also taken issue with what they feel is criticism of an overly literal interpretation of the illness model. These authors argue that what has been borrowed by psychology from medicine is not the notion of physical pathology but merely some assumptions about underlying causes and some terminology. Like Brown and Long, Sarason and Ganzer view the attack on the illness or disease aspect of the medical model as a specious one stemming largely from an interprofessional rivalry and the chafing of psychologists under an established professional structure which has the physician at the top.

The other two ways in which Brown and Long find the medical model being used are also related to power issues. In one case, these authors feel the term describes the way in which mental health services are organized and administered, with a physician or psychiatrist inevitably serving as director and other professionals being ancillary members of the service team. Finally, Brown and Long believe that the medical model is often used to refer to the formal or "establishment" structures that have grown up in the mental health fields around the ways in which diagnostic and treatment services are rendered. Thus some settings may be run in such a way as to exclude psychologists and others may exclude psychiatrists. Both established forms resist change, and Brown and Long feel that to alter their form would require not only an attitude change but also a change in the entire social system.

Although interprofessional power struggles no doubt have played a role in the concern expressed by community psychologists about the medical model, it would be an oversimplification to assume that such issues account for all these expressions. Turner and Cumming (1967) point out, for example, that a corollary of the analogy that is drawn between mental and physical illness is the retention of the typical one-to-one doctor-patient relationship. In this relationship the patient's role is seen as an active one only insofar as he takes the initiative in seeking help; but once in the doctor's office he becomes the passive, sick individual waiting to be ministered to. The doctor's role requires him to wait passively for the patient to seek him out, at which time he can become authoritative and active.

In their descriptions of the medical model, both Bloom (1965) and Cowen (1967) speak of its disease orientation, but they also acknowledge the centrality to the model of the dyadic relationship between a passive-receptive authority and a "sick" individual who seeks him out or is brought to him. Both the disease aspect and the passive orientation of the medical model have been called into question.

The illness or disease model, whether taken literally or figuratively, is considered to be misleading and even damaging in the area of mental health. For example, Rieff (1966) points out that the working-class individual views mental illness as the diametric opposite of mental health, a threatening term reserved for only the most extreme behavioral deviations. The working class, therefore, has difficulty accepting the idea that lesser behavioral problems can fall within the province of the professional who deals with mental illness. Thus, severe mental disturbance is viewed as an illness to be treated by some kind of doctor while less severe emotional disturbances are attributed to undue environmental pressures or moral weakness which should be dealt with by one's minister or mastered through self-control. Attitudes of this kind pose obvious challenges for a community mental health approach.

The validity and utility of the disease model has also been criticized recently by practitioners, notably Szasz (1960), who are not identified with community psychology or community psychiatry movements. Szasz feels that in work with individual patients the notion of mental illness or disease is both misleading and damaging. Illness is seen as deviation from some norm. Since ideal physical health can be described by physiological and anatomical indexes, physical illness can be readily recognized as a deviation from this ideal. Assessment of mental illness, however, is not so straightforward. The norms from which the mentally ill deviate are psychosocial, ethical, and legal ones. Adherence to a disease model commits the mental health profession to seeking medical remedies, presumably free of ethical values. Thus a basic contradiction exists between the way the behavioral disorder is defined and the way we attempt to alleviate it. This, Szasz believes, has serious detrimental consequences. It allows people to avoid facing their problems, since they can blame their failures on their mental *illness*.

Szasz' position may be criticized on the grounds that one of his major objections to the medical model is based on his discomfort with the carrying over of medical terminology into the mental health field. Thus, for example, "etiology" is used instead of "cause," and "symptom" is used instead of "sign." This, however, does not necessarily imply that practitioners regard behavior disorder as analogous to physical illness. Youngsters attend baseball and basketball "clinics," and some garages "diagnose" mechanical problems in their automobile "clinics," and no one regards such settings as medical in any way. Szasz would probably counter this critique by arguing that many medically trained mental health workers are, in fact, committed to biological bases of many behavior disturbances. Furthermore, in an effort to remove the social stigma from many disorders, they have been popularly characterized as being akin to physical disease. As a result, even if the therapist accepts purely psychological causation, the patient is predisposed to present himself to the mental health practitioner in the same passive spirit assumed when he goes to a medical practitioner.

The passive orientation imposed on the mental health professional by the medical model has its own serious drawbacks. It limits his role to that of a "counterpuncher" with respect to behavioral disorder. If one holds literally to the notion, as many in community psychiatry seem to do, that one's exclusive function is to attend those troubled individuals who seek you out, the practitioner is in the position of only being able to react after a problem has emerged. In a world where therapeutic efforts would always be successful and where professionals could be trained in numbers sufficient to treat all who needed their attention, there might be little need for a service delivery approach other than the one dictated by the medical model. As we point out in the next chapter, neither of these situations pertain in the current mental health scene.

Thus, for the community psychologist and, indeed, the community psychiatrist who wishes to mount preventive programs, operating within the limits imposed by the medical model is detrimental. The disease aspect of the model, whether taken literally or figuratively, predisposes people who might receive mental health services to attitudes that interfere with their being able to use such services optimally. This is acknowledged by some professionals who use very traditional treatment approaches as well as by community psychologists. The passive role imposed on the professional by the model would tie his hands with respect to taking active steps to head off the development of behavior disorder even when many of the conditions for producing it can be identified.

Many might contend, with respect to the latter point, that the medical model contains within it a model of service that is devoted to the prevention of illness. This is the model followed by the public health physician who has been concerned with eliminating the source of diseases and with widespread programs of inoculation against disease. Medicine's success against disorders like typhoid and smallpox are products of public health medicine.

Unfortunately, until very recent times, the public health model in medicine has had little impact on the mental health professions. As early as 1908 Adolph Meyer (Lief, 1948) argued for the necessity of "aftercare" —the preparation for family and community to receive the discharged hospital patient, and follow-up efforts to prevent recurrence of mental disturbance in the recovered patient. Meyer believed that efforts made to prevent recurrence of mental disorder would lead naturally to an understanding of how to prevent mental disorder in the first place. Brand (1968) points out that social work began to develop in the early 1900s as a profession devoted to playing the kind of community role that Meyer envisioned in the aftercare movement. Despite these early stirrings of a preventive approach, little progress was made in this direction until the 1960s. The reason is that while a public health model was being championed in the mental health field, another much more exciting movement was developing. The psychodynamic discoveries of Freud were beginning to become well-known and popular, particularly in the United States, and they were applied within the aspect of the medical model (even, eventually, by social workers) that involved a healer-expert who waited for potential patients to come to him. Thus the public health model receded in significance among the mental health professions for several decades.

In addition to the fact that the public health aspect of the medical model has had little impact on the mental health field, it is necessary to point out that there are some fundamental differences between how the public health or preventive approach can be applied in medicine and in mental health. These differences arise from the attitudes held by the general public toward physical disease and mental disorder. Most people need little convincing that they are vulnerable to small pox, typhoid fever, and hepatitis and willingly cooperate with preventive programs of inoculation or improved sanitation. On the other hand, few can acknowledge their vulnerability to serious mental disorder and fewer still regard behavior such as irresponsibility, alcoholism, school failure, unreliable work habits, and the like, as involving mental or emotional factors. Thus, to mount preventive programs, the mental health professional must have a special kind of aggressiveness that is perhaps more characteristic of the crusading politician or social reformer than it is of one reared in the traditions of office or hospital practice remote from the community arena. In essence, while the medical model holds out a service delivery example that can be adopted with few alterations by mental health professionals, the public health model in medicine requires many modifications before it can be applied in the mental health field.

CONCLUSION

Community psychology is described as a relatively new approach to dealing with human behavior problems that stresses the role played by the environment in causing adjustment difficulties, and the necessity to manipulate environmental forces to alleviate man's problems. This approach requires the mental health worker to be an active interventionist instead of wait passively for problems to come to him.

A review is made of the changes in man's thinking about what mental disorder is and what causes it—a process involving periodic redefinitions of behavioral abnormality and one that has progressively broadened the scope of the field. Many such redefinitions have occurred since the late 19th century and have culminated in the movement known as community psychology. These redefinitions have involved the recognition of behavior of greater and greater subtlety as deriving from emotional and psychological causes and has extended the sphere of psychology into areas formerly considered relevant to other fields such as the law, the church, and education. The most recent redefinitions in the scope of the mental health field have led to a concern for the effects of social forces on psychological development and adjustment, and to a belief that in the process of growth the personality can be strengthened to withstand stresses.

Some consideration is given to the fact that traditional mental health role models fail to serve the community psychologist. The medical model, a service model from which traditional role models derive, is discussed and compared to the public health model, which better suits emerging professional roles.

THE ORGANIZATION OF THIS BOOK

This book is written in three parts. The first is concerned with definitions and establishing a historical and theoretical foundation for community psychology. It consists of the present chapter and the one that follows. The second is by far the most extensive and is devoted to descriptions of a variety of specific community psychology programs. Each program is discussed with reference to the type of problem with which it attempts to deal. The final section discusses the many problems faced in these emerging programs and the future prospects of the field.

References

Alexander, F. G., and Selesnick, S. T. *The history of psychiatry*. New York: Harper & Row, 1966.

Bellak, L. Community psychiatry: the third psychiatric revolution. In L. Bellak (Ed.) , *Handbook of community psychiatry and community mental health*. New York: Grune & Stratton, 1964. Pp. 1–11.

Bennett, C. C. Community psychology: impressions of the Boston conference on the education of psychologists for community mental health. *American Psychologist*, 1965, *20*, 832–835.

Bennett, C. C., Anderson, L. S., Cooper, S., Hassol, L., Klein, D. C., & Rosenblum, G. (Eds) . *Community psychology: a report of the Boston conference on the education of psychologists for community mental health*. Boston: Boston University Press, 1966.

Bernard, Viola W. Education for community psychiatry in a university medical center. In L. Bellak (Ed.) , *Handbook of community psychiatry and community mental health*. New York: Grune & Stratton, 1964. Pp. 82–122.

Bloom, B. L. The "medical model," miasma theory, and community mental health. *Community Mental Health Journal*, 1965, *1*, 333–338.

Brand, Jeanne L. The United States: a historical perspective. In R. H. Williams & Lucy D. Ozarin (Eds.), *Community mental health: an international perspective.* San Francisco: Jossey-Bass, Inc., 1968, Pp. 18–43.

Brenner, C. *An elementary textbook of psychoanalysis.* Garden City, N. Y.: Doubleday Anchor Books, 1955.

Brown, B. S., & Long, S. E. Psychology and community mental health: the medical muddle. *American Psychologist,* 1968, *23,* 335–341.

Caplan, G. *Principles of preventive psychiatry.* New York: Basic Books, 1964.

Caplan, G. Community psychiatry—introduction and overview. In S. E. Goldston (Ed.), *Concepts of community psychiatry: a framework for training.* Bethesda, Md.: U. S. Department of Health, Education, and Welfare, Public Health Service Publication No. 1319, 1965. Pp. 3–18.

Committee on Nomenclature and Statistics of the American Psychiatric Association. *Disgnostic and statistical manual—mental disorders.* Washington, D. C.: American Psychiatric Association, 1952.

Cowen, E. L. *Emergent approaches to mental health problems: an overview and directions for future work.* In E. L. Cowen, E. A. Gardner, & M. Zax (Eds.), Emergent approaches to mental health problems. New York: Appleton-Century-Crofts, 1967. Pp. 389–455.

Cowen, E. L., Gardner, E. A., and Zax, M. *Emergent approaches to mental health problems.* New York: Appleton-Century-Crofts, 1967.

Duhl, L. J. The psychiatric evolution. In S. E. Goldston (Ed.), *Concepts of community psychiatry: a framework for training.* Bethesda, Md.: U. S. Department of Health, Education, and Welfare, Public Health Service Publication No. 1319, 1965. Pp. 19–32.

Dunham, H. W. Community psychiatry: the newest therapeutic bandwagon. *Archives of General Psychiatry,* 1965, *12,* 303–313.

Erikson, E. H. *Childhood and society.* New York: Norton, 1950.

Freud, Anna. *The ego and the mechanisms of defense.* London: The Hogarth Press, 1937.

Gelfand, S., & Kelly, J. G. The psychologist in Community Mental Health: Scientist and professional. *American Psychologist,* 1960, *15,* 223–226.

Golann, S. E., & Eisdorfer, C. Mental Health and the Community: the development of issues. In S. E. Golann, & C. Eisdorfer, *Handbook of Community Mental Health.* New York: Appleton-Century-Crofts, 1972. Pp. 3–17.

Goldston, S. E. *Concepts of community psychiatry: a framework for training.* Bethesda, Md.: U. S. Department of Health, Education, and Welfare, Public Health Service Publication No. 1319, 1965.

Halleck, S. L. Community psychiatry: some troubling questions. In L. M. Roberts, S. L. Halleck, & M. B. Loeb (Eds.), *Community psychiatry.* Garden City, N. Y.: Doubleday, 1969. Pp. 58–71.

Hartmann, H. *Ego psychology and the problem of adaptation.* New York: International Universities Press, 1958.

Hersch, C. From mental health to social action: clinical psychology in historical perspective. *American Psychologist,* 1969, *24,* 909–916.

Holt, R. R. A review of some of Freud's biological assumptions and their influences on his theories. In N. S. Greenfield, and W. C. Lewis (Eds.), *Psychoanalysis and current biological thought.* Madison: University of Wisconsin Press, 1965, pp. 93–124.

Hume, P. D. Principles and practices of community psychiatry: the role and training of the specialist in community psychiatry. In L. Bellak (Ed.), *Handbook of community psychiatry and community mental health.* New York: Grune & Stratton, 1964. Pp. 65–81.

Joint Commission on Mental Illness and Health. *Action for Mental Health.* New York: Basic Books, 1961.

Jones, E. *The life and work of Sigmund Freud,* Vol. I. New York: Basic Books, 1953.

Jones, M. R., & Levine, D. Graduate training for community clinical psychology. *American Psychologist,* 1963, *18,* 219–223.

Kahn, A. J. Planning and practice perspectives on the boundaries of community psychiatry. In L. M. Roberts, S. L. Halleck, and M. B. Loeb (Eds.), *Community psychiatry,* Garden City, N. Y.: Doubleday, 1969. Pp. 173–191.

Lief, A. (Ed.) *The commonsense psychiatry of Dr. Adolph Meyer.* New York: McGraw-Hill, 1948.

Lindemann, E. Symptomatology and management of acute grief. *American Journal of Psychiatry,* 1944, *101,* 141–148.

Loeb, M. B. Community psychiatry: what it is and what it is not. In L. M. Roberts, S. L. Halleck, and M. B. Loeb (Eds.), *Community Psychiatry.* Garden City, N. Y.: Doubleday and Co., 1969. Pp. 235–250.

Mechanic, D. Community psychiatry: some sociological perspectives and implications. In L. M. Roberts, S. L. Halleck, and M. B. Loeb (Eds.), *Community psychiatry,* Garden City, N. Y.: Doubleday, 1969. Pp. 211–234.

Reich, W. *Character analysis,* 3rd Ed. New York: The Noonday Press, 1949.

Rieff, R. Mental health manpower and institutional change. *American Psychologist,* 1966, *21,* 540–548.

Rieff, R. Social intervention and the problem of psychological analysis. *American Psychologist,* 1968, *23,* 524–531.

Sabshin, M. Theoretical models in community and social psychiatry. In L. M. Roberts, S. L. Halleck, and M. B. Loeb (Eds.), *Community psychiatry.* Garden City, N. Y.: Doubleday, 1969. Pp. 13–30.

Sanford, N. Psychology and the mental health movement. *American Psychologist,* 1958, *13,* 80–85.

Sarason, I. G., & Ganzer, V. J. Concerning the medical model. *American Psychologist,* 1968, *23,* 507–510.

Srole, L. Selected sociological perspectives. In S. E. Goldston (Ed.), *Concepts of community psychiatry: a framework for training.* Bethesda, Md.: U. S.

Department of Health, Education, and Welfare, Public Health Service Publication No. 1319, 1965. Pp. 33–46.

Szasz, T. S. The myth of mental illness. *American Psychologist,* 1960, *15,* 113–118.

Turner, R. J., & Cumming, J. Theoretical malaise and community mental health. In E. L. Cowen, E. A. Gardner, and M. Zax (Eds.), *Emergent approaches to mental health problems.* New York: Appleton-Century-Crofts, 1967. Pp. 40–62.

Zax, M., and Cowen, E. L. *Abnormal psychology: changing conceptions.* New York: Holt, Rinehart and Winston, 1972.

Zilboorg, G., and Henry, G. W. *A history of medical psychology.* New York: W. W. Norton & Co., 1941.

2. *recent impetus for community approaches*

This chapter explores the question of why community psychology has begun to emerge at this particular point in time. The preceding chapter provides a broad overview of the field of abnormal psychology out of which the community movements have grown. It is asserted that periodic redefinition of the scope of the mental health field has accounted for the development of new theories and, to some extent, new treatment approaches. Moreover community psychology is considered to have resulted from the most recent redefinition of the mental health field. But why has this definition come about at this particular point in our history, and why is this new movement taking the particular form that it is?

No single factor accounts for the recent development of community psychology. Instead, a number of forces, events, and circumstances have, like a series of disconnected streams, joined to create a torrent. The more significant of these streams is discussed in this chapter.

RECENT DISSATISFACTION WITH TRADITIONAL FUNCTIONS

Psychoanalysis and psychoanalytic psychotherapy enjoyed widespread acceptance in the United States from the time of their introduction in the early 1900s (Shakow and Rapaport, 1964). The new treatment approach seemed to hold promise for effectively alleviating psychopathology. Professionals were eager to learn these techniques, which soon became basic to the armamentarium of the mental health worker. Psychoanalysis led to exciting discoveries about the way people function psychologically and, above all, seemed to offer the hope that man's psychological problems could be dealt with effectively.

Although other psychotherapeutic techniques based on theoretical principles at variance with those of psychoanalysis were introduced between the early 1900s and 1950, most mental health workers seemed to accept the basic notion that psychotherapy would solve our mental health problems. In 1952, however, the blind faith of the preceding 50 years was profoundly shaken by a paper by Eysenck which attacked the supposed effectiveness of psychotherapy. Eysenck surveyed a number of studies reporting on improvement rates as the result of various psychotherapeutic approaches. His general conclusions were that roughly two thirds of all patients improve, regardless of the form of psychotherapy undergone. Eysenck reasoned that the significance of such results could only be determined by comparing them to recovery rates among patients suffering problems similar to those treated by psychotherapists but undergoing other methods of treatment. He found two studies in the literature referring to such patient groups. One reported on severe neurotics who had been treated in the New York State hospital system between 1917 and 1934. In this group, roughly 72 percent of the patients were rated by their physicians as improved on discharge. Another baseline estimate of improvement without psychotherapy was provided in a study of 500 individuals making disability claims for psychoneuroses to an insurance company. These cases, taken consecutively from the files of a single insurance company, were from all parts of the country, represented all types of psychoneurosis, and all claimants had been ill for at least three months before the claims were submitted. Since each claimant was totally disabled, the psychoneurosis could be classified as severe. All of these patients were seen regularly by their own physicians and were treated with drugs of various kinds, as well as with reassurance, suggestion, and whatever stock the ordinary general practitioner might have available, but not with traditional psychotherapy. All of these cases were followed up for a period of at least five years and some for as much as ten years after the disability period had begun. Using the ability to return to work and to adjust adequately economically as recovery criteria, it was found that 45 percent of the patients recovered after one year and another 27 percent recovered after two years, making a total of 72 percent in all. Comparing the results of many studies of psychotherapy outcome with those of the two baseline studies of New York State hospital patients and of the insurance claimants, Eysenck concluded that psychotherapeutic treatment produced no better results than ordinary hospital care or the attention of a general practitioner. Thus psychotherapy was not demonstrated to be superior to other, more superficial approaches.

Furthermore, Eysenck compared studies evaluating the effects of long-term psychotherapy, such as psychoanalysis, to those involving more superficial therapeutic approaches. He found that, on the average, about 44 percent of those patients having long-term, intensive therapy improved, whereas 64 percent of those patients treated more eclectically and less intensively improved. Neither of these figures quite reached the improvement rate of 72 percent that was found with insurance claimants treated by general practitioners. Thus Eysenck's figures indicate an inverse correlation between recovery and psychotherapy; the more intensive the psychotherapy, the lower the recovery rate.

Eysenck (1952) has summarized the import of his data as follows:

"In general, certain conclusions are possible from these data. They fail to prove that psychotherapy, Freudian or otherwise, facilitates the recovery of neurotic patients. They show that roughly two thirds of a group of neurotic patients will recover or improve to a marked extent within about two years of the onset of their illness, whether they are treated by means of psychotherapy or not. This figure appears to be remarkably stable from one investigation to another, regardless of type of patient treated, standard of recovery employed, or method of therapy used. From the point of view of the neurotic, these figures are encouraging; from the point of view of the psychotherapist, they can hardly be called very favorable to his claims" (p. 323).

Eysenck's paper provoked considerable reaction from other professionals who questioned many of his assertion (De Charms, Levy, and Wertheimer, 1954; Rosenzweig, 1954; Cartwright, 1955, 1956; Bindra, 1956). Some denied the equivalence of the outcome criteria in the experimental and control studies cited by Eysenck, others took issue with the contention that the so-called control group did not receive psychotherapy. Still others attacked the logic of Eysenck's conclusions and to some extent the bolder implications of his paper, namely that not only was psychotherapy ineffective, but that it might actually be harmful. None, however, were able to disprove Eysenck's fundamental conclusion that convincing demonstrations of psychotherapy's effectiveness had yet to be offered. In fact, Eysenck's critique has been revised and updated since 1952 by Levitt (1957), who extended the survey to the outcome of work with children and by Eysenck himself (1961).

What seemed to be heresy at the time of Eysenck's paper has become fairly well accepted as fact in recent years. For example, Schofield (1964) was willing to state in the mid-1960s that ". . . we are still awaiting definitive research—we still do not have acceptable evidence that psychotherapy accomplishes significant reduction of neurotic symptomatology, let alone evidence that the several different forms of psychotherapy have different levels of efficacy" (p. 99). Thus the tendency to doubt the effectiveness of psychotherapy became fairly common after Eysenck's critique appeared. Furthermore, many in the mental health field began to express the thought that even if psychotherapy is effective, it is not a practical answer to the large-scale mental health problems of today's society. For example, Eisenberg (1962) has stated:

"The limitations of present therepeutic methods doom us to training caretakers at a rate that ever lags behind the growing legions of the ill, unless we strike out successfully in new directions in the search for cause and treatment . . . Society can ill afford today's precious overspecialization in which trainees may learn one method even superbly well but a method that ever lags behind the demands placed upon it, while they remain abysmally unaware of the problems besetting the bulk of the mentally ill" (p. 825).

From the foregoing, it is evident that there are many within the mental health field who question the overall efficacy of psychotherapy. In addition, others who, even in the absence of hard experimental evidence, feel that psychotherapy is effective, nonetheless feel that this approach cannot meet society's overwhelming mental health needs. Thus, regardless of the position taken on the issue of psychotherapy's effectiveness, many professionals are calling for new ways of dealing with our widespread mental health problems. Those who doubt the effectiveness of psychotherapy prefer wide-scale community preventive efforts. Those who retain faith in the utility of psychotherapy are seeking ways of making that approach more widely available through the use of nonprofessionals in programs like those to be described in the following chapter. Despite the failure of research efforts to document the overall effectiveness of psychotherapy, there may well be considerable merit in using some psychotherapeutic approaches with some types of people and problems. It would, therefore, seem premature to abandon all efforts at psychotherapy in the absence of a well established alternative. This position is supported by the fact that behavior therapy, which was developed after Eysenck's original critique, offers very encouraging results in dealing with certain types of behavior problems. Thus, it does not seem unreasonable that some community psychologists are turning away from psychotherapy while others are training nonprofessionals to engage in the practice.

The leaders of the mental health professions who participated as members of the distinguished commission established by President Eisenhower represented another major source of criticism and dissatisfaction with traditional approaches. This group, known as the Joint Commission (Joint Commission on Mental Illness and Health, 1961), was an interdisciplinary body established by the Mental Health Study Act of 1955 and was selected by the National Institute of Mental Health to evaluate the mental health needs of the nation and to recommend steps for meeting such needs. The opening statement of the Joint Commission report is as follows:

"We are tempted simply to take the position that there is a crying public demand and needs are easily observable in the difficulty many persons experience in seeking a psychiatrist when they feel the need of one, in the long waiting lists of mental health clinics, the small amount of treatment many clinic patients receive, the total absence of mental health workers and clinics in many communities, the overcrowding of public mental hospitals, and their professional staff shortages" (p. 3).

This report is particularly critical of the state mental hospital systems which it describes as largely "custodial and punitive" and whose very nature and existence are attributed to society's long-standing tendency to reject its mentally ill, a problem alluded to in the preceding chapter that has typified the attitudes of much earlier times.

Other critiques of the hospital system appeared in the 1950s, most notably that offered by Goffman (1961). He maintains that not only are many basic hospital practices employed primarily for the convenience of the staff rather than for the therapeutic benefit of the patient, but that many such practices are actually anti-therapeutic.

Another source of dissatisfaction with traditional mental health practices involves the blatant inequities that exist with respect to the delivery of mental health services. The Joint Commission report points out this fact particularly with respect to the state mental hospital system. That report states:

"When we confront the total problem of care of the mentally ill, we find that, despite much talk and some progress, the greatest shortage still occurs in the area where patients with major mental illness are concentrated —in state hospitals. . . . The inevitable result is that those States with the least available money have the fewest psychiatrists, and the average

State hospital continues to occupy its historic position in the forgotten corner of medicine" (p. 146).

Several large-scale surveys have also made it clear that traditional mental health services are distributed in a grossly inequitable way. Hollingshead and Redlich (1952) did a survey of mental patients in New Haven, Connecticut in which they hoped to answer two questions: (a) Is mental illness related to social class? (b) Does a mentally ill patient's position in the status system affect how he is treated for his illness? They found with respect to neurotic disorders that there is an inverse relationship between social class and the number treated in public agencies; that is, the lower the social class the greater the proportion of patients seen in public agencies instead of by private practitioners. This is explained readily by the fact that the lower classes can ill-afford to pay the fees of private therapists. On the other hand, the nature of the treatment received is also linked to social class. While individual psychotherapy is the predominant treatment mode in all classes, those in the lower classes are more likely than the higher classes to receive directive psychotherapy, shock treatment, lobotomy, or drug treatment. This difference pertains even within individual agencies. Also private practitioners tend to administer intensive analytic psychotherapy to members of higher social classes and the briefer, more directive therapies to the lower classes. Furthermore, within agencies the frequency with which the patient is seen is also related to social class, with the higher classes being seen more frequently and for longer periods of time than the lower classes.

Hollingshead and Redlich found similar inequities among psychotic patients where, holding diagnoses constant, a clear-cut relationship is found between social class and the type of treatment received. Among schizophrenics, for example, those of the higher social classes are most likely to receive psychotherapy whereas those of the lower social classes are most likely to receive custodial care.

Results similar to those of Hollingshead and Redlich were reported in a survey done in midtown Manhattan (Srole, Langner, Michael, Opler, and Rennie, 1962). In this study done to assess the prevalence of mental disturbance within a discrete area of New York City, nearly 2000 residents were interviewed intensively, and assessments were made of their mental condition. Among the data collected in this survey was information indicating whether an individual was a patient in the local mental health facilities. It was found that those high in socioeconomic status were more likely to receive treatment than those of lower status. Paradoxically, it was also found that mental impairment was highest in the lowest socioeconomic class and lowest in the highest income levels. Therefore, the social class receiving the most care from mental health agencies displayed the lowest rates of severely impaired subjects in the study. Despite their greater need, members of the low socioeconomic classes in New York City receive less attention from mental health professionals than do the higher classes.

Sanua (1966) has surveyed a number of studies that provide evidence of a relationship between sociocultural factors and the type of treatment received by mental patients. He found that lower class patients are less likely than those of the upper classes to enter psychotherapy, are less likely to remain in psychotherapy, and are more likely to leave treatment after a few interviews. The primary treatment that they are most likely to receive is some form of symptomatic therapy. Sanua's survey indicates that traditional approaches to mental health problems are not appropriate for the lower social classes, and that our system for delivering these services tends to consign members of the lower classes to the most superficial approaches. This trend may well be related to the tendency, as reported by Hollingshead and Redlich, for mental health workers to diagnose schizophrenia more readily among the lower social classes than among the higher classes. A diagnosis of this kind is prognostically pessimistic, and it is conceivable that once the patient is stigmatized by such a label, he tends to be abandoned to the less dynamic, custodial treatments.

Some might argue that the inequity in mental health services delivery is simply part and parcel of the inequity in the delivery of health services in general. From this view the aims of the community mental health movement may be considered as identical to those of the public health movement, providing more services so that the lower social classes will no longer be neglected. This analogy, however, is an oversimplification. Mental health practitioners use treatment approaches that have grown out of experience with members of advantaged social classes, and they are accustomed to treating behavior problems typically found in these classes. As a result, as Lorion's excellent review (1973) indicates, traditional mental health practitioners "turn off" members of the lower social classes, or reject them as unsuitable for psychological treatment. Whereas the medical practitioner can apply his traditional tools to low social class members if he can contact them, the mental health worker must make many changes if he is to be effective. For example, Lorion points out that when these patients stay in psychotherapy, the outcome is as good as or better than in the case of high social class patients. This suggests that the mental health worker should not automatically rule out psychotherapy as a treatment approach with the lower classes, as often occurs. Beyond such attitude change, however, the mental health worker is also called on to develop a new stock of therapeutic tools designed to service low socioeconomic patients who cannot resonate to traditional practices, and who pose problems that differ from those of the middle and upper classes.

LATENT NEED FOR MENTAL HEALTH SERVICES

During the past 20 years, several attempts have been made to assess the demand for mental health services within our society. Although it had been recognized that traditional clinics and hospitals were already over-burdened, it was also suspected that many individuals needing mental health services were not receiving them. Surveys like those of Hollings-head and Redlich gave an indication of the extent to which people were receiving traditional mental health care, but they provided no estimate of how many others might possibly need these services.

A preliminary report published in 1956 (Leighton, 1956) provided startling data concerning the prevalence of mental health problems in the general community. Leighton reported an epidemiological study conduct-ed by a Cornell University research group in a single county in Nova Sco-tia, Canada. Focusing on a small town of about 3000 within Stirling County, this research group determined that roughly 47 out of 1000 adults were receiving care in local hospitals and clinics as of a given date. To answer the further question of how many people were equally in need of service but were not receiving care, a random sample of approximately 20 percent of the town was drawn, and efforts were made to interview all members within this sample.

The reported data were derived from 283 respondents each of whom was interviewed from 45 minutes to several hours. Interviews were con-ducted by eight different individuals, two of whom were psychiatrists, who helped to train the others, and all of whom had experience in admin-istering sociological questionnaires. Subjects were questioned about their general health, about physical complaints such as gastrointestinal symp-toms or headaches, and about psychiatric symptoms, such as sleep diffi-culties, mood variations, anxiety, and the like. Other questions concerned the health of family members, general background such as schooling and marital status, and whether or not they came from broken homes. The in-formation taken from these subjects was augmented through interviews with the town's two general practitioners regarding their knowledge of each individual in the sample.

Each respondent was rated by four different psychiatrists on a four-point scale: Point A on the scale indicated the presence of symptoms that almost certainly indicated mental disorder (nervous breakdown, anxiety attacks) ; a rating of B reflected the presence of symptoms that *probably* indicated psychiatric disorder (asthma, ulcers, sociopathic behavior) ; C ratings were used for borderline cases (where a symptom such as "high blood pressure" was claimed but not corroborated by a physician) ; a D rating indicated that there was no evidence of psychiatric symptoms. In addition to the symptom rating, another significant judgment was made by each evaluator. This involved a rating of the degree to which the respondent was impaired by his symptoms. Again a four-point scale was used: *no* impairment was rated when there was zero to 10 percent impairment; a rating of *mild* signified that there was from 10 to 30 percent impairment; *moderate* signified that there was from 30 to 50 percent impairment; and a rating of *severe* indicated that there was greater than 50 percent impairment.

Leighton's results indicated that 37 percent of respondents received a rating of *A* for symptoms and were judged to be impaired more than 10 percent. A smaller percentage, roughly 7 percent, were also rated *A* for symptoms, but were judged to be impaired less than 10 percent. A total of 65 percent of the sample received symptom ratings of an *A* or *B*. Leighton estimated from these data that 370 individuals per 1000 of the population studied need psychiatric treatment whether they are receiving it or not. These findings of a latent need for mental health services are quite startling in terms of what they portend, as they demonstrate that the prevalence of mental disorder is roughly eight times the number of individuals being treated for mental disorder.

The Leighton study was not the only one to suggest an enormous latent need for mental health services. Another study was one commissioned by the Joint Commission staff. The University of Michigan Survey Research Center was engaged to determine what mental health problems American people have, what they do about these problems, and where they turn when they feel the need for help. In this study a large sample of Americans over the age of 21, representative of the total population of the country with respect to age, sex, education, income, occupation, and place of residence, were subjects. Institutionalized individuals were excluded. Thus the group that was interviewed constituted an accurately proportioned sample of normal, stable, American adults. Interviews were conducted by experienced interviewers and lasted approximately two hours.

Several findings of this survey are of interest in the present context. Roughly 25 percent of those interviewed reported having had problems in which professional help would have been of some use. One of seven of those admitting having such problems also reported that they had actually sought help of some kind. Particularly illuminating was the fact that of those seeking help, the majority did not consult any member of the established mental health professions. Whereas 18 percent of this group sought help from mental health professionals such as psychiatrists, psychologists, and social workers, and 10 percent received services from social agencies or marriage clinics, a startling 42 percent consulted clergymen and 19 percent turned to physicians. This study offers further evidence of the great potential demand for mental health services. This latent demand is reflected both in the large numbers who had problems with which they felt they needed help, but who did not actually see anyone, and in the numbers who actually sought out help, but who went to someone other than a mental health professional.

Another recent study attempted to assess the prevalence of untreated mental disorder in New York City (Srole, Langner, Michael, Opler, and Rennie, 1962). This survey was conducted in an area within midtown Manhattan. More than 1600 residents of this area were selected randomly and interviewed intensively. Interviews were conducted in respondents' homes by psychiatric social workers, clinical psychologists, social case workers, and social scientists. These interviews were guided by a schedule especially developed for this study and took an average of two hours to complete. Responses to the questionnaire were quantified through a rating scale applied by psychiatrists associated with the study who attempted to make an overall evaluation of the mental health of respondents, categorizing each as well, mild, moderate, severe, or incapacitated on the basis of reported symptoms.

The overall results of the Midtown study indicate that only 18.5 percent of the 1660 adults surveyed were classified as being well. On the other hand, 13.2 percent were seen to show marked symptom formation, 7.5 percent showed severe symptoms, and 2.7 percent were incapacitated. The latter three categories were combined to constitute an impaired group consisting of 23.4 percent of the total sample. The results of this study also indicate a very marked need for mental health services in the community at large.

Considering the fact that the mental health professions seem already to be working at or well beyond their capacity to deal with the problems that come to their attention, the results of studies like those cited above are, indeed, frightening. They suggest a huge potential demand for mental health services which, if manifest, would literally swamp the existing professions. For many in the mental health fields, these unmet needs demand change both in the manner in which services are delivered and in the types of services rendered.

MANPOWER PROJECTIONS IN THE MENTAL HEALTH FIELD

Granting that mental health workers are presently overworked and that the potential demand for their services threatens to overwhelm the relatively small cadres currently prepared to offer services, what are the prospects for the future? The most direct solution would seem to involve training more traditional professionals with the hope that they can be turned out in numbers sufficient to meet future needs. The potential for applying this type of solution to the manpower problem was explored in another study sponsored by the Joint Commission and carried out by Albee (1959). Albee's study concerned mainly the supply and demand for mental health workers such as psychiatrists, psychologists, psychiatric nurses, and psychiatric social workers.

On the demand side of this issue, Albee has pointed out that public agencies have operated for many years without sufficient professionals to provide an adequate level of care, so that shortages within hospitals and agencies are very long-standing problems. In addition, this situation has been aggravated in recent years by an enormously increased demand for mental health services by agencies such as schools, courts, and prisons, which traditionally failed to utilize these services, and by the fact that private practice is also absorbing greater numbers of professionals. Thus Albee's survey indicated that only one fourth of the positions budgeted for physicians and psychologists in state and county hospitals could be filled at the time of his study. Similarly, roughly 20 percent of the jobs available for psychiatric nurses and social workers were unfilled. Still another significant factor to be reckoned with in estimates of the demand for mental health services is this country's population expansion.

Albee surveyed the prospects for increasing the supply of mental health professionals to meet the growing demand for their services. Although he found that an increasing number of physicians are specializing in psychiatry, a very high percentage of these individuals enter private practice or devote much of their time to such practice. As a result, the badly understaffed state institutions for the mentally disturbed do not benefit from this increase, and continue to suffer serious professional shortages.

Over the past several years, the supply of psychologists has also increased considerably. This is deceptively encouraging, however, in that only about one third of all psychologists trained enter clinical psychology where their skills contribute to the care of the mentally ill. By far the largest number are employed as academicians. Prospects for relieving shortages in social work are even less promising than in psychology, because social work is not attracting nearly as many students as it must train. Because the social worker's role is not well defined for the general public, or even for the profession itself, many schools have not been able to attract as many students as they could accommodate. Albee estimated that an additional 50,000 social workers would be needed by 1960 and that schools of social work were training no more than 2000 per year.

Unlike the situation in social work, nursing is a profession that enjoys a good public image and continues to attract increasing numbers of trainees. However, shortages have existed within the nursing profession for many years because the supply of trainees has not kept up with the demand for their services, as a result of a 50 percent dropout rate occurring primarily because of marriage. The situation with respect to psychiatric nursing is even more serious. Although nearly one half of all hospital patients require psychiatric care, psychiatric nurses make up only about 5 percent of all those employed in hospitals. Thus prospects for the future would suggest that unless psychiatric nursing can begin to attract a much larger percentage of the total available pool, shortages in this profession will increase with time.

Albee also pointed out that the resolution of mental health manpower problems interacts with manpower problems in a variety of technical and professional areas, primarily because all professions draw on the same manpower pool—the young men and women who are being graduated from colleges. When any one profession is successful in attracting recruits, it necessarily creates a shortage in another field. Furthermore, to the extent that there is, as Albee suspected, a general depreciation of intellectual achievement within our society, all professions will suffer.

Albee's overall conclusions were exceedingly pessimistic. Assuming a goal of providing only "adequate" standards of health care, he foresaw that the mental health professions would continue to fall behind in attracting manpower. Population growth and increasing competition for manpower from new social agencies and educational institutions would increase manpower shortages. A reexamination by Albee of the manpower problem eight years after his original study (Albee, 1967) left him with little reason to alter his original pessimistic projections.

PUBLIC HEALTH MEDICINE

Another of the diverse streams contributing to the community psychology torrent is the example provided by public health medicine, which had its modern origins in the latter half of the 19th century. The public health approach was a significant instance of the community's mobilizing in the face of serious plagues and epidemics that threatened to wipe it out (Brown, 1969). Threat drew people together toward concerted action even in the absence of specific knowledge of the etiology of the diseases they were attempting to combat. Epidemiological studies dealing with the rates and distribution of disorders within a population provided some clues on which to act. A vivid example of this involved the 19th century cholera epidemic that swept London. Once several cases of the disease appeared, it became apparent to people who were charting their location in the city that most of those who were infected were drawing their water from a particular well. This finding of a relatively crude epidemiological study suggested an effective preventive procedure, even in the absence of a full understanding of cholera's etiology,—removal of the pump handle from the suspect well. Eventually the discovery of disease-causing microorganisms advanced the cause of public health medicine significantly. This fundamental example of a broad-gauge effort to uncover the cause of a disorder, and the mounting of energetic efforts to prevent it, is identical to the mission of the community psychologist.

PRESSURE FOR PREVENTING MENTAL ILLNESS

Growing pressure for concentrating on the prevention of mental illness has been another recent contributor to the development of the community psychology movement. The idea of attempting to prevent development of mental illness rather than only treating it after it has appeared is not a new one. It was proposed in the early 1900s by Dr. Adolph Meyer, one of the most influential psychiatrists of the 20th century (Meyer, 1948). Meyer was greatly concerned with educating the public regarding the nature of mental illness and the workings of the mental hospital. Furthermore, he strongly supported the idea that the hospital should extend its activity into the community, thereby breaking down the walls between the mental institution and the general public. He also spoke with enthusiasm about "aftercare," a practice, then common in Europe, of preparing a patient for going out into the community and for making his reentry as smooth as possible. In speaking to a hospital committee devoted to aftercare, Meyer foresaw how such activity would eventually lead to a preventive approach toward mental disorder:

"... I have always felt that the term 'after-care' in the name of a committee of this character is one that limits the field of interest below that which is actually the result. It is not only 'after-care' as it was established in England, that is to say, one or two months care for people who are discharged and need a boarding place or something of that nature, but it consists of finding occupation for patients who are leaving the institution and trying to live again in the community, and helping to make their reentrance into the community easy and safe against relapses. There we have the after-care movement turned into the prophylaxis movement; and anyone who once gets interested in the prophylaxis of recurrences cannot help but get interested in the prevention of the first attacks, and there you are in a center of what we must hope from this movement" (Meyer, 1948, p. 300).

Many of Meyer's comments regarding the need for aftercare, prevention, and a closer tie between the mental institution and the community, expressed over 60 years ago, have a remarkably modern ring. But, despite Meyer's early advancement of these ideas, the mental health fields did not utilize them until very recently. Even the example of the introduction of preventive approaches into general medicine failed to stimulate activity in Meyer's time toward the prevention of mental disorder. Rather than causing active resistance, the preventive approaches simply failed to arouse enthusiasm. At the same time that Meyer was speaking out for prevention, psychoanalysis and the psychodynamic approach was rising in prominence. In the choice between Meyer's approach and psychoanalytic procedures which promised to cure disorders that had been puzzling for literally thousands of years, the mental health fields found greater glamor in Freud. Thus the enthusiasm of mental health professionals, particularly in the United States, was invested in psychoanalysis and dynamic psychotherapies. Even the profession of psychiatric social work, which developed as an integral part of the aftercare movement, eventually moved away from its original mission in the community and followed the other mental health professions into the clinics and hospitals where psychotherapy was being practiced. Thus most elements of the preventive movement virtually disappeared from the mental health scene for many years.

It was not until the 1940s that a call for preventive approaches was again heard. In this reawakening of interest in prevention, Lindemann (1944) played an important role with his study of reactions to bereavement. Lindemann had contact with a number of individuals who were bereaved as the result of a fire in a nightclub in Boston during the early 1940s which killed approximately 500 people. From his observations of the bereaved victims of this catastrophe, Lindemann identified acute grief as a distinct syndrome that involves a set of reasonably consistent psychological and somatic symptoms. He also described a fairly regular process through which those successful in overcoming their grief worked through this syndrome. This process typically involves feelings of guilt, anger, depression, and various somatic upsets. Lindemann also noted that many individuals, threatened by the distress associated with this process of normal grieving, attempted to avoid the experience altogether by resisting "breaking down." Lindemann felt that such efforts to resist the discomfort of grief were an obstacle to the necessary working through process. So long as the individual avoids the process, he remains preoccupied with the dead person and his functioning is impaired. Lindemann, therefore, asserted that the bereaved person can prevent psychological maladjustment by permitting himself to engage in the normal mourning process. Outsiders were seen to be potentially helpful in assisting people in this process. Clergymen particularly, as well as other individuals in the community who normally provided human services of one kind or another, were seen by Lindemann as capable of playing a significant role in preventing mental disorder by encouraging the grieving process.

In 1948 Lindemann, with the assistance of private foundation support, established a community mental health program in Wellesley, Massachusetts which became a laboratory for testing broad preventive techniques. In the Wellesley program (Klein and Lindemann, 1961) service was offered to all who faced "crises or predicaments." These included threats to specific individuals such as the loss or potential loss of significant relationships, the necessity to deal with a new person in one's social orbit, and various types of transition in social status. In addition, groups of individuals about to embark on potentially stressful experiences, such as student nurses about to enter training and children about to begin kindergarten, were also offered group counseling.

By 1961, Caplan (1961) was able to report that 16 different studies had been devoted to the prevention of emotional disturbance in children. A few years later the same author (Caplan, 1964) wrote a textbook designed to help mental health professionals to establish preventive programs. In his definition of the term "preventive psychiatry," Caplan distinguished between the three types of preventive efforts. The first, called *primary prevention,* is intended to reduce the incidence of mental disorders of all types in the community. The second, termed *secondary prevention,* is aimed at reducing the duration of disorders that have already occurred. The third, *tertiary prevention,* seeks to reduce impairment that may have resulted from some manifest mental disorder.

Primary Prevention

To lower the overall rate of new cases of mental illness, it is necessary to understand the circumstances that produce such disorder and alter them before they have an opportunity to exercise their influence. In this respect it should be emphasized that primary prevention is a community concept. It does not seek to deal with the problems of a specific individual but, instead, to reduce the risk of mental disorder for an entire population. Its goal, therefore, is to create an optimal living situation for all members of a population so that they will be able to adapt constructively to whatever crises they encounter. Thus the primary preventive program must identify environmental influences that are harmful, as well as environmental forces that are useful for resisting adverse influences.

Caplan recognizes that to create optimally effective primary preventive programs, it would help to know as much as possible about the etiology of mental disorder. That is, one must have a pretty good idea of what environmental forces predispose one to particular types of disorder and how these forces can be manipulated to build resistance against such disorders. However, Caplan feels that primary prevention is feasible despite the fact that we know far less about the etiology of most mental disorder than is optimal. He points to examples in public health medicine in which many successful primary preventive programs were established before the etiologies of the illnesses that they prevented were well understood. Smallpox was prevented by vaccination, for example, long before the causes of the disease were well understood. Likewise, major advances were made in the control of infectious disease in cities long before the advent of the germ theory and the discovery of microbial agents. Thus Caplan believes that one can rely on the best current knowledge of factors that seem to be associated with the presence or absence of a disorder and build a program based on that knowledge. Again, looking to examples offered by public health medicine, Caplan points out that the smallpox vaccine was developed by Jenner who noticed that those who had previously contracted cowpox seemed immune to smallpox. The hygienic reformers of the 19th century acted on an unsophisticated belief that dirt and squalor were unhealthy and on their observation that epidemics of infectious disease tended to occur in congested cities but not in rural areas. The earlier cited example of London's 19th-century cholera epidemic, which was checked by removal of the pump handle from the well out of which most of its victims were drawing their water, is also illustrative of Caplan's point.

Given our imperfect knowledge of the etiology of mental disorder, however, some other basis for directing primary preventive activities must be developed. Caplan feels that a conceptual model must be designed to guide preventive efforts. In essence he sees such a model as resembling the small-scale map of a region that is useful to one using an automobile but does not provide the kind of detail that a person on foot prefers to have. Therefore, the model proposed by Caplan emphasizes certain major outlines and directions for primary preventive programs.

Caplan's Conceptual Model for Primary Prevention

A fundamental assumption in Caplan's model is that to avoid mental disorder every individual needs "supplies" appropriate to his particular stage of development. Three groups of supplies are specified in this model: physical, psychosocial, and sociocultural. Quantitative or qualitative deficiencies in these supplies can prompt disorder just as insufficient food or excesses of the wrong kind of food can result in malnutrition.

Physical supplies are necessary for bodily growth and development and for the maintenance of good physical condition. Thus food, adequate shelter, opportunities for exercising the body, sensory stimulation, and the like are fundamental. There is also a need for means to protect oneself from bodily harm.

By the term psychosocial supplies, Caplan refers to the cognitive and emotional stimulation received through interaction with other people, one's family, peers, and older persons. People have a variety of interpersonal needs that must be satisfied through interaction with other human beings. Failure to satisfy needs such as those for love and affection, for limitation and control, and for participating in social activities, can result in emotional disorder. An "unhealthy relationship," one in which the individual has little opportunity to satisfy his needs because the people he deals with don't respect them or use him to satisfy their own needs, can result in mental disturbance. Furthermore, the disruption of previously satisfactory relationships through death or disillusionment can also be traumatic.

The term sociocultural supplies refers to those forces deriving from the expectations of others around the individual regarding his place in the structure of society. These forces are determined by the customs and values of a culture and the social structure. The advantaged group in a stable society often inherit social roles that make it easy to develop a healthy personality. Being born in a disadvantaged group or in a society that is itself unstable may hinder development. Furthermore, those born in a group rich in cultural heritage are more likely to be taught to deal effectively with highly complicated problems of living. On the other hand, when a society is in a transitional phase—as our own seems to be in today—well tested ways of dealing with new problems are not likely to have been developed. Under these circumstances the individual is forced to rely heavily on his own resources.

In addition to the described needs for various types of supplies, the Caplan's conceptual model also views *crisis resolution* as playing a pivotal role in primary prevention. As we pointed out previously, crises are situations that can create mental disorder or can provide opportunities for further psychological growth. Personality development involves passing through a succession of different phases. The business of passing from one phase to another can be stressful, and is considered to involve "developmental crises." In addition, there are crises that arise from the ordinary hazards that everyone faces in life. These usually involve a sudden loss of supplies of one type or another or the threat of such a loss. Periods of upset characterized by situations of this kind are termed "accidental crises." The histories of many mental patients reveal that their disorder intensified and progressed after failure to master challenges posed at these transitional stages in their lives. This failure to adjust seems to have rendered the individual less capable of meeting future crises. Successive failures in resolution accelerate the maladjustive progression and the result is mental illness. On the other hand, many individuals who have faced significant crises and surmounted them have found such periods of life to be turning points on which greater strength and competence have been built. Efforts to assist the individual, therefore, to master crises, has considerable potential for later prevention of mental disorder. On the basis of this conceptual model, Caplan offered concrete suggestions regarding primary preventive programs.

Primary Preventive Programs

Caplan described two primary preventive approaches: social action and interpersonal action. Social action involves making changes in the community; interpersonal action attempts to make changes in particular individuals that will, in turn, have communitywide influence.

Social Action. The basic goal of social action is to improve the community so that it will provide needed physical, psychosocial, and sociocultural supplies and, at the same time, offer assistance to those facing crises. One example of a social action program involves efforts to bring about communitywide change through influence over political policies and legislative actions. In such a program, mental health consultation is offered to legislators and administrators and steps are taken to modify the general attitudes and behavior of community members.

To achieve the goal of adequate physical supplies, a number of programs can be established. A campaign to prevent the ingestion by slum children of paint containing lead is an example of a social action program focusing on physical supplies. The establishment of prenatal clinics and of encouraging the lower socioeconomic classes to use them is another example. The proper medical care that these clinics can provide reduces pregnancy complications which can lead to a variety of mental disorders. The apparent relationship between material deprivation and vulnerability to mental disorder suggests another avenue for social action through community planning. Mental health consultation to urban renewal programs can help to assure that the dislocated family is provided with adequate housing and opportunities for sensory stimulation and recreation conducive to mental health.

There are many examples of programs of social action aimed at providing psychosocial supplies. Since the most significant psychosocial supplies are received through family relationships, legislative and social programs that help to maintain family integrity have primary preventive impact. Legislators can be influenced to insure that heads of families have work opportunities allowing them to remain close to their families and to provide adequately for them. Employment regulations can be set up to permit pregnant women and mothers of the very young to have needed time off to care properly for their children. Welfare laws can be designed to allow families to remain together. Divorce laws can require the couple to consult with a mental health specialist before a divorce is granted.

Homemaker services can be provided to families whose integrity is threatened by serious illness. Hospital policies can be shaped to minimize periods of separation between mother and child when either is seriously ill. Public education programs can be provided for parents to increase their understanding of their children's needs.

Social action can most directly provide for cultural supplies through influence over the educational system. For instance, as rapid technological advance reduces the need for unskilled labor, schools might be encouraged to develop programs for young people that will better prepare them for the more exacting requirements of the new industries. Furthermore, the community's responsibility for educating its members need not necessarily end with high school.

Another way for the mental health specialist to increase sociocultural supplies is through community organization efforts to overcome apathy and to increase the effectiveness of citizen groups. Social action efforts can provide sociocultural supplies for groups vulnerable to mental disorder because of social isolation, such as the aged. The community can be encouraged to provide stimulating social and recreational facilities as well as proper living arrangements. Legislators and administrators can be influenced to be flexible concerning the age at which an individual must retire. The elderly can be encouraged to remain interested in the broad aspects of community life and to participate in social, political, and recreational programs.

Social Action in Crisis Situations. Caplan identified two ways to prevent maladjustment resulting from reactions to crisis. The first involves attempting to anticipate situations that promote crises and to deal wih them before they can have a negative influence. The second involves providing services for those already facing a crisis to foster adaptive coping.

To lessen the impact of stressful situations, it is necessary to anticipate where and when such situations are likely to arise. Caplan makes the assumption that developmentally transitional periods engender stresses that are likely to result in crises. He, therefore, recommends that special attention be given to those beginning school, starting a college career, becoming engaged, being married, becoming pregnant, having children, experiencing the climacterium, or retiring. In addition, individuals who are physically ill or are undergoing surgical operations which threaten bodily integrity, those who are bereaved or suffering from separation from a loved one by hospitalization, or those experiencing a broken marriage can also be presumed to be particularly vulnerable. Concentrations of people facing many problems of this kind are often found in specific community agencies. These include prenatal clinics, hospitals, divorce courts, nursery schools and kindergarten, the primary grades of the public schools, college dormitories, and the offices of the clergyman. Providing consultation services in settings such as these can have primary preventive impact through lessening crisis stress.

Services that help foster healthy crisis coping are generally administered through agencies or professionals who are themselves often untrained in mental health work. To enhance such services, consultation must be offered to these agencies and groups. Obstetricians, for example, can be encouraged to be more sensitive to their patient's psychological needs. Agencies can be encouraged to abandon traditional routine, which imposes long time spans between initial appeals for help and the time when concrete service is provided. Since these social approaches are intrusive and often ask agencies and professionals to broaden their service goals, they are difficult to apply.

Another avenue for helping individuals to withstand crises is through education. Children can be taught to analyze the causal factors behind situations and to plan effective responses based on complete understanding. Likewise, the "character building" aspects of certain forms of training may be useful to better prepare people for handling future crises.

Interpersonal Action. Primary prevention through interpersonal action involves face-to-face contact between a mental health professional and individuals or small groups. Although the immediate focus in such interaction is the individual, the impact of the mental health workers' efforts hopefully will be communitywide. To maximize that likelihood, the targets of the mental health worker's efforts are chosen judiciously. Key community members whose role tends to affect the mental health of many others are highly desirable choices.

The interpersonal action approach can be used both to insure the provision of basic supplies as well as to assist in healthy crisis-coping. An example of a program focusing on basic supplies is the identification and amelioration of disturbed relationships between mother and child. Such a program could be based in a well-baby clinic where mother-child interactions can be observed. Often it can be determined that a mother is relating to her child on some basis that satisfies her own maternal needs but ignores the needs of the child. Counseling intervention before the baby's development has been adversely affected by this relationship can serve an important prevention function.

Mothers of young children are not the only group in a position to supply the basic needs of others. Many who exercise authority, such as the foreman in an industrial plant, officers in the armed forces, the warden of a prison, and the administrative leaders of a community are in a position to provide basic supplies to those within their jurisdiction. The best intentioned of these individuals may be unaware of the implications of their actions for the mental health of their subordinates. Others in such key positions may use their role to resolve their own problems. In either case, one has an opportunity to institute primary preventive measures through interpersonal action directed at such authorities.

The education of community leaders concerning mental health needs is another opportunity for the use of interpersonal action to increase the supply of basic needs in the community. Changing attitudes among key community leaders or important influence groups such as parents or professionals can have significant primary preventive impact. Such interpersonal action approaches obviously overlap with what has been described as social action.

Interpersonal action can be directed toward crisis-coping as well as toward increasing basic supplies. This can be done either by intervening directly with individuals who are in crisis or by consulting with care-giving professionals who often deal with individuals and families facing crises. To intervene directly in crises the mental health specialist must make contact with individuals confronted by critical circumstances in community locations to which they are likely to be drawn. Prenatal clinics, hospitals, divorce courts, and the freshmen dormitories of the university are all examples of locations. In these settings efforts must be made to identify those failing to adapt well to crisis and to assist them while the crisis is still in progress. This is the method that was described by Lindemann (1944) in his work with the recently bereaved.

To broaden the scope of a crisis-coping program, the efforts of the mental health professional can be extended by enlisting the cooperation of *community care-givers*. Care-givers are community agents whose role it is to foster the well-being of community members but who are not necessarily considered to have a mental health function. Physicians, nurses, social workers, teachers, lawyers, and clergymen are all examples of professionals who fulfill a care-giving role in the community. To extend preventive efforts through these individuals, the mental health professional must educate as well as consult and support care-givers. Caplan sees the support provided to the care-giving professional by the mental health specialist as an altogether crucial ingredient in primary prevention through interpersonal action.

Secondary Prevention

Secondary prevention involves reducing the rate of psychological disability in a population. Usually these efforts are directed toward lowering the prevalence of specific disorders. Prevalence refers to the rate of established cases of a disorder at a given point in time. For many disorders, a specific population within the community is the target. For example, if one is concerned with secondary prevention of involutional depression, the target population would be menopausal women, or men who are experiencing the climacteric.

A reduction in the prevalence of any disorder can occur either because factors causing the disorder are effectively eliminated, thereby diminishing the rate of new cases, or because the rate of old cases is lowered by early detection of the disorder and effective treatment. The first of these approaches is, of course, primary prevention. Secondary prevention tends to focus on the latter course. It is obvious, however, that successful primary preventive efforts necessarily have secondary prevention impact.

It might be argued that early diagnosis and effective treatment of any mental disorder is simply a part of what has long been regarded as good mental health care, since successful treatment of any individual with a mental disorder removes him from the pool of established cases of that disorder and, to some extent, lowers its prevalence. However, removal of a few cases from the prevalence pool may have very little effect on the overall prevalence figure if the pool is a very large one. In such instances, to have significant impact on the prevalence of the disorder, large numbers of individuals must have their illnesses shortened. Therefore, to qualify as a secondary prevention program, preventive efforts must deal with disorders on a large scale and must make recognizable differences in overall community rates. The reach of the mental health worker must extend not only to those troubled individuals who seek him out but to wherever such problems are found in the community. Ways must be found of locating these problems and of extending mental health expertise to treat them.

Essential to any secondary preventive program are procedures for detecting the presence of a disorder as early as possible. This may well require specialized techniques for detecting specific disorders, since traditional diagnostic tools offer relatively little in this respect. Screening procedures that focus on certain behaviors or on demographic characteristics may be suitable in many cases.

Sharpening early detection procedures and sensitizing individuals to making early referrals must be accompanied by programs preparing treatment agencies to deal with these problems. Public information programs aimed at encouraging early referral must include information as to where individuals can be referred. Furthermore, barriers between the agency and the community must be reduced to facilitate referral. The agency itself must be located close to the population from which referrals are likely to be made, and the bureaucratic red tape that ordinarily delays treatment must be reduced. In recent years, "walk-in clinics" have been established precisely to achieve this result. These are open on a 24-hour basis to receive anyone who comes to the door. Certain settings, such as schools and the armed forces, lend themselves more readily than others to large-scale screening programs and to the development of secondary prevention programs.

Tertiary Prevention

The focus in tertiary prevention is on the individual who has suffered mental disorder, has been treated, and is trying to readjust to community life. The goal is to eliminate residual effects of mental illness and to strengthen the individual so that he can contribute to the general quality of life in his community. The rehabilitation of the recovered mental patient is, therefore, the primary aim of tertiary prevention. Of course, primary preventive or secondary preventive programs also serve this end and, therefore, overlap considerably with tertiary prevention.

Caplan believed that a variety of large-scale efforts toward reducing residual defect in individuals who have suffered mental disorder are possible. One program of this kind involves public education about the nature of mental disorder. Frequently people living with someone who has become mentally ill are most familiar with his behavior in the early stages of the disorder, when he may have appeared at his worst. During hospitalization, his gradual change toward a more normal state is not readily observed; stereotyped fantasies develop regarding what his behavior is apt to be like when he has returned home, so that the people around the ex-patient may apprehensively expect to see again the bizarre behavior that took him to the hospital in the first place. Programs of public education and consultation with family members can help to short-circuit fantasies and misguided expectations about the patient's condition, and assure that he will be received in an optimally helpful atmosphere.

Another problem that the returning mental patient faces is that once he has left his social setting for a while, the social system to which he belonged tends to readjust in a way that transfers his old roles to others in the system. As a result, on returning, the ex-patient often finds it difficult to resume his former place in his family, at work, and among his social peers. At a time when his security has been weakened by having had to go to a hospital, he finds further uncertainty in not having his old role to return to. The seriousness of this problem can be lessened by minimizing the period of hospitalization and by maintaining close contact between the patient, his family, his friends, and his co-workers during the period of illness. Furthermore, professionals working with the patient can make it clear to those concerned that he will be returning and that he should be expected eventually to resume his former roles.

A most significant contribution toward tertiary prevention can be made by the mental institution itself. It has become obvious in recent years that living conditions in the typical mental hospital often contribute toward the deterioration of patient behavior that would be adaptive outside of the hospital. Hospitals serve a useful function for society by removing nuisances from the community and by keeping them from public view;

however, they often fail to meet the needs of the patient who hopes to return to the community. A rethinking of the goals of hospitalization and the methods used to achieve them can make a very significant contribution to tertiary prevention.

Another approach to tertiary prevention involves setting up institutions that are midway points between the sheltered hospital and the community. The demands of the mental hospital environment and that of the general community may be so disparate that some patients have difficulty adjusting readily. Their adjustment can be assisted by discharge to transitional institutions such as halfway houses, day hospitals, night hospitals, and the like. Such institutions can wean the patient away from dependency on a highly protective environment. Special clubs formed by ex-mental patients, akin to Alcoholics Anonymous, fulfill a similar purpose.

Another obvious tertiary preventive approach is occupational rehabilitation. In these programs the patient's job aptitudes and capacities are assessed, usually during the latter part of his hospital stay, and are compared to existing work opportunities. Retraining is provided where new skills will better fit the patient into the local labor market. Many communities sponsor sheltered workshops within which discharged patients can work for a period of time free of the demands of ordinary employment, but where they can have an opportunity to build up their capacity under supervisors who know of their problems and are careful not to overburden them. Locating job opportunities for discharged patients is another service provided by rehabilitation programs. In many instances this may be facilitated by offering consultation to the employer regarding the handling of such workers.

CONCLUSION

This chapter begins with the question of why community psychology is emerging at this particular time. The answer is not a simple one. A number of forces, converging at roughly the same period of time, seem to have contributed. Involved in this development are such factors as a dissatisfaction with traditional functions, the recognition of the serious inequities in the way mental health services are distributed in our society, the growing awareness of huge potential demands for mental health services far beyond those that are already manifest, and a hopelessness with respect to our capacity to train traditional mental health manpower to meet society's needs, as well as the new directions that are pointed to by those espousing more energetic efforts to prevent mental disorder. The combination of all of these forces has produced an energetic movement toward creating community-oriented programs to deal with a variety of mental health problems. The next section of this book describes many of these programs.

References

Albee, G. W. *Mental health manpower trends.* New York: Basic Books, 1959.

Bindra, D. Psychotherapy and recovery from neuroses. *Journal of Abnormal and Social Psychology,* 1956, *53,* 251–254.

Brown, B. S. Philosophy and scope of extended clinic activities. In A. J. Bindman, & A. D. Spiegel (Eds.), *Perspectives in community mental health.* Chicago: Aldine Publishing Co., 1969. Pp. 41–53.

Caplan, G. *Prevention of mental disorders in children: Initial explorations,* New York: Basic Books, 1961.

Cartwright, D. S. Effectiveness of psychotherapy: a critique of the spontaneous remission argument. *Journal of Counseling Psychology,* 1955, *2,* 290–296.

Cartwright, D. S. Note on "changes in psychoneurotic patients with and without psychotherapy." *Journal of Consulting Psychology,* 1956, *20,* 403–404.

Cowen, E. L. Emergent approaches to mental health problems: an overview and directions for future work. In E. L. Cowen, E. A. Gardner, & M. Zax (Eds.), *Emergent approaches to mental health problems.* New York: Appleton-Century-Crofts, 1967. Pp. 389–455.

Cowen, E. L., & Zax, M. The mental health fields today: issues and problems. In E. L. Cowen, E. A. Gardner, & M. Zax (Eds.), *Emergent approaches to mental health problems.* New York: Appleton-Century-Crofts, 1967. Pp. 3–29.

De Charms, R., Levy, J., & Wertheimer, M. A note on attempted evaluations of psychotherapy. *Journal of Clinical Psychology,* 1954, *10,* 233–235.

Eisenberg, L. Possibilities for a preventive psychiatry. *Pediatrics,* 1962, *30,* 815–828.

Eysenck, H. J. The effects of psychotherapy: an evaluation. *Journal of Consulting Psychology,* 1952, *16,* 319–324.

Eysenck, H. J. The effects of psychotherapy. In H. J. Eysenck (Ed.), *Handbook of abnormal psychology.* New York: Basic Books, 1961. Pp. 697–725.

Goffman, E. *Asylums.* Garden City, N. Y.: Doubleday, 1961.

Hollingshead, A. G., & Redlich, F. C. *Social class and mental illness: a community study.* New York: Wiley, 1958.

Joint Commission on Mental Illness and Health. *Action for mental health.* New York: Basic Books, 1961.

Klein, D. C., & Lindemann, E. Preventive intervention in individual and family crisis situations. In G. Caplan (Ed.), *Prevention of mental disorders in children.* New York: Basic Books, 1961. Pp. 283–306.

Leighton, Dorothea C. Distribution of psychiatric symptoms in a small town. *American Journal of Psychiatry,* 1956, *112,* 716–723.

Levitt, E. E. The results of psychotherapy with children: an evaluation. *Journal of Consulting Psychology*, 1957, *21*, 189–196.

Lindemann, E. Symptomatology and management of acute grief. *American Journal of Psychiatry*, 1944, *101*, 141–148.

Lorion, R. P. Socio-economic status and traditional treatment approaches reconsidered. *Psychological Bulletin*, 1973. *79*, 263–270.

Meyer, A. After-care and prophylaxis. In A. Lief (Ed.), *The commonsense psychiatry of Dr. Adolph Meyer*. New York: McGraw-Hill, 1948. Pp. 300–311.

Rosenzweig, S. The effects of psychotherapy: a reply to Hans Eysenck. *Journal of Abnormal and Social Psychology*, 1954, *49*, 278–304.

Sauna, V. D. Sociocultural aspects of psychotherapy and treatment: a review of the literature. In L. E. Abt, & L. Bellak (Eds.), *Progress in clinical psychology, Vol. III*. New York: Grune and Stratton, 1966. Pp. 151–190.

Schofield, W. *Psychotherapy: the purchase of friendship*. Englewood Cliffs, N. J.: Prentice-Hall, 1964.

Shakow, D., & Rapaport, D. The influence of Freud on American psychology. *Psychological Issues*. Vol. IV, No. 1. New York: International Universities Press, Inc., 1964.

Srole, L., Langner, T. S., Michael, S. T., Opler, M. K., & Rennie, T. A. C. *Mental health in the metropolis*. Vol. I. New York: McGraw-Hill, 1962.

3. community programs for traditional problems in schools, clinics, and hospitals

In keeping with many of the definitions of community psychiatry quoted in Chapter 1, the programs described in this chapter take cognizance of the fact that community forces are central to the development or perpetuation of many psychological disorders, or that the community can be used more effectively in treating these disorders. Essentially these programs focus on already manifest emotional disturbance. As such, they represent efforts to improve methods of dealing with psychological disorder, and within the preventive framework, they represent tertiary prevention. The locus for these programs has been quite varied, including the mental hospital, the public schools, and the outpatient treatment setting. One of the pioneer community programs of this type was developed by Dr. Margaret Rioch in 1958.

THE HOUSEWIFE PSYCHOTHERAPIST

In 1958, Rioch, concerned by the manpower shortages in the mental health fields, embarked on a program to use community resources more effectively in treating established mental disorder (Rioch, 1967; Rioch, Elkes, Flint, Usdansky, Newman, and Silber, 1963). Rioch and her co-workers reasoned that manpower shortages were not going to be resolved by encouraging young people to choose careers in the mental health fields. She recognized that even if one could successfully attract young students to mental health, it would be at the expense of luring them away from careers in other fields, such as general medicine or teaching, where critical manpower shortages also exist. Rioch's program, therefore, focused on the development of a heretofore untapped source of manpower. The group she chose to concentrate on would not ordinarily enter any of the professions but might, nonetheless, possess talent for mental health work—housewives whose children have grown and who are ready for second careers.

The truly bold and innovative feature of Rioch's program was that she intended to train housewives to practice what had been regarded as the most complex of the mental health worker's activities, psychotherapy. She set out to train housewives in a relatively short and untraditional program that focused specifically on psychotherapeutic practice. Since she was dealing with women who could not be full-time students, might not have the educational background to qualify for traditional graduate training, and would certainly feel threatened at having to compete with bright youngsters after many years away from school, Rioch felt that an entirely unique training program was necessary. Because she doubted that the two-year training program that she envisioned could produce a broadly skilled psychotherapist, Rioch and her collaborators decided to emphasize training for work with patients from a single age group. The readily available pool of adolescents found in the locale where the program was conducted prompted a focus on this subject group and, incidentally, their parents who were approaching middle age.

Recruits for Rioch's program were solicited through community leaders, PTA groups, women's associations, and other organizations likely to produce suitable applicants. Despite the fact that no assurances of future employment could be given, approximately 50 serious applicants responded. Since only eight students were desired, the selection task was difficult. A preliminary screening procedure was developed in which each applicant wrote an autobiography of about 1500 words and participated with staff members in groups of from eight to ten in four- or five-hour discussions on a variety of topics. Each group was required to take up one particular question and arrive at some consensus on it. They also listened to a tape-recorded interview and discussed their impressions of it. On the basis of impressions formed of each applicant from these activities, the staff eliminated more than half the group. Those who remained took psychological tests and were interviewed individually by the staff.

The general criteria of trainee selection included high intelligence, reliability, psychological stability, nondefensiveness, ability to relate well to others, and sensitivity to psychological subtlety. Other practical factors, such as the prospect of geographical stability and the freedom to work a flexible 20-hour a week schedule, were also taken into consideration. The nature and amount of the applicant's previous education was not consciously regarded as an important criterion. Ultimately, eight women, all middle-class mothers, were selected. One was a widow and the rest were married to professionals or executives. All were college graduates, three having earned advanced degrees, and half the group had undergone more than two years of psychoanalysis or psychotherapy.

The training program consisted of a combination of practical work and supervision as well as lectures and seminars on personality development, adolescence, family dynamics, and psychopathology. Clinical work and supervision took place at the National Institute of Mental Health, Bethesda, Maryland, the base for the program, and in nearby community clinics. Trainees also observed others conducting individual, group, and family therapy. The practical aspects of the training program were instituted very early, and considerable concrete experience was acquired before formal theory was taught.

Two types of program evaluations were utilized. At the end of one year's training, tape-recorded interviews done by each student and recordings of students' self-criticisms of their own interviews were sent to experienced psychotherapists for evaluation. These evaluators, who knew nothing of the project, were asked to rate the adequacy of the trainee's work along a five-point scale. The average of these ratings fell around the middle of the scale indicating satisfactory performance. At the end of the second year, three outside examiners were invited to spend three days evaluating the program by listening to taped interviews done by each trainee, reading the case reports written by each, and interviewing each trainee for one hour. These examiners agreed in rating all trainees highly. Another more tangible indication of the success of the program was that immediately on its conclusion, all students were offered jobs, most of them by agencies in which they had done field training. In a follow-up done approximately four years after graduation, all trainees were found to be employed at least half-time.

Two other formal evaluations of Rioch's first group of trainees have been reported. In the first of these (Golann, Breiter, and Magoon, 1966) a filmed 30-minute interview conducted by a psychiatrist with a female patient was viewed by Rioch's trainees, groups of first-year psychiatric residents, and second- and third-year psychiatric residents, senior medical students, freshman medical students, and hospital volunteer workers. All subjects were asked to make ratings of the patient's background, present status, prognosis, and dynamics. Mean ratings of each group were correlated with the mean ratings of a criterion group consisting of five experienced members of the psychiatric faculty of a large medical school. The performance of the Rioch trainees was found to be significantly poorer in these comparisons than that of advanced psychiatric residents, but significantly better than that of freshman medical students and hospital volunteers and on a par with that of first-year psychiatric residents and senior medical students.

In the second of these evaluations (Magoon and Golann, 1966) a three-year follow-up of the job performance of Rioch's trainees was done. Individual supervisors rated all trainees as average or above in comparison to referrent groups of either new therapists or newly trained social workers. Interviews were also held with co-workers, and nearly all expressed very positive opinions of the trainees' skill.

In the second program established by Rioch and her co-workers, eight women were trained as counselors to mothers of young children. The orientation in this approach was preventive in contrast to the therapeutic orientation of the first program. It was envisioned that the counselors would work with underprivileged women whose children were receiving services from child health clinics, nursery schools, or day-care centers. Significantly, none of these are traditional mental health agencies.

The second group of trainees, selected through procedures similar to those used for the first group, was quite similar in background to the women selected in the first study. As in the first program, training was at first clinically oriented, and throughout the program considerable practical experience was emphasized. A major problem in this program was role definition. While it is reasonably clear what is expected of a psychotherapist in a traditional mental health setting, the role of a mental health counselor in a setting primarily devoted to other than mental health functions is bound to be fuzzy. This is true in spite of the fact that in the typical child health clinic an obvious need exists for someone who can listen to mothers' problems and counsel with them. Traditional personnel have neither the time nor the training to perform this function. Still, the person who enters the child health clinic must outline a role that is distinct from that of the others in the setting. Furthermore, since the clinic patients were of different sociocultural backgrounds compared to the women training to be counselors, communication became a very serious problem. Thus, this second program of Rioch's went forth with a considerable feeling of uncertainty and frustration on the part of both students and program staff.

From the beginning of the training program, students placed in child health clinics interviewed mothers, took histories, and counseled with women referred by clinic staff or who, on the basis of casual contact in the waiting room, seemed to need someone to talk to. Interviews with these women focused on a variety of topics such as housing problems, lack of clothing, unemployment, inadequate education, or marital discord. In this work, trainees found that referral to other agencies such as psychiatric clinics, welfare agencies, or speech and hearing clinics was an important part of their function. Although prevention was their primary goal, the trainees often found it necessary to deal with the immediate problems of the parent and sometimes an older child before it was possible to attend to the child who was the primary clinic patient. In many instances trainees had only a single contact with mothers in the child health clinic, so that as much as possible had to be done within a very limited period of time. Eventually students built up a case load of mothers who came back repeatedly and who could be counseled more intensively. Clearly trainees seemed to find their greatest gratification in such cases. In addition to their child health work, trainees also had part-time placements in other settings, such as nursery schools, where they observed children, counseled with mothers, and consulted with teachers. Other placements were made in maternity clinics, family and child service agencies, and neighborhood centers.

As in the first program, field training was accompanied by case seminars and individual supervision. Course work was taken throughout the two-year program in child development, personality development, community resources, and brief courses were given on a number of special topics such as mental retardation, family dynamics, the techniques of school consultation, psychological testing, prenatal care, and medical problems frequently encountered in children.

The overall impact of Rioch's second program was not evaluated as extensively as the first. The staff's impression was that trainees in this program displayed remarkable flexibility in their approach to problems. From the experience of being limited to very few sessions with counselees, they learned to use time optimally. Physicians in charge of clinics in which trainees were placed were unanimous in positively evaluating the trainees' services. All expressed the wish that trainees could remain in their clinics as counselors. A further sign of the success of the program was the fact that, at its conclusion, seven of the graduates took work as mental health counselors.

This pioneering work of Rioch demonstrates that there are heretofore untapped sources of manpower that can be used to perform badly needed mental health services even of the most complex variety. In addition to an obvious contribution to meeting immediate mental health needs, such individuals can have an important primary preventive impact as well. By providing an exciting and important role for people at a time when they are faced with a reduced sense of importance, as may occur with a woman whose family has grown up, such a program can help the trainee to feel useful once again. Its potential advantages are obvious for groups such as the retired, the physically handicapped, and many others with the time and a need to give human service. Both helper and helpee have much to gain.

UNDERGRADUATES AS GROUP THERAPISTS

The work of Rioch in the late 1950s has stimulated a search for other manpower sources for traditional mental health functions. Poser (1966) has reported one such effort in which he questioned the validity of the assumption that considerable professional training was necessary to practice group psychotherapy. Poser compared the effects of group psychotherapy of hospitalized schizophrenics carried out by experienced professionals (psychiatrists, social workers, and occupational therapists) with the effects of therapy groups led by untrained college undergraduates. Patients undergoing psychotherapy were matched for age, severity of illness, and length of hospital stay. Groups of patients undergoing only ordinary hospital care were matched with those receiving therapy, to provide a no-group therapy control group. Patients in the study had a median age of 47 and all were chronically ill, having a minimum of three uninterrupted years of hospitalization. The trained psychotherapists had a minimum of five years experience, and all but one had previous experience as a group psychotherapist. Untrained therapists in the study were female undergraduates between the ages of 18 and 25, most of whom had never even taken a course in psychology.

The psychotherapy program involved a one-hour meeting, five days per week, throughout a five-month period. Therapists, both trained and untrained, conducted sessions as they desired. Some engaged only in verbal communications; others arranged group activities such as party games, dances, public speaking, and communal painting. All therapists stressed group interaction.

Poser used several criteria to evaluate the effects of the group therapy. These included: two psychomotor tests, tapping speed (TAP) and visual reaction time (RT), two perceptual tests, digit symbol test of the Wechsler-Bellevue Scale I (DS) and a color work conflict test (Stroop); two verbal tests, a test of verbal fluency (VF) and a word association test

(VAL) ; and, for some patients, ratings on a scale measuring adjustment to the hospital. Before and after measurements were taken with all tests and ratings. In addition to being matched in the various therapy and control groups for age, severity of illness, and length of hospitalization, patients were also matched for pretreatment test and rating scores.

After treatment, patients in groups led by untrained therapists were compared on the six criterion tests to the no-treatment controls to which they were matched. They were found to do significantly better on four of these tests (speed of tapping, digit symbol, reaction time, and color word conflict test). These results are depicted in Table 1.

Comparisons of the groups treated by trained therapists to their no-treatment control groups revealed significantly better performance by the treated group on only two criterion tests (digit symbol and color word conflict test). These results are shown in Table 2.

Most interesting, however, were the direct comparisons between the posttreatment performance of patients treated by untrained therapists with those treated by trained therapists as set forth in Table 3. Here it was revealed that the patients of untrained therapists performed significantly better than patients of trained therapists on three of the six criterion tests (speed of tapping, verbal fluency, and reaction time). Ward ratings had been made only on the patients of the untrained therapists by nursing supervisors and by ward attendants who knew particular patients best. The results of these ratings were equivocal, with supervisors' ratings indicating significant improvement after therapy and attendants' ratings reflecting no change.

Table 1.   Covariance Adjusted Posttherapy Scores of Untreated Patients and Those Treated by Lay Therapists (from Poser, 1966)

Treatment		TAP	VF	VAL	DS	RT	Stroop
Untreated controls	Mean	45.763	11.699	26.218	20.428	.169	2.508
(N = 63)	SD	9.772	4.449	6.580	7.204	.054	.768
Treated by lay therapists	Mean	49.735	12.600	28.786	24.135	.197	1.025
(N = 87)	SD	10.222	4.370	8.264	6.812	.063	.698
	t	2.308[b]	1.295	1.801[a]	2.922[d]	2.613	2.336[c]

[a] $p < .10$.
[b] $p < .05$.
[c] $p < .02$.
[d] $p < .01$.

Table 2.   Covariance Adjusted Posttherapy Scores of Untreated Patients and Those Treated by Professional Therapists (from Poser, 1966)

Treatment		TAP	VF	VAL	DS	RT	Stroop
Untreated controls (N = 63)	Mean	45.763	11.699	26.218	20.428	.169	2.508
	SD	9.772	4.449	6.580	7.204	.054	.768
Treated by professional therapists (N = 145)	Mean	46.372	10.948	28.104	23.187	.154	.835
	SD	9.894	3.061	6.950	5.612	.049	.579
	t	.387	1.148	1.427	2.313[a]	1.688	2.903[b]

[a] $p < .02$.
[b] $p < .01$.

Table 3.   Covariance Adjusted Posttherapy Scores of Patients Treated by Lay and Professional Therapists (from Poser, 1966)

Treatment		TAP	VF	VAL	DS	RT	Stroop
Treated by lay therapists (N = 87)	Mean	49.735	12.600	28.786	24.135	.197	1.025
	SD	10.222	4.370	8.264	6.812	.063	.698
Treated by professional therapists (N = 145)	Mean	46.372	10.948	28.104	23.187	.154	.835
	SD	9.894	3.061	6.950	5.612	.049	.579
	t	2.331[a]	2.899[b]	.588	.930	4.998[c]	.356

[a] $p < .05$.
[b] $p < .01$.
[c] $p < .001$.

The findings in this study by Poser are quite paradoxical. Rioch had demonstrated that intelligent housewives could be trained in a two-year program to do psychotherapy. Poser's findings indicate, however, that at least in working with chronic schizophrenics, altogether untrained therapists achieved better results in group therapy than trained professionals. Poser has speculated that the "naive enthusiasm" of the untrained undergraduates might have resulted in greater flexibility to patient mood shifts than did the "professional stance" of experienced therapists. This is supported by the fact that groups led by untrained therapists engaged in less stereotyped activities than did those run by professionals. It is also worth noting that there was greater variability in post-treatment scores of patients in lay therapist groups than in professionally led groups. This siggests that some patients in students' groups responded very well while others showed little or no improvement. By contrast, improvements among patients in professionally led groups seemed to be more evenly distributed among all group members.

Another program in which untrained college students have been used as group therapists with hospitalized patients has been reported by Rappaport, Chinsky, and Cowen (1971). In this program an attempt was made to gauge the effectiveness of group therapy offered by untrained college students supervised by graduate students. Two hundred and fifty-six chronic hospital patients were divided into 32 matched groups, half of which were led by male and half by female therapists. Groups met for a total of from 26 to 33 one-hour meetings distributed over a five and a one-half month period. The criteria for evaluating the effects of this treatment included psychomotor, verbal, perceptual and perceptual-motor tasks, as well as cognitive measures and behavior ratings. The outcome of this study indicated that male patients in groups led by females improved significantly more than no treatment control groups. No significant differences were found for the remaining groups (male patients with a male leader, female patients with a male leader, female patients with a female leader). Although this study did not compare the therapeutic effects of the work of professionals with nonprofessionals, it does lend some support to Poser's finding that effective group therapy can be carried out by relatively untrained group leaders.

COLLEGE STUDENT COMPANION PROGRAMS

Since the mid-1950s a number of mental hospital programs have emerged involving college student volunteers. The first of these appeared in 1954 when a student volunteer program was organized in the Boston area as an outgrowth of a very small social service program of the Phillips Brooks House Association at Harvard (Greenblatt, 1962; Umbarger, Dalismer, Morrison, and Breggin, 1962). Approximately 500 students from various colleges in the Boston area visited either Metropolitan State or Boston Psychopathic Hospital during the academic year 1954 to 1955. About 40 percent of this group made 10 or more visits, some on a weekly basis spending from one and one-half to three hours per visit with patients. Each visit was generally followed by a discussion with staff of what had taken place that day.

In this program no screening was used to eliminate volunteers, since it was felt that a self-selecting process would take place whereby those who were unfit for the role would drop out of the program on their own. Those who remained with the program were simply instructed to be themselves with patients. No further preparation was offered. Volunteers were assigned specific days for visiting and, in time, specific projects were planned and project leaders were appointed to organize each day's activities. The position of daily unit coordinator was created to provide someone to take charge of the day-to-day operations of the different volunteer teams. A sense of the variety of activities engaged in by volunteers is provided in Figure 1.

10/9   Six of us altogether; we spent two hours in E-3 talking with the patients. Organized an art class which proved to be great success with many of the patients, who wish it to be continued. We asked to take patients to the courtyard, but were not allowed to, because the male patients were already using it.

10/16   Five people out tonight; two took some patients bowling, and rest stayed on ward playing bingo, singing, doing jigsaw puzzles, drawing and talking. It would be hard to be too enthusiastic about the responsiveness on E-3 this evening, the patients greeted us eagerly and participated with remarkable interest and gusto in all activities.

    The supervisor of the ward expressed delight at the success of this evening's work, and praised the activities. Especially pleasing to her (and to us) was the responsiveness of one who laughed and talked with enthusiasm for the first time in many months.

    The only complaint was that we should come out earlier.

    Next week one girl is going to bring equipment to give haircuts, and another will bring her guitar.

    We all enjoyed ourselves tonight, and many patients came up to us afterwards and told us that they had had a good time.

10/30   Seven people out tonight; activities included piano and singing, checkers, puzzles, horse shoes, beanbags, and talking.

    Sometimes in E-3 we can see the silhouettes of men from D-3 pressed against the door, as though they wanted to have a feeling of association or participation with our activity. So we decided to open the door, and see if they really were amenable to joining us for games, talking and other pastimes. As it happens, they weren't amenable last night. I think, though, they might be if we try a few more times.

11/10   Attended a group meeting with the resident doctor and the E-3 attendants. Both the other volunteers and myself participated actively in the discussions, all our comments were well received.

12/4   First time out after two week lapse for exams. Enthusiastic reception, with several break-throughs to formerly uncommunicative or inactive patients.

12/18   Excellent results with lipstick applications and the lipstick to keep as a bingo prize. Established communication with patient who has never spoken to us before; she accepted a lipstick application from another patient and seemed pleased at the compliments she drew.

2/26   I spoke to a group of patients tonight and asked them what they thought of the idea of putting on some sort of play. They seemed genuinely interested and made their own suggestions as to what kind of play they wanted—opinions ran high for a comedy, especially a light musical comedy.

Some of our volunteers came from Emerson College; they will approach the Theater Arts Department there for help in getting scripts.

Figure 1. Excerpts from Adult Unit Diary (Umbarger et al., 1962, p. 26) .

On one ward the volunteer project involved physical beautification and the organization of group activities. Drab hospital walls were painted brightly, floors were carpeted, and bright paintings were hung on the walls. When some patients remained unstimulated by these environmental changes, efforts were made to reach them directly. Students tried to be especially friendly through the vehicle of group table games, such as bingo and cards, which would force social interaction. On a children's unit, student volunteers organized sports activities and formed one-to-one relationships with children who seemed starved for affection. With a group of adult patients who seemed capable of leaving the hospital, a "case-aid" program was organized in which students worked with individual patients throughout the year to facilitate his or her transition from hospital life to community life. This involved taking patients on trips, meeting their families, and checking out job placement possibilities, as well as visiting in the hospital.

Beck, Kantor, and Gelineau (1963) have reported a study evaluating the changes in clinical and social status of hospital patients who participated in the case-aid program. Between 1954 and 1961 a total of 120 case-aid patients were seen. Follow-up interviews were done with relatives of every patient who left the hospital during this period to evaluate their personal and social adjustment, recent work history, and symptoms.

It was found that 37 of the 120 patients left the hospital while they were being worked with by students and, of these, 28 of the 37 were still out at the time of follow-up (for an average of 3.4 years). The 9 returnees had remained out of the hospital an average of 1.4 years. Seven more patients had left the hospital some months after they were seen for case-aid work, and all remained out at follow-up (for an average of 1.2 years each). Of the 35 patients who were out of the hospital at the time of follow-up, 2 were considered to be unimproved, 10 were adjusting marginally, 18 were considered improved, and 5 were apparently well. Considering that the case-aid volunteer was working with a chronic hospitalized patient averaging in excess of 4 years of hospitalization, the authors of this program contend that the program was successful, and attribute this success to several factors. First, relationships with patients were maintained for long periods of time. Second, the role definition of the case-aid worker was a relatively loose one permitting him to engage in a wide range of activities and to deal gradually with anxiety provoking material. Finally, the activity of the case aide extended beyond the hospital walls and included helping the patient to find employment and to adjust to family life.

Partially as a result of the case-aide experience, a need was recognized for a transitional institution, or halfway house, midway between the hospital and the outside world. Many patients were seen to require the support of such an institution before they could reintegrate themselves into general society. Therefore, volunteer students and a hospital social worker planned and developed a transitional dwelling called Wellmet House (Kantor, 1962; Kantor and Greenblatt, 1962; Umbarber et al., 1962). A house was rented and funds raised to cover rent, maintenance costs, and the salaries of a resident couple. Financial support came from several sources. One was a $1000 yearly room and board charge to students who could reside with the patients at Wellmet, which was operated as a cooperative. State and government agencies provided additional support. Medical and psychiatric consultants were available for consultation, but perhaps the most important feature of Wellmet was that it provided ex-patients with an opportunity to live and develop spontaneous friendships with normal members of the community. Eight patients lived at Wellmet during its first year of operation. Within the year, four were able to return to full-time employment, three of whom took up their own residence.

It is apparent from this capsule description of the Boston program that this pioneering student participation effort developed despite the lack of well-organized goals and plans for reaching those goals. All of the projects that have been developed can be considered to have a tertiary preventive aim. The focus has not been on direct psychotherapy, as was the case in Poser's program, but on efforts to prepare the patient for living outside of the hospital and to maximize his chances of staying out once he left.

Following the example set by the Boston group, many other college student companion programs have appeared in mental hospitals (Holzberg, Whiting, and Lowy, 1964; Klein and Zax, 1965). In several of these programs tertiary preventive goals have been well articulated from the outset. Holzberg et al. (1964) have directed the focus of a companion program toward the socially isolated, "forgotten" patient. In addition to the potential good that a companion might do for the patient, however, Holzberg and his associates expected that the companion program would have primary preventive impact by modifying the personality of the student companion (Holzberg and Knapp, 1965). A study was done, therefore, of the effects on the student companions of participation in a program involving them with hospitalized patients. The results showed that companions developed greater self-acceptance and became significantly more tolerant in their judgments of sexual and aggressive behaviors than students who had not participated in the hospital companion program (Holzberg, Gewirtz, and Ebner, 1964; Holzberg, Knapp, and Turner, 1967).

SCHOOL PROGRAMS FOR THE DISTURBED CHILD

Community programs are beginning to appear in which seriously disturbed children are treated within a school or school-like setting rather than placed in hospitals. Two prominent examples of such programs are those developed by Donahue and Nichtern (Donahue, 1967; Donahue and Nichtern, 1965) in Long Island and Project Re-ED (Hobbs, 1966; Hobbs, 1968; Lewis, 1967) in Tennessee.

Reasoning that placing children in hospitals or residential treatment settings is a damaging rejection of the troubled child which isolates him from home and peers, Donahue and Nichtern set up a project to deal with the seriously disturbed child within the public school system. They felt that dealing with the child in his own community would reflect acceptance of his problems within a truly empathic, growth facilitating climate. Acknowledging that the seriously disturbed child is often not capable of coping with the demands of the ordinary classroom, Donahue and Nichtern created a special educational program that was aimed at helping him learn and grow within the system until capable of returning to the ordinary classroom.

This type of educational program was thought to require a warm, understanding teacher who could work with a child on a one-to-one basis.

The potentially high cost of such an approach was minimized by recruiting volunteers from among the retired teachers who were housewives in the community in which the program was developed. In the selection of these teachers, demonstrated adequacy as a mother was a prime criterion. The unpaid "teacher-moms" worked two mornings per week under the supervision of the educational staff and a psychiatrist. To further limit program costs, donated space at a local community center was used. The Board of Education provided transportation, books, and necessary professional support.

Two teacher-moms, working with a given child two mornings per week, provided a total of four mornings of individual instruction. Teaching teams were briefed concerning the problems of their child, were given appropriate educational materials, and were assisted by a teacher who took care of supply and transportation problems. Teaching programs were highly individualized to meet both the emotional and educational needs of the child, and efforts were made to integrate the activities of all of the children, to use all modalities (motor, visual, auditory, tactual) in the teaching process, and to limit distractions. It was hoped that a warm, interpersonal relationship would develop between the child and his teacher-moms that would facilitate the learning process. A typical session for a child and his teacher-mom is described in Figure 2.

A typical morning for a child and his "teacher-mom" follows:

The teacher-mom meets her project child as he gets off the station wagon, escorts him to his assigned room and helps him stow his gear and clothing. She then takes him to the "good-morning" room, where the professional teacher-in-charge is waiting to conduct the opening group exercises. These consist of the salute to the flag and a short reading and discussion period. The reading and discussion evolves from what the teacher-in-charge has written on the blackboard, or from "show and tell." She tries to include sentences at the reading level of each of the children which, when put together, make a paragraph about the day's weather, or a holiday or an event, or something with which the children are familiar. Discussion is encouraged. The opening exercises may last a very few minutes or as long as fifteen, contingent upon the manageability of the group that day.

While this is going forward the teacher-mom has secured the books, games, and equipment she plans to use that morning, and is in her assigned room ready to receive her child when he returns from the opening exercises. She sits next to, and close to, the child, and the day's work begins.

She may begin with reading, usually using the reading series and supplementary materials available to the professional teachers of the district. She is encouraged to follow the teacher's manual more closely than a professional teacher, because the manuals are well developed guides and provide comprehensive directions on how to teach the series with which she is working. From reading she moves to other subject areas, such as arithmetic, spelling, language skills, social studies, science. These activities, interspersed at her discretion with games, or talk, or a walk, listening to records, go forward until 10:30 A.M., at which time there is a snack break. She takes her child to a large room with a long table and benches. One of the children and his teacher-mom have laid out the cookies and milk beforehand—which is done on a rotating basis. All the children as a group sit down and have their snacks under the supervision of the professional teacher-in-charge.

While the children are having their snacks, the teacher-moms usually assemble in the kitchen for coffee and cookies. Here there is much discussion of the project children, although sometimes it is more social conversation than professional. The snack-time and coffee break takes fifteen or twenty minutes, at the end of which the teacher-mom returns to her room to continue work with her child, following the plan for the day as agreed upon with the teacher-in-charge. If other group activities are scheduled they usually occur during the time between the end of snacks and the end of the morning. At 11:45 the teacher-mom begins to get her child ready to go home. At this point she completes her log of what transpired with the child that day, and leaves it with the teacher-in-charge so that it is available for her teammate teacher-mom.

In the course of the morning she has probably been visited by the teacher-in-charge, who provides on the spot direction and suggestions for furthering the child's educational program.

Figure 2. A Typical Morning for a Child and His "Teacher-Mom" (from Donahue & Nichtern, 1965, pp. 53 to 55) .

The children participating in the program suffered a variety of problems. Some had been diagnosed as schizophrenic, others were thought to suffer mild brain damage, or were neurotic or mildly defective. Some examples are found in Figure 3. The average stay in the program was about two years during which time the goal was to prepare the child educationally and emotionally to return to the ordinary classroom. Readiness for such return was assessed by a team of mental health professionals. When a child was thought to be ready, a review was made of the various teachers at the child's grade level throughout the county system, and the judgment was made as to which teacher and which class might best suit him. Return to the classroom was gradual with some children beginning with only one-half day per week. Teacher-moms ordinarily stood by in the

child's new school in case they were needed while he was becoming accli-
mated.

Donahue (1967) has reported that of 21 severely disturbed children
treated in this program, 11 were able to return to regular classes where
they made normal progress both in their studies and in their interpersonal
relationships with peers. Considering the severity of the disturbance of
these children and the bleak future that youngsters of this kind ordinarily
face, such an outcome is impressive. Furthermore, the program cost is
trivial when compared to the high cost of residential treatment centers
and hospitals. Some descriptions of improvements in specific children are
found in Figure 3.

D. C.—Male—7 years, 5 months. His diagnosis was schizophrenic reaction of
childhood. The situation was complicated by considerable pathology in the
total family situation. His mother had been hospitalized for mental illness, and
his father was also disturbed. The child developed much better controls, a longer
attention span, real enthusiasm for the work and learning situation, and a
positive relationship to his "teacher-moms" and some of the other children. His
hyperactivity was greatly reduced, and coordination showed marked improvement. He was phased into a regular first grade of twenty-eight children and is
now in sixth grade.

B. T.—Female—7 years, 7 months. Her diagnosis was mild cerebral palsy and
mental retardation, poor coordination, short attention span, little interest in
other children, poor hand-eye coordination, distractibility, and hyperactivity.
B. T. progressed to the point that she could handle a pencil and produce basic
forms. Her attention span increased, and her interests broadened. She acquired
some impulse control, completed the readiness program, learned to identify
and write her name, developed arithmetical concepts of most-least, first-last,
sequence, bigger-smaller, etc., and left to right progression. She is now successfully functioning in one of the district's classes for the educable, mentally
retarded.

J. A.—Male—8 years, 8 months. His diagnosis was schizophrenic reaction of
childhood with the severe regressive symptom of soiling. He was hyperactive,
harmful to others, and so disruptive that he could not be contained in the regular
classroom. In addition, there was considerable family pathology. His parents
would not cooperate with the therapeutic proposals offered by the local mental
health center. When placed in the educational-therapeutic milieu, this child
progressed rapidly, both academically and socially. His soiling ceased. His

relationships at home improved. He began to relate well to the other children in the program and was phased into a regular third grade on a half-time program. J. A. is now functioning well in sixth grade.

C. M.—Female—8 years, 1 month. An aphasic child with organic involvement and extensive emotional problems, this child was known to many clinics in New York City as well as to some local mental health facilities which advised that she was completely hopeless and should be totally exempted from school. C. M. was a completely withdrawn child. She now enjoys physical contact. She has improved impulse control and appears to be a happy, attractive little girl who plays with others and occasionally assumes a leadership role. She was initially phased into a second grade, in the middle group in reading in her class, and is now in sixth grade where she is reading on a sixth-grade level. She is anxious to learn and writes and spells appropriately for her age. Most important of all, she speaks— in fact, at times she is a chatterbox. Though not always easy to understand, she has a sizable vocabulary and a desire to communicate.

R. L.—Male—8 years, 1 month. Diagnosed as a schizophrenic child with bizarre behavior, violent at times, he hurt other children, did not participate with the group, did not respond to reasoning, and was egocentric, autistic-like, immature, demanding, given to extreme temper tantrums, and sulking. R. L. was physically large and poorly coordinated. He now has positive relationships with his peers, and particularly with adults. His coordination is improved. He has lost much of his impoliteness and is receptive to suggestions and authority. He tries to play successfully with other children and sometimes shares willingly and voluntarily. He has a high degree of academic ability, particularly in mathematics and science. In mathematics he can solve problems mentally that most of us need pencil and paper to solve. His resistance to reading has been overcome, and he is reading on grade level. He is now in a junior high school program in a residential setting.

C. C.—Male—8 years, 9 months. C. C. was diagnosed as a schizophrenic child who on the surface would appear to be a severe behavior problem. He demonstrated gross distortions in conceptualization and visual-motor perceptualization and extreme unevenness of performance. His deficits inhibited his adjustment in all areas. When he was entered in the special program, it was necessary to start his academic program at the beginning. He needed much repetition and variety of approach. He progressed to a fourth-grade level and is now functioning with competence in a regular seventh grade; this despite a family with much pathology, including severe marital discord and extreme inconsistencies in the handling of the child.

Figure 3. Case Vignettes about Specific Children (from Donahue, 1967, pp. 380 and 381).

Project Re-ED (Hobbs, 1966, Hobbs, 1968; Lewis, 1967) is another program for the school child who would normally be excluded from the regular classroom because of his emotional problems. Unlike Donahue and Nichtern's program, project Re-ED is a partially residential program in which children live at the school five days each week and at home on weekends. Re-ED was started in 1961 as an experiment because of the manpower shortages in the mental health fields, and because its originators questioned the effectiveness of traditional approaches to treating children's disorders. It represents an attempt to set up a "total education milieu" for disturbed children. Unlike the typical residential hospital which provides a few hours each week of professional attention but long periods of relative inactivity, project Re-ED creates an atmosphere within which a child's entire stay is oriented toward the goal of returning him to the community.

Teachers for the Re-ED program are selected for teaching competence, unusual resourcefulness, and interest in working with the emotionally disturbed. The 13 elementary school teachers who participated at the beginning of the program, were selected and trained for nine months—two quarters of academic work plus a three-month internship in a residential unit for emotionally disturbed children. When their training is concluded, this program's teachers become known as teacher-counselors and are assigned to a residential school. Within such a school, eight children are assigned to two teacher counselors who design a comprehensive program for each child based on his needs and problems, and the shared objectives of his family, the referring agency, and the Re-ED schools. The emphasis throughout is on education rather than mental health. The language of the clinic and hospital are avoided and, while the staff are sensitive to emotional problems, the belief that education can serve as a helpful force in the adaption of the disturbed child is uppermost.

Rather than traditional psychotherapy, Re-ED emphasizes setting up concrete goals that can be reached in a short time. For example, the child with a reading problem is often regarded as needing long-term psychotherapy with concomitant counseling for parents. But in the Re-ED program it is assumed that a certain percentage of children with reading problems will improve as the result of direct educational approaches. Therefore, an educational approach is taken, and efforts are made to teach the child many of the basic attitudes and skills necessary for living successfully in society. Reading, the ability to remain in a classroom for long periods of time, the ability to get along peaceably with peers, and the development of trust in adults are examples of such goals.

Referrals to the Re-ED program come from schools, family agencies, or clinics. The history and current status of the newly referred child is reviewed in a conference generally held with the referring agency. At this conference concrete goals are set up for creating the kinds of behavior changes that will make it possible for the child to return home promptly. When project Re-ED was begun, severe psychotics, the brain injured, and the mentally retarded were excluded. Eventually it was found that diagnosis was not an important admission criterion, so that the likelihood a child's specific problem could be ameliorated by the educational and community program offered in Re-ED became the most significant determinant of whether a child was accepted. Thus a wide range of diagnostic groups within the age range of 6 to 12 years is now being treated.

New arrivals for the Re-ED schools are assigned to groups, and individualized educational and social living programs are designed for them. Other group members are prepared for the newcomer and generally receive him warmly. The typical school day runs from 9 A.M. to 3 P.M. during which basic skills such as reading and arithmetic are emphasized. Specific content is determined by the particular needs the child has for a given skill. Nonacademic parts of each day are used to teach socially useful skills that are undeveloped, such as kicking a football, roller skating, swimming, bike riding and, in the evenings, learning to live harmoniously with peers and adults. Periodic reviews are made of each child's progress with discharge being arranged as soon as he is functioning well enough to cope with home and community demands and seems likely to continue his growth.

The key personnel in project Re-ED are the teacher-counselors who have the major responsibility for planning each child's program, and who, by far, spend the most time with the child in the program. They manage his day-to-day educational, emotional, social, and recreational needs. At the same time they must recognize that the Re-ED program is merely a way station for the child who must return eventually to full-time community life.

Since one of Re-ED's fundamental assumptions is that the child is inevitably a part of a social system—an ecological unit including his family, school, neighborhood, and community—other professionals must be involved in the overall treatment program. Thus a liaison teacher responsible for maintaining communication between the program and the child's own school in the community is part of the Re-ED program. The liaison teacher helps to prevent alienation of the child from the system that he has left and to optimize conditions for his return to a regular classroom when he is ready. Another important professional in the Re-ED program is the social worker who, like the liaison teacher, deals with aspects of the ecological unit such as the family, community agencies, and any individuals who may be able to help the troubled child. The three types of personnel in the Re-ED program, therefore, combine to influence all significant elements in a child's social system, the child himself, his school, his family, and any other relevant agencies within his community. This contrasts sharply with traditional psychotherapy approaches which tend to be directed mainly toward the child.

A variety of evaluations of the Re-ED program have been undertaken. At a simple cost level, Hobbs (1966) reported that the Re-ED school costs about $20 to $25 per child per day. This was, at the time, about one third the cost of other forms of residential treatment and approximately four times the cost of custodial care. However, since the child tends to remain in the Re-ED program for a far shorter period of time than in custodial care, the Re-ED cost per child served ($4000) is considerably less than that of custodial care.

Granting that the Re-ED program is less expensive than traditional approaches for treating the disturbed child, the question of its effectiveness remains. Weinstein (1969) has reported a study addressed to this issue. Several approaches were taken to evaluate the Re-ED child's status after discharge. One involved asking the following question of the referring agency, which has had continuing contact with the child or his parents: "Compared to enrollment is the child's adjustment now worse, the same, slightly improved, moderately improved, or greatly improved?" The same question was asked of the child's parents six months after he returned home. The results of this evaluation effort indicate that in excess of 80 percent of the children are regarded as having improved greatly or moderately by the referring agency, the mother, and the father. In a further effort to assess parent views of the child's behavior, mothers and fathers were asked to rate the child's behavior both before enrollment and again at 6 and 18 months after discharge from Re-ED. The instruments used were a symptom checklist that included problem behavior such as crying, temper tantrums, running away, a social maturity scale, and a discrepancy score from a semantic differential instrument on which the parent describes the way the child behaves, and the way the parent would like him to behave. On all of these instruments both mothers and fathers indicated that Re-ED children had shown significant improvement. The semantic differential instrument indicated that the children were less tense, less aggressive, and more dominant than before they engaged in the Re-ED program. In addition, mothers regarded their children as more outgoing.

To assess Program effects on school performance, prior to the child's leaving his own school, teachers were asked to fill out a series of questionnaires and to make ratings of many aspects of his behavior. On the child's return from the Re-ED program, teachers were again asked to fill out these instruments. Analyses of these data indicate that after the Re-ED program the children improved significantly in their capacity to fulfill their role as students, were less disruptive, suffered fewer feelings of personal distress, were able to face new situations, had better work habits, and related better to other children.

Despite these impressive changes following the Re-ED program, the question remained as to whether it was the content of the program itself or the mere passage of time that accounted for the change. To deal with this issue, Weinstein (personal communication) identified a sample of disturbed children similar to those in the Re-ED program with the help of teachers in schools where referrals had been made to Re-ED. These children had remained within the school system with no special treatment. By using the same instruments on which Re-ED children were evaluated, teachers rated this control group on three occasions: at the time the children were selected, and again one and two years later. The results indicated that the untreated children had remained either substantially the same with the passage of time or had become significantly worse.

INNOVATIVE COMMUNITY PROGRAMS SPONSORED BY MENTAL HEALTH CENTERS AND HOSPITALS

A number of innovative treatment programs emphasizing the importance of community forces in the rehabilitation of the mental patient have appeared in recent years. Bierer (1964), who originated many of these programs, points out that community approaches to treating the mentally disturbed are very old indeed. Occupational and recreational therapies date back to Egyptian times. The Greeks prescribed useful work, music, and good diet for the mental patient and were opposed to restraints of any kind. Galen, the famous Roman physician, attempted to treat the patient's family as well as the patient. More recently the establishment of the colony of Gheel in Belgium is an example of a remarkable community effort to deal with mental illness. According to legend, the hospital at Gheel was built as a shrine to Dymphna, an Irish princess who had devoted her life to God. At her mother's death, her father, not satisfied with other prospective wives, proposed an incestuous marriage to Dymphna. She fled from him in panic, and he followed, catching up with her in Gheel and killing her when she refused to go along with his plan. For literally hundreds of years children and adults have been brought to Gheel for treatment and have been boarded with the local farmers who have played a central role in the treatment program. Many of the modern programs we describe, therefore, are simply current versions of a variety of community efforts that have been made in the past to treat the mentally disturbed.

The Day Hospital

The day hospital originated in Russia in 1933 as a facility to which patients came during the day for a full range of treatment programs. During the 1940s similar institutions were established in Canada and Great Britain, and by the late 1940s they began to appear in the United States in private institutions such as the Yale Psychiatric Clinic and the Menninger Clinic. Since 1950 more than 150 programs of this kind have developed throughout the country.

The rationale for the day hospital is that it provides relief for the acute shortage of hospital beds. Frequently patients are discharged from hospitals before they are quite ready because their bed is needed for the more acutely disturbed. The day hospital provides a gradual transition from institutional to community life. In addition, the day hospital has been used for screening patients. By admitting a seriously disturbed patient to the day hospital it becomes possible to observe him over long periods of time and thus to make a better judgment regarding the necessity for 24-hour hospitalization.

In addition to reducing treatment costs because they require fewer personnel and are less expensive, day hospitals have other advantages. Those treated in a day hospital are spared the shock of admission to a mental institution, avoid being stigmatized as mental patients, and are maintained in their home environment making it less likely that they will be abandoned by their family. Furthermore, the patient's family is likely to be included in the treatment program so that he is less likely to become overly dependent on the institution. Finally, day treatment helps to educate the community concerning psychological abnormality and demonstrates that even the seriously disturbed can be treated outside of a 24-hour hospital.

The Night Hospital

Like the day hospital, the night hospital is a part-time hospitalization facility. It serves two types of patients, the first being the patient who has already undergone hospitalization and who may find the step from the hospital to the community too burdensome to take all at once. The night hospital allows him to establish himself in the community while it provides the shelter and many of the treatment programs that supported him in the hospital. For this type of patient the night hospital diminishes the likelihood of a need for a quick readmission. The second type of patient who benefits greatly from the night hospital is the disturbed individual who is still capable of working. Originally the night hospital was designed in the early 1950s in Great Britain (Bierer, 1964) with the expectation that it would reduce the number of lost working days due to mental disorder.

Many night hospitals offer a variety of treatment programs between 6 and 10 or 11 P.M. Beds are also available for an occasional overnight stay. Specific types of treatment services vary from facility to facility.

Foster Home Care

The idea of placing mental patients in the care of foster families originated, as indicated above, many centuries ago in Gheel, Belgium. Over the years it has been adopted in a variety of countries such as Norway, for example, where almost one half of the country's mentally disturbed patients live with foster families. The growth of the family care plan in the United States has been relatively slow. However, many Veterans Administration hospitals are now moving in this direction.

Foster home care is thought to have a variety of potential benefits. First life within a foster family setting is inevitably more like normal living than life on a mental hospital ward. In addition, it is less expensive and requires fewer personnel, the patient is not subjected to the overcrowding that typifies hospital life, and it provides an opportunity for adjustment to the community for patients whose own families are unable or unwilling to accept them. For many patients it also represents a halfway house where their capacity to adjust in the community is tested before they are thrust out entirely on their own.

Home Treatment Services

The prototype for this type of service has existed in Holland for approximately 30 years. It is a service available 24 hours a day to evaluate and treat the mentally disturbed in their own homes. Home treatment was originally created to reduce the demand for hospital beds. The call for help is responded to as soon as possible and visits usually are short. Most treatment involves drug administration and, in Holland, no psychotherapy is administered in home treatment.

In the United States a few home treatment services have been established such as one set up in 1957 in Boston. In the Boston program, supportive psychotherapy as well as drug treatment are fundamental features. A number of patients who would ordinarily have required hospitalization were found to be treatable at home. From this experience, it is estimated that at least one half of those who would ordinarily be hospitalized can be treated in such a program. Another feature of the home service program is that it provides staff with an important training ground in community psychiatry and psychology. Furthermore, through home treatment it is possible to appreciate the significance of the family's role in the patient's illness, and to enlist the family in the overall treatment program.

Aftercare Services

Many hospitals are instituting after care services as a means of lowering the readmission rate. These services include various kinds of follow-up care for the newly discharged mental patient. One approach is to work through the family doctor who is brought into the case as an active member of the treatment team. This is particularly effective when the doctor has had a close relationship with the family before the patient entered the hospital. A second approach to aftercare involves enlisting the cooperation of visiting nurses associations, or the public health nurses in the patient's neighborhood. Through collaboration with the personnel of a hospital or clinic, such nurses can extend the type of care that they offer to include assistance to those with mental disorders. They visit homes on a regular basis, observe the patient's progress, and can consult with clinic or hospital personnel. Continued supervision by the mental health facility is an essential feature of this type of aftercare program.

An aftercare program can involve establishing "satellite" clinics in populous sections of the city. Ideally clinics of this kind are staffed by personnel who have treated the ex-patient in the hospital. Still another approach to aftercare is through an active social work program in which home visits are made by psychiatric social workers affiliated with the institutions in which the patient has been hospitalized. This brings a trained mental health worker into contact with the patient in his home context where impact can be made on the family and the entire environment around him.

Ex-patient Clubs

Clubs for former mental patients began to be formed in New York City in the late 1940s. Many of these clubs have been set up throughout the country since that time to serve a variety of purposes for the ex-mental patient. They attempt to find jobs, to set up foster home placements, to provide educational opportunities and, in addition, to offer a recreational outlet as well as consultation for a variety of problems. For many patients these clubs serve the useful purpose of easing them back into social relationships and community life within the shelter of an understanding, helpful social organization.

Educational and Consultation Programs with Key Community Care Givers

Another service being extended to the community by a variety of mental health centers and hospitals involves consultation with individuals in the community who, by virtue of their professional role, come into contact with many individuals suffering psychological disturbance. Prominent among these are clergymen who are probably more often consulted by people with psychological disturbance than is any other professional group including mental health workers. Other professional groups contacting many individuals with emotional problems are the police, lawyers, and general medical practitioners. A variety of services has been extended to these professional groups, ranging from highly structured course offerings to consultation services with respect to the specific problems dealt with from day to day.

CONCLUSION

A broad spectrum of approaches have been developed in recent years to deal with community forces believed to be significant in the etiology of mental disorders, and to better use community forces in treatment. These approaches range from training new manpower sources to perform highly traditional functions, through using well-intentioned but relatively untrained people to develop beneficial relations with the mentally disturbed, to interceding in the community itself to make it a healthier place for those suffering mental disorders. Many of those community programs are associated with new types of institutions (e.g., the Re-ED school and comprehensive community mental health centers), but some are simply new programs undertaken in long-established settings (e.g., the public schools and mental hospitals). In addition, some programs have few ties to established agencies. Whatever their locus or sponsorship, all of these programs indicate a far more comprehensive conception of what causes mental disorder and what can be done to treat it than has ever been held before.

The programs discussed promise to reshape many traditional institutions as well as to establish new forms of service agencies. In addition they are bringing to the fore a hitherto unheard of type of service worker —the nonprofessional. This development carries with it a train of problems and consequences, many of which are elaborated on in succeeding chapters. One obvious consequence is the important implications that the appearance of nonprofessionals have for the role of the professional. Removed from the front rank of service workers, the professional must become a program organizer, recruiter, trainer, and supervisor of nonprofessionals. The prospects for what can be done through such roles are most exciting, but require that experienced mental health professionals learn ways of functioning very different from what they have been accustomed to, and that training programs for new professionals take into account these new role requirements.

References

Beck, J. C., Kantor, D., & Gelineau, V. A. Follow-up study of chronic psychotic patients "treated" by college case-aid volunteers. *American Journal of Psychiatry*, 1963, *120*, 269–271.

Becker, A., Murphy, N. M., & Greenblatt, M. Recent advances in community psychiatry. *New England Journal of Medicine,* 1965, *272*, 621–626; 674–679.

Bellak, L. The comprehensive community psychiatry program at City Hospital. In L. Bellak (Ed.), *Handbook of community psychiatry and community mental health,* New York: Grune & Stratton, 1964. Pp. 144–165.

Bierer, J. The Marlborough experiment. In L. Bellak (Ed.), *Handbook of community psychiatry and community mental health.* New York: Grune & Stratton, 1964. Pp. 221–247.

Donahue, G. T. A school district program for schizophrenic, organic, and seriously disturbed children. In E. L. Cowen, E. A. Gardner, and M. Zax (Eds.), *Emergent approaches to mental health problems.* New York: Appleton-Century-Crofts, 1967. Pp. 369–386.

Donahue, G. T., & Nichtern, S. *Teaching the troubled child.* New York: Free Press, 1965.

Golann, S. E., Brieter, D. E., & Magoon, T. M. A filmed interview applied to the evaluation of mental health counselors. *Psychotherapy,* 1966, *3*, 21–24.

Greenblatt, M. A role for the voluntary organizations in the work of mental health institutions. In *College student companion program: contribution to the social rehabilitation of the mentally ill.* Hartford, Conn.: Conn. State Department of Mental Health, 1962. Pp. 10–19.

Hobbs, N. Helping disturbed children: psychological and ecological strategies. *American Psychologist,* 1966, *21*, 1105–1115.

Hobbs, N. Reeducation, reality, and community responsibility. In J. W. Carter, Jr. (Ed.), *Research contributions from psychology to community mental health.* New York: Behavioral Publications, Inc., 1968. Pp. 7–18.

Holzberg, J. D., Gewirtz, H., & Ebner, E. Changes in moral judgment and self-acceptance in college students as a function of companionship with hospitalized mental patients. *Journal of Consulting Psychology,* 1964, *28*, 299–303.

Holzberg, J. D., & Knapp, R. H. The social interaction of college students and chronically ill mental patients. *American Journal of Orthopsychiatry,* 1965, *35*, 487–492.

Holzberg, J. D., Knapp, R. H., & Turner, J. L. College students as companions to the mentally ill. In E. L. Cowen, E. A. Gardner, & M. Zax (Eds.), *Emergent approaches to mental health problems.* New York: Appleton-Century-Crofts, 1967. Pp. 91–109.

Holzberg, J. D., Whiting, H. S., & Lowy, D. G. Chronic patients and a college companion program. *Mental Hospitals,* 1964, *15*, 152–158.

Kantor, D. Impact of college students on chronic mental patients and on the organization of the mental hospital. In *College student companion program: contribution to the social rehabilitation of the mentally ill.* Hartford, Conn: Conn. State Department of Mental Health, 1962. Pp. 28–38.

Kantor, D., & Greenblatt, M. Wellmet: halfway to community rehabilitation. *Mental Hospital,* 1962, 146–152.

Klein, W. L., & Zax, M. The use of a hospital volunteer program in the teaching of abnormal psychology. *Journal of Social Psychology,* 1965, *65,* 155–165.

Lewis, W. W. Project Re-ED: educational intervention in discordant child rearing systems. In E. L. Cowen, E. A. Gardner, & M. Zax (Eds.), *Emergent approaches to mental health problems.* New York: Appleton-Century-Crofts, 1967. Pp. 352–368.

Magoon, T. M., & Golann, S. Nontraditionally trained women as mental health counselors/psychotherapists. *Personnel and Guidance Journal,* 1966, *44,* 788–793.

Poser, E. G. The effect of therapist training on group therapeutic outcome. *Journal of Consulting Psychology,* 1966, *30,* 283–289.

Rappaport, J., Chinsky, J. M., & Cowen, E. L. *Innovations in helping chronic patients.* New York: Academic Press, 1971.

Rioch, Margaret J. Pilot projects in training mental health counselors. In E. L. Cowen, E. A. Gardner, & M. Zax (Eds.), *Emergent approaches to mental health problems.* New York: Appleton-Century-Crofts, 1967. Pp. 110–127.

Rioch, Margaret J., Elkes, C., Flint, A. A., Usdansky, B. S., Newman, R. G., & Silber, E. National Institute of Mental Health pilot study in training of mental health counselors. *American Journal of Orthopsychiatry,* 1963, *33,* 678–689.

Umbarger, C. C., Dalsimer, J. S., Morrison, A. P., and Breggin, P. R. *College students in a mental hospital.* New York: Grune and Stratton, 1962.

Weinstein, Laura. Project Re-ED schools for emotionally disturbed children: effectiveness as viewed by referring agencies, parents and teachers. *Exceptional Children,* 1969. *35,* 703–711.

Weinstein Laura, Personal Communication, 1970.

4. *restructuring the hospital community*

Interestingly, mental hospitals, which for many years lagged behind in the development of advanced treatment approaches, were the site of some of the earliest patient-care programs emphasizing community forces. The humanitarian reformers of the late 18th and early 19th centuries, men like Phillipe Pinel and William Tuke attempted to benefit patients by making fundamental changes in the hospital environment. They removed physical restraints and introduced freedoms that made hospital life more like life outside. In addition, they encouraged kindness and understanding on the part of hospital personnel, attitudes that they believed would be therapeutic.

Hospital reforms were widely adopted, particularly in the United States during the first half of the 19th century where an approach known as *moral treatment* (Bockoven, 1956; 1957) prevailed. Bockoven points out that the term moral treatment was intended to convey both the idea that the insane must be treated in accordance with their moral rights as individuals and that treatment revealed to the patient the moral of his life story as it related to other individuals. In actual practice, moral treatment was by no means a highly prescribed procedure characterized by a single technique. Still, it had a definable goal—"arousing the dormant faculties of the mind." It stressed using every minute of the day therapeutically to awaken feelings of companionship in the patient. This end was sought through a communal life between patients and hospital personnel. Every effort was made to engage the patient in activities such as work, recreation, and religious worship that took him outside of himself and prompted cooperation with others.

Attention was paid to the small details of hospital life, and serious attempts were made to provide meaningful activities for the patients. Each patient had a private room, and each ward had sitting rooms and dining rooms. There were game rooms and shops equipped with tools. Church services were held regularly, and evening lectures were given on a variety of topics. Patients were provided with a variety of recreational opportunities such as the use of horses and carriages, hunting and fishing, gardening, and assisting in farmwork. The hospital administrator assumed that a patient's mental health would be best served by the variety of experiences that was important in preserving his own mental health. In a very real sense, the physician regarded the patient as a member of his own family and, in fact, in annual reports to the state the patients were referred to as "our family."

A careful review by Bockoven (1956) of the outcome data reported by mental hospitals practicing moral treatment, leads him to conclude that it was a singularly successful approach. At least 66 percent, and in some instances as many as 90 percent, of the patients treated were judged to be fully recovered or improved. Paradoxically, though, despite these impressive statistics, moral treatment virtually disappeared from the scene by the middle of the 19th century to be followed by "the void of custodial care."

Rosenhan (1973) has recently reported a fascinating study of modern mental hospitals in which eight experimenters (four of whom were mental health professionals) gained admission to 12 different mental hospitals by feigning psychotic symptoms, but once admitted behaved in their usual "normal" fashion. While in the hospital these "pseudopatients" took extensive notes on their experiences, resulting in an absorbing commentary on life in such institutions. Despite their asymptomatic, sane behavior, the pseudopatients were hospitalized an average of 19 days each (range from 7 to 52 days). Interestingly, during the first three hospitalizations, when a count was kept, 35 out of 118 *patients* on admissions wards detected that the pseudopatients were sane and expressed suspicion concerning their presence on the ward. Despite their apparently normal behavior, on discharge all but one pseudopatient was diagnosed as being a schizophrenic in remission.

One reason for staff failure to recognize the pseudopatients' sanity seemed to be that the staff had extraordinarily little contact with patients. Attendents spent an average of only 11.3 percent of their time outside of the ward staff station; daytime nurses emerged from the staff station only 11.5 times per shift (including times when they left the ward entirely) ; and physicians appeared on the ward an average of only 6.7 times per day. Staff appearances on the ward were primarily for caretaking—administering medication, conducting a group meeting, or instructing or reprimanding a patient. Direct questions or requests of staff by pseudopatients generally drew brief responses, while the staff member was "on the move," or no response at all.

Many examples are given of hospital practices and encounters with staff that prompt a sense of depersonalization and powerlessness in the patient. Included among these is the fact that the eight pseudopatients were administered nearly 2100 pills (representing several different drugs) , while only actually swallowing two of them. The remainder were pocketed or flushed in the toilet where the medications of other patients were often found. Occasional instances of unprovoked harsh or even brutal behavior on the part of staff also contributed to a feeling of powerlessness and depersonalization. At times, that feeling took on such proportions as to make the patient feel so trivial as to be invisible. Having to submit to physical examination in a semipublic room with staff coming and going is one example of an incident prompting such an extreme in feeling.

The experiences of Rosenhan and his fellow experimenters reflect the swing taken by the modern mental hospital away from the spirit of the moral treatment institution. This study documents the degree to which the average mental hospital has become an impersonal, custodial institution, despite the fact that Rosenhan can say of the staff, "our overwhelming impression of them was of people who really cared, who were committed and who were uncommonly intelligent."

Several factors probably account for the decline of moral treatment, not least of which is the fact that many of the inspired leaders of the movement passed on with no one to replace them. The successful practitioners of moral treatment trained very few disciples who could carry on their work. Another significant factor was the infusion into American psychiatry of the dominant European theory of the day that mental disorder was physiologically based. Insanity was regarded as a brain disease, usually degenerative. This viewpoint was encouraged by experience with large numbers of paretic patients, and Darwin's work suggested that mental illness was one of nature's ways of eliminating the unfit from the human species. In essence, the mentally ill were viewed as lacking the attributes that typify a human being.

As this viewpoint took hold, hospital statistics were reexamined and reports of improvement and cures were questioned. Bockoven has detailed these efforts and has pointed out obvious weaknesses in the reasoning of those disputing the worth of moral treatment. Nonetheless, such criticisms were accepted in their time, and gradually hospitals grew in size with less and less money being devoted to patient care and fewer and fewer physicians choosing to work in these custodial settings. The mental patient was no longer regarded as a member of his physician's family. Instead, he was an inmate of a "prison-asylum." Institutional life was reduced to a meaningless empty routine. Maintaining the patient's life became the main purpose of the institution because neither the laws nor medical ethics permitted ending it. Within the hospital the patient retained only the right to live. It took nearly a hundred years before widespread efforts were made to revive moral treatment approaches.

THE THERAPEUTIC COMMUNITY

An early example of a return to a program akin to moral treatment was described in 1930 by Harry Stack Sullivan, who attempted to create an optimal treatment environment for the acute schizophrenic (Sullivan, 1931). He set up a six-bed ward detached from all hospital services except those devoted to occupational rehabilitation and recreation. In particular, the traditional nursing service was eliminated. Sullivan stressed that the mental hospital must become "a school for personality growth, rather than a custodian of personality failures," and held strongly that the schizophrenic's growth could only be facilitated by people who are extremely sensitive to his interpersonal needs and fears. Traditionally trained doctors and nurses, he believed, have their interpersonal sensitivities blunted by their training. Sullivan, therefore, used as his primary treatment agents attendents who displayed a deep intuitive grasp of what schizophrenic experience was like, possibly because they themselves had some potential for becoming schizophrenic. These therapeutic agents were seen as "assisting in the growth by experience of a body of *relatively undeveloped* tendencies to interpersonal relations; the situation is one of education, broadly conceived, not by verbal teaching but by communal experience—good tutoring."

A more recent and better known innovative hospital program than Sullivan's was initiated just after World War II by Maxwell Jones (1953). Jones embarked on a new venture in hospital treatment, called the "therapeutic community," with the conviction that, in adopting the principles

and practices of general medicine, traditional mental hospitals were failing to meet the needs of psychiatric patients. In his own words:

*"Psychiatry has, in my opinion, paid far too much attention to the
model created by general medicine. This is inevitable so long as doctors,
nurses, and other professionals associated with psychiatry take their undergraduate training in general hospitals, whose social organization is
geared more to the needs of surgery than of psychiatry. The omnipotence
of the medical leader, the absence of two-way communication, and the
rigidly-defined status differentiation, which often excludes the patient as
a person, are only a few of the extreme characteristics of this setting."
(Jones, 1968, p. 126).*

For Jones, as for Sullivan before him, the most significant force in treating and preventing mental illness is the social environment, and it is precisely that force on which traditional hospital structures fail to capitalize.
Therefore, Jones set out to create an environment within which all of the
patients' hospital time would be therapeutic. In line with these goals, the
hospital was regarded as a microcosm of the larger community around it.

Jones' innovative program had as its immediate forebear the "Northfield Experiment." In 1943, two English physicians, Bion and Rickman,
were sent to the Northfield Military Hospital to restore order in one section of the institution after conditions there had become "unruly"
(Kraüpl-Taylor, 1958). They went about their task by imposing on the
patients, who chafed at Army discipline and wished only to return to ci-
vilian life, the responsibility for managing their own community life. The
doctors in charge of the hospital relinquished their traditional authority
and let the men know that their choice was between living in a chaotical-
ly unstructured community or organizing it themselves into a structure
with which they could be comfortable. This practice removed the Army
as a convenient scapegoat when things went wrong.

The administrative innovations of Bion and Rickman were eventually
extended to the entire Northfield Hospital. This example stimulated the
development in England of a variety of group approaches to behavioral
problems.

Jones' first therapeutic community was directed not toward psychotics
but toward chronic neurotics and character disorders who suffered extremely poor social and occupational adjustments. These included psy-
chopaths, schizoid personalities, drug addicts, and sexual perverts, all
sufferers of disorders that have been notoriously difficult to treat. Jones'
early patients were hard-core unemployed individuals and, therefore, his
program was supported by the British Ministry of Health, Labor, and
Pension. The project had five distinct aims: (1) to study the clinical
characteristics of the patient group; (2) to render appropriate psychiatric

care; (3) to find what job would be best for each patient; (4) to pave the way for the patient's to return to the community; and (5) to followup patients to evaluate long-range program effects.

A basic feature in the therapeutic community is the assignment of each patient to a job that he is expected to perform faithfully. In the selection of employment, primary emphasis is placed on semiskilled jobs, which are plentiful in the community surrounding the hospital, instead of on training patients for high-level trades. Also patients are not permitted to make things for themselves but, rather, are expected to produce things that will be of social value.

Another basic element of the therapeutic community is a daily one-hour morning meeting for all patients and as many staff as can attend. In Jones' early program the content of this meeting varied with the day of the week. On Mondays a "gripe" session was held where patients might make constructive suggestions regarding the program. The Tuesday meeting was typically a didactic one in which films on job training, social problems, and rehabilitation were viewed. Wednesday and Thursday meetings were staff-led discussions of sociological problems deemed to be of current interest to the patient groups, for example, "should married partners work?" or "should husband and wife spend leisure time together?" Such discussions were intended to stimulate and encourage patients' interest in important life issues. To further this end, role playing and psychodrama were utilized whenever they seemed appropriate for dramatizing an issue. Friday mornings were devoted to psychodrama sessions in which a problem or situation from the past life of a particular patient was depicted. The patients themselves volunteered the content of such sessions, wrote a play to depict the content, and chose a cast to dramatize it. Half hour presentations were attended by all patients, staff, and visitors to the hospital, followed by a physician-directed discussion of the production. A description of a group meeting (see Figure 1) following the theft of some money well characterizes these meetings.

For this meeting it was decided again to use a projection technique. It was felt that the difficulty in confessing should be highlighted as otherwise we could only treat the individual concerned indirectly as an unknown member of the community.

A family scene was enacted with the psychiatrist as the son, the Unit Sister as the mother, and two nurses as the sisters. The mother suggested that as it was a holiday they should go for a picnic, but the son would have to be left behind as he was not well enough for such an outing. The son did not object and the mother praised him excessively and stressed how he was always such a good boy. When the others had gone the son sat reading for a while and then, on looking up, noticed his mother's purse and helped himself to half-a-crown. Then the family returned tired but pleased after a successful trip. The mother needed some money, took her purse and noticed with surprise that half-a-crown was missing. She asked the girls if they knew anything about it but they did not; however, they told the mother that their brother had remarked recently that he needed some money. The son immediately denied having opened his mother's purse. The psychiatrist now turned to the audience and asked for comments. It was suggested that the son was resentful because the family left him alone; also that the sisters were trying to exclude him from the family group and would be glad to incriminate him in the theft, etc. Eventually, Mr. M. suggested that the son (played by the psychiatrist) should confess. He went to the family to confess, but in fact he did not. This provoked consideration of the difficulty in any confession and the audience seemed to warm up. Someone suggested that the mother was a difficult person who by forcing a "good" role on her son made it difficult for him to confess. Some patients felt that it would be best to confess, but others disagreed. Mr. M. suggested that the son should put the money back without anybody knowing. This was then acted out and it was demonstrated that the sisters' suspicion persisted and the family still quarrelled. The audience again discussed why it was difficult to confess. The son was advised to try and make the mother's attitude towards him more realistic. This was acted out, the son telling her that he was not so good as she thought, and pointing out that her attitude made everyone expect too much of him and also annoyed his sisters. The son then appeared to be on the verge of confessing when he broke off and turned to the audience. The latter was by now participating freely at a feeling level and urged the son to confess: this seemed to be clearly the feeling of the community as a whole. The son now returned to the family and confessed; and the family's reactions were demonstrated and discussed. Some patients pointed out that until the thief confessed suspicion would tend to fall on the innocent. These patients came from the ward which was associated with the recent thefts. The psychiatrist (who had played the role of the son) now summed up and pointed out that the thief in our midst had been asked to play the difficult role of the confessor; nevertheless it seemed to be the only constructive thing for him to do and the only way in which the "family" tension could be eased. He pointed out that the confession had been made more difficult because the son had been looked on as the "good boy." Mr. M. pointed out the difficulty of confession for those who were "bad boys" and were expected to do wrong.

At the 9:45 A. M. meeting of the staff everyone felt that the audience had wanted the thief to confess, but it was also clear that a public confession of this kind would be extremely difficult for the person concerned; also that secrecy would be difficult to obtain or maintain. The psychiatrist felt that he had achieved his objective in obtaining the patients' participation and their expressed need to have a confession in order to relieve the family tension. At this point he thought it might be better on future occasions to let a patient, or several patients, playing the part of the son, do the confessing. Such acting out might have established a pattern of behavior and made it easier for the real thief to confess. Moreover, he thought that the family should have received the confession with relief and brought out some underlying motives for the theft so that the idea of understanding and "treatment" rather than punishment was stressed. This had not been done because the family scene had only been roughly sketched with the staff before the 9 A. M. meeting and there had been no actual rehearsal or elaboration of a definite goal.

One therapeutic group discussed the 9 A. M. meeting spontaneously. They felt sorry for the boy who was left behind when the family went to the seaside. The whole group tended to reproach the family for the son's theft. One patient felt that the son had stolen in order to get more attention from his family. Nurse asked if the same explanation might apply to the individual who had stolen the Unit's funds. This was discussed at length and it was felt that the culprit might feel that the community here was too permissive and nice, and had wanted to disturb it or to attract attention to himself.

Another group also raised the topic of the 9 A. M. meeting spontaneously, and said that they had developed a good understanding of the reasons for confession but found it difficult to picture themselves actually doing this if they were personally involved.

Two groups declined to discuss the 9 A. M. meeting.

Figure 1. A Group Meeting in the Therapeutic Community (Jones, 1953, p. 172).

In addition to group meetings and work activities, the patient in the therapeutic community has a few free hours each day with the option of leaving the hospital if he is well enough to do so. Finally, from 7 to 9 P.M. each day, organized social programs are arranged by a patient committee. These include concerts, dances, dancing classes, art classes, and play reading groups.

Staff roles in the therapeutic community are different from those in the typical mental hospital. The largest staff group carries the title of nurse, but only a few have had traditional nurse's training. The small group of trained nurses is responsible for caring for the physically ill. The remainder are typically young girls with social science degrees or girls planning social work careers. In Jones' program many were Scandinavians. Their foreign origin seemed to make them more approachable for patients who commonly considered themselves as outsiders.

The new nurse is placed on the ward without receiving any special training and is expected to have three major roles. First, she is an authority who mediates quarrels between patients, and reports moderately severe patient infractions. Her second, and perhaps most important role is a social one. She is expected to become acquainted with each patient and to spend time with them according to their individual needs. In so doing, she is required to guard against using relationships to satisfy personal needs by spending time with those she likes rather than with those who need her most. Finally, the nurse has a therapeutic role requiring her to "interpret or transmit the unit culture to the patient" rather than becoming involved in a one-to-one relationship. The more she absorbs and accepts the culture, the better she is at stimulating patients to take part in the social, occupational, and special activities of the community.

The doctor in Jones' therapeutic community consciously dissociates himself from the role of remote magician thrust on him by society. He accomplishes this partly by avoiding many of the trappings of the medical doctor in the typical hospital—the white coat, the stethoscope and percussion hammer protruding from pockets. The doctor's role in the therapeutic community has five components. First, like all other staff he has a social role that he fulfills by participating in social situations. Second, he supports and encourages patients who are making social or occupational progress. Third, he participates in daily discussion groups where he serves as an example of one who can face and accept the anger of others without losing his own control or having to retaliate. Fourth, he encourages patients to deal actively with their own problems and sometimes uses psychodrama to allow them to try out active roles. Finally, the doctor interprets for patients the significance of and reasons for many of their feelings and behaviors.

In the therapeutic community the physician is also a disciplinarian. In this role he attempts to convey the importance of the rules of the culture and, together with the patient, he tries to understand why infractions have been committed. When rule breaking persists despite these efforts, discharge from the community is considered. The doctor takes such action only after considerable discussion with others involved with the patient, and invariably such discharges serve as the topic for one of the daily discussion groups.

Doctor-nurse relationship in the therapeutic community are much more informal than they are in the typical hospital. The staff eat together regularly and generally doctors are on a first name basis with nurses, although the title "Doctor" is retained particularly in the presence of outsiders. Staff meetings are continually devoted to a review of doctor-nurse relations and, at times, arouse considerable tension.

Jones (1968) has stressed that the leader's role in a therapeutic community is "to make optimal use of the potentials of all patients and staff." Therefore, decision making is, insofar as possible, the joint venture of all who are involved. To facilitate decision making by consensus, communication at all levels of the therapeutic community is made as efficient as possible. Jones believes that the most important attribute of the leader in the social community is a capacity to preserve the totality of the organization while encouraging flexibility, self-examination, social learning, and change within its members. When things are going well, therefore, he can be relatively uninvolved. Thus the phrase that best describes the leader's role in the therapeutic community is "leading from behind."

An evaluation was done, six months after discharge, of the social adjustment of 104 of the patients in Jones' original therapeutic community. Overall adjustment was measured by combining 11 indexes based on information and impressions deriving from six-month, follow-up interviews of 82 discharged patients. Impressionistic measures, judgments of the patient's health, value on the labor market, social adjustment, and standard of living, were quantified through rating scales. Other criteria, such as number of days worked in the past six months, wages earned at time of visit, average length of job and salary in the past six months, were already quantified. Weights for each measure were computed based on the degree to which each related to a general adjustment factor consisting of all 11 measures combined. It was found that 44 percent had adjusted satisfactorily and that 22 percent were making a fair adjustment. The remainder, 34 percent, were adjusting poorly. Considering that the patients in this experiment had been chronically maladjusted through much of their lives, these results are encouraging. Another measure of the success of Jones' experimental program is the number of new hospital programs that is stimulated (Fairweather, 1964; Fairweather, Sanders, Cressler, and Maynard, 1969; Greenblatt, York, and Brown, 1955; Sanders, 1967; Sanders, Smith, and Weinman, 1967) .

THE MASSACHUSETTS MENTAL HEALTH CENTER PROGRAM

An innovative hospital program, similar both to the old hospital of the moral treatment era and to the therapeutic community of Maxwell Jones, was described in the 1950s by Greenblatt, York, and Brown (1955) . This report details a series of changes, involving virtually every aspect of hospital procedure, that was introduced over a period of years in the Massachusetts Mental Health Center (MMHC), formerly the Boston Psychopathic Hospital, an institution for the treatment of acute mental disturbance.

Traditional admissions procedures at MMHC as well as many other hospitals were characterized by having the patient come to an old office at the rear of the hospital, where he was received in a bare, undecorated room by an admissions officer who asked a series of abrupt, impersonal questions. From there patients, sometimes manacled, were taken to a seclusion section of the ward through back stairs. Typically they were forced to bathe, their clothing was removed, and they were deprived of such personal articles as eyeglasses, dentures, money, and jewelry. Small wonder that new patients, already disturbed, developed an additional set of fears stimulated by the institution itself. Therefore, the new program restructured the admissions procedure to make it more tolerable. Admissions office furnishings were made more attractive, admitting personnel were instructed to take more time with the admissions procedure, female attendants or nurses were assigned to take the patient to the ward with a male attendant in the background. Once on the ward, the patient was asked if he wanted to take a bath. He was allowed to keep his own clothing and personal possessions, and he was shown around his new surroundings and instructed in the use of available facilities.

Within the hospital itself a number of procedures that presumably had been instituted as security measures underwent serious scrutiny. For example, seclusion rooms at the back of the ward, a commonplace at the time the program was set up, were often occupied by unclothed, hostile, or withdrawn patients, living in their own excrement. Most patients resisted being put in seclusion so that they were often overpowered physically and dragged, kicking and screaming, through the wards, an unnerving procedure for personnel and other patients. In the new hospital program a concerted effort was made to reduce the use of seclusion rooms as well as lesser forms of restraint. This was successfully achieved through several means. First, hospital administrators asserted that the practice of secluding patients could be diminished, and they encouraged ward personnel to do so. It was pointed out that many disturbances displayed by patients were prompted by the procedures used to manage them rather than by their mental disorder and that many other institutions had successfully eliminated the use of seclusion and other restraints. A second factor contributing to the reduction of restraints was the bringing of ward attendants into the treatment program. Staff-professional-led group sessions were held for attendants in which fears and frustrations about the job could be expressed, and the attitude that the attendant must be a participant in the planning of patient care was conveyed. These meetings helped attendants realize that they were essential cogs in the treatment procedure, and their former disinterested, routine approach to patient care was replaced by a genuine interest in engaging patients in various activities. The third factor that helped eliminate restraint as a method of dealing with disturbed patients was that every effort was made, once the patient was released, to interest him in some sort of diversionary activity. Ordinarily the ambivalent patient released from restraint feels that he has reentered the hospital with a reputation as a troublemaker. If left to flounder in surroundings he feels to be unfamiliar or threatening, his behavior quickly deteriorates again. Therefore, structured activities such as games, sports, occupational therapy or work programs were developed.

Once it was demonstrated that the problem of security was not nearly so significant as it had been thought earlier, interest shifted toward improving patients' appearances. It was obviously desirable for patients to dress in other than the bathrobes, slippers, and heterogeneous apparel ordinarily provided for them. Efforts were, therefore, made to obtain more suitable clothing, initially through gifts from the staff and friends and, eventually, from a variety of unsolicited sources such as the families of patients themselves. Having better clothing, patients began to show pride in their appearance, were careful about the way they dressed, and cared for their clothing. Such behavior signified to personnel that patients retained their self-respect and prompted still further staff efforts to change hospital routine so as to encourage further patient growth.

The pride exhibited by patients in things that they valued prompted staff interest in making the physical environment more attractive. With the help of contributions from relatives and interested friends of the hospital, draperies and pictures were hung, new furniture was installed, and the typically dull ward environment was brightened considerably. Walls were painted in attractive colors and, in some cases, talented patients decorated them with murals.

To combat the debilitating desocialization process typically occurring on the hospital ward, strenuous efforts were made to promote social behavior among patients in the MMHC program. Recreation equipment to promote socialization was provided. Playing cards and games that might ordinarily be found in a home were excellent vehicles for bringing patients together. The introduction to the ward of a radio and later a phonograph and piano also promoted socialization. Patients selected their own programs, and formed groups to discuss programs of special interest. Another revolutionary move involved bringing men and women patients together for various activities. The practice was at first resisted by personnel who feared that it would prompt the release of aggressive sexual responses. The result of this practice, however, was an improvement in patient behavior. Men became more conscious of their dress and grooming, and women took pride in their personal appearance. The introduction of a variety of evening activities such as parties, outings, sports events, movies, lectures, and concerts was still another innovation. Mealtime routines were altered to resemble those practiced in most families. Patients helped serve food and clean up afterward and eventually took over this chore altogether. Meals were leisurely and social. Smoking was encouraged. Efficient handling of mealtimes became less important to staff than making them enjoyable social events.

Another important feature of the MMHC program was patient government. This aspect of the program grew out of a survey among patients concerning hospital living conditions that uncovered many strong negative feelings and numerous suggestions for change. Several of these suggestions were discussed with hospital administrators, who took steps to make appropriate changes. Eventually, the patients on one ward held meetings concerned with the improvement of living conditions, and this activity came to be known as patient government. The nurse on this ward became the representative of the hospital administration to the patient government. Ultimately the patient government took over housekeeping functions and the organization of dormitory living. Six months after this procedure was instituted on one ward, it was adopted on another because of the favorable patient reaction to the improvements resulting from it. As patient government spread through the hospital, nurses, occupational therapists, social workers, and psychologists became regular visitors to meetings. To insure continuing patient government leadership in spite of a high discharge rate, a number of major offices and several committees were set up, making a large number of patients responsible for the ongoing work.

Since most self-governing bodies raise and spend money, the patient government was allowed to solicit funds from friends and relatives, make collections at annual dances, and use the profits from the candy and cigarette machines around the hospital, thus acquiring a substantial amount of money. Hospital administrators were satisfied, after some observations, that this money was used wisely.

It became a common practice for patient government to inform the assistant superintendent by letter after each meeting of the requests and points that had been made during the meeting. A point-by-point response was always made within a week. In this way the patients could see the concrete effects of their deliberations and requests. Many felt that the most significant effect of patient government was that patients found that they were held in genuine esteem as people capable of functioning democratically toward reasonable ends.

In addition to encouraging patient growth, efforts were made to maximize the therapeutic potential of personnel. Procedural rules were downgraded and the use of "intuition, imagination, initiative, judgment" was encouraged. The attitude was stressed that change should be accepted as a possibility in all cases if it came about through discussion and argument. All personnel on the hospital hierarchy, low or high, were encouraged to use creative imagination. Since attendants represented the largest single staff group, they received special attention. Weekly meetings were held with ward attendants some of which were attended by the hospital administrators. Initially the meetings were didactic in nature; however, they also provided an opportunity for attendants to discuss problems they were having on the ward. Eventually these discussions became the major ward meeting activity. Attendants learned a great deal and grew emotionally as a result of having the opportunity to discuss feelings about their job.

The second largest group of hospital ward personnel were student nurses. To help nursing affiliates develop a better understanding of their own motivations and those of patients, therapy groups were set up. One specific problem frequently discussed in these groups was the nursing affiliate's tendency to play favorites among patients. In the general hospital where the nurse's role is highly structured, she can relatively easily attend equally to all patients. In the mental hospital, however, the nurse is encouraged to interact spontaneously with patients and, in so doing, she comes naturally to prefer some over others. Such issues as why certain patients are favored and why others seem to repel personnel were discussed in these therapy groups. In many instances, it was found that superficial antipathies toward some patients could be strongly influenced by the group therapeutic process. Another issue explored in the group therapy sessions related to the optimal role of the psychiatric nurse. Typically, the student nurse is taught to obey superiors unquestioningly, to be seen rather than heard, and to carry out technical procedures quickly and efficiently. In the restructured psychiatric hospital, spontaneity, freshness, and enthusiasm are valued more than rigid obedience. The therapy group, therefore, helped the nursing student change the way she had been taught to function in a general hospital to an approach that was seen to be more suitable in a psychiatric hospital.

Concerted efforts were also made to make the head nurse on the typical ward a more integral part of the treatment team. In her traditional role, the nurse was responsible for carrying out the physician's orders. Since these frequently involved restrictive measures, she came to be viewed by patients as a punishing authority. As restrictive practices were eliminated, the nurse was able to play a more significant role in thinking and planning ward activities that brought her closer to patients. Thus she could help improve ward furnishings, organize crews for beautifying the immediate surroundings, find clothing for patients, and so on. Such roles as well as the more active part that she could take in planning recreational and occupational programs caused the head nurse to consider herself as being more responsible for ward morale than ever before. This inevitably brought her into closer contact with patients and with physicians who came to be looked on more as colleagues than ever before. In addition, weekly "classes" were set up for head nurses led by the director of nursing. These offered a channel for communicating about all matters related to the nursing service, for discussing administrative issues, and for griping about frustrations.

Because the entering patient's anxiety is provoked in large measure by the hospital's reputation in its community, and because the support received by the hospital is also, to some extent, determined by that reputation, efforts were made to better inform the community about the Massachusetts Mental Health Center. One direct way of acquainting the community with the hospital was through the friends of hospital employees. Unfortunately, for many years most attendants, nurses, and residents lived in the MMHC. This limited their community contacts and isolated them from the community. Therefore, personnel were encouraged to live in the community as most workers do. Furthermore, they were encouraged to invite friends to visit the hospital and to learn about treatment first hand. This open door policy attracted many community groups to the hospital. Requests came from schools, colleges, churches, parent-teachers associations, and clubs of various kinds. At first, visitors' tours were conducted by staff members, but later patients took over this role.

As another means of educating the public about the hospital, staff members participated in panel discussions about mental illness and its treatment. Another means of growing closer was the development of a volunteer auxiliary group including people representing schools, colleges, organizations such as the Junior League, social agencies, and even former hospital patients. These volunteers were placed in various hospital departments to participate in treatment programs. Relatives of hospitalized patients were invited to group meetings to ventilate feelings and to learn more about the hospital and its programs. Finally, a study was made of patient interactions with visiting relatives. As a result, it was recommended that personnel should take time to show new visitors around the ward. Furthermore, personnel were encouraged to monitor visitor-patient interactions and to obviate difficulties that seemed to be arising. Fundamentally, the position taken was that the visitor plays a central role in the patient's treatment and must neither be ignored nor kept away.

The effects of the MMHC program are reflected in a number of different measures. One fundamental index is discharge rate. A review of hospital records indicate that during the 1920s and 1930s newly admitted psychotic patients tended to stay in the hospital from about 10 to 20 days with about 35 percent being discharged to the community. The remainder were transferred to state hospitals for further hospitalization. With the institution of the program described above, more intensive treatment was offered, and the length of stay in the hospital increased to an average of 80 to 90 days. The discharge rate of newly committed psychotic patients, however, rose to between 80 to 85 percent during the 1950s. In addition, it was noted that patients were better behaved in the hospital than they had been in the past. In fact, the mutinous, repetitive behavior that characterized the catatonic schizophrenic and that is thought to be a response to a threatening environment virtually disappeared.

Another significant program effect was a change from the pessimistic attitude of hospital personnel concerning patients' futures to one of optimism and a willingness to trust patients to try their wings in the community. The therapeutic forces in the patient's home environment were considered much more seriously than ever before. Outpatient facilities were increased, and contact was maintained with discharged patients. Flexible treatment plans involving a day or night hospital (see Chapter 4) were adopted. Work programs were developed within the hospital to prepare patients to become wage earners when they were discharged.

To gauge the long-term effects of the MMHC treatment program, 100 patients committed after June 30, 1946 were followed for five years. It was found that after treatment 70 were discharged to the community, 29 were transferred to other mental hospitals, and one died. The average hospital stay was 75 days. At the end of the first year 72 of the original 100 were living in the community and 20 were hospitalized. Four had moved and were lost to the study, and four had died. At the end of the second year 76 were living in the community, a figure that remained stable for the remaining three study years. Overall, 45 of the original group were never readmitted to a hospital during a five-year period. Although the entire group of 100 spent an average of 18 percent of their time in a hospital during the five-year period, most of this time was accumulated by a small group of 10 or 12 patients. These had relatively few remissions, showing only brief periods of improvement.

To assess the quality of the patient's community adjustment, 106 patients were studied three years after their hospital commitment. Interviews with the patient and his family probed their degree of satisfaction with the patient's work adjustment, family life, and community activity. Both the patients and their families generally agreed that the occupational adjustment of the ex-patient was satisfactory. Eighty percent of the patients were working, most at full-time jobs, and 74 percent were self-sustaining, or nearly so. Despite satisfaction at the patient's being employed, some dissatisfaction was expressed concerning his financial status, probably because debts incurred during hospitalization put a strain on the patient's financial situation. Overall family adjustment was considered to be barely adequate, however, and community adjustment was regarded as almost unsatisfactory. Such findings have begun to shape the more recent forms of the hospital program. For example, length of hospitalization is kept to a minimum to reduce financial burdens on the patient and his family, family problems are studied intensively by staff professionals working with the patient, and efforts are being made to improve the patient's community relationships.

SOCIO-ENVIRONMENTAL TREATMENT

Sanders' program (Sanders, 1967; Sanders, Smith, and Weinman, 1967) (established in a mental hospital that had long been regarded as a dumping ground for the mentally ill) is an innovative hospital program based on "socio-environmental" treatment and also includes a study of the differential effects of programs varying in degree of structure. The purpose of all program elements is to encourage social interaction between patients. The term "structure" refers to the extent to which a given patient's program forces him into interaction with fellow patients and others. The socio-environmental treatment program has three major components: the social living situation, the interaction activity program, and various group experiences.

The Social Living Situation

To establish a social living situation, patients are moved out of large dormitory buildings into smaller ones having private rooms. Game rooms and living rooms are provided, and each patient has a key to his own room and is responsible for its daily care. Meals are served "family style" in a dining hall maintained and operated, at least, in part, by the patients themselves.

Formal meetings are held with staff to instill the attitude that the chronic patient is capable of being rehabilitated through social interaction, and staff members are encouraged to help patients assume responsibility for their own social community. To further stimulate patient social life, organizations such as a model railroad club and a personal grooming club have been established. Another organization called the Alumni Club has been set up for patients preparing to leave the hospital or for those who have already left. The treatment goal for all patients is placement outside of the hospital. All patients understand that they will live in the therapeutic community no more than 12 months, and that all program activities are preparing them for living outside the hospital. As adjustment to unit life progresses and the patient demonstrates that he can care for his own room, is able to look after his personal grooming, can participate in assigned activities, and can manage a regular work assignment, he is granted regular visits to the city. With this privilege comes the responsibility for learning how to travel on one's own and to become acquainted with community resources. Furthermore, he is encouraged to contact community agencies that might help maintain him in the community after discharge.

The Interaction Activity Program

The interaction activity program involves small, relatively permanent groups that meet approximately one half of each day in relaxing interpersonal situations such as enjoying music and engaging in recreation, as well as in complex social situations in which specific skills are taught. Among these skills are the fundamental techniques for meeting and interacting informally with others, etiquette, and social dancing. Many aspects of unit life such as social events, cooperative living, and family-style dining are used as opportunities to practice the skills patients are learning in the activity program. The activity program also prepares patients for living outside the hospital through discussions, and trips into the community. Instruction is offered in such fundamentals as personal grooming, preparing food, community facilities and resources, and how to use the want ads of the newspaper or the resources of employment agencies.

The interaction activity program is conducted by a group leader called a "social therapist," a role filled by staff members from various services in the hospital. Social therapists are trained to use group psychological pressures and support to ameliorate interpersonal problems, to teach patients to adapt better to one another, and to prepare the patient for leaving the hospital.

Group Experiences

Two group experiences, group therapy and patient government, are utilized to "broaden and intensify the resocialization process." Group therapy is seen to augment the interaction program while patient government enriches the social living situation. In group therapy, patients ventilate feelings, discuss attitudes, and reflect on current interpersonal experiences. Adaptive behavior is encouraged and the reasons for maladaptive behavior are discussed. Patient government gives patients the responsibility for managing their own living unit. Officers and a council are elected, regular problem-solving meetings are held, and through this vehicle the daily routine of the living unit is managed. Frequent elections are held in which election rules permit virtually all patients to serve in leadership roles.

Research Design and Evaluation

Not all patients participate in all aspects of the program as described. Because Sanders and his colleagues were interested in determining the degree of social interaction resulting in the greatest therapeutic benefit, three different types of "structure" were utilized and compared in a later study of treatment outcome. The various treatment conditions are depicted in Table 1.

This table shows that program content which forces on the patient different kinds of social interaction increases from the minimally to maximally structured treatment condition. All groups have individual work assignments, cottage meetings, and conferences with unit administrators. In addition, the partially structured and the maximally structured groups participate in the interaction programs with group therapy provided only for the maximally structured group, which also participates in patient government.

Only chronic patients with some potential for leaving the hospital within 12 months were selected for the program, while the severely regressed or physically incapacitated were screened out. The males in the program ranged in age from 19 to 72 years (median age was 45). Eighty-two percent of these patients were diagnosed as schizophrenic and had been hospitalized from one to 36 years (median of 8.6 years). Seventy-one percent of this group had never married, 61 percent had failed to complete high school, and most had worked at unskilled jobs such as dishwasher, laborer, hospital orderly, or factory worker. Female patients in the pro-

Table 1.　Treatment Units, Living Situation, and Content of Therapy Program Associated with Each Treatment Condition (from Sanders, et al., 1967)

Treatment Condition	Male Units	Female Units	Living Situation	Content of Therapy Program
Maximally structured	A	E	Therapeutic community with patient government	Group therapy Interaction program Individual work assignment Cottage meeting Conference with unit administration
Partially structured	B	F	Therapeutic community	Interaction program Individual work assignment Cottage meeting Conference with unit administration
Minimally structured	C	G	Therapeutic community	Individual work assignment Cottage meeting Conference with unit administration
Control	(D)	(H)	Regular ward environment	Regular ward program[a]

[a] May include work assignment, occupational therapy, group recreation, etc.

gram were similar to the males in most characteristics except that only 36 percent had never married and their median length of hospitalization was seven years.

Both long- and short-term criteria were used to evaluate "socio-environmental" treatment effects. Short-term effects, determined immediately after a patient had concluded the program, were assessed by global social behavior, awareness of others, verbal interaction, and spontaneous social behavior.

Global social behavior refers to the degree to which a patient interacts socially. Observations were made in the patient's living situation, work situation, special social activities, and in his contact with hospital staff. Behavior was rated on a scale anchored at five points by descriptions of behavior that differentiated different levels of social functioning. For example, at one end of the scale the description read "communicates freely with relative ease in groups in face to face situations. Participation is appropriate. Seeks out opportunities to interact." At the other end of the scale was the description "Markedly isolated. Uncommunicative. Withdrawn. (Highly inappropriate)." The scale was divided into 15 equal intervals, but behavioral descriptions were distributed unequally on the vertical scale, anticipating a negative bias in the distribution of ratings. Ratings of social interactions were made by clinical psychologists within the first two weeks of the treatment program and at the completion of treatment 6 to 12 months later. It was found that male patients in the two structured treatment programs displayed greater social behavior than those in the minimally structured program. It was also found that for the male patient the longer the illness duration, the higher (better) were the scores attained in post-treatment global social behavior. For females there was no relationship between global social behavior and degree of program structure, age, or length of illness.

Awareness of others was thought to relate to the degree of interaction between patients. It was reasoned that before two people interact they must become aware of each other's identity. Thus a simple measure of the patient's ability to identify fellow patients from recent photographs constituted the "awareness of others" measure. Patients were simply required to identify by first, last, or nickname, the photos of other patients who were currently in the various treatment units. The Photo Naming Test (PNT) was used to measure the patient's ability to identify other patients within his own treatment unit; to identify male patients in other groups; and to identify females in the experimental groups. Administration of the PNT to all male patients at from two to four weeks after the beginning of the treatment program and again at its completion revealed that all three treatment conditions prompted increased awareness of other patients, but that patients in the maximally structured condition surpassed the other two groups. Younger males in the maximally structured condition tended to show greater awareness of other male patients than did older patients in that condition.

Since the program was aimed at reducing social isolation, degree of verbal interaction was regarded as an important index. Group leaders were, therefore, asked after each session to rate patients with respect to three aspects of verbal interaction: the amount of talking done by a particular patient in comparison with others during a session; how much of a patient's conversation was directed toward the group leader and how much toward other patients in the group; and the number of other patients to whom the patient spoke during a given session. For each aspect of verbal interaction group leaders made a frequency rating on a four-point scale with a total verbal interaction score being obtained by adding individual scores on the three items. Statistical analyses of these scores revealed that degree of program structure and level of reactivity are not related to verbal interaction during treatment. However, older male patients in the maximally structured treatment condition improved more in verbal interaction than did older male patients in partially structured programs. Also in the partially structured program the younger male patients showed more improvement in verbal interaction than did the older patients. Among females, improvement in verbal interaction was not related to degree of program structure or level of reactivity.

In addition to social behavior manifested when the program forces such behavior, Sanders and his colleagues were interested in spontaneous displays of social behavior. Such behavior was observed and measured at the monthly socials planned by the patients themselves. Typically, a number of structured activities occurred at such events but in the intervals between these activities patients could converse freely with others, take refreshments, dance, and the like. During these intervals, patients' behavior was systematically observed and weighted in terms of certain assumptions made by the experimenters. For example, interaction with the opposite sex was seen to represent a higher order of social behavior than interaction with one's own sex and personal forms of interaction were regarded as more significant than relatively impersonal ones. Thus a spontaneous social behavior scale was developed that listed a number of specific behaviors with various weights. Those receiving the highest weight included dancing with the opposite sex, talking with the opposite sex, eating with the opposite sex, and engaging in a game with the opposite sex. Similar behaviors engaged in with a member of the same sex received a slightly lower weighting. Eating alone, or not participating, received still lower weightings. On this scale it was found that patients in the maximally structured condition increased spontaneous social behavior the most. Patients in the partially structured condition actually declined in spontaneous social behavior, while those in the minimally structured condition showed little improvement.

The long-range effects of the treatment program were assessed two years after the completion of each patient's treatment. A follow-up was done on 101 patients residing in the community. Of this group, 31 had been in the maximally structured program, 28 in the partially structured program, 19 in the minimally structured program, and 23 in the control group. Interviews conducted with these patients focused on five areas of adjustment: living situation, work, leisure time, interpersonal relations, and psychiatric condition.

Since the patients in this study had long, continuous periods of hospitalization, their family ties were fragmentary, and the majority (about 75%) were living apart from relatives, making it possible to assess their degree of independence. A measure was developed of the degree to which the patient was financially responsible for his own housing and for obtaining and preparing his own food. More than 50 percent of the patients were found to be assuming more than minimal responsibility for their own needs. Patients were also rated for the adequacy of their judgment with respect to how they spent their money, with the finding that 42 percent of the sample used good judgment, 35 percent manifested fair judgment, and 23 percent showed poor judgment.

Work adjustment was a difficult problem for these patients. Most of them had poor premorbid histories (lack of job skills, low educational levels, poor work records) and their long hospitalizations during which they had done little meaningful work further decreased their desirability in the job market. Therefore, it is not surprising that approximately 61 percent of the group was unemployed after 24 months outside of the hospital. Approximately 30 percent held full-time positions. Those who were working held jobs requiring considerably less skill than was necessary for the jobs they had held before becoming mentally disturbed, because while in the hospital their job skills had declined.

Since such a large percentage of this sample was not employed full time, community adjustment was measured by a catalog of the number and types of leisure-time activities engaged in. On the average, the patients engaged in 5.9 leisure-time activities, but only 1.8 of these involved other people. The largely nonsocial character of the leisure-time pursuits of these patients suggests a rather barren, isolated existence. To some extent, high-frequency activities such as watching television, listening to the radio, reading, taking walks, or visiting others were probably engaged in because these activities were free and the ex-patient had only limited financial resources.

One attempt to assess the quality and quantity of interpersonal relationships involved an evaluation of (a) the number of contacts (by mail, phone, or visits) toward first-order relatives (parents, siblings, spouse, and children) not living with the patient; and (b) an assessment of attitudes toward these relatives. Of the 101 subjects in the community, 93 had at least one relative with whom a contact could be made. Of the 86 patients on whom family contact information could be obtained, only 48 percent had contact at least once per week. Twenty percent had no contact during the entire year preceding the interview assessing this variable. A significantly greater number of females than males made weekly contact with family members (65 and 35%, respectively).

Patient attitudes toward family members were rated as positive, negative, or indifferent; for 74 subjects, 69 percent were seen to have generally positive attitudes. For the most part, patients with positive attitudes toward relatives were living with their families. Seventy-three percent of the 30 females who were not living with families indicated positive attitudes, but only 35% of the 17 males not living with their families felt positively toward them.

Another index of the degree to which patients were socially anchored in the community was the number of friendships they had developed in their immediate surroundings. Any community members the patient could name and with whom he had regular contacts were considered to be "his friend," excluding those he associated with through some functional relationship (e.g., fellow workers or landlord). On the basis of patients' self-report, there was a striking inability to establish friendships. Thirty percent of the group were unable to name a single friend, 25 percent could name only one, and only 45 percent could name two or more.

Another measure of social adjustment was the number of community groups with which the ex-patient was affiliated. It was found that ex-patients attended very few group activities on a regular basis. Only 27 percent of the sample attended a community group apart from the Alumni Club established at the hospital. Those that did attend group activities went to church socials, "Y" activities, and activities for former mental patients conducted by a variety of organizations.

On the basis of the sum total of follow-up interview protocols, ratings of general psychiatric adjustment were made with 31 percent of the sample characterized as being essentially abnormal, 44 percent showing limitations, and 25 percent being judged as essentially abnormal. Overall, it was felt that the ex-patients were extremely limited in the degree to which they maintained responsibility for their situation. Although more than half of the sample were able to house and feed themselves, the majority were unemployed and were supported by welfare or social security benefits. Those who were employed earned marginal livelihoods, and their leisure-time activities reflected little or no involvement with other people. Group affiliations were practically nonexistent. It was apparent from Sanders' survey of ex-patients' status that if the ex-patients had had to take complete responsibility for maintaining themselves in the community, the majority would have had to have been rehospitalized. They apparently managed to maintain themselves by remaining relatively inconspicuous, avoiding demanding situations, and being satisfied to function at a level well below their premorbid adjustment.

All of the foregoing analyses were done on the entire group of discharged patients regardless of their hospital treatment program. Separate analyses compared patients who had experienced the various types of treatment programs as well as the control condition. Among these analyses, only living situation failed to reflect the influence of previous treatment.

Socio-environmental treatment proved to be a significant factor in vocational adjustment. Those experiencing the two more structured programs were found to have significantly better judgment with respect to vocations, perhaps because these programs provided educational content that had a significant impact on this factor. Further analyses indicate that females showed better vocational judgment than males and that differences were not attributable to age. Employment rates for patients who had experienced the four different treatment conditions were: 48 percent for those in the maximally structured situation, 37 percent for those in the partially structured situation, 42 percent for those in the minimally structured situation, and 23 percent for those in the control condition.

Social adjustment also reflected differences related to the hospital treatment condition. Dichotomizing the distribution of friendships at the median, it was found that significantly more friendships were formed by patients in socio-environmental treatment than by those in the control condition. Measures of group affiliation reflected a program by age interaction. Young patients from the control or minimally structured treatment groups showed the poorest attendance at group activities while the young patients in the maximally and partially structured conditions showed significantly higher attendance. Social participation ratings differentiated between the control group and the three socio-environmental treatment groups at a level just short of statistical significance with controls participating more poorly than other groups. Age and sex differences were also found with respect to the social participation ratings; older patients surpassed younger patients significantly, and females participated more actively than males.

The psychiatric status scores indicated that patients in the three socio-environmental treatment programs were in better psychiatric condition than those in the control group. Also, younger ex-patients were found to be more disabled psychiatrically than older ones with the younger members of the control group showing the most marked disability.

Although, as a group, Sanders' patients displayed relatively poor community functioning, it does seem clear that socio-environmental therapy and particularly the more structured forms of it did have salient effects. Considering these patients' degree of pathology and long years of hospitalization, it is encouraging that a relatively short period (from six months to a year) of socio-environmental treatment had some impact on their work and social adjustment. These findings are encouraging enough to suggest that a reorientation of the hospital milieu to include elements of socio-environmental treatment over long periods of time might well produce far more effective changes in hospitalized patients than have traditional treatment programs.

THE "LODGE" PROGRAM

Fairweather (1964) describes another approach to the treatment of the chronic mental patient that combines elements of the therapeutic community and some entirely innovative features. Along with many others who have been interested in the more effective treatment of the chronic mental patient, Fairweather believes that one major problem is that behavior adaptive to hospital life is not adaptive to community life. Fairweather's own research demonstrates that discharged patients who had been living successfully in the hospital are often promptly rehospitalized and readjust quickly to the hospital. Despite their success in the hospital, they had apparently not been well prepared to live outside. Thus, to be maximally therapeutic, the hospital must train the patient in community-relevant roles. In addition, however, Fairweather recognizes that hospital life is sheltered and far less demanding than community life so that something must be done to help bridge the gap between the two.

Fairweather's innovative program devolved from his notion that the ideal way of reconciling hospital and community roles would be through the establishment within the hospital of small social reference groups that could function as organized units within the hospital and, later, outside of the hospital as well. Thus an entire group of patients would be returned to the community at one time to continue to function as a single social unit. Having successfully adopted a social role within the hospital, their role-change necessary for life outside would be minimized. Therefore, the hospital program must create a social unit in which community-relevant roles can be practiced, and a separate program must establish the unit outside of the hospital and help maintain it there.

The within-hospital program emphasized establishing social settings affording patients the opportunity to solve problems and to assist others in doing so. Therefore, small autonomous problem-solving groups were formed. To evaluate this group approach, experimental patients experienced the same ward program as those in the traditional hospital program except that they met as a group for two separate one-hour periods each day. In the first of these they engaged in ward housekeeping, and in the second they participated in a group discussion in which decisions and recommendations were made concerning each of them. The patient new to a problem-solving group proceeded through four distinct stages with the entire group responsible for each member's progress.

The new patient was oriented minimally by the staff and referred to the patient group, which provided a fuller orientation. In the first stage, the patient was required to care for personal needs, to be punctual for assignments, and to participate in orienting other new members for which he received $10 and a one-day pass each week. In the second stage, the patient was required to take a job and handle it acceptably, and during this period he was paid $15 per week plus an overnight pass every other week. During the third stage, the patient was required to perform stage one and two requirements satisfactorily and to demonstrate that he could manage his own money and passes. He was allowed to draw as much as $20 per week plus as many as three overnight weekend passes per month. In the final program stage, the patient was not limited in any way concerning his funds or freedom to leave the hospital, but he was required to begin making plans for his discharge from the hospital.

On four weekday meetings task groups met among themselves to work on one another's problems and to evaluate each other's progress. The staff was occasionally invited to these meetings but only to serve as resource people to provide needed information. A fifth meeting was held with the staff each week at which the group made recommendations concerning how each member's problems were to be solved. The staff accepted or rejected these recommendations, using this mechanism to convey the idea that action-oriented solutions were preferable to ones that did not result in action.

A follow-up study compared patients who had experienced the task groups to those who underwent traditional treatment and found that task group patients left the hospital significantly sooner than those receiving traditional treatment. In a follow-up six months after discharge, however, it was found that approximately 50 percent of both groups had been readmitted. Significantly, a preponderance of those readmitted were chronic cases. This emphasizes the need for the second component in Fairweather's program, the out-of-hospital setting that maximizes community adjustment.

Fairweather, Sanders, Cressler, and Maynard (1969) have reported extensively on the extra-hospital program for the discharged chronic mental patient. Patients were released in groups to live in "lodges" and were compared with matched controls who were released individually to participate in traditional outpatient mental health programs. Patient status was assessed at six-month intervals through a 40-month period. The authors were interested in: how long the discharged patient could maintain himself outside the community; his employment status; and patient self-evaluations as well as evaluations by a friend, relative, or acquaintance. Patient self-evaluations were intended to reflect satisfaction with living conditions, leisure activity, and community life. Respondents familiar with the patients' life situation rated them for the number of friends they had, the amount of communicating they did verbally, the presence of symptom behavior, their drinking behavior, their activity level, their leisure activity, and their degree of social responsibility.

The results of this study indicated that the lodge group remained in the community and was employed significantly longer than controls (see Figures 2 and 3).

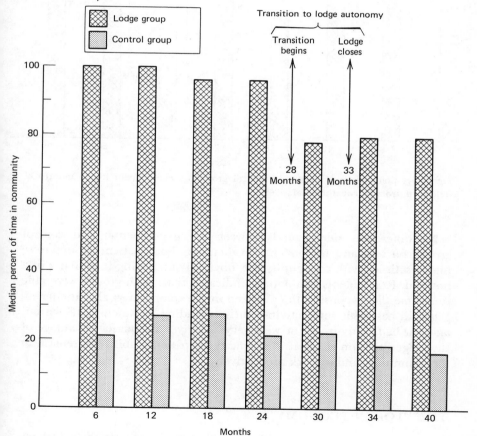

Figure 2. The comparison of lodge and control groups on time in the community for 40 months of follow-up (from Fairweather et al., 1969).

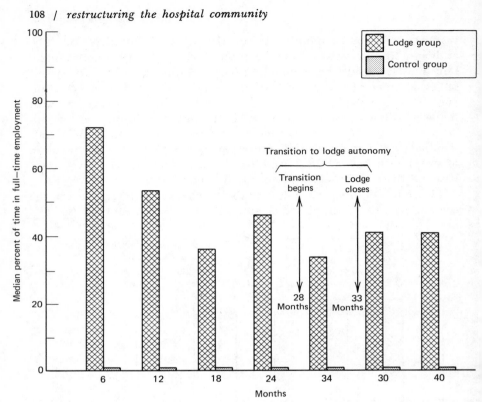

Figure 3. Comparison of lodge and control groups on employment for 40 months of follow-up (from Fairweather et al., 1969).

No differences were found between the experimental and control groups on self- and respondents' evaluations. Both patient groups were highly satisfied with community life, obviously preferring it to living in a hospital. Respondents' evaluations indicated that: both groups were able to assume the responsibilities of living in the community; all patients engaged in passive leisure activities such as reading or watching television; and few had many frends or were very talkative. The major advantage of the lodge situation was that it enhanced the patients' ability to remain in the community and to work productively.

THE "TOKEN ECONOMY"

Another recent approach to the hospital care of seriously disturbed patients that places great emphasis on the significance of hospital culture for patient behavior has resulted in a program known as the "token econo-my" (Ayllon and Azrin, 1968). Token economy programs owe less to the tradition of moral treatment and the therapeutic community than does the program previously described. Instead, these programs grow out of Skinner's theories of learning based on operant conditioning. The theoretical position involved in this paradigm is well described by Ullmann and Krasner (1969), who term the treatment procedure that follows from operant conditioning, *sociopsychological treatment.*

From the operant conditioning viewpoint, all behavior, psychotic or otherwise, is learned as the result of reinforcement patterns. A reinforcement is defined operationally as any stimulus associated with the increased emission of the behavior that precedes it. All behavior results from learning, defined as the acquisition of a functional relationship between an environmental stimulus and some response on the part of the organism.

Two learning paradigms are identified. The first is the classical Pavlovian conditioning situation in which a stimulus precedes the response and actually elicits it. The pairing of an unconditioned stimulus, such as food, with a neutral stimulus, such as a bell, is an example of this. The food alone elicits salivation, and the association of the food and the bell eventually makes it possible for the bell alone to produce salivation. This is known as *respondent conditioning.* In the other learning paradigm, called *operant conditioning,* the sequence of stimulus and response is reversed. In operant conditioning, the organism emits a response that has certain environmental consequences which, if reinforcing, will cause the operant behavior to be repeated. Responses to most social stimuli seem to be operant responses. In other words, they are shaped by the reactions that they receive from others. To make a socially "proper" response one must be attentive to stimuli, respond to them, and be reinforced for the responses one makes. Abnormal behavior is considered to be behavior that is unexpected, probably because it is in response to cues that most people are inattentive to. This gives abnormal behavior an upsetting and unpredictable quality. A schizophrenic, for example, is seen by Ullmann and Krasner to behave as he does because he is attending to a different set of cues than most other people. Attention itself is regarded as an operant behavior that is shaped by reinforcements.

Ullmann and Krasner emphasize the role played by the hospital in maintaining and even promoting behavior that is regarded as schizophrenic. The hospital is a large impersonal institution that looks on mental disorder as a physical disease. As such, it fosters in the patient behavior such as cleanliness, quiet, and passivity. The patient is viewed as not being responsible for his behavior, a position that absolves him from blame but that also regards him as not to be trusted with matches, belts, shoelaces, and the freedom to move about the institution. Since very few staff professionals are available for a great number of patients, the attendant becomes very significant in the patient's life. The hospital attendant has the most direct contact with patients and must organize and control large numbers of individuals. Reinforcements are, therefore, given when patients are quiet and conforming. Since the attendant can influence the patients' position with respect to the doctor and other patients, he is a very powerful source of reinforcement: he can provide desirable jobs, more comfortable living arrangements, minor luxuries, privacy, and prompt attention to special requests.

Because the attendant is a powerful reinforcer, the behavior he encourages is very readily learned. Unfortunately, much of the patient behavior that pleases the attendant is maladaptive in community life. The good patient helps with daily routine, and remains otherwise unobtrusive in a dull, drab environment where he is denied comforts, privacy, and stimulation. Self-assertion, which serves very well outside the hospital, is extinguished. Even efforts to have contact with a physician who might help with one's problems are looked on as disruptive. Thus, withdrawn, passive compliance which, incidentally, is often considered a hallmark of schizophrenia, is encouraged in the hospital. Ullmann and Krasner go so far as to suggest that the behavioral consistency attributed to the schizophrenic process is actually caused by the methods used to treat it instead of by anything inherent in the "disease."

A number of studies have been done to validate many of the assumptions basic to the reinforcement approach (Ayllon and Michael, 1959; Isaacs, Thomas, and Goldiamond, 1960; King, Armitage, and Tilton, 1960; and Ayllon, 1963). In these studies, isolated responses were either reinforced or extinguished in short, relatively infrequent sessions. Such studies demonstrated that the behavior of even very disturbed patients can be shaped through judicious use of reinforcement, but they did not provide a treatment model applicable to an entire ward. Therefore, Ayllon and Azrin (1965) set out to develop a behavior modification program that could be used in the average hospital setting. Such a program required a plan for determining what responses should be modified, defining reinforcements that would be used to promote desired behavior, and setting up a study to test program effectiveness.

The responses selected for modification were those deemed by the experimenters to be "necessary or useful to the patient." Such choices are, of course, arbitrary. In their experimental program, Ayllon and Azrin focused on responses like serving meals, cleaning floors, and sorting laundry. It was required that the responses selected be objectively measurable, and be performed only at certain times of the day so as to make measurement more convenient. Floor mopping, for example, was a good choice, since it could only be done when a mop was available.

The selection of reinforcers for desired behavior proved to be a particularly difficult problem. The reinforcements used in previous studies were unique to each individual whose behavior was being shaped. Typically, experimenters observed the patient over a period of time to learn what reinforced his behavior effectively. Such a procedure, however, would be entirely too unwieldly on the average hospital ward. To surmount this problem, Ayllon and Azrin observed the behavior of a group of patients over a period of time to determine what behaviors occurred with a high frequency. They reasoned that whatever a group of patients frequently did could be used as a generalized reinforcer for all of them. Six classes of behavior were identified as being potentially reinforcing: privacy, freedom to leave the ward, social interaction with staff, attendance at religious services, recreational opportunities, and the opportunity to purchase items at the commissary. Because the immediate reinforcement of desirable behavior is considered to be very important from the point of view of operant conditioning, and since the reinforcers described could only be delivered at specified times, Ayllon and Azrin decided to use a conditioned reinforcer as a bridge between the desired response and the primary reinforcement. This conditioned reinforcer consisted of metal tokens that could be spent later for whatever primary reinforcers were desired. As a result, this program was labeled a "token economy."

In a series of experiments on a single hospital ward, Ayllon and Azrin were able to demonstrate that: (1) their reinforcement procedures were more effective in determining patients' choice of jobs than any reinforcement intrinsic to the job itself; (2) when primary reinforcers became freely available with no work requirements, very little work was done; (3) job preference was more closely related to the amount of token reinforcement associated with it than to patients' liking for the task. This study provides an impressive demonstration of how significant patient behavior can be elicited through the systematic use of reinforcement. It also helps validate the learning principles described by Ullmann and Krasner.

The work of Ayllon and Azrin has stimulated the development of token economies in other hospitals and in other settings. One example is the token economy that was set up by Atthowe and Krasner (1968) on an 86-bed open ward of a Veterans Administration hospital for chronic psychiatric cases. These authors reported that after one year of a token economy, approximately 90 percent of the patients changed dramatically with respect to self-care, attendance at available activities, interacting with others, and sense of responsibility.

Ayllon and Azrin feel that one of the significant features of the token economy is that it is an environment within which disculturation (the deterioration of behavior important for living outside of an institution) is forestalled. They point out that even if the behavior disorder that necessitated hospitalization is cleared up, patients are often unfit for discharge because of disculturation, a process that causes families to lose interest in the patient. They feel that the "community psychiatry" movement represents a partial recognition of this problem.

A COMMUNITY BASED OPERANT LEARNING ENVIRONMENT

Horizon House is a community-based program for treating psychotic men which combines some of the features of Fairweather's "lodge" program with the "token economy" system of Ayllon and Azrin (Henderson, 1971; Kelley and Henderson, 1971; Samuels and Henderson, 1971). The goal of this program is to enhance the psychotic's community adjustment by eliminating symptomatic behavior, improving interpersonal skills, and providing literacy and occupational skills. Since the program was conceived of as an alternative to state hospital treatment, patients reside in a house within the community rather than in a hospital and are called residents instead of patients. A token economy system is utilized to promote behavioral change, and programs for bridging the movement of the patient from the experimental facility to the community are developed.

This token economy utilizes a reinforcer called a "grickle" which exists only on paper but which can be exchanged for primary reinforcers such as food, candy, cigarettes, passes and other privileges, admission to recreation, and the like. Grickles are awarded for a variety of desirable behaviors by making an entry on the program card carried by each resident in the facility. All earnings and expenditures are entered daily, thus maintaining a running balance. Chits are used to provide immediate reinforcement in cases where a specific treatment regimen is designed to eliminate symptoms peculiar to a given individual. Chits are not immediately convertable to primary reinforcers but are, instead, collected periodically and recorded as a corresponding number of grickles.

When facility residents become capable of working in the community, they are issued bridging cards. Grickles are then awarded for behaviors such as grooming satisfactorily and being punctual and, where employers are willing to cooperate, the bridging card is used for reinforcing good interpersonal relationships with co-workers and satisfactory work performance. Besides indicating how many grickles have been earned by a particular patient, the program and bridging cards are graphic records of the activities the patient has engaged in and indicate the adequacy of his performance. Partly on the basis of the data provided by the program and bridging cards, weekly summaries are prepared for each resident, and these are reviewed at a clinical conference concerned with decisions regarding program changes, discharge, referrels to other facilities, and the like.

Two treatment programs are designed to remove undesirable behaviors and to substitute acceptable responses, the intensive workshop and the interpersonal relations laboratory. Shortly after entering the institution, an individually planned treatment program is designed for the new resident that is directed toward behaviors deemed to be impairing his functioning most significantly. At *the intensive workshop* the emphasis is on the development of work-related behaviors as a preparation for entering a general work program. Behavior is observed continuously in the intensive workshop and reinforcers are applied liberally. Chits and, in some instances, primary reinforcers are awarded for positive behaviors. Three times a day chits are collected and converted to grickles. Bonuses are awarded whenever a resident increases his reinforcement earnings over a previous daily high. The resident is promoted from the intensive workshop to a general work program when his output is satisfactory and he displays a favorable ratio of positive to negative behavior.

The interpersonal relations laboratory functions in much the same way as the intensive workshop except that it emphasizes developing interpersonal skills. Residents attend this laboratory five days each week for 90-minute sessions. Interpersonal activities related to appropriate social behaviors such as group games, group discussions, and role playing are reinforced in the laboratory. Group discussions, for example, provide an opportunity to reinforce rational, coherent speech. Role-playing situations are used to condition increasingly sophisticated behaviors. One series of roles directed toward a gradual refinement of social behavior might begin with "asking a clerk for information" and progress to the point of "asking the boss for a raise."

Once symptom-displacing responses are established and stabilized in the intensive workshop and interpersonal relations laboratory, they are maintained on intermittent reinforcement schedules in the facility's general work, instructional, and recreational programs. In each of these activities, observations are made at regular intervals and reinforcements are awarded whenever a resident is engaging in behavior appropriate to the context. For the most part, however, a resident's earnings are related to his output on a job rather than to his display of countersymptomatic behavior and, as in the real world, reinforcement is delayed.

In the institution's work program every resident receives an assignment (kitchen work, household maintenance, or some special project), and is paid on a prearranged scale. Assignments are based on previous work experience and current functioning level, and promotions depend on performance as reflected in weekly work earnings. Work assignments are divided into job units each of which carries a fixed payment. The pay scale is used to maintain work behavior, and the program design mandates a gradual lengthening of the interval between work response and reinforcement. Both daily and weekly bonuses are provided for the satisfactory completion of a specific number of job units per day and per week, in order to encourage persistence. Recreational activities such as excursions into the community, films, discussion groups, dances, and the like are conducted every evening and on weekends. Residents pay an admission fee to participate, and prizes are available for competitive activities such as games. The residents cast ballots for each other to identify those seen as contributing most to the activity's success, and the number of ballots received by each resident is reinforced with a grickle payment. This is another means of encouraging social interaction.

Residents who are below the fourth grade level in reading, spelling, or arithmetic are assigned to appropriate instructional programs. These programs supersede work assignments for one or two 45-minute periods per day. Programmed materials are used for instruction and, at the conclusion of each session, grickle reinforcements contingent on output are awarded. Specified numbers of grickles are also awarded for satisfactory test scores on achievement tests or for the demonstration of acquired skills.

A *bridging* system has been developed to facilitate the transfer of the social and vocational skills developed within the operant environment to the world outside. Bridging is attempted when the resident is functioning satisfactorily at his highest work level, when his interpersonal skills seemed to have stabilized, and when displays of negative behavior are rare and not so disruptive that they might prevent his functioning in the community. Part of the bridging system involves assigning the patient to job hunting which restricts his opportunity to earn reinforcements within the institution, but offers, instead, substantial rewards for participating in job interviews and telephoning to prospective employers.

Once a resident finds a job he is promoted to night status and moves to a part of the facility called the "penthouse." The penthouse, the top floor of the facility, accommodates five residents and two staff members. The role of staff members in the penthouse is to promote good social relations, and to assist residents with budgets, apartment hunting, and the like. Penthouse residents meet periodically with members of an Alumni Club, who are graduates of the operant facility. Alumni help to encourage recently employed residents and even offer material assistance to those who are about to establish an independent life outside the institution, such as helping in apartment hunting, coaching them concerning job interviews, or providing leads for potential employment. When a patient demonstrates that he can maintain appropriate vocational and social behavior, he is discharged from the facility and becomes a member of the Alumni Club, through which he maintains continuing contact with the program until such time as he no longer feels the need for it.

Program Evaluation

Samuels and Henderson (1971) have reported on a study of the effects of the community-based operant environment for psychotic patients. The sample study includes psychotic men ranging in age from 18 to 55 years who were originally seen at a state psychiatric facility. Excluded from the sample were patients who were suicidal, assaultive, homosexual, addicted to alcohol or drugs, mentally defective, or suffering organic brain disorder. Such exclusions were made to minimize incidents of anti-social behavior, since the experimental facility was located in the center of a residential neighborhood. Random assignment of patients were made either to a state hospital, the psychiatric ward of a municiple hospital, or the experimental operant facility. For a total of 40 subjects, 21 of whom had been treated in the operant facility and the remainder in either the state or municipal hospital, follow-ups were done 18 months after each subject's admission to a treatment facility. Workers who collected follow-up data were uninvolved with the patients during the treatment phase and only became acquainted with them after their discharge from the initially assigned facility. Preliminary outcome data are shown in Table 2.

This table indicates that although the average number of days of initial hospitalization is higher for the operant group than for either of the other groups, the average total time of hospitalization is lower for the operant groups. A considerably smaller percentage of operant patients were rehospitalized (28%) as compared to rehospitalized state (50%) or municipal (66%) patients. Furthermore, rehospitalized state and city patients spent a considerably longer period in the hospital on their return than did rehospitalized operant patients. Differences in percentages of time spent in the community by patients treated in the various facilities were not large. However, those treated in the operant program were employed an average of 34 percent of their time in the community whereas city and state facility dischargees were employed only an average of 29 percent and 14 percent of their time, respectively.

An evaluation was done of the status of all subjects at the conclusion of the 18-month follow-up period. These data, reported in Table 3, indicate that in comparison to state and city hospital patients, fewer operant subjects are in hospitals, more of them are known to be in the community, and a higher percentage are working.

Data were also available for an additional 77 subjects who had not been in the program long enough for an 18-month follow-up. Analyses were done combining the follow-up data for these 77 patients with that

Table 2. Initial Hospitalization, Rehospitalization, Community Tenure and Employment During the Follow-up Period (549 Days) for Subjects from the Original Sample (from Samuels and Henderson, 1971)

Variables	Facility of Initial Assignment					
	Operant, *N* = 21		State, *N* = 10		City, *N* = 9	
	Days	Percent	Days	Percent	Days	Percent
Initial hospitalization (including transfers)						
Mean days	167		156		99	
% of follow-up period		30		28		18
Total hospitalization						
Mean days	180		249		202	
% of follow-up period		33		45		37
Time in community						
Mean days	369		300		347	
% of follow-up period		67		55		63
Employment						
Mean days	125		42		99	
% of time in community		34		14		29
Rehospitalization	*n* = 6		*n* = 5		*n* = 6	
Mean days	45		178		154	
% of follow-up period		8		32		28

Table 3. Status of Subjects' from Original Sample at Completion of Follow-up Period (from Samuels and Henderson, 1971)

Variables	Facility of Initial Assignment					
	Operant, *N* = 21		State, *N* = 10		City, *N* = 9	
	n	%	n	%	n	%
Subjects in hospitals	3	14	2	20	2	22
Subjects in community	17	81	7	70	6	67
Status unknown	1	5	1	10	1	11
Subjects working	11	52	2	20	3	33

available for the 40 subjects previously reported. For this group totaling 117, the range of involvement in the program was from 5 to 18 months with the average at 14 months. The findings with respect to this group are reported in Table 4.

The data in this table indicate that the city hospital patients had a shorter initial hospitalization than did those from the operant or state facilities. Total hospitalization was greater for the state hospital group than for either of the other two, with the city hospital group again showing the shortest period. The operant group showed to best advantage with respect to the percentage of subjects who were able to work during the follow-up period and the percentage who were able to work for more than one month. When rehospitalization was necessary, operant subjects also demonstrated superiority by remaining in the hospital for shorter periods of time than did the state and city patients.

Table 4. Initial Hospitalization, Total Hospitalization, Rehospitalization, Community Tenure, and Employment for Subjects of All Groups When Examined Two Years after the Inception of the Project (from Samuels and Henderson, 1971)

	Facility of Initial Assignment					
Variables	Operant, $N = 58$		Combined State, $N = 24$		Combined City, $N = 35$	
Initial Hospitalization (including transfers) Mean days	130		142		95	
Total Hospitalization Mean days	168		180		143	
Time in Community Mean days	274		235		288	
Employment Mean days	174		136		196	
No. of Ss who worked during follow-up period	32	55%	7	29%	16	46%
N of Ss who worked over one month	27	47%	6	25%	13	37%
Rehospitalization	$n = 20$		$n = 6$		$n = 13$	
Mean days	92		151		142	
Percentage of Ss rehospitalized during 2-year period		34%		25%		37%

This operant program for seriously disturbed patients conducted in a facility located in the community, is a very interesting and hopeful departure in the treatment of serious mental disorder. Like many other programs that are deeply concerned with the debilitating effects of long periods of institutionalization, its aim is to keep patients in close touch with the community and to bolster the patient's interpersonal skills, particularly those that will help him to adapt to community life. The primary tool in this effort is the operant technology that has proved to be successful in shaping behavior within institutions. The extension of this technology to settings within the community and even to actual work settings is a most interesting and potentially fruitful departure.

THE MENTAL HOSPITAL AS A RESORT

A fundamental assumption in many of the hospital programs described, as well as in the writings of contemporary observers of the hospital scene such as Goffman (1961), is that the patient is a victim of a set of forces that he is powerless to oppose. Recently, Braginsky, Braginsky, and Ring (1969) have reported a series of studies done in a mental institution that leads them to conclude that the patient is far from an entirely passive victim of hospital forces. These authors believe that patients exercise a counter power that gives them considerable control over their own fate. Because the schizophrenic is looked on as differing from the rest of humanity, as suffering a disintegrative disease impairing virtually all psychic functioning, and as being an involuntary victim of an uncontrollable illness, Braginsky et al. feel that it is difficult to recognize that patients are capable of a rational life-style in the hospital which provides many personal satisfactions.

Some studies were directed at the patients' tendency for "impression-management," a term referring to one's capacity for managing expressive behavior in such a way as to control the impressions that others form of him. One simple study demonstrated that patients who thought they were responding anonymously to a questionnaire concerning hospital conditions gave significantly fewer ingratiating responses than patients who knew that their responses could be identified. In a more elaborate study two groups of patients, a recently admitted group and a group hospitalized, at least, three months (most of this group had been hospitalized for more than three years), were asked to respond to the same instrument. For half of each group the test was called a "mental illness test" and for the other half it was labeled a "self-insight test." Those experiencing the mental illness condition were told that high scores would heighten a person's chances for remaining in the hospital for long periods of time.

Those who took it as a self-insight test were told that high scores would reflect inner mental health and would lessen the likelihood of a long period of hospitalization. It was hypothesized that patients who had already been in the hospital for a long time had some wish to remain whereas newcomers would be looking forward more eagerly to discharge. As hypothesized, significant differences were found between old-timers and newcomers depending on whether the test was taken as a mental illness test or a self-insight test. Old-timers scored significantly higher on the "mental illness" test and significantly lower on the "self-insight" test than did newcomers.

To test the effectiveness of patient impression-management as a counter-power tactic, three groups of patients were asked to respond for two-minute periods to the question: How are you feeling? One group was advised that the interviewer was interested in assessing readiness for discharge; a second group was told that the interviewer was interested in determining whether the patient should be living on an open or closed ward; the third group was told simply, "I think the person you are going to see is interested in how you are feeling and getting along in the hospital." Psychiatrists were asked to rate tape recordings of each of the two-minute segments for the degree of psychopathology and the amount of hospital control needed by the patients. Since all patients had long periods of hospitalization, it was hypothesized that they would be motivated to remain in the hospital, but that they would want to retain open ward privileges. Results indicate that patients in the open ward condition were regarded as the least mentally disturbed and requiring the least control, patients in the discharge condition were rated as suffering the greatest degree of psychopathology and needing the greatest amount of control. Ratings of patients in the third group, who were asked merely to reflect how they were feeling and getting along, fell between the other two groups.

In another series of studies, Braginsky et al. identified three specific adaptive styles among hospital patients: spending much time on the ward; spending a great deal of time at some work assignment; and becoming a "mobile socializer." These styles were associated with age, attitudes about hospitalization and patienthood, goals, and interests. Although psychopathology was not related to these adaptive modes, each style led to different hospital outcomes with respect to how much and what type of information was acquired about the hospital, the length of hospitalization, discharge rate, and involvement in therepeutic programs. The authors concluded from these studies that patients can successfully use their environment to their own satisfaction by maintaining personally valued life-styles even when such styles depart from institutional values.

A further study was directed toward the "invisible" patient, a type about whom little is known by hospital staff. It was assumed that the patient who is not well-known to staff actively seeks anonymity. Results indicated that patients vary considerably with respect to visibility within the hospital, and that this variability is a function of patient-initiated approach or avoidance of the psychiatrist. Visibility was also found to be unrelated to psychiatrist's ratings of psychopathology. It was related to discharge, however, with the more visible patient being more likely than the invisible ones to be discharged.

On the basis of these studies, Braginsky et al. likened time spent in the hospital to time ordinarily spent on weekends or vacations and drew an analogy between the mental hospital and the vacation resort. In the community, leisure time is the exception whereas within the mental hospital it tends to be the rule. Thus a study was done to demonstrate that the newly admitted mental patient's way of life is more similar to weekend life outside of the hospital than it is to the weekday routine. The conclusion drawn was that the hospital is used as a "resort" to satisfy patients' hedonic needs. Furthermore, the authors demonstrated that newly admitted patients having friends who were ex-patients entered the hospital with attitudes more similar to long-term patients than first-admission patients without such friends. That being the case, some newly admitted patients were suspected of entering with the *intention of* satisfying hedonic needs. In line with this hypothesis, it was demonstrated that several patients admitted from a given town were much more likely to be living in close proximity before entering the hospital than would be expected by chance. The authors presume thereby that many prospective patients learn beforehand about the institution and may even enter to be with old acquaintances.

Such data suggest that the mental hospital is seen as a resort. It is not necessarily one where patients "are holding hands and frolicking merrily across the hospital grounds." However, it is like a resort in that the hospital imposes minimal external demands, offers residents attractive physical settings with many social activities, does not expect residents to be productive, and maximizes the opportunity for them to choose a personal life-style. Both institutions, the mental hospital and the resort, attempt to replenish residents so they will be better able to meet life's demand.

These studies have led Braginsky, Braginsky, and Ring to suggest a model hospital program. They believe that since patients actually use the mental hospital as either a temporary or permanent refuge, society should face up directly to this fact and provide opportunities, through means other than mental hospitals, for withdrawal and renewal. In essence they propose that each community set up a small institution offering its members an opportunity to get away from it all without being degraded as mental patients. Such retreat facilities are already available for the wealthy so that what is primarily needed are similar institutions for the less affluent. Braginsky et al. expect that if retreats of this kind existed many of the traditional "symptoms" of mental illness would disappear altogether. Since people would understand that there was no need to appear mentally ill in order to remain in the institution, they would no longer act "sick." Those feeling the need to withdraw permanently might find employment in these retreats as staff members. Central to this plan is the idea that these retreats are not hospitals to deal with illness, but places of refuge for those who need a break from daily routine. Giving everyone the opportunity to get away at times should, furthermore, make life more bearable for all members of society. Visits to these retreats would serve as a shot of "social adrenaline," enabling people to become more fruitful and productive citizens.

CONCLUSION

The revolutionary changes brought about in hospital care during the late 18th and early 19th centuries were in response to a recognition of the importance of the environment on the mental state of the hospitalized patient. This was followed in the United States by a period characterized by "moral treatment" in many mental hospitals, an approach that placed great stress on the therapeutic community forces within the hospital. Paradoxically, during the latter half of the 19th century a renewed emphasis was placed on the theory that serious mental disturbance was entirely constitutional, and as a result a drastic change in hospital practice occurred. Since constitutional factors were thought to be paramount in the etiology of mental disorder, there was little need for concern about the patient's hospital environment. Institutions could be managed more economically if they were larger and were manned by a staff concerned primarily with the patient's survival needs.

Many of the recently developed hospital programs appear simply to be revivals of the old moral treatment approach. Stress is laid on patients' doing useful work, assuming responsibility for managing their lives, and having the recreational opportunities and freedoms that characterize life outside of an institution. In addition, some of these programs are beginning to take a very detailed look at the hospital as a social setting and how it fails to prepare the patient for successful life outside. Many of these programs are being carried out within theoretical frameworks undergoing empirical test. Treatment approaches are being carefully evaluated, and studies are being done to better understand the impact that the hospital environment has on the patient. These very positive steps may lead to important structural and functional changes in the mental hospital.

In some measure the greater "openness" characterizing innovative hospital programs in which physical restraints are minimized and patients have increased freedom may have become possible because of the widespread use of tranquilizers. While the typical patient may have always been capable of more self-restraint than he was usually given credit for, the fact that tranquilizers were in use undoubtedly encouraged some hospital personnel to attempt a more open hospital atmosphere. As the experience of Rosenhan (1973) would suggest, however, in many hospitals the use of tranquilizers has, no doubt, made it possible for hospital personnel intent on doing a purely custodial job to have only minimal contact with patients, a practice that leads not to greater openness but, if anything, to psychological stagnation. On a hospital ward where patients might lose control at any moment, an aide would simply not be able to spend only an average of 11 percent of his time among his charges, as Rosenhan found. The aide would inevitably be with patients most of the time he was on duty, would interact with them considerably, and would come to know them very well as people. Hence, the advent of the tranquilizer is a mixed blessing.

The various approaches to the open hospital we describe have in common an intense involvement of all personnel with the patients. Open hospital programs demand considerable sensitivity to patient experience and a constant questioning of environmental impact on behavior. As such, it is most demanding of those individuals having the most direct contact with patients. This calls for a considerable upgrading of the skills of traditional aides and nurses, and even for the development of new types of personnel. Associated with this shift is an alteration of the status hierarchy of the hospital. Where formerly the physician, who had minimal contact with patients, was considered the institution's primary therapeutic agent and the ultimate authority in patient disposition, in the open hospital many of his prerogatives must be shifted to personnel who live more closely to the patient. In effect, this reduces the physician's status from the all-powerful authority to that of a technician.

The development of new cadres of therapeutic agents, training them, supervising them, and making a career possible for them in an organizational structure having rigid traditions are some of the important issues facing community psychology. Reshuffling the power structure of a long-established institution that has received shockingly little public support is an additional problem of no mean proportion. Its major ally in the task it faces is the blatant failure of traditional practices and the persistence of an aroused public conscience.

References

Atthowe, J. M., Jr., & Krasner, L. Preliminary report on the application of contigent reinforcement procedures (token economy) on a "chronic" psychiatric ward. *Journal of Abnormal Psychology,* 1968, *73,* 37–43.

Ayllon, T. Intensive treatment of psychotic behavior by stimulus satiation and food reinforcement. *Behavior Research and Therapy,* 1963, *1,* 53–61.

Ayllon, T., & Azrin, N. H. The measurement and reinforcement of behavior of psychotics. *Journal of the Experimental Analysis of Behavior,* 1965, *8,* 357–384.

Ayllon, T., & Azrin, N. H. *The token economy-motivational systems for therapy and rehabilitation.* New York: Appleton-Century-Crofts, 1968.

Ayllon, T., & Michael J. The psychiatric nurse as a behavioral engineer. *Journal of the Experimental Analysis of Behavior,* 1959, *2,* 323–334.

Bockoven, J. S. Moral treatment in American psychiatry. *Journal of Nervous and Mental Disease,* 1956, *124,* 167–194, 292–321.

Bockoven, J. S. Some relationships between cultural attitudes toward individuality and care of the mentally ill: a historical study. In M. Greenblatt, D. J. Levinson, and R. H. Williams (Eds.), *The patient and the mental hospital.* Glencoe, Ill: The Free Press, 1957. Pp. 517–526.

Braginsky, B. M., Braginsky, Dorothea D., & Ring, K. *Methods of madness: the mental hospital as a last resort.* New York: Holt, Rinehart & Winston, 1969.

Fairweather, G. W. *Social psychology in treating mental illness: an experimental approach.* New York: Wiley, 1964.

Fairweather, G. W., Sanders, D. H., Cressler, D., & Maynard, H. *Community life for the mentally ill.* Chicago: Aldine Publishing Co., 1969.

Goffman, E. *Asylums.* Garden City, N. Y.: Doubleday, 1961.

Greenblatt, M., York, R. H., & Brown, Esther, L. *From custodial to therapeutic patient care in mental hospitals.* New York: Russell Sage Foundation, 1955.

Henderson, J. D. A community-based operant learning environment I: Overview. In R. D. Rubin, H. Fensterheim, A. A. Lazarus, & C. H. Franks (Eds.), *Advances in Behavior Therapy.* New York: Academic Press, 1971. Pp. 233–238.

Isaacs, W., Thomas, J., & Goldiamond, I. Application of operant conditioning to reinstate verbal behavior in psychotics. *Journal of Speech and Hearing Disorders,* 1960, *25,* 8–12.

Jones, M. *The therapeutic community.* New York: Basic Books, 1953.

Jones, M. *Beyond the therapeutic community.* New Haven: Yale University Press, 1968.

Kelley, K. K., & Henderson, J. D. A community-based operant learning environment II: Systems and procedures. In R. D. Rubin, H. Fensterheim, A.

A. Lazarus, & C. H. Franks (Eds.), *Advances in Behavior Therapy*. New York: Academic Press, 1971. Pp. 239–250.

King, G. F., Armitage, S. G., & Tilton, J. R. A therapeutic approach to schizophrenics of extreme pathology: an operant-interpersonal method, *Journal of Abnormal and Social Psychology*, 1960, *61*, 276–286.

Kraüpl-Taylor, F. A history of group and administrative therapy in Great Britain. *British Journal of Medical Psychology*, 1958, *31*, 153–173.

Rosenhan, D. L. On being sane in insane places. *Science*, 1973, *179*, 250–258.

Samuels, J. S., & Henderson, J. D. A community-based operant learning environment III: Some outcome data. In R. D. Rubin, H. Fensterheim, A. A. Lazarus, & C. H. Franks (Eds.), *Advances in Behavior Therapy*. New York: Academic Press, 1971. Pp. 263–271.

Sanders, R. New manpower for mental hospital service. In E. L. Cowen, E. A. Gardner, & M. Zax (Eds.), *Emergent approaches to mental health problems*. New York: Appleton-Century-Crofts, 1967. Pp. 128–143.

Sanders, R., Smith, R., & Weinman, B. *Chronic psychoses and recovery: an experiment in socio-environmental therapy*. San Francisco: Jossey-Bass, 1967.

Sullivan, H. S. Socio-psychiatric research: its implications for the schizophrenia problem and for mental hygiene. *American Journal of Psychiatry*, 1931, *87*, 977–991.

Ullmann, L. P., & Krasner, L. *A psychological approach to abnormal behavior*. Englewood Cliffs, N. J.: Prentice-Hall, 1969.

5. programs for infants and preschool children

The previous chapter described treatment or teritiary prevention programs. Although innovative in a variety of ways, these programs continue to reflect the traditional mental health orientation toward the amelioration of identified psychological disturbances. This chapter is principally concerned with interventions designed to reduce the incidence of psychological dysfunction. The programs discussed fall under the primary prevention model in that they concentrate on, "identifying current harmful influences, the forces which support individuals in resisting them, and those environmental forces which influence the resistance of the population to future pathogenic experience" (Caplan, 1964). More specifically, the present chapter focuses on programs for infants and preschool children whose environments are thought to provide inadequate resources for facilitating growth and development. Stated in positive terms, the interventions to be discussed seek to provide high-risk children with the opportunity to develop necessary skills for living.

The choice of the infancy or preschool period as the temporal point for intervention reflects several assumptions. The young child is a rapidly changing organism who may be particularly susceptible to positive influences; his acquisition of life skills at this time forms the foundation for future adaptation; and he has not yet learned many of the maladaptive behaviors that would have to be unlearned first if intervention were to occur later in his life (Bloom, 1964). Moreover, many theories of human development hypothesize that there may be "critical periods" for the acquisition of certain types of responses, and that it may be difficult or even impossible to fully compensate a person for the absence of facilitative experiences that should have been available but were not.

Although the potential advantages of very early intervention are evident, implementation of primary preventive programs involves serious conceptual and practical difficulties. A major problem arises from the fact that the specific environmental antecedents of most psychological disorders are not known. No one can yet say with certainty what, if any, early life experiences contribute to the later appearance of a complex behavior dysfunction such as schizophrenia. As a result, many workers in early prevention have set conservative goals for their programs, often centering around the enhancement of cognitive development (Tizard, 1970). The narrowness of professed goals does not rule out the possibility, however, that these programs will ultimately be shown to have substantial impact on the general well-being of the individual. Hunt (1961) has argued, for example, that the unfavorable environmental conditions that impede cognitive growth may also create generally unmotivated and emotionally deficient people. A practical difficulty associated with early intervention is the problem of reaching the target population. High risk infants and preschoolers cannot be identified through the public educational system as a rule. Furthermore, it is not always easy to convince parents, caretakers, or funding agencies that intervention is desirable with children who have not yet manifested signs of disturbance.

The first programs we discuss involve children who are institutionalized and who are, therefore, relatively easily reached. Not only is it comparatively convenient to set up programs of service for children gathered in institutions, but it is also possible, in some instances, to control and to observe environmental effects fairly thoroughly as a means of refining intervention techniques.

PROGRAMS FOR INSTITUTIONALIZED CHILDREN

Substantial evidence has been accumulated over the years indicating that children raised in orphanages and similar institutions often suffer severe emotional and intellectual damage (Dennis and Dennis, 1941; Spitz, 1945; Provence and Lipton, 1962). In 1939, Skeels and Dye mounted a program in an institution that was well ahead of its time and that, in retrospect, may be seen as providing an early model for primary prevention programs using nonprofessional helping agents.

Skeels and Dye did not plan their intervention on the basis of a full understanding of the possible effects of institutionalization, nor on the basis of a well-founded preventive strategy. Their efforts were the results of an accidental observation. Two infants in an orphanage, aged 13 and 16 months, had been adjudged to be feebleminded and were moved to an institution for retardates where they were cared for largely by teenage female inmates. A psychologist observing the two children on the ward about six months later noted striking changes in their apparent developmental level. The children were retested using a childrens' intelligence test and were found to have gained 31 and 52 IQ points since their transfer. Intrigued by this observation, Skeels and Dye arranged to have 13 other "feebleminded" children placed in the care of the brighter retarded girls in the institution.

The 13 transferred children ranged from about 7 to 36 months of age and had an average IQ of 64.3. A control group of children with a higher mean IQ was selected from among children who remained in the regular orphanage program. The experimental children remained in the special setting for periods ranging from 5.7 to 52.1 months. As is indicated in Table 1, these children all showed substantial gains in IQ. While the experimental group gained an average of 27 IQ points, the control children actually lost an average of 26 points over similar time spans. Skeels and Dye concluded that the enriched stimulation and one-to-one relationships provided by the retarded women were the operative factors in the dramatic intellectual gains made by the experimental group children.

Obviously, the long-term effects of any program directed at very young children cannot be evaluated for many years. The research initiated by Skeels and Dye provides one of the few examples of a program begun far enough in the past to provide us with data on the adult status of the children served. Skeels (1965) was able to locate all of the children who had originally been studied. The only subject lost from the sample was a child in the control group who had died. Skeels found that none of the children in the experimental group were receiving institutional care, while four of the controls were in institutions for the retarded or mentally ill. Furthermore, 11 of the experimental subjects were married and 9 had children. Only 2 of the original controls were married at the time of the follow-up study. These findings while not conclusive, suggest that the intervention may have enhanced not only cognitive development, but general social adequacy as well.

Table 1. Mental Development of Individual Children in Experimental Group as Measured by Kuhlmann-Binet Intelligence Tests Before and After Transfer (Skeels and Dye, 1939)

Case Number [a]	Before Transfer Test 1		Chronological Age, Months, at Transfer	After Transfer Test 2		After Transfer Test 3		After Transfer Last		Length of Experimental Period, Months	Change in IQ, First to Last Test
	Chronological Age, Months	IQ		Chronological Age, Months	IQ	Chronological Age, Months	IQ	Chronological Age, Months	IQ		
1	7.0	89	7.1	12.8	113			12.8	113	5.7	+24
2	12.7	57	13.3	20.5	94	29.4	83	36.8	77	23.7	+20
3	12.7	85	13.3	25.2	107			25.2	107	11.9	+22
4	14.7	73	15.0	23.1	100			23.1	100	8.1	+27
5	13.4	46	15.2	21.7	77	32.9	100	40.0	95[b]	24.8	+49
6	15.5	77	15.6	21.3	96	30.1	100	30.1	100	14.5	+23
7	16.6	65	17.1	27.5	104			27.5	104	10.4	+39
8	16.6	35	18.4	24.8	87	36.0	88	43.0	93	24.6	+58
9	21.8	61	22.0	34.3	80			34.3	80	12.3	+19
10	23.3	72	23.4	29.1	88	37.9	71	45.4	80	22.0	+7
11	25.7	75	27.4	42.5	78	51.0	82[b]	51.0	79	23.6	+7
12	27.9	65	28.4	40.4	82			40.0	82	12.0	+17
13	30.0	36	35.9	51.7	70	81.0	74[b]	89.0	81[b]	52.1	+45

[a] Arranged according to age at time of transfer from youngest to oldest.
[b] Stanford-Binet IQ.

The Skeels and Dye findings were not well received at the time of their original publication. Indeed, some experts derided their evidence because it challenged the then popular theoretical bias that IQ was hereditarily predetermined and could not be altered. Not all the criticism of the Skeels and Dye research was based on theoretical objections, however. There were undoubtedly methodological problems with the study, including the fact that the experimental and control children were not completely comparable prior to the intervention. The higher initial IQ of the control group may have meant that the control children had more room to drop in IQ whereas the experimental group had more room to improve. In any event, the research did not permit the identification of the precise environmental factors that could have accounted for the observed effects of the intervention.

Rheingold (1956) reported a somewhat different effort to modify the environment of institutionalized infants. Unlike Skeels and Dye, the author herself became the new element in the child's milieu, and it was thus possible for her to specify fairly precisely what experiences had been added. An even more important distinction between Rheingold's study and the earlier research is to be found in the description of program goals. Rheingold was relatively disinterested in raising the IQ scores of the children. Her goal was to increase their responsiveness to social stimuli. Relying on accumulated evidence (such as the findings of Dennis and Dennis, 1941, and Spitz, 1945) that institutionalized babies show inadequate emotional and interpersonal behavior, Rheingold offered herself as a surrogate mother figure who would partially replace the multiple institutional caretakers and, thereby, increase the child's opportunity to develop appropriate interpersonal attachments.

The children Rheingold studied were 16 infants residing in an orphanage hospital. The infants were six months old at the outset and were selected to exclude children with known physical or mental defects of any significance. In choosing children with no identified deficiencies, Rheingold was employing a true primary preventive strategy (in contrast to Skeels and Dye whose work might be regarded as having secondary preventive goals). Eight of the infants were designated as controls, and were matched with eight experimental infants for age, IQ, and pre-intervention social responsiveness.

In the experimental condition, Rheingold was the sole caretaker of each infant for a total of 300 hours distributed over eight weeks. She tended to the child's physical needs, talked to the child, and otherwise provided social stimulation. The control infants were cared for by the usual retinue of institutional workers. Both control and experimental children were, however, tested weekly during the eight weeks and for four weeks thereafter. The tester was a person unfamiliar to both groups of children (at least, initially), and the responses were recorded by an observer who was kept uninformed about the experimental design.

The chief measuring instrument was a response checklist for recording the child's behavior when he was approached by an adult. The examiner was instructed to engage in a two-part series of standardized behaviors intended to elicit social response from the infant (see Figure 1). In addition to being observed with the designated tester, the child was also scored for his performance with Rheingold and with a complete stranger. Thus, by varying the degree of familiarity of the adult in the test interaction, Rheingold was able to determine whether any changes in social responsiveness were generalized as opposed to being simply a function of increased familiarity with the particular adult figure.

The results of the study supported the general hypothesis that a brief period of increased interaction with a single caretaker could increase the

---

The four situations in Part A were as follows:

1. The adult stood approximately three feet from the child's crib, smiled at the child, but did not speak.

2. The adult went to the crib, leaned over the child, smiled, and said warmly, "Hello, baby, how are you?" which could be repeated a second time.

3. The adult tried by any means to get the child to smile, and as soon as the child smiled, frowned and scolded him in an angry tone of voice, saying, "You naughty baby, what did you do?" These words too could be repeated but only once.

4. After the lapse of at least 15 minutes (in order that the baby might forget the scolding), the adult, concealed by a sheet thrown over the side of the crib, called to the child, saying, "Hello, baby," or "Come on, baby."

The three situations in Part B were as follows:

1. The adult stood at the side of the crib, smiled, and talked to the child as in Part A, 2.

2. The adult picked the child up, walked to the center of the room, held him in her arms so that the top of his head was level with her shoulder, smiled, and talked to him as in Part A, 2.

3. The adult returned the baby to his crib, placed him on his back, and stood at his crib, silent, and not looking at him.

Figure 1. Experimental situations used to assess infants' social Responsiveness (Rheingold, 1956).

social responsiveness of institutionalized infants. The experimental group of infants showed generally greater interest and more positive behavior toward the examiners than did the control group. The experimental infants were particularly responsive to Rheingold herself, indicating that some specific attachment had developed in addition to the general increase in social interest. It had also been hypothesized, however, that children in the experimental group, as they became more attached to Rheingold, would become more fearful of strangers and this prediction was not confirmed. The two groups of children continued to differ in social responsiveness throughout the four-week period following the discontinuation of Rheingold's visits with the experimental children. No significant differences between the groups were found on measures of intellectual or motor performance.

In 1959, Rheingold and Bayley (1959) presented the results of a follow-up study in which 14 of the original 16 infants were revisited about a year after the last previous contact. Virtually no residual effects of the intervention could be found. None of the experimental children gave evidence of recognizing Rheingold or of special responsiveness to her. No differences were found to distinguish the control and experimental children, except that the experimental children seemed to engage in more spontaneous vocalization. Optimistically, Rheingold and Bayley sought to explain the apparent absence of lasting effects by noting that all of the children seemed to be doing well and that most had been adopted, thus gaining the chance to develop socially to a degree that would naturally obscure the effects of the brief intervention. Even so, this follow-up study may be viewed as providing one of the earlier indications that the effects of intervention in infancy might be dramatic but short-lived. The follow-up done by Skeels (1965) does, however, suggest that under certain conditions an early intervention may have a long-range impact.

The two efforts described in this section provide several illustrations of the distinction between a preventive intervention and a "treatment" modeled on the approach of the physician. One important difference is found in the fact that both projects neglected the first step in general medical practice, that of waiting for the referral of the service recipient. Despite the impossibility of self-referral by an infant, it would still have been possible for Skeels and Dye or Rheingold to have waited for the institutional caretakers to present their wards as cases needing treatment. In fact, however, Rheingold selected children adjudged to be free of defect, while Skeels and Dye chose children seen as having a defect that was thought to be irremediable. Thus both projects directed aid at individuals not already judged to require treatment. Furthermore, the two programs omitted the next step prescribed by the treatment model, the establishment of a firm diagnosis carrying implications for the appropriate ameliorative or curative procedure. Skeels and Dye and Rheingold, rather, began with the hope or assumption that no defect existed in the children that might not be related to the inadequacies of the institutional environment, and that it would be senseless to seek to identify the hidden flaw in the children when it might be possible instead to alter their surroundings. A third deviation from the medical approach is found in the nature of the interventions themselves. Neither program involved the selection of a "specific," that is, a remedy specially suited to the cure of a particular disorder, to be administered by a highly trained professional. Rheingold was content to offer her experimental infants an experience that any competant mother might have provided, while Skeels and Dye placed their children in the hands of women who could hardly have been able to understand, much less carry through a sophisticated treatment procedure. To a greater or lesser degree, the preventive programs to be discussed in the remainder of this chapter and in others that follow will similarly illustrate deviations from the treatment model of general medicine. Concepts of referral, diagnosis, and discovery of a specific may simply be inappropriate where the source of psychosocial inadequacy is perceived as lying in the nature of the community, and where the helping approach is aimed at preventing these forces from impacting on individuals to his or her subsequent detriment.

INTERVENTIONS CENTERED IN SPECIAL SETTINGS

Most preschool children are not, of course, institutionalized. The majority of children whose environments provide inadequate early experience are probably the children of the poor. Reaching these children is far more of a challenge than reaching the children who are already gathered in public institutions. The mental health worker must often choose between the relative efficiency of creating special children's centers and the possibly greater benefit of entering the home setting itself. In this section we focus on programs involving the establishment of special preschool environments.

At first glance, the strong movement to provide special settings for very young children would appear to be one of the most successful aspects of the prevention movement. However, much of the impetus for early intervention comes from an altogether different source. Changing economic conditions and new conceptions of sex roles have led many women to seek reentry to the job market while their children are still young. This has led to strong public pressure for the government to support day-care facilities and other forms of child care that enable women to work. As day-care facilities have proliferated, the community psychologist has conveniently gained access to a population that might otherwise have been difficult to reach. This phenomenon of the mental health worker capitalizing on the opportunities provided by general social changes is exemplified in many other programs described in this book. Even where the community psychologist cannot himself initiate wide-scale programs of service, he may be able to introduce a psychological perspective into projects initiated primarily to fill other needs.

Currently, the most massive program of preschool intervention is *Project Head Start,* initiated in 1964 by an act of Congress. As with the day-care movement the perceived need for this project was only partially related to mental health considerations. *Project Head Start* was founded as a part of the war on poverty in an effort to break the cycle that leads to generation after generation of people who can find no useful economic role in our technological society. This mandate was hastily translated into a network of preschool centers administered with a considerable degree of local autonomy (White, 1970).

Despite the ultimately economic objectives of *Head Start,* the immediate goals of the program included several types of psychological impact. The effects that were sought included aiding the emotional and social development of the child, increasing his sense of self-worth, and improving family-child interactions by influencing both. Thus the project demanded an interdisciplinary effort to aid children in matters of health and educational readiness, but placed considerable emphasis on psychological development.

By 1970 more than three million children had participated in the *Head Start* program. It is no simple matter to describe what this participation has entailed, however, since the program has been made up of literally thousands of separate and unique efforts. Some programs have offered only summer experiences, others have provided year-round half-day enrichment, and still others have offered full (school) day sessions year-round. Furthermore, the specific goals of the individual centers have differed. A major study of *Head Start's* impact was conducted by the Westinghouse Learning Corporation in conjunction with Ohio University. The Westinghouse/Ohio study (1969) involved a sample of 104 Head Start centers scattered throughout the country. Among other things, the government-sponsored researchers asked the directors of the centers in the sample to specify the degree of stress placed on eight different objectives. About one-half of the directors ranked improvement in the child's sense of self-worth, self-acceptance, and confidence as their most important objective. On the other hand, 20 percent of the directors ranked the improvement of grammar and vocabulary as their highest priority goal. Four of the remaining six objectives were ranked first by, at least, one director. It is evident, therefore, that no single statement adequately expresses the priorities of *Head Start,* nor will any single set of criteria serve as an adequate basis for evaluation.

The child populations served by the centers also were found to vary when examined by the Westinghouse/Ohio team. One of the centers studied enrolled children at a median age of 42 to 47 months, while three of the centers reported comparable figures of 78 to 83 months of age. Thus it is not even entirely correct to specify Head Start as being solely for preschool children. In general, the children in the centers were found to include an over-representation of nonwhite youngsters, with black children constituting more than a half of the full-year program participants and more than a third of the summer program enrollees. Socioeconomically, about 58 percent of the full-year children and 50 percent of the summer enrollees were found to come from families with yearly incomes under $4000. Fewer than 8 percent of the parents of Head Start children were found whose own parents held jobs beyond the unskilled worker category.

A potentially important finding of the Westinghouse/Ohio study, discovered through interviews with parents concerning parent-child relationships, was that about 56 percent of Head Start parents seldom or never play with their children. This finding lends support to the widely held belief that the deficits observed in disadvantaged children may at least partially be attributed to inadequate stimulation.

Assessment of the impact of Head Start is clearly a difficult task, and one that is still in its formative stages. The Westinghouse/Ohio study, already mentioned, constitutes the most ambitious attempt to date to discover what effects, if any, the project has had. After selecting 104 "representative" Head Start programs, the Westinghouse/Ohio team chose about 2000 children in these programs who were then in one of the first three years of elementary school. The children were matched with an approximately equal number of children attending the same schools who had never been enrolled in Head Start. Although the control children had to be potential eligibles for the program, it was not possible to match them perfectly with the children who had actually participated. The control group was found to be of slightly higher economic status and was composed of children who were more capable than the experimental sample; this mismatch between experimental and control children necessitated later statistical adjustments intended to compensate for the effects of initial differences.

The Head Start children and their controls were compared on a wide variety of instruments including IQ and school achievement tests, tests of linguistic abilities, self-concept measures, and questionnaires to evaluate the child's attitude toward home, school, peers, and society. The children were also compared on an inventory of classroom behavior that was based on teacher ratings. It was concluded from these many comparisons that the Head Start children were not demonstrably superior to the control sample in either cognitive or affective development. The few scattered indications of a favorable program impact were all attributable to children from full-time as opposed to summer Head Start experiences. When findings were compared according to regions of the country, however, the data did suggest that Head Start had positive effects on the most disadvantaged children, notably Southeastern Negroes. In their conclusion, the Westinghouse/Ohio study group offered suggestions for improving Head Start, including the proposal that summer programs be eliminated and the suggestion that intervention might begin even earlier in the children's lives.

The Westinghouse/Ohio report has been widely criticized on a variety of grounds. White (1970) questions the sampling procedure by which subjects were selected and comments on the possible invalidity of some of the research instruments. Much of the criticism leveled at the report is concerned with the statistical procedures by which the data were made interpretable. Campbell and Eriebacher (1970) attempted to show that the statistical methods used by the study group tend to bias the findings in such a way as to make the intervention look less effective.

Head Start has also been defended on the grounds that the Westinghouse/Ohio report did not explore some of the possible benefits of the program. For example, a survey conducted by Kirschner Associates (1970) purports to show that the program had very positive effects on the attitudes and public participation of the poor. Whatever the worth of these conclusions, it must still be admitted that the direct and pervasive benefits for children have yet to be demonstrated.

The essentially negative overall findings on Head Start do not eliminate the possibility that some programs within the network of centers have provided demonstrably useful services to children. Certain Head Start facilities, for example, have made substantial efforts to provide mental health services to children who might otherwise receive no attention. In parts of New York City the Head Start Centers have been able to enlist child psychiatrists to act as consultants in the preschool projects (Hotkins, Hollander, and Munk, 1968). The long-range benefits of such an arrangement remain to be demonstrated, but this type of effort may readily be seen to facilitate the goal of extending the reach of the mental health establishment to previously neglected areas of the community.

The scope and diversity of the Head Start project make it an important one for study. It should be evident, however, that the determination of why effects do or do not occur is difficult when dealing with so vast a project. For this reason, it may be useful to examine a more modest program of preschool intervention outside the home.

In the early 1960s, Gray and Klaus (1965) established a program intended to prevent the progressive retardation often occurring in culturally deprived children. This program actually served as one of the models in the planning of Head Start. The group of children originally involved in the Gray and Klaus study comprised 88 black preschoolers living in two cities of a middle Southern state. Gray and Klaus selected presumed high-risk children on the basis of parental occupation, education, income, and housing. Most parents were unskilled or semiskilled workers whose family incomes were below the poverty level. The average parental education was eight years of schooling, but Klaus and Gray (1968) found that many of the mothers were functionally illiterate. In one third of the homes no father was present.

The 88 children in the project who were nearly four or just four years old at the outset were divided into four groups. One group of children (N = 22) was pretested at entry in the study and then enrolled in a "summer school" for three consecutive years, after which tests were again administered. In addition to the summer sessions, the children in the first group were visited at home weekly during the period when sessions were not being held. A second group of children (N = 21) received the same type of enrichment experience as the first group, but the intervention began one year later so that each child was trained and visited for two instead of three years. A third group consisted of 18 control children who were tested at the same times as the experimental children, but who received no special training. Another control group was made up of 27 children from another city.

The summer sessions provided for the two experimental groups were conducted over a 10-week period each summer, with five 4-hour sessions each week. Hence, children in the first group had a total of 600 hours of enrichment, while children in the other experimental group received 400 hours. The summer session attempted to instill attitudes believed to be relevant to later school achievement, such as persistence and a capacity to delay gratification. The summer program also provided specific skills such as spatial perception and concept formation. The home visitor program was conducted by two trained teachers who attempted to stimulate parental interest in the child, provided materials, and aided the mother in caring for the child. The home visitors also collected data on the child's progress.

The first reports from the project (Gray and Klaus, 1965) gave definite evidence of the positive short-term effects of the intervention. In Figure B the four groups of children are compared in terms of mental age (MA) , a measure which, in this instance, is perfectly correlated with IQ. Group T_1 is comprised of children who had their first summer experience in 1962; as is indicated in the graph (Figure 2) , this group immediately

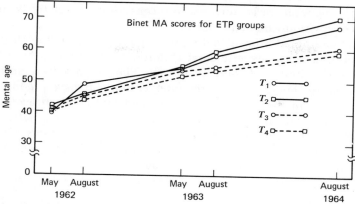

Figure 2. Binet MA scores for training $(T_1$ and $T_2)$ and control groups $(T_3$ and $T_4)$ (Gray and Klaus, 1965) .

gained an advantage in MA over the other groups. Group T_2 had its first summer experience in 1963 and showed a gain similar to that observed with group T_1 the previous year. Following the summer of 1963, both of the experimental groups had a higher average MA than either of the control groups, T_3 and T_4. Moreover, the slope of the graphs for the two experimental groups is steeper than for controls, indicating a more rapid rate of mental growth. Findings with respect to mental age were closely paralleled by comparisons between groups on linguistic abilities.

A follow-up study (Klaus and Gray, 1968) was performed five years after the initial intervention, by which time the children had entered school so that a broader range of evaluative instruments was appropriate for assessing program effects. Results were again encouraging. The experimental groups continued to hold their lead over controls on tests of aptitude and language skills. The trained children were also superior on tests of readiness for academic work and on tests of achievement. Furthermore, the experimental children were less impulsive and had a more positive self-concept (although other measures of attitudinal stance did not differ) .

In 1970, Gray and Klaus (1970) published a third report on the progress of children in the program which included the results of tests administered to the children as late as their fourth year of school. At this point the effects of the intervention were less apparent. The experimental children were narrowly, but significantly, superior to the controls on the intelligence tests. The experimental children were not, however, significantly superior to controls on tests of vocabulary and school achievement.

These results were interpreted as reflecting the inevitable decay of gains made through an early intervention consisting of relatively limited periods of environmental enrichment.

An interesting additional finding was also reported in the 1970 study —the siblings of the experimental children were found to have higher IQ's than the siblings of control children. These data led the authors to suggest that the home visitor in the intervention may have produced beneficial changes in the parents of the experimental children leading to a "vertical diffusion" of positive program effects. Such speculation leads naturally into the consideration of a final group of programs where the home is the locus of the intervention, and the parents are sometimes intentionally placed in the role of helping agents.

HOME CENTERED INTERVENTIONS

Home intervention programs are of two types: the first type brings trained workers into the home to work directly with the youngsters; the second relies on trained personnel primarily as educators to the parents. Despite differences in approach, both types of intervention probably influence the way in which the parent-child relationship develops. It seems virtually inevitable that the presence of a program in the family dwelling will have effects on parental behavior, even where the parents may not be required to participate actively.

A good example of a home-based intervention program using trained personnel as change agents is that reported by Schaefer and Aaronson (1970). Through canvassing two lower socioeconomic neighborhoods in Washington, D.C., a sample of 64 Negro male infants were selected. Infants were chosen whose families earned less than $5000 per year, and whose mothers had less than 12 years of schooling and were unskilled or semiskilled workers (if employed). Otherwise eligible children whose homes were not suitable as a location were excluded. This selection procedure illustrates one of the limitations inherent in home-based programs; crowded conditions, disruptive siblings, or poor physical environment may all too often prevent intervention in the very homes where it might be most needed.

The goals of the Schaefer and Aaronson program were to promote intellectual functioning and language skills, toward the ultimate objective of raising later academic achievement. Based on the belief that infantile behavior patterns, maternal behaviors, and mother-child relationships are relevant to cognitive growth, Schaefer and Aaronson sought to evaluate these factors as well as the actual intellectual and language development of the children.

The 64 infants were divided into an experimental and a control group of 31 and 33 infants, respectively. Initial differences were slight and tended to favor the controls. All infants were given intelligence tests at 14, 21, 27, and 36 months of age. Ratings of mother and child behavior were made only for the experimental group at intervals throughout the training process and at 36 months.

Beginning at 15 months of age, experimental group children received one hour of tutoring five days a week until the child reached 36 months of age. Control children received no special attention other than periodic intelligence testing.

The tutors were a carefully selected group of college graduates, many having regular jobs relevant to their role in the program. Interviews, written applications, and experimental background were considered in selecting the tutors. Part of the rationale for selecting a highly skilled group of individuals was that development and assessment of the innovative program would require workers with exceptional qualifications. It was not assumed that the service role itself would require so select a group of people. The tutors who were chosen received didactic and practicum training to augment their existing skills and experience. Didactic experiences included lectures, readings, and discussions. Practicum training included observation of infants in special settings, practice sessions with infants, and forays into the target community to actually select the infants to be used in the study. Schaefer and Aaronson emphasized their efforts to build and maintain a high level of enthusiasm among the tutors, an emphasis founded on their belief that a highly dedicated tutor would be most effective in relating to the child, and that the quality of the relationship would determine success.

The specific techniques and materials employed in the tutorial sessions have been described in unusual detail in an Office of Education publication (OE-37033-A) on the government sponsored project. Figure 3 is an

---

Methodology: Specific Examples

The tutors wrote up a number of activities which they tried during the course of the experiment, and which they felt were successful. Some of these are described or quoted here, along with the name of the tutor contributing each.

A. A number of objects, with which the child has become familiar, are placed in paper bags. These might include toy cars and animals, pencils, buttons, brushes etc. A game is played, in which the child must reach into the bag, handle the objects, and name them sight unseen. The child is allowed to remove and play with those objects he can name. The tutor guides him or provides hints to enable him to name the remaining objects (Lucille Banks).

B. Since the most frequently stated aim of the project has been to stimulate verbal development, I have concentrated on singing in my presentation of music. I have selected a few songs which have simple words, appealing melodies and rhythms and, most important, are repetitive. I have repeated these songs until they have been mastered by the babies.

Two of the babies have expressed a strong preference for one particular song. In these caes, I have attempted to include the favorite song in each singing session, since the babies become very excited and responsive when it is sung. From this song, I have moved to less familiar songs, hoping that the initial enthusiasm stimulated by hearing and singing a familiar song will carry over. The babies appear to derive much satisfaction from their increasing familiarity with and ability to perform these songs.

Figure 3. Excerpts from a Tutor's Log (OE-37033-A).

---

excerpt from one of the detailed logs kept by the tutors to describe their activities with children. This extensive accounting of interventive strategy has not been present in the reports of many of the projects already described, thus the Schaefer and Aaronson research may be particularly useful as a model for future work because it does provide an explicit procedure to be followed.

Although conducted in the home, the tutorial sessions did not require the active participation of the mother. Her participation was encouraged, but no pressure was exerted when she seemed reluctant. Some mothers evidenced little interest in the sessions and appeared to tolerate the intervention only because the program involved a small payment to participating families. Other mothers became actively engaged in the tutoring process and also sought out the tutors as sympathetic listeners.

Results of the short-term assessment of program impact (Schaefer and Aaronson, 1970) were generally positive. The IQ's of the tutored infants were significantly higher than those of controls at 21, 27, and 36 months. Tests of language development administered at 36 months also showed the tutored children to be superior. It was found, however, that the gains made by the children were correlated with ratings of the quality of the mother-child relationship. The greatest improvement was found for children whose mothers appeared to be relatively nonhostile toward the child, while children whose mothers were rated as hostile or disinterested benefited relatively less. Thus the impact of the intervention and the effects of relatively stable patterns of child rearing were additive. This finding substantiated the argument for interventive approaches that seek to affect the family situation more directly.

A pioneering effort to accelerate infant development by intervening in the mother-child relationship was reported by Irwin (1960). Working class mothers (not a poverty group) were instructed simply to read stories to their children for 20 minutes a day. This process was encouraged from the time the children were 13 months old until they reached 30 months of age. Irwin's criterion measure, the number of speech sounds spontaneously produced by the children, revealed that, compared to controls, the experimental group children engaged in significantly more vocalization.

A more ambitious program with a focus similar to that of Irwin's project is reported by Levenstein (1969). Levenstein sought to stimulate intellectual growth in preschool children by altering the mother-child relationship. Her total sample consisted of 54 mother-child dyads drawn from public housing and of low socioeconomic status. The children in the dyads were either two or three years old when the intervention began. In the experimental group, consisting of 33 dyads, mothers were trained to interact with the child around verbally oriented play utilizing toys and books supplied by the project. A "toy demonstrator" came to the home regularly to model appropriate behavior for the mother. The visits were made over a seven-month period after which the children were retested by using instruments that had been used in a pretest.

Levenstein compared the experimental group with two types of control groups. The first control group consisted of nine dyads that received home visits from a professional who expressed interest in the family but did not suggest or model parent-child interactions. A second control group received no visits, but was tested at the same times as the other groups.

The experimental group showed a significantly greater gain in both IQ and vocabulary than did either of the control groups. Contrary to Levenstein's expectation, however, the experimental children who were first seen when they were two did not benefit more than the children who were three when the home visits occurred. This result is reminiscent of the findings of Gray and Klaus (1965) where the earlier intervention did not produce differential results. It should be observed, however, that both the present study and that of Gray and Klaus involved interventions occuring earlier than in programs such as Head Start.

A final program to be considered resembles Levenstein's project in many ways, but adds one important element. To affect maternal behavior, Levenstein chose to send a visitor into the home itself. Where the visitor should be a trained worker, this approach must inevitably be a costly one, since the worker can serve only one family at a time. Karnes, Teska, Hodgins, and Badger (1970) chose the alternative strategy of bringing the mothers into the project center for training in parent-child interaction. The original sample consisted of 20 mothers whose children ranged in age from 13 to 27 months, with a mean of about 20 months. A control sample of 20 mothers was matched with the experimental group in both maternal and infant characteristics. One important difference, however, existed between the experimental and control mothers. The control group mothers were not asked whether they would be willing to participate in the training program. Thus the control mothers may have included women who would have refused the training because of disinterest in the child or other factors. To offset the possibility that an initial difference between experimental and control mothers could account for later findings, six control children were added to the study who were the older siblings of children whose mothers had agreed to enter the experimental training. Test data on these older siblings was collected when they were about the same age as the younger child would be when the maternal training was terminated. It was reasoned that if the older siblings were found to have been inferior to the children who had an opportunity to be effected by the maternal training it would demonstrate that the mother's willingness to enter training did not simply indicate that she had been a more effective parent initially.

The 20 mothers to be trained were divided into two groups and were given $1.50 for attending a two-hour lecture and discussion session each week. Lectures emphasized the importance of parent-child respect, positive reinforcement, and patient step-wise teaching. Parents were also advised to be tolerant when the child did not choose to interact with them. In addition to the lectures, the mothers were also provided with toys for use with the children. Training sessions were broken into seven and eight-month periods with a lapse of two months between semesters. After the first training period, five of the mothers decided not to continue and no posttest was done on their children. Program assessment was based, therefore, on a sample of only 15 children whose mothers had participated in a total of 15 months of training. From the standpoint of community impact, the 25 percent dropout rate may be regarded as a negative finding that does not appear in the formal test results.

Results of intelligence and language testing done on the children of the trained and untrained mothers following the intervention period showed the children of trained mothers to be significantly superior in both tests. Table 2 shows a comparison between the experimental group and the 20 nonsibling controls on the Binet intelligence test and the ITPA language test. The chronological age of the children in the two groups did not differ significantly, but mental age (MA) and language age of the children of trained mothers was significantly higher (language age is shown as a deviation from the general test norm, so that the negative score indicates that both groups were still subpar, but the experimental group was less so). In

Table 2. Experimental $(N = 15)$ and Matched Control $(N = 15)$ Groups, Stanford-Binet and ITPA (Karnes et al., 1970)

Variable	Binet CA (Months)		Binet MA (Months)		Binet IQ		ITPA Total Language-Age Difference Score (Months)[a]	
	Experiment	Control	Experiment	Control	Experiment	Control	Experiment	Control
Mean	37.9	38.3	41.8	35.5	106.3	90.6	−0.8	−5.9
Standard deviation	3.92	3.45	6.84	5.43	12.46	9.87	6.59	5.42
Difference	0.4		6.3		15.7		5.1	
t[b]	0.24		2.72		3.70		2.25	
Level of significance	N.S.		.01[b]		.0005[b]		.025[b]	

[a] To relate ITPA language age and chronological age and to compensate for slight differences in mean chronological ages between groups, a language-age *difference score* was computed by subtracting each child's chronological age at the time of testing from his language-age score. For example, a child who was 36 months old with a total language-age score of 32 months received a difference score of −4 months. All ITPA data are presented in this form. Children who scored below the norms provided for the ITPA total were arbitrarily assigned the lowest total language-age score (30 months). This score convention was required in three instances in the experimental group and in seven instances in the matched control.

[b] One-tailed test.

comparison with the sibling controls, the experimental group children were again found to be superior, suggesting that the training had a positive effect and that the experimental mothers had not simply been more adequate parents before their training than were the control mothers.

Unfortunately neither Levenstein or Karnes and their associates conducted their home-focused interventions long enough ago to allow for a post-intervention follow-up. Schaefer (1970) concluded on the basis of his review of early childhood intervention research that family-centered interventions may be necessary to produce lasting positive effects. Certainly, it is logical to suppose that long-term benefits are most likely where the intervention produces a permanent change in the home environment in which the child will spend most of his early life.

Findings (Karnes et al., 1970) and speculation (Schaefer, 1970) on the relationship between the effects of interventive programs and the breadth of their impact on the child's environment raise an important point concerning the value of early prevention programs as a means of gaining understanding of the operation of community forces. Much of the research on the impact of environmental deficiencies has been essentially observational, for example, the work of Dennis and Dennis (1941) with institutionalized children. It is likely, however, that observational research can only suggest, but never prove, how particular environmental factors affect development. This is because the possible variations in natural environments are so numerous that it is virtually inconceivable that one could ever find two settings differing in only one respect and, hence, permitting definitive conclusions as to the impact of a particular circumstance. Observational research must, therefore, leave problems in deciding where to lay blame and to attempt modification. For example, the observation that infants in institutions do poorly in a number of respects permits a multitude of plausible explanations: poor genetic makeup for children who are institutionalized, prenatal problems in cases where the mother must give up the child, poor diet in the institution, institutional sameness, lack of affection from caretakers, lack of adequate educational experiences, and so on. Interventive programs, on the other hand, by introducing controlled variations into children's environments may provide solid clues as to the importance of various environmental factors.

Consider the findings of Skeels and Dye that infants raised by retarded women could show intellectual gains over their performance under institutional care. These results strongly imply that cognitive growth in infancy is not mainly dependent on the ability of the caretakers to model highly intelligent behavior. Or consider the findings of Karnes et al. that children with relatively caring mothers gain more from a stimulation program than do children with less concerned mothers; the clear implication emerges that the emotional tone of the parent-child relationship may interact with the availability of learning experiences in determining whether children develop optimally. The interventive programs described in this chapter, others not mentioned and, hopefully, those yet to be attempted, may ultimately derive their greatest worth from the understanding to be gained about environmental forces by synthesizing the findings of numerous efforts to modify specific experiential factors through programs of applied research.

CONCLUSION

The programs directed at infants and young children provide illustrations of several principles that are gaining acceptance in the field of community psychology. First, these programs reflect the assumption that intervention is best attempted before manifest signs of psychosocial disturbance are evident. This assumption rests on the belief that high-risk populations can be identified on the basis of observed relationships between early experience and later maladaptation. The programs for young children also show that primary preventive efforts may have a positive rather than a negative emphasis. In Caplan's (1964) terms, the intervention may be aimed at providing appropriate "supplies" when they are needed, in contrast to the goal of removing an interfering disease entity. Finally, the programs described illustrate the notion that effective early intervention need not be restricted to improving psychological functioning directly; programs that provide the person with skills for meeting the demands of the society more successfully are assumed to increase thereby the likelihood that the individual will be psychologically adequate.

Many of the projects cited in this chapter offer the promise that effective and practical programs of early intervention are possible. Also, it is clear that most efforts to date have fallen short on issues of effectiveness, reach, or ease of implementation. Despite this failure, the value of continued research in this area cannot be overemphasized, given the worth it may have in helping us to identify the effects of varied environments on young children. Ultimately, an understanding of these effects might permit the community mental health worker to predict with confidence what changes in the environment will reduce the incidence of human dysfunction. Without a systematic exploration of the effects on the young of induced variations in community processes, the preventionist may be doomed to a future of building his plans on hopes, guesses, and prayers.

References

Bloom, B. S. *Stability and change in human characteristics.* New York: Wiley, 1964.

Campbell, D. T., & Eriebacher, A. How regression artifacts in quasi-experimental evaluation can mistakenly make compensatory education look harmful. In J. Hellmuth (Ed.), *Disadvantaged child.* Vol 3. New York: Brunner/Mazel, 1970. Pp. 185–210.

Caplan, G. *Principles of preventive psychiatry.* New York: Basic Books, 1964.

Dennis, W., & Dennis, M. G. Infant development under conditions of restricted practice and minimum social stimulation. *Genetic Psychology Monographs,* 1941, *23,* 149–155.

Gray, S. W., & Klaus, R. A. An experimental preschool program for culturally deprived children. *Child Development,* 1965, *36,* 887–898.

Gray, S. W., & Klaus, R. A. The early training project: A seventh year report. *Child Development,* 1970, *41,* 909–924.

Hotkins, A. S., Hollander, L., & Munk, B. Evaluation of psychiatric reports of Head Start programs. In J. Hellmuth (Ed.), *Disadvantaged child: Head Start and early intervention.* Vol. 1. Seattle, Wash.: Special Child Publications, 1968. Pp. 137–172.

Hunt, J. McV. *Intelligence and experience*. New York: Ronald Press, 1961.

Irwin, O. C. Effect of systematic reading of stories. *The Journal of Speech and Hearing Research*, 1960, *3*, 187–190.

Karnes, M. B., Teska, J. A., Hodgins, A. S., & Badger, I. D. Educational intervention at home by mothers of disadvantaged infants. *Child Development*, 1970, *41*, 925–935.

Kirschner Associates. *A national survey of the impacts of Head Start centers on community institutions*. Report prepared for US Department of Health, Education and Welfare, 1970.

Klaus, R. A., & Gray, S. W. The early training project for disadvantaged children: A report after five years. *Monographs of the Society for Research in Child Development*, 1968, *33*, 1–66.

Levenstein, P. Cognitive growth in preschoolers through stimulation of verbal interaction with mothers. Paper presented to the 46th annual meeting of the American Orthopsychiatric Association, New York: April 1969.

Provence, S., & Lipton, R. C. Infants in institutions: *A comparison of their development with family infants during the first year of life*. New York: International University Press, 1962.

Rheingold, H. L. The modification of social responsiveness in institutional babies. *Monographs of the Society for Research in Child Development*, 1956, *12* (2) (whole).

Rheingold, H. L., & Bayley, N. The later effects of an experimental modification of mothering. *Child Development*, 1959, *30*, 363–374.

Schaefer, E. S. Need for early and continuing education. In V. H. Denenberg (Ed.), *Education of the infant and young child*. New York: Academic Press, 1970. Pp. 61–82.

Schaefer, E. S., & Aaronson, M. Infant education research project: implementation and implications of a home tutoring program. Unpublished manuscript, 1970.

Skeels, H. M. Some preliminary findings of three follow-up studies on the effects of adoption on children from institutions. *Children*, 1965, *12*, 33–34.

Skeels, H. M., & Dye, H. B. A study of the effects of differential stimulation on mentally retarded children. *Journal of Psycho-asthenics*, 1939, *44*, 114–136.

Spitz, R. A. Hospitalism: An inquiry into the genesis of psychiatric conditions in childhood. *Psychoanalytic Study of the Child*, 1945, *1*, 53–74.

6. *primary prevention in the schools*

The school offers a promising operating base to the psychologist interested in reducing the prevalence of psychological dysfunction. Nascent problems may be spotted in the classroom, evaluated and, hopefully, eliminated through appropriate intervention. In the next chapter we shall provide examples of this secondary preventive approach. In this chapter we consider attempts to pursue an even more ambitious goal, that of reducing the original incidence of psychological disturbance. Stated positively, the common goal of the projects to be discussed is to make the schools more effective in providing the child with the resources that will help him develop into a psychosocially adequate human being.

The pursuit of the goal of primary prevention rests on the assumption that the school is more attractive as a base than a community clinic. The school experience is assumed to be a vital force in the child's life that has the potential to prepare him well or badly for the challenges of existence. Although its influence may be indirect and unrecognized, the school

147

must inevitably affect the way the student regards himself, his abilities, value as a person, and chances of success (Mosher and Sprinthall, 1970). From this perspective the function of the school as a place of learning cannot be separated from its function as a place in which the personality is formed (Biber, 1961). The further implication of this position is that the school as an institution must be engineered to serve the total needs of its students if it is to affect their psychological well-being optimally.

In maximizing the positive impact of the school on psychological development, the community psychologist faces two tasks: first, he must determine, or hypothesize, what types of experiences are likely to promote the acquisition of skills for effective living. Second, the preventionist must act as a "change agent" for a societal institution that has been molded by the traditions, biases, philosophies, and politics of the society in which it exists. The social scientist cannot be effective if he enters the school with the naive belief that he can or should totally reshape it in line with his own ideals.

To some extent, the community psychologist must always alter established institutions when he attempts to intervene. With respect to primary prevention in the schools, however, he encounters particularly serious difficulties. Primary prevention is not directed at the existing dysfunctions that may often motivate the educator to seek solutions. Further, the intervention may seem burdensome or threatening to school workers, whose goals do not necessarily include striving to provide for positive mental health (Caplan, 1961). Teachers may be poorly trained in personality development, overburdened, and prompted to concentrate primarily on students who perform readily within the existing school structure (Bower, 1961). The difficulty of instituting primary prevention programs in schools is attested to by the numerous efforts at intervention that have been rebuffed or quickly killed. It has even been suggested by one worker (DeCharms, 1971) that "intervention" as such is actually impossible, since only changes that school personnel perceive as originating with themselves can be expected to persist.

Aside from the questions and difficulties raised by the nature of the school as an institution, the preventionist must also come to grips with concerns that reside in the community at large. A central issue often encountered is whether the school should attempt to shape the personality development of children, or whether intentional efforts in this direction should be the prerogative of parents. This issue may encompass two separate types of concern. On the one hand, community members may fear that psychological engineering in the schools will foster developments in children that offend parental beliefs or thwart their child-rearing objectives. This issue has been salient in recent years with regard to efforts to introduce sex education into the schools. Some parents have argued, and not without impact, that the school must inevitably convey a value orientation toward sex in attempting to treat the subject; even a highly factual and mechanical presentation, by its omission of moral and ethical considerations implicitly provides children with an attitudinal stance. Where parents hold strong beliefs that sex should be treated within the context of a particular ethical framework, some are bound to feel threatened by any program, however strong an attempt is made to find an approach that is minimally offensive. As in the example of sex education, any primary preventive effort in the schools could potentially be regarded as offensive by parents who do not share the orientation of the interventionist. A second related area of community concern is whether environmental engineering may be objectionable in principle, even where the general goals seem acceptable. A civil libertarian might well hold that the schools already do too much to level and standardize the functioning of their students. Might not the well-intentioned psychologist only worsen this problem by giving educators the means and motivation to make students conform to someone's ideal of "mental health"?

There is still another perspective from which the community or segments thereof may oppose primary prevention efforts. To many citizens, the school exists mainly, if not solely, to impart socially useful skills and information to children. Goals of emotional growth have sometimes been seen as inconsistent with the primary task of the school. Indeed, it has sometimes been alleged that vaguely defined objectives of psychological development are actually invoked to rationalize the failure of educators to fulfill their true mandate of imparting specific knowledge.

The community concerns cited above cannot be lightly dismissed. They demand a careful consideration of the potential benefits of school-based primary prevention and a weighing of these benefits against substantial objections. The most obvious benefit of introducing primary prevention into the schools is that virtually everyone might be reached by such programs. Insofar as the community psychologist takes as his ultimate aim the maximum reduction of the incidence of environmentally related psychological disturbance, no more promising location is now available for directing his efforts. A second advantage, previously noted, is that the schools already inevitably shape the personality development of children. In response to the citizen who fears the control exerted by the interventionist in the school, it has been argued that schools can either control children through unsystematic efforts of unknown effectiveness, or through rationally planned and empirically tested methods; the psychological impact of the school is real in either case (Madden, 1972). Clearly, from this perspective, preventive intervention may be viewed as less potentially destructive and conflictful with parental wishes than existing approaches that already shape growth, but without the benefit of a public plan or assessed effect. Indeed, because the behavioral scientist is obliged to make known his goals and methods, it might be argued that he poses less of a threat to civil liberties than do those who shape behavior without acknowledging (or perhaps even realizing) that they are doing so. A final issue concerns the question of whether primary preventive efforts enhance or threaten the educative function of the school. As we show in several of the programs described in this chapter, the goal of helping schools to effectively teach culturally valued skills can be an integral part of the prevention program. From the positive stance of promoting mental health, the acquisition of learning that promotes later social adaptation may be viewed as essential. Thus, in answer to those who regard mental health programs as an interference with the true objectives of the school, it may often be possible to demonstrate that the innovative interventionist shares the concern that the school experience be educational, in the narrow sense, as well as beneficial in a broader psychological context.

In the final analysis, it may be necessary for citizens and psychologists alike to suspend judgment on the worth of primary prevention projects in the schools until more data are available. Meanwhile, however, the adversary role taken by many community members may actually serve a useful purpose by requiring the interventionist to take a true community perspective. Any community in which substantial numbers of people are interested enough to oppose programmatic efforts provides the mental health worker with the impetus and means for examining the general viability of his approach. Consistent with the model of public health medicine, an intervention cannot be deemed truly useful unless it can provide benefits on a wide scale. Projects that elicit community resistance to the extent that they cannot be implemented or quickly disappear enable us to learn both about our techniques and about the nature of the community.

Whatever the philosophical and practical problems of initiating innovative primary prevention in the schools, obviously the specific nature of the program will be a primary factor in its acceptability and effectiveness. The programs in this chapter exemplify a variety of approaches differing widely in their assumptions, goals, strategies, and methods. For purposes of organization, these examples are grouped according to which aspect of the school environment they seek primarily to influence. Roen (1967) has distinguished between programs aimed at altering the general atmosphere of the school and those that focus on alterations in the school curriculum. To these two categories a third will be added in this chapter to include projects aimed at altering the basic methods of teaching and behavior control.

PROGRAMS WHICH EMPHASIZE TOTAL SCHOOL ATMOSPHERE

The common feature of programs in this category is that the interventions are aimed at altering the school setting in a variety of interrelated ways with the objective of creating a total environment that promotes adequate human development. The basic premise of one such program, the Bank Street Project, exemplifies the assumption fundamental to projects of this type: "That it is necessary to formulate a program through which mental health principles will be infused into every school process and relationship" (Biber, 1961, p. 348). Given this objective, it is obvious that programs in this category involve a coordinated set of specific actions that will presumably have a beneficial cumulative effect. The specific interventions in a given setting will vary according to the nature of the existing institution and the community it serves. For these reasons, projects of this type are often better defined by their stated goals than by a single action strategy or set or techniques.

The Bank Street Project stands as a pioneering effort in the total school approach. The Project, based at the Bank Street College of Education in New York City, involved an ongoing effort to integrate research and action (Biber, 1961). Its philosophy rests on the thinking of modern educators like Dewey and the psychodynamic personality theorists like Freud, and the viewpoint of 20th-century humanism (Biber, 1961). The psychological goals of the educational process are stated to be: (1) positive feeling toward self, (2) realistic perception of self and others, (3) relatedness to people, (4) relatedness to the environment, (5) independence, (6) curiosity and creativity, and (7) recovery and coping strength. Techniques for achieving these goals have been described and given a rationale. For example, to increase openness to the environment, Biber (1967) has suggested giving children guided observation of potentially fascinating events such as the construction of a building.

The Bank Street team has been conservative in implementing its philosophy. Projects have been undertaken to facilitate the infusion of mental health principles into existing schools through group consultation with teachers and parents. However, the ultimate goal of establishing and testing the Bank Street approach, which requires the creation of a school integrally structured around the philosophy (Biber, 1961), has yet to be achieved. Indeed, it is not clear that the less ambitious efforts to affect existing schools have had much impact; Roen (1967) asserts that the influence of the Bank Street program has been limited to a few private schools.

Given that the ultimate test of the Bank Street approach must rest on the unrealized and lofty goal of creating a totally new school, the Bank Street team has performed research that provides less direct and less conclusive evidence of the validity of its philosophy. In a naturalistic study, Minuchin, Biber, Shapiro, and Zimiles (1969) sought to compare the effects on children of existing schools differing in their degree of resembalance to the Bank Street ideal. The research team carefully selected four schools that were adjudged to fall at different points along a continuum from "modern" (best exemplifying the Bank Street philosophy) to traditional. Figure 1 shows some of the specific differences in educational emphasis that were the criteria for evaluating schools on the modern-traditional dimension. An attempt was made to select schools that differed in educational philosophy, but served pupils of similar socioeconomic back-

---

1. Stimulation of Intellectual Processes

Active exploration and discovery by child	Direct transmission of information and skill from teacher to child
Child's ability to formulate and search for varied solutions to problems	Teaching devices that raise teaching and learning efficiency
Sustaining critical questioning and probing of ideas	Learning tasks with detailed directions for children to follow
Mastery through child's ability to discern relationships among facts and learn to deal with higher-order concepts	Amount and rate of mastering factual information
	Tendency to drift from pursuit of ideas to moral precepts

2. Variety of Learning Modes

Creative expression is integral to intellectual development	Creative arts are supplemental to academic program
Variety of media for expressive activities	Creative activities as skill subjects
Developing techniques to integrate expressive and analytic modes	Reliance on the verbal mode as the proper instrument for learning

3. Sources of Motivation: Children

Stimulation of interest and self-investment in learning activities	Use of established symbols as measure of accomplishment
Use of techniques for making learning individually meaningful and satisfying	Use of an approval-disapproval code of evaluation
Concept of a school climate that matches qualities and impulses of children	Encouragement of comparative-competitive processes

4. Sources of Motivation: Teachers

Enjoyment of spontaneity and curiosity of children

Sense of competence derived from depth and vigor of children's response to learning activities

Sense of personal worth derived from choice and initiative afforded by administrator

Identification with school's leadership position in the profession

Pride in high achievement scores attained by children

Ability to control and discipline valued highly as part of sense of competence

Dependence on administrator's approval as measure of competence

Opportunity for extra-classroom activities

5. Encouragement of Teacher Autonomy

Autonomy extended to teachers as part of general view in which the individual's independence and initiative is highly valued

Teachers encouraged and supported in innovative, creative approach to curriculum

Teachers made participants in some aspects of decision-making for school as a whole

Autonomy more a by-product of minimal supervision and absence of common value system

Teachers expected to follow a directed course in implementing objectives as interpreted by the administration

Figure 1. Differences in educational emphasis of schools on modern-traditional continuum (Minuchin et al., 1969).

ground. It is clear, however, that the schools were not altogether well matched on variables other than the social class of the student population. The most striking failure to control other variables arose from the fact that no public school could be found that was evaluated as falling toward the extremely modern end of the continuum. Thus the study included three public schools and a small private school; it is conceivable that the distinguishing characteristics of the children in the most modern school were related to the factors that led their parents to place them in a private institution, instead of to the effects of the school itself.

Within the four schools, Minuchin and his co-workers focused their attention on 105 fourth-grade children. The children selected were studied quite intensively, with information being gathered through the use of school informants, direct classroom observation, parental informants, and test data collected in the course of five individual sessions. The great wealth of data collected by these means defies brief summarization, so that only a few of the findings most relevant to primary prevention can be included here. Essentially, the basic hypothesis that the psychological characteristics of the children in the different schools would differ received moderate support. Children in the most modern school were found, for example, to be better able to accept their negative feelings and were less future oriented than their peers in the more traditional schools. It was not found that the cognitive skills of the children were directly related to the modern-traditional dimension but, if anything, the data suggested that children in the traditional schools achieved better on standardized tests. Children in the most modern school consistently scored below the other groups on tests of intelligence and achievement, although the authors attribute this difference to test-taking attitudes and motivation. In the interpersonal sphere some evidence was collected which suggested that the character of the school affected the way the children saw others; however, the findings must be evaluated with regard for the numerous failures to find differences. Sexual identity was another area studied where school philosophy seemed to have an impact. Children in the most modern school continued to evidence sex-linked personality features, but these children were less likely to exhibit the stereotyped sex-role distinctions than were children from the more traditional schools.

The complex findings of Minuchin and his associates certainly do not provide unequivocal evidence that a particular school philosophy is preferable from the standpoint of promoting mental health. The research does not prove that the future lives of children in the more modern schools will be happier or more stable than the lives of children receiving a more traditional educational experience. At best, any conclusions must combine the evidence presented with the observer's own biases as to what childhood traits are desirable. In addition, the naturalistic approach taken by Minuchin et al. does not speak to the issue of creating or modifying schools so as to produce the desired effects. Zimiles (1967) in evaluating the research argues, however, that studies of this type will ultimately guide us in the shaping of environments when it becomes technically possible better to identify influential factors and their interactions.

The Bank Street approach rests on a broad conceptualization of the school emphasizing the educational philosophy around which the institution is built. A different, but similarly broad model for conceptualizing school characteristics is to be found in the work of Kelly and his associates in Michigan. By drawing on the biological concept of an ecological system, Kelly (1968) has adapted several principles to make them applicable to social environments: (1) functions within a social unit are interdependent; (2) resources within a social system may be recycled and emerge as a productive output or may be absorbed by the system itself; (3) the environment affects styles of adaptation; and (4) natural communities evolve, with changes in membership and function occurring. Operating from these principles, Kelly (1967) sought to predict how students at two high schools would differ as a function of different rates of student turnover at the two institutions. Kelly identified a "fluid" school with a turnover rate of about 42 percent and a "constant" school with a rate of only 10 percent. Differences in turnover rate were primarily attributable to greater geographical mobility of the families served by the fluid school. Attending only to this known difference between the schools (although other differences were also known to exist), Kelly was able to make several predictions that were supported by observational and student interview data. Evidence supportive of predictions included the findings that new students were more readily accepted in the fluid school, that personal development was more valued in this setting, and that student groups were more stable and inviolable in the constant school. Kelly's data also showed that the school administrations, as aspects of an interlocking system, differed in their operating styles and professed standards.

The practical implication of Kelly's preliminary conceptualizations have already stimulated efforts to approach the task of primary prevention from an ecological perspective. Carroll, Bell, Minor, and Brecher (1973) have attempted to maximize the position impact of inner city parochial schools in Philadelphia by an intervention "focused upon certain key interlocking psychological systems and component subsystems rather than upon individuals per se" (p. 1). A particular project emphasis was to promote positive relationships between children and teachers despite the fact that the children live much of their lives in a "street" system which is, in many ways, in conflict with the school as an institutional system. Toward the goal of affecting both teachers and children concurrently, the researchers organized small groups including teachers and children in which consultants encouraged discussion by the children while teachers acted as participant observers. Similarly, project consultants aided teachers in establishing systematic contacts with parents in the community. The mental health team trained teachers to act as small group facilitators so as to bring into the ecosystem of the school the skills for perpetuating the new programs after the withdrawal of the outside consultants.

A recent report by Minor (1972) describes the deployment of the ecological model in a way that differs slightly in emphasis from the work of Kelly and his associates. Whereas Kelly recognized the ecological significance of the total community but attempted to intervene primarily with school personnel, Minor and his co-workers in the Philadelphia school system offered themselves as liaisons between the school and the other subsystems in which the child operates. In a case example, Minor describes how a community consultant contacted the family of a child who had been found by the teacher to be carrying pictures that the teacher considered pornographic. The consultant was able to piece together a picture of the total ecosystem in which the child was operating, and to formulate a plan of action that considered the interlocking aspects of the home and school situation.

Although the ecological model has yet to be widely applied, this conceptualization may have implications for an issue that we have already discussed. From an ecological viewpoint, school interventions may be doomed to failure if they are not planned with attention to the repercussions that any program will produce throughout the system. Thus preventive efforts that offer great promise may be impossible to implement or sustain if their effects on key subsystems in the institution or community are negatively regarded. One possible response to the danger that a program will fail because it ignores or offends elements of the scholastic community is to design multifaceted programs which expand over time as resistances diminish and demand develops. The remaining programs in this section exemplify this strategy. Naturally, those that evolve as a function of the unique characteristics of a particular school will inevitably lack the conceptual unity of an approach like that of the Bank Street Project. In fact, the projects to be discussed are sufficiently diverse in their interventive actions that they cannot be wholly encompassed under the category of primary prevention. Many of the specific functions of the workers in these programs would best be described as having secondary or even tertiary prevention as their goals.

The work of Sarason, Levine, Goldenberg, Cherlin, and Bennett (1966) provides an excellent example of a project shaped by the discerned needs and tolerances of the school settings to be served. Sarason and his associates wished to mount interventive efforts in elementary schools located in the New Haven area. Their first steps toward this goal were cautious ones, based on a recognition that the services they were preparing to offer would not be universally welcomed within the institutions. Meetings were arranged with teachers and administrators to introduce ideas, but more importantly to gain a sense of the way in which the outside consultants were viewed by the school staff. Through these meetings, the consultant team was able to identify the problems in entering the institution and to determine their next move toward developing a helpful role in the setting. Based on the observations made in initial meetings, the consultant team moved next into a passive observer role in the classrooms. By observing the classes, the consultants hoped to help school personnel recognize the willingness of the consultants to learn how things really happen in the actual "front line" work of the teacher. The observation sessions in some instances led to rapid breakthroughs in staff acceptance, as occurred when a consultant was able to help concretely a teacher and principal confronted with a child throwing a frighteningly impressive temper tantrum. In most cases, however, acceptance was gained less dramatically as a few teachers would begin to approach the consultant for help.

The operating style of the consultants, once they gained acceptance, was based on the observation that teaching is a lonely profession where the teacher must generally rely almost solely on his own resources, even in situations for which he has little preparation. The consultants made themselves available to the school staff as trustworthy, politically (school politics) disinterested fellow professionals with a useful new perspective to provide. Indeed, the consultants primarily viewed their own helping skill in terms of their ability to aid teachers in changing their perceptions of problem situations. It was hoped, and anecdotally verified, that when teachers could gain new perspectives on the problem that their own resources would enable them to solve the dilemma and effect a solution. Note that in contrast to the traditional role of the psychologist in the system, the program consultants did not act as "stand-ins" to take over when the teacher had "failed." The consultants labored to become a useful part of the working team in the school, sympathetic to the mental health needs of pupils and teachers alike.

It might be readily inferred that the consultants did not always, or even frequently, serve as true primary preventionists; the case material provided by Sarason et al. suggests that secondary prevention was more often the need for which the consultants were sought. Nevertheless, there were instances in which the consultants intervened where the problem situation was not necessarily created by an existing psychological disturbance in the child. Figure 2 represents an example of a situation where the

---

Example 6. A first-grade child was a saucy and mincing young lady who would sometimes move slowly and deliberately in rather theatrical fashion, making everyone wait on her. She also did not do her work in class, tending to daydream away her time, or complain that she was too tired. The consultant and teacher both knew that the little girl had experienced much illness in her family and that, in fact, in her own household she was a little prima donna. The teacher, a highly competent individual who shared some of the child's prima donnishness, found herself reacting almost with rage to this little girl. One afternoon, seeing the consultant in the building, she asked for a conference, during which she expressed the frustration and anger she felt with the little girl. After having permitted herself the rather uninhibited expression of her feelings, the teacher found herself amazed at the intensity of her reaction to the child and expressed guilt and shame about the situation. The consultant was able to be quite supportive of her in the situation, and throughout the rest of the term the teacher never again felt quite so distressed as she had on this one occasion.

Figure 2. Example of consultant's work with a teacher (Sarason et al., 1966, p. 85).

mental health of the child may have been fostered by helping a teacher work through feelings that might have led her to be destructive toward the student. In general, by helping the teacher to handle difficult situations, the consultants may have permitted him to have more positive impact on his students generally.

A project reported by Morse (1967) resembles the New Haven program to the degree that the consultation model was employed and teachers were the primary consultees. The Morse project placed greater emphasis, however, only on goals of true primary prevention. The present effort, as with the New Haven project, began with careful steps to gain entry to the schools, in this instance, elementary and junior high schools located in Michigan. The project workers went so far as to create a "hospitality index" to assess the degree of resistance to the intervention. Based on this index, schools falling at different points along the hospitality dimension were selected as the target institutions. The consultants entered each school prepared to offer whatever services were initially desired. From this starting point, formulated to respect the idiosyncracies of each institution, the project consultants worked to evolve an increasingly comprehensive helping role for themselves. In many instances the services of the consultant involved direct service to children with a secondary preventive emphasis. The Michigan project also included, however, services to teachers having primary prevention as their objective. These services included didactic presentations on topics like personality theory; more uniquely, the services included group sessions, for self-selected teachers, that approached the character of group therapy.

The goals of group meetings included such things as enhancing the self-esteem of the teachers so as to enable them to become more confident and direct in their classroom interactions. Assessment data, based on self-perception inventories administered to teachers, was found to show that participants in the group programs gained in their sense of competence as had been hoped. Newer teachers were found to be particularly affected by the experience. In addition, children in the classes filled out questionnaires on the perceptions of their classrooms. Here, the data were generally positive, but less clearly so than the data on the teachers themselves.

The final project we describe in this section is chosen primarily for the uniqueness of its consultant team. This effort, involving schools in two Texas school districts, is described by Iscoe, Pierce-Jones, Friedman, and McGehearty (1967). The consultants in this project were school psychology graduate students who, as part of their training, acted as "child behavior consultants" for half a day once a week in 14 diverse schools. The student consultants, whose previous training had included psychotherapy experience, were prepared for their new role through orientation to the theories of crisis intervention (the concept being that teachers seeking consultation should be viewed as people in crisis) and had ready access to supervisors. Despite this preparation, Iscoe et al. found that their students experienced many problems in adapting to their new role, partially as a result of their new role, partially because of their preconceptions about the way a psychologist must function.

The child behavior consultants functioned primarily as helping agents for the school personnel; direct service to children was not a major part of their function. Consultants were, however, given latitude to vary their style of operation according to the characteristics of the school in which they were placed. Preliminary findings of the two-year program showed that about 600 consultations had been conducted, with initial differences between the rate of utilization by schools in different districts. In particular, the schools servicing minority groups solicited fewer consultations. About 41 percent of the school personnel eligible for the service across districts did make one or more uses of the consultants. Of particular relevance to this chapter is the finding that almost two thirds of the children for whom assistance was sought did not display major psychological problems; thus, the program was not mainly useful for secondary prevention. A particular value of the program in Texas would seem to be that it demonstrates consultants can enter the schools, can be utilized with reasonable frequency, and can service the needs of children not already experiencing substantial psychological difficulty. The fact that the project operated in a reasonably large number of schools, 14, makes it useful for generating hypotheses about which institutional and community variables may determine whether a program of this type will be accepted and optimally utilized.

PROGRAMS AIMED AT CURRICULUM IMPROVEMENT

The programs just described suggest that interventions directed at the school as a total system may be a promising means for achieving primary prevention. Doubts must remain, however, as to just how much impact these interventions may have and, also, as to how widely such efforts can be implemented. One of the problems with the total school approach is that it generally requires the extensive use of professional or preprofessional workers; given manpower resource limitations it is doubtful that most schools could be served in the ways previously described. For this reason, among others, some workers have focused their efforts on an approach that might require less psychological manpower to implement— the strategy of developing curricula that schools might adopt as a means of promoting the mental health of students. The curriculum approach, in addition to its possible efficiency, is also attractive because it requires a form of change within the school that is more familiar to educators and potentially less threatening. The programs to be discussed are based on the assumption that children can be taught to understand themselves and the psychological environment, and that such learning will promote the development of psychosocial adequacy. These programs should not be confused with projects to introduce a social sciences curriculum into the schools (such as that proposed by Farris, Kent, and Henderson, 1970) where the goal is simply to introduce children to the fundamentals of an important new science.

The Bullis (Bullis and O'Malley, 1947) curriculum for classes in human relations is a pioneer preventive program intended for children in the late elementary or early secondary grades. Starting in 1941, Bullis and his colleagues began to develop a fairly well specified sequence of lesson plans for a course to augment the usual range of class activities. The program goal was clearly stated: "in the past our schools have put all the emphasis on developing children intellectually and physically. We want them to grow up with robust personalities, able to go through life in an even keel" (Bullis and O'Malley, 1947; pp. 1–2). The specifically preventive nature of the project is underscored by the fact that statistics on psychiatric hospitalization, psychological disability, and antisocial behavior are presented as compelling reasons for instituting the human relations courses.

The Bullis curriculum places heavy emphasis on active student participation. The teacher's role is primarily to introduce evocative material and to facilitate class discussion. Many of the lesson plans include short stories which the teacher reads to introduce topics such as the arousal of emotions or the means for handling defeat. The curriculum also provides briefing for the teacher regarding the major psychological issues toward which each lesson is directed. Teachers who implement the program are not assumed to begin with any particular sophistication in psychology or the technique of group discussion leadership.

The relatively limited demands made on the teacher and the minimal time requirements of the course (one class per week) certainly make the Bullis program an easy one to implement. Even so, Bullis and O'Malley are forced to note that adding a single class in human relations cannot, in itself, have much impact, and that greater degrees of effort on the part of teachers and administrators may be required to create a meaningful program. Thus even the Bullis curriculum may fail or succeed as a function of total school situation.

Evidence on the effectiveness of the Bullis curriculum is sparse. The originators offer only anecdotal data indicating that the program was well accepted by the children and played an early secondarily preventive role for some children showing signs of disturbance. Given the program goals, a real test of the efficacy of the Bullis curriculum would require a longitudinal study following children who had experienced the program into adulthood to determine whether their coping ability had been strengthened. Research of this kind has not been done, and one study casts doubt on even the short-range value of the Bullis approach.

Leton (1957) compared the effects of four different mental hygiene programs on ninth graders who had scored poorly on an adjustment inventory. The four treatments were the Bullis human relations course, a series of mental hygiene movies, sociodrama and role playing, and a hobby and crafts activity group. Each experimental treatment group was matched with a sample of children receiving no special attention. The basic framework of the experiment is shown in Table 1. As may be seen, the experiment was done twice in two succeeding years with different samples of students. Results of the Leton study failed to demonstrate that any of the interventions were superior to no treatment as measured by pencil-and-paper tests of adjustment, school grades, or school attendance. In two respects, however, the Leton study may not be a fair test of the Bullis program. First, the Bullis curriculum was conceived as a primary preventive tool; the inclusion of only students who were already experiencing problems may have excluded the group most likely to benefit from the program (Carter, 1965). Second, the single semester weekly classes may have been too little or too late to substantially affect the adjustment of students already at the high school level.

A second curriculum centered approach to primary prevention in the schools was developed by Ojemann and his associates. Dating back to the early 1940s like the Bullis project, this effort has been based at the University of Iowa. A considerable amount of evaluative research has been

Table 1. Framework of the Leton Experiment (Leton, 1957, p. 527)

Ninth Grade Second Semester 1952 to 1953					Ninth Grade Second Semester 1953 to 1954				
School method	Grade N^a	N	N_1	N_2	Method	Grade N	N	N_1	N_2
1 Activity	236	48	13	13	Sociodrama	231	45	13	13
2 Bullis	254	52	13	13	Movies	259	43	13	13
3 Sociodrama	110	26	13	13	Activity	128	24	12	10[b]
4 Movies	447	113	13	13	Bullis	322	72	13	13

[a] Grade N is the number of students in the ninth grade class, N is the number of students with deviant scores, N_1 is the experimental sample, and N_2 is the control sample.

[b] Two students from this control group dropped out of school before the experiment was completed.

done on the Ojemann approach over the years, a fact that may be partially attributable to the nature of the program goals. Unlike the projects already described, the Iowa program has fairly definite objectives that are more easily operationalized than such broad, vague goals as improved adjustment or better self-image.

The focus of the Iowa intervention has been on the way in which children learn to perceive and interpret human behavior. Ojemann (1960) distinguishes between a causal approach, in which behavior is viewed as having antecedents that must be considered before action is taken, and the noncausal or punitive orientation where reasons and motives are disregarded. Ojemann argues that the punitive approach leads to dissatisfying human relationships and that such relationships often lead to mental illness. His observation of typical schools led Ojemann to conclude that children were being trained toward a noncausal orientation. Teachers were seen to model the punitive approach when they punished students for misbehavior without questioning the reasons for the transgression. School textbooks were also found to be faulty in their emphasis on the "facts" of human events without examination of the motivations that shaped those occurrences.

Ojemann's operational strategy involved modifying the existing school curriculum to make it more relevant to issues of human behavior (Roen, 1967). The means for implementing curriculum change has been the training of teachers and the creation of new teaching materials in various subject areas. In addition, the program includes consultation with the trained teachers throughout the school year (Ojemann, Levitt, Lyle, and Whiteside, 1955).

A typical procedure for training teachers to give children a causal orientation (Ojemann et al., 1955) begins with the selection of teachers through consultation with school officials. The teachers chosen, undoubtedly a superior group, receive one month of triweekly training sessions during the summer vacation period. Training is focused on the study of normative developmental problems, indoctrination in the causal approach, discussion of techniques for dealing with classroom problems, and the preparation or modification of teaching materials. In addition, teachers receive about 20 hours of group therapy over the summer. Beyond the summer program, teachers engage in trimonthly consultations with project personnel to discuss materials, specific pupils, program evaluation, and further issues in child development. The variegated nature of the teacher training makes it difficult, of course, to specify what elements of the procedure are influential in producing any observed results.

In a study of how effectively the program influenced the causal orientation of children, Ojemann (1960) compared four elementary school classes taught by trained teachers with four classes led by untrained instructors. Children in experimental and control classes were matched on IQ, while teachers were matched on age, sex, experience, and education. Prepost measures on a test of causal orientation, the Problem Situations Test (PST), showed the children in the experimental classes to have become significantly more causally oriented than students in the control classes. The data from this test is shown in Table 2, with a low PST score indicating a more causal orientation. Recognizing that this difference might be attributed to initial differences between teachers who entered the program and those who did not, Ojemann used a self-control design (that is, a comparison of an individual with himself) to show that two of the teachers were significantly better at instilling a causal approach after having been through program training than they had been before they were trained.

The demonstration that Ojemann's program leads to better causality scores does not indicate that it enhances mental health. Several studies, however, have attempted to relate the causal curriculum to various indexes of psychological status. Levitt (1955) examined the effects of the program on authoritarianism and responsibility in elementary school children. Three classes, a fourth, fifth, and sixth grade, were taught by teachers who had been trained in the causal approach. Two matched control classes whose teachers had not been so trained were selected for each experimental class. Posttest comparisons showed the experimental groups to be less authoritarian than the controls with no differences between groups on the responsibility measure. It should be noted, however, that no pretesting was done, and the differences in authoritarianism might have been due to initial unrecognized variations between the classes.

Bruce (1958) conducted a study to determine the effects of the Ojemann program on three variables often regarded as indexes of adjustment: anxiety, security, and self-ideal-self-discrepancy. Two sixth-grade classes were exposed to trained teachers for a single year and two for a period of 2 years. Control classes matched on several variables were se-

Table 2. Mean Pretest and Posttest Scores on the PST (Ojemann, 1960, p. 332)

Grade	Experimental				Control			
	N	IQ	Pre	Post	N	IQ	Pre	Post
4th	19	110.89	5.05	3.74	16	106.31	5.81	7.47
5th	19	108.47	4.95	2.32	16	109.94	4.50	5.13
6th (I)	19	111.74	4.74	2.00	16	108.63	6.63	6.06
6th (II)	19	105.68	5.95	1.53	16	107.88	4.56	4.06
Total	76	109.20	5.17	2.39	64	108.19	5.38	5.67

lected, and posttest comparisons were run that found the experimental group to have lower anxiety scores and higher security scores. Self-ideal-self-discrepancy did not differ significantly between the groups. In a more detailed study, Muss (1960) used six mental health scales and four tests of causal orientation. Subjects were members of three sixth-grade classes, one of which received 1 year under the program, one 2 years, and the third no time in the program. The group that received only 1 year of treatment was not found to be superior to the no treatment controls. The group that received 2 years in the program was more causally oriented than the controls and also did better on three of the scales reflecting mental health (they were less authoritarian, more tolerant of ambiguity, and more aware of the probabalistic nature of events).

The data supportive of the Iowa approach are impressive, but two cautions are in order. First, most of the instruments used to assess program effects were paper-and-pencil tests and the children in the experimental classes may have been inadvertantly influenced by the trained teacher to recognize the socially desireable nature of the "healthy" response. In the absence of observational data, it is impossible to say that the children in the experimental groups actually behaved differently in any way other than test-taking behavior. Second, the intervention involved a variety of procedures with teachers, and it is not clear that the causal curriculum orientation was the most potent factor producing the changes. It is conceivable, for example, that the group therapy experienced by the teachers improved their outlook sufficiently to make their psychological impact on the children a more positive one irrespective of the curriculum used. The only data bearing directly on this issue is that of Ojemann et al. (1955), which shows that program teaching materials employed by untrained teachers did not make the teachers more effective than controls without the materials. Thus Ojemann's own work suggests that the formal curriculum itself is not sufficient to produce an effect, but what precisely is remains in doubt.

The issue of the effective elements in the Iowa training program is of considerable practical importance. As Roen (1967) has observed, the program has not had widespread impact because the training procedure is difficult to master and the structure of the training does not fit existing curriculum structures in schools of education. If the Iowa program of teacher training is to have greater national impact, it will undoubtedly be necessary to pare the training procedure to its essential elements.

The final program discussed in this section constitutes a more narrowly delineated curriculum modification than is exemplified by the Bullis or Ojemann approaches. Roen (1967) proposes a behavioral sciences curriculum for the elementary schools which structurally resembles the kind of course outline that might be used to teach any subject. Indeed, part of the goal of Roen's program is simply to introduce another area of science into the schools. Roen also argues, however, that the behavioral sciences curriculum could serve as a tool for early prevention. The psychological benefits of the program are said to derive from the ego-enhancing effect of acquiring a new type of knowledge and from the increased comfort in the school setting that the child might gain by studying the various influences involved in the learning process.

The behavioral sciences curriculum has been tested in Massachusetts fourth grade classes and in a residential treatment center for children. The time demands of the program seem quite modest, with one school allotting 45 minutes per week to the new course of study.

While data on the didactic success of the course is shown by Roen to be impressive, the evidence on the mental health benefits of the program is slight. Roen cites an unpublished study done in 1965 by Bartolo Spano designed to test the psychological impact of the behavioral sciences program. The children taking the new course were students in two fourth-grade classrooms of differing socioeconomic composition. Two control classes were matched on the basis of the economic background variable, IQ, age, and achievement level. Spano employed several tests of psychological adjustment and personality orientation in evaluating the effects of weekly 50-minute classes conducted over a five-month period. Findings showed the experimental group children to be superior to controls on measures of causal thinking and democratic behavior. On a number of other instruments, however, the groups were not found to differ significantly.

The special virtue of Roen's program, if it can be shown to be effective, is the relative ease with which it can be implemented. The techniques needed to employ the new curriculum can be learned in a single college seminar; one such seminar has already been developed. The school time required to teach the curriculum is minimal, and teaching aides can assist the teacher in enlivening the program.

PROGRAMS TO MODIFY TEACHING TECHNIQUES

The programs that follow represent attempts to modify very specific aspects of the way in which teachers conduct their classes. These programs are not founded on a stated philosophy concerning the validity of teaching goals or the value of curriculum content. Instead, the programs in this section seek to provide teachers with techniques to achieve whatever ends they seek. These techniques are founded (their proponents assert) on the application of psychology as an empirical study of observable behavior and the laws by which it is modified. The techniques involved often have their foundation in studies of animal behavior, particularly in studies of operant conditioning.

The movement into the area of intervention grounded in learning theory requires a shift in perspective if the goals of the investigators are to be understood. Ulrich, Stachnik, and Mabry (1970) speak explicitly of the behaviorist becoming involved in the business of prevention, but they do not speak of the prevention of mental illness as such. Rather, they see the behaviorist as designing programs that will prevent relatively circumscribed, readily specifiable problem behaviors. That these behaviors may be designated as mental illness by other psychologists is of no particular interest to the committed behaviorist, because he assumes that all behaviors (except, perhaps, those produced by bodily dysfunction) develop from, are maintained by, and can be modified through the usual principles that govern behavior.

Although behavioristic interventive approaches rest on a philosophy which differs from that of the projects discussed previously several similarities exist between the varied approaches. A broad similarity is that all of the behavioristic programs to be discussed share the primary preventive orientation toward making the school a positive influence in children's lives. Ulrich, Stachnik, and Mabry express this positive approach in noting that: "To the extent that a youngster acquires and engages in skills which are valued by our culture, there is a concommitant decrease in problem behavior" (p. 287). Also the behavioristically oriented approaches are similar to the more humanistic efforts in that the differing approaches converge on certain critical points, for example, the understanding that the child should be given an optimal chance to experience success in the scholastic setting. Indeed, less orthodox behavior modifiers may even be willing to phrase their goals in fairly humanistic terms. Witness Madden's (1972) observation that, ". . . children who habitually act out or disrupt a class tend to be unhappy, unpopular, and low in self-esteem" and that "Positive reinforcement offers these children a chance to find academic and peer-group success in a friendly open environment" (p. 105). Yet, it would be absurd to overstate the similarities between programs of behavioristic intervention and some of the humanistically oriented programs cited earlier. The behaviorist, with his technology for shaping behavior through the maintenance of a precisely regulated set of contingencies, obviously would find little virtue in the Bank Street Project's emphasis on minimizing the school's control over the activity of the child so as to release his creative energies.

Thomas, Becker, and Armstrong (1968) entered a middle primary school to test and demonstrate the effects of teacher approval or disapproval on ordinary children. The subjects were 28 children, ages six or seven, in a group regarded as a "good" class. The independent variable in the research design was the frequency with which the teacher responded to the child's appropriate behavior with approval and to inappropriate behavior with disapproval. The independent variable was manipulated by instructing the teacher to withhold approval for a period of days and to give frequent disapproval on other days; periods of baseline behavior (approval predominant) were interspersed between the manipulated conditions. The independent variable was the frequency with which disruptive behaviors, recorded by classroom observers using a time sampling procedure, occurred during each of the experimental periods.

Findings of the study showed that when the teacher stopped giving approval, the frequency of problem behaviors returned almost to baseline level. The frequency of disruptive behavior reached a peak during the period in which the teacher gave no approval for positive acts but much disapproval for negative behavior. The implications of these results are clear for the teacher whose objective is to encourage task orientation and prosocial behavior in the classroom. Contingent positive reinforcement in the form of teacher approval reduces or keeps low the frequency with which children will engage in behaviors that frustrate the teacher's goals.

An important point to observe in the study by Thomas and his associates is the fact that the researchers actually instituted situations in the classroom that they had reason to believe would produce negative effects. To demonstrate that teacher approval is crucial to maintaining low levels of disruptive behavior, the authors had the teacher deny all approval over a period of days. By instituting the ineffective condition (low approval for positive behavior) and returning later to a more desirable condition, it was convincingly demonstrated that the rate of teacher approval actually controlled the rate of disruptive behavior. Such a powerful demonstration technique could hardly be employed with a complex intervention like the Iowa causal curriculum; it is very unlikely that any researcher would institute a noncausal, punitively oriented program to demonstrate that subsequent exposure to the causal curriculum could reverse the negative effects. The behaviorist, by playing for lower stakes than the overall mental health of the child, that is, specific target behaviors, gains a freedom to manipulate conditions that is unavailable to the traditional interventionist. Conceivably, the more definitive results that the behaviorist can produce to substantiate the value of his intervention, the greater the likelihood of his selling his ideas in the schools.

Another example of behavioristic experimental intervention in the classroom is Packard's (1970) work using token reinforcements to control student attention. The subjects in this study were children in kindergarten and the third, fifth, and sixth grades. The dependent variable was the percentage of time spent by students in behaviors indicative of "paying attention" to the teacher and the assigned work. The principle, experimental conditions were: (1) baseline, (2) instructions to attend unaccompanied by other reinforcements, and (3) a special group contingency regimen in which the teacher gave tokens or privileges to all the children when criterion levels of class were showing attentive behavior. An observer was also present to record attentional behavior of specific children in the group. Although the actual experimental conditions were fairly complex and variations existed between the precise methods used at different grade levels, the basic findings are readily communicable. The group contingent reinforcement was found to be effective at all grade levels in increasing the percentage of time spent attending. When reinforcement was discontinued, attention dropped; when reinforcement was reinstated, attention levels rose again. The instructions-only condition produced attention levels above baseline for some classes, but where it occurred, the increase was less dramatic than that shown with the reinforcement. Packard noted the encouraging fact that the teachers were able to measure the occurrence of the target behavior and did not need the help of an outside observer to know when to give reinforcements.

One might well ask at this point whether a school intervention to demonstrate ways of reducing disruptive behavior or increasing classroom attention is really relevant to the prevention of psychological disturbance. Chandler (1971) offers two affirmative lines of reasoning. She suggests that when a child performs poorly in school, he is likely to receive negative labels such as "lazy" or "immature." This outcome in itself could have detrimental effects on the child's self-esteem and relations with others. Yet, if appropriate classroom management techniques can increase the probability that a given child will perform within accepted norms, the risk that negative labels will be applied is reduced. Furthermore, the behavioristic intervention may enhance the future well-being of the child by increasing his chances of acquiring the skills he will find useful in later life. To the extent that academic and vocational success are relevant to adjustment, any intervention that enables the child to acquire the skills for such success will positively affect future psychological adequacy.

The two projects described as examples of contingency management in the classroom are actually experimental studies rather than organized prevention programs. The issue remains as to whether the approach illustrated by these studies can be implemented on a wide scale. We have already mentioned that the behavioristic approach has the advantage of yielding concrete evidence of effectiveness which may sell the program to school personnel. It may not be enough, however, for the psychologist to produce graphs and tables to show that a technique has proved useful in an experimental study. Abidin (1971) notes that attempts made by school psychologists to implement behavior modification programs often fail for one or more of several reasons. One reason is that the teacher may not find truly effective reinforcers promptly, and may prematurely conclude that the approach does not work. Another reason for failure cited by Abidin is the tendency for the mental health worker to oversell his ideas to a degree that he seems to be denigrating traditional teaching skills, thereby alienating the teachers whom he wishes to accept his suggestions.

Chandler (1970) describes an actual school consultation program designed to train teachers to use behavior modification techniques. In discussing this program, she emphasizes how the nature of the school as a social system must be considered in the attempt to implement programs. For example, she notes that the psychologist is a potentially threatening outsider in the school who cannot expect success if he overwhelms educators with his own jargon or fails to recognize that his goals and those of school personnel may not be identical. Furthermore, Chandler argues that just as reinforcement may be the key to changing the children's behavior, it may also be necessary to reinforce appropriate behaviors on the part of the school workers themselves if changes are to occur and persist. In a sense, Chandler's approach represents a synthesis between the techniques of the behavior modifier and the systems analysis approach of people like Kelly. This type of synthesis may offer promise for establishing primary prevention programs that are both demonstrably effective and capable of large-scale implementation.

ALTERNATIVE SCHOOLS

In closing this chapter, it is appropriate to mention an action strategy for bringing children a psychologically positive school experience which evades the difficulties of entering existing institutions. The effort here is to create new schools that immediately embody the principles believed to be desirable. Projects to create schools that offer a substantially different environment than is found in the typical public facility have been spurred on by the work of educators like Neil (Summerhill School), Montessori, and Dennison. The innovative programs of these workers and others have been increasingly imitated in recent years. Most of the schools founded recently seem to represent an effort to provide a school setting that encourages cooperation over competition and loosens the structures that constrain the child's choice of activity. According to Areen (1973) the number of these schools has grown from about 25 in the late 1960s to more than 600 at present. Areen argues that recent legal challenges to the public educational establishment and its near monopoly over tax revenue for education raise distinct possibilities that innovative schools will eventually begin to receive more public support and will, at least, partially supplant the state-run institutions. Whether or not this happens, clearly the movement toward alternative schools is significant enough to provide a counterpoint in a chapter heavily laden with discussions of the difficulty involved in changing existing institutions.

CONCLUSION

The goal of establishing primary prevention programs in existing schools is difficult to achieve, but is worthwhile to pursue. The two challenges facing the interventionist are the need to demonstrate that his efforts will have substantial positive effects, and the need to implement his approach by gaining entry into an institutional setting where workers may fear or discount his efforts. Although several of the programs described in this chapter offer evidence of positive effect, none has been widely sought or accepted within the educational community. Successful future efforts may depend on an increased sophistication in the techniques of analyzing the social system of the school and of designing preventive interventions that fit the needs and tolerances of school personnel. In a larger sense, the success of efforts to improve the psychological environment of the schools may depend on an understanding of the entire community as it functions to maintain or alter its institutional subsystems, like the schools. Conceivably, alternate schools may ultimately supplant some of the existing facilities, thereby sidestepping some of the problems of providing children with new types of learning environments. Barring this possibility, however, the community worker will continue to be confronted with the multifaceted task of proving that he can design school environments that truly foster psychological development and then of finding a way to actualize his principles.

References

Abidin, R. R. What's wrong with behavior modification. *Journal of School Psychology.* 1971, *9*, 38–42.

Areen, J. C. Alternative schools: Better guardians than family or state? *School Review*, 1973, *81*, 175–193.

Biber, B. Integration of mental health principles in the school setting. In G. Caplan (Ed.), *Prevention of mental disorders in children.* New York: Basic Books, 1961. Pp. 323–352.

Biber, B. A learning-teaching paradigm for integrating intellectual and affective processes. In E. Bower and W. G. Hollister (Eds.), *Behavioral science frontiers in education.* New York: Wiley, 1967.

Bower, E. M. Primary prevention in a school setting. In G. Caplan (Ed.), *Prevention of mental disorders in children.* New York: Basic Books, 1961. Pp. 353–377.

Bower, E. M., & Hollister, W. G. (Eds.) *Behavioral science frontiers in education.* New York: Wiley, 1967.

Bruce, P. Relationship of self-acceptance to other variables with sixth grade children oriented in self-understanding. *Journal of Educational Psychology,* 1958, *49,* 229–238.

Bullis, H. E., & O'Malley, E. E. *Human relations in the classroom.* Wilmington, Del.: Hambleton, 1947.

Caplan, G. *Prevention of mental disorders in children.* New York: Basic Books, 1961.

Carroll, J. F. X., Bell, A. A., Minor, M. W., & Brecher, H. An ecological analysis of and prescription for student dissent. In W. L. Claiborn and R. Cohen (Eds.), *School intervention.* New York. Behavioral Publications, 1973. Pp. 110–121.

Carter, J. W. *Research contributions from psychology to community mental health.* New York: Behavioral Publications, 1968.

Chandler, G. E. Providing training in behavior modification for school personnel. Paper presented at the University of Maryland-Syracuse University Symposium in Community-Clinical Psychology: School intervention, 1971.

Cowen, E. L., Gardner, E. A., & Zax, M. *Emergent approaches to mental health problems.* New York: Appleton-Century-Croft, 1967.

Davis, J. A. *Education for positive mental health.* Chicago: Aldine, 1965.

DeCharms, R. Intervention is impossible: A model for change within. Paper presented at the University of Maryland-Syracuse University Symposium in Community-Clinical Psychology: School Intervention, 1971.

Farris, H. E., Kent, N. D., & Henderson, D. E. Teaching behavioral science in the elementary and junior high school. In R. Ulrich, T. Stachnik, & J. Mabry (Eds.), *Control of human behavior* (Vol. II). Glenview, Ill.: Scott Foresman and Co., 1970. Pp. 309–314.

Iscoe, I., Pierce-Jones, J., Friedman, S. T., & McGehearty, L. Some strategies in mental health consultation. In E. L. Cowen, E. A. Gardner, & M. Zax (Eds.), *Emergent approaches to mental health problems.* New York: Appleton-Century-Crofts, 1967. Pp. 307–330.

Kelly, J. G. Naturalistic observations and theory confirmation: An example. *Human Development,* 1967, *10,* 212–222.

Kelly, J. G. Toward an ecological conception of preventive interventions. In J. W. Carter (Ed.), *Research contributions from psychology to community mental health.* New York: Behavioral Publications, 1968. Pp. 75–99.

Leton, D. A. An evaluation of group methods in mental hygiene. *Mental Hygiene,* 1957, *41,* 525–533.

Levitt, E. E. The effect of a "causal" teacher training program on authoritianism and responsibility in grade school children. *Psychological Reports,* 1955, *1,* 449–458.

Madden, P. C. Skinner and the open classroom. *School Review,* 1972, *81,* 100–107.

Minor, M. Systems analysis and school psychology. *Journal of School Psychology,* 1972, *10,* 227–232.

Minuchin, P., Biber, B., Shapiro, E., & Zimiles, H. *The psychological impact of the school experience.* New York: Basic Books, 1969.

Morse, W. C. Enhancing the classroom teacher's mental health function. In E. L. Cowen, E. A. Gardner, & M. Zax (Eds.), *Emergent approaches to mental health problems.* New York: Appleton-Century-Crofts, 1967. Pp. 271–289.

Mosher, R. L., & Sprinthall, N. A. Psychological education in secondary schools: A program to promote individual and human development. *American Psychologist,* 1970, *25,* 911–924.

Muss, R. E. The effects of a one and two-year causal learning program. *Journal of Personality,* 1960, *28,* 479–491.

Ojemann, R. H. Sources of infection revealed in preventive psychiatry research. *American Journal of Public Health,* 1960, *50,* 329–335.

Ojemann, R. H., Levitt, E. E., Lyle, W. H., & Whiteside, M. F. The effects of a "causal" teacher-training program and certain curricular changes on grade school children. *Journal of Experimental Education,* 1955, *24,* 95–114.

Packard, R. G. The control of "classroom attention": A group contingency for complex behavior. *Journal of Applied Behavior Analysis,* 1970, *3,* 13–28.

Roen, S. R. Primary prevention in the classroom through a teaching program in the behavioral sciences. In E. L. Cowen, E. A. Gardner, & M. Zax (Eds.), *Emergent approaches to mental health problems.* New York: Appleton-Century-Crofts, 1967. Pp. 252–270.

Sarason, S. B., Levine, M., Goldenberg, I. I., Cherlin, D. L., & Bennett, E. M. *Psychology in community settings.* New York: Wiley, 1966.

Thomas, D. R., Becker, W. C., & Armstrong, M. Production and elimination of disruptive classroom behavior by systematically varying teacher's behavior. *Journal of Applied Behavior Analysis,* 1968, *1,* 34–45.

Ulrich, R., Stachnik, T., & Mabry, J. *Control of Human Behavior,* Vol. II., Glenview, Ill.: Scott Foresman, 1970.

Zimiles, H. Preventive aspects of school experience. In E. L. Cowen, E. A. Gardner, & M. Zax (Eds.), *Emergent approaches to mental health problems.* New York: Appleton-Century-Crofts, 1967. Pp. 239–251.

7. *secondary prevention in the schools*

The school programs described in preceding chapters either involve primary prevention (attempts to optimize the learning conditions for all children), new types of treatment, or tertiary preventive efforts. In this chapter we emphasize programs that seek: (a) to identify as early as possible the child who is likely to suffer school maladjustment or more serious disturbances; and (b) to prevent the progress of the disorder. Several programs of this kind have appeared recently, focusing, for the most part, on children in the earliest school years. Both components of secondary prevention (early identification and prevention) are not always present in these programs, as we shall learn.

THE ST. LOUIS PROJECT

One of the pioneering school secondary preventive programs was originated in St. Louis in 1947 as a small project sponsored by an organization of educators and laymen called the St. Louis Council for Parent Education (Gildea, Glidewell, and Kantor, 1961, 1967). During its modest beginning, this program was based in two schools in which teachers identified certain problem children on the basis of their classroom behavior, and invited the mothers of these children to participate in group therapy (Buchmueller, and Gildea, 1949). Social workers assigned to the project schools interviewed prospective group therapy participants to learn about the family, to encourage ventilation of feelings (about the school, the child, the teacher), and to broach the idea of group therapy. This emphasis on intervention with the mothers of the problem school child has been a hallmark of the St. Louis program over the years. Buchmueller and Gildea (1949) reported that 75 percent of the children whose mothers participated in the group therapy were judged by teachers to have improved in their school behavior, whereas about 80 percent of comparable children whose parents were not seen were judged to be unimproved. Unfortunately, the design of this study was such that teachers who acted as judges were reporting their ratings to parent group leaders, and their ego-involvement in the success of the program could have been a source of bias.

The apparent success of group therapy prompted a program expansion to include several other schools, using a variety of workers as group leaders. As the program broadened, it became apparent that the group therapy approach was not uniformly successful. In some schools, most notably all-black schools, the service was decisively rejected. Project leaders hypothesized that the early success of the program probably resulted from the fact that it dealt with middle class mothers who understood and accepted mental health concepts. The program failed in schools where parents seemed to have a poorer understanding of these concepts and were not ready to accept their significance. Therefore, it seemed necessary to prepare the school and the parents to accept secondary preventive intervention by instituting a broad mental health education program. In some respects, this aspect of the St. Louis program involved primary prevention as this was considered to be necessary to make possible a more intensive involvement with the parents of problem children.

The broad-gauge education program was carried out by a group of volunteers who led group discussions, generally centering around ideas provoked by mental health films. These lay discussion leaders were trained in workshops by professionals. Little effort was made initially to screen applicants for leader roles. To a certain extent, volunteers selected themselves in that many failed to complete training and others dropped out after leading a few groups, since they felt poorly suited to such work. Discussion leaders worked in pairs at schools, PTA's, mothers' clubs, churches, service clubs, and wherever else they were requested. Thus the two mental health services being offered in concert were the parent group therapy program and the broad-scale mental health education program.

Although early evaluations of the effects of the St. Louis program were encouraging, a more rigorous evaluation seemed necessary (Gildea, 1959; Rae-Grant and Stringer, 1969). The design of such an evaluation required the development of instruments for assessing the adjustment of the child and the attitudes of the mothers who were the prime target of the preventive program (Glidewell, Mensh, and Gildea, 1957). The major evaluation study was done across 15 schools, using 30 third-grade classrooms which were divided into experimental and control classes. A total of 830 families were involved in the first year of the study. The considerable attrition that occurred by the conclusion of the study two and one-half years later reduced this figure by one half. Two experimental conditions were evaluated: the volunteer lay education program, and the combination of the volunteer program plus the consultation of a mental health professional. In addition, a no-treatment control condition was set up as a baseline for comparing the effectiveness of the two experimental programs to no special program at all.

Children and their mothers were assessed on three different occasions, the last occurring two and one-half years after the first. The battery of instruments used with the children included a symptom checklist filled out by the mother, teachers' ratings of the child's emotional state, sociometric indexes on which children evaluated each other, and semiprojective tests. Mothers' attitudes were studied on a 17-item questionnaire.

The results of this evaluation were disappointing. Over the three-year period during which the children were followed, teachers ratings indicated that all children got worse and that the children in the experimental groups seemed to worsen more markedly than controls. The experimenters regarded this finding as positive from one viewpoint. It conceivably indicated that teachers, as a result of the program, had become more sensitive to emotional adjustment in children.

On the other hand, mothers, who were asked to evaluate the children, felt that the children improved behaviorally. However, no difference was found between the ratings of experimental and control mothers in this respect. Also, no differences were found between experimental and control mothers with respect to attitudes toward child rearing. There was a small positive correlation between change in mothers' reports of symptoms and change in their attitudes, reflecting a correspondence between mothers' impressions of improvements in the child and the examiners' impressions of improvement in mothers' attitudes. However, this change was unrelated to the type of mental health program experienced. Clearly, the overall results of this evaluation of the St. Louis program are not encouraging.

In its most recent phase, the St. Louis program has begun to emphasize very early detection of potential for school problems and the development of programs for preventing such disturbance (Rae-Grant and Stringer, 1969). This program phase emerged after the recognition by a senior school mental health worker that the practice of automatic or "social" promotions for all children regardless of achievement was not working out well. School records clearly demonstrated that the achievement of many children steadily worsened from year to year through the elementary grades, and that little was being done to deal with the problems prompting this decline. For this reason an instrument called the Academic Progress Chart (APC) was developed (Stringer, 1959). The APC is an objective index of a child's academic progress as reflected in his scores on standardized achievement tests generally used in schools, and it can provide a graphic picture of the contrasting results of social promotions and retention in a grade. The chart is a grid with chronological age on the horizontal axis and grade level on the vertical. A diagonal line plots the grade level at which the achievement test is administered and a child's median score on the test battery is also plotted relative to test grade level. Thus easy comparison can be made between a given child's actual progress and the progress that he should be making (based on national achievement test norms). Figure 1 provides examples of the APC's of two different children.

The APC was also recognized as a potential screening tool for detecting early school maladjustment. A research study using this instrument demonstrated that 61 percent of the cases eventually referred to school mental health services could have been referred on the basis of their APC anywhere from one to eight years earlier.

Later, when a sizeable group of mothers participating in research interviews concerning their children were found to derive considerable personal benefit, the idea arose of conducting such interviews with every mother whose child was entering school. It was felt that the interview could deal with already existing problems and might help to innoculate the child against future problems. This prompted development of a new preventive program called "Mothers As Colleagues in School Mental Health Work." Most recent informal evaluations of this program indicate that it is working well and that it is promoting understanding between school and mental health personnel.

Associated with the preventive program focusing on mothers of entering elementary students has been a trend for increased consultation with teachers by school mental health workers. This, too, has a generally preventive impact through the education that it provides for teachers. Future programs of the St. Louis group will undoubtedly expand in this direction.

THE CALIFORNIA STATE EDUCATIONAL DEPARTMENT PROGRAM

Bower and his associates (Bower, 1960; Bower and Lambert, 1961) did an elaborate study in California on the early identification of emotional disorders in school children. Although their work focused on only one component of a secondary preventive program, it has provided means for identifying emotional handicaps in youngsters in the early school grades that have been used in other secondary preventive programs (e.g., the Rochester Primary Mental Health program to be described later).

Bower's ambitious early identification program was conducted in 75 California school districts with screening data collected for approximately 5500 children, 207 of whom were identified as emotionally disturbed. This designation was made by mental health workers in the school districts from which the children were chosen. Workers were asked to select a number of emotionally disturbed children representative of the disturbed children in their district. The purpose of this study was to determine the extent to which information available to the teacher in the normal course of instruction could be used to identify children recognized by experienced clinicians as emotionally disturbed.

Teachers were asked to collect data on the children in their classes without knowledge of the study's purpose, or the awareness that certain of their pupils had been designated as emotionally disturbed. The following information was collected: (1) the child's chronological age, (2) the number of absences in a four-month school period, (3) father's occupation, (4) standardized test scores in reading and arithmetic achievement, (5) a group IQ test score, (6) a score on a personality self-measure entitled "Thinking About Yourself", (7) a score on a sociometric device entitled "A Class Play," and (8) the teacher's rating on each child's physical and emotional characteristics. On the test called "Thinking About Yourself" (TAY) the child was given an opportunity to describe himself as he felt he was and as he would like to be; test scores measured the discrepancy between the self- and ideal images. In "The Class Play," each child was rated by his peers through the vehicle of casting positive and negative roles for a hypothetical play that the class was to put on. Each child's score was the percentage of negative role selections made for him by his peers. Analyses compared the emotionally disturbed children with their nondisturbed peers on each of the eight measures taken.

It was found that the emotionally handicapped children were older and more frequently absent than their classmates, but these differences were not significant. While there were no differences between the groups on socioeconomic status, significant differences favoring the nondisturbed group were found on reading and arithmetic achievement test scores (at

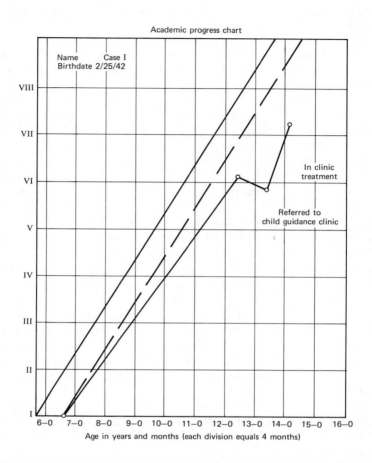

Academic progress chart

Name   Case I
Birthdate 2/25/42

In clinic
treatment

Referred to
child guidance clinic

Age in years and months (each division equals 4 months)

I. He was given to copying work of his classmates. Since he was a recent transfer to the school, no test data were available for his earlier years, but at sixth grade he was lagging by 0.7 grades, and in seventh grade his lag increased to 2.0 grades. The mental health counsellor had meanwhile talked with the mother, who accepted referral to the Child Guidance Clinic for diagnostic evaluation of the boy. Clinic study, completed during the summer vacation, led to an offer of clinic treatment for the boy, and this was begun as the next school term began. By the end of that year (eighth grade) he had decreased his lag to 1.5 grades, had clearly reversed his earlier downward trend, and seemed well on the way to making up all of his earlier loss (Stringer, 1959 12-19).

II. A behavior problem, he was considered bright and had done well in his grade, but then his mother died, and he was left to the care of elderly and over-indulgent grandparents. He beame obese and increasingly aggressive and dis-

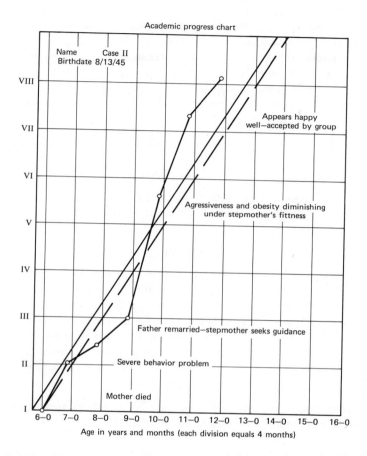

Academic progress chart

Name   Case II
Birthdate 8/13/45

Appears happy
well—accepted by group

Agressiveness and obesity diminishing
under stepmother's fittness

Father remarried—stepmother seeks guidance

Severe behavior problem

Mother died

Age in years and months (each division equals 4 months)

ruptive, and his 0.2 lead at first-grade level became a 0.4 lag at second grade, a 0.8 lag at third grade. Then his father remarried, and the stepmother, warmly concerned to help the boy, sought contact with the mental health counsellor and made good gains in learning to understand the child and in developing a positive relationship with him, even while setting limits to his acting-out. In the next year he made a remarkable gain, moving from below the normal line to above it, jumping 2.6 grade levels in one year; and in the following year this gain was further increased. Meanwhile his obesity and aggressiveness were subsiding toward normal levels, and at the end of the sixth grade he was a well-accepted member of his class, and in some respects a leader (Stringer, 1959, p. 19).

Figure 1. Examples of APCs of two different children (from Stringer, 1959).

the fourth-, fifth-, and sixth-grade levels) and on group intelligence tests. However, intellectual differences were not found when IQ was measured by individually administered tests. Bower explained this discrepancy by pointing out that the group test emphasizes school-related material more than the individual intelligence test. Self-perception scores, as measured by the TAY, indicated that emotionally handicapped children are more dissatisfied with themselves, showing a greater discrepancy between self-

---

A CLASS PLAY

Prepared by Eli M. Bower and Carl A. Larson
California State Department of Education

SECTION I

Just suppose your class was going to put on a play and you are selected as the director. When you turn the page you will find a list of some of the parts in this play. As director of the play, you have to pick a boy or girl in your class for each of the parts. In order to make your play a successful one and a lot of fun, you will need to pick a boy or girl who you think would be best able to play the part. Since many of the parts listed are small ones, you may, if you wish, select the same boy or girl for more than one part. Do not choose yourself for any of the parts. You will have a chance to do this later.

Make your choices carefully and if you have any questions about the meaning of a word or anything else be sure to ask your teacher.

THINKING ABOUT YOURSELF
Prepared by Carl A. Larson and Eli M. Bower
California State Department of Education, Sacramento

The questions in this booklet will make you think about yourself. Because all of you like different things, each of you will probably answer the questions differently. What you say will help us to find out what boys like you are thinking and wishing. Do your best to make your answer to each question tell what you really think and really wish.

HOW TO ANSWER THE QUESTIONS IN THIS BOOKLET

This is an EXAMPLE of the questions you will be asked to answer: This boy is usually picked first to play on a team.	Always	Fre-quently	Seldom	Never
1. Are you like him?	1	3	5	7
2. Do you want to be like him?	2	4	6	8

In answering the first question, "Are you like him?"—you can place an X in any one of the four boxes. If you feel you are like this boy always, place the X in Box 1. If you feel you are like this boy frequently, place an X in Box 2. If on the other hand you are like this boy seldom, place the X in Box 3. If you feel you are never picked first to play on a team, place the X in Box 4.

In answering the second question, you have to think about what you want to be and put an X in the box which would be more true for you. If you would like to be someone who is picked first always, place the X in Box 5. If you would like to be picked first frequently, place the X in Box 6. If on the other hand you would like to be this boy seldom, place the X in Box 7. If you don't care at all and would never like to be chosen first, place an X in Box 8.

Now try to complete the two examples below—

This boy likes to do daring things.	Always	Fre-quently	Seldom	Never
1. Are you like him?	☐	☐	☐	☐
2. Do you want to be like him?	☐	☐	☐	☐
This boy worries about tests.				
1. Are you like him?	☐	☐	☐	☐
2. Do you want to be like him?	☐	☐	☐	☐

If you still don't understand how to answer the questions, raise your hand. Also, if you need help later on, raise your hand. Your teacher will give you the help you need.

Now turn the page and begin.

Figure 2. Instructions for "A class play" and the TAY (from Bower, 1960).

and ideal-image than their nonhandicapped peers. Likewise the emotionally handicapped children were assigned negative roles on "The Class Play" significantly more often than the nonhandicapped. Finally, teachers' reports indicated a far bigger percentage of the emotionally handicapped group displayed negative classroom behaviors than did their peers who were not seen as handicapped.

This study demonstrated that a variety of measures taken in the ordinary classroom can differentiate emotionally handicapped children from nonhandicapped children. This indicates that wide-scale screening procedures can be done within the ordinary classroom that would identify, as early as the fourth to sixth grades, children who need help with emotional problems.

THE PACE I. D. CENTER PROJECT

The Pace I. D. Center, an agency established with federal funds in the Northern part of San Mateo County, California is also concerned with the early identification and prevention of emotional disorders in school children (Brownbridge and Van Vleet, 1969). The Pace program focused on a population of approximately 6000 school children in the kindergarten through fourth grade in both the public and parochial system of northern San Mateo County. In this population, a sample of 354 were identified as needing the preventive services of a social worker. The primary instrument used for identifying these children was the AML Behavior Rating Scale. This instrument, used by the teacher, is an 11-item checklist having five aggression items (A), five moodiness items (M), and one learning disability item (L). Aggression items describe fighting, restlessness, disruptiveness, obstinacy, and impulsivity; moodiness items decribe children who are unhappy, prone to becoming ill, sensitive to criticism, in need of coaxing, and are moody. The teacher rates each item on a five-point scale ranging from seldom (1) to always (5). Four scores are derived from this scale: the aggression score, the moodiness score, the learning disability score, and a total score. The range of scores is from 11 to 55. The children included in the Pace I. D. prevention study were those scoring in the highest 10 percent of their prospective school districts on the AML scale who were under 10 years of age as of July 1, 1966, and whose families were not on the active roster of a social agency at the time the child was screened. The 354 children meeting these criteria were assigned randomly to an experimental (E) or control (C) group matched according to grade level, sex, and the AML learning disability score.

The preventive program was carried out by the school social worker.

Five social workers served on the Pace staff and serviced approximately 30 children in each of the E schools. As soon as a project E child was identified, teachers and other school personnel were notified. Typically, the Pace social worker was invited to the school to discuss the program and to get to know the teachers. Other essential aspects of the social worker's role were to develop a relationship with the principal, and to become acquainted with other key school personnel to maximize cooperation. An early problem in dealing with teachers and other school personnel was to explain why some children were receiving special attention while others were not, and to fend off efforts to have the social worker deal with children who were immediate problems for the school but were not part of the Pace project.

The Pace social worker's role included responsibility for informing principals of all developments concerning individual children, teachers, and parents. Social workers were also required to have close contact with teachers through formal or informal conferences, depending on the individual teacher's style. Thus some meetings were quite formal while others were held over coffee, at lunchtime, and occasionally in school corridors as people were moving from one place to another. Finally, within the school, the social worker directly observed the Pacer both in the classroom and in other school situations to become better acquainted with his behavior and reactions to stressful situations. The combination of these observations plus knowledge concerning the child's home background frequently made it possible for the social worker to help teachers understand a child's behavior.

Once the worker had become well acquainted with the Pacer and school personnel, it became essential to make contact with the child's family. In cases where the child was an overt problem to the school, there was little difficulty in making such contact. In other cases, however, in which the child was not viewed as a serious problem by principal and teacher, there was resistance to approaching the child's parents. As a result, the worker was required to continue observing the child until an opportune time arose to intervene. The social worker's approach to families was highly flexible and was shaped mainly by the needs of the child, the needs of the school system, and the attitude of the parents. There was also considerable flexibility concerning the time and place of meetings with the family: some meetings took place in the home, but others were held at places of employment, in the park, in the library, or at a bar. Wherever possible a worker attempted to see all of the important people in the child's immediate home environment. In each case the social worker attempted to secure parental interest and involvement without disrupting what might be a delicate family equilibrium. To fully understand the child's problems, it was necessary to become acquainted with the myriad of problems that beset the family as a unit, because the child's difficulty often stemmed from an overall adjustment problem suffered by the family.

Another component of the Pace program involved the use of three psychiatric consultants serving as collaborators with the social workers engaged in the front line program operation. The consultants, all trained child psychiatrists, helped with understanding the dynamics of specific cases, and in setting up specific intervention plans. In addition, they were concerned with social workers' style of interaction with the school system and other relevant community agencies. The consultant also helped with the general problem of role definition for the social worker.

Evaluation of the effects of the Pace program was based on essentially four types of instruments: (1) the AML Behavior Rating Scale, (2) achievement test scores, (3) the Bender-Visual Motor Gestalt Test, and (4) the Draw-A-Person Test. The AML was administered on five different occasions in the two years during which the project was conducted. Comparisons of E and C groups for change over that two-year period demonstrated that there was a significant difference on the M subscale, indicating that the E group was less moody after the treatment than the C group. Similar results were found with a subsample of E subjects who had received particularly intensive attention from the social workers. Significant differences were also found on the A subscale, as E subjects showed a significantly greater pre-post decrease in aggression than did C subjects. Although the E group gained significantly more than the C group on the arithmetic achievement tests, neither group achieved the expected gain of one school year. No significant differences were found between the two groups on the Bender or on the Draw-A-Person Tests. Overall, these results reflect some significant E group improvement in the Pace program.

Qualitatively, the Pace staff was able to identify retrospectively several factors that seemed to contribute to positive change in the children with whom they worked. These included a low case load, allowing a flexible and intensive effort with particular children, the individualization of programs in line with the problems and needs of the child, consultative support, and the coordination of school services with family and community resources.

THE ROCHESTER PRIMARY MENTAL HEALTH PROJECT

Like the St. Louis project the Primary Mental Health Project of Rochester, New York is a program that has spanned several years and has passed through several stages (Cowen, Izzo, Miles, Telschow, Trost, and Zax, 1963; Cowen, Zax, Izzo, and Trost, 1966; Zax and Cowen, 1967;

Zax and Cowen, 1969). While the general objectives of this program have been the early identification and prevention of emotional disorder in school children, a basic feature of this program's approach has been the utilization of nonprofessional manpower in the schools.

The impetus behind the development of the Rochester program stems from two frequently made observations. First, teachers commonly recognize that a large percentage of their class time is taken up by the need to work with relatively few youngsters. Second, school mental health workers often find that referrals increase markedly during the transition period from elementary to high school, a time when resources for dealing with serious problems are relatively meager. Furthermore, the school records of youngsters referred at this point in their academic career often indicate that many early signs of school maladjustment have been ignored. Thus it seemed worthwhile to concentrate mental health services in the very early school grades in an effort to promote prompt identification of signs of impending disorder and to take preventive measures that might make later referral unnecessary.

In the early stage of the program a psychologist and a social worker concerned with the early identification and prevention of emotional disorders were assigned full time to the primary grades of one elementary school. The experimental (E) school was in a neighborhood that was socioeconomically upper-lower class and was ethnically fairly representative of the city at large except for the fact that black and Jewish families were underrepresented. Two demographically comparable schools from contiguous neighborhoods were used as control (C) schools in connection with the assessment of project outcome.

The early identification phase and the prevention phase were two clear-cut components of the Rochester program, with the early identification phase remaining stable through many program stages. The social worker interviewed the mothers of all first graders to learn about the child and his development, family patterns, family attitudes toward education, and to open a line of communication with the family so that the social worker might be used later as a resource if necessary. Classroom observations were made of all children, teachers reported on classroom behavior, and some psychological testing was done with the first graders. On the basis of these data, a clinical judgment was made concerning each child. Those already manifesting problems or seeming to have great potential for doing so in the future have been called the Red-Tag (RT) group. Those doing well and thought likely to continue to do so have been called the Non-Red Tag (NRT) group. While percentages have varied across groups and from year to year, roughly about 30 percent of entering first graders have been labeled RT. Later research on factors contributing to the RT designation has indicated that data uncovered in the social worker's interview contribute heavily to the judgment, and that the overall quality of family life seems to be the most influential factor in determining whether a youngster will be designated RT or NRT. Furthermore, from this research it has been possible to develop a continuous instead of a binary judgment concerning the potential for a child's having school difficulty (Beach, Cowen, Zax, Laird, Trost, and Izzo, 1968).

To evaluate the effectiveness of the early identification procedure, RT and NRT children were compared when they reached the third grade, more than two years after they were originally classified. Two independent sets of evaluations were done in 1961 and 1962. Groups were compared on a variety of school record measures, that is, nurse referrals, attendance, grade-point average, and achievement test scores, as well as on several adjustment measures, that is, teachers' ratings, the Children's Manifest Anxiety Scale (CMAS), a rating by the mental health clinical team, Thinking About Yourself (TAY), and The Class Play (CP). The results of these comparisons are listed in Table 1.

This Table shows that NRT children surpassed the RT children on a variety of indexes in both sets of comparisons, although the 1962 data showed many more differences between the two groups. Within two years, NRT children were achieving higher than RT children, were rated by teachers as better behaved and better adjusted and, for the 1962 group, were regarded more positively by their peers as measured by CP. The adjustment measure used by the mental health clinical team also showed significant differences. This judgment was contaminated, however, by the team's knowledge of which students were RT and NRT.

Stability of differences between RT and NRT groups was tested by a further follow-up of the 1961 to 1962 samples when the children had reached seventh grade, about six years after they were originally diagnosed and four years following the first evaluation. By the time of the seventh-grade evaluation, group sizes were diminished by attrition but, since no significant differences on third-grade measures were found between pupils leaving the E school and those still present, the group remaining was viewed as representative of the original group. A summary of comparisons on which significant differences were found among the seventh graders is listed in Table 2.

The data from this table indicate that by seventh grade the NRT children were still surpassing the RT children in school achievement, and in adjustment as rated by teachers and peers. Again, these findings were consistent for the two independent samples. To determine whether the achievement and adjustment of RT children had progressively worsened between the third and seventh grades, the difference scores between third and seventh-grade measures for RT and NRT children were compared. No significant differences were found in these analyses, indicating that al-

Table 1. Comparisons of RT and NRT Groups Tested in 1961 and 1962 (from Zax and Cowen, 1969)

Criterion Measures	1961					1962				
	RT		NRT			RT		NRT		
	X	N	X	N	t	X	N	X	N	t
School record measures										
Nurse referrals	1.40	40	.82	67	1.81	1.93	29	.65	71	4.13[b]
Cumulative nurse referrals	4.11	35	4.16	55	.05	6.69	29	1.76	71	5.67[b]
Attendance	8.40	40	10.57	68	1.08	11.94	31	9.76	72	1.10
GPA	20.23	40	22.54	68	2.20[a]	21.35	31	24.65	72	3.37[b]
SRA comprehension	52.03	39	63.66	62	2.29[a]	42.77	30	56.34	70	2.67[b]
SRA vocabulary	51.83	39	60.09	61	1.52	48.88	30	56.56	70	1.39
SRA reasoning	—	—	—	—	—	49.13	30	60.73	70	1.99[a]
SRA concepts	—	—	—	—	—	43.10	30	40.97	70	.45
SRA computation	—	—	—	—	—	30.38	30	42.73	70	2.18[a]
Achievement–Aptitude D score	2.82	38	3.08	61	1.24	2.70	29	3.25	55	2.57[a]
Adjustment measures										
Teachers' ratings (total)	12.30	40	8.61	68	2.23[a]	7.03	30	2.66	71	5.40[b]
Teachers' ratings (overall)	3.25	40	2.69	68	2.55[a]	2.57	30	1.75	71	4.32[b]
CMAS A	19.90	40	19.60	62	.17	21.83	29	19.41	71	1.52
CMAS L	4.10	40	4.37	62	.68	4.31	29	4.10	71	.17
MHCS rating	3.13	40	1.22	68	13.14[a]	4.48	31	1.19	72	32.90[b]
TAY D score	—	—	—	—	—	34.00	28	33.38	61	.24
CPI	—	—	—	—	—	57.71	31	44.04	72	2.30[a]
CPII	—	—	—	—	—	32.33	30	21.14	72	2.03[b]

[a] $p < .05$.
[b] $p < .01$.

Table 2.   Significant Differences in Seventh Grade Data between RT and NRT Children for 1961 and 1962 Groups (From Zax and Cowen, 1969)

| | 1961 | | | 1962 | | |
| | RT | NRT | | RT | NRT | |
Criterion Measures	X	X	t	X	X	t
Nurse referrals, fifth grade	2.18	.92	2.26	—	—	—
Nurse referrals, seventh grade	—	—	—	1.81	.31	3.58
Nurse referrals, total	—	—	—	8.13	3.71	2.78
GPA, fourth grade	—	—	—	3.28	4.09	2.53
GPA, fifth grade	—	—	—	3.22	4.13	3.40
GPA, sixth grade	3.65	4.10	2.32	3.06	4.02	2.91
GPA, seventh grade	3.35	3.88	2.17	3.10	3.87	2.96
GPA, total	—	—	—	3.12	4.10	3.17
SRA, seventh, language arts, grammar usage	30.18	34.90	2.54	33.00	36.82	2.02
SRA, seventh, language arts, spelling	—	—	—	13.93	18.15	2.32
SRA, seventh, arithmetic, concepts	12.42	15.34	2.24	—	—	—
SRA, seventh, arithmetic, reasoning	18.33	22.19	2.19	—	—	—
SRA, fifth, arithmetic, reasoning	23.27	27.87	2.11	—	—	—
SRA, fifth, arithmetic, concepts	—	—	—	9.92	11.97	2.19
Teachers' rating (total)	13.95	5.61	3.41	—	—	—
Teachers' rating (overall)	3.48	2.51	3.20	3.31	2.39	2.76
CPI	65.05	44.73	2.35	58.07	34.59	2.40

though the RT children were performing consistently more poorly than NRT children in a number of respects, their performance had not worsened over the years. They seem to have made a poor start in school and to have never caught up with their better adjusted peers.

The preventive aspects of the Rochester Primary Mental Health Project have gone through, at least two distinct phases. The initial program was broadly gauged and directed primarily toward school personnel and parents. Fundamental to the preventive program described, as well as to the form adopted later, was the reshaping of the mental health professional's role from one of a direct service-giver to children to that of consultant and resource person for others who provide service to children. Every effort was made to bring mental health personnel closer to teachers and school administrators. At the beginning of the school year, informal luncheon conferences were held with first-grade teachers during which they could talk about children who were causing concern. Often the school principal, the nurse, the attendance teacher, and various other special teachers were present. These conferences later assumed sufficient im-

Table 3. E and C School Comparisons for 1961 and 1962 Third Grade Groups

Criterion Measures	1961 E School X	1961 E School N	1961 C School X	1961 C School N	1961 C School t	1962 E School X	1962 E School N	1962 C School X	1962 C School N	1962 C School t
Schol record measures										
Nurse referrals, third grade	.95	151	1.04	107	0.50	.88	65	1.51	65	2.02[a]
Cumulative nurse referrals	2.87	47	4.14	90	1.90	2.52	65	3.41	22	1.23
Attendance	9.60	176	9.77	108	0.13	10.72	65	12.76	65	1.01
GPA	21.46	176	21.69	108	0.38	24.95	65	20.98	65	4.37[a]
SRA comprehension	52.78	172	59.17	101	1.83	56.59	65	45.20	59	2.54[a]
SRA vocabulary	53.57	171	56.88	100	0.91	57.88	65	51.02	59	1.37
SRA reasoning						62.72	65	60.71	59	0.39
SRA concepts						42.86	65	41.51	59	0.29
SRA computation						43.91	65	39.48	58	0.97
Achievement-aptitude D score	2.97	161	2.98	99	0.50	3.47	65	2.59	65	5.95[b]
Adjustment measures										
Teachers' rating (total)	9.56	175	10.03	108	0.42	3.62	65	3.30	64	0.43
Teachers' rating (overall)	2.60	175	1.26	108	2.07[a]	1.94	65	2.69	64	4.41[b]
CMAS A	19.62	102	21.85	169	2.06[a]	19.61	63	22.47	65	2.03[a]
CMAS L	4.21	102	4.66	169	1.75	3.76	63	4.63	65	2.23[a]
TAY D score						33.60	57	32.31	64	0.62
CP I						46.25	65	55.46	65	1.69
CP II						24.25	65	29.61	61	1.39

[a] p < .05.
[b] p < .01.

portance to warrant hiring substitute teachers to replace the regular classroom teacher while she participated. While teachers learned a great deal about specific children, they also acquired much knowledge and useful experience for better dealing with a variety of general classroom problems. The consulting psychiatrist who served with the project over a period of many years was often present at these conferences and helped both with the understanding of specific children and with the general problems inherent in the teacher's role.

Also basic to the early program were special meetings for parents and teachers to discuss various mental health relevant topics (e.g., child development and functioning, human motivation, and the emotional and psychological needs of the young child). After-school meetings for teachers were led by specialists on topics in which teachers had particular interest. Six evening meetings for the parents of primary grade children were devoted to the emotional and social development of children and were also led by specialists in these areas.

Direct service to children was provided in an after-school program to which teachers assigned students who needed extra attention. This program was designed to provide a meaningful interpersonal experience in a relatively informal setting. Groups were limited to 10 children. The mental health clinical team selected leaders, teachers in the E school, on the basis of their interest in children and their problems, demonstrated effectiveness in working with the socioeconomically handicapped, and the attribute of being a good mother or father figure. Groups met for one hour a week for 20 weeks, engaging in activities as diverse as woodworking and baking cookies.

E and C school children completing third grade in 1961 and 1962 were compared as a means of evaluating the effects of the prevention program. The results of these comparisons are reported in Table 3.

For the 1961 group, the only significant differences found were on the teachers' adjustment rating and the CMAS A scale. The A scale results indicate that E school children reported significantly less anxiety than did C schoolers. However, teachers' ratings indicate the reverse of what was expected in that the E school children were rated as more maladjusted than C school children. The results for the 1962 group indicate significant differences between E and C school on seven measures, all favoring the E group. E school children were found to have fewer absences, higher SRA comprehension and vocabulary scores, better achievement records relative to their aptitudes, more favorable teacher ratings, and significantly lower anxiety scores on the CMAS.

A follow-up study was done of the 1961 group when it reached seventh grade. Original E school children who were still available in the school were compared to available C school children on 46 different measures taken from their several years of schooling. Table 4 depicts the results of these comparisons.

Fourteen of the 46 comparisons between E and C school students reflected significant differences, although the pattern of differences is not clear-cut. The E school children were found to have lower grades, were more likely to be underachievers, and had poorer attendance records than C schoolers. On the other hand, they were less anxious at the seventh-grade level and scored higher than C school children on several standard achievement tests. It was not possible to do an adequate follow-up for the 1962 group because of the high degree of attrition in those classes. Thus the results of this fairly long-term follow-up did not lead to definitive conclusions. The relatively weak follow-up findings may be the result of program inadequacies or the high attrition rates. Whatever the reasons, the positive effects of the preventive program were not demonstrated to be enduring with respect to the measures used.

Partly because of these inconclusive findings and partly because those children identified early as RT youngsters continued to lag behind their NRT peers by seventh grade, despite the fact that they had experienced the preventive program, the form of the Rochester primary mental health program was altered. One major problem was that it provided relatively

Table 4. Significant t Tests Resulting from Comparisons of E and C Subjects in the 1961 Group (from Zax and Cowen, 1969)

Criterion Measures	X (E)	X (C)	t
School record measures			
Nurse referrals, fourth grade	1.56	.94	2.25[a]
Nurse referrals, seventh grade	.58	1.38	2.92[b]
Attendance, 61–62	10.53	7.84	2.23[a]
Attendance, 64–65	9.95	5.83	2.50[a]
Attendance, total	39.32	28.43	2.53[a]
Grades, fifth grade	395.52	421.10	2.08[a]
Grades, sixth grade	370.92	430.70	3.82[b]
Grades, total	382.64	411.46	2.26[a]
SRA, fifth grade, work study, charts	15.70	13.86	2.67[b]
SRA, fifth grade, arithmetic, concepts	12.98	11.72	2.72[b]
SRA, seventh grade, arithmetic, reasoning	21.14	18.02	2.98[b]
SRA, seventh grade, arithmetic, concepts	14.55	12.97	2.25[a]
Achievement–Aptitude D score—seventh grade—seventh grade Otis	364.05	445.87	5.91[b]
Adjustment measures			
CMAS anxiety, seventh grade	13.51	15.82	2.17[a]

[a] $p = .05$.
[b] $p = .01$.

little direct service to children. To provide that service, it was recognized that considerably more manpower had to be bought into the program. This led to the recruitment, training, and supervision of a group of non-professionals who were interested in working with young children. Taking a cue from the work of Rioch, a group of housewives who had demonstrated their own success as mothers and who expressed a strong desire to work with young children were recruited for work as "teacher aides" (TAs). Initially six trainees were selected on the basis of their flexibility, interest in and positive attitudes toward children, and their demonstrated success as mothers. None had a college degree, and one had not even completed high school. Their training was limited to a five-week program intended to provide only a few psychologically technical tools to help alleviate some of their anxiety and uncertainty. The program relied heavily on the natural reflexes and personal qualities of the TA.

At the outset, new TAs were assigned to a specific primary grade classroom to assist with children who required more attention than the teacher could provide. When one year of experience with this format proved too trying both for teachers and aides alike, a new format was adopted and has been maintained for several years. In the new setup the TA operates outside of the classroom accepting referrals from the teacher. One consequence of this change has been more constructive TA-teacher involvement around the problems of specific children—as the new system avoids the conflict engendered by the ambiguous responsibilities of the two roles when operating in the same room. Typically, in this system, the teacher brings specific problems to the attention of the school mental health team, a psychologist and a social worker, who have overall program responsibility. In concert with the TA, the teacher, and often a mental health consultant to the project, devise a set of objectives and a plan of action for each child. Once this is done, the TA begins to see the child, perhaps for several one-half hour periods a week. Continual feedback occurs among the TA, the teacher, and the mental health clinical team. Progress is regularly evaluated and goals are revised.

In her work with the child, the TA often begins by focusing on school work. In the background, however, a major emphasis is placed on developing a meaningful relationship that is emotionally supportive for the child and that will hopefully foster better school adjustment. Most contacts between TA and child are individual but, where it seems likely to be beneficial, small groups have been formed. Such groups might be established for children who are particularly timid about peer relationships. Thus the children receive assistance with academic problems plus the opportunity to form a beneficial peer relationship in a less complex and less threatening environment than the classroom. TAs are also used to deal with children who face specific crises that cannot be handled easily by the teacher in a large classroom.

Another component of the revised preventive program is an after-school day-care program staffed by undergraduate college volunteers. The teachers or the school psychologist or social worker select children for the after-school program who seem to need such an experience. Typically, these children manifest problems similar to those that prompt teachers to refer a child to a TA, that is, acting out, undersocialization, or poor achievement. The format for the after-school program has varied somewhat over the years. At its inception, each child was assigned to an individual college student volunteer who visited him in the school about three times every two weeks for approximately one and one-fourth hours immediately after the end of the school day. Contacts took place in the school or on the school grounds, where use of many of the school's facilities such as the auditorium, gymnasium, shops, home economics room, or music room made possible a variety of activities. As in the case of the TA program, it was expected that major benefits would derive from the relationship with an interested, energetic, enthusiastic, young person who could, hopefully, provide support as well as a model for the youngster to emulate. In a more recent program development, small groups of children, particularly undersocialized ones, have been assigned to single volunteers.

Although a detailed evaluation of the new form of the Rochester Primary Mental Health Program has not been made, some measures that bear on its effectiveness are available. Four of the original six housewife TAs are still with the program after seven years of operation. Referral rate to the TAs has grown to a point where waiting lists have become necessary. Indeed, in one school with a total primary grade enrollment of fewer than 200 children, referrals have approached 50 per year. Another measure of the program's acceptance and success is the fact that the school system in which the program originated on an experimental basis has hired TAs, with its own funds, to function in several inner-city schools.

One objective study has been done to evaluate the effectiveness of the TA and after-school programs (Cowen, 1968). In this study, primary grade children matched for age, sex, and other relevant variables were assigned randomly to TAs, to the college student after-school program, or to a control condition. Children in the experimental groups averaged from 25 to 30 contacts with TA or a volunteer. Program effects were evaluated by a rating on a seven-point scale filled out independently by teachers and TAs, which evaluated the child's status for the period of time covered by the program (from very much improved to very much worse). The correlation between TA and teacher ratings was .62, which was reasonably high, considering that they were based on observations in different situations. Comparisons of ratings of the three groups indicate that the greatest improvement took place in children seen by TAs, followed by those seen in the after-school program. The youngsters in the control condition remained essentially unchanged. Ratings of TA-seen youngsters were not significantly better than those in the after-school program but were significantly better than those in the control group. Children in the after-school group did not show significantly greater improvement than the control group. In a later study, children participating in the after-school program for five and one-half months (Cowen, Carlisle, and Kaufman, 1969) showed significant improvement as judged by teachers and TAs.

In its most recent phase, the Rochester Primary Mental Health Program has concentrated on training school mental health professionals to adopt the role model established in the program. The preventive program has been extended to 11 schools, 6 in the city of Rochester, and 5 in neighboring county school districts. The location of these schools ranges from the inner-city ghetto to the affluent suburbs. This program should provide valuable information concerning the differences in approach and types of personnel that will be most effective in the various settings. In its latest form, about 55 nonprofessional child aides have been trained with approximately one full-time psychologist, one full-time social worker, and 10 TAs available for each 2 schools in the program. In addition to extending the old program, the new one is intended to develop primary intervention approaches. These can come about through studies of the nature of the school and classroom structure, through efforts at building psychological strength and resources in children, by reinforcing curiosity or altruistic responses, and through improved means for handling crises (Zax and Cowen, 1972).

THE SUMTER CHILD STUDY PROJECT

The program developed in Sumter County, South Carolina in the early 1960s (Newton and Brown, 1967) was concerned with preventing adverse emotional reactions to a particular crisis faced by all young children —school entry. Basically the program's aim was to identify children likely to have the greatest difficulty in managing the crisis and to assist them in overcoming it. The program was based on the assumption that what become serious problems for children frequently had originated from a failure to adapt adequately to some crisis situation such as that involved in beginning the school experience.

The Sumter Child Study Project began in 1963 with the support of the National Institute of Mental Health. The program's purpose was to serve as a model of crisis intervention in the preschool and early school years. It had three phases: (1) an early detection phase in which all children were evaluated in the spring before entering school, on the basis of which predictions were made concerning their ability to cope with the stresses of the early school years; (2) an intervention phase devoted to planning and carrying out procedures for helping a particular child with the stresses to be encountered; and (3) an evaluation phase concerned with measuring the effectiveness of planned interventions.

The preschool evaluation phase of the project involved two 45-minute examination periods. The first was directed toward the child who was observed in a structured situation and tested by a psychologist while his parents were interviewed by a psychiatric social worker. The second 45-minute period involved a meeting of the evaluative team members whose individual impressions were distilled into a final team-summary concerning the particular child. Later, each team discussed the child's record with a group of consultants consisting of a regular project staff member, a pediatrician, and a child psychiatrist. Each team was required to make a rating that predicted the capacity of each child for adapting to the school situation. A four-point scale was used: (1) exceptional, (2) typical, (3) weak, and (4) trouble.

Interventions were designed at times for the entire project sample, at times for specific subgroups within the total, and at times for specific children. One example of an intervention directed toward a group of children involved several youngsters who had been identified as being immature and so deficient in adaptive skills as to be particularly unprepared for entering the typical school situation. These children were placed in a six-week summer program in the school they would attend in the fall. In this program a teacher attempted to work with them to promote the kinds of social skills and competencies in handling feeling that would be required in a larger group of more adequate peers. Another subgroup consisted of children having speech difficulties. The parents of these youngsters were advised to provide their children with remedial therapy prior to the child's entering school. The striking benefit of this intervention for many children eventually led to the hiring of two full-time speech therapists by the school system. A third group of children who were identified as lacking in important social skills were dealt with through their parents. These parents were guided in using informal neighborhood play groups, church programs, family outings, separation experiences within the family, and the pooled efforts of groups of parents as enrichment experiences for their children. Finally, socioeconomically disadvantaged parents who could not afford private kindergartens or who could not devote much of their own time to enhancing the preschool readiness of their children were assisted through the city recreation department, which established a program for preschool children that was aimed at fostering essential social skills in children from deprived neighborhoods.

Many children with unique problems were dealt with in programs especially designed for them. Part of the preschool workup by the project team involved offering three or more suggestions for enhancing the child's readiness for entering school. These suggestions were conveyed to the parents, and follow-up interviews were scheduled to discuss the outcome of suggested interventions. Parents were very involved in this process and only a few of them (2%) failed to meet their appointments for the follow-up interviews. An example of a program to meet the needs of a specific child is described in Figure 3.

(Lemar)

Preschool Checkup. A walking index of poverty, undernourished, cleaned up for the school visit, speech incomprehensible, suspected mental defective, impulsive, functioning well below norms in all areas. A grim mother determined that her child succeed in school, suspicious of rejection and easily antagonized. Married at sixteen to a man twenty-five years older; after five children is tired and worn at twenty-six. Husband is currently unemployed and in jail; family has moved four times in the last year, is currently living in three rooms, and obtains water from a neighbor. Parents quit school by the fifth grade. Little resources beyond existence and impulsive moments of pleasure; known to welfare sources to be in a chronic state of crisis. Team predicted little chance of school success without major interventions. Most significant strengths are child's energy and mother's determination for school success.

Needs. So excessive in all areas the problem will be to remain focused on school readiness and a realistic school program, rather than to become overwhelmed by family needs.

Interventions

Alerted welfare sources managed to supply immediate food need. The first step was to select a simple, easily attained intervention that responded to urgent needs but did not promise more than could be delivered and was in line with basic aims. Achieving the preschool physical at the local county health department was effective in establishing a working relationship between mother, school, and interventionist, as well as a build-up of body health as a readiness resource. The following list of interventions focused on key behavior agents using existing or specially developed resources.

1. Prior to School.

(a) Communication of Project and school efforts toward Lemar's school readiness stimulated renewed welfare interest leading to mother's employment and later, minimal welfare contacts.

(b) Speech evaluation by state speech and hearing team helped parents to be more realistic (if not more helpful) about speech handicap, and mobilized school efforts for therapy (school system hired two full time speech therapists).

(c) Development of a new city recreation department program for preschool children provided Lemar's first supervised social experiences as well as enrichment and learning opportunities.

(d) Development of the new preschool summer program (six weeks) in the school he would enter provided: (1) a gain in school behavior orientation, (2) easily reached goals to build up achievement skills, and (3) maintenance of mother's positive motivation. His IQ was raised 15 points according to brief testing

2. During School Entry.

(a) Place Lemar with teacher accepting of seriously deprived children; he may need special tolerance and handling at first; parents' needs are excessive, their negative feelings easily aroused; except need to handle communication distortions.

(b) Enrolled in the Junior League "Big Sister" program, aimed at early attack on school dropouts by interest in deprived elementary children (facilitated by the pilot program of current Project). Lemar received human interest and strategic resources, for example, extra dental attention and a birthday cake.

(c) School nurse checked on regular visits to his school to build up hygiene and body health; initiated a vitamin program from free physician samples.

(d) Interventionist was available at regular intervals to teacher and parent, especially if distress signals occurred.

Outcome. School entry was minimally adequate, but significantly no behavior problems or distress signals occurred from family or school. Difficulties arose with family-school communication but were resolved. Dramatic progress gradually occurred with speech handicap. Repeated first grade; now in second grade, functioning as a slow learner but clearly not mental defective. Is happy and well-motivated, never misses school. Father remains unchanged, mother attends PTA regularly and continues to progress with employment; family remains off welfare rolls.

Figure 3. An Intervention program for a specific child (from Newton and Brown, 1967, pp. 518, 519, and 520).

The evaluation of the program is partly objective and partly impressionistic, as described by Newton and Brown (1967). Follow-ups have compared children whose global rating predicting school success was either 1 or 2, reflecting that they were either exceptional or typical, with children whose ratings were 3 or 4, indicating they were weak or in trouble. Children regarded as typical or better completed twice as many of the first grade reading requirements as those seen as weak and in trouble. Only 2.9 percent of the children rated as typical failed to complete reading readiness primers whereas 28 percent of the children seen as weak failed. Furthermore, the higher rated children had significantly fewer school absences, and 94 percent of them were promoted whereas only 66 percent of the children with poor ratings were promoted. Children rated as weak were found by the assessment teams to have revealed in the psychological tests either negative or unrecognizable feelings concerning school and seemed to have particularly unrealistic impressions or concepts about school. They were also found to be lower in initiative, were either over- or underresponsive to adult wishes, displayed less independent behavior, were less satisfied concerning their own age status, were lower in curiosity, and were consistently seen as poorer in functional uses of the body and social development than were their better rated peers. They were not regarded as less intellectually capable, however.

Most of the above-mentioned findings support the validity of the early detection procedure. The success of the intervention is reflected in the parents' very positive reaction to the program. Also, demand for services increased in time, and the number of interventions per child seen in the preschool checkup increased substantially in the second year of the program.

On the basis of their experience with the program, the designers of the Sumter Child Study Project believe that they have helped validate the general principle that confronting stress and developing techniques for coping with its effects are building blocks for maturity. They see the "management" of stress as being more effective than "treating" it. Management is distinguished from treatment in that it involves bringing to bear on the child's problems the resources of all the individuals who interact with him in his daily life, such as parents and teachers, instead of abdicating responsibility for dealing with his problem to some outside "expert." In line with this emphasis on managing rather than treating the child is the conviction that helping the child develop spontaneous coping behavior in the arena where stress naturally occurs is more conducive to promoting future adaptive skill and resourcefulness than is the development of insight in the conventional treatment situation.

CONCLUSION

The school system has been the locus of significant secondary preventive efforts with children; early identification has received major stress in a few instances and prevention has been the prime thrust in others. In many cases, programs have emerged as almost frantic efforts to stem the flow of clinical referrals to vastly overburden school mental health workers. Many of these programs seem to have proceeded on the blind faith that early intervention is worthwhile, even though some question this assumption and few have been able to offer pragmatic ideas about how to intervene at the outset.

The oldest secondary preventive programs have undergone several metamorphoses as a function of specific experiences. Many of these programs have produced convincing evidence that children with problems can be identified quite early in their school careers and that such problems tend to endure. These findings affirm the worthwhileness of attempting to develop effective secondary preventive programs, a point that might have been disputed a few years ago when some argued that a child's problems are so ephemeral as to be unworthy of preventive efforts.

One might well ask, however, given the experience of the programs described in this chapter: Where do we stand with respect to the potential for preventing early identified disorder? Clearly, the programs surveyed have not yet produced results that are sufficiently conclusive to encourage complacency. Program efforts might be focused on any one of three targets or on some combination of all of them—that is, parents, teachers, and the children themselves. The St. Louis program concentrated largely on parents and created a format, group psychotherapy, that seemed beneficial to a certain class of parents. On the other hand, a similar format with other social classes produced very disappointing results. Although other programs have made weak attempts to reach parents, for the most part, we are still without a widely applicable model for a secondary preventive program in which parent involvement is extensive. Most of the secondary preventive programs described here have done relatively little direct work with teachers. Consultation with teachers by mental health professionals in the course of carrying out a secondary preventive effort does take place; however, no program is involved in truly systematic efforts to work with teachers as has been done in the behavior modification programs discussed in the previous chapter. Clearly, this is another aspect of secondary prevention that could benefit by the creation of new program models and research into their effectiveness.

It is with respect to direct work with children manifesting school problems that the programs described have contributed the most. The Rochester Primary Mental Health Project as well as the PACE program, and the Sumpter Child Study Project have all provided the model of a professional role which is more active than that of the traditional school mental health worker. It is a role model that encourages intervention, and a variety of efforts to bring beneficial forces to bear on the child. The Rochester project has also provided the model of a teacher aide who can provide a great deal of attention to the child who needs such help. Extensive work has proved this model to be altogether feasible, and even should the long-range results of such a program be less successful than desired, new types of programs will very likely adopt the teacher-aide model as a means of bringing concerted attention to the problems of the young child.

In summary, the secondary preventive programs that have been reviewed are far from finished products in which to repose all of our faith. On the other hand, they do represent some interesting beginnings suggesting that many innovations are possible for dealing with the troubled school age youngster when his problems are first recognized rather than only after they have become exacerbated to the degree that referral to a clinical facility becomes necessary.

References

Beach, D. R., Cowen, E. L., Zax, M., Laird, J. D., Trost, M. A., & Izzo, L. D. Objectification of a screening procedure for early detection of emotional disorder. *Child Development*, 1968, *39*, 1177–1188.

Bower, E. M. *Early identification of emotionally handicapped children in school.* Springfield, Ill.: Charles C. Thomas, Publishers, 1960.

Bower, E. M., & Lambert, N. M. *A process for in-school screening of children with emotional handicaps.* Sacramento, Cal.: California State Department of Education, 1961.

Brownbridge, R., & VanVleet, P. (Eds.) *Investment in prevention: The prevention of learning and behavior problems in young children.* San Francisco: Pace ID Center, 1969.

Buchmueller, A. D., & Gildea, M. C.-L. A group therapy project with parents of behavior problem children in public schools. *American Journal of Psychiatry*, 1949, *106*, 46–53.

Cowen, E. L. The effectiveness of secondary prevention programs using non-professionals in the school setting. *Proceedings, 76th Annual Convention, APA*, 1968, *2*, 705–706.

Cowen, E. L., Carlisle, R. L., & Kaufman, G. Evaluation of a college student volunteer program with primary graders experiencing school adjustment problems. *Psychology in the Schools*, 1969, *6*, 371–375.

Cowen, E. L., Izzo, L. D., Miles, H., Telschow, E. F., Trost, M. A., & Zax, M. A mental health program in the school setting: description and evaluation. *Journal of Psychology*, 1963, *56*, 307–356.

Cowen, E. L., Zax, M., Izzo, L. D., & Trost, M. A. The prevention of emotional disorders in the school setting a further investigation. *Journal of Consulting Psychology*, 1966, *30*, 381–387.

Gildea, M. C.-L. *Community mental health: a school centered program and a group discussion program.* Springfield, Ill.: Charles C. Thomas, 1959.

Gildea, M. C.-L., Glidewell, J. C., & Kantor, M. B. Maternal attitudes and general adjustment in school children. In J. C. Glidewell (Ed.), *Parental attitudes and child behavior:* Springfield, Ill.: Charles C. Thomas, Publisher, 1961. Pp. 42–89.

Gildea, M. C.-L., Glidewell, J. C., & Kantor, M. B. The St. Louis mental health project: history and evaluation. In E. L. Cowen, E. A. Gardner, & M. Zax (Eds.), *Emergent approaches to mental health problems.* New York: Appleton-Century-Crofts, 1967. Pp. 290–308.

Glidewell, J. C., Mensh, I. N., & Gildea, M. C.-L. Behavior symptoms in children and degree of sickness. *American Journal of Psychiatry,* 1957, *114,* 47–53.

Newton, M. R., & Brown, R. D. A preventive approach to developmental problems in school children. In E. M. Bower, & W. G. Hollister (Eds.), *Behavioral science frontiers in education.* New York: Wiley, 1967. Pp. 499–527.

Rae-Grant, Q., & Stringer, L. A. Mental health programs in schools. In M. F. Shore, & F. V. Mannino (Eds.), *Mental health and the community: problems, programs and strategies.* New York: Behavioral Publications, 1969. Pp. 83–102.

Stringer, L. A. Academic progress as an index of mental health. *Journal of Social Issues,* 1959, *15,* 16–29.

Zax, M., & Cowen, E. L. Early identification and prevention of emotional disturbance in a public school. In E. L. Cowen, E. A. Gardner, & M. Zax (Eds.), *Emergent approaches to mental health problems.* New York: Appleton-Century-Crofts, 1967. Pp. 331–351.

Zax, M., & Cowen, E. L. Research on early detection and prevention of emotional dysfunction in young school children. In C. D. Spielberger (Ed.), *Current topics in clinical and community psychology.* New York: Academic Press, 1969. Pp. 67–108.

Zax, M., & Cowen, E. L. *Abnormal psychology: changing conceptions.* New York: Holt, Rinehart, & Winston, 1972.

8. *prevention in the college community*

In the preceding three chapters we discussed programs of preventive intervention aimed at children or young adolescents. There are impressive reasons, both theoretical and practical, for arguing that a greater percentage of our mental health resources should be committed to providing services for the very young. However, somewhat older populations also present a picture of need and an opportunity for impact that warrant the development of innovative programs of prevention. The population of college students is one in this category (armed services personnel may be another). College students, as a group, may be subject to an unusually great number of stresses. Generally, the student is made anxious by doubts and conflicts over matters such as occupational choice, sexual behavior, and separation from his home community (Reid, 1970). Also, unlike his working peers, the college student is subject to the academic demands of his school and, often, to the confusion arising from a situation in which parents, college staff, and the student himself may be uncertain as to whether to view the student as a child or an adult. Given these conditions, it is reasonable to suppose that the psychological resources of the student may be greatly enhanced or sadly damaged by the nature of the experiences that occur during the college years. The community psychologist may be well justified, therefore, in viewing the college population as deserving relatively high priority for efforts at prevention.

The portrayal of the college student population as a "high-risk" group is based on more than speculation about the stresses of college life. Statistics on the rate of identified emotional disorders among students indicate that the rate of incidence is higher than for the population at large (Reid, 1970), although these data may be misleading because of inequities in the processes by which problems are identified in the college community as opposed to other communities. There can be no doubt, however, that the incidence of psychological disturbance among college students is substantial. Based on the findings of campus mental health services offering comprehensive programs, Farnsworth (1966) has estimated that for every 10,000 students, up to 1650 may be impaired to the degree that they require professional help or cannot function effectively as students, up to 20 may attempt suicide, and up to 25 may require treatment in a mental hospital. When one considers that the United States Census Bureau figures placed the college population at almost 7 1/2 million as of 1970, rates such as those cited above would indicate that hundreds of thousands of individuals will experience substantial distress during their college years, not to mention the unknown number of students who will leave college before their problems are identified, or who will experience later problems because of the adverse effects of an inadequate college experience.

The existence of a substantial need for mental health services in the colleges does not in itself imply the need for innovative programs of prevention. The concept of preventive psychiatry for student populations dates back to the early decades of this century (Farnsworth, 1966), and mental health facilities are hardly novelties on the current American campus. Yet it is doubtful that existing programs are adequate to meet present and future needs. On one hand, the actual demand for psychological services may be increasing. Reifler, Lipzin, and Fox (1967) found, for example, that the number of students seeking help from the student mental health services at the University of North Carolina increased from about 18 per 1000 in 1956 to about 44 per 1000 in 1965. Manpower resources in the mental health fields may simply be insufficient to meet increasing demands for service under the usual plans for delivery. On the other hand, existing services, even if sufficiently available, may not be designed to reach a substantial portion of students who could benefit from psychological assistance, but who would not seek out the types of services traditionally offered by campus agencies. Kysar (1966), for example, argues that the college facilities may be reaching too few students whose "psychosocial difficulties" lead to their dropping out or flunking out of school.

Beyond the issue of need there is another standpoint from which the college campus represents a logical setting for programs of prevention. The campus may provide an excellent laboratory for discovering and demonstrating the means for effective psychological intervention (Leveridge, 1957). Larson, Barger, and Cahoon (1969) have cited three ways in which the college setting lends itself to the work of developing a paradigm for community mental health services generally. First, the college community provides a relatively small, homogeneous and stable population on which research data may be collected with comparative ease. Second, the college is already well staffed with helping agents, such as chaplains, residence hall advisers, and administrators, whose functions might be altered to reflect the new concepts of service undergoing trial. Third, the college community as a setting for experimental interventions is ideal for training workers among the population of preprofessional students, and these workers could then carry their insights into other communities where new modes of service may be needed.

The idea of using the campus as a proving ground for principles of community intervention raises the question as to whether the campus is an appropriate analogue for communities generally. In certain respects, even the large residential campus differs from other types of communities; only part of the population lives within its confines, most of the residents retain other home addresses, and the student population is committed to only a limited, predetermined period of community membership. Nevertheless, the campus structure permits the identification and study of most of the features on which all communities vary. Klein (1965) has conceptualized a number of community characteristics relevant to programs of community mental health, including physical size, population density, location and resources, guiding values, distribution of authority and power, and patterns of communication. On all of these dimensions, and others, college campuses may vary widely. Kelly (1966) has proposed that human communities be viewed as ecological systems, whose attributes as such a system will determine the feasibility and impact of interventive efforts. Insofar as this is true there is one further perspective from which the campus may be a uniquely desirable target for the community psychologist. Given that many, if not most, community psychologists operate out of universities, it is to be expected that they are particularly apt to grasp the complex realities of their university community. It is somewhat ironic, therefore, that so few efforts, relatively, have been directed by community psychologists at their own base of operations, and so many efforts have been directed at communities with which the professional is likely to be relatively unfamiliar.

Perhaps one reason why the university-based community psychologist has not always sought to work in his own institutional community is that his more intimate knowledge of the setting may be negated by the unique problems in acting as change agent for a system of which he is an integral part. Brigante (1965) has described various ways in which campus mental health workers may be viewed by other members of the college staff as usurpers of prerogatives or narrow stereotypical figures who implicitly belittle academic concerns by their emphasis on hidden motivations for behavior. Moreover, Brigante notes that, as with any community, the goals of the mental health worker may be regarded by others as superfluous or even contrary to the goals of institutional leaders. For example, he cites the possibility that the community psychologist may be viewed as fostering dependency or excessive emotionality in an institution where academicians may feel independence and a capacity for detached intellectual assessment of problems should be fostered.

Whatever the virtues and drawbacks of attempting to develop innovative programs of preventive mental health in the colleges, the fact remains that relatively few projects have been reported in detail. Many programs may not appear in the literature because they are exclusively service oriented and are not intended to serve as models. It must also be suspected, however, that there have been a number of other programs that have earned obscurity because they could not be implemented or failed to demonstrate positive impact. Indeed, some of the projects to be described in this chapter hardly qualify as great successes on the basis of their effects and longevity. They will, however, provide a valuable lesson to the reader who asks a few appropriate questions as he considers the reasons for the different outcomes. Who instigated the project and what was their prior relationship to the community? To what extent did the plan of intervention reflect a concern for the unique characteristics of the campus social system? How broadly did the project seek to alter the workings of the community? Finally, were the potential service recipients in the community given input into the program as planners, workers, or advisers, or did they merely constitute the target of concern.

The development of this chapter partially reflects an editorial effort to ask and answer the questions above. Initially, the programs described are those that only minimally illustrate a sophisticated consideration of community intervention issues. Progress through the chapter, to a point, provides illustration of programs involving more recognition of the questions that community workers may be obliged to face in their efforts to innovate. The last part of the chapter deals with some projects that derive a special status from the fact that they were staffed or instigated from within the segment of the community which was the target group for service.

Webster and Harris (1958) reported a program that, like many of its successors, represented an effort to reach freshmen entering college, in this instance, a male population at Massachusetts Institute of Technology. The program was seemingly intended to have both primary and secondary preventive functions, and the report described three years of program operation, from 1953 to 1956. The program was hypothetically open to all incoming students who chose to volunteer for what was presented as an "experiment in group psychodynamics." Of 3000 students admitted to the college during the project's first three years, 650 volunteered to participate in the "experiment." Of these volunteers, 227 were assigned to participate in group experiences led by several psychiatrists or psychiatric residents. Of these, 45 never attended a single session, because of scheduling, administrative problems, or a change of heart. Volunteers who had not been randomly selected to participate in the first semester groups were regarded as control subjects.

The groups varied in size, but a membership of 10 was typical. The groups had autonomy with respect to frequency of meetings with the result that the number ranged from 4 to 27 sessions during the semester. Group leaders were instructed to present the meetings as an opportunity for the students to become acquainted, share thoughts, and engage in discussion of ways of relating to each other. Webster and Harris reported impressionistic data that discussions tended to focus on school related matters and did not strongly resemble the interactions of a psychotherapy group.

Efforts to determine the impact of the project on participating freshmen were made, but research emphasis focused on the question of what determined whether a student would volunteer and what determined whether a given volunteer would attend meetings regularly or irregularly. Researchers had access to a variety of data on all incoming freshmen, including their college grades, personality ratings (based on assessment of admissions interviews and materials), names of students dropping or flunking out during or after the first year, and the names of students who sought individual psychological attention.

Three types of comparisons were made in attempting to determine the effect of the program and which students were being reached by it. First, the experimental and control groups of volunteers were compared. Second, all volunteers were compared with the general norms for their freshman class. Finally, volunteers who had been assigned to groups were divided according to frequency of actual attendance into high and low attenders and compared.

The findings of this early study did not show that the intervention was effective in improving academic performance as measured by discrepancy between predicted and actual grades in the first year. The experimental and control groups were essentially similar on this dimension. It was found, however, that the controls tended to seek more psychiatric help than the experimental subjects or the average freshman. Retrospective analysis of this finding led to the conclusion that the control subjects were not more disturbed than most of their peers but, instead, that they were more inclined toward seeking psychological help than were the nonvolunteering students. Generally, the volunteering and nonvolunteering students were found to be similar except for the difference just mentioned. In comparing high and low attenders among the experimental subjects, it was found that students predicted to do exceptionally well academically tended to be in the extreme groups with respect to attendance; that is, they either attended no sessions at all or they attended six or more. Students of lesser presumed potential were more often found to attend one to five of the sessions.

Although the MIT project did not demonstrate that a brief, professionally led series of discussion groups would markedly enhance the adjustment of college freshmen, it did provide valuable information for the planning of future interventions. In particular, the results of the Webster and Harris study suggested that self-selected volunteers for programs of psychological intervention may not be more needful of services than nonvolunteers, but may be more psychologically minded individuals who would more likely seek some form of counseling than the average student. The practical implication of this finding seems to be that volunteer discussion groups may not meet the total community needs for some form of preventive intervention, but lessen the demand for individual counseling by meeting the felt needs of students otherwise inclined to seek these services.

Despite its innovative aspects, the MIT project retained two significant features of more traditional approaches. The front line workers in the intervention were highly trained professionals, and the project was structured without any particular regard to the specifics of student life within the institution. A more recent effort (Wolff, 1969) was somewhat more traditional with respect to both the personnel and the structure of the intervention.

As with the MIT project, Wolff's program was directed at male college freshmen. Again the experimental group students, in this case at the University of Rochester, were volunteers invited to participate in discussion sessions focusing on interpersonal relations. In the Rochester project, however, the groups were led either by dormitory resident advisers or graduate students in clinical psychology as opposed to the more experienced leadership in the earlier effort. Furthermore, the Rochester intervention involved natural groupings of students, specifically groups of students living in close proximity to one another along a corridor in a dormitory.

Student volunteers for the groups at Rochester were solicited from among the populations of 10 residence hall corridors. On two of the corridors the volunteering students were told that the group experience would not be available, and this group became the nontreatment control for the study. An additional control group of nonvolunteers were recruited to take the test instruments without participation in any group experience. Each control group consisted of 15 students.

Volunteers from the remaining eight corridors became eligible to participate in the group experience. Of the volunteers from these corridors, 13 were ultimately eliminated from the study because they did not complete the research questionnaires or failed to attend more than half of the group sessions. The final experimental sample consisted of 58 students. Each corridor had a group of its own with 8 to 10 participants. Four of the corridors had groups that were led by the clinical psychology graduate students. The groups on the other four corridors were led by their resident advisers.

The resident advisers who were given responsibility for group leadership were not an unselected sample. Like all such advisers, these individuals were junior or senior students who had received some initial didactic training for their job as dormitory personnel. The four chosen advisers, however, were men who were rated as being more effective by the dormitory administrators than the advisers on the corridors with groups led by graduate students or the advisers on the control corridors. The four advisers who led the groups had not had prior formal group experience nor were any of them psychology majors.

A central focus of the Wolff study was the impact of the group experience on the social interactions and mutual perceptions of the corridor residents. Prior to the first meetings of the groups, all of the students on all of the 10 research corridors were asked to complete a sociometric instrument shown in Figure 1. In addition, students who had volunteered for the groups or who had agreed to fill out the test instruments were asked to complete questionnaires on their extracurricular activities, their ways of spending their time, and their personal values. A final assessment device required the students to make predictions about the behavior of an unknown individual given increasingly greater amounts of information on his past behavior; this last device was intended as a measure of interpersonal perceptivity.

The groups met for the first time at the beginning of the second semester and continued until ten 1 ½ hour sessions had been held, which required about three months. Following the intervention, the test instru-

Your Name ————————

Instructions: For each of the categories below place the names of as many members of your dormitory corridor who fill the description.

1. Would want as a roomate:
2. Would want in a club that you belong to:
3. A warm person:
4. Involved with others on your corridor:
5. Cooperative.
6. Keeps to himself:
7. Trouble Maker:
8. Hard to get along with:
9. A cold person:
10. A person you try to avoid being involved with:

(Wolff, 1969; Appendix)

Figure 1. Sociometric Instrument used in the Wolff Study (Wolff, 1969).

ments were again administered, including the sociometric measure given to all corridor residents. The members of the four research groups (experimentals) with graduate student leaders, experimentals with resident adviser leaders, volunteer controls, and nonvolunteer controls) were compared on the basis of change scores for the prepost measures.

The principle findings of the Wolff study related to the sociometric ratings of the group participants as compared to controls. The experimental groups showed a significantly greater increase than did controls in the percentage of "favorable" choices by peers where the person was not the first choice listed. The percentage of unfavorable roles to which group participants were assigned as nonfirst choices declined more for the two experimental groups and the nonvolunteer controls than for the volunteer controls. There was also evidence to indicate that fellow group members were particularly apt to rise in the estimation of group participants. In general, the sociometric data suggested that the group experience had positively affected the way in which participants were perceived by both participating and nonparticipating peers. The fact that this increase in favorable judgments were detected only for nonfirst choices may have indicated that the group members did not achieve the more favorable ratings by becoming unusually salient members of their corridor peer group.

Some prepost change score differences were also detected in comparing the two experimental groups. In particular, students in the graduate student-led groups tended to show a greater increase in the value that they attached to status. This finding might be interpreted to suggest that the opportunity to participate in groups led by less familiar, preprofessional leaders was apt to be more status enhancing than was participation in groups with resident advisers as leaders, with a concommitant increase in the value of status by those who had experienced such gains.

A final finding of the Wolff study seems to parallel one of the findings of the Webster and Harris research at MIT. The frequency with which group members sought individual counseling at the student health service was found to be unusually low. As in the MIT study, the possibility is again raised that freshmen given the opportunity to engage in group discussions with peers in a structured program may be less likely to seek traditional psychological services than would be the case in the absence of such a program. Thus the Wolff study demonstrates that the discussion group approach can improve the interpersonal relations of male freshmen, and possibly, can reduce their demand for more costly types of services. However, neither the MIT nor the Rochester program was found to significantly affect the academic performance of participants. The next program we describe was explicitly designed to improve scholastic functioning as opposed to the interpersonal adjustment goals that were central to the two programs discussed above.

The psychological relevance of a program to improve the academic performance of college students may be twofold. Kysar (1967) has pointed to the psychological damage that may accrue from the experience of failing to meet the challenges of scholastic life. On the other hand, the occupational skills, living skills, and confidence that may result from the student's ability to complete his schooling successfully may do much to prevent the occurrence of later psychosocial failures. Cognizant of these factors, Spielberger and Weitz (1964) initiated a program at Duke University designed to aid students believed to represent a high-risk group with respect to the possibility of academic failure.

Basing their premise on earlier research, Spielberger and Weitz believed that highly anxious incoming freshmen were likely to experience considerable difficulty in performing up to their academic potential. The Duke researchers believed that these students might often become college dropouts or troubled marginal cases. Spielberger and Weitz sought, therefore, to direct their efforts toward anxious incoming freshmen males selected through an exhaustive screening of new students. All incoming male freshmen were required to complete an adapted version of the Minnesota Multiphasic Personality Inventory scored for two scales of anxiety, and a test of scholastic aptitude. Eligible for the program were students who scored in the upper 30 percent on one anxiety scale, the upper 50 percent on the other, and the upper 75 percent of the aptitude test. This last criterion was employed because of earlier findings that low aptitude students tended to become marginal performers regardless of anxiety.

The Duke program was first tested in the 1959 to 1960 academic year and was partially replicated in the following year. In the first year of operation the selection criteria identified 112 anxious freshmen; in the second, it identified 124. In both years the eligible freshman received an invitation early in the first semester to participate in the "Academic Orientation Program" or AOP. Fifty percent of the students selected in the first year accepted the invitation and a somewhat higher percentage accepted the following year. The students who thus elected to participate were then divided into two matched groups of approximately equal size. One group each year was immediately offered the opportunity to participate in discussion sessions intended to facilitate adaptation to college life; the remaining students were told that they would have to wait until the second semester to participate. In this way, experimental and control groups were constructed with 26 and 27 students in 1959 to 1960 and 34 and 38 students in 1960 to 1961 (there was some attrition from the original sample of volunteers).

Freshmen in the experimental condition were divided into smaller discussion groups with six to nine participants in the first project year and a somewhat larger number in the second year. All groups were led by the authors, faculty members with doctorates in psychology and a substantial amount of experience in group psychotherapy. Each group met for one and one-half hour weekly sessions. The total number of sessions in the first semester groups ranged from 8 to 13. The two project years differed as mentioned above in that the second year groups were somewhat larger; the second year groups also met a slightly greater number of times because of an earlier start in the semester.

As with the two programs discussed earlier in the chapter, the group sessions were not uniformly attended by different students. Spielberger and Weitz divided participants into high and low attenders according to whether a student had participated in seven or more sessions or a lesser number. Data on scholastic aptitude and academic performance were analyzed with regard to attendance category. In 1959 to 1960 there were no significant initial differences between the high attenders, low attenders, and controls. Grades for the first semester showed the high attenders doing significantly better than the controls. Low attenders, however, did least well on first semester reports. In the second year partial replication, there were significant prior differences between the three categories of subjects, with the students who were high attenders having the best aptitude scores, followed by the controls and, then, the low attenders. In ranking the groups on first semester grades, the same order was noted; when initial differences were partialed out, the difference in grades did not prove significant, although a trend remained. Interview data collected from the group participants showed that the high attenders regarded the sessions as having been helpful in developing their approach to studies and their way of relating to faculty, while the low attenders did not stress these factors as frequently. Both categories of participants tended to report that the most helpful aspect of the experience was the chance to see that they were not unique in their anxiety over scholastic performance.

Because of the ultimate interest of the authors in the program as a method for reducing academic failures and dropouts, the freshmen subjects were followed through their first and second college years. The high attenders were found to have the lowest rate of academic failure, followed by the low attenders and the controls, but these differences were not significant. Moreover, all three groups had low rates of academic failure, raising the question as to whether the selection procedures had been adequate for identifying students who would be likely to end their college careers prematurely. In comparing all of the students who had been identified as anxious, however, it was found that they did drop out more frequently than less anxious students. Unfortunately, the greatest number of severe underachievers was found among the anxious students who had never volunteered for the program. Once again, empirical support for voluntary group discussion programs was demonstrated, but it was also shown that such a program may not reach the very students who most need the help. Commenting on this possibility, Spielberger and Weitz concluded that a substantial need may exist for programs that more effectively reach out to the student population, perhaps through consultation with college personnel who habitually come in contact with students experiencing difficulty.

The programs at MIT, Rochester, and Duke are all illustrations of one innovative principle that may deserve wider deployment: all of these projects reached out to their clients. The need to abandon the passive stance typical of traditional mental health programs may be a major consideration in the formulation of new and better campus interventions (Falk, 1971). Yet, it is striking that all three projects failed, at least partially, to reach, engage, and help the needful members of the community. Conceivably, this fact might be explained by weaknesses in the technology of the intervention. A careful consideration of the programs in toto, however, seems to point to a different level of assessment. None of the programs cited appear to have rested on a prior analysis of the particular features of the campus community in which they were to operate. In none did the plan of action involve a flexible strategy to alter broadly the student's environment. Finally, these programs did not engage the creative participation of the population to be served. In some measure, the projects described repeated the traditional sequence of the professional worker attempting to bring to a community a treatment technique determined by his own preferences, applying the technique without particular concern for its impact on the system as a whole, and finding that the cooperation and response to treatment in the target population are limited.

These three programs should probably be categorized as primary or secondary prevention. Certainly, the project at Duke, dependent as it was on early detection has the features of a secondary preventive effort. Until programs of early prevention can be made both effective and readily implemented, however, a significant number of college students will continue to experience relatively severe psychosocial crisis during their schooling. An innovative program of tertiary prevention was developed at Kansas State University for providing services to students whose problems had reached the severe or chronic stage during their college careers (Sinett, Wiesner and Frieser, 1967; Sinnett and Niedenthal, 1968).

The Kansas State program centered on the formation of a halfway house for students whose needs were seen to exced those that could be met by the traditional student mental health services. The troubled undergraduates were nominated by the personnel of the campus counseling center as being individuals requiring extensive help in addition to their ongoing therapy. Sinnett, Wiesner, and Frieser (1967) comment that the clientele thus defined was not so deviant a population as might be found in a halfway house for former patients of state mental hospitals. Even so, the disturbed students represented a group with a poor prognosis for college completion and a fair chance of hospitalization. The residents of the halfway house also included a substantial number, in fact, a majority, of "normal" students loosely selected on the basis of nominations by deans, residence hall directors, and school counselors. No professional mental health workers were residents in the halfway house, although they were available as consultants on both a crisis and routine basis.

Early experience with the counseling center referral mechanism indicated that about 50 to 70 students per year would be identified as appropriate for the project. Of these nominees, only unmarried full-time students were generally invited to participate. The first occupants of the halfway house consisted of 20 disturbed students divided equally between males and females, and 40 other residents including the volunteer students and some administrative personnel (Sinnett et al., 1967). As of the third semester of operation (Sinnett and Niedenthal, 1968), 28 students referred by the counseling center had been residents in the house.

The student volunteers in the project were initially paid a small stipend for their participation and given the title of "resident fellows." This practice was discontinued when it was found to produce jealousy and to increase social distance between the disturbed students and the volunteers. The actual living experience tended to blur the status distinctions. One volunteer commented as follows:

"Perhaps the distinction between clients and volunteers has appeared to be quite precise. However, in actual living within the project, this is not the case. Each individual is aware of his own position, but is not necessarily aware of each other person's designation. While this is sometimes relatively apparent, at other times there is no obvious behavioral distinction between the two categories. A volunteer is not always a helper nor is a client consistently receiving help. There is no real status difference in functioning either as a client or as a volunteer. Each person is aware that at times he has problems, some of which he can handle more effectively than others. Likewise, some individuals can consistently handle situations more effectively than other students can. However, both of these statements refer to any individual in the project, not to persons in one group or the other" (Sinnett and Niedenthal, 1968; p. 237).

In addition to the usual features of college dormitory living, the halfway house offered a number of special activities. The residents met periodically in planned group sessions, ad hoc meetings were held, and consultations with project consultants were available. The counseling service clients in the house also continued to receive their individual psychotherapy (Sinnett et al., 1967). The in-house activities were said to emphasize the value of communicating feelings as a means toward exposing and resolving interpersonal conflicts.

Early data from the program were found to be encouraging. In the first semester of the halfway house's operation, none of the resident clients left the school. Findings reported after three semesters of operation (Sinnett and Niedenthal, 1968) showed that 6 of 28 clients had left the college, a rate that was considered relatively low but that was not significantly lower than the rate for controls, who had been referred and were not admitted to the halfway house. All students in the project were asked to rank the various experiences associated with program participation according to their helpfulness. Both clients and volunteers tended to agree that the informal contacts with other students engendered by the living arrangements were among the most useful aspects of the experience. Thus the basic fact of bringing the two types of students into a situation where they might interact was found to have been a highly positive element in the program as judged from subjective reports. It should be mentioned that the presumed fate of many of the client residents would have involved quite the opposite experience, that is, extrusion from the community or campus peers into the outside world or the world of the mental hospital

The Kansas State project may be viewed as an effort to create a therapeutic community within the larger community of the university. This illustrative program naturally raises an important question: Is it possible to create a therapeutic milieu that encompasses the entire campus by altering crucial features of the total institution? If such an approach were feasible, the potential advantages would be substantial. In particular, a total community approach would be more apt to reach needful students, whereas it has been shown that more limited interventions may fail to include students whose needs are great but whose motivation to participate is low. Furthermore, a project aimed at substantially altering the college experience by redesigning aspects of the institution would be capable of serving as true primary prevention. Several programs are now described that illustrate the kinds of efforts that have been made to study and alter relevant features of the campus operation in the interests of preventive psychology.

Reifler, Lipzin, and Fox (1967) engaged in a program of limited scope that still managed to produce an observable change in the college operation. They studied the rate of psychiatric usage of students at the University of North Carolina and found that nonresident students, especially freshmen, tended to seek more service. As a result of their finding being reported to the school administration, a rule was established requiring that all freshmen live on campus. (This outcome may have been desirable but probably did not increase the esteem in which the consultants were held among the students.)

An earlier effort to employ a total community approach was reported by Leveridge in 1957. As in the North Carolina project, mental health consultants attempted to study the scholastic institution and to provide suggestions as to changes that would help improve the milieu psychologically. Leveridge and his associates studied two types of features of Goddard College, a small college in Vermont. First, the researchers studied the students of the institution, their backgrounds, needs, values, and the like. Second, they employed psychometric instruments to determine the patterns of group influence within the student population. Based on their findings, the mental health team provided feedback to faculty and administrators; at the same time these staff members were solicited as participants in further efforts to study the campus. The Goddard project was intended primarily to demonstrate that the college setting could be a laboratory for applying the behavioral sciences to the task of restructuring the milieu of a sociocultural institution. No data were reported to indicate whether this demonstration ultimately had an impact on the well-being of the students in the institution. Obviously, evidence of this kind would have been difficult to obtain for a project of this breadth. Even if an overall change in the adjustment of Goddard students had been shown to coincide with the period of the study and consultation, it would have been virtually impossible to prove that factors other than the program (such as cultural shifts in student values) could not account for the observed changes.

The final program considered in this chapter represents the most diverse and ambitious effort to introduce public mental health principles on a college campus. The mental health program at the University of Florida (Barger, 1963; Barger, Larson, and Hall, 1966) was designed to meet the goals of primary, secondary, and tertiary prevention by approaches that would not overtax manpower resources. As of the 1966 report the staff of the program consisted of three psychiatrists, three psychologists, one psychiatric nurse, clerical assistants, and graduate students in training.

In the interests of primary prevention, research was conducted to determine the sources of environmental stress that confronted the student (Barger, 1963). One study focused on the degree of congruence between the values and attitudes of students and the normative goals of the institution; it was hypothesized that low congruence would be a source of stress. Another study plotted the help-seeking efforts of students over the school year to identify the particular scholastic activities that contributed to the buildup of tension among students or served to release tension. Findings of this research revealed that such things as difficult courses became a major source of student distress around the examination periods. On the other hand, opportunities to participate in athletic events were found to be sources of relief. A third study was designed to identify background and personality variables associated with the ability to adapt to student life at the University. Findings from these research projects were utilized in programs of consultation with faculty and administrators. Some concrete changes were attributed to the work of the mental health team, including improvements in the freshmen orientation program and the introduction of pre-enrollment questionnaires by which incoming students and their parents could provide information on the student's readiness for college (Barger et al, 1966).

Secondary prevention efforts focused on the development of means for the early identification and treatment of students' psychological disturbance. Toward this end new students were given MMPI's and individuals showing disturbed profiles were offered opportunities for counseling. About 10 percent of the incoming students were found to be deviant on the test, but only one third of these accepted the offer of treatment. Another major aspect of the secondary prevention program involved the establishment of communication between project personnel and "signal receivers," such as faculty members and residence hall personnel, who were in a position to spot the early signals of disturbed behavior (Barger, 1963).

In the category of tertiary prevention, the program included facilities for several modes of treatment, including group psychotherapy, individual therapy, psychodrama, chemotherapy, and crisis hospitalization. A specifically preventive feature of these services was that they were offered on a no-waiting basis. Students seeking help were immediately seen by the psychiatric nurse for screening; the nurse then recommended a course of treatment or referred the client on for further evaluation. It was found that about 33 percent of the students entering the screening procedure required significant amounts of treatment, while about 60 percent needed to be seen only briefly (Barger et al, 1966).

Multifaceted interventions such as the program at the University of Florida certainly seem to represent promising actualizations of many principles of community mental health. These programs do, however, face a number of problems. As Brigante (1965) has noted, members of the academic community may not universally welcome mental health programs, and efforts requiring widespread participation by college staff are likely to meet considerable opposition. Another problem lies in the fact that the effectiveness of programs aimed at significantly altering the campus environment is more difficult to demonstrate than is the case with smaller programs having narrower goals. This latter difficulty is a problem both with respect to "selling" the intervention and, also, with respect to making refinements based on the assessment of impact. Even so, the potential value of major campus programs for demonstrating community mental health principles and for serving people would justify further efforts to develop programs of this kind.

The project at the University of Florida clearly stands out as one of the best examples of an effort to develop and apply a true community intervention strategy in a university setting. Barger and his associates made definite attempts to analyze the specific characteristics of the community, to select the best places to focus interventive actions, and to involve large segments of the community in the program. It is not clear, however, that the project solicited much student participation at the level of planning or service delivery. There was student input, as collected through the research efforts, but of the various segments of the campus community the students apparently played the smallest role in the operation of the new services. In contrast, a number of campus programs have appeared in recent years that are primarily or solely staffed by students.

Of the student-staffed service instrumentalities some, but not all, are incorporated into a professionally managed campus health facility. At a convention of counseling center directors in 1971, a study group polled 135 directors about the use of paraprofessionals in their operations. Of the 63 directors who responded to the survey, 60 percent reported that they use undergraduate help in some phase of their efforts (Crane and Anderson cited in Steenland, 1973). In some instances, the student workers were said to be serving in clerical positions or as written test administrators. More than 40 percent of the student-staffed projects, however, involved hotlines or drop-in centers and peer counseling. Thus professionally run campus counseling centers have, with some frequency, sought to use undergraduates as a source of direct aid to their peers. There are still other operations, similar in purpose and approach, that were started by students and that remain separate from other existing mental health facilities on campus. A few of these true "grassroots" efforts have been instigated by and for special interest groups in the college community, for example, homosexuals. The majority of student-run programs probably do not differ radically from the professionally managed programs in their areas of concern. There may, even so, be an important philosophical difference.

Whereas professionally instigated programs using undergraduates as helping agents generally are conceived as mental health test projects, the student initiated programs are often oriented almost totally toward service. Not surprisingly, therefore, it is relatively hard to find published reports on the methods or impact of student-run programs. Some evidence (McColskey, 1973) suggests that programs of this type may rapidly become professionalized or cease to function. What is central to many student initiated projects is not a concept of community mental health intervention but, rather, a humanistic philosophy and a zeal to be humanly useful.

A pioneering example of the professionally organized project utilizing students as helping agents in their own community is the Campus Crisis Center founded at Southern Colorado State College in 1958 (Tucker, Magenity, and Vigil, 1970). The crisis center was founded to serve three major purposes: to supplement inadequate counseling services, to permit anonymous discussion of embarrassing problems, and to bring help closer to the person in crisis. Given these aims, the strategy of a telephone hotline was employed. Volunteers to staff the hotline were sought from among the faculty and administration of the college as well as the student body. Undergraduate students predominated in the sample of volunteers who ultimately became front line workers.

The volunteers received 24 hours of training which involved orientation lectures, listening to taped telephone conversations, and role playing. Once on the job, the hotline helpers had access to professionals who could be consultants or could take over on occasions when the volunteer felt his skills would not suffice. Volunteers were instructed to keep worksheets on each call to record essential facts about the interaction. Monthly meetings were held to discuss problems and ways of improving the operation of the hotline.

As is shown in Table 1, the campus hotline did not serve the campus

Table 1.   Sex and Educational Status of 246 Callers
(Tucker et al., 1970, p. 345)

Group	N	Percent
Female	142	55
Male	104	45
Total	246	100
College student	89	36
Unknown	57	26
High school student	48	19
Nonstudent	44	16
Junior high student	8	3
Total	246	100

population exclusively, although the student callers represented the largest group of users. Telephone hotlines cannot feasibly restrict their services to members of a particular community, given the need to assure the
dissemination of information about the service. Thus, the Colorado State
hotline handled calls from other segments of the larger community, and
was also subject to a fairly high percentage of wrong number or no answer calls (about 37 percent). The calls tabulated above represent the
data collected for the first three academic quarters of the hotline's functioning. These data indicate that, even from its inception, the service provided a substantial amount of aid, with much of it being given to the students of the college.

Table 2.   Problem Areas Mentioned by 183 Callers
(Tucker et al., 1970, p. 345)

Problem Area	N	Percent
Dating	66	29
Family	40	19
Loneliness	28	12
Pregnancy	22	9
Classes	21	9
Finances	8	3
Marriage	7	3
Drugs	6	2
Alcohol	5	2
Other [a]	28	12
Total	231	100

[a] Obesity, insomnia, selective service, employment, religion,
housing, etc.

On their worksheets the volunteers attempted to record the problem areas mentioned by their callers. Table 2 shows the types of problems brought to the volunteers by some of the callers who used the service in the first three semesters. As may be seen, the most frequently mentioned problems were those related to social relationships or the lack thereof. Interestingly, none of the calls were classified as involving threats of suicide. This is notable, because the pioneer work in the area of nonprofessionally staffed hotlines was framed in the context of suicide prevention (Helig, Farberow, Litman, and Shneidman, 1968). Clearly, the usefulness of the service extended by the Colorado State program was in other areas, many of which closely parallel the types of complaints that bring clients into face-to-face counseling situations. The concept of crisis intervention does not, however, involve the notion of long-term efforts to correct chronic adjustment problems.

At American University in Washington, D. C., a structurally similar hotline operation was started through the instigative efforts of a small group of students (McCarthy and Berman, 1971). These students sought out professional guidance in their efforts, but remained the primary organizers. They originally conceived of their hotline as a referral service that would inform callers of helping agencies on or near the campus. The concept also came to include direct service to callers in crisis. A multidisciplinary board of advisers (including lawyers, psychologists, and obstretricians) was recruited by the student founders. Berman and McCarthy, who reported the program, were given the responsibility for training the volunteers. Thus professional advice and training was utilized, but the program remained essentially in the hands of the students. The student government financed operation of the crisis center.

A core of hotline workers was selected from among the students in a University course on crisis intervention. Enrollees in the course were carefully screened for emotional stability, integrity, and receptivity to learning. Core workers in the project received about 30 hours of training, which included didactic presentations, discussions, and role playing. The cadre of workers trained in this way later served as trainers for new volunteers.

Hotline phones were manned from late afternoon and through the night on weekdays; on weekends the service functioned continuously. Publicity for the service originally took the form of posters on campus, newspaper advertisements, and calling cards. When methods of this sort seemed to be achieving less than optimal visibility for the program, a film was created for showing at appropriate campus gatherings to explain and illustrate the center's function. It should be noted that publicity efforts of this type would be regarded as ethically questionable in the case of professionally staffed traditional mental health facilities. Such ethical constraint imposed on mental health professionals would be inimical to the creation of effective outreach efforts, but did not interfere with the work of the student-run hotline.

As in the Colorado State project, hotline personnel attempted to record relevant information about the calls received. The problem areas mentioned by some of the early users of the service are shown in Table 3. As was true at Colorado State, problems in social relationships were common, but the American University hotline serviced more drug problems and several calls were classified as information seeking instead of help seeking. Whether these differences reflect variations in the expressed purpose of the two operations, the populations they served, or the system for recording the nature of the calls is difficult to say. It is again obvious that the hotline provided aid in a variety of situations and could not be aptly regarded as a suicide prevention agency.

It is evident that the evaluation of hotline effectiveness poses special problems. Campus hotlines like those described offer to their users, as one of their attractions, the opportunity to remain anonymous. Follow-up reports on the outcome of the intervention are available only where the user chooses to provide such feedback, and those who do may include an overrepresentation of satisfied users. Thus few programs can provide any direct evidence of their impact on the campus community. A study to evaluate hotline services by an indirect means was conducted in the Washington, D. C. area (Bleach and Claiborn, 1974. In press) in 1972. Four hotlines serving college or high school students and staffed by non-professional volunteers of similar age were compared along several di-

Table 3. Breakdown of Problem Areas Mentioned by 59 Callers (McCarthy and Berman, 1971, p. 527)

Problem Area	Number of Callers
Drugs	6
Dating	2
Emotional[a]	6
Lonely	12
Legal	5
Sex	1
Academic	1
Peer	2
Suicide	1
Other	9
Information	11
Prank	3

[a] Depression, anxiety, etc.

mensions. Data were collected by having experimenters call the services purporting to be experiencing difficulties in one of four areas: possible pregnancy, loneliness, parent conflicts, or drug related problems. Calls to the hotlines were rehearsed to assure uniformity. Hotline workers were advised that the experimental calls were to be made, but were not given information that would enable them to identify the simulated requests for help. In total, 96 calls were made to the hotlines, with each service receiving 6 calls of each type.

The experimental calls to the hotlines were recorded so as to facilitate evaluation. Responses by hotline workers were scored on several scales aimed at rating the amount of information provided, the style of information giving and the interpersonal skills of the volunteer. Results of the study indicated that the four hotlines differed significantly in the effectiveness of their interventions. In addition, some differences were found to be related to the type of problem posed by the caller. Of particular relevance to this chapter's discussion is the finding that the hotline which showed generally superior performance was the one that was staffed exclusively by college students. This service was also known to be unique in the intensity of its screening and training procedures. Bleach and Claiborn (1974, In press) did not offer validity data to verify a relationship between the measures used and the actual effectiveness of the hotline interventions. However, some of the scales used had been related to counselor effectiveness in earlier studies of other types of therapeutic interventions. It is not farfetched, therefore, to conclude tentatively that the research provided indirect evidence for the effectiveness of a well-planned, college-centered, and student-staffed hotline.

To an extent, the campus telephone crisis centers illustrate the principles underlying projects described earlier in the chapter. In particular, they represent another approach toward reaching out into the college community to provide services to those who might be reluctant to come to a traditional mental health facility. In some respects the student-run centers illustrate an approach not seen in other programs. First, they tap the creative abilities and helping skills of the very population that the services are intended to serve. Second, they may serve the worker students themselves by providing them with an opportunity to provide their peers with a psychologically useful service. Finally, these programs may speak rather directly to the problem of sensed alienation among college students by providing a source of aid that may be viewed as less threateningly "establishmentarian" than existing mental health programs. In this last aspect, the campus crisis intervention projects may have a general impact on the college milieu. Yet, realistically, the existence of a number to call on campus for nonprofessional help can hardly be assumed to constitute a radical alteration of the campus as a living environment.

This chapter would not be complete without mentioning the ways in which some campuses are changing in fundamental ways in response to student pressures for an improved psychological milieu. A prominent move in this direction is the establishment of coed dormitories with relatively relaxed rules about heterosexual intermingling. This experiment in making the college community more nearly resemble the community at large may be as important for the philosophical changes it reflects as for the immediate effects on student mental health. In the introductory portion of this chapter we mention that a source of stress for college students is the ambiguity of their status; they are neither given full adult privileges nor the right to be as irresponsible as children. American college administrators have typically operated on the assumption that the staff in the college community must function as surrogate parents to their students. The establishment of coed dormitories, which challenge the student to make more of his own decisions regarding sex and life-style, may reflect a philosophical shift toward viewing the student as an adult who can and should be allowed to make his own mistakes. This shift may also be occurring on campuses where systems of competitive grading are being abandoned or substantially altered. In the University of Florida project (Barger, 1963) previously described, one of the findings of the preliminary research was the fact that anxiety over difficult courses and the threat of poor grades were major sources of stress among the college population. The alteration or abandonment of traditional competitive grading systems may, therefore, prove to be a most important instances of a stress-reducing environmental change (although this innovation may also have its drawbacks) .

Changes in institutional policies relating to factors such as grades and living arrangements often have resulted from expressions of student dissatisfaction or even from instances of radical protest action (Feldman, 1972) . It would be incorrect to suppose that the community psychologist has thus far played a major role in the instigation of campus experiments favored by activist students. Despite this fact, the opportunity clearly exists for the behavioral scientist to study and, perhaps, have an impact on student initiated programs of campus reform. As with other programs discussed in this book, efforts to implement principles of community mental health need not always be restricted to projects instigated by the professional worker. Indeed, pessimists in the community mental health field have been known to argue that "change agentry" from outside a community may be a near impossibility, whereas the professional can often have influence where he capitalizes on the spontaneous movements within the community and joins to become another force for change from within.

A final comment is warranted concerning innovative alterations of the college community. To this point, nothing has been said of efforts actually to create new institutions of higher learning to serve better the human needs of community members. Such efforts are not unknown, although they face great obstacles and have often been doomed to failure (Wolfe, 1970). One of the newer developments on this front has been the emergence of the "free university" as an entity within or without the settings of established collegiate institutions. One model for such innovative educational establishments has been provided by the example at Berkeley, where students dissatisfied with the standard curriculum initiated the development of a set of courses markedly different from the usual University offerings, including, for example, "Theory and Practice of Meditation" (Bilorusky, 1972). While few if any of the free university programs seem at present to offer a full and independent alternative to existing institutions, they do point toward a model for student-structured college communities that might be founded, given the necessary resources and sufficient interest on the part of potential enrollees. It remains to be seen, however, whether such radical innovation is truly necessary or if current academic communities can change to become more broadly responsive to their members' wants and needs, thus obviating the reason for the establishment of totally new learning environments.

CONCLUSION

The college community represents an obvious and logical choice for the trial of programs of innovative mental health service delivery. The need for service is evident, and existing models may be inadequate. The community offers the human resources and ecological characteristics to make possible the establishment and study of new environmental features. Finally, the campus offers a community that the mental health professional already understands to some degree and, thus, one where he need not start from scratch in conceptualizing the needs and possibilities for change in the setting. Despite these reasons for selecting the college community as the locus for intervention, actual efforts to intervene have been relatively rare. The difficulties of working within one's own system may partially account for this fact. Perhaps another reason may be the general societal pressure for professionals to redirect their efforts away from the relatively privileged members of society, such as college students, and toward the troubled and "troublesome" poor.

The programs discussed in this chapter spanned a wide range with regard to degree of innovativeness and extent of intended impact. Initially, programs with relatively narrow focus and fairly traditional techniques are described. These programs derived their innovative quality primarily from the newness of their effort to reach out into the community to provide service. In reaching out, such efforts inevitably functioned to change subtly one basic aspect of the campus environment; they made students aware of an active concern for their human functioning. These narrow programs did not, however, prove highly effective even within their areas of primary concern.

Subsequent to the description of programs utilizing a small set of techniques to reach out to the campus community, we discuss several programs that exemplify a broader effort to understand and to alter the social milieu of the campus. The program at the University of Florida is cited as a particularly striking example of an effort that was keyed to the characteristics of the particular community and was actively responsive on a broad range of fronts. The ultimate worth of these "total community" approaches is, however, considered to be lacking in empirical support because of the problems of assessing multifaceted, broad-goaled projects.

A characteristic shared by both the broader and narrower programs is the general lack of input from the segment of the community most often seen as the target of the intervention, the student body. Therefore, the concluding program examples are projects that were unique in their attempts to utilize students as resources, on the front line as workers, or even at the project roots as initiators and administrators. These programs were committed in varying extents to the use of the creative potential of the student population. They are found to be relatively primitive in most cases with respect to sophistication of technique and evaluation. Nevertheless, the student-run or student-initiated projects are viewed as contributing the possibly vital concept of the necessity to involve all segments of the community in the process of community change.

In general, the concepts, methods, successes, and failures of programs in the colleges seem to have enough value as lessons for community psychologists to justify continued innovative efforts. The programs described here, many of which were less than wholly successful in providing useful human services, may nonetheless eventually prove worth their cost for the understandings they may contribute to the theory and practice of community psychology. This will only happen, however, if experimentation and innovation continue, thus eventually providing enough data to allow us to discern the general principles and specific strategies that facilitate interventions in communities of varied characteristics.

References

Barger, B. The University of Florida mental health program. In B. Barger and E. Hall (Eds.), *Higher education and mental health*. Gainesville: University of Florida, 1963. Pp. 27–46.

Barger, B., Larson, E. A., & Hall, E. Preventive action in college mental health. *Journal of the American College Health Association*, 1965, *15*, 80–93.

Bilorusky, J. A. Selection of student initiated courses: Student autonomy and curricular innovation. In K. A. Feldman (Ed.), *College and student: selected readings in the social psychology of higher education*. New York: Pergamon Press, 1972. Pp. 453–462.

Bleach, G., & Claiborn, W. L. Initial evaluation of hotline telephone crisis centers. *Community Mental Health Journal*, 1974. In press.

Brigante, T. Opportunities for community mental health training within the residential college campus context. *Community Mental Health Journal*, 1965, *1*, 55–61.

Falk, R. B. Innovations in college mental health. *Mental Hygiene*, 1971, *55*, 451–455.

Farnsworth, D. L. *Psychiatry, education, and the young adult*. Springfield, Ill.: Charles C. Thomas, 1966.

Feldman, K. A. Recommendations, innovations, experimentations and reform. In K. A. Feldman (Ed.), *College and student: selected readings in the social psychology of higher education*. New York: Pergamon Press, 1972. Pp. 435–442.

Helig, S. M., Farberow, N. L., Litman, R. E., & Shneidman, E. S. The role of nonprofessional volunteers in a suicide prevention center. *Community Mental Health Journal*, 1968, *4*, 287–295.

Kelly, J. G. Ecological constraints on mental health services. *American Psychologist*, 1966, *21*, 535–539.

Klein, D. C. The community and mental health: an attempt at a conceptual framework. *Community Mental Health Journal*, 1965, *1*, 301–308.

Kysar, J. E. Preventive psychiatry on the college campus. *Community Mental Health Journal*, 1966, *2*, 27–34.

Larson, E. A., Barger, B., & Cahoon, S. N. College mental health programs: A paradigm for comprehensive community mental health centers. *Community Mental Health Journal*, 1969, *5*, 461–467.

Leveridge, D. The college as a laboratory for applying findings and methods of the behavioral sciences. *Group Psychotherapy*, 1957, *10*, 64–70.

McCarthy, B. W., & Berman, A. L. A student-operated crisis center. *Personnel and Guidance Journal*, 1971, *49*, 523–528.

McColskey, A. S. The use of the professional in telephoning counseling. In G. A. Specter & W. L. Claiborn (Eds.), *Crisis intervention*. New York: Behavioral Publications, 1973.

Reid, K. E. Community mental health on the college campus. *Hospital and Community Psychiatry*, 1970, *21*, 387–389.

Reifler, C. B., Lipzin, M. B., & Fox, J. T. College psychiatry as public health psychiatry. *American Journal of Psychiatry*, 1967, *124*, 662–671.

Sinnett, E. R., & Niedenthal, L. The use of indigenous volunteers in a rehabilitation living unit for disturbed college students. *Community Mental Health Journal*, 1968, *4*, 232–244.

Sinnett, E. R., Weisner, E. F., & Freiser, W. S. Dormitory half-way house. *Rehabilitation Record*, 1967, *8*, 34–37.

Spielberger, C., & Weitz, H. Improving the academic performance of anxious college freshmen: A group counseling approach to prevention of underachievement. *Psychological Bulletin Monographs* (whole, no. 590), 1964, *78*, 20 pp.

Steenland, R. Paraprofessionals in counseling centers. *Personnel and Guidance Journal*, 1973, *51*, 417–418.

Tucker, B. J., Megenity, D., & Vigil, L. Anatomy of a campus crisis center. *Personnel and Guidance Journal*, 1970, *48*, 343–348.

Webster, T., & Harris, H. Modified group psychotherapy, an experiment in group psychodynamics for college freshmen. *Group Psychotherapy*, 1958, *11*, 283–298.

Wolfe, A. The experimental college-noble contradiction. *Change*, 1970, *2*, 26–32.

Wolff, T. Community mental health on campus: Evaluating group discussions led by dormitory advisors and graduate students. Unpublished doctoral dissertation, University of Rochester, 1969.

9. prevention programs in the greater community

The programs described up to this point have been carried out within specific community agencies, particularly school systems. These agencies are good natural sites for prevention programs, since they bring together large concentrations of people striving toward a common end. The establishment of prevention programs for adults in the community at large has probably been hampered by the fact that there are relatively few such natural sites. Still, there are several recent examples of community programs, and the fascinating history of the helping services by Levine and Levine (1970) details many community programs developed more than 50 years ago that have a surprisingly modern tone.

The Salvation Army, for example, an organization that had its origin in 19th-century England, is essentially a community program for rehabilitating the poor. Its express aim is to train the indigent to become self-sufficient. The essential components of this program involve giving a man shelter and honest work with the hope that he will lose his "more repulsive habits" and accept work willingly. Early in the Salvation Army's history it was envisioned that once an individual acquired work skills and proper attitudes, he would be given a portion of land to work. This plan was actually put into practice in the United States where, by the beginning of the 20th century, colonies existed in California, Colorada, and Ohio involving approximately 200 workers. Perhaps better known is the work of the Salvation Army in developing residences, schools, orphanages, employment bureaus, legal aid societies, life insurance companies, day nurseries, halfway houses for prisoners, a youth corps, and a number of other services for the urban poor. Thus the Salvation Army is a rare example of a community program established many years ago that exists even to the present day.

THE SETTLEMENT HOUSE MOVEMENT

Levine and Levine (1970) have described the settlement house movement, involving a variety of community programs, that appeared in many large urban areas during the late 19th and early 20th centuries. This was a period when the United States was receiving vast numbers of immigrants who settled in urban areas, particularly those on the eastern seaboard where most lived in hardship, poverty, and considerable ignorance of the new society that they had entered. The industrial revolution taking place at the time created further changes in the social order and prompted the need for community agencies to serve those whose important needs went unmet by the established society.

Settlement houses first appeared in England in response to the problems created by the industrial revolution occurring there. The English programs focused on providing education for the working man. Idealistic intellectuals from the universities would typically come into working class neighborhoods to teach in programs that were forerunners of university extension courses. As an outgrowth of the education programs, concern developed for gaining a better understanding of the general life and problems of the working class. To achieve this understanding it was thought necessary actually to live in working-class neighborhoods and to experience day-to-day life there. Thus the English settlement movement progressed from a concern with education to an attempt to alleviate a broad range of the problems besetting the lower classes. In England the British Labor Party received considerable impetus from the settlement house movement, since some of its leading figures such as Clement Atlee and Stafford Cripps moved from the movement into politics with an eye to solving social problems through national political action.

In the United States the church played a role in the early settlement house development despite its relatively conservative nature in the 19th century. Most churchmen supported the status quo, but some were critical of the business ethics of the day. Because the Protestant churches felt a need for new methods to attract the workingman, religious settlements and missions were established. These agencies had programs similar to those of the YMCA and the Salvation Army. The religious settlements and missions were cost-free institutions offering the services of a resident minister, kindergartens, athletic and recreational facilities, classes, lectures, schools, and a variety of other potentially beneficial community services.

Perhaps the most significant feature of the settlement house movement was that it attracted the contributions of a number of young, very well educated women of the late 19th century. This was the first generation of women managing to acquire higher education. Many of these women were idealistic, socially conscious, ardently feministic, and deeply committed to justifying their intellectual advantages through useful works. Among these women, Jane Addams, Lillian Wald, Florence Kelley, Julia Lathrop, Alice Hamilton, Grace and Edith Abbott, Mary Simkhovich, and Vida Scudder stand out. The settlement house movement thus grew out of a set of complementary needs. Many young, educated people were seeking a useful outlet for their ideals and talents, and masses of needy people were living in urban slums created by the waves of immigration and were experiencing the upheaval of the industrial revolution.

The earliest American settlement houses were established in the late 1880s and early 1890s in New York City. Creating a settlement house involved renting space, sometimes no more than an apartment, in the neighborhood where service was to be provided. Settlement house workers, typically young people of independent means, would move into these apartments or houses to live among those they wished to help. They offered a wide variety of services to their neighbors, ranging from providing public baths to establishing libraries, organizing clubs, taking in the sick, and offering a mother and her children sanctuary from a drunken husband. One early settlement house worker, Lillian Wald, was a trained nurse and, hence, her settlement house emphasized nursing care. It was from this "Nurses Settlement" on Henry Street in New York City that the Visiting Nurse Service was established.

Perhaps the most famous of the settlement houses was Hull House, established in Chicago in 1889 by Jane Addams. The mission of the Hull House group was to share their cultural advantages with Chicago's immigrants to help create a fuller life for these people. This sharing involved diverse activities such as washing newborn babies, preparing the dead for burial, nursing the sick, acting as midwives at illegitimate births, and sheltering the 15-year-old bride who was being beaten regularly by her husband.

The settlement houses had a stream of young residents who came for a time to work in impoverished neighborhoods for many reasons. Some were scientists and medical students, others were ministers or graduate students, many were ardent feminists or people interested in social action. Novelists, reporters, and writers commenting on the times came to the settlement house in search of material. Living in the squalor of the urban ghettos prompted a variety of philosophical concerns. There was guilt among settlement workers concerning their own prosperity in comparison to the poor and uneducated, as well as frustration at being able to do so little to change the lives of the impoverished. Many discussions were held about broad issues such as social reform, the problems of neighborhood organization, and the problem of lifting the cultural level of the neighborhood. The settlement house was more than just an important intellectual influence on its time, however. It was also a moving force for social reforms. Child labor laws, sanitation codes, building codes, improvements in schools, and the establishment of juvenile courts all came about as the result of the efforts of settlement workers.

Some settlement houses led the fight to clean up neighborhoods. This involved pressuring city officials to improve garbage collection and disposal services as well as organizing neighborhood groups for the improvment of sanitation. Projects of this kind brought settlement house workers into the arena of local politics where they faced the conflict of whether to enter the political scene themselves or to try to educate already established political bosses. Also the era of the settlement house coincided with the rise of the labor movement, and many settlement houses lent significant support to the efforts of the working class to organize. Finally, settlement house workers were at the forefront of many social welfare measures such as the reform of the county poorhouse system and relief for the aged, the development of sheltered workshops, and the establishment of workmen's compensation and unemployment insurance.

Within many settlements the essential organizational unit was the club. These were formal organizations for individuals having special interests. Holden (1922) has described the way in which a boy's club might be developed (see Figure 1).

This type of club might engage in a variety of activities, and Holden (1922) has indicated many ways in which the group took the club organizer as a model with whom to identify. In such a manner many who came to the settlement house grew to appreciate a variety of educational, recreational, and cultural activities.

The financial problems faced by the settlement houses resulted in ex-

A certain group of boys averaging about fifteen or sixteen years got the reputation of being "the toughest bunch on the block!" They used to stand around drug stores and side doors of saloons smoking very cheap cigarettes and catcalling at the girls who passed by. They had a scorn for the conventional type of hats and affected big caps pulled over their ears at curious angles. They had a peculiar way of spitting out of the corners of their mouths. They punctuated their sentences with words like Jesus and damn and hell, and others not so nice in their original meaning. They spent their evenings provoking trouble and hunting for excitement. One night they visited the neighborhood dance in progress at a settlement (Admission 5 cents). Two of them were kicked out for refusing to take off their caps, another was evicted for a rough house that ended in breaking a chair, a fourth was put out for using profane language. Three remained. They were engaged in conversation by a very large man they later learned had been a famous football player at Princeton. They were interested in the gymnasium equipment. The idea came to them that basketball could be played by boys who didn't go to high school. They asked if they could play. They were told that if they formed a club and had a director that they could play. They asked the big man to be their director and said they would get the rest of their "bunch." But the rest of the bunch resentful over having been put out, refused to come in. They asked the big man if he would come and talk to the others. He did. He spent an evening with them. Where they went he went also, but they noticed that he didn't catcall after girls and that he didn't wear a cap.

They came to the settlement house again and asked him to spend another evening with them. The big man said he didn't much enjoy dancing on cellar doors and proposed that they should go to a show. Two of them hadn't any money and asked him to wait while they "swiped a nickel off the soda and candy man at the corner." He said he'd lend them the money. They said that would be all right that "they'd swipe it later." They noticed that he took off his hat when he went into the movie house. They asked if they couldn't form a club and play basketball. He helped them start their club.

Figure 1. Description of formation of a boy's club (quoted from Holden, 1922, pp. 67–69).

periences that are enormously instructive for the organizers or modern-day community programs. Not infrequently people or agencies who support programs like settlement houses attempt to exercise control over their functions. The settlement houses found that they depended on private sources for most of their support. These sources, however, might give funds only for specific purposes, or the patron might disapprove of certain settlement house activities and withdraw support. At times, support was offered in the form of a bribe with money available only if efforts to bring about a certain kind of legislative or social change would be suspended. Funds of this kind had to be refused. In essence the problem was that the settlement houses depended for support on an establishment that they were attempting to alter in many fundamental ways.

The settlement house movement waned as the social need out of which it grew declined. The masses of immigrants gradually became assimilated in life in America and left the ghettos, which themselves became more orderly places. The interest of eager, idealistic intellectuals declined, and the work of the settlement houses began to be taken over by trained professionals who were concerned with narrower problems than the sweeping issues that had inspired the early workers. In recent years there has been a resurgence of broad social needs akin to those that stimulated the settlement house development in the 19th century. The aims and purposes of many recent community programs are strikingly similar to those of the early settlement houses. Therefore, much can be learned today from a study of the experiences of the settlement house movement.

A pioneering community effort to control juvenile delinquency, a problem commonly encountered in the settlement houses, was mounted in the mid-1930s by a varied group of professionals. The Cambridge-Somerville study (Powers and Witmer, 1951) operated out of an established mental health framework that was unlike that of the settlement house.

THE CAMBRIDGE-SOMERVILLE YOUTH STUDY

The Cambridge Somerville Youth Study, a program developed in the mid-1930s for preventing the development of delinquency (Powers and Witmer, 1951) is of great significance for community psychology. This program was inspired by Dr. Richard Clarke Cabot, a retired member of the faculty of the Harvard Medical School. Concerned with delinquency and the reformation of the criminal, Dr. Cabot firmly believed that the absolutely necessary condition was "that someone should come to know and to understand the man in so intimate and friendly a way that he comes to better understanding of himself and to a truer comprehension of the world he lives in" (Powers and Witmer, 1951, p. v). Cabot, therefore, planned to identify predelinquents and to recruit a group of people to work with these youngsters in the hope that a friendly, big brother relationship would deter the tendency toward antisocial behavior. The opportunity to relate to and identify with a good example of a social being,

Dr. Cabot believed, would be the salvation of the potential delinquent. In his own words "what is it that keeps any of us straight unless it is the contagion of the highest personalities whom we have known?" (Powers and Witmer, 1951, p. x).

In addition to creating a treatment program, Dr. Cabot designed the program in such a way that its effects could be evaluated. Therefore, two groups of 325 boys each were selected. The groups were carefully matched with one group serving as an untreated control for the other which would receive regular counseling in addition to whatever other services school and community agencies could provide for it or its control. It was intended that the project would span a 10-year period, with boys being brought into the program as young as possible (the median age at the start of the treatment turned out to be 10 $\frac{1}{2}$ years). Ideally each boy in the program would work with only one counselor throughout the period. Evaluations were to be done at the conclusion of the program. In many respects the counselor's role as envisioned by Dr. Cabot was similar to that of the social case worker, but it differed in two important ways. First, the approach was an intrusive one in that it sought out the client rather than waiting in some agency to be approached by him. This is, of course, a characteristic of most preventive programs and more will be said of the general issue in later chapters. The second difference was that the role model that is stressed was that of a "big brother" instead of the highly professional social worker.

Early Identification

The early identification aspect of the project was accomplished with the help of the school system. In June 1935, after explaining the intent of the proposed program to personnel of the Cambridge, Massachusetts public schools, a list of behaviors typical of the delinquent youngster was submitted to principals and teachers who were then asked to designate children below the age of 10 displaying these characteristics. Included in this list were truancy, persistent rule breaking, stealing, sexual delinquency, excessive lying, repeated disobedience to authority, undesirable gang activities, cheating, and the like. Because teachers were relatively slow to refer the names of boys meeting these criteria, it was decided that a group of nondelinquent children should also be included in the study, largely as a public relations tactic. Thus both the experimental and the control groups included boys who were termed "average" as well as serious predelinquents. In an effort to attract the requisite number of subjects quickly, in the fall of 1937 the school system of Somerville, Massachusetts, a city adjoining Cambridge, was approached as another source of referrals. The referral period ended in 1938 with about three fourths coming from the public schools. Other referral sources included community organizations, police departments, playground supervisors, and social agencies.

Once referrals were collected, home visits were made to gather information concerning the home situation of each child. Interviews in the home were guided by a "home visitor schedule" filled in by social workers who visited the homes of the 839 boys. The schedule included a developmental history of the child, the mother's description of the child's habits, recreational outlets, attitudes towards school, religion, and general personality. The schedule also furnished background data to the parents. On the basis of the interview, visitors made a rating of the likelihood that the family would cooperate with the study in the years to come, as well as a rating of the likelihood that the child was headed for a delinquent lifestyle. This latter rating was made on an 11-point scale that was to be used by the selection committee later. Only 8 families out of 839 refused to be interviewed. Some were uncooperative at first but subsequently did give adequate information.

Descriptions of the child's behavior were also obtained from school teachers who used behavior checklists and a series of rating scales. Some children were tested by psychologists as well. Teachers were personally interviewed concerning many children to encourage a frank appraisal. Finally, each child was given a physical examination; probation records of each child and those of his family were reviewed; social service records were surveyed, the boy's neighborhood was rated for the amount of delinquency normally found there; and some boys (only 47) were taken on a series of overnight camping trips where their behavior was observed. Ratings were made of each boy's potential for a delinquent career on an 11-point scale ranging from $+5$ to -5 with high potential rated in the minus direction. These ratings were made by the home visitor, a staff psychologist, the teacher interviewer, the physician, and the nurse or others on the staff.

Out of a total of 1953 screened cases, 782 were retained for the study. The final classification of each of these boys was made by a committee consisting of a psychiatrist and two social workers, all of whom had had experience with criminals and delinquents. Examples of descriptions by several judges of children who were rated as predelinquent are found in Figure 2.

Of the 782 cases selected as possible subjects in the study, 361 (46%) were rated as potential delinquents, and 334 (43%) were viewed as unlikely to go this direction. The remaining 87 subjects (11%) were rated in the middle of the prognostic scale. An elaborate matching procedure paired boys who were similar on a number of variables (physical health, intelligence, the relationship between the amount of personality tension

Example A. In this case the boy gave the appearance of a predelinquent. The committee members rated him—3 or —4 with a final rating of —3 (a high delinquency rating, for the extreme —5 rating was seldom used). This boy, later placed in the treatment group, did not become delinquent at least up to the age of 18.

Judge 1:—3. A highly neurotic boy emulating the neurotic behavior of the mother by whom he is defended on every occasion. A serious behavior problem at school, where he is recognized by several teachers as a potential source of continued difficulty, which may be expressed in several types of delinquency (truancy to escape unpleasantness, fighting as immediate reaction to any restraint, and so on). Several siblings neurotic. One brother has court record for assault and battery. There are now charges pending against boy for assault on teacher. Boy undisciplined and out of control in home. Home situated on margin of one of principal delinquency areas, and home during previous five years located in one of worst delinquency areas. Some of the outward appearance of disorder in home situation must be discounted because it is due to an habitual excess of emotionality in facing all situations. Boy may be expected to encounter greater difficulty as he meets responsibility of increasing age.

Judge 2:—3. Poor pattern in both parents. Mother distinctly neurotic and children are taking on her self-excusing impulsive traits with physical symptoms. Father is obviously evading. Boy undisciplined and shielded by mother. On the streets much in delinquency area. Is acquisitive and "cashing in" on an attractive, glib personality in the easiest way. Can't stand discipline.

Judge 3:—4. A thoroughly undisciplined youngster, son of a highly neurotic, aggressive mother who speaks little English. One brother already on probation for assault and battery. Boy a problem in home and school. Recently assaulted teacher who tried to restrain him. Mother also attacked teachers. Is handsome and spoiled. Few, if any, assets and many liabilities.

Example B. This boy, in spite of treatment, became a very serious delinquent and was finally sentenced to state prison for a term of five to eight years for armed robbery when he was 18 years, 8 months old. Each member of the committee independently rated him on the delinquent side at —2 on the scale.

Judge 1:—2. An unsupervised boy in a home broken by separation of parents. Boy a frequent truant and is developing anti-authoritarian attitude at school where he is leader, mischievous, lies, suspected of stealing; bold, impudent. Good neighborhood and home furnished well, but little security offered by home. No criminality.

Judge 2:—2. Colored boy long without supervision at home and resents authority. Has built up poor work habits and evasive methods. Already truants much—possibly steals. Is aggressive enough to get into trouble. Mother, while well-meaning, works and will gradually lose control. Father's influence in the broken family too far removed.

Judge 3:—2. Negro, age 11, the youngest of four children in a home broken by separation of parents (no details) and further handicapped by need of mother working out, and hence inadequate supervision. Fair district, though one case of delinquency in same house or next, and a sister may have had illegitimate child. Boy has average intelligence and is in Grade V. Bright but not interested in anything but manual training. Has truanted at least 20 times this year and is leader of clique of four Negroes; a fighter and liar.

Figure 2. Two representative examples of rater descriptions of bases for judgments (quoted from Witmer and Powers, 1951, pp. 56 and 57.)

displayed by a boy and the number of desirable tension outlets available, the prognostic rating of the selection committee, an evaluation of the delinquency stimulation found in the boy's home, and the neighborhood in which he lived). Once boys were matched in pairs, assignment to treatment or control group was determined by a coin flip.

The Treatment Program

The 325 treatment cases were seen by a cadre of nine full-time counselors and one half-time worker. These were primarily social workers although a few were psychologists or nurses. Each counselor was asked to submit a statement of preferences and prejudices with respect to cases that he might take on, and assignments were made in keeping with these feelings. Each full-time counselor saw approximately 35 cases and the half-timer saw 18. It was hoped that each counselor would see a case continuously for a 10-year period. Actually, relatively few boys were seen by a single counselor for the entire program period.

Several obstacles had to be overcome by the counselors at the outset. First, they were offering help to people who had not requested it. Thus there was the problem of winning acceptance from the boy and his family. The constraints of the research design imposed further problems on the counselor. Often the project child in a given family had a sibling more in need of help than he was. The counselor was still required to concentrate on the research subject. Case load size was another problem. Befriending 34 or 35 boys and their families seemed to be an insurmountable task. Another limitation imposed by the program designers was that no effort should be made to change the boy's environment. Counselors were, therefore, forbidden to initiate community projects or to organize clubs that might have general impact on the neighborhood. Instead they were required to focus entirely on the project case.

Certainly a very major problem for most counselors was "breaking the ice" with the families they were to see. Reactions to the program ranged from eager acceptance to marked suspiciousness and, in a few cases, outright rejection (only about 1% of the cases). The brief descriptions of reactions listed in Figure 3 depict the various degrees of acceptance encountered.

I. An Eagerness to Be Included in the Study (about 33 percent of the cases).

"Will Jeffrey be accepted by the Study?" his mother asked anxiously. The counselor explained that Jeffrey had already been selected. She almost screamed with delight and called the boy into the room. She said how glad she was that it was really true. (The boy's father was dead; the mother was working and trying to support her own mother and father as well as this boy who was then only 12.) She said she felt the need of having some man take an interest in her son. "What is the first thing you are going to do?" she asked eagerly. The counselor had in mind helping the boy with his studies, as he had been having difficulty in school. The mother, going beyond the counselor's aspirations, said to the boy, hugging him to her side, "Just think, Jeff, they will help you in your schoolwork and when you grow up, they will send you to college!"

2. An Interest in the General Idea and a Willingness to Hear More about It (comprising about 25 percent of the cases). Visiting Maurice's home for the first time the counselor met a rather incredulous woman. The record states:

She shuffled to the door in her slippers and what looked like a nightgrown. She had light red hair, looked very pale and ill, and her manner was not cordial. I introduced myself and asked if she could conveniently give me a few minutes time to tell her about the Study and that Maurice had been invited to be one of the 325 boys to join. Ungraciously she said, "I don't know what more information I can give you. . . ." (Evidently referring to the first home visit and the questions asked then.) She added she had been sick in bed. I tried to persuade her to let me return another time when she felt better and more like talking. Somewhat mollified she said, "Now that you're here you may as well say what you want." I explained then that we were interested in boys and wanted to have a chance to know a few specially selected ones, whose parents were interested. We thought it was going to be a good deal of fun and expected that there might be some situations in which we might be able to help a boy develop his own special ability. She seemed to relax and become more and more pleased. She raised the question of what it would cost, saying she couldn't pay anything. She added that she had had to stop another son's music lessons, so certainly couldn't afford to spare any additional expense for Maurice.

Shortly the mother was talking about her own ill health. She said, "I have bronchial asthma and it has been wearing me out for nine years." The counselor then discussed her problem. She became more interested. Several interviews followed and the counselor became acquainted with the boy. The mother called upon the counselor for help many times during the ensuing years and a great deal of time was spent with the boy.

3. An Attitude of Indifference (about 16 percent of the cases). Lester's father was home when the counselor made his first call. "It is okay with me," he said, returning to his newspaper and showing no further interest or curiosity concerning the counselor's plans.

4. A Suspiciousness about the Purpose of the Study (about 25 percent of the cases). The counselor stated in Hank's record:

Mr. F. answered the door. He is a short, thin, wrinkled man with seamed face. He speaks broken English and seems quite suspicious of me. He impresses me as shrewd, sly, taciturn and reserved—he glared suspiciously at me. I started to explain my interest in Hank and the reason for my visit. He listened a bit and then said he had been out of work all year and didn't want anything to do with it. He called in another son, who was 24 years old. The young man asked suspiciously what it was that we wanted to do. I explained this in terms of various interests that the boys might have and in terms of our connection with the schools, etc. He said quite frankly that it sounded screwy to him. "Listen, Buddy, I've been around a hell of a lot but never heard anything like this. Just tell me one thing you can do for Hank!"

The suspicion lingered for some time until the counselor was able to show the family that he was sincere in his attempt to be helpful and that the program would not involve any cost.

5. A Rejection or Unwillingness to Hear More about It (about 1 percent of the cases). On the first visit to Rudolph's home the mother questioned the value of the Study. She kept interrupting the explanation of the counselor by asking why the counselor assumed that there must be something wrong with Rudolph. If he had to be examined by a doctor, she reasoned, he must be in poor health. Why did he have a mental test if we did not think there was something peculiar about him? She went to the school to inquire why the study was interested in her boy. She rejected the explanation of the master of the school who tried to reassure her of the counselor's sincere interest. She felt that the counselor was hiding something. She concluded that she did not want her boy "to serve as a guinea pig." The counselor then talked to the father who shared the suspicions of the mother. The father said, "There's no reason for you to be interested in my boy, especially as there are so many boys needing special attention." The father became belligerent in his attitude and said, "Every time one of you people come around the boy's mother is a nervous wreck afterwards. I want to get at the bottom of it." He said he would see the school superintendent. (The parents got in touch with the school and with the help of the teachers some cooperation was obtained, although the case never became an active one.)

Figure 3. Types of response to counselors' first visit (quoted from Powers and Witmer, 1951, pp. 107, 108, 109) .

In 1939 the program became operational with counselors being asked to project a general plan for each of their cases. The goals of the counselors included the following: "to supply a masculine ideal"; "to be a person to whom the boy will turn for service that he believes is important to him"; "to be available to the boy and family when needed"; and "to discuss family problems and work out plans with some continuity." These, however, were broad goals and reviews of counselor records indicated that the following types of concrete activities were actually carried out: "arranging for physical examinations, interpreting to the family, and so on," "taking a boy on educational trips to 'see things,'" "finding employment for boy and family," "giving specific tutorial help in school subjects," "procuring legal advice for family," and "getting much needed clothes for the boy."

As the project progressed its original objectives were reformulated. The program had been concerned initially with preventing delinquency. It was found, however, that although many children did not seem likely to become delinquents, they were developing other problems such as neuroses. Thus a restatement of program objectives emphasized "continuing social, physical, intellectual and spiritual growth" rather than delinquency prevention. Another important change came about because counselors were greatly overburdened by their case load. A particular problem for these counselors was the "average" boy in the treatment group. These boys, included largely for public relations purposes, were not expected to become delinquent and were not manifesting serious problems. Working with them proved trying for the counselors who were at a loss to find ways of being helpful to such boys. Therefore, in 1941 and 1942, 65 average boys were retired from the treatment program.

Further attrition in the original study sample arose as time wore on. In the early 1940s the effects of World War II were felt in the project. Younger members of the counseling staff entered the armed forces necessitating the introduction of new counselors and some shifting of cases. As the project boys grew older, some became uncooperative and had to be dropped. Some families moved out of the area to distant locations making it necessary to terminate their children. Finally, older boys in the program became eligible for draft or entry into the armed forces and left the program for that reason. Thus, in 1943, all 17-year-old boys were terminated unless there was some special reason for continuing them. These boys had a minimum of five years or more of treatment. The Cambridge-Somerville study terminated formally at the end of 1945 at which point 75 boys were still in the study. Table 1 below taken from Powers and Witmer (1951, p. 152) describes the disposition of the original 325 cases in the study.

Table 1. Disposition of the 325 Cases (from Powers and Witmer, 1951, p. 52)

Retired in 1940 and 1941		65
Dropped before the end of the program		113
A. Died during the treatment program	2	
B. Moved outside the field of operations	25	
C. Boy and/or family uncooperative	9	
D. Taken over completely by other agencies	2	
E. Mental retardation too great a handicap	4	
F. Following the reclassification during the war when the Study could not retain an adequate staff, it was necessary to drop cases that were relatively less able to profit from the treatment program	71	
Terminated: Most of the boys who had passed their 17th birthdays in 1944 and 1945		72
Closed: Carried through the entire treatment program		75
Total		325

Evaluation

Following the conclusion of the Cambridge-Somerville program in 1945 an evaluation was made of its effects. It was determined that on the average each of the 325 project boys received 4 years and 10 months of treatment. The 75 boys who remained in the program to its official termination received about 6 years and 9 months of treatment. Boys who had been dropped from the program earlier received an average of only about 2 ½ years of attention. In the treatment group only about one third of the boys who appeared to be pre-delinquent at the outset actually became delinquent in any serious sense. Relatively few (less than one sixth) were actually committed to correctional institutions. The counselors estimated that they had substantially benefited about two thirds of the boys they saw. More than one half of the boys in the treatment program acknowledged that they had been helped by their association with the study.

The crucial comparisons, however, were between the treatment and the control groups. Here, the findings with respect to delinquency behavior were disappointing. For example, more treated boys appeared before the Cambridge Crime Prevention Bureau than control boys. More treated boys were taken to court than control boys regardless of age or the number of years in the study. Even treated boys who had received the most intensive efforts of the counselors were found to have more official contact with the police department than matched controls. No differences were found between groups with respect to seriousness of criminal offences committed. The one encouraging finding was that the more frequent offenders and those committing the more serious crimes were more often in the control group than in the treatment group suggesting that, although the project failed to prevent the early stages of delinquency, it may have curtailed the delinquent careers of some youngsters.

In 1955, 10 years after the Cambridge-Somerville project terminated, a follow-up study was done of the participants in that program by Mc-Cord, McCord, and Zola (1959). The results of these analyses were as disappointing as were those of the original study. McCord et al. concluded that the study failed to prevent delinquency or adult criminality either in terms of number of crimes committed or of number of boys becoming criminals. The treatment and control groups committed the same types of crimes at about the same ages, and treatment did not seem to prevent crimes of violence, sexual offenses, or drunkenness. Roughly equal numbers of boys from both groups went to reform schools and committed crimes after release from these institutions. The length of treatment did not seem to affect the likelihood of being convicted of a crime, nor was having one counselor through the entire treatment period an important factor in limiting the crime rate.

Stanfield and Maher (1968) have done a relatively recent follow-up of the data from the Cambridge-Somerville study. Their concern was with the adequacy of judges' predictions of the likelihood that subjects in the study would manifest delinquent behavior. Stanfield and Maher's conclusion was that the clinical predictions of later delinquent behavior made by the judges in the study were somewhat *less* accurate than were predictions that could have been obtained by using actuarial methods based solely on statistical base rates. Several reasons were suggested for the unimpressive results of the attempt at clinical prediction: (1) judges seemed to be predicting to "social maladjustment" instead of to the more narrow criterion of arrest for criminal behavior; (2) judges seemed to prognosticate with respect to psychological disorder rather than socially problematic behavior, the standard used in the study to evaluate subjects; (3) clinical predictions were based on written records of the subjects based on reports by teachers, parents, and the like rather than on personal contact.

Summary

In summary, the Cambridge-Somerville study stands as an ambitious, early landmark in community psychology. Despite its failure to produce positive results, it merits attention as an isolated attempt at secondary prevention appearing long before its time. It is a good example of how such a project should be carried out and evaluated, and even its negative results are useful for plotting the course of future programs. These results suggest that future efforts at delinquency prevention might better focus on environmental change than on direct counseling with individuals.

RECENT COMMUNITY EFFORTS

In many respects, recent conditions in large urban areas are similar to those at the turn of the century when the settlement house movement developed. Just as in the late 19th century when there occurred a massive influx of immigration, in recent years large masses of people have again streamed into the urban areas (Zax and Cowen, 1972). The growth of American inner cities has not occurred this time because of immigration from other countries but, instead, reflects a marked population shift within the United States. Whereas in 1910 more than 80 percent of all American Negroes lived in the South, today fewer than 50 percent reside there, and more than a third live in the crowded ghettos of our large northern cities. This population shift has undoubtedly been provoked by the same need to seek a better life that earlier motivated the European immigrant. Also, like the immigrants of an earlier time, southern blacks are not finding that their lot in life has improved significantly in the northern city. In fact, for many, it was probably worsened. As a result, the large urban ghetto dweller is beset by a variety of problems that inevitably affect all of society. The frustration resulting in the urban riots of recent years are dramatic examples of these problems, but there are many others such as rising crime, alcoholism, and drug addiction rates and massive unemployment. Thus, recently many community psychology programs have been developed that are directed at the problems of the inner city.

The Lincoln Hospital Neighborhood Service Center Program

One approach for dealing with the mental health problems of the inner city has been to establish Neighborhood Service Centers (NSCs) that, in some ways, are a throwback to the settlement houses of an earlier period. The idea for the development of NSCs originated with a group at the Lincoln Hospital, part of the Albert Einstein College of Medicine in New York (Peck, Kaplan, and Roman, 1966; Peck and Kaplan, 1969). Lincoln Hospital had to provide mental health services to the entire South Bronx region, an area with a population of about 350,000. On almost any index reflecting psychopathology, the residents of this area are extremely high. They have significantly less education than residents of other parts of New York City, and have lower incomes, live in poor housing, have higher homicide and suicide rates, more juvenile delinquency, venereal disease, divorce or separation, and unemployment. The problem, therefore, of providing for the mental health needs of this area is a staggering one. Existing public and private mental health agencies in the area had been entirely overwhelmed by the problems they faced. Residents of the South Bronx area were relatively uninvolved and apathetic. Like the agencies, they felt that the prospects for change were hopeless.

The Lincoln Hospital group determined that one obvious starting point for dealing with the area's problems must involve broad social change. They decided to attempt to produce such change through a two-pronged effort involving both existing institutions and the residents of the area. Consultations held with various community agencies as well as departments within Lincoln Hospital such as medicine, pediatrics, and obstetrics indicated that the need for help with mental health problems could potentially overwhelm all available mental health staff. Such profound need in the face of relatively meager resources inspired the idea of a multi-purpose clinical facility.

Organization and Goals

The organization and staffing of the clinic facility that came to be known as the NSC was based on interesting reasoning. Instead of registering alarm at the appalling statistics of the South Bronx, the NSC originators were amazed at the fact that these statistics were not worse considering the conditions of life in the area. This led to a recognition that despite the fact that the community seemed disorganized, it must have some unique, informal organizational structure for treating and rehabilitating its members that operated at least as effectively as the community mental health agencies. Therefore, it was felt that the NSC should attempt to learn more about this informal community network and should bring it to bear on community problems. Concern was also felt about the fact that the bureaucratic structure of mental health agencies makes it difficult for potential clients to find points of entry to make their needs known and to contribute to agency planning and operation. Since the NSC stressed community participation, it was set up as a relatively simple agency based in the neighborhood served. The first NSC was established in early 1965 in a storefront. The operation of this center and others like it, which were set up later, have been described by Reissman (1967) and Hallowitz and Riessman (1967).

The character of the NSC and the services it offered are well depicted as follows.

"*The NSC escapes the office atmosphere, shortens intake procedures and makes them less formal, has no waiting lists, accepts any problem in any form, does not require continued visits, catches people at the point of crises, uses treatment agents recruited from the population itself who can be informal, personal, and friendly. It helps people with concrete, present-oriented problems and provides directive advice and assistance (i.e., it does not demand that the individual do it himself). Its staff is willing to make home visits at any time and participates in all types of activities including funerals, outings, helping people to move, and extinguishing fires in apartments*" *(Riessman, 1967, p. 163).*

The broad goal of the NSC was to promote positive mental health and thereby to limit the development of pathology. Three subgoals served this larger goal: (1) providing prompt mental health services, broadly defined; (2) increasing social cohesion within the neighborhood served to provide community members with a sense of power and group involvement; (3) promoting changes in community agencies and institutions to improve their services. An important means of achieving these goals was *community action*. Riessman (1967) contrasts community action to social action as described by Caplan (1964). Social action produces social change through the influence of mental health specialists on legislators and administrators. By contrast, community action involves influencing those at the lower levels of society to make what changes they can on their own and to pressure administrators for other necessary changes. In the NSC program, individual services were offered as an "entering wedge" into the community through which broader social changes eventually could be brought about. To the neighborhood the NSC was, therefore, held out as a place to which any kind of problem can be brought.

The NSC Staff and Program

The typical NSC was staffed by 5 to 10 nonprofessional mental health aides indigenous to the neighborhood served and by one or two professional mental health specialists who directed center operations. The nonprofessional staff played so central a role in the operation of the NSC that an elaborate selection procedure was set up to attract the best qualified personnel. Ultimately, those selected were rated by various professionals as being highly empathic, having good attitudes toward authority, being comfortable in group situations, being able to communicate ideas and feelings, being flexible, having a capacity for self-awareness, reacting adaptively to stress, manifesting relatively little personal pathology, and having relevant work and life experience. Workers underwent a three-phase training program. The first phase was conducted by NSC staff professionals and was based at the Lincoln Hospital Mental Health Clinic. This three-week training period involved making community surveys, doing door-to-door interviews with families, assisting in hospital intake, and visiting community agencies such as the welfare department, police department, and the schools. Role playing concerning many aspects of the job was also engaged in as part of this phase. During the second three-week training phase, aides actually worked at an NSC for two weeks. Half of the time spent at the NSC was used to render direct service to area residents, and the other half was used to discuss on-the-job experiences with supervisors. The third training phase was a continuous process that took place during the routine operation of the center. Roughly one day per week was spent on systematic training to develop

Miss Martinez

Miss Martinez came to the Center reporting that she was eight months pregnant and that her common-law husband had deserted her last month. She worked until two weeks ago, but had been forced to stop working and had to move into a basement apartment with a brother and his family. The few dollars she had accumulated were now gone and she had applied to the Welfare Department for assistance. They had rejected her at intake because they contended that she must know the whereabouts of her common-law husband: they couldn't believe that she could live with a man for two years and not know more about him.

The aide, who spoke Spanish, explained to Miss Martinez why Welfare had to make an investigation and encouraged her to tell whatever she could about her husband. All she knew was that he worked for a cab company, but didn't know which company or where he had lived prior to their getting together. The aide suggested to her that they go together to the police station to see if it were possible to locate her husband. (The aides have had excellent relations with the Police Department—they have visited the police station on a number of occasions, and various policemen have dropped in at the Center to chat and keep warm). The captain of the station, upon hearing the details of the case, dispatched a member of his staff to the central taxicab bureau. There it was discovered that the woman's husband was in fact a cab driver, that he was wanted on charges, but could not be located and had disappeared. These facts were then reported to the Department of Welfare Intake Unit, who felt that they were sufficient to warrant opening the case for further investigation.

When the aide checked with the investigator assigned to the case shortly afterward, he was told that the field supervisor would not fully accept the evidence that was presented and still could not believe that the woman didn't know where her husband was.

Uncertain of what his role should be at this stage, the aide turned to his professional supervisor. The latter, in the presence of the aide phoned the investigator and subsequently the Department of Welfare supervisor. The aide was able to observe his supervisor moving from the stage of reasonable discussion to the point of righteous indignation, pointing up that the record was clear, that the woman had worked and was self-maintaining during eight months of pregnancy, that our aide had visited the home and had observed the living conditions and found they were as the woman had reported them, that it was not atypical for a woman in these circumstances not to know more about the husband than she did and the very fact that the Police Department couldn't locate the husband should be proof enough of her cooperativeness, her dependability and reliability.

That afternoon the investigator stopped by the Neighborhood Service Center to talk further with our aide. The aide indicated that we wanted to work cooperatively with Welfare, that we didn't want to serve as a pressure group and pointed up all of the things which the aide had done prior to raising this issue. The investigator agreed that the woman could receive Welfare assistance, arranged for an emergency allocation including back payment for carfares; the grant also included money for a layette and for future carfare which would enable her to take advantage of the prenatal service at Lincoln Hospital.

The aide then helped Miss Martinez find more adequate living quarters. On the day she moved, which happened to be a Saturday, the aide assisted her with the moving, helped her to wash down the walls, hang curtains, etc. (This is highly significant as the nonprofessional is now providing a model to the helpee, the client—a model which seems to say that helping people even outside the line of duty, not on a work day, is a good thing. The nonprofessional was functioning as one neighbor helping another and was implicitly suggesting a model whereby the helpee in the future might help another neighbor. He was persuading by example in line with our goal of transforming clients into helpers and citizens.)

Shortly after delivery of the baby, the woman stopped by the Center to see the mental health aide. She was relaxed and friendly and obviously enjoying the baby. She indicated to the aide that in a couple of months she would like to return to work. There was a neighbor who could care for the baby during the day at a modest stipend. She complained to the aide that her problem is that she has no marketable skills. She has taken some commercial course work when she was in high school, but these skills were very rusty. The aide was able to arrange a modified training program for her while she was at home with the baby. This was worked out in cooperation with the Department of Welfare. When she is ready to return to work, both the aide and the social investigator will attempt to find suitable employment for her.

Figure 4. The example of a case seen at an NSC (quoted from Hallowitz and Riessman, 1967, p. 769).

new skills, to further understanding of mental illness, and to work through on-the-job problems.

Since institutional change through community action was a basic objective of the NSC, the program focused on a segment of the community that has traditionally been difficult to arouse. Other programs (Haggstrom, 1964) have appealed to the militant poor who recognize injustices, are willing to engage actively in conflict, and who feel capable of affecting change through their own actions. The NSC program, however, was directed at the apathetic poor, a very large segment of the community which, feeling powerless, is unable to identify with the militant position. To organize them the NSC program first offered concrete assistance with specific individual problems. Once attracted to the NSC on this basis, th normally apathetic individual could more readily be drawn into informa groups run by people they knew from the neighborhood, in which the n cessity for social change was discussed. Eventually such groups begin tak ing concrete steps to improve community services and to pressure for ir stitutional changes. Examples of community action programs stimulate by the NSC were voter registration campaigns, block cleanup program antiviolence and antidrug campaigns, protests about poorly run loca agencies, and collaboration with school, welfare, and housing organiza tions to improve area life. Hallowitz and Riessman (1967) have offere a good example of the way in which NSC aides could help a troubled in dividual (see Figure 4).

What NSC organizers spoke of as community action often encom passed what can be labeled as *political action*. Voter registration cam paigns, efforts to force the improvement of community services, and pro tests over the quality of local agencies all constitute attempts to influenc the political process to serve better a constituency's needs. It seems inevi table that community psychology programs, especially those located i the greater community, should become embroiled in political issues. Thi occurred in both the English and American settlement house movements which promoted much social legislation and were training grounds fo many socially concerned politicians. Philosophically community psychol ogy views social problems (crime, addiction, and poverty) as bein caused by unfavorable environments, so that political action aimed a changing or alleviating adverse settings is appropriate.

From this viewpoint, community psychology, although interested ir helping the ghetto dweller to avoid a criminal career and to acquire ar education and the means for leaving the ghetto, is equally concerned witl eliminating the ghetto itself. Accomplishing this requires political actior to a large extent. The interspersing of expensive and low-cost housing ir newly planned communities is one means of forestalling the developmen of a ghetto. In long-established communities the aim of urban renewa programs can be to replace ghettoes with safer, more comfortable, anc growth-enhancing settings.

It should be emphasized, as the example of the NSC also demon strates, that the target problem of the community psychology program is usually not a traditional one for mental health workers. Thus, even a suc cessful solution to such a problem may have little immediate effect on schizophrenia rates or the prevalence of psychoneurosis. In fact, im proved social conditions leading to reduced crime rates might conceivably result in increases in certain types of mental disorders. Preventive models must, therefore, be targeted specifically to the behaviors to be modified.

Evaluating the effects of the NSC program is not easy, particularly over the short term. The basic problem is that it is very difficult to establish a direct relationship between NSC activities and their eventual effects on the community. Over a long period of time, the demonstration of dramatic changes in the negative demographic characteristics of the NSC area, in the absence of other apparent community forces to account for them, would speak to the beneficial effects of the NSC program. There are, however, bases for a current evaluation. First, it was extremely economical (Riessman, 1967). The total operating expenses for one of the early centers, including the salaries of the professionals, nonprofessionals, a secretary, rent, and other expenses, totaled less than $50,000 per year. Since centers were expected to serve communities populated by 50,000 people, this represents a cost of only about one dollar per person. Furthermore, in terms of center utilization, Riessman (1967) reports that during a six-month period when two NSCs were in full operation, they averaged 1037 cases per month. Projecting these figures, approximately 6200 would be treated at each center per year. Since the average family size of individuals served by the centers was approximately 3.9, each NSC affected the lives of roughly 25,000 people per year. When one adds the potentially beneficial effect of the NSC on scores of others through the institutional changes it stimulated, it is possible to predict a profound impact on many social problems.

The Residential Youth Center (RYC)

Goldenberg (1971) has described the development, operation, and evaluation of a short-term residential setting designed to promote personal growth in culturally deprived adolescents and their families. Strongly emphasized in the project is the development of an institution realistically capable of promoting this growth. In creating a new type of institution, Goldenberg rejects many basic assumptions of other programs, such as the Job Corps, that attempt to deal with inner city youth. One Job Corps assumption is that the poor can best be rehabilitated in settings different from those in which they live. Rejecting this, the RYC bases its program in the same neighborhood where the client must live and adapt. A second common assumption of many programs is that mental health professionals make the best staff in programs dealing with the culturally disadvantaged. Rejecting this assumption, the RYC staff consists largely of indigenous nonprofessionals. A third common assumption in the development of most institutions is that the leaders should specify the goals and values of the institution. In the RYC the views of both staff and residents enter into goal setting and decision making.

Organizationally, a pyramidal administrative structure was avoided in the RYC. Such a structure was seen to reflect a number of assumptions detrimental to RYC functioning. These include the notion that a man wi avoid work unless he has a boss, that he prefers being led to taking pe sonal initiative, that he is self-centered and insensitive to the needs of th organization, and that there is nothing instrinsically fulfilling about th work that he does. Concern that functioning under a pyramidal structur would lead RYC workers to believe and to accept these assumptior about themselves and to behave accordingly, led to the adoption of a ho izontal organization. Such an arrangement permits the staff to learn fror one another, to develop a collective clinical sensitivity and perspective, t accept personal responsibility, and to develop an open and trusting a mosphere.

At a practical level the horizontal structure requires that each sta member, regardless of his title in the organization, assume a case loa with total responsibility for all decisions and interventions concerning resident and his family. Other staff might attempt to influence decisior concerning a particular case, but the final determination is always mad by the member responsible for that case. Along with clinical duties, al RYC staff shares in the work of other members. Thus, although differer staff members hold different titles and perform functions for which the are best suited, they also share functions wherever necessary. On th cook's day off other staff members take turns preparing meals. Althoug there is a regular live-in staff, other staff members are expected to reliev them on days off so that everyone takes turns living in. Administrative du ties are distributed to several different staff members. Each is expected t inform the others about his administrative functions, but administrativ power is not concentrated in the hands of any one person.

Despite the fact that the RYC program was ultimately directed a neighborhood youth, considerable emphasis was given to staff growt and development. It was felt that personal growth on the part of sta would render them better able to provide optimal service to the youn people treated at the RYC. Therefore, staff selection and the staff train ing program was a central feature.

Formal background or training was considered to be relatively unim portant for potential staff. Instead, commitment to the work to be don at the RYC, and previous experience working with the types of boys wh would be serviced by the RYC were the qualities sought in prospectiv staff members. Those designated as director and deputy director of th RYC interviewed applicants for staff positions. No tests of any kind wer administered. The interview included an explanation of the RYC pro gram, invited the applicant's reactions to what he had heard, and encour aged a frank discussion of the problems faced by the program. A recogni tion of community problems and a willingness to voice dissatisfactior with existing conditions were qualities sought. In many respects, such in dividuals had been looked on as troublemakers by other community agencies. The RYC program director kept a diary of reactions to interviewees, and Figure 5 depicts one particular interview.

Of the original RYC staff, eight males and a female secretary, five were white and four black, and all were indigenous to the inner city. Virtually none had had formal training in psychology, sociology, or social work and only one had earned a professional degree. Most were high school graduates. Their occupational experience was diverse and included an automobile mechanic, an X-ray technician, a supermarket employee, a professional singer, a policeman, a baseball player, a book de-

---

Interview 12: May 1966

Today, Scotty and I interviewed Jack T. I think we both knew, even before the session was over, that we wanted Jack as one of our RYC workers. As soon as he left the office we kind of looked at each other, both of us knowing, almost without a word, that Jack was the man for the job.

So far, Jack is the only guy we want to hire who is not a work crew foreman. Although Scotty has known him for some time, I never met Jack until today. At the present time Jack is a Neighborhood Worker working out of the Newhallville area. He is a Negro, 34 years old, married, and has four children, Prior to coming to work for CPI he was a packing house worker.

Jack came a few minutes late for the interview and as soon as he came in he greeted Scotty, nodded to me, and took a seat from which he could look out of the window and onto the street.

Scotty and I began in the usual way. We told him about the job and about the RYC program as a whole. We gave him the usual spiel about it going to be a program "unlike any program ever run"; about how we wanted to work with kids and families in ways which were different and unorthodox; about how we wanted to create a program that would allow the staff to develop their own talents and would encourage and help people to assume the total responsibility for working with a client; and how, when I left in January, nobody would be brought in from the outside to run the program, but that movement would come from within the staff. It was the usual pitch.

During the whole time that we, mostly I, explained the program to Jack he never once looked at me. All he did was nod occasionally and continue to stare out of the window. I got the feeling that Jack either didn't believe what we were saying or that he just plain didn't care. But if he didn't care why was he down here in the first place? It couldn't be because of the salary that the job would carry because no one knew what it would be. And even if he knew that the job might involve an increase in pay there were still a lot of other openings in CPI and we sure didn't put on a big advertising campaign to get people to apply.

I think that my most vivid impression of Jack and of the whole situation was that I was sitting and talking to a man who acted as if he had heard all this before, had been "put on" many times by stories that stressed "growth, responsibility, and advancement," and just couldn't care less about "words." When we asked him about what he was doing at CPI, he responded by saying: "Officially or on my own?" Naturally, we said: "Both," and Jack took it from there. He told us in a somewhat bored way about his "official" duties as a Neighborhood Worker and about how he is supposed to contact and recruit people for the Employment Center but not to get "too involved with them" on a personal or counseling basis. He told us about how he drives people to and from appointments, offers them "support," and does some follow-up work after they have been placed on jobs or in training programs.

The only time he kind of lit up was when he began telling us about his "on my own" work. With a bit of a glint in his eye (I must have imagined this because I rarely saw his eyes, what with him almost constantly staring out of the window) he told us about his nighttime activities; about how he works with "shook-up kids" from his neighborhood; how he spends all his time talking with them on street corners and in their homes; and how he tries to keep them out of trouble by involving them with him in a makeshift judo program (Jack T. is a black belt in judo).

Although he never said so, I got the feeling that one of the reasons Jack enjoyed his night work was that he was able to function in some of the very ways in which he could not work during the day. In other words, at night and informally, he could, indeed, get close to his "clients," counsel them, become deeply involved with them, and deal with their problems in a direct and unrestricted manner.

I also got the feeling that Jack was a fairly angry guy. He mentioned once or twice, always in passing, about how little he felt "the professionals" with whom he worked and who now supervised his activities knew about slum kids. He made no effort to hide the fact that he was somewhat disillusioned and unhappy about the way the War on Poverty was going. Despite what seemed to be his strong feelings he remained outwardly calm and completely self-possessed.

It was a strong interview in many ways. I guess mostly because the more Jack spoke about his concerns and reservations about all CPI programs (and, by implication, the RYC program), the more convinced I became that I wanted him on the staff.

When the interview was over, and as Jack was leaving the office, I said to him: "Jack, if we hire you as an RYC worker in our program do you think there's a chance that some day you'll look me straight in the eye and not stare out a window when you talk to me?" He almost, but not quite, smiled and said: "Maybe, we'll see."

Figure 5. Notes from an interview with an applicant for an RYC staff position (quoted from Goldenberg, 1971, pp. 136, 137, and 138) .

partment manager, and a packing house worker. What they did share was a good knowledge of the workings of the inner city. Besides the full-time staff members, six part-timers—Yale University students using their RYC experience as part of their training—were also part of the staff.

The first RYC clients were young people who had had extensive experience with traditional agencies and had been given up by these organizations. The first 20 RYC residents came from families suffering chronic unemployment, serious disorganization, and considerable interpersonal conflict. Most of the boys had police records, had served time, and were doing poorly in an elementary job training program sponsored by a local community action agency. A few were thought to be capable of success but were regarded as being held back by their poor home situation. None of the boys had completed high school, and all had been involved in local community action programs. Twelve of the first 20 youngsters were black and 8 were white; they ranged in age from 16 to 20. They averaged 2.9 arrests per individual for offenses such as loitering, trespassing, petty theft, breaking and entering, burglary, and assault. Only 3 of the 20 had never served time in prisons, reformatories, or institutions for the mentally retarded or emotionally disturbed. Nearly one half of those institutionalized had spent more than a year at the institution.

It was hoped that the RYC program would bring a youngster and his family together under circumstances permitting mutual growth. To that end, the youngster's worker attempted to dispell the idea that the family was losing the child to the agency or that the agency was assuming parental responsibility. Instead the worker attempted to serve as a "catalytic agent."

At any one time the RYC housed 20 boys and worked with their families, hopefully to become a "therapeutic lever in their lives." The formal program goals were straightforward: (1) to help the boy and family members to find work or to enter employment opportunity programs of interest to them; (2) to help the youngster and his family to overcome the problems that prevented their having a more fulfilling life; and (3) to make it possible, within a short time, for the youngster either to return to live with the family or to set up his own apartment. During the days, RYC residents were expected to be working outside of the center. During this period, the case worker visited families to become acquainted with them. Special weekend and evening programs were organized for residents and their families, and eventually the entire community. These programs were based on special staff interests such as carpentry, automobile mechanics, judo, remedial education, municipal government, athletics, and group sensitivity sessions. To avoid the institutional aura, visiting hours were unlimited, and the family or residents were encouraged to come to the center at any time of the day or night. Residents paid rent and were permitted to go home whenever they wished. It was hoped tha the center would be regarded as a place in which people, not patients worked and lived and grew, as they might in any good family.

Because the RYC staff felt the need for a vehicle for facilitating com munication, group meetings were held three times weekly for all full-time staff and clinical psychology interns. Called sensitivity training, these meetings differed in many respects from T-groups in which participants are encouraged to express a great deal of emotion in the presence of group members who will not be seeing each other in the future. Instead the sessions at the RYC served a number of important local purposes One of these was to deal with the problems that would inevitably arise out of the program's organizational and interpersonal features. For exam ple, the horizontal organizational structure was bound to create problems for people who are accustomed to hierarchical organizations. Further more, the fact that in the RYC a racially mixed group of individuals were living and working together in an emotionally close relationship led to the expectation that considerable interpersonal tension would arise among the staff. The group meetings were also expected to provide an opportun ity for self-reflection which could help prevent the RYC's becoming dom inated by its own structure. The group experience was intended to con tribute to the growth of staff as clinicians by increasing their sensitivity to human feelings and interpersonal problems. Finally, the group was used as a forum for mutual decision making and for the development of a feel ing of mutual trust, and to provide continual feedback on what was hap pening in the institution.

The RYC program utilized three forms of sensitivity training, each tai lored to the organization's specific needs: *individual sensitivity, group sensitivity,* and *special sensitivity.* The individual sensitivity approach was used for one meeting per week. The remaining two meetings could be de voted to any one of the other types as seemed necessary at the time. The most personalized of the meeting formats, individual sensitivity, was di rected at providing a randomly selected individual with feedback con cerning how he was coming across to others. Some attention was also de voted to the way in which the group was reacting to this particular indi vidual. Group sensitivity sessions were "open meetings" where any staff member could bring up a problem that he felt was affecting any individu al's functioning or the group as a whole. Thus if one staff member began to sense that he was finding it difficult to relate to another, he could raise this issue without waiting for an individual sensitivity session devoted to that other person. Group sensitivity sessions could also involve attempts to gain perspective on the program, the staff members involved, and how both were changing over time. Special sensitivity sessions were held infre quently, usually only once in six months, and were primarily devoted to taking a long-range perspective on program progress. When major crises arose, special sensitivity sessions were used as emergency "cabinet" meetings.

The center was located in an area of New Haven that had once been mostly middle-class and largely Jewish. The character of this neighborhood, however, had begun to change during World War II and by the time of the program's conception, it was populated largely by lower and lower-middle class families (approximately 60% white, and 40% black). The building housing the center was an old 15-room Victorian house standing on the corner of two main streets. Originally a single family home, it had undergone several changes as the neighborhood declined. Its metamorphoses included use as a boarding house and, later, as a "house of pleasure." Immediately before being taken over as the RYC, the building had been a rooming house for transients and was in a state of considerable disrepair.

To evaluate the effects of the RYC program, boys were chosen as controls at the time the original residents of the RYC were selected. Subjects were selected for both groups by having each of a number of community social agencies provide a list of the 50 boys within the required age range whom they regarded as their most difficult cases. Those boys found on the lists of several agencies were regarded as the most difficult, and those found on the fewest number of lists were regarded as least difficult. The first 25 of the most difficult boys were placed in the experimental group, with 20 being admitted to the RYC, and the remaining 5 available as substitutes for dropouts from the original group. The group of 25 who were regarded as least difficult constituted the control group. Thus the two groups were not equivalent in social deviance, but they were matched with respect to age and race.

Outcome evaluation was based on occupational adjustment, attitude changes, and community adjustment as reflected in involvement with legal authorities. With respect to occupational adjustment, it was found that prior to initiation of the RYC program control subjects attended work approximately 86 percent of the time whereas the RYC boys were working only approximately 60 percent of the time. After nine months of participation by experimental subjects in the RYC program, these differences were dramatically reversed; the RYC boys were attending work approximately 97 percent of the time while the controls were attending only 56 percent of the time, a statistically significant difference. Vocational status changes paralleled these changes in work attendance records. Boys in the RYC program showed a sharp decrease in unemployment rates (39.7%) and a sharp increase (30%) in full-time employment. Small changes were found in the control group on these categories. Income also reflected the beneficial effect of the RYC program. On entry into the

RYC, the experimental group boys averaged $25 per week as compared with $29 per week for the control group. Nine months later the RYC group was earning an average of $45 per week as compared with $20.72 for the control group.

With respect to community behavior, the average number of arrests per RYC youngster in the six-month period before entering program was 1.87 as compared with 1.70 for the controls. For the six months after they entered the center program, the RYC residents averaged only 0.96 arrests as compared with 2.08 for the control youngsters, a highly significant difference statistically. Similarly, during the nine-month period prior to the opening of the RYC, experimental group boys spent a total of 153 days in jail as compared with 140 days for the control group. For the nine-month period following initiation of the RYC program, experimental group boys spent a total of 70 days in prison as compared with 258 for the control group, another statistically significant difference.

Attitudes were measured by a variety of questionnaires designed to tap feelings of alienation, and attitudes toward authoritarianism, trust, Machiavellianism, and social desirability. Comparisons between experimentals and controls at the initiation of the RYC program showed no differences on these measures. Six months later, however, the RYC group was found to have become significantly less alienated, and to have decreased in feelings of authoritarianism as compared with the control group. The RYC boys also showed a tendency toward greater trust as compared with the controls, but this difference was just short of significance.

These initial findings of the RYC program effects are very impressive. If long-range follow-ups substantiate the differences already reported, the RYC program would appear to hold considerable promise for dealing with some of society's most difficult problems. Besides rehabilitating the youngster set on a course of serious social maladjustment, the program has the advantage of being relatively economical. The RYC is run on an annual budget of approximately $150,000. Since approximately 50 youngsters can be served in any given year (at an average of 5 ½ months of residence per boy) the average cost is only $3000 per resident. Since the costs of dealing with a boy in juvenile court is higher, and the cost of supporting a youngster who remains on the welfare rolls over a long period of time can be infinitely higher than this figure, the RYC approach would seem to be a very compelling one, both from economical as well as humane viewpoints.

Community Programs for Delinquents

Behavior Modification in the Storefront Laboratory

Several reports in recent years have described attempts to diminish delinquent behavior through the use of behavior modification principles

(Schwitzgebel, 1963, 1964, 1967; Schwitzgebel and Kolb, 1964; Slack, 1960, 1963). The model for this approach originated in a study on the dynamics of hostility. Seven male adolescent delinquents were hired to participate in interviews and to take some psychological tests for the purpose of this study. Surprisingly, it was discovered that the scientist-subject relationship had positive behavioral effects on the delinquents. Slack (1963) has described his relationship as a collaboration in which the adolescent and the experimenter regard themselves as scientists doing a "job for the community." The job in this case is attempting to lower the crime rate. Schwitzgebel (1963, 1964, 1967) describes extensively the approach used in such a program.

Prospective "employees" are actively solicited from among individuals frequenting pool halls, street corners, or any location where adolescents with records of delinquency seem likely to congregate. Once it is established that the boy has a police record, he is offered a job as an experimental subject. He is told that he can earn spending money simply by showing up at the storefront laboratory and talking into a tape recorder. A typical conversation from a first contact is described in Figure 6.

Bill and his friends gathered around a pinball machine on which I had just won nine free games. After I had given Bill several free games, the following conversation was recorded as nearly as possible by a friend who had come along for this purpose. I had not met Bill previously.

Experimenter. Have you ever been in trouble with the cops?

Bill. No, not me. How come you ask? [Bill is caught off guard by the direct question. He thinks perhaps this guy is a cop.]

Experimenter. Well, that's too bad because if you'd been in some trouble I might have a job for you. [Bill is really surprised now. Maybe this guy is some new kind of cop. Or maybe he's a queer. Anyway, things are getting interesting.]

Bill. What do you mean? Do you want me to roll drunks or what?

Experimenter. No, it's a different kind of job. We're trying to find out how come kids get into trouble and what to do about it. So the only way to find out is to ask them. You just talk into a tape recorder about anything you want, but mostly about yourself. You can get up to two dollars an hour. You don't get rich 'cause you only work a couple of hours a week, but it's good pocket money. We want to find out why kids get into trouble so we ask them and they tell us.

Bill. You're not a cop, are you? [Bill doesn't really believe the experimenter. Who ever heard of a "straight" job that required a police record?]

Experimenter. No, we don't want to know names or places or anything like that. Just what's happened to you, and what you think about things. I'd like some coffee; let's talk about it over here. [Both walk over to the lunch counter on the other side of the amusement center and order coffee. Experimenter pays for both.] It's a job. We're doing research. It's an experiment, and you get paid for being one of the guys in it. I know it sounds corny. We've got a little white rat at the lab and we're teaching him to do tricks. That's his part in the experiment. Other people do other things. Your job would be talking into a recorder.

Bill. You mean I'm a guinea pig? [He is beginning to get the idea of the job. He is also a little pleased that some one is seeking him out for a legitimate job.]

Experimenter. That's right. Some of the guys call it guinea-pigging. Most all of them like it, and bring their friends around for a job; but we like to start with new guys who don't know us.

Bill. Say, you're not a bug doctor, are you? [Fear of the psychiatrist is intense. To associate with one voluntarily in gang territory would immediately cause the loss of gang prestige and protection.]

Experimenter. No, I just help out. I'm a student. There's other people like me, and there's Dr. Slack. He's the big man who runs the outfit. He's a prof. at the school where we run the experiment.

Bill. You're not a bug doctor, huh? If you are, I won't go.

Experimenter. No, I just help out with the experiment. You get paid in cash, and you can quit whenever you want to. You've really got to see the place before you make up your mind. It's a pretty good deal, and it's on the level. But maybe you don't have a bad enough record, because we need kids who've done time. You look like you've been around.

Bill. I've done time.

Experimenter. Good. Let's take a look at the place. You can bring your friend along. Look it over, then make up your mind. Nothing to lose, and it's something to do.

Figure 6. Example of the first contact with a prospective subject (quoted from Schwitzgebel, 1964, pp. 14 and 15) .

Typically the experimenter brings the new employee to the laboratory, often with a friend, for the first session. On arrival the delinquent is generally reinforced with soft drinks, food, or a cigarette. If the boy comes to the laboratory on his own the first time, at the conclusion of the session he is invited to return the next day at the same time. If he was met on the street, the next meeting is arranged for the next day in the same location, and he is again brought to the laboratory. A boy initially met on the street often presents a problem about returning. If he fails to do so within several hours of an appointed time, the experimenter returns to the neighborhood where he was found and tries to seek him out. If not found on one day, he is sought the next day. In particularly noncooperative cases, a procedure called "shaping" is used. In this procedure the boy is met at locations successively closer geographically to the laboratory. Each time a boy is met, whether late or not, he is immediately rewarded by the experimenter, most often with a cigarette or candy bar. Eventually most boys began coming to the laboratory on their own.

The initial task in this program is to induce boys to come to the laboratories for their meetings, even if several hours late. Once this is accomplished, efforts are made to encourage punctual arrival. This is done by introducing a system of paying for the full hour's work only if a boy arrives roughly on time. If he is late, he is permitted to work only the remaining part of the scheduled hour and paid only for the portion worked. A system of bonuses may also be introduced whereby prompt arrival is occasionally reinforced with extra gifts such as money, or tickets to a baseball game.

The "work" engaged in by the adolescents consists, simply, of talking into a tape recorder. It is explained that the experimenters are interested in learning about teenagers who have had trouble with authorities and are not attempting to reform the boys. The boy is encouraged to join in the experimenter's efforts to learn about why adolescents have problems with established authority. Experimenters are completely candid about the purposes of the project and its operation and the boys are, therefore, encouraged to ask as many questions as they wish and to read any publications or correspondence related to the project. The impression of one subject (see Figure 7) in this study after only three weeks in the project indicates the impact this simple procedure can have on delinquents.

In an early evaluation of this "street corner research" Schwitzgebel (1954) compared 30 boys who had been seen in the laboratory for a period of six months or more to a control group of boys formed by matching members of the experimental group with male offenders having records in the Department of Probation and Parole and the Youth Service Board of the Commonwealth of Massachusetts. Matching was done on variables such as the first major offense, nationality, city of residence, and amount of time spent in reform school and prison prior to February 1959. On the average, both experimental and control group subjects committed their first offense at about age 13 1/2 and had been incarcerated for approximately 15 months before the experiment began.

One postexperimental index on which the two groups were compared was the mean number of arrests three years after their involvement with the program. The experimental group had an average of 2.4 arrests while the control group had 4.7, a difference that is statistically significant. A total of seven (35%) experimental subjects and nine (45%) control subjects had been incarcerated during the three-year follow-up period, a nonsignificant difference. There were, however, significant differences between the groups in the number of months spent in institutions as the

I have been a part, material wise, in the program at Harvard University, titled "Research Center in Personality and Rehabilitation" for a period of 3 weeks. The person in that department I work with is——[the experimenter]. Who is a Jesuit priest finishing a degree in Sycology at this University. Now the main purpose of this program is to get material and also at the same time, help troubled people who have delinquently dealt with the law, who naturally have many different types of problems. Myself being a person under that description can be of use to this program. I must honestly state, that in my such short period attending here so far, I have never since I can remember, felt greater mentally. Although it has only been a short period of time, as I mentioned, I feel a great decrease in my trouble with facing reality. I hope it is possible for me to continue my attendance for quite awhile. Because I still have much more information to give to this program about myself, and different things. I also feel there is much more knowing I can receive about myself here. I have, as most troubled people, always thought that I would never straiten things out. But now since attending these visits I have put a whole new light on everything concerning life and myself. And the light is on the good side, one hundred per cent. After finding this information out on such a short visit here, I am sure enough of everything, to say that the outcome of this will be excellent, not only for me but everyone else that attends this program. If this program was greatly increased I feel both sides would benefit greatly. I hope I have expressed myself as well as I wanted to about this matter.

Figure 7. One subject's reaction to experimenter subject therapy (quoted from Schwitzgebel, 1954, pp. 54 and 55).

result of offenses committed, with the experimental group averaging 3.5 and the controls 6.9 months. Even though roughly equivalent numbers of experimental and control subjects committed crimes leading to incarceration, the fact that significantly fewer crimes were committed by experimental subjects and that they spent significantly less time in penal institutions is quite encouraging.

In a later evaluation, Schwitzgebel (1967) compared the effects of an experimental procedure in which boys received positive reinforcement for arriving at work on time and for making statements of concern about other people with a procedure in which boys received negative reinforcement for negative statements about people and positive reinforcement for socially desirable nonverbal behavior that reflected social tact or desirable employee qualities. A third group in this study was a no-treatment control group in which subjects participated in only 2 interviews spaced over a period of two to three months, approximately the same amount of time experimental subjects participated in the study. Experimental subjects had a total of 20 interviews in the course of a two to three month period. The posttest results of this study indicated the experimental group that was reinforced for prompt behavior was significantly more likely to arrive near the starting time than the experimental group that did not experience such reinforcement. Likewise, the same group, which had been reinforced for positive statements about other people, showed a significantly greater increase in these statements than did the experimental group that was negatively reinforced for hostile statements. The experimental group receiving negative reinforcement for hostility decreased in their average frequency of such statements but, although the decrease in this group was larger than in the other two groups, the differences were not significant.

Measures were also taken of various social behaviors that might reflect tact and consideration for others. Two of these tests yielded significant differences. One involved the amount of food that a subject would order at a restaurant when limited to a maximum of one dollar. On the average, all three groups showed an increase between the pre- and posttest on this behavioral measure (meaning their total was closer to the one-dollar limit on posttest), but the experimental group that had been reinforced for displaying desirable behaviors showed a significantly smaller increase than did the other two groups. The other behavioral measure on which significant differences were found involved a test in which subjects were asked to list, for five minutes, all of the bad things that they might do and then later all of the good things that they might do. A ratio was taken between the number of thoughts that could be offered in the two 5-minute segments. The experimental group that had been positively reinforced for socially desirable behavior showed a significantly greater increase in the number of good thoughts than did either of the other two groups.

The efforts and achievements of these examples in street-corner and storefront experimenter-subject collaborations are impressive. Such a program reaches out to a social problem, the significance of which is incontestable involving, as it does, young people set on a course where their own lives will be wasted and society will be everburdened. Because of its significance as a social problem, juvenile delinquency has been the object of many early community efforts, most of which have failed despite ambitious and energetic programs (e.g., the Cambridge-Somerville study). The results of the work of the storefront laboratory are hopeful and should be extended and tested further.

Modeling Procedures with Juvenile Delinquents

The creation of learning situations designed to meet the special needs of delinquents has also been used to deal with juvenile delinquency. Sarason

(1968) and Sarason and Ganzer (1969) have pointed out that as one who has been rejected by the mainstream of his culture, the delinquent is deficient in socially acceptable and adaptive behaviors. These experimenters have, therefore, set about to provide opportunities in which the delinquent can directly observe and learn socially useful behavior.

The rationale for this approach is that delinquents need to be exposed systematically to models with whom they can identify who display socially appropriate behavior in situations relevant to the delinquent's life experience. Pilot studies using modeling approaches have been carried out at the Cascadia Reception-Diagnostic Center in Takoma, Washington where all children committed by the juvenile courts of the state of Washington are sent. Preliminary work was devoted to determining what model situations should be presented, how models should behave toward delinquents to maximize the effects of the observations, and to experimental issues such as the controls that must be used to evaluate such a project and what types of dependent measures are necessary for assessing program effects.

It was concluded that relatively objective and uncomplicated modeling situations must be used, and that good rapport between models and subjects was vital if the program was to have significant impact—models must be people with whom the delinquent *wants* to identify. Eventually a series of 15 situations were designed that could be modeled for delinquent boys. Each, presented in a single session, provided opportunities for delinquents to learn adaptive responses to problems they were likely to experience. Session themes involved situations such as applying for a job, resisting peer pressure to engage in antisocial behavior, approaching a teacher or parole officer with a problem, and putting off immediate gains in favor of long-range gratification. Efforts were made in each modeling example to stress the generality of the lesson to be learned from the specific situation. A typical example of a modeling situation involving application for a job is presented in Figure 8.

Six people attend each modeling session. Two are models (advanced clinical psychology graduate students), and the other four are delinquents typically ranging in age from 15 to 18. One of the models introduces the topic for the session and describes the theme which everyone present will ultimately play. The two models act out the scene which is structured carefully beforehand. Following this example, a pair of delinquents is invited to act out the same scene. Afterward a round of soft drinks is served, and a discussion is held on various aspects of what was observed and acted out. Later the boys who have not already done so act out the scene. In discussions following the job interview modeling example, four points are emphasized: (1) a boy takes initiative in these scenes rather than waiting for things to happen to him; (2) a delinquent must often deal with the fact that he has a record; (3) feeling anxious at a job inter-

Job Interview Scene

Introduction: Having a job can be very important. It is a way that we can get money for things we want to buy. It is a way we can feel important because we are able to earn something for ourselves through our own efforts. For this same reason, a job can make us feel more independent. Getting a job may not always be easy. This is especially true of jobs that pay more money and of full-time jobs. A job may be important to guys like you who have been in an institution because it gives you a way of showing other people that you can be trusted, that you can do things on your own, that you are more than just a punk kid. However, because you've been in trouble, you may have more trouble than most people getting a job. In the scene today you'll have a chance to practice applying for a job and being interviewed by the man you want to work for. Being interviewed makes most people tense and anxious because interviewers often ask questions which are hard to answer. After each of you has been interviewed, we'll talk about the way it felt and about what to do about the special problems that parolees may face in getting jobs.

Scene I.a

A boy who is on parole from Cascadia is applying for a job at a small factory in his home town. He is 18 and has not finished high school but hopes to do so by going to school at night. Obviously, the boy has a record. This will come up during the interview. Pay careful attention to how he handles this problem. This is a two part scene; first, we'll act out the job interview, then a part about another way of convincing an employer that you want a job.

(Mr. Howell is seated at his desk when George knocks on the door.)

Howell. "Hello. Have a seat. I'm Mr. Howell, and your name?"

(Mr. Howell rises—shakes hands.)

George. "George Smith."

Howell. "Have a seat, George."

(Both sit down.)

"Oh yes, I have your application right here. There are a few questions I'd like to ask you. I see that you have had some jobs before; tell me about them."

George. "They were just for the summer because I've been going to school. I've worked on some small construction jobs and in a food processing plant."

Howell. "Did you ever have any trouble at work, or ever get fired?"

George. "No trouble, except getting used to the work the first couple of weeks. I did quit one job—I didn't like it."

Howell. "I see that you have only finished half your senior year in high school. You don't intend to graduate?"

George. (showing some anxiety) "Yes, I do. I intend to go to night school while I'm working. It may take me a year or so, but I intend to get my diploma."

Howell. "How did you get a year behind?"

George. "I've been out of school for a while because I've been in some trouble. Nothing really serious."

Howell. I'd like to know just what kind of trouble you've had, serious or not."

George. "Well, I was sent to Cascadia for six weeks but I'm out on parole now. I just got out a couple of weeks ago. One of the reasons I want a job is to help keep me out of trouble."

Howell. "What kind of trouble were you involved in?"

George. "A friend and I stole some car parts and parts off an engine. I guess we were pretty wild. I'm not running around like that any more though."

Howell: "You sound like you think you can stay out of trouble now. Why do you think so?"

George. "In those six weeks at Cascadia I thought about myself and my future a whole lot, and realized it was time to get serious about life and stop goofing off. I know I haven't been out very long yet, but my parole counselor is helping me with the problems that come up. I'm trying to stay away from the guys that I got into trouble with. I really think that if I could get a job and be more on my own it would help a lot."

Howell. "Yes, I think you're probably right—but, I'm afraid we don't have any openings right now. I'll put your application on file though and let you know if anything turns up. I have several other applications too, so don't be too optimistic."

George. "All right. Thank you."

(George stands and starts to leave as he says this line.)

Scene I.b

Introduction: It is now two weeks later. George has called back several times to see if an opening has occurred. He now stops by to check again.

(George knocks on Mr. Howell's door.)

Howell. "Come in."

George. (enters room while speaking) "I stopped by to see whether you had an opening yet."

Howell. "You certainly don't want me to forget you do you?"

George. "No sir, I don't. I really want a job, I think its the best thing for me to do now."

Howell. "You know, I believe you. I wasn't so sure at first. It's pretty easy for a guy who has been in trouble to say that he's going to change and then do nothing about it. But the way you've been coming here and checking with me so often, I think you're really serious about it."

George. "Yes, sir, I am. I started night school this week. I think I'll be able to get my diploma in a year. So, if I had a job now I'd be all set."

Howell. "Well, I've got some good news for you, George. I have an opening for a man in the warehouse and I think you can handle the job if you want it."

George. "Yes, very much. When do you want me to start?"

Howell. "Tomorrow morning at 7:30."

George. "O.K."

Howell. "I'll take you out there now and introduce you to Mr. Jones, who will be your supervisor."

Scene I.c

Introduction: Same as Scene 1b.
(George knocks on Mr. Howell's door.)
Howell. "Come in."
George. "I stopped by to see whether you had opening yet." (enters room while speaking)
Howell. "You sure are persistent. Have you tried other places?"
George. "Sure, I'm checking back on them too. Getting a good job isn't easy."
Howell. (uncomfortably) "Ah, well, look. We're not going to have a place for you here. I wouldn't want you to waste your time coming back again. We can't use you."
George. (rises to go) "Well . . . (pause) . . . O.K. Thanks for your trouble. Look, what's up? I know that your company is hiring other fellows like me right now."
Howell. "Er . . . that's true. Uh, I'm afraid that we have a company policy not to hire anyone with a record."
George. "How come? That doesn't sound fair to me."
Howell. "Well, er, ahem . . . that's just the company's policy. I'm sorry, but my hands are tied. There's nothing I can do about it."
George. "Well, I would have appreciated knowing that right away."
Howell. "I'm really sorry. I can see you're trying . . . I hope you get a job.
George. "Well, do you know of a place that could use me? Since you're in personnel, maybe you've heard something."

Figure 8. Example of a modeling situation (quoted from Sarason, 1968, pp. 260, 261, and 262).

view is quite understandable; (4) persistence is a trait that is valued by employers.

Sarason (1968) has reported two pilot studies to assess the effectiveness of modeling procedures. In one, subjects in modeling sessions were compared with two control groups: one that received no special treatment and another in which boys spontaneously enacted roles similar to those used in the modeling situation, but which had not been modeled for them. In a later pilot study, modeling sequences were followed by a detailed group discussion in which great emphasis was placed on the personal meaning of group meetings to subjects. Experimental-control comparisons were based both on self-report indexes and on behavioral ratings provided by the institution staff. One of the self-report procedures required subjects to describe themselves as they felt they were and as they would like to be. Behavioral measures focused on table manners, lying, peer relationships, staff relationships, and performance on weekly details. These measures were made during the boys' first 10 days at the institution and, again, just prior to discharge.

Initial evaluation efforts have yielded several interesting findings. First, boys participating in the modeling groups tend to show a greater discrepancy between "me as I would like to be" and "me as I am now" than do control subjects. This indicates that those experiencing modeling become more dissatisfied with themselves the longer they stay at the institution. This stirring up of self-dissatisfaction may well be a necessary precursor to important behavioral changes. A further finding was that boys in both experimental groups, the modeling group as well as the role-playing group, changed behaviorally and attitudinally to a greater degree than did matched controls who had no special treatment program. These differences were most marked in the subjects who participated in modeling. A further analysis indicated that boys who were characterized by the greatest amount of anxiety responded most favorably to the modeling situations.

The promising findings in these early studies of the effects of modeling on the behavior of juvenile delinquents have prompted an extension of this work. Studies are now being devoted to increasing the power of the modeling situation through the use of closed circuit television, thereby providing greater observational opportunities. New kinds of control groups are being introduced to more closely approximate psychotherapy groups. And, finally, research is being done on the personal characteristics of the most effective models.

The New Careers Movement

A relatively new approach for dealing with the myriad of problems suffered by the impoverished is the New Careers Movement, which is dedicated to improving economic conditions among the poor through creating career opportunities in the service professions. In addition to improving the material state of the impoverished, such careers should help diminish the powerlessness felt by the impoverished and should enhance their self-image. Thus the New Careers Movement has a significant potential for preventing mental disorder.

Pearl and Riessman (1965) have written movingly of the necessity for developing new careers for the poor. They point out that in a highly technologically advanced society even the skills of the well-trained professional rapidly become obsolete. At an early stage of technological development the poor, traditionally society's least well educated group, had one important resource that gave them a toehold on the economic ladder, their capacity to perform unskilled labor. For many, this opening was sufficient to permit their children to advance to higher stations in society through advanced education or business enterprise. For a long period of time, technological advance stimulated the economy and provided still more and more openings for the unskilled. Advancing automation, however, has gradually been eliminating the need for the unskilled labor traditionally provided by the poor. Thus other avenues for advancement are now needed by the impoverished. Through the service field, Pearl and Riessman envision that the poor can find one such avenue. Their faith is well stated in the introduction to their book:

"The central thesis of this book is that in an affluent automated society the number of persons needed to perform such tasks (services in the health, education, welfare, and recreation fields) equals the number of persons for whom there are no other jobs" (Pearl and Riessman, 1965, p. 6).

Basic to the new career concept is the creation of jobs out of activities that have traditionally been carried out by highly trained professionals but that can be done at a technician level, or the creation of new jobs to provide needed services that are not currently available. In either case, these jobs should be established at a level permitting easy entry for the relatively untrained and unskilled. Beyond this first step of creating jobs suitable for the poor, it is also necessary to enable an adult to have a career in a given field. Thus permanency and an advancement ladder must be built into the job. These requirements necessitate considerable rethinking of the functions of the typical professional and demand much administrative and legislative reorganization. While these aspects of the new careers concept are ambitious and difficult to implement, another aspect further compounds this difficulty.

In addition to making possible limited advancement within a new career, without the necessity for extensive additional training, it is also basic to the new careers concept that substantial professional advancement be possible for those who are capable and willing to work for it. Therefore, one might enter a profession at its lowest levels with relatively little training. Job experience plus further education in junior colleges and colleges might then provide one with the skills to perform at a higher level within the profession. Ultimately it is envisioned that the new careerist can aspire to the highest station within the profession. Thus, where up to now one has entered a field such as medicine, psychology, or education only by acquiring very high level training before going to work, it is proposed in the New Career Movement that the opportunity to achieve the highest professional levels be created for those who enter with no skills and work their way up gradually within the field. In medicine, therefore, one might begin as a hospital aide, advance to a medical assistant, eventually proceed to being a medical associate in which more demanding relationships with patients are engaged in under a physician's supervision, and then take on increasingly more significant challenges until, ultimately, one reaches the status of the medical doctor. In a sense this concept calls for a return to a time when people entered professions as apprentices, attaching themselves to an established professional who served as their tutor over a period of years. They entered with virtually no training and eventually, through experience, achieved the status of a full-fledged professional. This avenue has been closed with the development of high level professional schools. Unfortunately, the poor have little access to these schools, and those who champion the New Careers Movement feel that something like a return to the old tutorial system is necessary if the poor are to have a genuine opportunity to advance. Thus the entry level to the service profession should not require extensive training and education which the impoverished lack, and the opportunity for advancing through work and training in the profession should exist.

The new careers concept has stimulated the development of a wide variety of service jobs for the poorly educated and impoverished. Riessman and Popper (1968) have described potential and actual programs offering career opportunities for the poor. These are found in social welfare agencies, in schools, in various health services, as well as in the corrections and police agencies around the country.

One of the pioneering efforts in the New Careers Movement was a program developed at Howard University in Washington, D. C. (Fishman, Klein, MacLennan, Mitchell, Pearl, and Walker, 1965; Fishman, Denham, Levine, and Schatz, 1969; Klein, 1967; MacLennan, Klein, Pearl, and Fishman, 1966). This program was designed to provide ego-enhancing employment in the human service field for young people facing a seriously limited future because of their lack of skills, poor education, and police records. If successful, such a program would have two major dividends: it would help to alleviate serious manpower shortages in the human services field; and it would convert a young person, who would otherwise become a liability to society, into a productive citizen.

Trainees for the Howard University New Careers Program were recruited through a variety of community agencies and sources, some traditional, such as the United States Employment Service, the Division of Vocational Rehabilitation, and neighborhood development centers of the Community Action Program, and some untraditional, such as the Probation Department, news stories, posters, and word-of-mouth contacts. The application procedure involved merely filling out an application form, undergoing a physical examination, and participating in an interview. Elimination of those applicants failing to meet minimal requirements left a far larger number than could be worked with; hence, several selection procedures were adopted to reduce the size of the group. One procedure simply involved random selection from the total pool of acceptable candidates. In other instances, the interview was used as a device for selecting applicants with certain special qualities. Still another way of selecting applicants involved choosing on the basis of sex or some desirable personal characteristic. Differences in selection procedure came about because trainees were being selected to work in a variety of different settings. In many settings no special characteristics were required so that random selection was possible. Others required certain minimal qualifications, necessitating the creation of priorities for people possessing them. Mainly the selection program was keyed to *screening in* applicants rather than screening them out.

Overall, the Howard program trained a total of 136 people, ranging in age from 16 to 35 years, with the majority (89%) under 26. Most (about 2/3) were married and 58 percent were males. All but two of the trainees were black, with more than 50 percent having been born in the District of Columbia. Over 90 percent had had previous job experience but only 7 percent were employed at the time that they entered the program. Thirty-nine percent were high school dropouts. The majority of the group (65%) had been arrested. Thirty-five percent had between 1 and 5 arrests for offenses ranging from simple misdemeanors to burglary, housebreaking, and assault. Figure 9 describes a typical trainee.

Aide X finished the tenth grade at a Washington D.C. high school before quitting school altogether. He is somewhat small in stature and, when first seen, his tendency to wear clothes one or two sizes too large only accentuated this fact. He gave the impression of being an extremely wary and guarded individual who hardly ever looked at or spoke directly to whomever he was addressing. In the early days of the program, he was quite critical of it, and openly questioned the possibility of its having any effect on the behavior of the group members. At the same time, he was quick to point out positive directions for action and to assume leadership. He is one of five children, and has lived for 17 years at the same address (a public housing project). His mother is a housewife, and his stepfather, a post office employee. In recent years, Aide X has tried to become more self-sufficient, at least in part because of a conflict with his stepfather. He has alternated between living at his parents' home, an aunt's apartment, and an apartment of his own. His employment record includes a series of low-paying, unskilled, temporary jobs, the most recent of which was a one-dollar-an-hour kitchen helper. Aide X's delinquency arrest record includes charges of robbery and truancy. For both of these, he was confined to a correctional institution (Fishman et al., 1965, p. 14).

Figure 9. Description of a typical new careers trainee at Howard University (quoted from Fishman et al., 1965, p. 14).

The Howard University program prepared trainees to work in a variety of roles: teachers' aides, recreation aides, welfare aides, and the like. Since different trainees were being prepared for many different jobs, one element of the training program was an on-the-job experience designed to teach the specific requirements of a given setting. Also, specialty instruction was offered to provide the skills and knowledge necessary for a particular job. Common to the program of all trainees, however, was the Core group. This was a vehicle designed to help trainees assimilate the "values and expectations of the world of work" and to see the relevance of their own efforts to other people. The Core group was defined in the Howard program as:

". . . a training group in which its members would learn how society, small groups, people in general, and they themselves felt, functioned, and developed. Within this group aides learn how to analyze personal, social and particularly job-related problems, make their own decisions, try on various roles and attitudes for size, and learn to cope more effectively with people and the world around them.

"Starting from their own experience, the members of the Core group are encouraged to examine the process of their immediate lives and the problems of living in a poor area of the city. As the group progresses, it draws upon experts to examine with it areas of knowledge of common concern to all. These include: problems of human development, i.e., family life, childhood, adolescence, normalcy and deviance; community institutions and resources; special problems of the socially deprived; health care; labor and employment; the law and legal aid; credit unions, insurance and medical care; and general problems of working with people" (Fishman et al., 1965, pp. 18–19).

Core group sessions were held daily for the first half of the three-month training program and ranged from one to three hours as a function of the topic under consideration. During the latter half of the training program it met only twice a week, allowing increasing amounts of time for on-the-job experience.

Once training was completed, the Howard University Program designers played a major role in job placement. Also many trainees were hired by agencies in which they had trained.

A follow-up evaluation was done with 106 out of the 136 new careerists trained at Howard, based on trainees' job experience since leaving the program. Follow-ups were done no less than 6 months or more than 2 ½ years following completion of training (Fishman et al., 1969). In this group 92 (87% of the sample) were employed at the time of follow-up, and those employed had held their present job for an average of 9 months with the majority (about 53%) having had only a single job since training. The remaining interviewees had held from 2 to 4 jobs. The major follow-up findings showed that among trainees who were employed when interviewed, viturally all were still working in the human service field. Approximately one half of the job changes taking place were for reasons beyond the trainees' control. Also most job changes resulted in salary increases. Approximately one third of the interviewees sought further schooling after their new careers training. Of considerable significance was the fact that only 8 out of the 102 follow-up trainees reported conflicts with law-enforcement agencies. A total of 15 offenses were reported by these trainees. Five were for traffic violations and the remaining 10 were for somewhat more serious offenses. This record is in marked contrast to that reported in the pretraining period when approximately one third of the trainees reported a total of 79 delinquent acts.

The overall results of the Howard University program are extremely impressive, particularly when one considers the nature of the trainee population. This example of a successful program for converting people who are ordinarily a liability to society into human service workers has stimulated a variety of new career programs throughout the country. Such programs are, of course, beset by a number of difficulties, but have the potential for solving some of society's most serious problems.

Mental Health Consultation

Still another approach designed to grapple with community mental health problems is the wider practice of consultation by mental health specialists. Typically, such consultation is offered to professional groups that, although having little specialized training in the mental health fields, nonetheless, in the ordinary course of their work, deal with many people experiencing mental health problems. Nurses, teachers, general practitioners, clergymen, probation officers, policemen, and welfare workers are professionals of this kind. Caplan (1964) and Bindman (1959) have written about consultation practices with these groups. Bindman defines mental health consultation as follows:

"Mental health consultation is an interaction process or interpersonal relationship that takes place between two professional workers, the consultant and the consultee, in which one worker, the consultant, attempts to assist the other worker, the consultee, solve a mental health problem of a client or clients, within the framework of the consultee's usual professional functioning. The process of consultation depends upon the communication of knowledge, skills, and attitudes through this relationship, and therefore, is dependent upon the degree of emotional and intellectual involvement of the two workers. A secondary goal of this process is one of education, so that the consultee can learn to handle similar cases in the

future in a more effective fashion, and thus enhance his professional skills" (Bindman, 1959, p. 473).

Caplan (1964) has described four types of mental health consultation. The first, "client-centered case consultation," focuses on the consultee's problems with a specific client. The primary goal is to help the consultee deal most effectively with the client, but a secondary goal in this, as in most consulting approaches, is to improve the consultee's functioning so that he will be better able to handle similar cases in the future.

The second type of consultation, "program-centered administrative consultation," deals with the problems encountered in administering or creating programs for preventing, treating, or rehabilitating the mentally disabled. These problems typically relate to the planning and administration of services and to the formulation of high-level policies concerning the most effective recruitment and use of personnel. An example of such a consultative procedure is a psychiatrist's being called in by a city health department to advise on establishing a mental health program.

A third type of consultation, "consultee-centered case consultation," focuses on the consultee rather than on the client or clients with whom the consultee is having difficulty. Hopefully, consultee benefits derived from this approach will be translated into gains for the client as well. In this interaction much of the consultant's time is spent in talking about the client with the goal of detecting the distortions and omissions in the consultee's perceptions that account for the difficulty he is experiencing. Once these problems have been identified, attempts are made to help the consultee master his own problem with the case. A variety of personal deficiencies such as inadequate understanding, inadequate skill, inability to remain objective, or a lack of self-confidence may account for the consultee's difficulty. The consultant is called on to determine the basic problem and to provide whatever is necessary to enable the consultee to be more effective.

The fourth type of consulting relationship, "consultee-centered administrative consultation," has the goal of helping consultees deal with the problems of setting up and maintaining agencies for treating emotional disturbance. This type of consultation is often directed toward administrators, as is often true of program-centered consultation, and this type of consultant should be a mental health specialist with administrative experience.

Consultation practices expand the mental health specialist's sphere of influence. Within the large urban area they have considerable potential for reaching large numbers of individuals who may never approach a mental health professional directly. A consultant's efforts with school teachers, lawyers, physicians, policemen, welfare workers, and the like can have enormous impact on the mental health problems of the people of any community. Rieman (1969) has argued that mental health consultation is also a particularly effective way to deal with the mental health problems of the small community. In such areas because of the dearth of mental health professionals, members of the health, educational, or legal professions often must provide necessary mental health services. These "caregivers" need the assistance of trained professionals. The consultation program described by Rieman involved what Caplan has called program-centered administrative consultation. The consultant helped to plan and set up an overall mental health program for a small urban area. Spielberger (1967) has also described a preventive consultation service in a rural area. In Spielberger's program client-centered case and consultee-centered case consultation predominated. Groups of physicians, teachers, clergymen, and nurses met with a consultant in a case seminar format and presented specific problem cases to the consultant who responded with understanding, advice and, at times, specific recommendations. Beyond helping with the specific case, the consultant's efforts were directed toward educating consultees with respect to the nature of mental health problems and the means by which they are best treated.

Bard (Bard, 1969; Bard, 1970; Bard, 1971; Bard and Berkowitz, 1967) has described a mental health consultation program for police officers. He points out that while middle and upper class people tend to turn to lawyers, clergymen, and marriage counselors for help with family problems, the lower classes are far more likely to call on the police for help in times of crisis. Some estimates indicate that 90 percent of a police officer's function is devoted to activities such as intervention in family problems that are related to controlling crime or enforcing laws. It is also found that most serious crimes occur within families or among people who know each other, rather than among strangers. Therefore, Bard feels that it is worthwhile to train policemen to discharge more effectively the service function that they are forced to perform in many everyday crisis situations.

Bard organized a demonstration project within a single precinct of New York City responsible for an area that includes about 85,000 people. A group of 18 patrolmen were selected from among 45 volunteers for the program and were trained intensively in behavioral principles for a one-month period by using on-campus course work, field trips, laboratory exercises involving role playing, and human relations workshops aimed at sensitizing the police officers to their own values and attitudes. In its operational phase, Bard's program continued for a period of about 21 months during which time one radio patrol car manned by his trainees was always available for dealing with family crises arising in the precinct. All complaints identifiable beforehand as involving family disturbances were referred to this particular car. Mental health backup support was provided through weekly discussion groups for 6 men at a time and by one-hour weekly consultations with an advanced clinical psychology student. This aspect of the program was mutually beneficial to the police officer who was thus provided with mental health expertise and to the student who derived from the interaction an opportunity to learn about the community.

The available information on the evaluation of this project (Bard, 1970; Bard, 1971) indicates that during the 21 months that it functioned, Bard's unit intervened in 1375 incidents involving 962 families. Despite the fact that intervention in family crisis situations ordinarily involves a relatively high risk of injury to the police officer, not one single injury was sustained by any member of the consultation program unit. During the same period, three patrolmen who were not part of the program but who worked in the same precinct did sustain injuries while responding to family disturbances. Community response to the unit appeared to be very positive as measured by a variety of indirect sources. Although homicides in New York City increased during the project period, there were none within the families dealt with by the unit. The number of assaults in the demonstration area was reduced, and the number of arrests for assault during the project period dropped. The apparent success of this demonstration project has led Bard (1971) to propose that a program of this kind be extended by developing police specialists to deal with problem groups such as adolescents and psychotics.

CONCLUSION

This chapter provides a sampling of the programs that have emerged in recent years to deal with the mental health problems of society. The few examples provided of very early "community" programs in urban areas suggest that recent efforts are far from novel. The urban problems of a large immigrant society, which characterized the United States at the turn of the century, are in many respects duplicated in modern urban areas where large numbers of disadvantaged individuals have migrated from other parts of the country. Crime, alcoholism, failure to take advantage of educational opportunities, and the like, typified the late 19th-century urban ghetto as much as it does the urban ghetto of today.

What is novel about current community efforts is that they are being spearheaded by mental health professionals. In the past the church, the sensitive, concerned members of the advantaged social classes, or the occasional politician were responsible for efforts to improve the lot of the impoverished and poorly educated. Currently the mental health specialist is becoming involved in the business of dealing with community problems, and the programs described are, in many instances, proliferating throughout the country.

Many of these programs involve other than traditional mental health problems and require other than a traditional role of the mental health worker. Often, political action aimed at improving destructive or growth-limiting environments, or the reorganization of social structures to make them more growth facilitating is required. Historically, workers in early community programs found it necessary to enter the political arena more or less directly to promote needed legislation and to struggle for social change. For the mental health professional, politics, dominated primarily by members of the legal profession, is a vast wilderness. And even if he is able to find his way around in this wilderness and to achieve some success, he is likely to find that the political model is useful for dealing with some problems, and is entirely ineffective with others that require a more purely psychological approach.

It is far too soon to judge which of the programs reviewed will be most effective and useful in the long run. Hopefully all will undergo careful testing and refinement, and will eventually become firmly established. As entirely new institutions, or in many cases, drastic modifications of older institutions, they face an uphill battle. Their acceptance will inevitably depend on their proven effectiveness as well as a willingness on the part of society to accept changes. More will be said about these issues in the chapters that follow.

References

Bard, M. Extending psychology's impact through existing community institutions. *American Psychologist*, 1969, *24*, 610–612.

Bard, M. Alternatives to traditional law enforcement. In E. F. Korten, S. W. Cook, & J. I. Lacey (Eds.), *Psychology and the problems of society*. Washington, D. C.: American Psychological Association, 1970. Pp. 128–132.

Bard, M. The role of law enforcement in the helping system. *Community Mental Health Journal*, 1971, *7*, 151–160.

Bard, M., & Berkowitz, B. Training police as specialists in family crisis intervention: a community psychology action program. *Community Mental Health Journal*, 1967, *3*, 315–317.

Bindman, A. J. Mental health consultation: theory and practice. *Journal of Consulting Psychology*, 1959, *23*, 473–482.

Caplan, G. *Principles of preventive psychiatry*. New York: Basic Books, 1964.

Fishman, J. R., Denham, W. H., Levine, M., & Shatz, E. O. *New careers for the disadvantaged in human service: report of a social experiment*. Washington, D. C.: Howard University Institute for Youth Studies, 1969.

Fishman, J. R., Klein, W. L., MacLennan, B. W., Mitchell, L., Pearl, A., & Walker, W. *Training for new careers.* Washington, D. C.: President's Committee on Juvenile Delinquency and Youth Crime, 1965.

Goldenberg, I. I. *Build me a mountain: youth poverty, and the creation of new settings.* Cambridge, Mass.: The MIT Press, 1971.

Hallowitz, E., & Riessman, F. The role of the indigenous nonprofessional in a community mental health neighborhood service center program. *American Journal of Orthopsychiatry,* 1967, *37,* 766–778.

Holden, A. C. *The settlement idea: a vision of social justice.* New York: Macmillan, 1922.

Klein, W. L. The training of human service aides. In E. L. Cowen, E. A. Gardner, & M. Zax (Eds.), *Emergent approaches to mental health problems.* New York: Appleton-Century-Crofts, 1967. Pp. 144–161.

Levine, M., & Levine, A. *A social history of the helping services.* New York: Appleton-Century-Crofts, 1970.

MacLennan, B. W., Klein, W. L., Pearl, A., & Fishman, J. R. Training for new careers. *Community Mental Health Journal,* 1966, *2,* 135–141.

McCord, W., McCord, J., & Zola, I. K. *Origins of crime: a new evaluation of the Cambridge-Somerville youth study.* New York: Columbia University Press, 1959.

Pearl, A., & Riessman, F. *New careers for the poor.* New York: Free Press, 1965.

Peck, H. B., & Kaplan, S. R. A mental health program for the urban multi-service center. In M. F. Shore, & F. V. Mannino (Eds.), *Mental health and the community:* problems, programs, and strategies. New York: Behavioral Publications, 1969. Pp. 123–142.

Peck, H. B., Kaplan, S. R., & Roman, M. Prevention treatment and social action: a strategy of intervention in a disadvantaged urban area. *American Journal of Orthopsychiatry,* 1966, *36,* 57–69.

Powers, E., & Witmer, H. *An experiment in the prevention of delinquency.* New York: Columbia University Press, 1951.

Rieman, D. W. Midway: a case study of community organization consultation. In M. F. Shore, & F. V. Mannino (Eds.), *Mental health and the community.* New York: Behavioral Publications, 1969. Pp. 41–58.

Riessman, F. A neighborhood-based mental health approach. In E. L. Cowen, E. A. Gardner, & M. Zax (Eds.), *Emergent approaches to mental health problems.* New York: Appleton-Century-Crofts, 1967. Pp. 162–184.

Riessman, F., & Popper, H. I. (Eds.). *Up from poverty: new career ladders for nonprofessionals.* New York: Harper & Row, 1968.

Sarason, I. G. Verbal learning, modeling, and juvenile delinquency. *American Psychologist,* 1968, *23,* 254–266.

Sarason, I. G., & Ganzer, V. J. Social influence techniques in clinical and community psychology. In C. D. Spielberger (Ed.), *Current topics in clinical and community psychology.* New York: Academic Press, 1969. Pp. 1–66.

Schwitzgebel, R. L. Delinquents with tape recorders. *New Society*, 1963, *1*, 11–13.

Schwitzgebel, R. L. *Streetcorner research*. Cambridge, Mass.: Harvard University Press, 1964.

Schwitzgebel, R. L. Short-term operant conditioning of adolescent offenders on socially relevant variables. *Journal of Abnormal Psychology*, 1967, 7, 134–142.

Schwitzgebel, R. L., & Kolb, D. A. Inducing behaviour change in adolescent delinquents. *Behavior Research & Therapy*, 1964, *1*, 297–304.

Slack, C. W. Experimenter-subject psychotherapy: a new method of introducing intensive office treatment for unreachable cases. *Mental Hygiene*, 1960 *44*, 238–256.

Slack, C. W. Score—a description. In *Experiments in culture expansion*. Sacramento, Cal.: California Department of Corrections, 1963. Pp. 59–64.

Spielberger, C. D. A mental health consultation program in a small community with limited professional mental health resources. In E. L. Cowen, E. A. Gardner, & M. Zax (Eds.), *Emergent approaches to mental health problems*. New York: Appleton-Century-Crofts, 1967. Pp. 214–236.

Stanfield, R. D., & Maher, B. A. Clinical and actuarial predictions of juvenile delinquency. In S. Wheeler, *Controlling delinquents*. New York: John Wiley, 1968. Pp. 245–270.

Zax, M., & Cowen, E. L. *Abnormal psychology: changing conceptions*. New York: Holt, Rinehart & Winston, 1972.

10. *the creation of growth – enhancing settings*

Each community program we have discussed thus far has been established within the confines of an ongoing community structure. Some programs have attempted to change the structure to improve the lives of all community members. More often, they have been directed toward individuals already manifesting either incipient or blatant signs of behavior disorder. In this chapter we examine actual attempts to create essentially new social structures. In some instances the motivation for these ambitious endeavors is fueled by utopian or religious ideals; in others the motivation derives from a wish to apply newly developed technology, both psychological and otherwise, to establishing living situations that will lead to an improvement in the quality of man's life.

The dream of building an ideal living situation is probably nearly as old as civilized man. Man's earliest conceptions of an afterlife in some heavenly domain very likely contained in them the seeds for later active attempts to create ideal living situations here on earth. Many literary figures, dating back hundreds of years, have described plans for ideal or utopian societies. Fairfield (1971) identifies the earliest actual attempt at establishing a utopian society as that of the Essenes, a solitary group living on the shores of the Dead Sea, between the second century B.C. and the second century A.D. This was a group of celibate men who worked at their own particular specialties but who pooled ownership of their property. Members of this Judaic sect lived separately in dwellings scattered through a number of towns and villages but shared and consumed the products of their labors collectively. Between the 11th and 17th centuries in Europe a number of other minor religious sects formed communal living societies, drawn together by the persecution of outsiders, where they shared ideals and values.

In the United States during the 19th century occurred a number of experiments in communal living designed to satisfy utopian ideals. Kanter (1972) has identified three forms of dissatisfaction with organized society that prompt the quest for a utopian community. The first concerns the failure of the typical society to live up to certain religious ideals. Many who have been drawn to utopian communities have wished to be with others whose religious values coincided with their own, and to share their lives in harmonious coexistence. A second source of dissatisfaction relates to the political and economic character of established institutions. For example, the 19th-century socialist communities were, in many cases, reacting against the growing factory system, the dehumanization they sensed in the competitive economic system of the United States, and the fact that a large number of individuals worked extraordinarily hard for the primary benefit of relatively few. The third type of dissatisfaction that has caused the development of new communities, particularly in recent years, centers around unhappiness with society's psychosocial character. Individuals thus concerned are distressed about the alienation and loneliness experienced in modern society. They feel that people are out of touch with each other and even with their own basic inner nature. For this reason, soceity's heavy emphasis on achievement is rejected in favor of "self-actualization" or "personal growth" as central ideals. Man is seen to need liberation from society's typical constraints, and must be freed to achieve intimacy, psychological growth, and to "do his own thing."

Another significant social development of recent years is a move toward the planning and creation of entire communities to house, in some instances, literally thousands of people. These planned communities are inspired less by utopian ideals of a religious, political, or psychosocial nature than they are by an awareness that the typical city, which developed haphazardly in response to a variety of unplanned forces, does not present the best type of living situation for modern man. Instead, it is believed that by combining man's best efforts with respect to architecture, various types of technology, and sociological and psychological understanding, entirely new communities can be built that will be more comfortable, healthier, and happier places in which to live than is the city or town as we know it.

We are concerned here, then, with both types of new communities, the utopian society as well as the planned community. Each represents an effort to create an optimal living situation. Each has the goal of helping man to grow more strongly and to live more happily than he is able to do in modern-day society.

PERSPECTIVES ON COMMUNAL LIVING SITUATIONS

Kanter (1970, 1972) has reviewed and compared the experience of a large number of 19th-century utopian communities. Her work provides a valuable backdrop for classifying and understanding the commune movement as it is developing today, and the problems it faces.

Kanter views the utopian community as stemming from a particular set of ideals concerning man and the possibilities for his living a healthy, rewarding social life. The first of these ideals is the notion that human perfectability is possible. Most basic to this belief is the idea that whatever tensions, conflicts, and disharmonies exist in social situations, they stem not from man's inner being but are inflicted on him by the social conditions in which he must live. Thus the creation of a better society will free him and allow him to live on a higher plane than he had ever known. A second ideal is a tremendous faith in the value of order. General society is seen to be chaotic, purposeless, and wasteful in many of its functions, and it is believed that the carefully planned utopian community can coordinate human affairs in such a way that every member's welfare will be assured. In some of today's communes this value is emphasized through the title "Intentional Community." In the utopian community, therefore, all events have purpose and contribute toward the group's shared values.

A third significant value in the utopian community is brotherhood. Man's social world is thought to be potentially harmonious with the universe's natural laws and, analogously, individuals are thought to be capable of living harmoniously with one another. Such harmony is enhanced by removing the "artificial" barriers between people that result in competition, jealousy, and conflict and prevent the development of natural relationships. Erasing these barriers entails substituting community property for individual possessions, the sharing of necessary work and, perhaps, even the sharing of family and love life.

A fourth value of the utopian society is the merging of physical and intellectual-spiritual pursuits. Thus physical labor holds high status in the commune and is even considered to be a basic condition for mental well-being. In fact, many utopians have believed that intellectual or spiritual experiences could only be expressed through bodily states. A fifth value for builders of utopian societies is experimentation. Since the establishment of the utopian community is itself a drastic experiment, compared with the usual way people live, a marked predisposition exists for experimenting within the community. Consequencely, practices are occasionally initiated that are illegal in the larger society. This exposes the utopian community to potential confrontation with law enforcement officials. Nonetheless, a wide variety of experimental practices are found in utopian communities; these include dietary experiments, the use of drugs, and the practice of yoga or astrology. A final value characterizing most utopian communities is pride in the community's uniqueness and coherence as a group. Commune members are acutely sensitive to their place in history and to their own particular boundaries. Unlike people in the larger society who are only vaguely aware of who belongs in their social community, in most utopian communities members know precisely who belongs, what the community stands for, and how it is different from the outside community.

In many instances the ideals impelling the development of communal societies prompt utopians to return to the land where they can carve out a circumscribed area separated from the larger society. There, they can achieve a simpler, more natural life than is found in the more complex urban setting. In the farm setting, the necessary physical labor is seen by utopians to help to integrate the body and the mind. Since special skills are not required in such a setting, jobs can be shared, thus eliminating specialization and the development of a status hierarchy based on individual talents. The rural living arrangement fosters an idealized harmony and brotherhood and also helps the group to maintain a clear identity, and to distinguish itself from the surrounding society.

Between the Revolutionary and Civil wars almost 100 utopian communities were established in the United States. A few were to survive many years (one more than a century), while others dissolved in less than a year. By using survival for an extended period as a criterion of success, Kanter (1972) has compared 9 successful 19th-century utopian communities (surviving, at least, 33 years) with 21 unsuccessful communities established during the same period (existing for less than 16 years). The difference between the successful and the unsuccessful community is considered by Kanter to reside in the degree to which they are capable of building commitments among their members. Commitment is, in turn, affected by the organizational structure through which the work necessary to meet both a community's survival needs as well as the ideals that prompted the establishment of the community gets done. In the long run, therefore, the success of the community demands its members' commitment to necessary work, to the community's basic values, to each other, and to the degree to which members are willing to give up their own independence when it interferes with group interests. Because the utopian community has separated from a larger social order, there is constant competition for the loyalty of members between the new community and the larger society. Maintenance of good communal relations requires that what the person is willing to give up to the group, both behaviorally and emotionally, and what the group requires of him be closely coordinated and mutually reinforcing.

Commitment Mechanisms Characterizing 19th Century Communes

Kanter identifies six processes that built commitment to communal groups in 19th-Century communes. They are sacrifice, investment, renunciation, communion, mortification, and transcendence.

Sacrifice

The process of sacrifice requires the recruit to give something up as his price for becoming a group member. Presumably the more he must give up, the more valuable will he regard his membership in the group. A variety of sacrifices were required for membership in 19th-century communities. Abstinance from alcohol, tobacco, coffee, tea, and rich foods or meat are examples. In modern-day communes similar sacrifices are sometimes seen such as the requirement that one abandon drug use or adopt a vegetarian diet. Forms of sacrifice such as sexual abstinence, and avoidance of personal adornments like jewelry and attractive clothing were also practiced in the 19th century. Yet another was a commitment to an austere life-style devoid of comforts and luxuries. One measure of the austerity of its life was whether the community built its own dwellings. Activity of this kind involves considerable struggle and commitment, and at its conclusion concrete signs of a communal effort remain. Table 1 compares successful and unsuccessful 19th-century communes with respect to these various sacrifice mechanisms.

Investment

The individual who makes a heavy investment in the group has a serious stake in its future. Such an investment can consist of material that would make it costly for him to leave the group, but it also can involve intangibles such as time and energy. Thus the utopian community should not have nonresident members who share in group benefits without being totally active participants. One must be either "in" or "out" of the group.

Members of successful communes became integrated with the group's economic system by donating their money to the group, assigning any

Table 1. Proportion of Successful and Unsuccessful 19th-Century Communes Having Sacrifice Mechanisms at Any Time in Their History (from Kanter, 1972).

Sacrifice Mechanism	Successful Communities		Unsuccessful Communities	
	n/N^a	Percent	n/N^a	Percent
Abstinence				
Oral abstinence	7/9	78	11/20	55
Celibacy	9/9	100	2/21	9
Other abstinence	5/7	71	4/14	28
Austerity				
Built own buildings	9/9	100	18/21	83

[a]N represents the number of communities for which the presence or absence of the mechanism was ascertainable; n represents the number in which the mechanism was present.

property that they might own to the community, and transferring to the community anything they earned while members. Furthermore, these investments were emphasized by their irreversibility. In many communities records were not even kept of what was donated by individual members. Also, if a member elected to leave the group, the successful community rarely reimbursed him for any material things that he had brought into the group or for what he had contributed by his years of service and labor. Table 2 compares successful and unsuccessful 19th-century communes with respect to investment mechanisms.

Renunciation

Since relationships outside of the group as well as within group subunits threaten to disrupt group commitment and cohesion, successful communal groups of the 19th-century tended to require the renunciation of these diluting influences. As a member's options for relationships outside of the group decrease, the potential for his gaining his primary satisfaction within the group increases. In the ideal case he becomes completely dependent on the group for all satisfactions. Renunciation processes can involve the world outside of the communal society, the couple within the group, and the family.

Successful 19th-century utopian communities limited the amount of contact with the outside society. One way of enforcing such a barrier was through geographic isolation. Many 19th-century communal societies were, at least, five miles away from neighbors or towns. Access to the community was made difficult, and outsiders lived far from the immediate

Table 2.   Proportion of Successful and Unsuccessful 19th-Century Communes Having Investment Mechanisms at Any Time in Their History (from Kanter, 1972)

Investment Mechanism	Successful Communities		Unsuccessful Communities	
	n/N^a	Percent	n/N^a	Percent
Physical participation				
Nonresident members prohibited	6/7	86	7/17	41
Financial investment				
Financial contribution for admission	4/9	44	9/20	45
Property signed over at admission	9/9	100	9/20	45
Group-assigned property received while member	4/7	57	6/14	43
Irreversibility of investment				
No records of contributions	4/8	50	4/14	28
Defectors not reimbursed for property—official policy	3/7	43	5/12	42
Defectors not reimbursed for property—in practice	2/6	33	0/6	0
Defectors not reimbursed for labor—official policy	6/7	86	7/13	54
Defectors not reimbursed for labor—in practice	6/7	86	3/9	33

$^a N$ represents the number of communities for which the presence or absence of the mechanism was ascertainable; n represents the number in which the mechanism was present.

area. The community became an entirely self-sustaining unit. Language and dress styles became distinctive and served to create boundaries for separating the community from the outside. In successful communities, movements across their boundaries were carefully controlled so that regular members tended to leave the community less frequently than once a year. Likewise, the presence of nonmembers in the community was very carefully regulated. Rules were established to restrict interactions between members and visitors.

The regulation of two-person intimacy was also regarded as extraordinarily necessary in successful communities. Two-person attachments, particularly those involving sexual attraction, were seen to represent serious competition for the devotion of the members' energies and loyalties to the group. Thus communities that managed to survive had strict policies about intimacy which were designed to restrain the formation of dyads. Two extremes were commonly practiced: at one pole complete celibacy was enforced, whereas at the other free love, including group marriage, was practiced. In the latter case, every group member was expected to be intimate sexually with every other group member. Private ties were minimized and, in a free love situation, any signs that one particular couple were becoming overly attached to each other were counteracted by the requirement that each circulate among other group members.

Just as the dyad threatened group cohesion, so did the family. Thus in a high proportion of successful communes families did not live in a single dwelling as a unit. Children were separated from parents, often to be raised in a separate children's residence by community members assigned to this task. Table 3 compares successful and unsuccessful 19th-century communes with respect to various renunciation mechanisms.

Table 3. Proportion of Successful and Unsuccessful 19th-Century Communes Having Renunciation Mechanisms at Any Time in Their History (from Kanter, 1972)

Renunciation Mechanism	Successful Communities		Unsuccessful Communities	
	n/N^a	Percent	n/N^a	Percent
Insulation				
Ecological separation	9/9	100	21/21	100
Institutional completeness (medical services provided)	7/7	100	10/18	55
Special term for outside	4/7	57	0/17	0
Outside conceived as evil and wicked	2/7	28	0/19	0
Uniform worn	8/9	89	5/17	30
Foreign language spoken	5/9	56	3/21	14
Slang, jargon, other special terms	2/9	22	2/19	11
Outside newspapers ignored	3/6	50	1/16	6
American patriotic holidays ignored	3/4	75	4/6	67
Crossboundary control				
Average member rarely leaving community	2/2	100	0/7	0
Rules for interaction with visitors	3/7	43	1/15	7
Renunciation of couple				
Free love or celibacy	9/9	100	6/21	29
Controls on free love, celibacy, or sexual relations	7/9	78	1/21	5
Renunciation of family				
Parent-child separation	3/8	48	3/20	15
Families not sharing a dwelling unit	3/9	33	1/20	5

$^a N$ represents the number of communities for which the presence or absence of the mechanism was ascertainable; n represents the number in which the mechanism was present.

Communion

The term communion refers to a sense of belonging, a sense of being part of the group as a whole and an immersion of oneself in the group to the degree that one has an equal opportunity both to contribute and to benefit. The "we" feeling is strong when a true sense of communion exists and former social ties are completely severed so that one becomes totally absorbed in the community.

The feeling of communion was fostered in successful 19th-century communities by several factors. One was the homogeneity of the background of many who made up these communities. Often they shared a common religion, had similar social or educational roots, or were of the same national or ethnic origin. Less successful groups were more heterogeneous collections of individuals banding together in response to an impersonal notice such as a newspaper advertisement.

Another factor that fostered a sense of communion was the enforced sharing of all goods and property. Generally, in the successful community all property was turned over to the group, which owned the land, the buildings, the furniture, the tools, and any equipment used by the community. In some cases, even the clothing worn by members was regarded as community property and was drawn from a common pool with little regard for sizes or styles.

Another factor promoting a sense of communion was the fact that all group members rotated through all necessary jobs and received equal reward for their efforts. Specialization was not permitted in most successful communities where admission was not based on preferences for special types of skills, artistry, intelligence, or technical knowledge. Rotating jobs had the effect of eliminating the concept of a career among community members.

Another communion-fostering technique was the regularization of group contacts. Members were rarely left alone, and frequent group meetings were held requiring the attendance of all members. In successful utopias such meetings might convene as often as once a day. Associated with these structured group contacts was the development in successful communities of group rituals. Many successful utopias emphasized group singing, even writing their own songs. Special community occasions were celebrated, for instance, significant dates in the community's history.

Finally, the persecution suffered by many of the 19th-century experimental communities at the hands of the larger society also was a force for creating communion among its members. Facing a common enemy tended to bind group members together. The persecution inflicted on such experimental communities ranged from public denouncement in the newspapers to economic discrimination and, at times, even to physical force through mob violence.

Table 4 compares the communion mechanisms characterizing successful and unsuccessful experimental communities of the 19th century.

Table 4.   Proportion of Successful and Unsuccessful 19th-Century Communes Having Communion Mechanisms at Any Time in Their History (from Kanter, 1972)

Communion Mechanism	Successful Communities		Unsuccessful Communities	
	n/N[a]	Percent	n/N[a]	Percent
Homogeneity				
Common religious background	8/9	89	10/20	50
Similar economic and educational status	7/8	88	10/16	63
Common ethnic background	6/9	67	3/20	15
Prior acquaintance of members	8/8	100	17/20	85
Communal sharing				
Property signed-over at admission	9/9	100	9/20	45
Group assigned property received while member	4/7	57	6/14	43
Land owned by community	8/9	89	16/21	76
Buildings owned by community	8/9	89	15/21	71
Furniture, tools, equipment owned by community	8/8	100	15/19	79
Clothing and personal effects owned by community	6/9	67	5/18	28
Legal title in name of community (not individuals)	7/8	88	18/21	83
Communal labor				
No compensation for labor	8/8	100	7/17	41
No charge for community services	7/7	100	9/19	47
No skills required for admission	7/8	88	13/17	77
Job rotation	3/6	50	8/18	44
Communal work efforts	7/7	100	7/14	50
Regularized group contact				
Communal dwellings	3/9	33	14/21	67
Communal dining halls	5/9	56	15/19	79
Little opportunity or place for privacy	2/9	22	2/16	13
More than two thirds of typical day spent with other members	5/8	63	3/13	23
Regular group meetings	9/9	100	13/16	81
Daily group meetings	5/9	56	1/16	6
Ritual				
Songs about community	5/8	63	2/14	14
Group singing	7/7	100	8/11	73
Special community celebrations	5/6	83	5/10	50
Persecution experience				
Violence or economic discrimination	5/8	63	10/20	50

[a]N represents the number of communities for which the presence or absence of the mechanism was ascertainable; n represents the number in which the mechanism was present.

Mortification

The term mortification refers to the destruction of one's sense of a private ego in favor of a new identity whose meaningfulness is based on group membership. As a result of mortification, self-esteem derives from one's commitment to group rather than to personal standards. From this viewpoint, to be worthwhile one must live up to the model offered by the community. The mortification process entails stripping away a person's earlier identity, making him dependent on authority, and making him insecure in his role until he has learned what the group expects of him. In religious groups this process is related to a concern with erasing the "sin of pride." Often individuals come to experimental communities precisely to have their identity changed and may refer to this process by terms other than mortification, for example, "personal growth." Within the community itself the mortification procedure is felt to be proof of the fact that the group cares about the individual, about what he thinks and feels.

Mechanisms for promoting mortification include confession, self-criticism, and mutual criticism among group members. Many successful 19th-century communes encouraged the individual to "bare his soul," to admit weaknesses, and to confess his imperfections. The group was permitted to pry into the most intimate matters relating to the individual. In many instances, new members were required to confess misconduct engaged in before joining the community. Not uncommonly these confessions were made before the entire group.

Public punishment was another mortification process. It was, of course, embarrassing and impressed on each member that his status in the organization was always in question. Publicly visible sanctions were carried out against deviants from the group in most successful communities.

Still another mortification mechanism practiced in successful 19th-century groups was the awarding of status to members on the basis of how well they were able to live up to group standards and to identify with the community. In a sense, this distinguished members on spiritual-moral grounds. Those considered to be more spiritual, more moral, or more zealous received greater respect from the group.

Finally, the mortification procedure also involved reducing all members to a single common denominator to encourage group identity. The use of uniform dress styles was one mechanism for achieving this commonality as, similarly, were communal dwellings and dining halls.

Table 5 contrasts successful and unsuccessful 19th-century communes with respect to mortification mechanisms.

Table 5. Proportion of Successful and Unsuccessful 19th-Century Communes Having Mortification Mechanisms at Any Time in Their History (from Kanter, 1972)

Mortification Mechanism	Successful Communities		Unsuccessful Communities	
	n/N^a	Percent	n/N^a	Percent
Confession and mutual criticism				
Regular confession	4/9	44	0/20	0
Confession upon joining	4/8	50	0/19	0
Mutual criticism or group confession	4/9	44	3/19	26
Mutual surveillance	2/7	29	0/17	0
Surveillance by leaders	3/7	43	1/17	6
Sanctions				
Public denouncement of deviants	6/9	67	3/16	19
Removal of a privilege of membership	2/8	25	2/16	12
Participation in a community funcion prohibited	3/8	38	2/15	14
Deviants punished within community more often than expelled from it	4/6	67	2/5	40
Spiritual differentiation				
Members distinguished on moral grounds	5/9	56	3/20	15
Formally structured deference to those of higher moral status	4/9	44	1/20	5
No skill or intelligence distinctions	9/9	100	15/17	88
Instruction in community doctrines	3/8	38	2/11	18
Learning of rules and dictates required	2/8	25	2/11	18
New members segregated from old	2/7	28	0/17	0
Formal probationary period with limited privileges for new members	5/8	63	8/15	53
Deindividuation				
Uniform worn	8/9	89	5/17	30
Communal dwellings	3/9	33	14/21	67
Communal dining halls	5/9	56	15/19	79
Same meals eaten by all	3/7	43	4/10	40

[a]N represents the number of communities for which the presence or absence of the mechanism was ascertainable; n represents the number in which the mechanism was present.

Transcendence

The term, transcendence, refers to man's need to consider himself as a part of some comforting, all-embracing structure along with others who feel similarly and who recognize his individual existence. Kanter points out that achieving this sense of transcendence requires the feeling that the community is the repository of great power and meaning. To some extent a feeling of this kind is communicated to group members by a charismatic leader. Successful 19th-century communities tended to invest power in leaders who possessed awe-inspiring qualities. Furthermore, demands made on group members were often seen to emanate from a higher principle or power such as justice, the people, nature's will, or God's will.

One way of institutionalizing awe to maximize the sense of transcendence was to maximize the distance between the higher level decision makers and the ordinary members who might participate in making day-to-day decisions. Another means was to cloak the administrative apparatus in mystery to encourage moral conviction and absolute obedience. Charismatic leaders were often assumed to possess special sources of power and to be a link between members and some higher repository of wisdom. To encourage this feeling, leaders of successful communities often lived apart from the rest of the community, enjoyed privileges not available to the ordinary membership, and were addressed by special titles.

Another mechanism for encouraging the sense of transcendence was the establishment of rigid order over the lives of community members. Most successful communities had fixed daily routines throughout their history. Philosophical guides for behavior were provided. Free time and recreation was programmed in line with the group's ideals. In some groups the program extended all the way to the procedure to be used in dressing oneself.

Another mechanism to enhance transcendence was the requirement that members undergo a conversion to the ideology of the movement. Most successful 19th-century communities require a "test of faith" before one could join.

Finally, transcendence was facilitated by traditions. It was an asset, therefore, if a particular community could build on a prior organization of some duration that provided a ready-made tradition.

Table 6 compares successful and unsuccessful communities with respect to transcendence mechanisms.

Issues Raised by Kanter's Study

The first question that might be raised about Kanter's study of 19th-century communal living situations is whether longevity is a proper crite-

Table 6. Proportion of Successful and Unsuccessful 19th-Century Communes Having Transcendence Mechanisms at Any Time in Their History (from Kanter, 1972)

Transcendence Mechanism	Successful Communities		Unsuccessful Communities	
	n/N^a	Percent	n/N^a	Percent
Institutionalized awe (ideology)				
Ideology explained essential nature of humanity	9/9	100	16/19	84
Ideology a complete, elaborated philosophical system	8/9	89	15/20	75
Power invested in persons with special, magical characteristics	7/9	78	4/21	20
Demands legitimated by reference to a higher principle	9/9	100	11/19	58
Special, magical powers imputed to members	8/9	89	3/20	15
Possession of special powers as evidence of good standing	6/8	75	2/19	10
Ideology related community to figures of historical importance	8/9	89	5/21	24
Values formed ultimate justification for decisions	6/7	86	7/17	41
Institutionalized awe (power and authority)				
Authority hierarchy	4/9	44	8/20	40
Top leaders were founders or were named or groomed by predecessors	9/9	100	10/20	50
No impeachment or recall privileges	7/8	88	7/12	58
Special leadership prerogatives	7/9	78	3/18	16
Special leadership immunities	5/8	63	3/18	16
Separate, special residence for leaders	6/8	75	1/15	7
Special forms of address for leaders	6/9	67	2/19	10
Irrational basis for decisions	4/7	57	3/20	15
Guidance				
Fixed daily routine	6/6	100	8/15	54
Detailed specification of routine	4/6	67	2/15	13
Personal conduct rules (demeanor)	5/8	63	6/19	31
Ideological conversion				
Commitment to ideology required	5/9	56	4/21	19
Recruits expected to take vows	7/8	88	6/21	29
Procedure for choosing members	6/8	75	13/17	77
Prospective members often rejected	3/6	50	6/11	54
Tests of faith for community children to receive adult membership status	7/9	78	5/21	24

Tradition

Community derived from prior organization or organized group	7/9	78	13/21	62
Prior organization in existence at least 10 years before	5/9	56	1/21	5

[a]N represents the number of communities for which the presence or absence of the mechanism was ascertainable; n represents the number in which the mechanism was present.

rion of success. Clearly it is an easy one to measure, which makes it immediately attractive in an area where criteria of success are ordinarily very complex. Kanter argues that such a criterion for evaluating 19th-century utopian societies is valid simply on the grounds that the overriding goal of many of these communities was little more than to exist. Enormous energies were devoted to simply creating a viable social organization embodying a particular set of ideals. Another argument for the validity of such a criterion is that since members had a free choice to join or leave the experimental communities, the fact that they remained within a given community for a very long time is, at least, an indirect indication that they were receiving within that society the satisfaction of many of the needs that had brought them there.

Another very significant aspect of Kanter's study that merits close consideration is the set of forces leading to the dissolution of these utopian communities. Even the most successful of the 19th-century communes eventually were disbanded. The reasons for their dissolution rarely involved an inability to cope with the hardships and problems of communal life. More generally, the group was unable to cope with the dilemma posed by longevity itself. Sometimes the ideals that originally inspired the formation of the community were dissipated by the practical demands of existence. In other cases it was not possible for a community to adapt to the demands of a changing environment and still maintain its integrity. Most communities suffered an erosion of membership because their founders grew old and the second generation did not stay with the group. Several factors played a role in the breakup of even successful groups.

Natural Disasters, Financial Problems, and Internal Disagreements

Many unsuccessful 19th-century communes failed because they could not withstand a variety of problems that more successful communities managed to overcome. In one case an epidemic of fever led to a commune's end whereas a long-lasting community survived severe bouts of malaria. In other cases, fires that caused serious material damage resulted in an end to utopian experiments. In some instances the pressure from neighbors forced groups to scatter and leave an area, and the motivation and energy to regroup was not forthcoming. Successful communes were often forced to move and yet managed to maintain their integrity as a group. Among the internal problems leading to the destruction of some groups were the growth of schisms within the group, major dissension among its members, and challenges to established leadership. Most problems of this kind were overcome in successful groups without leading to the community's early demise.

The Changing Environment

Inevitably environments change and the original members of communal groups grow old. Failure to adapt to environmental change can make the group obsolescent and lead to its eventual death. To survive, the group must find a way of dealing with the changes that take place in the external society. A variety of options are possible. Changes may be ignored entirely, or efforts may be made to incorporate them. Dealing with change by ignoring it involves the risk that it will not be possible to keep change from intruding on the group. Technological advance, for example, leading to improved transportation and better communication systems, inevitably threatened the isolation of many 19th-century utopian communities. Ignoring these factors led to much discontentment among group members, and a failure to deal with them eventually caused erosion of the basis for the community. The alternative approach of attempting to incorporate external changes into the group is fraught with its own dangers. The adaptations necessary for accommodating to a changing environment often drastically alter the community in a way that undermines the communal base. In some instances it led to the gradual introduction of goods, life-styles, and fashions from the outside world along with a tendency to be drawn away from the community and toward the individualism and materialism characteristic of the surrounding society. Early 19th-century communities had the advantage that they existed at a time when external change was relatively slow. Modern-day communes are confronted by a rapidly changing society and for survival must attempt to develop techniques for dealing with them.

The Problems of Aging, Recruitment, and Maintaining a Hold on the Second Generation

The obvious fact that people grow old and die confronts the utopian society with a problem that may be faced in one of several ways. One is to decide that the group will not outlast the life of its last member. From this viewpoint, the group's existence clearly is time-limited, but it must struggle with the problems of a steadily aging population and the difficulties a group of this kind encounters in maintaining itself. The growing infirmities of group members, for example, makes it necessary to bring outsiders into the community to perform the physical tasks necessary to maintaining life.

If a group wishes to survive beyond the life span of its oldest members, it has two options: it can attempt to recruit new members, or it must raise its own children to perpetuate the community. Both approaches presented difficulties for 19th-century utopias. The Shakers who managed to survive more than 100 years, despite the fact that they were a celibate community, recruited new members very actively and sometimes took in entire families or orphans. Most reports indicate, however, that many of the children taken in and raised by the community refused to remain in it when they were old enough to have a free choice. The second generation simply failed to maintain the commitment to the community that characterized their parents who had entered out of free choice. Apparently they failed to share the needs drawing their parents into the communal society and, in many cases, they resented commitments that their parents had made for them.

Recruiting outsiders for the community poses its own special problems. Not infrequently recruits were dissident members. Sometimes they challenged the established leadership of the group. In addition, the recruiting effort itself can consume much time and energy. Furthermore, often the social problems that had prompted the group's original members to band together were sufficiently mitigated that the life in the utopian community was in a less favorable position to compete with life outside.

Aging also posed problems for those communities whose survival depended on the leadership of a charismatic founder. Some communities succeeded in many respects without being able to outlive the death of their first great leader.

The Conflict Entailed in Trying to Serve Two Facets of Social Life

The twofold aims of the 19th-century utopian communities were to provide a rich interpersonal experience full of meaning and significant values while they also fulfilled all of the practical, political, economic, and physical needs of their members. Because, in some measure, this combination of aims is inherently contradictory the term utopian itself has come to connote impracticality.

Kanter indicates that the tension created by the pulls toward the two somewhat contradictory aspects of the community's life was a factor in virtually all of the 19th-century communes she studied. Most communes were not content to exist as simple agricultural societies but tried also to produce enough goods and services to enter into commercial and political relations with the larger society. This introduces several problems. To deal with external systems requires an organizational structure reaching out to the larger society. Commercial ventures must be informed about the environmental system in which they will be dealing. Entering into large-scale businesses requires labor, often more than can be provided by commune members alone. This means that outsiders must be brought across the boundaries of the experimental community, and the resulting boundary permeability conflicts with some of the commitment mechanisms necessary for maintaining the community's integrity. Furthermore, as it becomes easier to pass in and out of the system, experts must be introduced to run certain facets of the business, and their goals will primarily be the success of the venture rather than the values that promoted the development of the experimental community in the first place.

For many 19th-century communes, even the successful ones, commitment could be maintained at its highest level during the building stage when production and trade with the environment was of secondary importance. Once the community had managed to establish itself, however, commercial and political interchange with the larger society grew in importance and eventually "conducting business" began to supersede and to conflict with the maintenance of community feeling. By the time even successful experimental communities had run their course, most of their commitment mechanisms had disappeared, and members no longer maintained allegiance to the group.

Prosperity and the Decline of the Community

Another problem that contributed to the decline of many utopian 19th-century communities was, paradoxically, their own material success. Financial prosperity, not uncommonly, helped hasten decline not only because it was associated with the growth of an efficient commercial organization, and all of the problems that that entailed, but also because a prosperous community tended to attract members who are more interested in prosperity than in the community's original ideals. Furthermore, financial prosperity led to competitiveness among individuals and families and to a preference for private rather than shared ownership.

THE 20TH CENTURY UTOPIAN COMMUNITY

The experimental communities of the 20th century, particularly those in the United States, are mainly phenomena of the 1950s and 1960s. A much older movement, and one that in many ways closely parallels those of the 19th century is the kibbutz movement in Israel. The oldest of the Israeli kibbutzim has been in existence for more than 60 years.

The Israeli Kibbutz

In many respects, the kibbutz, as described by Spiro (1970), closely parallels in form as well as in guiding ideals many successful 19th-century utopian communities. A kibbutz is usually an isolated agricultural community with firm boundaries which hold its members tightly within the fold. It is a community in which physical labor and, particularly, the most onerous of physical chores, are held in the highest esteem. All property is held by the community, with members usually contributing all the worldly goods they own when they join the group and take from it only what they need. In some cases even clothing is community property and members draw what they need from a central supply responsible for a communal laundering operation. Group members are not encouraged to have contact with the outside community and relationships with visitors are limited.

The significance of family structure in the kibbutz community is played down. In many kibbutzim, children are regarded as children of the community, and are not raised by their parents but by workers assigned to such duties in a communal nursery.

In the kibbutz described by Spiro the terms marriage, husband, and wife are not used because they connote a tie between individuals that might interfere with ties to the group. Instead, men and women who wish to live together are regarded as having become a "pair." Instead of acquiring a husband, a woman acquires a "young man" or a "companion." Likewise the man acquires a "young woman" or a "companion." Divorces might occur frequently, but they entail few hardships since no legal problems are involved.

In the kibbutz, moral values are indistinguishable from group values. Maintaining the group and group processes in the kibbutz are regarded as the highest moral ends toward which anyone can strive. This requires that the individual subordinate all of his own interests to those of the group. Furthermore, when individual needs conflict with those of the group, it is the individual who must give way. This applies equally to vocational interests as well as to ideological values. All of an individual's motivations are expected to be directed toward promoting the group's interests. Thus each individual is responsible for the welfare of the kibbutz as a whole.

Another aspect of this attitude toward the group is that to wish for privacy is regarded as "queer." Much more highly valued are group living and group experiences. The ultimate criterion of whether a kibbutz has achieved success in its organization is the degree to which it radiates group spirit.

Eisenstadt (1967) has discussed recent changes which are taking place in the social organization of kibbutzim. Some of these changes seem peculiar to the situation of the kibbutz in Israel; however, others are reminiscent of many described in Kanter's discussion of 19th-century American utopian societies. The Israeli kibbutzim enjoyed an elite status at one time because they fostered the settlement of a yet undeveloped country, because they formed defensive outposts of the new state, and because they served an important need by absorbing new immigrants to the country. As Israel developed as a nation, the significance of the original roles filled by kibbutzim diminished and to some extent, their elite status was weakened. In addition, however, the kibbutzim have experienced economic changes that have had significant effects on their organization.

A most significant factor in contributing to the change of kibbutz structure was that through a gradual transition the kibbutz, which was once populated almost exclusively by young men and women, came to be made up mainly of middle aged family units with a sprinkling of old, mostly retired people, and youngsters representing the second and even third generation of community members. Thus the population changed from a relatively homogeneous one with respect to age to one that was widely heterogeneous. These changes in the makeup of kibbutz membership are considered by Eisenstadt to have altered many traditional kibbutz values such as equality, the allocation of rewards according to needs, the simplicity and modesty of life, the place of manual labor in the social system, the status of collective production and consumption, and the direct-democracy form of government.

Originally, in the kibbutz goods were distributed on a highly uniform basis with each member assured that no other member would receive more than he did. By 1960, members were given annual budgets of equivalent size which they could use to purchase goods from a general store. Thus individual choices became possible whereby individual members could decide for themselves how austerely they would live in some respects and how extravagant they might be in other respects.

With respect to productivity, whereas the kibbutz once valued agriculture and manual labor as major ends for their own sake, material achievement has begun to receive growing recognition and to this end greater and greater agricultural diversification has been introduced. Industrial ventures have been undertaken in the kibbutz, and the profitability of these enterprises has come to take on significance to the community.

Along with these changes, have come changes with respect to the types of jobs performed by kibbutz members. Formerly, no member was supposed to be identified with a single specialty. Workers rotated through all jobs that needed to be done. Eventually a need arose for specialists, and only those jobs requiring managerial skills or low level service functions were rotated. Eisenstadt reports that, in time, even this distinction began breaking down. Leadership positions, which are still allocated largely by elections, do rotate, but only among a very small group of members. Likewise, service functions such as kitchen and laundry work, work in the general store, and in the children's house are more and more falling to the same people for increasing periods of time.

With the economic expansion of many of the kibbutzim, another problem involving the hiring of outside labor has been introduced. Formerly, this practice was strictly forbidden by kibbutz ideology. Economic expansion, however, resulted in a constant shortage of labor, so that hired help had to be brought in from the surrounding areas.

The sheer physical growth of the kibbutz has made it necessary to abandon the "general assembly" form of government which typified its early days. Decision making has fallen into the hands of specialists and elected officials, with the general assembly now functioning mainly as a forum for receiving information and for communicating ideas.

Early attempts by the kibbutz to diminish the role of the family in the social structure have also been reversed. It was originally expected that a weakening of the family structure would cause the second generation to identify more closely with the collective than with the family unit. This, according to Eisenstadt, has not turned out to be the case, with more and more kibbutzim finding new functions and values in family life. Children seem closer to parents than they once were, and although they still do not sleep at home in a family unit, a family spirit is clearly present, and families are increasingly coming together for meals and other private occasions.

All kibbutz children receive a similar education and all complete high school regardless of their special talents. The best students are sent on for higher education outside of the kibbutz with the hope that they will return to the community to become teachers. Eisenstadt reports that, on the whole, the second generation has remained faithful to the kibbutz movement and its ideals. There are some notable exceptions, however. Many of the younger generation prefer to organize their own kibbutzim in line with their own pioneering values. Others abandon the kibbutz in favor of city life because of conflicts with kibbutz ideals or with their parents. In some instances they leave to seek a higher standard of life and the possibility of a specialized career.

It is difficult to predict what the eventual fate of the kibbutz movement in Israel will be. Clearly these experimental communities served a vital role in the growth of the country and in the lives of those who elected to join them. It does appear, however, that, in Kanter's terms, the commitment mechanisms are weakening and the boundaries between the kibbutz and the larger society are becoming more permeable. Although from Kanter's viewpoint, many of the kibbutzim are successful communities, they are displaying many of the weaknesses that led to the demise of even the most successful of the 19th-century communes.

Modern-Day Communes in the United States

Kanter finds many parallels between 19th-century social circumstances which prompted the development of utopian communities and the 20th-century situation which is again impelling many to seek new forms of social life. Widespread social movements are appearing that are concerned with issues similar to both periods: women, blacks, and even temperance, although in the latter case it is with respect to drugs rather than alcohol. Similar dissatisfactions are expressed concerning the capitalistic economic system in both periods. In both periods anarchists resistant to any form of social structure, and spiritualists obeying their messiah's commands have been prominent. Just as in the 19th century, large numbers of people wander from one commune to another. And in both periods a concern with individual fulfillment, which tends to lie at the bottom of all reform impulses, has been expressed.

A major difference between the two periods, however, is that in the 19th century the concern with fulfillment was often expressed in religious terms, for example, as "salvation." In the 20th century this concern finds expression in psychological terms. The seeker after an ideal social living situation is concerned now about his "personal growth," or the opportunity to "do his own thing." This is a most significant difference between the two periods. The major concern of the present-day utopian is with his own personal growth rather than with social reform, sweeping political and economic change, or the overall welfare of the community. This emphasis on the personal fulfillment theme has led to the appearance of a number of communes that are nonutopian in character. Instead, they are living situations in which property is shared, interpersonal relationships are close, but an ideology is lacking. Kanter points out that these collections of people represent more of an extended family than they do a utopian community. In many respects, the contemporary commune is a temporary living situation, a way of "making do" during a particular phase of a person's life, rather than a permanent social structure. In such communities behavior is not guided by a long-range vision of an ideal form of existence but, instead, by one's intuitive feel for the quality of life at the moment. Thus success in these communities is measured in terms of immediate personal fulfillment, the "vibes," rather than by group cohesiveness and endurance.

Instead of looking toward the future and building on a sense of history as did the 19th-century utopian, today's commune dweller looks to a romanticized past and prefers to ignore the perspective to be gained from the broad sweep of historical movement. There is nostalgia for the small town, for the simple life, for the crafts of the rural societies, for natural foods, and for dress styles, hair styles, and even the tools and equipment of an earlier age. Along with this is a yearning to return to the innocence and simplicity of a childhood free of obligations.

Although these characterizations do typify the majority of present-day communes, a few attempt to continue the utopian tradition. Some are organized around charismatic leaders of a religious stripe. Still others are dedicated to serving a vital need of society.

Whether the communes of today strive to create a utopian society or merely a temporary family, they face similar problems in establishing a group. In many respects, these problems are more difficult than they were for 19th-century community builders because boundaries are not easily maintained. In the 19th century, physical boundaries could be readily set up. Isolation was easily accomplished, and since technological needs were slight, contact with the outside world could be minimized. Life in the 19th century offered fewer options ranging all the way from the choice of a career to the choice of a life-style. The environment of the 20th century constantly intrudes, forcing its way through the border of groups. Communication is instant, more people wish to remain in cities to enjoy the advantages of urban life, and advanced technology diminishes the likelihood that any single group can become entirely self-sufficient, or can develop an economic base making it a complete production unit. New ideas and stimuli constantly disrupt the establishment of a distinctive set of beliefs. Casting about for a new way to determine boundaries, most groups seem to have settled on either affirmative or negative principles for boundary establishment. Affirmative principles define the group by what it accepts; negative principles define it by what it rejects.

On the basis of these two principles, Kanter has created two broad classifications of modern-day communes. Those whose boundaries are based on negative principles she calls "retreat" communes. These are small groups, anarchistic in nature, that tend to dissolve easily. While some urban communes fall into this class, most are rural groups involving young members. The goals of "retreat" communes are limited to interpersonal relationships, and they tend to be very permissive, inclusive, and temporary. Communes having affirmative boundaries choose to interact more broadly with the wider society through service. Their boundaries are erected around a "mission," and they may be either urban or rural and usually have a strong core group that holds the community together.

Retreat communes tend to be isolated geographically, avoid technological advance, and dwell on a nostalgic view of an idyllic past. Its members live in remote locations, often without modern plumbing or electricity, and purposely seek a primitive life-style. Many "hip" communes described by Fairfield (1972) are examples of retreat communes. Members of those groups reject organization, the use of work schedules, and even the necessity to earn money. Material needs are met by relatives, welfare, or whatever is brought in by new members. The events of the outside world are ignored as much as possible. This anarchistic character of the retreat commune defines the group largely by what it rejects and is not conducive to building a strong community. Having rejected the forces in the larger society that make for order, the retreat commune cannot hope to have a strong, committed, stable group without introducing an alternative type of order. Although these groups may provide some individuals with rich and satisfying experiences for limited periods of time, they have considerable difficulty in enduring.

Groups established on the basis of affirmative principles are oriented toward serving a need of society. In marked contrast to the retreat commune, the missionary commune seeks out involvement with people and often settles in cities. In further contrast to retreat groups, these communes erect firm boundaries that encourage group coherence and evince a strong commitment in their members. In the missionary commune the values of the collective are maximized, and such groups are already demonstrating that they are capable of longevity.

Most service communes emphasize education. Such well-known colleges as Oberlin and Antioch had their beginnings in the 19th century as utopian communities. Similarly, many modern communes have organized themselves as schools of one type or another. Several of them have grown out of the human potential movement, and many regard themselves as "growth centers" or centers for the study of human relations. Some of these centers concentrate on teaching the Zen macrobiotic life-style, whereas others are dedicated to caring for the mentally handicapped or to rehabilitating drug addicts. Typically, service communes are made up of two types of membership: (1) a core group having a deep personal commitment to the community which takes responsibility for teaching functions; and (2) a transient group, having limited involvement, which is expected to move in and out of the group.

Perhaps one of the strongest and best known of the service communes is Synanon. From its founding, in 1958, Synanon has grown to include over 1200 resident members in urban communities in California, New York, and Puerto Rico. When founded, it was primarily a form of group therapy and a residential treatment setting for drug addicts. It has evolved into an intentional community with its own schools and businesses including gas stations and an advertising firm.

Twentieth century utopian communities may be classed among groups having affirmative principles. Perhaps the best known utopian society of this kind is Twin Oaks, which was established in the Virginia countryside in 1967 (Kinkade, 1973). The inspiration for this community came from the utopian novel, *Walden II*, by B. F. Skinner (Skinner, 1948). The society described by Skinner was based entirely on the behavioral principles that he had helped to develop in a variety of laboratory studies. Kinkade's account of the development of aspects of the social organization of Twin Oaks describes attempts to incorporate Skinner's principles into the functioning of the community. Her account is also an excellent record of the practical problems to be faced in arriving at an organization suitable for such a social experiment. For example, at Twin Oaks efforts were made to set up work assignments taking into account the desirability of each job for each individual member. Another problem concerned how to deal with those who did not wish to do necessary community work, or who wished to devote most of their time to highly personal pursuits such as writing poetry. Efforts were also made to equalize the income of individual members. Unlike 19th-century communes, Twin Oaks members were not required to give up their own financial resources on entering the community. Initially it was decided that any money a person had before he entered the community would stay in his own bank account with the community benefiting only from interest and dividends. After a three-year period this policy was to be reviewed.

The authority structure in Twin Oaks has remained a relatively loose one. Individuals are named as managers for various work areas. Overall decision making falls to the group of managers. Basic principles for running the community are taken from *Walden II* and attempts are made to stick with these as long as they seem to be empirically useful. As they seem to fail in a specific situation, they have been modified. Kinkade justifies these departures from Skinnerian principles on the grounds that, in many respects, Twin Oaks is a long way from the relatively ideal situation envisioned in *Walden II*. The physical plant at Twin Oaks is a modest one and per capita income is as yet low. Neither has the commune reached the point where every member does what he ought to do because that is what he wants to do. Such a situation is the goal toward which the Twin Oaks founders are striving, but they still find it necessary to use other governmental props such as rules and pep talks as substitutes for intrinsically natural reinforcers.

One problem with which the Twin Oaks commune has had much difficulty is the legitimate criticism of members' behavior. Eschewing the group criticisms that were practiced in many successful 19th-century communes and even in such modern groups as Synanon, the rule that eventually evolved at Twin Oaks was that if one was dissatisfied with the behavior of another, one had to discuss it with him privately. Prior to arriving at this rule, however, several other techniques were attempted, each of which achieved only partial success. At first a "generalized bastard" was appointed whose job was to collect complaints about other members and to relay them anonymously. Unfortunately, the person designated as the "generalized bastard" found that he had little stomach for the job. A later variant of this process involved the use of a "bitch box" in which written grievances could be placed by those without the courage to confront an offender. The latter technique was found to be successful with some members but not with others who were little moved by such complaints. Efforts to apply group criticism also foundered, primarily because those who were most subject to criticism often refused to attend group meetings. Since the community was loath to abridge anyone's right to stay away from meetings that he didn't care to attend, those volunteering for criticism tended to be the ones no one was angry with.

Marriage at Twin Oaks is a somewhat less stable institution than in the larger community. This occurs, not surprisingly, because there are fewer economic ties to force a couple to remain together. As a result, there appears to be some experimentation with a variety of coupling relationships. Essentially, however, lovemaking is regarded as a private thing at Twin Oaks, and little public affection is seen.

Thus far, the Twin Oaks community has not faced the problem of dealing with a new generation. It is expected that the first children will be born in Twin Oaks during 1973. In the meantime, outsiders with children will not be accepted until the children are a year or two old. It has been felt that three conditions must be met before the community will be prepared to deal with children. These include: (1) sufficient resources to build a nursery building separate from adult quarters; (2) enough stability in membership so that babies will be cared for by the same caretakers through their early years; and (3) a group of parents sufficiently committed to the ideals of the community so that they are not likely to leave.

Reflections on Utopian Communities as Growth Enhancing Situations

The basic idea behind the utopian community is an attractive alternative to the notion that social problems are caused by "sick" individuals. Instead of assuming that a healthy society can only emerge if each individual in that society is cured, the utopian notion suggests that structural reform must take place within the society itself and that a social world must be built in which the old problems can no longer appear. Thus social problems are considered to be a function of defects within society that can only be solved by reshaping social institutions.

The prospect of starting fresh with a group of dedicated individuals who are devoted to creating a new social order—one designed to fulfill important needs and to minimize the problems arising in ordinary society

—is extraordinarily attractive. The experience of literally hundreds of these ventures, however, in both the 19th and 20th centuries suggests that this approach is deceptively simple. Literally hundreds of well-meaning people have made gallant efforts to organize themselves into social groups in which healthy, satisfying lives can be lived, only to find severe limitations within the structures they have formed. As Kanter states:

"The life of communes, therefore, like other groups, has its limits and costs as well as its benefits and advantages. Utopian communities are not the answer to everything. They are difficult to create, even more difficult to sustain. They exact a dedication and an involvement that many people find unappealing. They sometimes have shortcomings that make them fail of the perfection they promise. But as thoughtful, concerned people have discovered, they do supply partial answers" (Kanter, 1972, p. 235).

Even the long-lived, successful communes of the 19th century seem to have provided sufficient satisfaction for large groups of members for only limited periods of time. Hence it appears that utopian groups met the very special needs of many of their original members over an extended period of time, but that these needs were not duplicated in others who were drawn to the group or in the young who grew up in the utopian society. For this reason the group eventually disbanded. The same seems to be occurring in most modern communes.

Fairfield (1971) is optimistic about the value of 20th-century communes. He rejects longevity or survival as a valid measure of a commune's success. Instead, he looks to the individual member's experience of a feeling of aliveness, a better awareness of himself and others, as a proper measure of the worth of a communal experience. From this point of view he believes that the present-day commune in America has been very successful. He views the commune as being in the forefront of a revolution that carries people out of a "private, intolerable, grasping, solitary self toward the cooperative, sharing, loving, universal self."

Fairfield lists five basic ideals of the commune movement that have important value for society as a whole. These include: (1) encouraging return to what is real and essential in life; (2) taking man away from the polluted city and getting him back to his natural habitat where the air is fresh, and he can till the soil; (3) escaping from the alienation that separates people in our society and bringing them back to shared human relationships; (4) allowing individuals to self-actualize, to find out as much as they can about their own potential; and (5) providing an example for the rest of society of how to live a better life.

On the other hand, even Fairfield is cognizant of the problems encountered in recent years in establishing stable communities. In large measure he accounts for these problems as deriving from the fact that utopians, as products of a competitive, overly intellectualized society are themselves "overly cerebral." He finds the great idea or ideal as often being meaningless and possibly personally harmful. He illustrates this with the example of a personal experience:

"To give another example, at a 4th of July party given by a community group in Boston, I noticed a friend of mine sitting in a corner, looking quite sad. Sad, he was, amid demonstrations in Hatha Yoga, animated conversations, wild dancing, a great variety of delicious food, good drinks, and even fireworks—a really great party. I couldn't imagine what was wrong, so I asked him. He replied, 'Sure, it's a good party, I guess. But we're not getting any closer to the community we want this way!' He was utterly convinced that a community had to be a particular place with a particular kind of behavior, so that he was unable to enjoy the present. He allowed his ideals to stand in the way of his enjoyment of the unplanned, unexpected pleasures of life" (Fairfield, 1971, p. 369).

Fairfield's example is intended to illustrate that a sense of community is possible even in the midst of the booming, buzzing confusion of the "really great party." On the other hand, one cannot help but sympathize with the sad friend who may have needed a different, more enduring relationship to feel a sense of community. The transitory nature of the communes that Fairfield describes suggests that these social organizations are extraordinarily limited in what they can provide. They may meet the specialized needs of a few individuals at a certain point in their lives, but they are not examples of living situations that can serve over a long pull. It is difficult to envision, too, how they can fulfill needs for intimacy, deep personal understanding, and self-actualization. Instead, like the party Fairfield describes, they seem to provide only an immediate high, temporary "kicks."

In the light of this survey, Sarason's pessimism concerning our present capacity for developing utopian societies seems well founded (Sarason, 1972). Sarason points out that man's experience demonstrates that no matter how firmly a group may share a set of basic values, and no matter how well motivated its members may be to unite in forming a lasting, rewarding social organization, such groups have failed to build enduring societies. Sufficient knowledge as to how organizations of this kind are to be created simply has not been available. Sarason feels that social relationships are so complex that man has vast distances to go before he will be able to think about designing an optimal social living situation. Thus Sarason's own efforts are devoted toward understanding the problems involved in creating the mini-social organizations that go toward making up an entire society.

Perhaps because of the discouraging results of the utopian societies of the past, today's experimental communities seem to start out with less of a sense of mission, of grand scope concerning the possibility of sweeping the entire society than was true in earlier times. The typical modern commune tends to be a small, modest venture, tailored to the needs of a particular group of individuals, caring little about long-range endurance. Kanter points out that the "grand visions of the past" have been taken over in the present day by real estate developers and city planners. While somewhat less grandiose than the utopian society builders, the city planners wish to create large communities, even cities, whose basic design can anticipate human needs, minimize stresses, and enhance the general quality of life.

PLANNED COMMUNITIES

Lemkau (1969), a psychiatrist, has described his participation in planning a new town, Columbia, Maryland, which is being designed and built to house more than 100,000 people. Along with a pediatrician, a biometrician, a health insurance expert, a health educator, a health economist, a social work educator, a specialist in chronic diseases, a public health dentist, an obstetrician, a public health administrator, a hospital service analyst, and a medical sociologist, he participated as a member of a Health and Welfare group to consider the way the physical structure of the community might contribute to the health of its members in the broadest sense.

Although, as social scientists, this group was given an unparalleled opportunity to embark on an extraordinarily exciting venture in social planning, the first problem that they struggled with was a political-ethical one concerning the degree to which they had the right to plan the lives of other people who would one day live in the town that they were helping to establish. How to avoid restricting freedom and maximizing the opportunity to grow was felt as an enormous responsibility. Since the community was to encompass a full range of socioeconomic classes, the problem arose of how to intermingle very expensive housing with relatively inexpensive housing without creating ghettoes. High value was placed on the availability of comprehensive health services for all residents of the planned community, but the question of whether a tax should be imposed to provide these services, even for those who did not want to have them, had to be considered.

A major issue quickly agreed on by the consultants participating with Lemkau was that one of the major drawbacks of the large city is its lack of the community feeling that typifies small towns. The city is simply too large and too disparate to allow for the development of a concern for the totality. One can acquire a sense of pride about a neighborhood or a smaller social unit, but not for a very large complex unit such as a city. This concern led to the conclusion that Columbia should be organized in such a way that identification might be fostered with small local geographical units. In planning the size of these units, a number of practical matters had to be considered. To support a small shopping center, for example, approximately 10,000 or 15,000 people are required. Such a number also is capable of supplying enough junior high school pupils to populate optimally sized schools. Thus the range of 10,000 to 15,000 population was set up as the ideal for a fairly self-sustaining social unit that would include various services, a recreation area, churches, and the like.

To accommodate those preferring to live in a downtown area rather than in suburbs, it was deemed necessary to plan a central city consisting of high-rise buildings and some of the population density and bustle that typifies the core of a large city. Many community services could be centralized within such an area, and thought was given to fostering a Columbia-wide identification with the city through the creation of some symbolic structure. Eventually, the idea of a single symbolic structure was abandoned because it was believed that the various cultural, educational, professional, economic, and recreation needs satisfied within the central core would be factors with which all neighborhoods could identify.

Much of the planning group's discussion revolved about the need for adult education. While it was anticipated that many residents would be working in the nearby Baltimore or Washington areas, it was hoped that the city would eventually attract light industry to support a significant proportion of local residents. Such industry might well require training programs and facilities for retraining workers.

Welfare planning was considered to some extent although it was not elaborated in great detail. Various "mortgage insurance" plans were recommended as part of the financing of homes so that emergencies arising through death or prolonged disability would not strain the capacities of families to support their housing needs. The reduction of this form of stress in time of serious emergencies was viewed by mental health planners as extraordinarily important. It was also recognized that through death and disability the city's welfare load would soon build. Thus planners anticipated a need for expanding the county welfare system.

Several other plans were introduced to promote mental health and to prevent the development of behavior disorder. These included a parent education program in child development as part of the nursery school program, as a segment in adult education, and as a basic aspect of programs in maternal child care. A fundamental aspect of educational planning included counseling backed up by psychiatric consultation when necessary. Local public health personnel, working closely with medical practitioners, were to be used to provide crisis information. Medical buildings that would include local health department representatives were to be placed close to schools to facilitate communication between such service givers and the school system. Prenatal care plans were introduced to anticipate physical problems in the newborn. The needs of adolescents were provided for with the development of suitable recreation opportunities and the development of part-time employment possibilities. Various part-time volunteer services for housewives were also planned.

Lemkau was careful to point out that all plans engaged in at Columbia, while prophylactic with respect to some disorders, could not be expected to succeed in erasing mental disorder. Mental retardation and other handicaps among children would doubtless appear in Columbia despite every preventive effort being made. Some of the elderly, while benefiting to a degree from the provisions made for them, would become senile and require special care. There is little evidence to indicate that engineering a particularly healthy environment has an effect on the rate of the occurence of schizophrenia. Furthermore, depression is a disorder that may be more common among the types of people who would live and grow up in Columbia than among an unselected population. Lemkau points out that depression arises more frequently in those who bear responsibilities well. To the extent that the Columbia environment fosters the development of a responsible, concerned citizen, depression may commonly be found among its residents in reaction to the grief instilled by the loss of old friends as well as by the stresses involved in making new adaptations. Finally, Lemkau points out that all consultants who participated in planning the Columbia community recognized that they were making their best guesses on the basis of experience and information assimilated in a myriad of ways. On the basis of this unsystematic accumulation of knowledge, they were forced to take action and to plan approaches depending only on subjective judgments. Not having the assurance the scientist would like to have on the basis of controlled study that his recommendations are likely to be highly effective, Lemkau points out that in the group in which he participated "one sat as an expert and hoped that he was."

Nunn (1971) has described a plan drawn up at the Urban Study Center of the University of Louisville for dealing with the poverty problems of this country through the design of new communities. In essence, the Louisville group drew up a prototype of a plan for designing and populating new communities that could be applied in a variety of areas throughout the country. They envisioned that these communities would be located just outside of medium-sized urban areas that are growing economically. Many such regions are impeded in their growth because of a lack of appropriate labor. Thus the new communities would be a source of manpower for developing urban areas and would provide needed work for people presently living in places where they cannot find it.

A major purpose of this plan is to redistribute the country's population so that needy segments can settle in areas where their needs for employment and a better life can be satisfied. The Louisville planners envision that the new communities would consist of approximately 20,000 families (80,000 people). They estimate that such communities would cost approximately half a billion dollars to finance but that private sources could manage this with no more than normal federal backstopping. The plan would require that approximately half of the families to populate the new communities would be the urban poor who would voluntarily decide to move and would be assisted in joining the new community. The attraction for these settlers would be an improved living situation and job opportunities. Such community residents would be prepared for specific jobs and would be oriented toward "the world of work" and the kind of life they could expect to lead in the new community as responsible, taxpaying citizens. The remaining settlers would be families not requiring assistance. They would be drawn to the community because of the availability of managerial and administrative positions. Many would be people already living in the area who would be simply attracted by the prospect of living in a new, planned community.

Similar to the Columbia plan, one aspect of the Louisville plan is to avoid creating a series of "poverty towns" or ghettoes. In some measure, this would be avoided by the fact that settlers who had previously lived on a poverty level would not remain poor. They would be trained for work and placed in rewarding jobs leading to a life different from that experienced in the ghetto. Another means of avoiding the development of a ghetto would be a deliberate mixing of the population to include various social, economic, and racial groups.

Among the concerns of the Louisville planners has been the development of a psychosocial environment that is maximally conducive to growth and a good life. In the planning, much attention is paid to the distribution of the population and to the various subgroups within it. The psychosocial planners specify, for example, that during any given period in the development of a new community, no more than 35 percent of the population should consist of families receiving assistance in establishing their residency. Recognizing that at the subneighborhood level residents might well wish to live in socioeconomically homogeneous clusters, it is recommended that clusters consisting of about 25 dwelling units of similar cost be set up within neighborhoods to produce socioeconomic homogeneity. Within a given neighborhood, consisting of eight clusters or about 200 dwelling units, and within each village, consisting of six or seven neighborhoods and approximately 1200 dwelling units, the plan calls for a variation in clusters to achieve population heterogeneity. It is further stipulated that no cluster, neighborhood, or village be permitted to consist solely of residents of one race, a single place of origin, or one income level.

Part of the Louisville plan includes an effort to encourage participation on the part of residents in the community's government. This is accomplished by setting up relatively small elective districts (consisting of 200 families). In addition, a series of monitoring boards are to be set up to evaluate community services. All service users will be asked to evaluate that service every two years. As a result of these evaluations it will be possible to depose administrators of a particular service that is poorly regarded. Overall, a marked effort is made toward distributing power widely and this is valued more than administrative efficiency. Wherever possible, local control at the village level is set up over service agencies.

It is still, of course, far too early to make any judgment about the success of the kinds of new communities envisioned in Columbia, Maryland, or by the Louisville planning group. Columbia is still in the building stage. The communities projected by the Louisville planning group are not yet off the drawing board. Clearly both enterprises are in some respects, more ambitious than the communes previously described and are, in other respects, more modest. As living situations that will accommodate literally thousands of people in entirely newly designed communities, they are ambitious. On the other hand, they do not pretend to alter the social living situation nearly as drastically as does the typical experimental community. Only time and experience can demonstrate whether the kinds of planning going into communities like Columbia, Maryland will enhance the quality of the lives of its residents and will prevent behavior disorders.

CONCLUSION

Long before the general idea of community psychology was even conceived, man was concerned about creating an ideal form of social organization to best meet his needs. Prior to the 20th century, such social experiments were generally impelled by values or ideals, often cloaked in religious terms, that prompted a group of like-thinking people to separate themselves from established society. In the 20th century, some social experiments have developed similarly, but many are emerging more as a rejection of the values of established society than as the affirmation of a new set of standards.

In 19th-century utopian communities, enormous value was vested in the group, the cohesiveness of members, and a devotion to group standards. At that time, it was felt that the ideals of individual members could best be served through developing an overall community spirit. For the most part, the 20th-century commune is less oriented toward the values of the group. Instead, individual development and satisfaction of the psychological needs of the individual member receive the greatest emphasis.

Another form of social experiment arising in the 20th century is the planned community. In the forefront of this development are the architect, the urban planner, and the real estate developer rather than the social scientist. Basic to the thinking behind the planned community is dissatisfaction with the quality of life in the typical city where the form and structure arise haphazardly over a period of many years. Community planners are not so bold as the utopians in striking out toward radical social experimentation, but they are quite bold in attempting to design living situations for literally thousands of people. Their emphasis is on organizing the subunits within the city, in distributing population groups, in arranging for the availability of needed services, and in planning for the recreational and work needs of residents. Careful planning for all these aspects of human life is seen to be a way of improving the quality of life and of preventing the development of behavioral disturbances.

Although the prospect of starting fresh by designing social living situations is enormously exciting for the social scientist, a review of the process of these experiments and their outcome indicates that they have failed to provide a model for a truly growth-enhancing situation. Neither the long-lived utopian communities of the 19th century nor the Israeli kibbutzim, which have existed for many years, are demonstrated to be enduring models of an ideal living situation that can accommodate the needs of a heterogeneous population. To endure, many of these groups were required to adopt commitment mechanisms that virtually ruled out any sense of individuality in their members. While such a living situation might have sufficed for a person who had little desire to build a personal career or to develop any specialized personal skills, it was clearly not a home for the person who wished "to do his own thing." Even the longest-lived utopian experiments eventually underwent changes in social organization because of contamination arising from contact with the outside society, and they eventually dissolved entirely. In many instances, these communities did not seem to be able to outlive their original founders.

The typical 20th-century commune is rarely dedicated to group values, and tends to require little sacrifice of its members. It allows much personal expression and a striving toward satisfaction of personal needs. On the other hand, the social organization that results in those settings appears to be extremely unstable. The modern commune seems to serve the needs of particular individuals temporarily and acts as little more than a brief way station in life.

Despite innumerable experiments with a variety of social organizations, one must conclude that we simply lack the social technology at this point to design new social living situations that will be optimally growth enhancing. It is probably also overly simplistic to expect that any single model will serve all types of people. Perhaps the major problem encountered by the more successful, more long-lived utopian societies was ultimately the fact that they could not adapt to changing external conditions and the changing character of their own population. It may well be that the practice appearing in Israel whereby the young kibbutznik leaves the kibbutz where he grew up to join others in starting a new kibbutz is a reasonable solution to the adaptation problem. It is, perhaps, unreasonable to expect that the needs that drew the original settlers to a utopian, communal living situation would be duplicated in new recruits who enter the community from an environment that is different from the one to which the original settlers of the community reacted. Furthermore, even the children born in the experimental community are not likely to be impelled by the same motives as their parents and caretakers. Thus many models specifically designed to meet many different clusters of needs may well be the only solution to developing truly growth-enhancing settings.

One can be somewhat more optimistic about improving the quality of life through planned communities. Clearly, it would seem that improvements can be made on the haphazard social arrangements arising in a city that develops over a period of many, many years in response to a variety of uncontrolled forces. To this point, there are too few planned communities and those that do exist are too few to permit any evaluation of how they serve man. Clearly, they allow a more flexible living situation than is true in many utopian social experiments, and by minimizing many of the stresses of urban life while maximizing the availability of services, they should enhance the quality of life. They should also have a much better chance of enduring than has been true of the utopian community.

Man will, of course, continue to dream, and certainly one of his noblest ambitions will be to create a better world in which to live. Hopefully these dreams will be guided by the experience of dreamers of an earlier time who attempted to build a reality modeled on their ideals. It is only through such a process that we can hope to see the creation of truly growth-enhancing living situations.

References

Eisenstadt, S. N. *Israeli Society*. New York: Basic Books, 1967.

Fairfield, R. *Communes U.S.A.: a personal tour*. Baltimore, Md.: Penguin Books, 1971.

Kanter, R. M. Communes. *Psychology Today*, 1970, *4*, 53.

Kanter, R. M. *Commitment and community: communes and utopias in sociological perspective*. Cambridge, Mass.: Harvard University Press, 1972.

Kinkade, K. Commune: A Walden-Two Experiment. *Psychology Today*, 1973, *6*, No. 8, p. 35 and No. 9, p. 71.

Lemkau, P. V. The Planning Project for Columbia. In M. F. Shore & F. V. Mannino, *Mental health and the community: problems, programs, and strategies*. New York: Behavioral Publications, 1969. Pp. 193–204.

Nunn, D. *Newcom, Volume I, Summary*. Louisville, Ky.: Urban Studies Center, University of Louisville, 1971.

Sarason, S. B. *The creation of settings: and the future societies*. San Francisco: Jossey-Bass, 1973.

Skinner, B. F. *Walden two*. New York: MacMillan, 1948.

Spiro, M. E. *Kibbutz: venture in utopia*. New York: Schocken, 1970.

11. *criticisms of changing mental health approaches*

The preceding chapters have depicted the development of exciting new ideas about mental illness and the need to foster mental health, as well a many of the organized efforts to operationalize these ideas. The purpos of this chapter is to give perspective on the extent to which communit psychology has gained a foothold on the current mental health scene and particularly, the problems it faces in attempting to maintain this foothol in the future. In essence, programs described in this book have been rela tively isolated efforts aimed at increasing reliance on community force that deal with already manifest mental disturbance, and at changing com munity forces in such a way as to prevent the development of psychologi cal disorder. They have involved an isolated mental hospital here o there, a particularly progressive school system in one locale or another an unusually forward-looking community mental health center, and th like. Unquestionably, the majority of mental health services available i this country still proceed in the traditional mold despite the heavy criti

314

cism directed toward that mold in recent years. Therefore, a central concern for the community psychologist must be the question of how broad-scale change can be brought to the mental health field. What can be done to shake up the old institutions and practices? As a first step toward answering these questions, this chapter is devoted specifically to describing and discussing the types of objections met in attempting to revise our orientation toward mental health problems.

The sources of opposition to change are pervasive. Anyone who has attempted to develop a community program in a traditional mental health setting can easily attest to the omnipresence of dissent at local levels. Distressingly, however, opposition is also met even at the highest levels of the mental health establishment. The Joint Commission on Mental Illness and Health was established in 1955 by President Eisenhower with a mandate to study the mental health needs of the nation and to recommend ways for meeting these needs. This commission, supported by 36 national organizations in the medical, public health, mental health, welfare, education, and social science fields included the leaders of American psychiatry, psychology, social work, education, and the social sciences. The conclusions and recommendations of this august body were based on a series of excellent studies of theoretical issues that concern positive mental health, methodological issues in epidemiological research, the economics of mental illness, mental health manpower problems, community resources in mental health, the role played by schools and churches in dealing with mental health problems, and recent developments in inpatient and outpatient care of the mentally ill. These conclusions, while acknowledging the need for greater community involvement in the treatment of the mentally disturbed, quite specifically resist movement toward attempting to prevent the development of serious disorder. The tone of these conclusions is conveyed well by this quotation:

"Here, of course, we reveal the bias of this report—and give a little discomfort to some of our colleagues who have a strong commitment toward practices and programs aimed at the promotion of positive mental health in children and adults. Indeed, a few members of the Joint Commission have found themselves in the position of affirming this final report as it relates to the treatment of the mentally ill and to research, but of rejecting the view that achievement of maximum effort in behalf of the mentally ill would require the minimizing of emphasis on the mental health of persons who are not ill or in immediate danger of becoming so. We have assumed that the mental hygiene movement has diverted attention from the core problem of major mental illness. It is our purpose to redirect attention to the possibilities of improving the mental health of the mentally ill. . ." (Joint Commission, 1961, p. 242).

It is of considerable significance, despite the Joint Commission's emphasis on better treatment for those already disturbed, that much federal legislation which followed the Joint Commission report was oriented toward the development of preventive programs (Caplan, 1964). Thus the lay public seemed to acknowledge the need for prevention and were more willing to adopt a new orientation than were the contemporary leaders of the mental health fields. Along similar lines a task force on the mentally handicapped, established by President Nixon in 1970 to take another overview of the mental health fields and to recommend necessary legislative action, was unequivocal in its commitment to prevention and gave high priority to the development of services for children, who were virtually ignored in the Joint Commission report (The President's Task Force on the Mentally Handicapped, 1970). Significantly, although the 1970 task force included representatives of the major mental health fields as well as education, many of its members were lay people affiliated with various mental health organizations throughout the country.

Given that opposition to a change in mental health orientation and practices persists in a variety of significant quarters, it is important to examine the grounds on which these objections are based, and to attempt to evaluate the adequacy of such grounds. What follows is, therefore, a rough classification of various bases for opposing community and, particularly, preventive approaches.

OPPOSITION BASED ON THE ASSERTION THAT WE LACK SUFFICIENT KNOWLEDGE TO ESTABLISH PREVENTIVE PROGRAMS

The objection that we lack sufficient knowledge to attempt to create truly preventive programs is well exemplified by the discussion of the Joint Commission on Mental Illness and Health (1961) on the mental hygiene movement. Clifford Beers, the energetic figure responsible for initiating the mental hygiene movement, was originally concerned primarily with improving the care of those already mentally ill. He is said to have been diverted in this aim by "his doctor friends of those days" who were more interested in attempting to prevent mental illness by following contemporary examples of the control of epidemic diseases. As a result, the movement concentrated on establishing child guidance clinics and on programs of public information for improving attitudes toward the mentally disturbed.

Although not quarreling with the broad aims of the mental hygiene movement, the Joint Commission dismisses them as unachievable. Grounds for this rejection are the lack of sufficient knowledge in many realms that would be necessary to succeed with such programs. For example,

"Even if we could agree on what kind of men and women we wanted to produce, we could not predict the outcome in a given family due to the multiplicity of uncontrolled variables—such as the mathematics of inherited characteristics. Thus, primary prevention of mental illness has remained largely an article of scientific faith rather than an applicable scientific truth" (Joint Commission on Mental Illness and Health, 1961, p. 70).

This report goes on to point out that we are neither able to control or even to agree on what would represent a proper psychological environment for children and closes its discussion of the topic by asserting that the results of establishing mental health education programs and child guidance clinics have been disappointing, with no convincing evidence available that they have actually kept people out of state hospitals.

Halleck (1969) is concerned that community psychiatry might draw the practitioner into the political decision-making arena for which he has poor qualifications and, frequently, little interest. He points out that it is not possible for a mental health worker to enter the community arena to attempt to deal with "the casualities of social conflict" without attempting also to change the conditions that produced the casualty. A policy of nonpartisanship or neutrality is not possible and being drawn into the community movement forces one to take a stand on political issues. Halleck is concerned that the mental health worker cannot differentiate between positions taken as private citizens and those having the force of authority as "medical scientists." As private citizens, Halleck feels, mental health workers both influence the community climate and, in turn, are influenced by it and have no special expertise to offer in this realm.

Dunham's well-known criticism of community psychiatry (Dunham, 1965) is also based largely on the grounds that we do not yet possess the requisite knowledge to have an effective community psychology or psychiatry. For Dunham, one of the essential implications of a community approach is the idea that the community is, in effect, the patient, and that techniques must be developed for altering its structure. Basic to this position is the notion that:

"Within the texture of those institutional arrangements that make up the community there exist dysfunctional processes, subcultures with unhealthy value complexes, specific institutional tensions, various ideological conflicts along age, sex, ethnic, racial and political axes, occasional cultural crises, and an increasing tempo of social change that in their functional interrelationships provide a pathogenic social environment" (Dunham, 1965, p. 306).

While Dunham acknowledges that the social milieu has long been recognized as an important force in shaping personality structure, he is far less certain that knowledge of this kind can be useful in work at the community level that is designed to treat mental and emotional maladjustment. He raises a number of questions for community psychiatrists or psychologists:

"Why do psychiatrists think that it is possible to treat the 'collectivity' when there still exists a marked uncertainty with respect to the treatment and cure of the individual case? What causes the psychiatrist to think that if he advances certain techniques for treating the 'collectivity,' they will have community acceptance? If he begins to treat a group through discussions in order to develop personal insights, what assurance does he have that the results will be psychologically beneficial to the persons? Does the psychiatrist know how to organize a community along mentally hygienic lines and if he does, what evidence does he have that such an organization will be an improvement over the existing organization?" (Dunham, 1965, p. 306).

Dunham goes on to assert that the only proper community role for the mental health worker is to assume public office as a private citizen rather than as a professional. In that role he can attempt to use his professional knowledge to bring about desired goals and, even if not successful, such experience would be useful in acquainting him with the complexities involved in dealing with the community as a patient.

As support for his position that the mental health worker has little to offer in the community arena, Dunham cites two projects organized several years ago to curb juvenile delinquency (one was the Cambridge-Somerville study described in Chapter 9) and the overall impact of the child guidance movement as examples of previous community programs that failed for one reason or another. He also describes the progressively broadening definition of mental illness that has taken place over the past 40 or 50 years, but does not view this process as coming about because of unmet social needs, the position taken in this book. Instead, he sees it occurring because the mental health profession has been unsuccessful in treating "bona-fide psychotics" and has, therefore, widened the "psychiatric net" to deal with people whose problems are more trivial and who are more amenable to existing treatment techniques. Thus the broadening definition of mental illness is a device constructed by the mental health professions as frustrations are met in dealing with "traditional mental cases." Mental illness is simply redefined periodically to encompass problems that presumably will be more amendable to current treatment approaches. Movement toward community approaches is viewed by Dunham simply as another effort of the mental health professions to find an arena where the prospects of success are better than they have been in the more traditional ones.

Dunham feels that some aspects of community psychiatry such as the reduction of the psychoanalyst's and hospital psychiatrist's isolation, may maximize treatment potentials. However, he is extremely dubious concerning community psychiatry's future:

". . . Here I am most skeptical concerning the adequacy of our knowledge to develop significant techniques for treating social collectivities or for developing techniques on the community level that will really result in a reduction of mental disturbances in the community. It seems that such expectations are likely to remove the psychiatrists still further from the bona fide cases of mental illnesses that develop within the community context. Much of his effort will be spent on dealing with the noncritical cases . . . Until we have a more sound knowledge which will indicate that the minor emotional disturbances are likely to develop into the serious types of mental disturbances we will be dissipating much of our collective psychiatric efforts" (Dunham, 1965, p. 311).*

The positions taken by the Joint Commission, Halleck, and Dunham are in one sense very difficult to refute. One rarely if ever reaches the point where he possesses all the knowledge that he would like to have about the phenomena he is dealing with in any scientific field. The situation in the human service field is no different, but the worker in that area suffers an even more acute dilemma. He is confronted by people badly in need of some form of help and must weigh the potential harm of a new treatment approach against the potential harm of not instituting such a program. In many cases, such weightings are extraordinarily difficult to arrive at because of the nature of the phenomena under consideration. None of this refutes the arguments of Dunham and others, however. The criticism that we are lacking in sufficient knowledge to be comfortable about proliferating all manner of community programs is well taken. There is a real danger that, carried away by enthusiasm for the new venture, the community psychologist will rush headlong into developing programs that are doomed to fail or that actually do harm because necessary preliminary studies were not done. This makes it incumbent on program organizers at this stage of community psychology's development to foster an investigative stance and to do careful evaluations of their programs. Perhaps an even greater need is more basic research devoted to understanding the naturalistic settings in which community psychology programs will be set up.

The community is, indeed, a mystifying, strange, awesome arena for the mental health worker accustomed to operating within the cloistered walls of the hospital or clinic where his function is clear and his status is assured by tradition. It might justifiably be asserted, contrary to Dunham's thesis, that the mental health worker has resisted engagement in the community for a good many years, despite many forces impelling him in that direction. These forces include the moral treatment movement within the mental hospital systems of this country during the 19th century, Adolph Meyer's attempt to develop an aftercare movement and to bring the mental hospital system out of its isolation and closer to the community, and the efforts of the mental hygiene movement to establish a truly preventive program. The failure of the mental hygiene movement to diminish mental illness rates through programs of public education, as cited by the Joint Commission, may be attributed, in part, to the fact that the mental health professions were not attracted to, and did not engage in, the preventive aspects of the mental hygiene program. They participated in the operation of the child guidance clinics set up by the movement, but in these settings they maintained a traditional role.

Dunham's citations of failure of previous preventive efforts also deserve scrutiny. Two of his examples, the Cambridge-Somerville Youth Study (Powers and Witmer, 1951), and the seeming failure of child guidance clinics to diminish the adult incidence rates of major psychoses, while preventive in aim, involved traditional approaches to dealing directly with behavioral problems. In the Cambridge-Somerville Youth Study the workers were specifically prohibited from attempting to manipulate the delinquent's environment. The study was a test of the benefits that might derive from the relationship between counselor and counselee. In the child guidance clinic, while problems are addressed early in the life of the individual, they are again dealt with in a traditional psychotherapeutic one-to-one relationship. Thus, while these examples represent attempts at prevention, they are not attempts in the spirit of the types of community programs that are currently evolving.

The third example of a previous preventive effort cited by Dunham involves the Chicago Area Project (Kobrin, 1959) initiated in 1930 to reduce delinquency among the lower class immigrant groups of Chicago. This study devised by a sociologist, Clifford R. Shaw, as described by Kobrin (1959), does have a great deal in common with many types of community projects that are emerging today. Its design was based on two aspects of sociological theory. The first was the assumption that most delinquency can be understood as a direct process of social learning where young boys are not able to find meaning in the institutions that have importance for their parents and have contact with a peer group manifesting a "vital tradition of delinquency." From this view becoming a delinquent is a way of assuming a respected adult role rather than simply being a product of antisocial strivings. The social change confronting the immigrant from a peasant or rural society to a large urban area leads to a breakdown of spontaneous social controls. This predisposses the immigrant's offspring to adopt delinquent behavior if that is a significant adaptive option. From this point of view, therefore, delinquency is a "reversible accident of the person's social experience."

The second basis for the Chicago Area Project program derived from two postulates related to sociological theory. The first states that a person's conduct is controlled by his natural social world. The rules of behavior that are valid for the individual are those that affect his daily sustenance, his status in primary groups, and his self-development. The second postulate holds that people truly support only those enterprises where they themselves play a meaningful role. The implications of these two postulates are that to prevent delinquency, a program must become an integral activity of the adults who participate in the youngster's natural social world. The aims of the program must also become the aims of the local population which must take up the cause as its very own. Furthermore, those who live in high delinquency areas must become integral parts of whatever constructive action is devised.

The program of the Chicago Area Project basically involved developing neighborhood welfare associations that were aimed at limiting delinquency. Specific programs in different neighborhoods varied depending on the character of the neighborhood, the type of local interest in it, and the facilities available in each neighborhood. For the most part, however, all area project programs include three elements: (1) a recreation program that, in some cases, included a summer camp, (2) organized campaigns for improving the local community, and (3) programs with police and juvenile courts for supervising identified delinquents, visiting those already committed to corrective institutions, working with neighborhood gangs, and offering assistance to adult parolees returning to the community. As in many modern community programs in large urban areas, project programs were based in storefronts, churches, police stations, and even the basements of homes.

Establishment of these programs required the identification and recruitment of local residents who held influential positions in the neighborhood and who might contribute usefully to program operation. Over the objection of professional social workers who disapproved of the use of untrained lay people, it soon became evident that employing individuals indigenous to the neighborhood had many advantages. The indigenous worker was well acquainted with the local society, was able to communicate more easily than outsiders, had more direct access to the community's delinquents, and his employment demonstrated to the local resident that the project organizers were confident that local residents could carry out the program in their own neighborhoods.

To set up specific neighborhood programs, the Chicago Area Project founders learned that they had to study local social organizations, become acquainted with the history of local institutions, and learn about the local power structure with its various conflicts and cleavages to be effective. The well-structured, stable neighborhoods were dominated by one or a few local institutions. In such circumstances efforts were made simply to operate through these established institutions. More often, neighborhoods were not well structured, making it necessary to operate through a variety of local neighborhood institutions such as churches, political organizations, businessmen's groups, or lodges. In many respects, ranging from the underlying theoretical orientation to the programs that have included the use of indigenous workers, the Chicago Area Project has a surprisingly modern ring and stands as an important pioneer of the community movement in urban areas.

Dunham's dismissal of the Chicago Area Project as an example to "point to some of the difficulties that are inherent in any proposal that emphasizes the development of psychiatric treatment techniques for the collective level" is based on the fact that, in attempting to evaluate the effects of the Chicago Area Project, Kobrin (1959) emphasized the problem of deriving precise measures of program effects. These methodological problems result from the reality that large community areas are subject to a variety of forces that cannot be experimentally controlled. It is, therefore, difficult to sort out program effects from the effects of a variety of other forces operating on an area's residents. Thus, Kobrin cautioned that a simple reduction in delinquency rates would not necessarily indicate program effectiveness. On the other hand, Kobrin asserted that "on logical and analytic grounds" the Chicago Area Project was a *success*. Its achievements included: (1) the demonstration that a viable youth welfare organization could be established among residents of delinquency areas; (2) that indigenous workers could make personal contact with normally unreachable boys; and (3) it succeeded in rendering less impersonal the urban society's legal machine for controlling and reforming the delinquent. Quinney (1970) concurs with this evaluation of the effects of the Chicago Area Project in his own recent book on crime. Although the methodological problems inherent in evaluation are difficult ones, they are potentially surmountable through the use of neighborhoods matched to program areas as controls and fail to warrant Durham's pessimism. Admittedly, the stated accomplishments are not the ultimate program goal, delinquency reduction, but are, instead, the means to such a goal. Still they do not sustain Dunham's claim that the program was a failure.

In summary, it would seem that while the mental health professions have no reason to feel sanguin about their gaps in knowledge concerning disease etiology, this lack need not block all efforts at establishing preventive programs and carefully studying them. Perhaps the difference between this view and that of Dunham is related to what are regarded as the forces impelling current community movements. Dunham asserts that psychiatry is moving into the community because it has failed in its traditional functions and is embarked on a trip, hopefully, to bolster the ego of a group of frustrated professionals. This seems to be a gross oversimplification. It greatly overestimates the degree of personal dissatisfaction experienced by the majority of mental health professionals concerning the invalidity of their techniques. Furthermore, it greatly underestimates the potential for denial among such professionals, most of whom are not engaging in community enterprises, are very content with traditional practices, are unmoved by research findings, and are relatively unconcerned about major social needs. Dunham's view also greatly underestimates the threat posed for any traditionally trained professional by the prospect of leaving traditional positions, where high status and good income are assured, in favor of entering a community arena fraught with all of the uncertainties that Dunham describes. From our point of view the impetus for current community movements can only be understood as stemming from the urgent need for more effective solutions to a variety of behavioral and social problems. These, like the cholera or typhoid epidemics that once sweep a community, demand that action be taken based on even fragmentary knowledge.

OBJECTIONS BASED ON WHAT APPEARS TO BE THE SHEER ENORMITY OF THE NEED AND ITS HIGH COST

Some who acknowledge the desirability of preventive approaches to mental health problems nonetheless oppose their establishment on the grounds that truly effective programs require major social change which is virtually impossible to bring about. From this viewpoint, preventing emotional disorders requires the abolition of all injustices, discrimination, economic insecurity, poverty, slums, and illness (Bower, 1969). Those who take this position feel that to do any less would be like attempting "to fell a giant sequoia with a toy ax." Efforts short of such formidable social changes are bound to be inadequate and, therefore, the most that can be done is to concentrate on immediate needs such as the diagnosis, treatment, and rehabilitation of those already manifesting mental disorders.

An argument against the establishment of preventive approaches that is associated with the issue of the enormity of the problem is their high cost (Cowen, 1967). Most preventive programs are, indeed, expensive, particularly in their developmental stage. They require high-priced professional personnel over long periods of time. Often the public is asked to support programs that are entirely exploratory in nature, have few if any precedents, and are without promise of an immediate payoff. The necessity of making expensive investments toward an often intangible outcome that may require years to assess tempers the enthusiasm of many people for preventive programs.

Admittedly, establishment of the ideal society which would minimize the development of emotional disorder is a remote ideal. On the other hand, our immediate needs are such that as Bower (1969, p. 6) puts it, "small beginnings, however, need to be made on many fronts." The problems encountered in managing those already identifiably disturbed emotionally is becoming so overwhelming for the mental health field that it is imperative that even small efforts be mounted to reduce the numbers succumbing to mental disorder.

The issue of the high cost of prevention programs is placed in perspective by Cowen (1967). He points out that costs currently entailed in managing many emotional disorders, which society is accustomed to bearing, are enormously high. Processing a single adolescent through the New York City juvenile court system costs $4000. The average costs to an urban community of an adolescent who drops out of high school and later enters the welfare roles is approximately $30,000. Residential treatment care for those suffering emotional disorders can cost in excess of $15,000 per year. Custodial, state hospital care for a long-term mental patient may cost as much as a quarter of a million dollars. Thus even the inadequate mental care system being supported today is an extraordinarily expensive one. From this perspective, investments in preventive programs that provide the hope of diminishing the long-range costs of emotional illness seem eminently worthwhile despite their obviously high initial cost.

OBJECTIONS BASED ON THE IDEA THAT PREVENTIVE PROGRAMS INVADE PERSONAL PRIVACY

Many are threatened by the possibility that community preventive programs in the mental health field will invade their personal privacy (Bower, 1969). In a free society each individual regards it as his right and privilege to mind his own business and to expect others to mind theirs. Halleck (1969) feels that the danger in community psychiatry of the use of "medical power" to control those with deviant political or ethical beliefs is very real. He recognizes that the growth of community psychiatry has encouraged the expansion of the concept of mental illness, and fears that it could come to include whatever behaviors are regarded as troublesome by the powers that be. Halleck points to the practice in the Soviet Union of pronouncing insane many who are regarded as dangerous to the state as an example of the type of abuse of mental health practices by which society is threatened. Another example he offers which strikes closer to home is the poll conducted by a national magazine during a recent presidential campaign asking 13,000 psychiatrists to judge the psychological fitness of one of the major candidates, whom none had ever examined. A more recent example that may be even more disquieting to those with Halleck's concerns is Clark's (1971) advocacy of the administration of behavior-controlling drugs to society's "power-controlling" leaders.

This type of objection to preventive programs and, in fact, to virtually any efforts that are advanced to regulate society in order to deal with a major problem, such as polio inoculation and water fluoridation, is firmly rooted in the individualism that characterized the frontier American. Admittedly, some societies have used the mental health fields and medicine in general as a means of controlling the behavior of its members, but this has occurred in societies with long traditions of state control over the individual. If such control had not been manifested through the mental health professions, it would probably have been exercised in some other way. The American tradition is characterized by a resistance to controls, including many that would seem to have obvious benefits for the society as a whole. The difficulty of passing gun control legislation and controlling concentrations of lead in the air are current examples of this phenomenon. Despite such resistance, it has been recognized that our survival and existence as a healthy society has demanded certain kinds of controls that necessarily require giving up some freedoms and a certain amount of privacy. These include regulations on the use of automobiles, school attendance, and physical hygiene and sanitation.

The fact that Americans "give grudgingly" in the face of the potential loss of personal freedoms or privacy is probably a strength that prevents the abuses of control found in other societies. Nonetheless, some individuality must be sacrificed when failure to do so will result in the persistence of social problems. Thus, from our viewpoint, the notion of a community psychology would be impossible were it not for the fact that, because of a variety of social problems, need is felt for it at a grass roots level. By contrast, those who are most concerned about the possible abridgement of personal freedom imposed by community psychiatry, such as Dunham and Halleck, seem to assume that the impetus for developing community programs derives from *above*, either in a state with the ulterior motive of intensifying its control, or in a profession like psychiatry that needs the community movement to bolster its ego. If this were truly the case, the movement would certainly founder in a society that jealously guards its traditional freedoms. Furthermore, community pro-grams generally require the active participation of the citizenry if they are to survive. Thus they are more subject to community wishes and needs than are traditional efforts which often are carried out with only passive community assent or even legalistic force as backing.

OBJECTIONS BASED ON A SOCIAL NEED FOR WINNERS AND LOSERS

There are some who would interpret our society's resistance to the solu-tion of many social problems as being rooted in the simplistic traditional view that people are either "good guys" and winners, or "bad guys" and losers (Bower, 1969; Eissler, 1955; Rome, 1969). According to this view, in a free, individualistic society each person begins with an equal opportunity and by conscientiousness, hard work, and good intentions he can be successful. He fails if he has not been conscientious enough, has been lazy, or has been badly intentioned. This is the theme of the popular movie western, and is the essence of the cops and robbers drama. A ma-jor value of this theme for society is that through overt success one proves for himself that he is one of the good guys. If there were few or no losers, or if losing was recognized often as being caused by starting out at a dis-advantage in the game, the satisfaction of winning or being successful would be tarnished.

Eissler (1955) in writing of delinquency in this country, questions whether society's problem controlling delinquency is mere accident. She hypothesizes that society may have a need for its criminals. In the service of such a need, therefore, some individuals are seduced into criminal be-havior, and efforts by others to prevent such behavior is resisted.

Rome (1969) describes our cultural values as setting the needs of the individual in opposition to those of society. Given these values, there is antagonism to social controls, resentment of paternalism, and insistence that all men must be treated as if they were equal. Furthermore, when not impeded by society, man is presumed capable of fulfilling his needs and wants provided that he applies himself to the task. Failure is prima facie evidence that he is weak or deficient in some important way. Such failure qualifies him for being taken care of by society but by no means at a level equal to what he could have achieved by succeeding on his own. Rome, terming this individualistic set of values "frontier psychology," be-lieves that the attitudes which glorify this approach are overidealized and unrealistic. The American frontiersman was often a hungry man and still more often a sick man. Few of his children survived infancy and quite commonly his wife died early as a result of childbirth complications. Still the romantic ideal persists, and frontier psychology characterizes the attitudes of many in our society. Some of the effects of its value system include "highly competitive territoriality, whose restrictive covenants, secret collusions, need for scapegoats, and consequent discrimination are witnessed in the disadvantaged states of women and of certain races and minority groups" (Rome, 1969, p. 39).

The attitudes that simplistically regard men as winners and losers are being challenged increasingly. Bower (1969), for example, points to mounting clinical and research evidence indicating that successful adults were successful as youngsters, and that those whose adult life is filled with frustration and failure tend to have had similarly unfulfilling childhoods. This shakes faith in the basic assumption of frontier psychology that everyone begins with the same chance. Likewise, as Rome indicates, the social problems provoked by an exploding population demand that conflicts be dealt with before they erupt into serious confrontations. This prompts a more realistic, careful look into their sources, and again points up the inequities within society. Thus the traditional individualistic barriers seem to give way, as they must, because of the very serious problems that will inevitably persist unless viewpoints and approaches change.

OBJECTIONS BECAUSE PREVENTION IS NONPALPABLE, FUTURE ORIENTED, AND OF UNPROVEN QUALITY

Cowen (1967) has pointed out that among the difficulties in arousing public and professional interest in prevention programs is the fact that they are nonpalpable and future oriented. Fund-raising programs for supporting preventive approaches must start with examples of visible suffering with which potential donors can identify. Campaigns to support research on polio, cerebral palsy, or muscular dystrophy lean heavily on posters displaying young, attractive children in braces, on crutches, or in wheelchairs. While most potential donors can readily identify with such physical disorders, or see them afflicting members of their own family or friends, they are less likely to be similarly aroused over the possibility of being stricken by mental illness. What dramatic poster display can characterize the neurotic or personality disorder in such a way as to induce strong support for preventive measures? The most dramatic example of immediate suffering caused by mental illness would be the severe psychotic. Generally, however, the lay public has extreme difficulty accepting the possibility that they are vulnerable to the plight of such unfortunates. Thus the need to prevent mental disorder has been a difficult one to impress on the general public, particularly when the payoff for such efforts tends to be in the distant future.

Associated with the nonpalpability and future orientation of the preventive program, is the further concern that prevention programs have not yet proved their worth. Lack of tangible evidence of the effectiveness of prevention programs was one of the reasons cited by the Joint Commission on Mental Illness and Health (1961) for their own emphasis on dealing with manifest mental disorder. Of course, the long-term nature of preventive programs and the fact that their effects cannot be assessed for some time makes it difficult to provide tangible evidence of success. Furthermore, these programs are often instituted in complex social situations involving a variety of forces, many of which cannot be experimentally controlled. Thus the methodological problems in providing good evaluations are, in truth, complex, as was pointed out by Kobrin (1959) in connection with the Chicago Area Project.

The objections to preventive programs cited here have, no doubt, impeded their development for many years. If traditional mental health approaches seemed at all adequate, it is highly likely that these objections would continue to prevent the establishment of preventive programs. The increasing demand for preventive approaches to a variety of problems speaks to the failure of traditional approaches. If already manifest problems could be treated successfully and quickly, prevention would have little or no appeal. Therefore, the willingness to delay gratification and invest in programs that cannot demonstrate their utility in the immediate future has become an absolute necessity.

OBJECTIONS BASED ON THE IDEA THAT PREVENTION WOULD RESULT IN POORER TREATMENT FOR THE IMPOVERISHED

Halleck (1969) points out that although one of the more exciting aspects of community psychiatry is that it holds out hope for providing better care for the impoverished, it may, paradoxically, merely intensify current inequalities in our service delivery systems. While he recognizes that community approaches would bring many new services to the lower classes, Halleck regards it as unlikely that these new approaches will include intensive psychotherapy. Instead, considerable environmental manipulation will be involved, and drug therapies, brief psychotherapy, and counseling will be stressed. Thus he suggests that a wiser approach might be to train more individual, group, or family therapists who could practice intensive psychotherapy.

This type of objection is based entirely on a value system that places individual psychotherapy at the top of a hierarchy of treatment for mental problems. One can only continue to maintain such a value system by ignoring, or denying a tremendous amount of evidence that would (a) question the general utility of intensive psychotherapy, and (b) regard traditional intensive psychotherapy as particularly inappropriate for the lower classes (Bernstein, 1964; Bredemeier, 1964; Reiff, 1966). Mental health professionals working with the lower classes have long recognized that the poorly educated and impoverished view their problems as immediate ones, requiring solutions that are as tangible and prompt as possible. The poorly educated, economically deprived patient has been notoriously impatient with and unresponsive to psychotherapeutic approaches stressing the need for insight into deep psychic needs. As a result, as Bredemeier (1964) has pointed out, the mental health professional has reacted by labeling such individuals as being inferior and unworthy of his attention. Training more intensive individual psychotherapists would not alter this state of affairs. Furthermore, Albee's research (1959, 1963) would indicate that we cannot possibly train individual therapists in the numbers required, even if the service they could provide were altogether effective. The answer to the problems of the poor inevitably lies in approaches that are different from those that have been traditionally practiced.

OBJECTIONS ROOTED IN THE THEORETICAL VIEWS OF THE CAUSES OF BEHAVIOR DISORDER

Traditionally, the behavioral sciences have attributed the major impetus for behavior in general and behavior disorder in particular to forces internal to the individual. The earliest approximations of personality theories were characterologies (MacKinnon, 1944) many of which focused on physiological makeup. In ancient Greece, broad personality characteristics were thought to be expressions of various internal combinations of four basic elements—earth, air, fire, and water (Rosenhan and London, 1968). Different combinations resulted in different temperamental types and these, in turn, determined the kinds of behavior a person would manifest. Although a developing sophistication over the years has prompted the rejection of ancient theories of temperament, there have been continuing attempts to associate personality characteristics with temperamental attributes rooted in the physiological makeup of the individual. Till the end of the 19th century, the idea that certain character types, particularly the socially deviant, were rooted in an inherited physiological structure was popularized in the writings of Lombroso and Krafft-Ebing. Later typologists such as Kretchmer and Sheldon conducted highly sophisticated research on the relationship between body types, temperament, and behavior.

Although many other psychological theorists rejected the idea of a direct relationship between constitutional makeup, heredity, and temperament, they did not reject the idea that the essential forces that determine the way the individual behaves are internal. Although Freud, for example, attributed great importance to a person's experience as a determinant of his behavior, thereby minimizing the significance of constitutional makeup, he regarded all behavior disorder as deriving from patterns that became fixed in the first five years of life and continued to exercise their influence throughout the remainder of one's life. Many other personality theories have differed in content from Freud's but have held to the basic idea that the earliest learning experiences set up predispositions that are carried throughout life and that play an inordinately important role in determining behavior. Traditionally, most psychotherapeutic approaches have involved attempts to derive greater understanding of the internal forces that propel the individual. Many brief psychotherapeutic approaches have continued to be influenced by psychoanalysis so that, while they probe less deeply, they nonetheless emphasize the past and its role in determining present behavior. Even in recent years, the development of the encounter group has involved an attempt to acquire deep understanding of one's own internal processes, presumably as a way of better understanding and regulating behavior (Zax and Cowen, 1972). Likewise, recently popular cathartic therapies (Janov, 1970) retain an emphasis on internal factors.

The emphasis on the role of *external* forces in determining human behavior has been a traditional focus of sociology, not psychology. In recent years, however, psychologists have become more and more concerned about the impact of external, often social, forces on the behavior of individuals. Hunt (1968), for example, has discussed competence—skill in symbolizing, in being able to solve problems, in being future oriented, and in being motivated to achieve and assume responsibility—as deriving from man's continuing interchange with the environment and other individuals. He musters considerable recent evidence to support the notion that intelligence, long regarded as a characteristic fixed by internal factors, is greatly affected by experience. This evidence is drawn from a multitude of sources including recent genetic theory, studies of the problem-solving ability of animals, studies of the psychological development of human infants, and cross-cultural studies using so-called "cultural-free" tests.

Behavior modification, an approach which is achieving greater and greater currency these days is another movement that places great emphasis on the effects of immediate experience in shaping and maintaining behavior (Ullmann and Krasner, 1969). From this viewpoint, man's immediate experience is far more significant in determining his behavior than his remote past. Operating on the basis of such a viewpoint, and through using certain laboratory derived principles of learning, very impressive behavioral changes have been demonstrated in individuals in a variety of settings including hospitals and schools.

Kahn (1968) has applied the implications of organizational research to mental health problems and concludes that, to be effective, therapy must be less compartmentalized, less separated from "other agencies of socialization." For him the classical therapist-patient model, with its isolation from the social context, is ludicrous. His point is well made by an analogy he draws involving a boxer and his adviser:

"The patient and therapist laboring in these circumstances are reminiscent of a prizefighter and his second caught in a nightmare situation. The fighter is taking a terrible beating under circumstances that the second is forbidden to witness, from adversaries that the second is forbidden to meet, and whose onslaughts he can do nothing to prevent. Nevertheless, the fighter returns to the second for a few minutes after each round for repairs and advice that he is allowed to get from no other source. To the student of human organizations, it is a terrible and marvelous conception" (Kahn, 1968, pp. 70 and 71).

Thus a growing trend within psychology emphasizes the significance of social and environmental forces in determining behavior. Nevertheless, very significant numbers of traditionally trained professionals think, almost reflexively, of deep-lying psychological forces as being the most significant factors in behavior, and will continue to operate on that basis. In his above-mentioned critique of community psychiatry, Halleck (1969) reveals the traditional bias toward emphasizing the importance of internal psychic forces by pointing out that the poor will undoubtedly receive inferior mental health care through community psychiatry because they will receive less intensive psychotherapy than they might if our resources were invested in training more therapists. This implicit bias among traditionally trained mental health workers favoring the search for deep-lying internal sources of behavior doubtless will impede development of community psychology.

DISSENT BASED ON THE THREAT TO THE PROFESSIONAL'S ROLE

Perhaps the most formidable resistance to community psychology resides in mental health professionals whose current professional roles are threatened by the new movements. Halleck (1969) exemplifies this point quite explicitly when he asserts that a major implication of community psychiatry is that it thrusts the psychiatrist into a number of administrative roles. He questions whether those roles are suitable for the physician with typical residency training and fears that the public will be the loser if the psychiatrist spends more of his time in "administration" and less in direct clinical practice where his primary training and expertise lie. Other observers, concerned about the same issue that Halleck discusses, take an entirely different view. They regard the tight specialization that Halleck believes serves the public best as a weakness. Rome (1969), for example, describes technological advances within medicine, which have inevitably been accompanied by greater and greater specialization, as a process that has fragmented interests and has led to a damaging compartmentalization of services. Emergence of separate structures has led to factional differences that have diverted professionals from pursuing their proper goals of high standards of practice and knowledge toward defending the social or business interests of their own particular specialty.

A somewhat similar concern over specialization dangers is expressed by Sarason, Levine, Goldenberg, Cherlin, and Bennett (1966). These authors speak of a "professional preciousness" which is one of the detrimental consequences of the parochialism of the mental health professions. This term refers to "the tendency to view what they are and do as unique, and to believe that they are the only ones who 'truly' understand, grapple with, and effect changes in individuals beset with problems in living and adjustment" (Sarason et al., 1966, p. 34). As an example, they cite the early years of the child guidance movement when the functions performed by the various members of the clinic team were rigidly differentiated. The psychiatric social worker was restricted to doing casework, the psychologist did psychological testing, and the psychiatrist was the team member responsible for treatment. Gradually these interprofessional boundaries were broken down and, in most clinics, psychotherapy is now practiced by nonpsychiatrists with no suggestion that treatment quality has suffered because it is performed by a nonmedically trained person instead of a psychiatrist. However, once psychology and social work won the psychotherapy battle, they, too, adopted a "precious" attitude toward other groups that might engage in this "holy" rite. Thus the guidance worker, the vocational rehabilitation counselor, the speech therapist, and a variety of professionals concerned with educational remediation are looked down on. Such individuals are regarded as engaging in a far less complex undertaking than the psychotherapist and, therefore, are thought to be in less need of psychological understanding and skill.

Sarason et al. believe that attitudes of this kind reflect a confusion between the typical level of training and practice of other professionals and the complexity of the problems with which they attempt to deal. Those who have looked closely at the situations with which the vocational counselor and guidance worker must cope recognize them as extraordinarily complex problems, equally as demanding of psychological skill as the usual clinic functions. The reason most mental health workers have failed to recognize this is because they are ignorant of the problems dealt with in settings other than traditional clinics and hospitals. As a result, established mental health professionals contribute little to the training or practice of many individuals attempting to cope with very serious and complex psychological problems.

Bredemeier (1964) has done a provocative market analysis of the relationship between the socially handicapped and traditional mental health agencies. Among the "costs" to agencies of accepting patients from disadvantaged backgrounds, he lists the potential obsolescence of the methods used by traditional personnel. Bredemeier points out that the professional skills and ideologies of typical agency people have been developed to deal with a client who is different from the one coming out of a disadvantaged background. Considerable reliance has been placed on the preexistence of a home and community that has built into the client the motivation to use the services and techniques offered by the agency. But what works pretty well with the middle class client does not work well with those from the lower classes. Middle class patients recognize that they have problems, are motivated to ask for help, and are involved enough to weather the routine of being referred from one professional to another before being offered help. Lower class clients fail to recognize problems in many cases, are afraid to approach the agency for help, and may be too confused or too poorly motivated to accept being shunted from one professional to another.

What is the price agency personnel must pay in attempting to change their techniques and approaches to accommodate to the needs and characteristics of the lower classes? Bredemeier identifies three types of costs. The first has to do with the professional's feeling of self-respect. To some extent, professional status is tied to the status of the client that he serves. The lower class client adds little to the status of the professional, and to treat him, the professional must risk the failure of his traditional approaches. Thus it is simpler to reject the lower classes as being somehow inherently inferior. As Bredemeier states:

"It is as if our hypothetical psychologist, upon finding that his techniques for reinforcing rats did not work with pigeons, hastened to assure himself and bystanders that pigeons are notoriously inferior creatures anyway, and he is not to be judged on the basis of his unfortunate association with them" (Bredemeier, 1966, p. 99).

A second price that the professional must pay in attempting to treat the lower classes relates to his investment in acquiring his clinical skills.

Considerable time and effort goes into the training that provides the traditional skills for dealing with psychological problems. To set these aside an attempt to acquire a new set of skills means writing off a considerable investment. Worse yet, to some degree, most professionals have begun to identify with their old methods. Writing off a hard-won well-practiced model of functioning is like giving up part of oneself. The resistance to doing so on the part of agency personnel is likely to be as tenacious as the resistance of the handicapped client to giving up the self-defeating behavior which is felt as part of himself.

The third factor that prompts opposition to moving toward new approaches is the fact that success is not assured by new methods. The absence of such certainty, in a realm where success is highly important, leads to the endowment of a magical quality to whatever methods are used. Thus the method becomes a "reassuring ritual" which is difficult to relinquish unless it can be exchanged for some other form of reassurance.

The resistance of professionals themselves, who must help bring about the changes leading to community psychology, is quite formidable. In many instances, professionals block initiation of community approaches. Equally damaging, they often operate in subtle ways to undermine already established programs. Considering the potential power of this form of resistance, the ever-growing numbers of community psychology programs that are emerging testify to the force of the social need impelling them.

CONCLUSION

This chapter attempts to summarize the types of objections to establishing a community psychology. The sources of this opposition are manifold. Some reside in the attitudes and values characterizing American society. Many others are found within the professional groups expected to take the lead in the community movement. The array of criticisms is so formidable that many would marvel at the fact that community psychology has managed to establish even the foothold it now enjoys. This can only be understood on the basis of very potent social needs that are felt quite intensely at the present time.

References

Albee, G. W. *Mental health manpower trends.* New York: Basic Books, 1959.

Albee, G. W. American psychology in the sixties. *American Psychologist,* 1963, *18,* 90–95.

Bernstein, B. Social class, speech systems, and psychotherapy. In F. Riessman, J. Cohen, & A. Pearl (Eds.), *The mental health of the poor*. New York: Free Press, 1964. Pp. 194–204.

Bower, E. M. *Early identification of emotionally handicapped children*, 2nd ed. Springfield, Ill.: Charles C. Thomas, 1969.

Bredemeier, H. C. The socially handicapped and the agencies: a market analysis. In F. Riessman, J. Cohen, & A. Pearl (Eds.), *The mental health of the poor*. New York: Free Press, 1964. Pp. 88–109.

Caplan, G. *Principles of preventive psychiatry*. New York: Basic Books, 1964.

Clark, K. B. The pathos of power: a psychological perspective. *American Psychologist*, 1971, *26*, 1047–1057.

Cowen, E. L. Emergent approaches to mental health problems: an overview and directions for future work. In E. L. Cowen, E. A. Gardner, & M. Zax (Eds.), *Emergent approaches to mental health problems*. New York: Appleton-Century-Crofts, 1967. Pp. 389–455.

Dunham, H. W. Community psychiatry—the newest therapeutic bandwagon. *Archives of General Psychiatry*, 1965, *12*, 303–313.

Eissler, R. Scapegoats of society. In K. R. Eissler (Ed.), *Searchlights on delinquency*. New York: International Universities Press, 1955.

Halleck, S. L. Community psychiatry: some troubling questions. In L. M. Roberts, S. L. Halleck, & M. B. Loeb (Eds.), *Community psychiatry*. Garden City, N. Y.: Doubleday, Anchor Books, 1969. Pp. 58–71.

Hunt, J. McV. Toward the prevention of incompetence. In J. W. Carter, Jr. (Ed.), *Research contributions from psychology to community mental health*. New York: Behavioral Publications, 1968. Pp. 19–45.

Janov, A. *The primal scream*. New York: G. P. Putnam's Sons, 1970.

Joint Commission on Mental Illness and Health. *Action for Mental Health*. New York: Science Editions, 1961.

Kahn, R. L. Implications of organizational research for community mental health. In J. W. Carter, Jr. (Ed.), *Research contributions from psychology to community mental health*. New York: Behavioral Publications, 1968. Pp. 60–74.

Kobrin, S. The Chicago area project—a 25 year assessment. *The Annals of the American Academy of Political and Social Sciences*, 1959, *322*, 19–29.

MacKinnon, D. W. The structure of personality. In J. Mcv. Hunt (Ed.), *Personality and the behavior disorders*, Vol. I. New York: Ronald, 1944. Pp. 3–48.

Powers, E., & Witmer, H. *Experiment in prevention of delinquency*. New York: Columbia University Press, 1951.

Quinney, R. *The social reality of crime*. Boston: Little, Brown & Co., 1970.

Reiff, R. Mental health manpower and institutional change. *American Psychologist*, 1966, *21*, 540–548.

Rome, H. P. Barriers to the establishment of comprehensive community mental health centers. In L. M. Roberts, S. L. Halleck, M. B. Loeb (Eds.),

Community psychiatry. Garden City, N. Y.: Doubleday, Anchor Books, 1969. Pp. 31–57.

Rosenhan, D., & London, P. Character. In P. London & D. Rosenhan (Eds.), *Foundations of abnormal psychology.* New York: Holt, Rinehart & Winston, 1968. Pp. 251–289.

Sarason, S. B., Levine, M., Goldenberg, I. I., Cherlin, D. L., & Bennett, E. M. *Psychology in community settings: clinical, educational, vocational, social aspects.* New York: Wiley, 1966.

The President's Task Force on the Mentally Handicapped. *Action against mental disability.* Washington, D. C.: U. S. Government Printing Office, 1970.

Ullmann, L. P., & Krasner, L. *A psychological approach to abnormal behavior.* Englewood Cliffs, N. J.: Prentice-Hall, 1969.

Zax, M., & Cowen, E. L. *Abnormal Psychology: Changing Conceptions.* New York: Holt, Rinehart & Winston, 1972.

12. *training for new professional roles*

Obviously, as preceding chapters have indicated, the psychologist who is creating and functioning in community psychology programs is assuming a variety of roles that are entirely new to him. For the most part, clinical psychologists have taken the lead in the evolving field of community psychology. Traditionally, their training has emphasized diagnosing and treating behavior disorders. Therapy has typically been practiced on a one-to-one basis, although in recent years group approaches have grown in prominence. Thus the traditional role for the psychologist who has led the way in community psychology has been shaped largely by the medical model. Although other professional groups, such as sociologists and social psychologists, have been concerned with community forces, they have been interested in researching and understanding these forces rather than in altering them. For virtually all, therefore, who would enter community psychology, it is necessary to adopt entirely novel roles.

While it is premature to assemble an exhaustive list of potential new roles that may be required of the community psychologist, several general classes can be identified. Spielberger and Iscoe (1970) have described three functions that community psychologists have performed in recent years: mental health consultation, participant conceptualization, and serving as agents of social change. Although these functions can be distinguished one from the other, they are not mutually exclusive so that, in a given program, a particular individual may function in more than one of these roles.

In the role of *mental health consultant,* the psychologist is primarily a resource for assisting community "caregivers" (Caplan, 1964), who are themselves professionals in a position to assist community members in dealing with various stressful situations, but who have little mental health training. Various types of consultative roles are discussed in a previous chapter.

The *participant-conceptualizer's* role requires the mental health professional to "help community leaders analyze and clarify mental health problems in terms of social system variables" (Spielberger and Iscoe, 1970, p. 233). Once the problem has been defined, the community psychologist may revert to the role of mental health consultant and thereby help in formulating programs for coping with it. An important requirement of the participant-conceptualizer role is the capacity to anticipate long-range consequences of problem solutions. Historically, mental health problems have been addressed after-the-fact, with solutions directed at the immediate situation but lacking perspective on potentially adverse long-range effects. To take the necessary long view, the participant-conceptualizer will very likely need to integrate the knowledge of a variety of areas such as community organization, sociology, urban planning, economics, and political science in solving problems. As a participant-conceptualizer, one must also anticipate the potential threat that any innovative solution to a problem will have for established community interests.

When a psychologist, through his professional activities, attempts to modify a social system, he is functioning as a *social change agent.* In the consultant role the psychologist tries to help caregivers provide better service to clients; as a participant-conceptualizer he attempts to help community leaders identify significant problems and to develop solutions for them; as a social change agent he takes direct steps to solve a problem that he has identified. A number of the programs described in the previous chapters of this book involve efforts on the part of mental health professionals to serve as social change agents.

As several writers have pointed out, the essence of community psychology is an emphasis on the significance of external forces as a determinant of behavior in contradistinction to the traditional intrapsychic emphases (Reiff, 1970; Roen, 1970; Levine, 1970). This shift in emphasis calls into questions the value for the community psychologist of much typical clinical psychology training, especially that portion devoted to theory, individual diagnosis, and one-to-one psychotherapy. As Levine (1970) states in discussing the new community approaches:

"The relevant theory has to do with group dynamics, with concepts such as role, with the study of institutions and organizations, particularly as these involve the control of deviancy, the study of the goals and values of a variety of social institutions and settings, the organization of helping services, the introduction of services into ongoing systems, the development of new service organizations, and the concepts of social and institutional change" (Levine, 1970, p. 76).

How, then, should the new community psychologist be trained?

GENERAL RECOMMENDATIONS FOR COMMUNITY PSYCHOLOGY TRAINING

The purpose of the Boston Conference of 1966 (Bennett, Anderson, Cooper, Hassol, Klein, and Rosenblum, 1966), which is often regarded as the birth of modern community psychology, was to discuss training for psychologists preparing to go into community mental health work. Understandably, at such an early stage in the development of community psychology, conference participants were reluctant to support a narrowly restricted training model. Community psychology was considered to be too poorly defined to permit rigid specification of any type of training program. Clearly accepted was the idea that the psychologist, and particularly the clinical psychologist, who was most likely to be drawn into community work, needed to broaden his horizons greatly and to become much more of a generalist than he had been heretofore. The psychologist who would function in the community was seen to need input from many of the social sciences, and recognizing the still fragmentary knowledge of community psychology functioning, it was felt that he should remain relatively open to new concepts and service approaches. The ideal role for the community psychologist was that of a "participant-conceptualizer." Thus, while he is embroiled in community processes, the psychologist must also conceptualize such processes within his framework. This entails, in a sense, pulling the field up by its bootstraps.

Discussion at the Boston Conference ranged widely. Recognizing that most community psychologists were converted from clinical psychology, one major issue concerned the necessity of basic training in clinical psychology for community mental health work. Some felt that skills acquired through clinical training were essential for many aspects of community psychology; others feared that the clinician's emphasis on individual pathology might impede functioning in community work. Conference participants tended to agree that the community psychologist required doctoral training and that such training was best provided in university settings. With respect to program content, it was generally agreed that the sociological aspects of psychology merited greater stress and, correspondingly, that the traditional clinical emphasis on neurological and somatic knowledge should be deemphasized. Areas such as social system theory, community organization, city planning, biostatistics, consultation methods, human ecology, and epidemiology were frequently stressed as necessary.

The necessity for field training for the community psychologist was accepted by all. It was agreed that this training should include participation in consultation, group programs not typically found in clinical internships, and community action programs. There was less agreement about the place of training for patient care in these field programs. Thus, once again, although the conference encouraged the establishment of a new field in psychology, it was ambivalent about the prospect of cutting the emerging specialty off from its clinical roots. Another base in psychology that the conference participants seemed most reluctant to abandon was the research tradition. Community psychology was considered to need scientific inquiry and a readiness to test procedures objectively to become established on a firm scientific footing.

The Boston Conference participants explored the relative merits of specialist versus generalist training and rejected the concept of a highly developed specialist. The developmentally primitive stage of the field of community psychology was viewed as discouraging rigidifying professional roles or training patterns. Instead, it was believed that a broad outlook on the place of man in his social context and the introduction of a variety of interventive practices for dealing with man's problems was necessary. Some opted for a shift from courses based on subdisciplines in psychology toward a training program focusing on necessary social changes, and the various approaches that might be used to bring these changes about. Diverse field placements and a broad sampling of social settings, social problems, and different types of clientele were recommended as optimal preparation for such efforts.

Finally, the necessity for having training program directors who could serve as role models involved in social-system change was stressed. The mandate for such leaders is to convey an "ecological model" and to protect the "inquiring innovative ecological stance" against the sterility that can follow the process of institutionalization. Many recognized, too, that, as relevant bodies of knowledge and skills developed, these would have to be transmitted to undergraduates as well as to graduate students.

In his discussion of the training requirements for mental health professionals entering the community field, Cowen (1967), like the members of the Boston Conference, recognized the difficulty of delineating the specific form that training programs should take. He pointed out that relevant course work is not yet well defined and, furthermore, that the field lacks sufficient identification models to make the necessary learning "come alive." He foresaw that the development of new training programs would be a drawn out process in which mistakes would be made and learning would have to come about through experience. A significant point made in Cowen's discussion was that even in the best program that might evolve, it would probably not be possible to prepare professionals for the "full spectrum of situations and challenges that they will be called upon to face in their subsequent careers" (Cowen, 1967, p. 440). However, Cowen asserted that a sense of skepticism concerning what might be the "proper" way of functioning, a focus on solving problems, and the establishment of a general set preparing one always to deal with the new and unexpected should be common to all professional training for community psychology.

Reiff (1966), in discussing the training of community psychologists and the retraining of clinical psychologists, expressed the need for a period of exploration before specifying the nature of training programs. He favored meetings between clinical psychologists and other social scientists, bringing together professionals who have stressed the significance of internal and external forces as determinants of behavior. He also favored empirical studies to generate data on which to base firm decisions. He suggested training social psychologists to do community mental health work and to experiment in various types of settings to determine which would be the best base for a community mental health program. Avoiding the issue of specialist versus generalist training, Reiff did take a stand for "training for versatility." Instead of being a generalist, the versatile professional would be capable of applying a variety of techniques in keeping with the needs of those he serves. In a later discussion of training needs, Reiff (1970) stressed the necessity for developing a body of theory and a set of practices that could distinguish community psychology as a separate school of psychology. Without a definition of the parameters of a new field, as a first step toward developing a body of new knowledge, he could not see how training programs might be developed.

Golann (1970) has recommended five principles to guide the development of community psychology training programs. The first concurs with the Boston Conference recommendation that generalists rather than specialists should be trained. The second recommends that training experiences should include collaboration with different professionals such as educators, political scientists, psychiatrists, and sociologists. The third specifies that training for consultative roles is necessary. Fourth, Golann indicates that a basic knowledge of social systems and the experience of being a participant observer under a supervisor's tutelage in more than one of the several systems is desirable. Finally, he recommends that the community psychologist be trained to evaluate mental health services.

Roen (1970) makes a number of recommendations concerning optimal training in community psychology, most of which relate to practicum experiences. He recommends that students be exposed early in their training to as broad a range of human problems as possible. For Roen, the ideal training facility would adhere to the neighborhood service center model rather than to a medical clinic model, and would be operated by the training institution itself. This facility would be affiliated with a specifically defined community that would be studied historically, topographically, demographically, and clinically to provide a data pool in the context of which the personal and social problems of community members could be best understood. Community psychology students would affiliate with this facility as soon as they entered training. Their activities and experiences would be graduated so that in the early stages of training they might simply assume the role of "case administrator" for as many as 10 to 20 cases. In this role they could become familiar with a client early in his intake phase and serve as his "ombudsman" by contacting him from two to four times a year to check on how a particular intervention was working. This would provide both a quasi-administrative experience and a longitudinal perspective on what happens to people who are being treated. Other early student experiences might include taking the phone calls or reading the letters representing the earliest contacts made by the client with the facility. Later experiences for the student would, of course, include specific contact with clients with respect to their problems.

The faculty in Roen's training facility would conduct conferences dealing with cases typifying the problems faced in such a center, and would devote a portion of their time to research. Faculty would supervise students in areas of special competence, and students would be encouraged to move flexibly from one supervisor to another as needed.

Along with his previously described position that relevant training for community psychologists should include group dynamics, a conception of roles, a study of institutions and organizational structure, and the development of new types of service programs, Levine (1970) has sketched an image of a model community psychology institution. His ideal institution, oriented toward urban problems, would essentially be a service commune. Two or three senior staff members and, perhaps even their families, would reside in the center along with approximately 20 others, most of whom would be graduate students. The graduate student group, drawn from a variety of disciplines, would include, besides community psychology students, sociologists, law students, city planners, economists, education students, medical students, and the like. In addition, some places would be reserved for indigenous workers as well as a journalism student, an artist, a poet, or a novelist. This type of mix is sought to guard against the insularity that characterizes many professional groups.

Each resident in the center would be responsible for identifying a "problem in living" in the area served, and for creating a program to deal with that problem. Resident staff would be expected to encourage the student to treat each program of this kind as a research opportunity through which a specific ameliorative approach can be related to a broader conceptual framework. Course work for students would be kept to a bare minimum, perhaps, including only courses in statistics and research design. Students would be certified primarily by examinations testing their knowledge of a set of readings specified by the graduate department. At the heart of the training program would be three experiences provided at the training center itself. The first would be a seminar where students would present their ideas and discuss their work. University faculty with expertise relevant to specific problems grappled with by the group would be invited to speak. Course credit would not be given for the seminar, but participation in it would be required of all residents at the training center to make intellectual exchange a vital aspect of the life situation.

The second basic training experience would be some combination of group sensitivity training and psychotherapy. This experience would be designed to assist in the self-development of group members. Hopefully, this experience would provide an understanding of one's personal impact on others, for Levine a vitally necessary insight for one intending to lead community programs.

The third training experience at the center would be a regular meeting devoted to dealing with the problems arising in life within the institution. All residents would participate equally in policy decisions, in allocating the center's resources, and in the everyday problems of maintaining and caring for the building. Thus, every resident would have the opportunity to handle the mundane administrative matters that beset any leader.

Graduate departments sending students to the center would be required to do so with the understanding that no feedback would be forthcoming concerning an individual student's progress without his consent. The institution's residents would select students on the basis of interest, and each new resident would begin on a probationary status until the group decided whether or not the program was a suitable one for him. Once admitted to regular status in the program, all decisions about a student's continuation would be the responsibility of the group. Individual members would be encouraged in their own growth but, if the decision were reached that a person was not functioning well in the group, it would become a group responsibility to find a suitable alternative placement for him.

Levine emphasizes that such a training center must be financially independent. All too often he fears that those who provide funds attempt to exercise control over an institution's functioning, so that there would be a serious danger of having the goals of the center subverted by its financial supporters. Ultimately, he envisions that the best way to ensure the integrity of the institution and its goals would be for a portion of its funds to come from those who are served by its programs, which has the added advantage of helping to guarantee the relevance of programming.

Within the center's general service mission, each individual would ideally have the ultimate responsibility for any program that he develops. All decisions with respect to that program should be made by its developer with center residents exercising only an advisory role. Although some group control would prevail, since the allocation of funds would be a group decision, a resident would be free to seek funds from outside sources in instances where he disagreed with a group decision that might limit him.

This survey, while not exhaustive, represents much of the recent thinking of some of the more prominent figures in community psychology about training for work in that field. Unfortunately, the dominant feature in all of these recommendations is vagueness. Agreement with respect to certain general issues is evident, but specific guidelines for reaching desired goals are lacking. All seem to agree that a readiness to be innovative and flexible in coping with human problems is a prime requisite for the community psychologist. Many speak of the need for training a generalist. Those who propose specific programs, such as Roen and Levine, speak in visionary terms not readily translated into practical programs. A fair evaluation of the majority of these recommendations is that they point out some very general directions while they ignore many practical details that must be dealt with in developing specific programs. This is probably less a criticism of the general recommendations that have been made than it is a comment on the nascent state of the field. At such a stage it is easier to talk in idealistic terms and in broad generalities. The next section considers several examples of extant training programs in which developers have had to work through a variety of practical issues.

SPECIFIC TRAINING PROGRAMS FOR COMMUNITY ROLES

Specific training programs for community psychology have emerged in a number of different settings around the country. These programs may be classified, as is done by Iscoe and Spielberger (1970), into those that have been grafted onto already existing clinical psychology training programs and those that have developed in multidisciplinary settings. Community psychology training in clinical psychology programs is an attempt to make clinical psychologists broader, more versatile practitioners. Typically, community training is only one segment of the total program for the fledging clinical psychologist and is often provided after some of the basic clinical training is completed. Clinical psychologists are prominently present in multidisciplinary programs but are joined by graduate students from other areas such as education, sociology, psychiatry, nursing, philosophy, and even law and business.

Training Within Clinical Psychology Programs

The Program at George Peabody College

The community psychology program at George Peabody College (Newbrough, Rhodes, and Seeman, 1970) began modestly with a seminar in community mental health first offered in 1957 that was incorporated the next year into the doctoral program in clinical psychology. From its modest beginnings in what was a pioneering period for such programs, the Peabody program has passed through three developmental phases. Phase I, lasting from 1957 to 1963, started out with a primary focus on presenting content areas through a typical seminar format. Topics such as the major historical influences on community psychology, conceptual models of community psychology, understanding the community, and methodology in community psychology were covered. Midway through Phase One, practicum experiences were set up to augment classroom content, with the major practicum technique being consultation. Practicum experiences were coordinated with a course designed to teach students about various aspects of the consultation process. Field agencies used for the consultation program included nursery schools, private schools, the welfare department, a social work program in a housing project, the detention center of a juvenile court, and a neighborhood community center. Prior to engaging in these consulting experiences, students were given experience in administration and supervision through work with other graduate students in what was called a "verticle team" approach. Teams were set up consisting of from four to six students at varying levels of training. Each team functioned as an independent clinical staff with specific service responsibilities at a child study center. In each team a third-year clinical student took the major supervisory and administrative responsibility with the assistance of a faculty member. Thus each team member, when he advanced to the third year, came to assume an administrative, supervisory role.

Phase Two of the Peabody program, a brief one, lasted from 1964 to 1966. Some broadening of the original program took place during this period as the result of research study carried on by one of Peabody's faculty members. This study was devoted to describing patterns of discordant behavior in a high pathology neighborhood, and to studying ways in which the community dealt with its problems as reflected in the action of its agencies (the church, courts, welfare, schools, and the like). Among the by-products of carrying out this study was the increased contact among the participating agencies. A second important yield was the establishment of a neighborhood counseling center as an extension of an existing mental health center in Nashville. These developments were relevant to the community psychology program in two ways. First, they made available a resource through which training in community research could be provided. Second, and no less significantly, the interdisciplinary group that was brought together for the purposes of carrying out the study found it worthwhile to remain together once the study was completed. This group formed the nucleus for the eventual establishment of a Center for Community Studies at George Peabody College. During Phase II also occurred the extension of the community psychology program into small urban communities having limited professional resources, and its further extension to consultation with community caregivers such as nurses and ministers.

In the third and most recent phase of the George Peabody program, beginning in 1966, the community psychology program was developed as a separate entity within the psychology department coordinate with other departmental programs. It still remained most closely related to the clinical training program but became available to students in other departmental programs such as counseling, school psychology, educational psychology, and the like who could benefit from community psychology training. In addition, this independent status provided the community psychology program with an opportunity to develop its own unique form.

Presently training in Peabody's program includes two seminars given in alternate years entitled "An Introduction to Community Mental Health," and "Community Action and Community Development." In addition, there is a series of three to four field placement semesters structured according to the level of the student's experience. In the field placement from four to six hours per week are spent in the setting and two hours are devoted to a seminar in which students' experiences are reviewed. The most elementary field experience involves the study of some aspect of the local community. Field work is spent in collecting information, with the assistance of a community volunteer, for a report on the particular aspect of the community under study. A second type of placement at a higher experience level involves consultation to a particular agency or program under the supervision of some staff member, often not a psychologist, in the agency. The third field experience at the most complex level requires participation in a program evaluation or research project in the community.

Another significant development in Peabody's third phase has been the development and articulation of a Center for Community Studies. This center includes faculty from departments of sociology, psychology, and psychiatry from a variety of colleges in the Nashville, Tennessee area, and has become affiliated with many centers and schools equipped to make relevant contributions to the center's functions. These functions include primarily descriptive and evaluative research that deals with the impact of community programs on the local scene. As a coordinator for this research, the center is in a position to provide community field experiences for students as well as paid research assistantships.

The University of Rochester Program

Cowen (1970) describes the community mental health training that has been introduced in the clinical program at the University of Rochester. In this program some didactic materials on community psychology are introduced in an early seminar in psychopathology, but the primary vehicle for community psychology training is a yearlong practicum usually taken when the student is in his final year of training. On the average, a student spends about eight hours per week in his community mental health practicum.

Unlike the typical psychotherapy practicum in which the student is assigned a certain number of patients, in the community mental health practicum, a series of programs are conducted to address specific problems found in the local community and, typically, students are assigned in pairs to programs in which they have special interests. While the student's primary responsibility is toward his own program, he is expected to assist in the functions of others when they require extra manpower. Thus he may assist in screening prospective nonprofessionals or in helping with the training of nonprofessionals who are working in a program other than his own. The individual student's training is also broadened through a weekly meeting held for all the students engaged in the particum. Here students and instructor exchange information and chew over current problems.

In any given year the programs serviced through the community mental health practicum are, in part, holdovers from previous years, programs initiated by an earlier group that have, to some extent, become institutionalized and, in part, new programs being introduced for the first time. Inevitably, the new program requires broader participation on the part of the trainee, since routines have not been worked out and many unanticipated problems must be faced. The established program tends to require only the energy for looking after current program operations and, possibly, the refinement of some details of the way the program has been run in the past, with relatively little opportunity for creative, conceptual problem solving. Ideally, therefore, optimal training might result through the initiation of entirely new programs each year. In the real world this is not practical, however. Existing programs may be treating real-life problems for important segments of society and must be maintained, especially if their existance has potential for modifying an ongoing social system in a beneficial way. Another reason for continuing with existing programs is to refine them so that they can be improved over a period of time. Finally, the problems associated with mounting entirely new programs is extraordinarily complex, and the task of initiating many at one time may well be too impractical within the framework of a practicum.

A major advantage of having a variety of programs conducted concurrently along with the regular introduction of new programs is that the trainee becomes attuned to grappling with different types of problems in many different ways. This may be the best way to train students for the flexible adaptation to the varying demands of new situations that Reiff (1966) regards as essential for the community psychologist.

Some notion of the variety of social problems addressed in the Rochester Community Mental Health practicum can be provided by specifying some of the programs that have been operated through this training experience. One has been an after-school day-care program for primary grade school children who were referred by teachers as needing more attention from adults than could be provided in the ordinary school situation. To provide interested adult companions for these youngsters, members of the graduate practicum recruited volunteers from among college students who were training to teach at the elementary grade level. This volunteer target group was selected both because it seemed like a group that should be capable of meeting many of the emotional and cognitive needs of children, as well as being one that might benefit greatly from close contact with an emotionally needy child outside of the classroom context. Hopefully what could be learned in relating to the troubled child might enhance the classroom effectiveness of the volunteer once he or she became a teacher.

In this program the undergraduate volunteer was assigned to a single child with whom he met for one hour on each of two afternoons a week.

Graduate students in the program served as supervisors and resource people for groups of six to eight undergraduates and met with their groups immediately after each session between volunteer and child.

A second project through which University of Rochester clinical students received community psychology training was based in the settlement house. This project involved setting up a counseling program for 6- to 8-year-old children using 14- to 17-year-old indigenous youths as counselors. The program was based in the settlement house, and the staff of the agency referred youngsters to the program on the basis of their knowledge of the youngster or his family situation, and also participated in helping decide about counselor-child pairings. Graduate students selected counselors, trained them, and then monitored their functioning in the program through a series of regular meetings that were held twice a week following periods of interaction between a counselor and the child to whom he was assigned.

A third type of program in the Rochester Community Mental Health Practicum used retirees as mental health aides in the public schools. It was felt that retired people had considerable potential for helping young children struggling to adjust in the school system and, also, might be benefited by being useful to others. Graduate students participated in conceptualizing this program, consulting with the school system, and in selecting, recruiting, and training the retirees. Later they implemented the program and supervised the aides' functions in the schools. Retirees worked three and one-half days per week with three aides and one graduate student being assigned to each school. Teachers were acquainted with the availability of the aide in the school to deal with youngsters who might need contact with an interested adult. Aides' activities included helping with school work, play activities, reading, and conversation. In many cases, aides introduced special activities related to their own areas of expertise or interest. Graduate students maintained close contact with the aides and served as liaison to school mental health and administrative personnel.

More recent developments in the Rochester program have included the establishment of a mental health practicum for undergraduates that is taught in part by graduate students. Concurrent with the didactic portion of the practicum, undergraduates have been placed in a variety of field settings including a local state hospital and the local school system. In these settings they function in programs that are supervised by the graduate students.

Community Psychology at the City College of the City University of New York

Singer and Bard (1970) describe a community psychology training procedure that is part of a clinical psychology training program which stresses many traditional functions. The primary focus of the community psychology thrust in this program is training for consultation. As described by Singer and Bard (1970, p. 128) :

"Consultation involves a contact with either an individual or a group and has as its function the preparation of the client for some more effective activity in the amelioration of difficulties in living for some other person or small group. This consultation is not ordinarily a matter of formal teaching, lecturing, or advice giving. It is essentially a clinical contact in which the client's emotional stresses, cognitive distortions, or other personal difficulties are dealt with, using the best knowledge of individual or group interaction techniques available."

The view of consultation as the application of the consultant's clinical expertise to the consultee's cognitive or emotional problems is relatively narrow compared to the consultant's role as described by Caplan in a previous chapter. Singer and Bard's conception of the consultant's function is also not far removed from the traditional role of the clinician, and avoids the broader activity of system change and the creation of entirely new service programs.

Another essential focus of the City College program derives from the belief that our society's increasing complexity and mobility requires the establishment of neighborhood psychological centers to help provide individuals with a sense of affiliation and a feeling of community. These centers are envisioned to provide a variety of services to the community in which they are located. In addition to traditional diagnostic and treatment services, neighborhood centers are expected to carry out ecological research assessing community characteristics, stress points, and the like. Consultative services to community leaders, architects, and urban planners in connection with community projects would be another potential neighborhood center role. Agencies or groups not customarily benefiting from mental health support such as the welfare department, police departments, visiting nurses associations, boys clubs, day-care centers, unions, and the public schools could also receive consultative services. In keeping with this imagined future role for psychological service centers, students in the City College program are exposed early in their training to the operation of a university-sponsored psychological center that operates within a circumscribed community. Considerable emphasis is placed on how the community must be studied and understood to optimize the research and consultative services offered by the clinician. An important dividend in such a training experience is the realization that the clinician cannot sit by passively waiting for patients to come to him. It is hoped that he will recognize that he must be more active in communicating with community members at many different levels and that he must become aware of how the personality of the individual client must be understood in the context of the client's specific community.

The City College clinical program provides general training at the predoctoral level. Its organizers have felt that specialty training is better acquired postdoctorally. However, in its attempt to provide a good broad general base in clinical psychology, the program does stress a developmental orientation. This orientation is reflected in the sequence of courses and training experiences offered the student in the three years of the program.

In his first year, the City College student takes course work and has practicum experiences that stress the developmental cycle from childhood through old age. From eight to ten hours per week are spent in the University Psychological Center where the student observes and rates the behavior of children, without any prior knowledge of the child's background. Once experience has been acquired in systematically observing behavior, the student reads the case material on a particular child and attempts to relate background experiences to current observations. Another important feature of the first-year program is the assignment of each student to a three-generation family—a family in which there are grandparents, parents, and children all living fairly close to each other. Students are expected to meet with their family on a regular basis and to observe them systematically over their three years of residence in graduate school, and to provide the family with advisory or consultative services. Another significant feature of the first-year program is the participation of all students in a group situation described as being midway between a T-group and group psychotherapy. The first-year class is divided into two groups, each of which meets for from 20 to 25 sessions with an experienced group leader. This experience is expected to provide an outlet for the anxieties normally associated with the first-year of graduate school and to be a model for later consultation experiences in the community that will be part of the student's work.

During the second year, course work and practicum assignments focus on diagnostic testing and personality assessment. Students do intake interviews at the Psychological Center, and in the latter half of the second year, as didactic materials are being presented in the psychotherapy course, students begin to counsel troubled college students. In their consultative functions, the City College second-year student is an advisor to an undergraduate group at the college organized to provide tutoring services to local Negro and Puerto Rican school children. Here the clinical student's role is to provide information concerning the cognitive capacities and limitations of the children, to improve teaching techniques, and to help tutors deal with their doubts and uncertainties concerning their efforts.

In the third year, the graduate student carries a case load of approximately three cases in psychotherapy drawn from the local college group. The third-year consulting program is more complex than those preceding it. A course is provided in "small group dynamics and family interaction process" to acquaint the student with the theory and research literature in the field. In addition, three types of consultation experiences are available. The first, a parent education project for mothers of children placed in day-care centers, involves group meetings including mothers, clinical students, and staff supervisors that are devoted to the problems of child care. In these sessions, mothers' attitudes, gaps in knowledge, and environmental stresses are dealt with particularly. A scecond consultation experience is directed toward teachers in the local school system. In this experience, examinations are made of teachers' attitudes toward the behavior of the typical slum child, the cognitive limitations of such children, and the teachers' feelings about themselves, their school, the administration, and the neighborhood in which they are working. The third type of consultation experience involves work with a special unit of policemen. This program initiated by Bard (Bard and Berkowitz, 1967) is described in detail in Chapter 10. In this program the graduate student helps to train police officers in a special family crisis intervention unit that intercedes in identifiable family conflicts. The students participate in T-groups with police officers and are consultants to them on a continuing basis. Students also do follow-ups of families contacted by this unit. They are thus in a position to identify potential sources of serious community problems and to offer families the opportunity for treatment through various established agencies.

Community Psychology at Yale

Sarason and Levine's discussion (1970) of community psychology at Yale is more a description of a training facility than a characterization of a training program. Apparently, the authors consider this facility, the Yale Psycho-Educational Clinic, and the activities it engages in, as the backbone of the community psychology training program. The clinic, an integral part of the department of psychology, is the setting for certain practica in the clinical training program as well as the internship setting for Yale students interested in community psychology. The core staff consists of six faculty members and three part-time psychologists who, although not teaching members of the faculty, are considered clinic staff members. Faculty members of the clinic staff participate voluntarily, agreeing to devote a minimum of three days per week to the clinic.

Unlike the typical psychological or psychiatric clinic, the Yale Psycho-Educational Clinic is not open to the general public and does not take referrals of specific individuals with problems. Instead, the staff spends most of its time away from the clinic in other people's settings designing and operating various types of preventive programs. Specific settings in which staff members work are presumably a function of staff interests and the potential host's cooperativeness. Institutions and agencies such as the elementary schools, the junior high schools, aspects of the local community action program, and regional centers for the mentally retarded have been sites for many of the projects emanating from the Yale Psycho-Educational Clinic. Formal characteristics of programs vary depending on where they are based, but they often include consultation services and group approaches to dealing with the problems of large numbers of people. Prevention is a major goal throughout, and in line with this goal there is considerable concern with the way in which organizational structures often tend to be self-defeating and harmful. Another major purpose of the Yale Psycho-Educational Clinic is to serve as a vehicle through which faculty members having broadly similar aims can test their prevention theories in practical settings where personal opinions may be altered or bolstered through empirical findings.

One full day each week is set aside at the Yale Psycho-Educational Clinic for bringing together all faculty and student staff for three different activities: a clinic-wide seminar, a faculty staff meeting, and a meeting with an outside consultant on group process. The seminar and the group process meeting represent the most formal aspects of training for students. The seminar is a general meeting open to as many people as can fit around a large table, typically a maximum of 20. A broad range of topics are discussed, from research studies to strictly theoretical issues. Any participant can suggest seminar topics, and guest experts are frequently invited both from within and outside of the university. At times, the faculty and students present their own work, and some meetings are left entirely agendaless. These seminars are characterized by spirited, freewheeling, interchanges not devoid of "wit and repartee." Outsiders participating in the seminar usually lunch alone with the interns, affording students considerable personal contact with visitors.

The other meeting attended by clinic trainees is devoted to group process. Originally established as a didactic seminar focusing on theoretical and practical issues related to therapy and discussion groups, some pressure has been exerted to direct group efforts toward self-study and away from its didactic aims. This has led to the development of two factions within the group, one preferring to emphasize sensitivity training and the other regarding this as an impossible goal, given the status differences between group members. This disagreement has proved to be useful in pointing up to all group members how the clinic organization itself and the conflicts deriving from it can effect ongoing functions.

Students can train at the clinic during their pre-intern, graduate years as well as for their internship. For pre-intern students, the major problem in working at the clinic is establishing a sense of identity. Typical preconceptions about what the clinical psychologist does and what he is supposed to know are simply not confirmed at the Yale Psycho-Educational Clinic, intensifying the identity problem to which all budding young professionals are subject. Of course, a major contributant to this confusion is the fact that the clinic staff itself is engaged in something of an identity struggle, since its members are moving into what is essentially new territory for the clinical psychologist.

For the intern, the confusion experienced by the pre-intern is duplicated if not compounded. The goals of the internship experience at the Yale Psycho-Educational Clinic are to give the student an overview of what various human service settings are like; how a particular administrative organization contributes to the problems it experiences; and to appreciate eventually the possibility for changing settings. Another goal of the internship is to provide the student with experience in several different helping modalities such as consultation, tutoring, individual, group, and family therapy, the supervision of nonprofessionals, program development, and participation in decision making. To achieve these ambitious goals, the student must be exposed to more than one agency at the same time so that he can compare different settings and acquire a sense of perspective.

For students, out from under the yoke of a structured didactic program for the first time, eager to have an impact on the real world and to become useful well-defined professionals, the experience at the Yale Psycho-Educational Clinic is chaotic and anxiety provoking at first. They meet many new people in several different physical settings at roughly the same time. They are greeted by some as honored figures of high status and are virtually ignored by others. Making sense out of these experiences is difficult, and the resultant confusion is disturbing. Adding to these problems are inevitable concerns that community psychology experiences are not preparing the student to be a traditional clinical psychologist and that this may leave him with no marketable skills. If not perturbed by these issues, the students may worry that as community psychologists they lack knowledge in sociology, anthropology, political science, and economics that will be essential to their functioning.

Supervision of the community psychology student presents special problems. In his high anxiety state, the student is also frequently angry, and the target of his anger becomes the faculty member who is considered to be responsible somehow for the anxiety. The student's hostility often takes the form of either subtle or direct attacks on the supervisor's qualifications, competence, and ethical responsibility. Since most faculty are also new to the community psychology field, they doubtless suffer considerable personal uncertainty about these issues so that such attacks on the part of the student can be telling. Another supervisory problem in community psychology is that it is often difficult, if not impossible, to arrange to have the faculty member observe the student. When both function together in a given setting, it is virtually impossible to disguise the fact that one is a student and the other is a faculty member, and the client's natural inclination is to ignore the student and direct his attention to the faculty member.

Not having an opportunity to observe a student's work directly, the faculty is forced to rely heavily on the student's report of his functioning. Reports can be solicited from the people with whom the student is working, but these are often biased in one way or another. In some instances, informants may not wish to say anything they feel might be damaging to the student because they like him. In other instances, a student with considerable competence and drive for taking action might be condemned by agency workers who prefer to maintain the status quo. Without a fairly accurate assessment of student performance, it is difficult to find ways to correct faults, to reinforce strengths, or to enhance overall effectiveness. One major asset in achieving perspective on an intern's reports is the supervisor's experience of having worked himself in the setting where the student has been placed. This familiarizes the supervisor with the background of the situation against which he can evaluate what the student reports.

An important supervisory technique in the Yale Psycho-Educational Clinic is the use of group supervision. One type of such group experience includes only interns or students on an equivalent experience level and the clinic director. In group sessions of this kind the clinic director may express opinions or suggest courses of action that are at odds with those of an immediate supervisor. Such differences can be used to reflect alternatives based on theoretical differences rather than as bases for resisting supervision. Within that framework the differences are useful in shedding light on basic issues. In a sense, therefore, this form of group meeting is an antidote to the authoritarian structure of the ordinary supervisory relationship. The second advantage of the group meeting is that it provides the student with a sense of belonging to a peer group among whom comparisons can be made and with whom an identity can be achieved. Third, these meetings provide students with an opportunity to learn what others are doing in similar settings and to become familiar with different settings.

Community Mental Health Training at the University of Colorado

The University of Colorado training sequence was initiated in 1965 with the hiring of a single faculty member to provide a new specialty within the clinical area (Bloom, 1970). A sequence of four new one-semester courses were set up to be given, one each semester, for a two-year period. Although they were intended to provide specialty training for clinical students interested in the community area, nonclinical graduate students were also welcomed. The courses, all given as seminars, were organized so that each could be taken as an independent unit without any prerequisite.

The first course entitled "Basic Issues in Community Mental Health" was concerned with many broad issues and programs. The topics covered include historical antecedents of the community mental health movement, the practices and concepts of public health, current developments in the organization of health and welfare services, issues in the provision of local mental health services, the role of the state in the organization and support of community mental health services, and the federal role in the support of community mental health services. The second course, "An Introduction to Community Mental Health Practice," included examples of primary, secondary, and tertiary preventive programs, and examined various community mental health programs outside of the United States. The third course, "Epidemiologic Methods in Community Mental Health," included general material on epidemiology plus reports of specific epidemiologic studies relevant to the mental health field. The fourth course was entitled "Research Problems in Community Mental Health" and covered topics such as biostatistics, the methodology involved in studying families, material on mental health program evaluation, and a discussion of psychiatric case registers.

Because students were interested in making their own contributions to course content, two course projects were developed. During the first semester the instructor and each student independently developed a format for analyzing a national mental health program. Toward the end of the first semester the various independent efforts were integrated into a single format. During the second semester each student selected a specific country and applied the format that had been developed in the first semester to a study of the mental health program of that country. The first phase of the University of Colorado program, therefore, entailed a four-course sequence in community mental health plus two special projects associated with the courses.

In the second phase of the Colorado program, field placements were introduced. The community mental health field placement served as one of two clinical practicum assignments that were required for the doctorate in clinical psychology. The types of field placements sought included community-based action programs in the mental health field, selected comprehensive community mental health centers, and entire communities where it was possible to study the power structure and decision-making processes as well as the organization of public and private health and welfare services. Nonclinical students were placed in agencies not requiring clinical functions such as guidance techniques, crisis intervention, brief psychotherapy, and mental health consultation. Experiences open to all students included activities such as community organization, work with interagency groups, community decision making, and preventive research programs for reducing the incidence of mental disorder. Field placements required 2 one-half days of work each week through the academic year.

Multidisciplinary Training Programs

The Program at the Harvard School of Public Health

One of the pioneering training programs for community mental health specialists was developed by Caplan (1959, 1965) at the Harvard School of Public Health. This was a multidisciplinary, postprofessional program drawing its students from psychiatry, clinical psychology, and social work. The program involved one year of training leading to the Master of Public Health (M.P.H.) degree or the Master of Science in Hygiene (S.M.Hy.) degree. For most community mental health students the S.M.Hy. degree seemed preferable because very few fixed requirements were associated with its attainment. The one course required of all students opting for the M.S.Hy., Biostatistics and Epidemiology, was designed to present fundamentals of the two disciplines regarded to be basic to the study of problems of health and disease at the community level. Beyond this requirement, didactic aspects of the program were quite flexible depending on the student's previous background.

Some course work was drawn from the regular offerings of the School of Public Health including examples such as "Principles of Public Health Practice," "The Organization and Administration of Health Agencies," "Factors in Health and Disease," "Principles Basic to the Practice of Maternal and Child Health," "The Human Community," "Research Methods in Community Health," and "Health and Illness in Cross Cultural Perspective." Out of the 40 credit hours per year required for the master's degree, roughly 25 to 30 were earned through already-established courses in the public health school and the remaining 14 or 15 units were earned in courses devoted strictly to mental health topics such as "The Epidemiology of Noninfectious Disease," and "Group Dynamics and the Control of Mental Disorders."

In addition to the course work described, students in the Harvard School of Public Health program participated in a series of field assignments at a set of field stations developed by Caplan and his staff. These field stations included three guidance centers located in diverse communities, one of this country's original mental health centers, established by

Eric Lindemann in Wellesley, Massachusetts, and the main office of the Massachusetts Division of Mental Hygiene. The purpose of the field activity was to provide front line experience in and training for consultation with professionals around a variety of problems with which they must contend. It was hoped that through consultation the mental health professional could have primary preventive impact on the community.

In 1964 the Harvard program was moved from the School of Public Health into a newly established Laboratory of Community Psychiatry within the Department of Psychiatry of the Harvard Medical School. Since that time the program has been unencumbered by the degree requirements of the Public Health School and has offered a certificate to its graduates instead of a degree. The program continues to integrate didactic learning with field training and still emphasizes the consultative role of the community mental health specialist.

Community Mental Health Training at the University of Texas

Iscoe (1970) has described a multidisciplinary graduate training program in community mental health originating in the Psychology Department of the University of Texas in 1965. The program's purpose is to provide graduate students in a variety of disciplines with a combination of course work and field experiences to enhance their understanding of the community and their skills in dealing with its complexities. Present methods of delivering mental health services are studied with an eye to improving them. Impulsive activism is restrained by the program's emphasis on the necessity for winning a community's acceptance before reconceptualizing its problems and introducing new approaches. The program is intended to turn out a community mental health specialist or a community psychologist with a broad view of mental health problems and an appreciation of the need for *relevant* behavioral science research in the community.

The Texas program accepts students from psychology (social, personality, or clinical), educational psychology, sociology, and anthropology. Entering students must have satisfied most basic degree requirements in their own departments or programs, including the completion of qualifying examinations, before entering the community mental health program. Typically, therefore, entering students have completed two years of graduate training and participate for one full year in the community mental health program. Clinical psychology students may continue their concentration by taking an internship in a setting with a heavy community mental health orientation. Students from other areas, particularly within psychology, have the option of taking a second year in the program. To date, most of the program's students have entered from the clinical psychology program.

The didactic side of Texas' community mental health program includes four required courses: "Mental Health Consultation," "Seminar in Mental Health," "Seminar in Community Mental Health," and "Seminar in Community Organization," taken at the school of social work. Several elective seminars and courses including "Human Ecology and Demography," "Sociology of Health Services," "Cultural Deprivation and Poverty," "Introduction to School Psychology," and "Computer Techniques of Programming" are also available.

Field training in the community mental health program is carried out in a variety of settings that have been selected for their relevance to program goals. In all but one field setting students' experiences are monitored by nonpsychologists, a strategy that is intended to broaden the student's horizon concerning the community and its subsystems.

The experience provided in three of the field settings used by the program seems to be primarily observational. These three settings include the Hogg Foundation for Mental Health, the Juvenile Court and Probation Department of Austin and Travis counties, and the Human Opportunities Corporation of Austin and Travis counties. The Hogg Foundation, a private foundation administered through the University of Texas, supports programs in mental health education, as well as action projects involving the application of behavioral science and psychiatric studies in practical settings, and the evaluation of these projects. Students are assigned to monitor specific projects, following them from intake, through staff review, and acceptance, rejection or consultative recommendations to the applicant. This experience provides some sophistication in evaluating proposed projects. Students also sit in on semiannual meetings of the foundation's National Advisory Committee where they meet prominent figures in the mental health scene and become familiar with mental health developments on a national level.

Experience in the juvenile court and probation department acquaints students with the goals and problems of such a setting. It familiarizes them with legal problems involving juveniles and with the duties and responsibilities of probation officers. Furthermore, the complicated interrelationship between the school system, the police department, the community employment picture, and the incidence of delinquency becomes apparent.

The Human Opportunities Corporation of Austin and Travis counties administers and monitors all community action programs in the area. Texas' community mental health students visit projects administered by the corporation to study the problems that they face, their relationships to the community, and the way cooperation with community forces is encouraged or impeded.

More active participation by community mental health students takes place in a mental health consultation program in the public school system, which is the program's fourth field training setting. This consultation experience is associated with a year-long seminar in mental health consultation. During the first three months of the seminar, students are exposed to lectures, readings, and literature reviews of the consultation process. They also observe others engaging in consultation through films and role-play consultation situations. Some time is also devoted to studying the organization and administration of the school system, and students attend school board meetings to become familiar with the way important decisions are made. Eventually the student is assigned to a school where he is confronted with many problems associated with the consultant's role. These include the problem of entering the system, the efforts on the part of teachers and administrators to inveigle the consultant into providing direct service to pupils, and thereby subverting his role, and the various ways in which personnel in each school choose to use its consultant in keeping with their own insecurities and misunderstandings.

Supervision for student consultants is provided by university staff members, and consultants meet as a group for a two- or three-hour session each week to review their activities and to compare experiences. Toward the end of the consultation experience, each trainee writes a description of the school in which he has worked, the problems with which he has had to deal, and how he has handled them. Principals and teachers using the services of the consultants are also asked to submit evaluations.

The Texas program is too new for a formal assessment of its efforts. Generally, reactions of school personnel toward the consultants have been quite favorable, and the reactions of students to their training and field experiences have been enthusiastic. Several students have already left the university to serve in settings where they can usefully exercise the skills acquired in the community mental health program.

Field Training in Community Psychology at Duke University

The community psychology experience offered at Duke University is comprised of a field training program that focuses on consultation to community caregivers in a rural county (Halifax County) in northeast North Carolina (Altrocchi and Eisdorfer, 1970). The program was made possible when the county health director approached a member of the Duke University faculty for help in setting up a county mental health program. When the program began in 1959, the consultant visited the county for a two- to three-day period each month to consult with key community members and with various professionals, including educators, welfare workers, clergymen, and public health nurses. Steady program growth has resulted in regular consultation visits on the part of 5 consultants and approximately 10 trainees. Consultation is now available to all of the county's schools, and to the general medical practitioners in the county. In addition, a suicide prevention service has been initiated through the consultation program.

Virtually from its inception, Duke University's consultation program has included graduate students from several departments, interns in psychology, residents in psychiatry, and colleagues outside of the Psychology Department. Students have been allowed to participate in every phase of the consulting program and, by entering it before it became a stabilized operation, many have had the valuable opportunity of participating in the "initial gropings" of the consultant.

The Duke program uses the apprenticeship model. Most of the student's learning is acquired by observing an experienced professional operating as a consultant. This requires the professional to be quite open about what he does, and to allow himself to be closely scrutinized, making his mistakes as well as his successes clearly visible. Typically trainees remain as relatively passive observers early in their field training but gradually participate more actively as they become comfortable. With time, the consultant turns over specific aspects of a problem to the trainee, so that through a series of graded steps the trainee moves from being a relatively uninvolved novice to functioning semiindependently as a consultant. Heavy program emphasis is placed on instilling the attitude that while the consultant has something to give the community he, in turn, has much to learn from the community and from the consultee. This has been found to be a requisite to a successful consultation program.

Most of the trainees in the Halifax County program have been psychology graduate students from Duke University, or interns in psychology at the Duke University Medical Center. A few psychiatric residents have participated in the program, some undergraduates taking honors programs have carried out special projects through the program, and various colleagues from psychology, psychiatry, psychiatric nursing, sociology, pediatrics, and public health have participated along with the consultants in the programs. Many of the graduate students interested in the program begin their involvement very early in their graduate training by accompanying consultants on their visits to the county. One limitation on the multidisciplinary aspect of this program is the feeling on the part of its members that clinical training is quite essential to the role carried out in the field. Thus advanced training has been restricted to third-year graduate students who have begun training in psychotherapy.

The Duke program includes relatively little formal course work. Seminars in community mental health are offered in the psychology and psychiatry departments, and staff members in the consultation program recommend various books and journal readings in community mental health so that, informally, a background in the literature of the area is acquired. Some students have been sent for summer training to mental health centers emphasizing community psychology. Associated with field training, is a twice-a-month meeting for all who are in the consultation program. This is an unstructured meeting in which trainees or staff may make presentations. Discussions are held of crises that may be arising, programs that are developing, or theoretical or research issues.

The activities engaged in by trainees are virtually identical to the range participated in by senior consultants. These include serving as group consultants with nurses, ministers, or policemen, consulting in the schools, and consulting with counselors working at a suicide prevention center. When he is first assigned to a particular setting, the trainee often performs some direct clinical service, since the agency is likely to press for this. Typically, of course, such services are directed toward the agency's most serious and long-standing problems. Each consultant, whether a staff member or trainee, encounters this type of pressure on entering a relationship with an agency, and must exert a counter effort to divert his role from that of a direct service giver to that of a resource for others who provide direct service.

Altrocchi and Eisdorfer (1970) have reported on their attempts to evaluate the Duke University training program after approximately 24 students had participated in it. Gratifyingly, virtually all found the training experience a significant aspect of their professional preparation. Members of this group anticipated that an average of approximately 35 percent of their time was or would in the future be devoted to community consultation. This is a higher percentage than the senior consultants devote to such efforts. Other criteria suggesting that the consultation program is having a significant impact is the fact that a doctoral dissertation is in process through this program and another is being planned. Furthermore, five psychology interns and three psychology graduate students were being trained in the program during the year that Altrocchi and Eisdorfer made their report.

Community Psychology Training at Boston University

In 1965 a training program in community psychology was developed at Boston University under the sponsorship of the Psychology Department and the Human Relations Center (Lipton and Klein, 1970). The Human Relations Center at Boston University was established to study human relations within a multidisciplinary context. It is not a degree-granting division of the university but one to which graduate students from a variety of departments can apply for one or two years of training. An essential feature of the community psychology program at Boston University is that it brings together students from many different fields, for instance, philosophy, theology, law, business, psychology, social work, sociology, nursing, and education. Students take time out from specialty training to apply for a fellowship to support one or two years of work at the Center.

Training in Boston University's program includes course work, field work, and research. A core requirement of the program is a two-seminar sequence that includes a practicum in Human Relations and a seminar on "Theories of Changing." The Human Relations practicum is organized as a modified T-group that attempts to provide the student with a sense of self-awareness as well as an understanding of group phenomena. Specific topics covered in this practicum include mutual trust, norm setting, inclusion-exclusion phenomena, communication processes, helping and collaborating, the emergence of leadership, and coping with authority relationships. The seminar on "Theories of Changing" is taught by an interdisciplinary faculty and is devoted to discussions of various change strategies.

Several optional courses are available to community psychology fellows. These include courses in evaluation research, psychological consultation, an advanced practicum in human relations, and various summer residential workshops covering human relations, intergroup dynamics, and community relations in community development. Field placements in the Boston University program include mental health and geriatric facilities, the public school system, a community self-help organization, a state commission against discrimination, and a leadership training and evaluation project run by an innercity voluntary organization. Little description is offered of the function of the fellow in the field setting.

Lipton and Klein acknowledge many of the disadvantages of multidisciplinary training. For the teacher, these include the problem that within a given student group there is apt to be a wide range of previous preparation for the material to be offered. For the student, there is considerable "emotional buffeting" as a result of the fact that within the student group there is a wide range of viewpoints concerning any particular issue. The complexity of this situation makes it difficult for a student to find a personal identity. Despite these disadvantages, multidisciplinary training is seen to have certain compelling advantages particularly for one who intends to work in the community. The diversity of approaches, viewpoints, and ways of conceptualizing problems that characterizes the training program is also seen to be characteristic of what will very likely be encountered in the community itself.

CURRENT STATE OF TRAINING IN COMMUNITY PSYCHOLOGY

The wide diversity found in the training programs described might suggest that their organizers got together and consciously designed them, keeping in mind the injunction of the Boston Conference participants against rigidifying training patterns. This, of course, is fanciful. The many programs reviewed have been developed at different times and in different settings. Not having well established examples on which to model themselves or to react to, the forms taken by the various programs have probably been a function primarily of available resources, and the talents and propensities of the particular program organizers.

All of the programs reviewed include some form of field training. In some cases, didactic offerings, as in the Colorado program, seem paramount, with the field training having been added later in the program's history. In other cases, the field training is the essential program feature as, for example, the programs at Yale and Duke universities. In the latter model, formal course work has a relatively insignificant place and considerable emphasis is placed on the type of field experience offered, supervision of the trainee in the field, and trainee-supervisor relationships. Programs emphasizing formal course work have relatively little in common in terms of types of courses offered, judging from titles alone. Although much is said about the need for acquiring a background in sociology, education, anthropology, and other social sciences, relatively few offerings of this kind are present in most training programs. Instead, most course titles sound like broad surveys of the community mental health field.

Considerably more overlap between programs is found with respect to field training. The professional activity receiving the most frequent emphasis by far is consultation. However, consultation practices vary from program to program. For example, in the Duke program consultants apparently spend some of their time providing direct service to clients, whereas in the Texas program such direct service-giving is assiduously avoided. In the City College program consultation has the aim of enhancing the emotional state of the consultee to improve his functioning with clients, whereas in other programs such as the one at the Harvard School of Public Health the consultation process is viewed much more broadly.

Only one of the programs reviewed, the Rochester program, seems to engage extensively in the creation of new types of service delivery. Consultation may lead to development of new service models in other training programs, but this receives little training emphasis. In many programs the beginning experiences in community psychology field training are passive and observational instead of involving active engagement in consultation, or program development.

In several programs that profess a multidisciplinary emphasis, two classes of citizenry seem to have been established. One class, with a background in a clinical area such as clinical psychology, psychiatry, social work, or nursing has been permitted to participate in phases of field training that involve activities bearing some relation to clinical functioning. On the other hand, educators, sociologists, anthropologists, and other social scientists who have participated in multidisciplinary programs have been prevented from participating in clinically oriented activities. Although the reasons for these distinctions are obvious, one cannot help but wonder if some of the value of the multidisciplinary program is not lost when members of certain disciplines are kept from participating fully in the field training program. Conceivably, some of the greatest multidisciplinary program benefits might derive from the insights occurring to the nonclinician, well schooled in a relevant content area, who is confronted by clinical problems that demand an immediate response. Admittedly, the supervisory burden in dealing with such trainees would be great, but the investment could prove to be worthwhile.

FUTURE PROSPECTS

In their summary of the current status of training in community psychology, Spielberger and Iscoe (1970) shy away from attempting to predict the new directions that community psychology may take. They point out that within a relatively short period of time a multitude of new roles for community psychologists have emerged. The prospects are that these roles will continue to proliferate. Also a great deal will be learned about communities and how to function within them. Perhaps this is another reason why training programs have taken diverse forms and why to date many of the field's leaders have preferred not to impose a great deal of structure.

The only type of structure that community psychology's leaders have been comfortable about imposing with respect to training is the requirement that community psychology programs produce generalists. In a sense, it has been specified by many that the community psychologist should not be a specialist. Very likely this stance has been a reaction to the rather highly specialized role that had emerged for the psychologist operating within the medical model. What has, therefore, been called for is a professional who can function in a much more flexible, general way than the clinic or hospital-bound psychologist. On the other hand, it is likely that as the field of community psychology progresses, greater and greater specialization will characterize training programs, as has been true in a variety of other fields. In its pristine state it is impossible to predict in what settings community psychology will become best established and what forms it will take. Once its development becomes clear, inevitably training programs will be targeted specifically to particular settings and particular types of functions. After all, there is a limit to the degree of versatility any professional, even a community psychologist, can manifest.

It might well be that once specialization sets in, the result will be a considerably more functional role for the other social sciences in the training programs. For example, in a community psychology training program preparing people to function within the public school system, it is likely that many offerings from the area of education will be highly relevant. For programs to train workers, for functioning in the inner city, probably sociology, economics, and political science will have much to offer to community psychologists. With specialization, too, will doubtless come greater homogeneity in training programs.

CONCLUSION

At present, training programs in community psychology reflect the mandate for producing a professional who can be a generalist, someone far more flexible than the traditional mental health worker. In an effort to produce such an individual, training programs have taken many forms and operate through a variety of field settings. Although a need for multidisciplinary input into these programs is recognized, this aspect of training has not yet become well established, or taken any clear form. Future prospects are for a continued period of experimentation very likely followed by the development of specialization within the field of community psychology. As this occurs, training programs can be expected to take on greater structure and to reflect more specific input from disciplines outside the mental health fields.

References

Altrocchi, J., & Eisdorfer, C. Apprentice-Collaborator Field Training in Community Psychology: The Halifax County Program. In I. Iscoe, & C. D. Spielberger (Eds.), *Community psychology: perspectives in training and research*. New York: Appleton-Century-Crofts, 1970. Pp. 191–205.

Bard, M., & Berkowitz, B. Training Police as Specialists in Family Crisis Intervention: A Community Psychology Action Program. *Community Mental Health Journal*, 1967, *3*, 315–317.

Bennett, C. C., Anderson, L. S., Cooper, S., Hassol, L., Klein, D. C., & Rosenblum, G. (Eds.), *Community psychology: a report of the Boston Conference on the education of psychologists for community mental health*. Boston: Boston University Press, 1966.

Bloom, B. L. A Psychology Department Graduate Course Sequence in Community

Mental Health. In Iscoe, & C. D. Spielberger (Eds.), *Community psychology: perspectives in training and research*. New York: Appleton-Century-Crofts, 1970. Pp. 163–177.

Caplan, G. An Approach to the Education of Community Mental Health Specialists. *Mental Hygiene*, 1959, *43*, 268–280.

Caplan, G. *Principles of preventive psychiatry*. New York: Basic Books, 1964.

Caplan, G. Problems of Training in Mental Health Consultation. In S. E. Goldston (Ed.), *Concepts of community psychiatry: a framework for training*. Bethesda, Md.: U. S. Department of Health, Education, and Welfare, Public Health Service Publication No. 1319, 1965. Pp. 91–108.

Cowen, E. L. Emergent Approaches to Mental Health Problems: An Overview and Directions for Future Work. In E. L. Cowen, E. A. Gardner, & M. Zax (Eds.), *Emergent approaches to mental health problems*. New York: Appleton-Century-Crofts, 1967. Pp. 389–455.

Cowen, E. L. Training Clinical Psychologists for Community Mental Health Functions: Description of a Practicum Experience. In I. Iscoe, & C. D. Spielberger, (Eds.), *Community psychology: perspectives in training and research*. New York: Appleton-Century-Crofts, 1970. Pp. 99–124.

Golann, S. E. Community Psychology and Mental Health: An Analysis of Strategies and a Survey of Training. In I. Iscoe, & C. D. Spielberger (Eds.), *Community psychology: perspectives in training and research*. New York: Appleton-Century-Crofts, 1970. Pp. 33–57.

Iscoe, I. The Graduate Training Program in Community Mental Health at the University of Texas. In I. Iscoe, & C. D. Spielberger (Eds.), *Community psychology: perspectives in training and research*. New York: Appleton-Century-Crofts, 1970. Pp. 181–189.

Iscoe, I., & Spielberger, C. D. *Community psychology: perspectives in training and research*. New York: Appleton-Century-Crofts, 1970.

Levine, M. Some Postulates of Practice in Community Psychology and Their Implications for Training. In I. Iscoe, & C. D. Spielberger (Eds.), *Community psychology: perspectives in training and research*. New York: Appleton-Century-Crofts, 1970. Pp. 71–84.

Lipton, H., & Klein, D. Community Psychology Training in a Multidisciplinary Setting. In I. Iscoe, & C. D. Spielberger (Eds.), *Community psychology: perspectives in training and research*. New York: Appleton-Century-Crofts, 1970. Pp. 207–214.

Newbrough, J. R., Rhodes, W. C., & Seeman, J. The Development of Community Psychology Training at George Peabody College. In I. Iscoe, & C. D. Spielberger (Eds.), *Community psychology: perspectives in training and research*. New York: Appleton-Century-Crofts, 1970. Pp. 87–98.

Reiff, R. Mental Health Manpower and Institutional Change. *American Psychologist*, 1966, *21*, 540–549.

Reiff, R. The Need for a Body of Knowledge in Community Psychology. In I. Iscoe, & C. D. Spielberger (Eds.), *Community psychology: perspectives in training and research*. New York: Appleton-Century-Crofts, 1970. Pp. 19–31.

Roen, S. R. New Requirements in Educating Psychologists for Public Practice and Applied Research. In I. Iscoe, & C. D. Spielberger (Eds.), *Community psychology: perspectives in training and research.* New York: Appleton-Century-Crofts, 1970. Pp. 59–69.

Sarason, S. B., & Levine, M. Graduate Education and the Yale Psycho-Educational Clinic. In I. Iscoe, & C. D. Spielberger (Eds.), *Community psychology: perspectives in training and research.* New York: Appleton-Century-Crofts, 1970. Pp. 143–162.

Singer, J. L. & Bard, M. The Psychological Foundations of a Community-Oriented Clinical Psychology Training Program. In I. Isoe, & C. D. Spielberger (Eds.), *Community psychology: perspectives in training and research.* New York: Appleton-Century-Crofts, 1970. Pp. 125–141.

Spielberger, C. D., & Iscoe, I. The Current Status of Training in Community Psychology. In I. Iscoe, & C. D. Spielberger (Eds.), *Community psychology: perspectives in training and research.* New York: Appleton-Century-Crofts, 1970. Pp. 227–246.

13. the "nonprofessional" in community psychology programs

Before we discuss the place of the nonprofessional in community psychology, we must specify what a nonprofessional is. This definition is far from obvious when we consider the diversity of the people who are referred to as nonprofessionals. Following Sobey's lead (Sobey, 1970), we define a nonprofessional as any individual who is recruited to provide mental health services without having completed customary professional training in one of the traditional mental health disciplines. As such, the nonprofessional may be paid or unpaid, and he may be a trained, practicing professional in some other field (nursing, law, medicine, or the ministry).

Perhaps one of the most striking aspects of the many community programs we have reviewed and in others that we might describe is the extent to which significant roles are played by nonprofessionals as we define them. Within the traditional mental hospital setting, many nonprofessionals, in the form of the college student volunteer, have served as companions to hospitalized mental patients (Holzberg, 1967; Klein and Zax,

369

1965; Umbarger, Dalsimer, Morrison, and Breggin, 1962), and even high school students have served as companions for adolescent and preadolescent hospitalized patients (Fellows and Wolpin, 1969). The mental hospital has also been a setting in which new kinds of personnel have been trained to play a very significant treatment role with patients. The "socio-environmental therapist" (Sanders, Smith and Weinman, 1967) and the "nurses" utilized in Jones' (1953) therapeutic community are examples of college graduates trained specifically for roles in innovative hospital programs who would ordinarily have no place in the mental health field.

There are several examples of the use of nonprofessionals in an activity reserved heretofore for only the most highly skilled professionals. Margaret Rioch (1967), for example, has trained housewives to do individual psychotherapy. Others (Poser, 1966; Rappaport, Chinsky, and Cowen, 1971) have employed college undergraduates as group therapists in mental hospitals. Carkhuff and Truax (1965a, 1965b) have trained hospital personnel, primarily attendants, to lead therapy groups. Kreitzer (1969) has trained college students to participate in a hospital behavior therapy program for emotionally disturbed children.

In the school setting, Donahue and Nichtern (1965) have recruited housewives who are former teachers to act as individual tutors for seriously disturbed children. Harris, Wolf, and Baer (1964) have programmed teachers to use behavior modification procedures as a means of increasing desirable behaviors and decreasing undesirable behaviors in disturbed nursery school children. Casework agencies have also begun to make use of nonprofessionals to assist in special programs. Johnston (1967) has reported the use of retired people as "foster grandparents" for children suffering from emotional disturbances, and Perlmutter and Durham (1965) have described a program using teenagers as nonprofessionals to supplement casework service with younger children. Youngsters no older than 10 have been trained to tutor still younger school children (Gartner, Kohler and Riessman, 1971). Several programs have involved training parents to do therapy with their own children (Fidler, Guerney, Andronico, and Guerney, 1969; Andronico, Fidler, Guerney, and Guerney, 1967; Wahler, Winkel, Peterson, and Morrison, 1965). A large number of programs, many of which have been described in preceding chapters, have trained nonprofessionals to fill vital roles in a variety of community mental health programs. Examples include the use of nonprofessionals as teacher-aides (Cowen, Izzo, Miles, Telschow, Trost, and Zax, 1963), the use of indigenous nonprofessionals to man neighborhood service centers (Hallowitz and Riessman, 1967), and to staff a residential youth center (Goldenberg, 1971), and the training of nonprofessional mental health aides for work in a hospital program in Harlem (Christmas, 1966). Hawkinshire (1963) has even proposed that a like peer group be trained to work with criminal offenders.

This diversity both in the types of roles being filled by nonprofessionals as well as in the types of people who are serving as nonprofessionals is impressive. However, the picture that these examples convey may well be a distorted one, implying as it does that nonprofessionals have truly arrived and are entirely well established on the mental health scene. Actually, many of the programs cited stand out dramatically just because they are unique structures on an otherwise unremarkable horizon. The subjective impression that programs making use of nonprofessionals are proliferating is undoubtedly accurate, but we lack data to indicate who these nonprofessionals are for the most part, what roles they are generally filling, what permanency their positions tend to enjoy, and the like.

Sobey's survey of 185 NIMH sponsored programs utilizing nonprofessionals (Sobey, 1970), indicates that virtually all of the nonprofessional's time in these programs is devoted to direct service. To be sure, Sobey found differences between the types of services rendered by professionals and nonprofessionals. Professionals did more individual and group counseling, and more screening of new patients than did nonprofessionals. Nonprofessionals participated more in tutoring, caretaking and activity-group therapy than did professionals. Still, the nonprofessional in the projects surveyed by Sobey participated heavily in the direct service programs of the agencies that employed them. This finding is somewhat at odds with that of Grosser (1969). Grosser's survey covered several programs sponsored by the Labor Department under the Manpower Development and Training Act which have largely utilized indigenous nonprofessionals. For the purposes of his survey Grosser has distinguished four types of service responsibilities assigned to nonprofessionals: direct service to clients, services ancillary to the professional services provided a client, service involving establishing ties with the target community, and services that are entirely separate from the professional services offered to clients (custodial and certain types of clerical assignments). He found that nonprofessionals are most often used to provide ancillary services. Such jobs involve clerical work, administrative functions, transport services, and the like. Also among these ancillary services Grosser includes jobs such as intake work, which is further along the continuum toward direct service than the functions mentioned but still falls short of it. Direct service responsibilities for clients is the least common type of work assigned to nonprofessionals, although Grosser asserts that in many instances the nonprofessionals are probably best suited for this role than for any other. In addition to finding that direct service is the role that nonprofessionals are least likely to be called on to provide in the programs he surveyed, Grosser also found that those nonprofessionals who were providing direct services were more likely to be *middle class* non-professionals rather than *lower class* indigenous nonprofessionals.

In their roles as agents for establishing bridges between the agency and the target community, the nonprofessionals surveyed by Grosser serve a recruitment and a follow-up function within the target neighborhood. These functions are accomplished through speaking to local groups, canvassing door-to-door, distributing leaflets, and the like. The discrepancy between the findings of Sobey and Grosser can probably be explained on the basis of the types of programs that each examined. Sobey's respondents undoubtedly represented the most innovative and willingly experimental agencies in the country, and it was on such a basis that they received NIMH funds. Grosser's survey probably covered the more typical agency, which depends on a variety of sources, local and national, for support, but which is not in the forefront of change in professional practice. The use of the nonprofessional in the latter type agency is apt to be made grudgingly and, unfortunately, agencies of this kind predominate in the mental health scene.

It is clear that the movement toward the use of nonprofessionals in mental health programs is well underway. It is also abundantly clear that nonprofessionals who have been pressed into service are extraordinarily heterogeneous with respect to age, social background, and educational background, and that the roles they are called on to fill may be quite varied, although frequently they may be limited to functions that fall short of providing direct service to clients. The rest of this chapter is concerned with the reasons why the use of nonprofessionals is becoming more prominent in recent years, the techniques that are used for selecting and training nonprofessionals, and the problems that must be overcome if nonprofessionals are to represent a significant force in the mental health movement in the future.

REASONS FOR USING NONPROFESSIONALS

To Meet Manpower Needs

The need for a means to bolster the inadequate manpower resources of mental health professionals is perhaps the most obvious reason for turning to nonprofessionals (Richan, 1967; Grosser, 1969; Harris, Wolf, and Baer, 1964; Rioch, 1967). The mental health manpower surveys done by Albee (1959, 1963) have shaken the complacency of professionals concerning their ability to meet mental health manpower needs within the framework of current practices.

The reflexive response to the recognition that mental health professionals are in drastically short supply, and probably will continue to be for many years given current training limitations, is to argue for energetic recruitment programs to attract talented young people and for a proliferation of professional training programs. Unfortunately, such an approach is difficult to implement. Expansion of professional training programs is extraordinarily difficult to bring about but, even worse, such a solution promises only to "rob Peter to pay Paul." Should the mental health field succeed in attracting talented young college students to enter the mental health professions, it will do so by luring them away from a variety of other professions that are also in short manpower supply, such as medicine, education, and the sciences. Thus the nonprofessional becomes a prime candidate for helping to meet the manpower needs of the mental health professions. The greatest benefit would accrue to society if nonprofessionals for the mental health field could be drawn from a segment of society that normally would not be contributing to the economy and might even be a drain on society's resources. Such individuals would include the retired, the young who are still students, housewives with time to spare, the delinquent, and the indigent. In fact, we have already demonstrated that many programs utilizing nonprofessionals have drawn liberally from these groups.

To Improve the Life of the Potential Nonprofessional

This basis for the development of large numbers of nonprofessionals in the mental health field was articulated very well by Riessman (1965) who termed it the "helper therapy principle." Riessman emphasized that giving help often is of as much profit to the helper as it is to the helpee. Benefits resulting from a variety of self-help organizations such as Synanon, Recovery Incorporated, and Alcoholics Anonymous are seen by Riessman to derive largely from this principle. Admitting that there was a lack of scientific evidence for the helper-therapy principle, Riessman, nontheless, felt that his observation of people functioning in a variety of different settings amply demonstrated that a principle of this kind was valid. Speculating on the potential mechanisms that might account for the validity of the principle, Riessman pointed to the fact that doing something worthwhile tends to improve one's self-image, that having to advocate a position often leads to a commitment to the position, that employment as a helper gives one a stake in a system, and that the sheer status associated with being a helper in a prestigeful endeavor is beneficial.

A number of people who have utilized nonprofessionals in mental health programs have been able to support Riessman's contention that the helper gains greatly from participating in a helping situation. Holzberg (1967) has done a series of comprehensive studies in this area involving college students acting as companions to disturbed mental patients. He found that participation in his companion program led to gains in knowledge, the development of more positive attitudes toward mental disorder, greater tolerance of sexual and aggressive behaviors, greater introspectiveness, and the feeling in his subjects that they knew a great deal more about mental illness, its causes and treatment, than they had before. Follow-up studies also demonstrated that as a result of their companion experience some participants had their interest in a mental health career confirmed, whereas others were helped to decide that such a career was not for them. Klein and Zax (1965) found similarly that participation in a companion program with hospital patients helped to firm up career plans for college students, attracting many to the mental health profession and convincing a few that such a career was not suited to them. Goodman (1967) has reported that the college students who served as companions to grade school boys who were described as "troubled" displayed "dramatically heightened interest" in children's behavior, in working with the emotionally disturbed, and in their own interactions with friends.

In reporting on a program utilizing retirees as mental health aides with children, Cowen, Liebowitz, and Liebowitz (1969) indicate that their retirees very much enjoyed their work as aides in schools, that they had learned many new things at their function, and that they were enthusiastic about continuing work in such a program. Dorr, Cowen, and Sandler (1972) report that housewives working as child aides in the primary grades of a public school evidenced greater understanding and less rejection of children's behavior after participating in the program for three and one-third months than did a set of control subjects who did not participate.

In many ways the new careers program that was described in a previous chapter has its roots in the helper-therapy principle. The idea advanced by Pearl and Riessman (1965) is that by giving the impoverished individual with relatively few hopeful options in life an opportunity to work at something that provides dignity and a sense of purpose can result in both useful service and important ego enhancement for the server himself. The Howard University program (Klein, 1967) which utilized indigenous youth, most of whom had serious delinquency records, as human service aides is a good example of a new careers program intending to provide both important new mental health manpower and to rehabilitate a segment of society that would normally be a drain on its resources.

To Capitalize on the Unique Assets of Nonprofessionals

Many nonprofessional groups that have been utilized in mental health service programs possess unique qualities which have been found to be important assets in their work. This case can be most easily made for the indigenous worker, particularly the lower-class worker serving the culturally disadvantaged. Gordon has stated:

"A second major advantage of the helping team is that it may include workers from the same milieu as the clients served by the team, and these workers could well be much more successful than the fully qualified professional in making contact with potential clients, in motivating them, and in interpreting the agency to the client. Where they have been well trained and well supervised, indigenous leaders have made important contributions which cannot be made by anyone else. There are dimensions of expression, voice inflection, gesture, body language, which are almost instantly recognizable as signs of class and ethnic origin. The indigenous leader can communicate instantly to the suspicious and distrustful client, avoiding noblesse oblige, in a way that many middle class professionals cannot do when dealing with disaffected, hostile, anomic youths who see the middle class agency worker as part of the system against which he is fighting" (Gordon, 1965, p. 340).

Reiff and Riessman (1965) emphasize many of the same ideas as does Gordon. They point out that the social position of the indigenous nonprofessional matches that of his client so that he is a peer in terms of background, language, and interests. As a result, the nonprofessional can do things that the middle class professional "expert" is not free to do. The nonprofessional can "belong" to the extent that he can be invited to weddings, parties, funerals—and he is free to go. As a peer of the client, such flexibility of behavior comes off quite naturally. For the professional, behavior of this kind would be awkward, and would doubtless make everyone uncomfortable.

Reiff and Riessman also points out that having been poor himself, the indigenous nonprofessional has developed a "know how" about dealing with the problems of poverty and can, through his personal experience, provide concrete, meaningful help. Furthermore, in terms of life-style, the assistance he offers is more likely to be action oriented, less involved with delay and talk than that characterizing the typical middle class professional.

Christmas (1966) has described a program serving a seriously deprived community in which she has found certain important assets in aides who had lower class roots but are now of the middle class. She emphasizes the potential benefits to clients of having contact with an aide who, on the one hand, is not far removed from the type of life that the client is experiencing but, on the other hand, is an example of one who has been able to surmount his initial disadvantages. As Christmas puts it:

"The talents and skills which may have come from advanced education

and employment may help patients (and other nonprofessionals) to de-velop their skills. Since most adult urban middle class Negroes are at the most a generation or two removed from the working class, those who are relatively free of conflicts around their current status and society may use this background for greater understanding of the patients" (Christmas, 1966, p. 410).

Grosser (1969) views the indigenous nonprofessional as serving an important function as a "bridge" between the agency and the deprived community. His interests are similar to those of the members of the target community, he talks their language, he lives among them, he shares their minority group status, and has a similar background. Furthermore, the indigenous nonprofessional is often hired because he has succeeded to some extent in "beating the game," in mastering problems of living in a urban slum. Thus he is in a position to teach program participants in a direct, immediate, and pragmatic way many important skills for coping with everyday life. He can advise the job trainee about how to deal with the foreman at work or suggest ways in which the welfare client can ob-tain larger benefits. The tactics involved may consist, to a certain degree, of rule bending, but this is seen by Grosser to be no different from the stretching of rules engaged in by agency administrators for expedience or economy.

Another advantage of the use of the indigenous nonprofessional in agencies is that it potentially upgrades the functions of agency profession-als (Goldberg, 1969; Grosser, 1969). Some observers have noted that professionals in agencies employing nonprofessionals feel they are con-siderably more effective in working with the poor than their counterparts in agencies that do not employ nonprofessionals. Grosser attempts to ex-plain this:

"Professional staff has probably been affected more than is generally acknowledged by the employment of nonprofessionals. For one thing, they find in the office, on their own side of the desk, as it were, attitudes, life-styles, and points of view which heretofore they saw only in clients and usually characterized as pathology. They are forced by their nonpro-fessional colleagues to justify their practice in client related terms" (Grosser, 1969, p. 144).

Thus far the emphasis has been on the assets of the indigenous non-professional. In programs where other types of nonprofessionals have been used, particularly college students, other important assets of the nonprofessional have become apparent. One significant feature, apparent in the early college companion programs for mental patients (Umbarger, Dalsimer, Morrison, Breggin, 1962), was the zest and enthusiasm of the college student that seemed to create an entirely different and beneficial atmosphere in the typical mental hospital. Some programs (Klein and Zax, 1965) attempted to capitalize on the college students' enthusiasm by having them work with patients who, although seemingly capable of establishing a life for themselves outside the institution, were lacking in motivation to do so. Poser (1966), in attempting to explain why his lay therapists (college students) seem to have done better with their patients than professionals therapists, also refers to their "naive enthusiasm." He saw their lack of a "professional stance" as allowing them to engage in less stereotyped behavior than typifies professionals and as giving them considerably more freedom to respond to the patient's particular mood of the moment. Rioch (1966) in commenting on Poser's results also refers to the freshness of viewpoint and the flexibility of the college student nonprofessional. She anticipates, however, that this may be a quality that wears off in time if the nonprofessional engages in the same activity over a long period.

Another advantage of the college student nonprofessional which should be mentioned is the suggestion by Rioch (1966) that patients find it easier to relate to and cooperate with people who are less imposing than professionals, and who are closer to the bottom of the social hierarchy, as they themselves are. Reinherz (1964) in describing a volunteer case-aide program for school children also commented on this quality of the college student nonprofessional. She noted that some children, who had been unreachable through traditional therapeutic approaches, were able to develop meaningful relationships with their case aides, who could serve as good identification figures.

SELECTION AND TRAINING OF NONPROFESSIONALS

Selection

Procedures for recruiting and selecting nonprofessionals have varied quite widely, even in different projects where nonprofessionals are used to perform relatively similar functions. Some of the early college student companion programs utilized any students who were interested, or those taking a particular course, and relied on self-screening for ultimate selection (Umbarger et al., 1962; Holzberg, 1967). In such cases the student came to the hospital for a few sessions before making a firm commitment to the program. It was expected that those who found, after brief exposure, that the program was not for them could bow out gracefully. Those who persisted were thought to be suitable to continue. In the college companion program described by Klein and Zax (1965), potential participants were interviewed in only a brief screening procedure to rule out those who seemed grossly unfit for taking part in the program. Similarly, Cowen, Zax, and Laird (1966) used a gross screening interview to rule out college students who "seemed either flagrantly maladjusted or grossly unsuited" to work with primary grade children suffering incipient emotional problems. Goodman (1967), on the other hand, reported a college student companion program with "troubled" youngsters in which a very careful selection procedure was followed. Applicants responding to campuswide advertisements were required to describe themselves via several psychological test instruments designed to elicit self-disclosing information, and to participate in a group assessment procedure which provided the major selection data. The group procedure is structured to encourage each member to reveal highly personal information about himself. On the basis of this performance in the group, each applicant rates his fellow applicants, and all are rated by three staff members for warmth, self-disclosure, empathy, rigidity, surgency, and the like. Applicants not viewed as warm, self-disclosing, and understanding by a majority of all raters, fellow applicants and staff included, were rejected.

In her program to train housewives to become psychotherapists Rioch (1967) used rather elaborate selection procedures. As previously mentioned, her mental health counselor trainees were recruited from among housewives recommended by community leaders, women's associations, PTA's, church groups, and college clubs. After turning up an abundance of applicants, a complex selection procedure was instituted. Each applicant wrote a 1500-word autobiography describing both the major facts of her life and her own view of her development. Applicants then were seen by two or three staff members in groups of eight or ten where they spent four or five hours discussing a variety of topics and asking questions about the program. Each group was assigned a particular question for discussion and was asked to arrive at a consensus concerning that issue. In some cases applicants were asked to discuss as a group a tape-recorded interview that all had jut listened to. A later procedure involved a group discussion of how members would feel if they were rejected for the program. The autobiography and group sessions were used to eliminate more than half of the applicants, and the remainder were seen individually by two interviewers on separate occasions. The subjects in Rioch's project were also administered psychological tests.

So that it will not be interpreted that Rioch's procedures were elaborate because the activity for which she planned to train her volunteers involved psychotherapy, it should be pointed out that several programs utilizing nonprofessionals as psychotherapists have used far less elaborate selection procedures. Carkhuff and Truax (1965b), for example, used student volunteers taking a graduate course in individual psychotherapy and lay hospital personnel who were volunteers but were otherwise unselected for the program. Poser (1966) used altogether untrained college undergraduates who expressed interest in the project but were otherwise unselected. Most of Poser's volunteers had never had course work in psychology, and none seemed even to be considering work in the mental health professions.

Similar contrasts in approach have been found among programs training indigenous workers for service in deprived neighborhoods. Reissman (1967), for example, has described a very elaborate procedure for selecting workers to serve in a neighborhood mental health center. Recruitment was done through local community agencies, radio stations, the state employment service, community meetings, and the like. The selection procedure involved several steps. First, a large meeting was held for all applicants where the job, the salary, and personnel practices were described, and where questions concerning the program were answered. In the next phase, 10 or 11 applicants at a time were interviewed as a group and observed by four judges, all professionals (a psychologist, a social worker, a psychiatrist, and a nurse). The two people conducting the interviews attempted to ascertain the attitudes of the candidates toward the neighborhood and the people living there, their attitudes toward welfare, discrimination, minority groups, emotional disturbance, and the like. All applicants were rated by the judges for empathy, attitude toward authority, comfort in a group, ability to communicate ideas and feelings, trainability and flexibility, capacity for self-awareness, reaction to stress, pathology, and relevant work and life experience. The large initial applicant group was winnowed down through this procedure, and another group session was held for those who remained. Ultimately individual interviews were held with any candidates about whom there seemed to be any question.

By contrast with Riessman's selection process, the procedure described by Klein (1967) for selecting human service aides indigenous to the neighborhoods in which they were to work was extraordinarily simple. Recruits for this program, conducted in Washington, D. C., were chosen from among individuals referred by several local agencies dealing with problem youth. Quite intentionally many of these recruits were seen as poor risks for the training program because of their previously poor employment records and histories of delinquency, and poor school achievement. Selection was done on an almost random basis from the pool of applicants that was generated. Every effort was made to include as wide a variety of individuals as possible rather than to rule out particular subgroups on the basis of preconceptions about who might or might not succeed.

Contrasting selection procedures are also found in programs involving nonprofessionals recruited to work in school mental health programs. Donahue and Nichtern (1965) recruited a number of "teacher-moms" without making a general announcement of their program. Their recruits were acquired "by personal contact." This procedure entailed, apparently, various members of the school system who were familiar with the project recommending women they knew to have had teacher training and who were thought to be suitable for the program. Although an educational administrator and a school psychologist interviewed recruits, the interviews were used to discourage those who had any doubts about participating in the program and to get to know the applicant better rather than for screening; and no applicants seem to have been rejected as a result of the interview. Zax and Cowen (1967) described a more elaborate procedure for selecting "teacher-aides" than that used by Donahue and Nichtern. Their recruitment was carried out through local professional groups and clergymen, both to avoid accumulating too large a number of applicants and in the hope that professionals would provide a type of prescreening that would identify a small group of very strong applicants. Functionally, this effort at prescreening was probably similar to that used by Donahue and Nichtern. However, in Zax and Cowen's program, each applicant was further required to participate in two interviews, one with the project directors, and a second one with the school psychologist who would be one of their direct supervisors. Ratings were made on a variety of personality characteristics by each interviewer, and ultimate selections were made on the basis of interview findings. Incidentally, prescreening and recruitment through recommendation by project professionals or nonprofessionals is reported by Sobey (1970) to be the most popular technique in the 185 programs she surveyed.

Few generalizations can be drawn from the foregoing concerning procedures for selecting nonprofessionals. Some criteria are, of course, obvious. Where an important part of the nonprofessional's function is to teach, as in Donahue and Nichtern's project, it is desirable that the recruit have teacher training. Where a program's target population is a social class that the traditional professional has difficulty reaching, it is desirable that the recruit be indigenous to that class. Programs intending to capitalize on the enthusiasm and commitment of young people naturally draw recruits from among college student groups. However, beyond choices involving these gross criteria, there are few commonly used guidelines. Some program designers acknowledge openly that they have little basis on which to establish rigid selection procedures and are comfortable to allow volunteers to self-select or to rely solely on a gross screening procedure for eliminating only the patently maladjusted. Other program designers begin with preconceptions of qualities that they feel will be desirable in their nonprofessionals and set up elaborate procedures to select for them. In the latter case, however, there is much reliance on intuition and personal predilections, since very little empirical data relating nonprofessional characteristics to performance in specific programs have been provided.

Rappaport, Chinsky, and Cowen (1971) have attempted to relate personality characteristics of their college student volunteers to their success as leaders of groups of chronic mental patients. They used a variety of measures including scales rating empathy, nonpossessive warmth, and congruence that were developed by Truax and Carkhuff (1967), the A-B scale developed for rating therapist characteristics (Betz, 1962), and a procedure known as the Group Assessment of Interpersonal Traits (GAIT) developed by Goodman (1967). Unfortunately none of the measures of volunteer characteristics predicted reliably to patient change. More recently Cowen, Dorr, and Pokracki (1972) have compared the personal characteristics of women selected to work as nonprofessional child aides with those rejected for this role. They found that the professionals' "liking" of the candidate was the most significant determinant of acceptance or rejection. These studies are relatively minor ones which have not produced important results, but they serve as models for the type of research that must be carried out extensively if greater sophistication is to be achieved in the selection process.

Training

Several who have dealt with the training of nonprofessionals have recommended that abstract, didactic programs be minimized in favor of on-the-job experiences and learning through doing. Reiff and Riessman (1965) emphasize that on-the-job training should begin virtually immediately. They feel that the longer the nonprofessional remains in a training phase without actually functioning at the job for which he is being prepared, the more anxiety he develops. Thus some aspect of the new job should be engaged in very early with the various tasks to be performed phased so that the simplest ones, which can be handled with little training, are introduced first. As training progresses, so can task complexity.

Another recommendation of Reiff and Riessman is that didactic sessions should stress doing rather than listening or writing. Role playing and role training are much perferred to lecturing. Teaching styles should be down to earth and clear, the student should have easy access to individual discussion or supervision, and nonprofessionals in training should be encouraged to develop a sense of group solidarity so that, feeling supported by their own group, they will not feel a need to imitate professionals. In line with the latter point, Reiff and Riessman believe that it is essential that the nonprofessional have the freedom to develop his own personal style of functioning.

Apropos of the latter point, Riessman (1967), in a later paper on training nonprofessionals, points out that nonprofessionals are usually selected because they possess characteristics such as informality, humor, earthiness, and neighborliness. On the other hand, they may also possess many other personal qualities that are less positive for adequate functioning in the human services field such as punitiveness, suspiciousness, and moral indignation. Thus training programs should attempt to build on personal traits that will serve well in the kind of work they are expected to do and should attempt either to control or to train out negative characteristics. In the same article, Riessman reiterates the need to provide only the most minimal degree of training necessary to permit the nonprofessional to begin work in a job, and to provide the training for more complex functioning while the trainee is actually functioning at his work.

Many of the points stressed by Reiff and Riessman are reiterated by Hawkinshire (1969). He stresses the need for making training clearly relevant to a job, providing continuing support for the trainee, and setting up a continuous on-the-job training program. In addition, he stresses the significance of "feedback" in the training process. By this term he refers to the necessity for allowing a two-way communication channel. Here, the trainer provides information in one channel while, in the other, the trainee has the opportunity to express his anxiety and, with the help of a supervisor, to adjust his performance to his own expectations.

An essential element of many training programs is, in fact, an organized group experience to provide the kind of "feedback" that Hawkinshire stresses. Klein (1967), for example, has described a "core group" which is essential to the training of human service aides in the Howard University program. This core group is defined as:

"... a training group in which its members would learn how society, small groups, people in general, and they themselves felt, functioned, and developed. Within this group aides learn how to analyze personal, social, and particularly job-related problems, make their own decisions, try on various roles and attitudes for size, and learn to cope more effectively with people and the world around them" (Klein, 1967, pp. 149–150.

Similarly, in Goldenberg's residential center for delinquent youth, a variety of group experiences that involve a form of sensitivity training are an essential part of staff training. These have been described in a previous chapter. Andronico, Fidler, Guerney, and Guerney (1967) have also described a semigroup thereapy experience that is fundamental to their training of parents to conduct filial therapy. Parents are taught to conduct play therapy sessions with their own children within the group but are also encouraged to use the group to explore their own feelings, so that the group session involves a combination of both didactic and dynamic elements.

Perhaps the most common training model of all that involve nonprofessionals is the one combining didactic training with supervised experience on the job (Sobey, 1970). Tremendous variation is seen, however, with respect to the nature of the mix between these two training elements. Rioch (1967), and Sanders, Smith, and Weinman, for example, have described training programs that have been quite long and heavily laden with didactic materials in addition to job experiences. Carkhuff and Truax (1965) have utilized a shorter training period to produce psychotherapists for work in a hospital setting. Their program involved approximately 100 hours of training extending over a period of about 16 weeks. Zax and Cowen's teacher aides (1967) participated in a 5-week training program that combined didactic sessions with classroom observation. Hallowitz and Riessman (1967) trained their neighborhood service center staff in a prejob period of only 3 weeks before placing them in the center for the continuation of their training while on the job. Johnston (1967) trained foster grandparents during a one-week orientation period before putting them to work, as Fellows and Wolpin (1969) did with high school students who served as companions to hospitalized adolescents.

Perhaps the primary commonalities among the recommendations and actual training programs for nonprofessionals are the acceptance of the notion that abstract, didactic material should be reinforced by actual experience on the job. Beyond this there seems to be relatively little commonality with respect to how much formal training should be provided. At times, one wonders if program organizers do not utilize extensive training periods to deal with their own doubts and insecurities about placing nonprofessionals in human service settings. Sometimes, as was directly stated by Zax and Cowen (1967), the training program is intended as much to allay the anxiety of the nonprofessional as it is to provide a background of information for doing the job. Clearly, the field could benefit from research programs designed to assess the merits of various nonprofessional training approaches.

In some respects the training programs described may be special cases in that they have been reported in the literature, often with the results of attempts to evaluate their effectiveness. In many of the federally sponsored programs surveyed by Grosser (1969), he reports that training is a neglected feature. One of the reasons for this is that funding agencies tend to prefer that the funds they provide be used for programs which provide visible service. Training programs for nonprofessionals do not eventuate in statistics indicating that services have been rendered, so that to maintain a flow of funds, training is neglected in favor of programs that produce quantitative results. Thus many agencies indicate that nonprofessionals are being trained in regular inservice training programs available to their total staff. In such agencies no formal orientation period is provided for the nonprofessional, and he is expected to learn what he can through staff mettings that are sometimes scheduled regularly and sometimes only sporadically. While feeling uncomfortable with this situation, many administrators seem to be resigned to living with it. There is a danger in such a neglect of training in busy agencies which is foreboding for the entire nonprofessional movement. Should nonprofessionals fail to learn quickly what they need to know, and fail to receive the backup support from experienced professionals which may be necessary for performing their function effectively, they may create more problems than they help to solve. In that event professionals may use these failures as a reason to abandon the use of nonprofessionals despite their own failure to have used them properly. The professional's readiness to banish nonprofessionals from agencies is provoked by a variety of problems that will be discussed in detail in the next section.

PROBLEMS IN THE USE OF NONPROFESSIONALS

Despite the many potential advantages cited in an earlier part of this chapter in using nonprofessionals, this movement is clearly not without its problems and disadvantages. These problems take a variety of forms ranging from those that derive from the reaction of professionals to the nonprofessional, through the many personal problems experienced by the nonprofessionals in working in a mental health field, to the practical problem of finding jobs and appropriate career opportunities.

The Reactions of Professionals to Nonprofessionals

MacLennan (1969) comments:

"Essentially it has to be recognized that the introduction of the indigenous nonprofessional into an agency puts a demand on all to change not only in terms of the organization of task and job but also through a need to review values and to reach out to each other so that good communication can be established. In such a situation some conflict is inevitable and it is only through a willingness to respect each other and to examine differences that these problems can be satisfactorily resolved." (MacLennan, 1969, p. 140).

The conflict MacLennan speaks of is doubtless a profound one whether the nonprofessional is indigenous or not, and probably accounts for a variety of the negative reactions emenating from the professional. Perhaps the professional's most common negative reaction is concern that the nonprofessional will not be able to render high-quality service (Goldberg, 1969; Grosser, 1969; Johnston, 1967). Many state that the mental health worker's job is simply too complex to be broken down into elements that can be handled adequately by untrained nonprofessionals.

Another cause for negative professional reaction is that the introduction of the nonprofessional into an agency poses a direct challenge to the status of professionals. Grosser (1969) points out that federal agencies which support programs involving the use of nonprofessionals frequently regard the nonprofessional as a change agent who will promote a reorganization of the agency's service pattern. Agency personnel, on the other hand, prefer to regard the nonprofessional as a facilitator of existing services. Thus the inertia that prompts agency professionals to resist attempts at drastically reorganizing their functions in favor of new, unfamiliar roles, at which they may fail, accounts for many negative reactions to nonprofessionals. It is difficult for a professional who has endured many years of training and built up a backlog of experience in a certain type of role to welcome with open arms nonprofessionals who are brought in either to take over their own jobs in part or to promote an entirely new way of functioning within the agency. Manifestations of professional resistance to nonprofessionals may take many forms. Grosser (1969) reports that nonprofessionals in many instances are not allowed to perform direct service functions. Those who are, tend to be members of the middle class rather than the lower classes. Another pattern is for the professional to treat middle class patients and to assign only lower class patients to nonprofessionals.

Reiff and Riessman (1965) recommend preparing professionals whose agencies are to utilize nonprofessionals very carefully before the program begins. These authors believe that the professional often is unclear about the capacities of the nonprofessional and the role that he is to serve. For Reiff and Riessman the success of a nonprofessional program will depend heavily on the flexibility of professionals and their capacity to understand the aptitudes and potential roles of the nonprofessional, and a willingness to reorganize their own jobs to take advantage of the nonprofessional's assets. Reiff and Riessman also warn that verbal expressions of acceptance are not sufficient and must be manifested in the professional's actual behavior. Reiff and Riessman's recommendations are echoed in great measure by Zax, Cowen, Izzo, Madonia, Merenda, and Trost (1966). These authors describe the introduction of teacher aides into the public school system and reflect on the problems created in the first year of their service because of the inadequate preparation of teachers to incorporate the aides into their functioning.

Reiff and Riessman also warn against the tendency to overemphasize the potential assets of the nonprofessional which thereby devalues the contribution that the professional can make. In a similar vein, Grosser (1969) comments on the tendency of some professionals to have a "somewhat romanticized reaction" to the nonprofessional and thereby to inflate the virtues of the untrained. This is seen by Reiff and Riessman as reverse alienation and must be guarded against by making it clear that nonprofessionals are not replacing professionals entirely; their employment merely requires the professional to alter his role to that of consultant, supervisor, teacher, and coordinator from that of a primary service giver.

The Nonprofessional Must Abandon an Established Life-Style

As MacLennan (1969) points out, often the nonprofessional must change his life-style dramatically when he becomes a mental health worker. Simply the fact of having a steady job, and not "hanging around" in the old neighborhood with the old group makes him a different kind of person. A regular income makes it unnecessary for him to perform delinquent acts, his contact with well-educated people opens up new vistas for him, and his view of himself undergoes a change. This change inevitably involves a certain degree of conflict for most indigenous nonprofessionals, and some are unable to persist in the face of it.

Another danger is that those who manage to persist and accept the change in their outlook and way of life, may begin to feel contemptuous toward the type of people with whom they grew up and whom they are now expected to serve. Goldberg (1969) points out that many nonprofessionals are criticized as not being empathic and understanding toward their own social class. Instead, they may look down on those who have managed less well than they themselves. Reiff and Riessman (1965) speak of this as "overidentifying with the agency." They suggest that this problem is likely to be a continuing one for nonprofessionals, and one that needs to be monitored carefully by agency professionals. The distance between the nonprofessional and his impoverished client is likely to increase the longer the nonprofessional works in the agency. Dealing with this problem is facilitated when the agency's attitude toward its underprivileged clients is genuinely positive.

The Nonprofessional's Newness to the Mental Health Role

Several problems have been identified by different observers that derive partly from the nonprofessional's newness to the mental health role. These problems also affect the fledgling professional; however, they may be more intense in the case of the nonprofessional. One problem concerns the issue of maintaining confidentiality. Reiff and Riessman (1965) point out that the indigenous nonprofessional who has grown up in a densely populated area where privacy is a rare commodity may be insensitive to the need of keeping a client's problems from becoming public. Living under circumstances where it is very difficult to maintain secrecy, may make one less inclined to attempt to achieve this. It may also be that fewer feelings of guilt and shame are engendered by behaviors the larger society would regard as negative, so that on this account the keeping of confidences seems unnecessary. In any case, the problem of maintaining confidentiality is one that Reiff and Riessman feel must be addressed directly in the case of the indigenous worker.

Riessman (1965) in his paper on the helper-therapy principle suggests that the nonprofessional may be especially prone to project his own personal problems onto his clients. He recognizes that such projection is a problem for anyone in mental health work, but professional training programs ordinarily attempt to grapple with this problem, either intellectually or through personal psychotherapy. Since the nonprofessional often fails to have extensive training, supervising professionals must be alert to the need to help the nonprofessional avoid projecting his personal problems onto those he is attempting to treat.

A third problem for many nonprofessionals, pointed out by Reiff and Riessman (1965), concerns the sense of defeatism that is apt to develop in the indigenous worker who approaches his work with considerable enthusiasm in the expectation that results will be promptly forthcoming. The nonprofessional's zest for his work is an asset. However, when change does not come about as rapidly as he might wish, he may become overly discouraged and pessimistic about the enterprise. Again, this is a problem that is common to fledgling professionals in the mental health field. The nonprofessional, however, is apt to be somewhat more impatient about this issue, is apt to be more easily frustrated by bureaucracy, and is more likely to blame the agency or the establishment for being apathetic and the reason for his lack of success. To forestall this problem, Reiff and Riessman recommend that a realistic timetable be laid out concerning the expectations of program achievements.

Power Struggles with Professionals

Reiff (1966) has pointed out that just as power struggles have existed among different professional groups within the mental health fields, similar struggles can inevitably be expected between professionals and the new nonprofessionals being introduced to the mental health field. If the nonprofessional is to "serve the function of doing what the professional cannot do," he must find a place within the mental health establishment without being absorbed by the existing structure. Thus he needs a power base of his own. Reiff feels that the most effective power base arises out of the development of a constituency, a group within the general population that feels the need for the type of services the nonprofessional can provide. As a direct service giver to the poor, the nonprofessional is often in an excellent position to develop such a constituency.

Grosser's survey of federally sponsored programs utilizing nonprofessionals (Grosser, 1969) indicates that, as Reiff asserts, nonprofessional staff do create serious tensions within agencies. They are viewed as being demanding concerning job placements and as tenacious concerning job development. Furthermore, they are often not content to operate within the boundaries of assigned tasks and are seen as wanting to "take over the entire agency."

The pressure exerted on agencies by federal fund granting programs to employ nonprofessionals is also seen to have forced many agencies to embark on such programs without really wholeheartedly favoring them. Many agencies seem particularly resentful of having to hire indigenous nonprofessionals. One agency administrator expressed the feeling that his project was "paying the price for a hundred years of discrimination by the entire community." Another complaint centering on power issues has to do with the feeling among professionals that, even in cases where a nonprofessional is essential to a successful treatment program, the agencies are seriously limited in how freely they can reassign or dismiss indigenous workers because of the threat of reprisal from the nonprofessional's constituency within the local community.

The power issues described present a serious problem that must be reckoned with in any program making extensive use of nonprofessionals. Essentially the nonprofessionals represent a new force within the mental health movement, which to be effective in its mental health role, must maintain its own identity and integrity. Failure to do so may easily lead to a dilution of that aspect of the force that is new to the mental health scene and that probably is its most potent element. Clearly, however, the establishment of such a force must create tension with forces already present within the mental health establishment. These tensions threaten to divert both professionals and nonprofessionals from what should be their primary goal, the provision of optimal service to those needing it. Only time and experience can lead to a good resolution of these conflicts. Recognizing the potential for their existence and anticipating them, however, should aid in an eventual resolution.

Finding Appropriate Jobs

Ultimately, the success of the nonprofessional movement will depend on the availability of positions for this type of mental health worker. Goldberg (1969) points out that many observers feel that the majority of nonprofessionals, who are essentially new careerists, should be employed in public health, educational, or welfare agencies. Agencies of this kind are, of course, the largest dispensers of human services; they tend to be chronically understaffed; and they serve the poor, the very clientele with whom many new careerists are thought to be particularly effective. Unfortunately, many of these agencies are organized along bureaucratic lines, with entry jobs and career lines clearly laid out in a way that makes the introduction of a very new type of worker, and particularly one who tends to be relatively poorly trained in the formal sense, difficult. There may also be considerable resistance within agencies to the restructuring of tables of organization in order to make room for nonprofessionals. To some extent, existing supervisors may be threatened by the possibility that their own status or prestige will be diminished if new entry-level staff are less poorly qualified and lower paid than was the case earlier. Administrators, too, may be threatened by the possibility that the introduction of personnel with relatively poor formal preparation will lower the morale of existing staff.

This state of affairs makes it imperative that, as Cowen (1967) points out, the nonprofessional be trained to perform a useful function in a specific setting, with administrators of potential recipient agencies contacted at the very beginning of the training program and encouraged to hire trainees. Trainers must maintain a continuing liaison with potential employers of the nonprofessional and must work toward the resolution of any practical problems that threaten to interfere with appropriate employment for the nonprofessional once his training is completed.

CONCLUSION

The introduction of the nonprofessional to the mental health scene is becoming prevalent. Many good reasons, besides the fact that it helps resolve manpower problems, support this movement. It is a movement, however, that is fraught with many problems. Some of them are concerned with the issue of how to select and how to train people who are to be employed for mental health functions. Relatively little systematic research has been done to solve these problems, and most programs have dealt with these issues arbitrarily. Many of the other problems inherent in using nonprofessionals in the mental health field are probably not soluble on the basis of research and systematic study. They involve the negative reactions of professionals to nonprofessionals, the personal problems that the nonprofessional is apt to bring to his work in the mental health field, the power issues that will inevitably arise within agencies taking in large groups of nonprofessionals, and the practical problems of reorganizing existing bureaucratic structures to permit the introduction of a nonprofessional who can find a career within an agency. Many of these latter problems will require considerable time and experience before they are resolved. The best that can be done at present is to anticipate what problems threaten to occur in a given program and to take steps to forestall or alleviate them once they arise.

References

Albee, G. W. *Mental Health Manpower Trends.* New York: Basic Books, 1959.

Albee, G. W. American psychology in the sixties. *American Psychologist,* 1963, *18,* 90–95.

Andronico, M. P., Fidler, J., Guerney, B. G. Jr., & Guerney, L. F. The combination of didactic and dynamic elements in filial therapy. *International Journal of Group Psychotherapy,* 1967, *17,* 10–17.

Betz, B. J. Experiences in research in psychotherapy with schizophrenic patients. In H. H. Strupp, & L. Luborsky (Eds.), *Research in Psychotherapy,* Vol. 2., Washington, D. C.: American Psychological Association, 1962. Pp. 41–60.

Carkhuff, R. R., & Truax, C. B. Lay mental health counseling: The effects of lay group counseling. *Journal of Consulting Psychology,* 1965, *29,* 426–431 (a).

Carkhuff, R. R., & Truax, C. B. Training in counseling and psychotherapy: An evaluation of an integrated didactic and experiential approach. *Journal of Consulting Psychology,* 1965, *29,* 333–336 (b).

Christmas, J. J. Group methods in training and practice: Nonprofessional mental health personnel in a deprived community. *American Journal of Orthopsychiatry,* 1966, *36,* 410–419.

Cowen, E. L., Dorr, D. A., & Pockraki, F. Selection of nonprofessional child aides for a school mental health project. *Community Mental Health Journal,* 1972, *8,* 220–226.

Cowen, E. L., Izzo, L. D., Miles, H., Telschow, E. F., Trost, M. A., & Zax, M. A preventive mental health program in the school setting: Description and Evaluation. *Journal of Psychology,* 1963, *56,* 307–356.

Cowen, E. L., Leibowitz, E., & Leibowitz, G. The utilization of retired people as mental health aides in the schools. *American Journal of Orthopsychiatry,* 1968, *38,* 900–909.

Cowen, E. L., Zax, M., & Laird, J. D. A college student volunteer program in the elementary school setting. *Community Mental Health Journal,* 1966, *2,* 319–328.

Donahue, G. T., & Nichtern, S. *Teaching the troubled child.* New York: Free Press, 1965.

Dorr, D., Cowen, E. L., & Sandler, I. Changes in nonprofessional mental health workers' response preference and attitudes as a function of experience. Unpublished manuscript. University of Rochester, 1972.

Fellows, L., & Wolpin, M. High school psychology trainees in a mental hospital. In B. G. Guerney, Jr. (Ed.), *Psychotherapeutic agents: new roles for nonprofessionals, parents, and teachers.* New York: Holt, Rinehart & Winston, 1969. Pp. 274–277.

Fidler, J. W., Guerney, B. G., Jr., Andronico, M. P., & Guerney, L. F. Filial therapy as a logical extension of current trends in psychotherapy. In B. G. Guerney, Jr. (Ed.), *Psychotherapeutic Agents: New roles for non-professionals, parents, and teachers.* New York: Holt, Rinehart & Winston, 1969. Pp. 47–55.

Gartner, A., Kohler, M., & Riessman, F. *Children teach children.* New York: Harper & Row, 1971.

Goldberg, G. S. Nonprofessional in human services. In C. Grosser, W. E. Henry, & J. G. Kelly (Eds.), *Nonprofessionals in the human services.* San Francisco: Jossey-Bass, 1969. Pp. 12–39.

Goldenberg, I. *Build me a mountain.* Cambridge, Mass.: The MIT Press, 1971.

Goodman, G. An experiment with companionship therapy: college students and troubled boys-assumptions, selection, and design. *American Journal of Public Health,* 1967, *57,* 1772–1777.

Gordon, J. E. Project cause, the federal anti-poverty program and some implications of subprofessional training. *American Psychologist,* 1965, *30,* 334–343.

Grosser, C. Manpower development programs. In C. Grosser, W. E. Henry, & J. G. Kelly (Eds.), *Nonprofessionals in the human services.* San Francisco: Jossey-Bass, 1969.

Hallowitz, E., & Riessman, F. The role of the indigenous nonprofessional in a community mental health neighborhood service center program. *American Journal of Orthopsychiatry,* 1967, *37,* 766–778.

Harris, F. R., Wolf, M. M., & Baer, D. M. Effects of adult social reinforcement on child behavior. *Young Children,* 1964, *20,* 8–17.

Hawkinshire, F. B. W. Training procedures for offenders working in community treatment programs. In B. G. Guerney, Jr. (Ed.), *Psychotherapeutic agents: new roles for non-professionals, parents, and teachers.* New York: Holt, Rinehart & Winston, 1969.

Holzberg, J. D., Knapp, R. H., & Turner, J. L. College students as companions to the mentally ill. In E. L. Cowen, E. A. Gardner, & M. Zax (Eds.), *Emergent Approaches to Mental Health Problems.* New York: Appleton-Century-Crofts, 1967. Pp. 91–109.

Johnston, R. Some casework aspects of using foster grandparents for emotionally disturbed children. *Children,* 1967, *14,* 46–52.

Jones, M. *The Therapeutic Community: New Treatment Method in Psychology.* New York: Basic Books, 1953.

Klein, W. L. The training of human service aides. In E. L. Cowen, E. A. Gardner, & M. Zax (Eds.), *Emergent Approaches to Mental Health Problems.* New York: Appleton-Century-Crofts, 1967.

Klein, W. L., & Zax, M. The use of a hospital volunteer program in the teaching of abnormal psychology. *Journal of Social Psychology*, 1965, *65*, 155–165.

Kreitzer, S. F. College students in a behavior therapy program with hospitalized emotionally disturbed children. In B. G. Guerney, Jr. (Ed.), *Psychotherapeutic agents: new roles for non-professionals, parents, and teachers.* New York: Holt, Rinehart & Winston, 1969.

MacLennan, B. W. Special problems in training the nonprofessional. In B. G. Guerney, Jr. (Ed.), *Psychotherapeutic agents: new roles for non-professionals, parents, and teachers.* New York: Holt, Rinehart & Winston, Inc., 1969.

Pearl, A., & Riessman, F. *Poverty and new careers for professionals.* New York: Free Press, 1965.

Perlmutter, F., & Durham, D. Using teenagers to supplement casework service. *Social Work*, 1965, *10*, 41–46.

Poser, E. G. The effects of therapists' training on group therapeutic outcome. *Journal of Consulting Psychology*, 1966, *30*, 283–289.

Rappaport, J., Chinsky, J. M., & Cowen, E. L. *Innovations in helping chronic patients.* New York: Academic Press, 1971.

Reiff, R. Mental health manpower and institutional change. *American Psychologist*, 1966, *21*, 540–548.

Reiff, R., & Riessman, F. The indigenous nonprofessional: A strategy of change in community action and community mental health programs. *Community Mental Health Journal*, 1965, Monograph No. 1, 3–32.

Reinherz, H. The therapeutic use of student volunteers. *Children*, 1964, *2*, 137–142.

Richan, W. C. A theoretical scheme for determining roles of professionals and nonprofessional personnel. In B. G. Guerney, Jr. (Ed.), *Psychotherapeutic agents: new roles for non-professionals, parents, and teachers.* New York: Holt, Rinehart & Winston, 1969.

Riessman, F. The "Helper Therapy" principle. *Social Work*, 1965, *10*, 27–32.

Riessman, F. A neighborhood-based mental health approach. In E. L. Cowen, E. A. Gardner, & M. Zax (Eds.), *Emergent approaches to mental health problems.* New York: Appleton-Century-Crofts, 1967.

Rioch, M. J. Changing concepts in the training of psychotherapists. *Journal of Consulting Psychology*, 1966, *30*, 290–292.

Rioch, M. J. Pilot projects in training mental health counselors. In E. L. Cowen, E. A. Gardner, & M. Zax (Eds.), *Emergent approaches to mental health problems.* New York: Appleton-Century-Crofts, 1967.

Sanders, R., Smith, R., & Weinman, B. *Chronic psychoses and recovery: an experiment in socio-environmental therapy.* San Francisco: Jossey-Bass, 1967.

Sobey, F. *The nonprofessional revolution in mental health.* Columbia University Press: New York, 1970.

Truax, C. B., & Carkhuff, R. R. *Toward effective counseling and psychotherapy: training and practice.* Chicago: Aldine, 1967.

Umbarger, C. C., Dalsimer, J. S., Morrison, A. P., & Breggin, P. R. *College students in a mental hospital.* New York: Grune and Stratton, 1962.

Wahler, R. G., Winkel, G. H., Peterson, R. F., & Morrison, D. C. Mothers as behavior therapists for their own children. *Behavior Research and Therapy,* 1965, *3,* 113–124.

Zax, M., & Cowen, E. L. Early Identification and Prevention of Emotional Disturbance in a Public School. In E. L. Cowen, E. A. Gardner, & M. Zax (Eds.), *Emergent approaches to mental health problems.* New York: Appleton-Century-Crofts, 1967.

Zax, M., Cowen, E. L., Izzo, L. D., Madonia, A. J., Merenda, J., & Trost, M. A. A teacher aide program for preventing emotional disturbance in the school setting. *Mental Hygiene,* 1966, *50,* 406–415.

14. *the role of the community and community psychology*

In the opening chapters of this book the point was made that community psychology has begun to emerge largely because the mental health professions, as they are traditionally practiced, have had little to offer in solving many pressing social problems. Furthermore, it has become very apparent that what the mental health professions have had to offer best suited the needs of certain privileged social classes. Hence, while one thrust of the community movement has involved an attempt to improve the services of traditional mental health settings, another has reflected a need to extend services to social classes previously ignored and to make service relevant to the types of problems experienced by these social classes.

In a provocative paper in which he does a market analysis of the socially handicapped and the agencies that must presumably deal with them, Bredemeier (1964) discusses some of the reasons why agencies have been relatively unresponsive to client needs. He contrasts the social agency with the typical business firm as a means of understanding this problem. The essential force that prompts the business firm to be responsive to consumer demands is competition. In a market where people have many alternatives, they have the freedom to sample and to settle on what product suits them best. This forces the business, as Bredemeier puts it, to "heads-up playing." The product must be altered and shaped to suit the demands and needs of potential consumers.

By contrast, in the social agency field, competition does not exist. Agencies are thoroughly professionalized, are very bureaucratic, and the competition among them is mainly for philanthropic dollars. In its role as a service provider, the agency is less dependent on its clients than it is on its employees. Agencies have a monopoly on services that are in short supply, so there is no dearth of clients. Professional manpower shortages make the acquisition and maintenance of sufficient staff much more difficult than the problem of attracting clientele. Therefore, agency personnel are often protected by the agency structure when they fail to be considerate of clients. The businessman or entertainer cannot afford to be insensitive to the wishes of his consumers because he suffers for it immediately and materially. The personnel of a social agency, however, are regularly sheltered from the effects of their own indifference to their clients.

Taking his analysis further, Bredemeier considers why agencies have avoided dealing with certain social classes manifesting what he calls "handicapped potential." One reason is that it is simply more costly in terms of time and money to develop the potentials of the handicapped than it is to develop those of more privileged classes. It may be necessary to establish more elaborate control over the environment of the handicapped to deal with them effectively. It may require the effort of ancillary professionals such as remedial reading teachers, social workers to visit in the homes, special classes in the schools, and the like. Costs of this kind cannot be met by the ordinary agency. Another, perhaps, more crucial cost is the obsolescence of the methods ordinarily used by agency personnel. The typical professional has been trained to deal with a very different kind of material than that which is presented by the lower classes. The professional who is predisposed to conceptualizing problems in terms of the Oedipal conflict is hard put to service a client "who knows that his mother's income from the welfare department depends on her producing more children."

In the light of this description of the situation that obtained under the old order, it is not surprising that a major issue for the emerging community movement has been the question of how best to create new agencies that are both sensitive and responsive to its clientele's needs. The answer to this question has been to speak of encouraging community involvement and even community control over the agencies that are to be created. Many reports are beginning to appear describing efforts to encourage community involvement and to incorporate residents of local communities on agency boards (Salber, 1970; Tischler, 1971; Whitaker, 1970). Clearly, creators of new agencies are in many respects becoming much more sensitized to the demand that their services be "relevant" to their clientele and are struggling to create a structure that will respond promptly to local needs.

Smith and Hobbs (1966), in setting forth guidelines for the new federally established comprehensive community mental health centers, assert, almost at the outset of their discussion, that "For the Comprehensive Community Mental Health Center to become an effective agency of the community, community control of center policy is essential" (Smith and Hobbs, 1966, p. 500). Their reasons for this recommendation go beyond the issues discussed heretofore. They point out that under our traditional mental health system, the "mental patient" was abandoned by his community. His mental disturbance was seen to be his own "private misery." One of the essential purposes of the new community movement is to affirm that serious emotional disorder stems from the "breakdown of normal sources of social support and understanding, especially the family." Thus, when a person becomes emotionally disturbed, it is not simply one individual who has gone wrong. His disturbance can be viewed as a symptom of a fault in the entire social system in which he is embedded. Therefore, the role of a treatment agency must include work with various components of the patient's social system to help it function in ways that will better sustain him. This requires a partnership between the mental health center and the community. The mental health center must become integrated into the life and the various institutions of the community it serves. In a sense, therefore, Smith and Hobbs' plea for more community involvement, and even control over mental health centers, is as much for the purpose of making the community more sensitive to its responsibility in the breakdown and rehabilitation of the emotionally disturbed as it is to sharpen the agency's sensitivities to the community's needs.

From the foregoing, it would seem that the argument for the community's playing an increasingly central role in the functioning of the mental health agencies is quite compelling. It is difficult to deny that traditional agencies have failed certain social classes badly. The insensitivity of the community to many serious disturbances is also easily documented. The seemingly obvious solution to these problems is to have the community run its own service agencies. This would seem to ensure that the community will have what it needs and wants and will become far better aware of its own role in the development of behavioral disorder. But will such a solution work? Simple solutions to complex social problems have often promised much only to produce disappointing results. In the rest of this chapter we consider some of the problems of implementing community involvement in and community control of mental health agencies, and discuss specific examples of efforts to surmount these problems.

SOME PROBLEMS WITH THE CONCEPT OF COMMUNITY CONTROL

Although the notion of encouraging greater community involvement in the operation of mental health agencies would seem to be a logical approach to correcting the insensitivity and neglect manifested by these agencies over the years, it takes little reflection to recognize that there are many problems in implementing that approach (see Figure 1). For ex-

---

Built on a former garbage dump that thrusts into Boston Harbor, the Columbia Point Housing Project has never been an appealing place. The stark, institutional-style buildings and their occupants—now mostly impoverished Blacks and Puerto Ricans, with a majority of white pensioners—are isolated both geographically and culturally from Boston proper. There are no private doctors in the project, and Boston City Hospital, is a long bus ride away.

The project's one bright spot since 1965 has been the Columbia Point Health Center, organized by Tufts University Medical School with federal funds, the center has provided a variety of high-quality medical and social services. After the clinic's first two years of operation a survey showed that 91% of the people thought that the medical care available to them was "good" or "very good." Now the 1,130 families are in danger of losing the clinic altogether. Reason: chronic and bitter controversy between professionals in the center and black community activists in an unstable environment. It is the kind of fight that occurs all too frequently in and around ghettos.

Tufts has abolished its department of preventive medicine, which originally sponsored the center, and has encouraged patients to look elsewhere for care. Four of the clinics's seven doctors and all of its social workers have quit out of fear and frustration. Though last-minute negotiations have stopped the other professional staffers from following, the center's chances for survival are dim.

Part of the reason is crime. Fear of robbery and assault—always a problem —has worsened to the point that many families have left. Their apartments often remain empty because of the project's reputation. In the past couple of years the threat of crime has become so serious that residents and doctors alike feel besieged. Says Dr. Sol Fleishman, a former medical director: "When I first came. I didn't hesitate to go out on calls even at night. By last year I thought twice before going out in broad daylight."

Even more damaging has been the political warfare, with Tufts and the medical staff on one side and militant critics from the community, most of them black, on the other. A loosely knit elected body called the Columbia Point Health Association often speaks for the clinic's opposition, though some attacks have come in the form of anonymous leaflets charging incompetence and insensitivity. The controversy reached a crisis point last spring after the then administrator. Leon Bennet-Alder, a frosty Englishman who had little rapport with the neighborhood, tried to cut costs and personnel he considered superfluous. He also attempted to fire a black business manager whom he accused of gross incompetence. Bennet-Alder became the target of threats by phone and leaflet. Then, on the way to work one morning, he was bludgeoned so viciously that his skull was shattered. There was no attempt to rob him, and the identity of the assailant remains unknown. Bennet-Alder recovered and left the center: the business manager still has his job.

Angry Wolves. One of the gut issues continues to be white-collar jobs for project residents. Dr. Jack Geiger, the center's creator, points out that pumping large amounts of cash—the current budget is $1.4 million—into a desperately poor area is risky. "It's like throwing a pound of meat to 50 angry wolves," he says. "They'll kill each other to get a bite." But racial pride and sensitivity about the condescending attitudes of some white professionals are also crucial factors. Gloria Nelms, a black former psychiatric counselor at Columbia Point who is among those responsible for the leaflet attacks, charges that "Bennet-Alder did everything possible to keep the Health Association from developing the ability to run the center. He also cut off training for paraprofessionals from the community." Opposition from some quarters in the community is virulent. Even some of the newer black administrators are being pilloried for "the same plantation mentality as the whites who came before."

Help has now arrived with the intervention of Action for Boston Community Development (ABCD), a city-wide agency that has replaced Tufts as the administrator of federal funds for the center. The group is heavily staffed with blacks and is determined to rally Columbia Point residents in support of the clinic. ABCD is trying to enforce some of the efficiency measures started by Bennet-Alder but is imposing them gradually. It has also hired a black as acting administrator and persuaded the remaining staffers to stay for a while. The agency, says ABCD Director Bob Coard. "is not about to retreat from involvement in Columbia Point because of a few faceless saboteurs." Coard may succeed, but for doctors like Fleishman, the retreat is final. "I got battle fatigue," says the physician, "after 61 years of hassles with everyone."

Figure 1. A Health Center's Problem with Community Involvement *(Time,* October 30, 1972, p. 71) .

ample, before one can speak of community control it is necessary that a definition of the community, or some way of identifying the community be settled on. Just what is the community of which we are speaking? Next, even if we define the community to our satisfaction, we face the question of where to find it. Does a particular geographical locale encompass the community? If so, do its boundaries conform closely to those of an area of responsibility of a particular agency? Going further, even if the community, elusive entity that it is, is identified and located, how are its representatives to be selected? Who speaks for the community? Finally, even if seemingly satisfactory representatives are selected to speak for the community, are they knowledgeable enough about the function of mental health agencies to play a meaningful part in their management? All of these are broad issues that must be dealt with to achieve perspective about the role that community members might be able to play in the functioning of mental health agencies.

Defining the Community

Defining the community is no simple matter because of the varied ways in which human groups organize themselves. Greer (1955) has traced the increasing complexity of man's social organization as his style of life has changed. He points out that primitive man tended to live in small groups sustained through hunting and grazing over circumscribed areas. Individual members depended on their group for their entire social existence. They lived in close physical proximity, status differentiations between them were based almost exclusively on age and sex, and they interacted with each other constantly and very intensely. For groups of this sort the definition of the community is a relatively simple one. The group one lives in is his community.

The invention of agriculture led to a tendency for humans to group themselves into villages involving a much more complex social system that was characterized by divisions of labor and a tendency toward development of specialized roles. As soon as a surplus of agricultural products was created, variations came about in the wealth of members of the village social group. The tendency to live one's life in one particular locale led to a wide integration of many groups, particularly extended family groups. Despite its increased social complexity, however, the village continued to exercise powerful control over the behavior of its members and remained a social group of a sort rather than an aggregate of individuals. This was because within the village, individual members depended on each other for status, access to production, a share of the surplus products of the group, and social and personal security. In many respects, the village remained a self-sufficient entity and its inhabitants depended on the world that it provided for most of their needs. Thus, in human groups organized along village lines, the problem of defining the community is still a relatively simple one. As Greer points out, the village, as a territorially defined entity having truly functional meaning for all its members, is very much a community. To be sure the village community does not order all of the behavior of its members in the same sense that the more primitive social group does, since other structures within the village, such as the extended family, differing age groups, or conjugal families, inevitably modify the village community's controlling power. Still, community controls are strong and result in behavior which is sufficiently uniform that the cultural anthropologist can justifiably study a few village members and feel secure that they well represent the relatively homogeneous world of village behavior.

Most societies, however, have gone beyond village communities. Heavy concentrations of people have grouped themselves into spaces so small that they cannot produce all of their own necessities; such concentrations characterize the city. The city sustains itself by exporting goods or services such as its manufactured products, military power, administrative order, financial credit, and the like and must import necessities like food and raw materials. Thus existence of cities becomes possible only after a number of agricultural villages are established that can produce enough of a surplus to maintain an urban population. An important characteristic of the city is a spectacular increase in occupational differentiation. In the cities, the professions, such as the clergy, the military, the government workers, the merchants, and the like develop. Even the ordinary population is absorbed in a variety of specialized work that is related to trade and industry. In addition to this occupational differentiation, the city is characterized by much physical and, to some extent, social mobility. People move around within the city far more than villagers do from one village to another. One effect of urban mobility is to insulate the individual socially, since a change in locale often allows him to escape from local "public opinion." Toffler (1970), in his book on "Future Shock," documents the increasing superficiality of interpersonal relationships resulting from technological advances that make movement over great distances very easy.

These complexities of urban society seriously complicate the problem of identifying or defining communities. The urban dweller is typically dependent on many different social groups for the fulfillment of different needs. He may depend on one group for his income, another for his recreation, a third for his religious needs, and so forth. Even his family, which in other societies is often depended on for a variety of these functions, may be relatively unimportant to him. Furthermore, the geographical bounds within which an urban dweller has most of his needs met become greatly broadened. He may live 15 to 20 miles from where he works, and may depend most heavily for his recreational gratifications on settings that are likewise far from the neighborhood in which he resides. This weakens the functional importance of his immediate neighbors and results in a decline of the urban neighborhood. In the big city a person's true neighbors are often likely to be those with whom he works and socializes and not necessarily those who live nearby. Thus the resident of the modern city is a member of that city in only a very limited sense. The citizen of a classical city-state, who was a member of a privileged minority, belonged to a definite social group, and knowing this, one could predict a great deal about his behavior. In modern times, knowing that a person is a citizen of New York City or Minneapolis, Minnesota, tells very little about how he is likely to behave.

In many respects, Greer's characterization of the difference between the primitive social organization and the modern city parallels the classic sociological distinction described by Tonnies between two extreme forms of social organization, the *Gesellschaft* and the *Gemeinschaft*. To quote:

"The theory of the Gesellschaft *deals with the artificial construction of an aggregate of human beings which superficially resembles the* Gemeinschaft *insofar as the individuals live and dwell together peacefully. However, in* Gemeinschaft *they remain essentially united in spite of all separating factors, whereas in* Gesellschaft *they are essentially separated in spite of all uniting factors. In the* Gesellschaft, *as contrasted with the* Gemeinschaft, *we find no actions that can be derived from an* a priori *and necessarily existing unity; no actions, therefore, which manifest the will and the spirit of the unity even if performed by the individual; no actions which, insofar as they are formed by the individual, take place on behalf of those united with him. In the* Gesellschaft *such actions do not exist. On the contrary, here everybody is by himself and isolated, and there exists a condition of tension against all others" (Nisbet, 1966, pp. 75–76).*

The complexity of modern human social organization, especially as it is found in the cities, makes it very difficult to define or clearly to identify a community. As a result, some settle for very broad definitions like that of Klein who regards the community as "patterned interactions within a domain of individuals seeking to achieve security and physical safety, to derive support in times of stress, and to gain selfhood and significance throughout the life cycle" (Klein, 1968, p. 11). This definition allows one to group individuals despite the fact that they do not share a common geographic locus. For example, according to this view all Jews who have lost their homeland would represent a community despite the fact that they may be scattered over the face of the earth. Furthermore, Klein's definition does not imply that those individuals who are concentrated within a particular locale necessarily are members of the same community.

In grappling with the question of what the community actually is, we have several times touched on the question of where it is located. This issue requires a more detailed examination, since it is a very practical concern for the mental health agency that must seek to identify the community it serves.

Locating the Community

From the discussion above it is apparent that in complex social organizations like those found in the modern urban area, geographic boundaries either fail to designate a specific community or may encompass many different kinds of communities or parts thereof. This factor creates serious practical problems for the modern-day community mental health center, which is assigned responsibility for specific "catchment areas." The catchment area is a delimited geographic area that is the responsibility of a single community mental health center. In setting up catchment areas, it was apparently assumed that all or most of an area's residents would have a great deal in common. From what has been said of the problem of defining the nature of the community, this position is only more or less true. Commonalities may exist, but diversity is perhaps even more the rule.

Panzetta (1971) points out that one condition which leads to a close commonality among the residents of a particular locale is a sense of oppression. In such communities housing is poor, crime and death rates are high, and infant mortality is a serious problem. These social conditions become the "symptoms" of a geographically defined community, and the community mental health worker may make them the logical targets of his efforts. Unfortunately, Panzetta asserts, even such seemingly tangible and highly logical problems are not necessarily soluble within the catchment area. As Panzetta states:

"The dilapidated house on Diamond Street is a complex phenomenon derived from City Hall, the money market, the suburban ethos as well as from events and people within the catchment area. If we choose to define our mental health goals in this grand dimension, they had better not assume a catchment area orientation in our programming" (Panzetta, 1971, p. 6).

Another way in which Panzetta locates the community is in terms of time. He points out that we are all aware that a sense of community may come and go. People unite to work toward some common goal over a period of time, and then disband when the cause that bound them together is adequately served. From a historical perspective it is apparent that social units as complex as entire civilizations are formed and dissolved in the same way that family structures are modified to a degree that greatly loosens the ties of its individual members. The problem of dealing with a time limited community is that one is hard put to predict to what degree a particular social phenomenon is time limited, and to make a response to it that is appropriate to its duration.

For Panzetta, the time-bound, or epiphenomenal, community requires two conditions for its existence, oppression and leadership. The members of such a community must share a sense of suffering and a commonality of values and goals, but without leadership they remain fragmented and isolated from one another. The leader articulates their commonalities and binds them together as a community.

One practical implication of Panzetta's viewpoint is that the urban community mental health center may well be able to recognize a sense of community or *Gemeinschaft* with respect to certain specific issues, and may attempt to relate to that sense of community. If the agency overestimates these commonalities and romanticizes the united spirit of the area residents, it will discover soon that its clientele reacts as a community only to those issues that are related to the oppressive conditions which bind them together, and that sustained community input will not be forthcoming with respect to any other issues. Thus only a very limited *Gemeinschaft* can be hoped for. Many centers that have been established in suburban areas operate as though little possibility exists for a sense of *Gemeinschaft* within its geographic area of responsibility and have concentrated on providing whatever services are needed by specific individuals or families. Panzetta asserts that in this case the *Gesellschaft* character of the community is being responded to quite appropriately, but the agency is essentially providing a traditional type of mental health service.

Who Represents the Community

Assuming that a sense of community can be identified within a particular area, successful community involvement or control of a mental health agency requires the identification of individuals who truly represent the spirit of that community. Hersch (1972) is extremely dubious about the possibility of locating such representative community members. Panzetta (1971) expresses similar doubts, and the experience of the Newark Medical School controversy (Duhl, 1969) reinforces these doubts. The notion that community representatives can be located who will not represent special interest groups is seen to be naive. Hersch believes that local leaders usually emerge because they are stronger, more vocal, or perhaps more clever than their fellows but that they are rarely produced by a democratic election process.

Going even further, Hersch is concerned that local leaders often turn out to be among the most pathological members of the community. He suggests that paranoid characteristics such as intensity, a readiness to sense persecution, a legalistic approach to issues, and a need to assert control over situations are the very qualities that often bring community leaders to the fore. This being the case, the power that is placed in the hands of community representatives is often not wielded for the community at large but, instead, to serve special personal interests. Efforts may be made to advance the cause of one's family members, or one's own ethnic group, despite the fact that the community as a whole would be best served by job candidates with better qualifications.

Worse yet, power may be used by community representatives for its own sake, or as a means of expressing feelings built up over years of intense frustration. When this occurs, anger is often directed at well-meaning professionals who are hard put to deal with these feelings. The professional who invites a community partnership often sees himself as a giving, liberal person who is trying very hard to be responsive to community needs. When he is challenged, mistrusted, and has questions raised about his competence and integrity, his liberal, giving stance is shaken. Not uncommonly an agency board consisting in part or entirely of community representatives may use its powers to actually destroy professional leadership. The distinction between the policy-making function of the board and the administrative functions of the agency executives is broken down, ending in the ultimate destruction of the agency.

Can Community Representatives Be Helpful to the Agency

Hersch (1972) points out that when the notion of community control was introduced, it was seized on by many professionals as a panacea. This seemed to be the ultimate mechanism whereby the poor could, at least, begin to get service that would be meaningful to their needs, and with which they would be comfortable. As a result, swept along on the lofty spirit of reform, professional judgment was played down in favor of the native wisdom of the disadvantaged. Few of the complications that have been described above were anticipated and, as they were encountered, much disillusionment set in.

Hersch feels that the primary problem with community control has been the mental health professional's tendency to romanticize the concept in the hope that he could play a savior's role with respect to a variety of extraordinarily vexing and complex social problems. The danger of disillusionment is that the community control concept will be rejected completely without preservation of its potentially useful aspects.

The bruises of enough agency battles indicate that there is little reason to believe that the disadvantaged, by taking matters entirely into their own hands, will be better able to solve their problems than were the mental health professionals who worked for so long in the absence of much contact with the lower social classes. For Hersch, the choice should not be between complete community control or complete professional control. What is necessary is a careful evaluation of what is to be gained from having community input and of how programs can be created to minimize the potentially destructive effects of community involvement.

Along somewhat similar lines, Panzetta urges that the mental health agency needs to define for *itself* those tasks for which it is best suited given the background and training of its professionals, and those for which it is not suited. Only after defining its own feasible goals, can the agency turn to the local community for some form of help in becoming aware of what the community's needs are. Thus the agency must be willing to accept realistic limitations to what it can accomplish.

THE LESSONS OF EXPERIENCE WITH COMMUNITY INVOLVEMENT AND CONTROL

The Lincoln Hospital Community Mental Health Center

The Lincoln Hospital Community Mental Health Center in Bronx, New York is a prominent example of the destruction of a celebrated mental health program by community participants. Reiff (1972) points out that the mental health program at Lincoln Hospital received the Silver Achievement Award of the American Psychiatric Association in October 1968 "in recognition of the unique combination of psychiatric services and major innovations in reaching out to the community," yet a short six months later a crisis over community issues resulted in the shutting down of center operations.

It is inaccurate to place the blame for the problems encountered at Lincoln Hospital at the feet of the consumers that it served. The crises encountered at that center were precipitated directly by indigenous nonprofessionals employed in large numbers by the center. An important facet of Lincoln Hospital's outreach program involved the development of neighborhood-based storefront service centers (described in a previous chapter), staffed largely by nonprofessionals. Lincoln hospital also collaborated with several community organizations in the development of service programs and thereby allied itself with those who strongly supported community control of mental health service centers.

The events leading up to the crisis that debilitated the program at the Lincoln Hospital Mental Health Center have been described by Roman

(1969). He indicates that the background out of which conflict was to grow including space problems, annoying bureaucratic delays, disagreements between professional and nonprofessional staff concerning performance evaluations, racial conflicts, and conflicts over ideological issues. The center was affiliated with the Albert Einstein College of Medicine, which had serious financial problems. Since the Lincoln program was administered by the medical school, medical school problems inevitably affected Lincoln Hospital. Personnel practices were poorly defined in the early years of the program, there were serious delays in the payment of the bills it incurred, petty cash funds necessary for dealing with family emergencies uncovered through the program were limited, and salary checks were either delayed or workers were shortchanged by mistakes in their paychecks. While these difficulties annoyed everyone, the nonprofessional staff tended to regard them as signs of exploitation and even racism, thus heightening their distrust of the white establishment.

Against this tense background of sensitivity, annoyance, and distrust an occasional incident occurred that seemed to foretell an eventual major confrontation between agency nonprofessionals and professionals. One such incident involved a conference that was to be set up concerning the use of nonprofessionals. The funds to support the conference were provided by the Office of Economic Opportunity, and the planning group included nonprofessionals. However, during the course of planning a question was raised as to "whose" conference this would be. Professionals were willing to assign major responsibilities for planning the conference to nonprofessionals, but were unwilling to relinquish the ultimate authority of final approval. The nonprofessionals started out insisting that they should be allowed to manage the conference but eventually demanded that they should be assigned complete responsibility for inviting guests, fixing the agenda, and operating the conference with no participation on the part of professionals. As a result of this impasse, the conference was canceled.

Roman regards the conflict over "whose" conference was being set up as quite basic to the more serious problems that were to develop later at the center. Essentially he views this conflict as a political question that exposed a basic ambivalence among agency professionals concerning the use of nonprofessionals. While openly lauding the nonprofessional and admiring his assets for performing mental health functions, few professionals were actually willing to give up their own privileged positions in a system that assigned them high status. One prerogative deriving from this system was the power to make decisions, and professionals were altogether unwilling to relinquish this. The nonprofessionals reacted by concluding that they could never share this power that was husbanded by the professionals short of seizing it through a dramatic coup. The resentment of the nonprofessionals over this issue was fanned, in Roman's opinion, by "unrealistic self-evaluations that had developed in the minds of the nonprofessionals." These misleading self-evaluations were encouraged by the "rhetoric" of the storefront program's first director who drummed into the nonprofessionals the idea that they could teach professionals more than they could learn from them.

The Lincoln Hospital nonprofessionals reacted to the power differential in several ways. One way was to resist passively any decisions arrived at by professionals. Another involved demands for access to professional credentialing that would make it possible for the nonprofessional to work his way up into the decision-making hierarchy. Eventually discouraged by the amount of time required to make even minimal changes in the desired direction, nonprofessionals began to demand status in the absence of experience or the opportunity to gain additional credentials. At this point, their primary criterion for replacing the white supervisor became a racial one. Blackness was regarded as the only mark of legitimacy.

Beginning in May 1968 the Lincoln Hospital Center began to experience a series of major confrontations that ultimately led to the demise of its service programs. One involved a sit-in on the part of nonprofessionals in the hospital business administrator's office where a series of demands, ranging from the resolution of grievances over payroll practices to the allotment of educational release time and free tuition for upgrading the skills of the nonprofessional staff, were issued. Two other serious confrontations involved the professional staff. In one case a demand was made for an internal reorganization that would delegate more authority to the professional staff. In the second instance a work stoppage was held following an announcement that salary increments would be limited.

When a plan for reorganizing the center's administrative structure to delegate more authority to service chiefs and project directors was presented to the total staff, it was met with considerable opposition because the reorganization was developed without the consultation of "all levels of staff." Thus a new committee was formed on which all disciplines, both professionals and nonprofessionals, were represented. The charge of this new group was to develop a policy planning and review board (PPRB). This body was to have veto power over the entire center program. The first few months of the new committee operation were spent in debate over what powers the PPRB was to have and how it would be composed. Some argued that it could only serve in an advisory capacity, since it could not usurp the power of the program's officially designated director. The nonprofessionals took the stance that the PPRB should consist primarily of nonprofessionals and that it should have veto and policy-making powers. In essence, this group felt that the PPRB should serve as the directing board of the agency until it was possible to form a board consisting of community consumers. The nonprofessionals justified their position on the grounds that they were of the community, they knew more about it than anyone else in the agency, and they were in a position to legitimately act for agency consumers until the community could form its own representative group.

Opposition to the formation of the PPRB in the image described by the nonprofessionals was based on the concern that the formation of such a board would actually retard the development of community control. Some doubted that the nonprofessionals would be willing to relinquish their newly acquired power to the community and, more important, it was felt that the nonprofessionals themselves, as service providers, should be responsible to a consumer board. Despite these objections, the Lincoln Hospital Center director supported the nonprofessionals' plan and sought the approval of the medical school dean in implementing it. That approval was refused on the grounds that the center's director did not have the authority to create such a board, and that setting up a body of this kind violated the contract that the agency had with the city of New York. Some nonprofessionals as well as professionals were relieved at this outcome since, they believed, the creation of such a board was simply a power grab for a militant minority. Many, however, reacted with considerable anger, feeling that the center's director had led them to believe that they were making some headway while he knew full well that the plan would be vetoed at a higher level.

This setback for the nonprofessionals was followed by a relatively quiescent period at the center that culminated in a major crisis in March 1969. During this period of calm, Roman points out, a power struggle was taking place within the community between a leader of the black militant faction, who happened to be a nonprofessional at the center, and one of the major leaders of the Puerto Rican community. In this struggle, the Puerto Rican leader emerged as the winner after a prolonged and bitter struggle. Roman believes that the defeats suffered by several of the Lincoln Hospital nonprofessionals who were involved in this power struggle intensified their need to establish a political base through the Lincoln program. The incident that touched off the crucial confrontation at Lincoln Hospital was the firing of a recently hired black nonprofessional. Although most workers seemed to acknowledge that the firing was appropriate, their leaders argued that agreed on procedures for dismissing an employee had not been followed by the administration. A search was made for additional issues on which to base a major confrontation, and there ensued a series of accusations against the administration concerning alleged racist practices, malfeasance, misuse of funds, and the like.

Amid the turbulance that followed, a work stoppage was declared, buildings were occupied, nonstrikers were locked out, and nonprofessionals took over as chiefs of the various services. Some professionals supported the "work-in," accepted the authority of nonprofessionals, and continued to work in their services as consultants. The program was declared "the people's Mental Health Center." Mark Rudd of Students for a Democratic Society (SDS) entered the scene to lend his support to the striking staff as did members of the Black Panthers. On the other hand, the Mental Health Workers Union refused to support the strike, regarding it as illegal, and it seems apparent that the movement received relatively little support from the local community, which was 70 percent Puerto Rican. One community organizer remarked, "Baby this is some peoples' revolution, you got white shrinks from Westchester, the VC flag, posters of Che and Malcolm, but there ain't a Puerto Rican button in sight."

On March 6, the Lincoln Hospital Mental Health Center director acknowledged the impossibility of maintaining a liaison between professionals attempting to maintain service at Lincoln and the administration in exile, and notified the City Hospital Commissioner that he could no longer accept responsibility for patient care. At 5 P.M. that day the city closed the mental health services at Lincoln.

In the next few weeks efforts were made to revive the center program, but these proved to be ineffective. The professional staff, including some of the psychiatrists who supported the strike, began to drift away to other jobs. At the time of Roman's report, efforts were still being made to revive the program at Lincoln Hospital, but clearly a program that had stood out as a beacon on the mental health center scene had crumbled, at least in part, as the result of its involvement with community members. Despite this, Roman continues to support the notion of community control and continues to find in it the only solution for the alienation of the ghetto dweller from the immediacy of life.

The Temple University Community Mental Health Center

Panzetta (1971) considers that there are two relevant roles that the community can play in its relationship to a mental health center. One is as the franchiser of the agency and the other is as a consumer. As a franchiser, the community essentially sponsors the agency and has effective control of its program, its personnel, and its funds. Despite the fact that this would seem to be an ideal way for the community to "confront" institutions that should serve it, Panzetta sees the franchiser relationship as generally not workable because communities rarely develop representatives who can speak authoritatively for the group as a whole. When community representatives fail to truly represent, the agency is simply under the control of a new special interest group that may not even serve community needs as effectively as professionally controlled agencies.

As consumers, Panzetta believes that the community can wield considerable influence. Since the agency goal is to provide services, the choice of using or rejecting these services can exercise a powerful control over the agency functions. On the other hand, for consumer power to be most effective, it must operate in a free market where the consumer has the option of accepting the services of one agency and rejecting the services of another. The catchment area principle, which is built into the community mental health center structure, although attractive because it clearly allocates responsibility for designated geographical areas to specific centers, actually denies the consumer the right of free choice. If he lives in a catchment area, he must go to the particular mental health center serving it. Thus his choice is between a given center or nothing, and as a consumer his power to influence agency function is greatly diminished.

Wearing the scars of his experience in a very forward looking mental health center in Philadelphia, Panzetta makes some specific recommendations about the way out of the dilemma of reconciling agency functions to community needs. He suggests first that the search for the "communtiy" be abandoned entirely. More important than locating the community, is having the center establish an identity of its own. That is, it must know before it opens its doors what it can and cannot do. Once a clear sense of identity is established, it should then turn to the community to make that identity known. Part of the process of establishing an internal identity should be a rational decision about the degree to which agency decision makers wish to balance their own views by including community members who may be identified as (a) residents of the area, (b) interested in the center's work, (c) able to conceptualize the problems faced and the potential solutions involved, and (d) , in participating, having a willingness to both disagree as well as agree. The incorporation of such community residents on the center's board is not thought by Panzetta to be entirely necessary. Some centers may not wish to have these board members and will very likely be less sensitive to area needs than they might otherwise be. While this is not an ideal situation, in the last analysis, agency professionals must perform the service, and they must do so under circumstances in which they are comfortable. One way centers may choose to maintain a sensitivity to area needs is by hiring area residents. Panzetta asserts that the indigenous nonprofessional may serve a more significant role in the agency because he can help sensitize it to area needs than because of the manpower function he fulfills.

Panzetta carefully underscores the point that the mental health professional must accept the fact that his professional skills prepare him to deal effectively with some kinds of problems but not with other kinds. He suggests that because the rise of the community movement has paralleled the black revolution, many professionals in the community have taken on the cause of the downtrodden blacks. While this is justifiable on some grounds, he feels that the enthusiasm and energy thrown into this movement has created a series of illusory goals that are only vaguely related to the concept of mental health. The community movement may, therefore, have stepped out of its proper arena and into one in which it is ultimately doomed to frustration. The black revolution is seen by Panzetta as a movement that affects deeply the entire fabric of our social structure, and professionals, as private citizens, may wish to play a role in it. The community approach to mental health is interpreted as a move from a narrow conception of the way mental illness comes about, and how it should be treated, toward a broader view, the borders of which are still ill-defined. The goals of each of these noble efforts Panzetta regards as separate and unique.

The Denver Model Cities Program

Whitaker (1970) has described his involvement in a Model Cities experiment initiated in Denver in the spring of 1968. Planning funds had been made available to develop mental health services appropriate for the urban poor. Ghetto problems were to be attacked from many different directions including education, employment, health, cultural expression, and physical planning. Furthermore, the ghetto residents whose problems were to be dealt with were to be allowed to participate in the planning of projects.

Initially, the professionals involved in the planning program met each week with officials of the city government while the residents who were to participate met separately. Eventually on "a lovely, warm day in the early summer at a recreational site in the countryside, replete with meals, a luxurious pool, and other recreations" (Whitaker, 1970, p. 2004), the first major meeting between professionals and participating residents was held. Despite the elegance of the setting, "anger, cynicism, and suspicion were the guests." The anger of the residents seemed ever ready to erupt at topics that they found controversial, though they might seem quite innocent to the professionals. For example, the use of the word computer by one white professional brought forth deafening shouts from some male black residents. Even more ominous was the failure of even a single resident to appear for a discussion of health planning.

After this initial meeting some professionals stressed the need for greater resident participation in the planning program, and a concerted effort was made to recruit residents to participate on 12 committees. At this point it became clear that the major problem the planning group faced was the apathy of the resident population. Militant groups such as the Black Panthers could become intensely involved, and were capable of working very energetically and constructively, as well as being destructive. Recruiting other residents, however, was difficult, and it also became apparent that professionals were apathetic about and poorly educated for the task of working with residents. Despite these obstacles, the difficulty in staffing committees was overcome, and even the health committee found enough members to pursue its task.

Whitaker became the technical adviser to the mental health planning committee, and much of his paper describes his experience in that role. Progress in the committee function was made inch by inch and only after cultivating the personal trust and understanding of individual residents. Movement was agonizingly slow and painful and, on many occasions, Whitaker was tempted to withdraw from the committee. One such occasion was prompted by the personal attacks of some residents that shook Whitaker's self-esteem. On another occasion, the rigidity and shortsightedness of establishment people seemed to be a permanent barrier to further progress. On still another occasion, the combination of the demands of other professional activities in addition to the committee work prompted the impulse to give up.

Whitaker compares the process engaged in by the committee to group therapy or to an encounter group where all participants are sometimes patients and sometimes therapists. He numbered among his own major therapists a half black and half Hispano woman who chaired the committee and was effective at getting a mixed group to work together. Another was a rugged black man who, although verbally articulate, displayed a persistent sense of goodwill and a deep intuitive understanding of personality. Despite the agonies of the process, Whitaker reports that a number of projects were planned that had considerable relevance for the problems faced in the ghetto community.

Whitaker's three major conclusions as a result of his experience is that the greatest challenge in effective planning for Model Cities programs that involve community participation is not a technical one. Instead, it is a challenge of interpersonal relationships. Empathy, a willingness to share power, strong motivation for social reform, and enormous patience are absolutely necessary for the effective use of technical skills. A second conclusion is that to promote maximum feasible participation by the community in planning, intensive efforts must be made to develop appropriate interpersonal skills among all who participate in the collaboration between residents and establishment people. Professionals must, therefore, receive some of their education in the ghetto as well as in the university. Whitaker's third recommendation is that the universities inject into formal education a considerably greater effort to develop value systems that encourage the development of socially constructive action. In the absence of such guidance, students have had to develop their own causes, and frequently these have led to distressing student uprisings. If faculty demonstrated a personal involvement in meaningful social issues, students might well identify with them and devote their energies to solving such important problems.

Community Participation in a Neighborhood Mental Health Center

Salber (1970) is a former director of a neighborhood health center that invited community participation in directing the agency. She has offered both her subjective impressions of these experiences and recommendations concerning how best to implement such a program. Salber identifies two extreme positions that may be taken with respect to community participation. At one extreme, involving minimal community involvement, a committee of residents is formed to meet infrequently with board members of the agency at a place outside of the neighborhood, and these residents simply provide advice concerning the facility that has been set up. Significant decisions are not made at such meetings, and the advisory committee's power is minimal. At the other extreme, neighborhood residents hold all or most of the administrative power in the agency. They control the budget, hire the staff, and contract with other agencies to provide necessary services. Salber's own experience leads her to favor a partnership model, a compromise between the two extremes. Here an *informed* neighborhood group serves along with a group of agency professionals who agree to share power and to operate as partners in making decisions.

A major problem faced by the newly established neighborhood health center is the unrealistic expectancies of both neighborhood residents and agency staff concerning what can be accomplished. Area residents are apt to think that at long last all of their physical illnesses will be cured, that unsanitary conditions in the neighborhood will be corrected, that alcoholism and drug problems will diminish, that landlords will repair their property, and that increased numbers of patrolmen will reliably protect them against muggings. They expect that agency services will be available night and day, that doctors will make house calls, that psychiatrists will be available when needed, that their children will be looked after in daycare centers, and that, being rich, the agency will be able to care for them without any financial constraints. Unrealistic expectations are not exclusive to the residents, however. The new agency's staff is often youthful and idealistic, deeply devoted to patients, but quite naive about the political and economic structure of society that determines both the future of the agency itself and, to a great extent, the life-styles of neighborhood residents who are their clients. Such professionals are usually working for relatively moderate salaries and expect their major rewards to come from the satisfaction of serving their fellow men who are deeply in need. Thus they are ill-prepared to cope with the militant or angry patient, or with patients who are lackadaisical about keeping scheduled appointments, who come in late, or who come in without appointments at all and expect to be seen.

Salber feels that it is essential to adjust these unrealistic expectations on the part of both neighborhood residents and staff by establishing better communication channels. But improved communication is not easily come by. One approach is to employ community residents as much as possible in the agency. The indigenous employee can educate the agency staff concerning the neighborhood and can also serve as a bridge from professional staff to the neighborhood and its residents. They also make the center more appealing and approachable for neighborhood residents. The lower classes often feel intimidated by middle class professionals and are less comfortable bringing complaints and requests for service to them than they are to staff members who are seen to come from their own social class. But the device of employing neighborhood residents does not entirely solve the problem of establishing effective communication between agency staff and area residents. To some extent, it creates additional problems. Resident employees often fail to adhere to middle class standards of punctuality, may be unaccustomed to a daily work routine, may have difficulty arranging for the care of their children while they are away at work, and may react badly to the criticism of supervisory personnel.

A major impediment identified by Salber in achieving effective communication between professionals and neighborhood residents is the fact that neither really listens to the other. Meetings between professionals and resident groups are characterized by much shouting and little reasoned argument on either side. Community residents are generally bitter over previous experiences with agencies which have made them suspicious and distrustful. Professionals often respond to this feeling with restraint but harbor their own sense of bitterness and frustration which they release only at private meetings of peer groups. A major reason for the gap between the professional and the community resident is that, when both groups do come together, the professionals regard themselves as service providers and the residents as service recipients. They do not meet on common ground as human beings either in a social context or as partners in the solution of a problem. For this reason, professionals often find it difficult to accept community members in either participatory or decision-making roles. On the other hand, community people tend to oversimplify the professional's job and often think that he can easily be replaced by people with no theoretical background or special training. Thus both agency professional staff and residents need extensive training in communicating with each other.

Salber recommends that the agency director establish a long-range educational program for the institutions that sponsor the center, the area residents who are selected to serve on advisory committees, and the agency staff. Sponsoring institutions can be acquainted with the neighborhood's problems by having their directors meet with area residents at the agency. Staff members' attitudes can be dealt with through in-service training programs and by participation in programs in which they must function jointly with community residents. Salber believes that the education of the area residents serving on boards is probably the easiest of the three programs to mount, since residents tend to be eager to learn and are drawn enthusiastically to the new opportunities offered them. Their training, however, must extend beyond the bounds of health matters into issues such as governmental structure and financing, the formation and function of committees, education concerning present health and delivery systems, some notion of how budgets are set up, and exposure to the job functions of different agency personnel.

Ideally, Salber feels that such a partnership between consumers and agency professionals should be developed before the center begins operating. This reflects the interest of the agency in the resident's participation and ensures that realistic goals will be set from the beginning. Also, the machinery for hiring and firing personnel and for handling grievances must be created in advance so that a common set of ground rules is established for all who are involved, thereby minimizing clashes over the mechanics of the operation.

The Hill-West Haven Experience

Tischler (1971) has described the community participation model developed at the Hill-West Haven division of the Connecticut Mental Health Center. This agency operates on the premise that because the service consumer has "savvy" about the world in which he has to live, because he recognizes the complexities of service agencies and is aware of the impact that these agencies can have on his own life situation, he is virtually obligated to participate in setting up community service programs.

At the outset at Hill-West Haven, the community residents had only an informal involvement with the agency. No clear authority was granted to community participants and, although their advice and opinions concerning program goals and policies were solicited, no powers were vested in community representatives. In part, this situation prevailed because the catchment area lacked the organization to participate in the regulation of health and social services. The initial task, therefore, required organizing the community through work with specific groups and other agencies to set up structures to represent the community with respect to health and social services. This phase required a period of about three years following which a consumer board was set up to which the agency became accountable. Board responsibility encompassed program development, personnel practices, and the establishment of service and research priorities. Any changes in the basic agency structure or direction required board approval which could initiate changes as well.

The impact of the shift from informal consumer participation in agency functioning to a formalized role involving consumer control was evaluated from two viewpoints, the structural and the functional. Structurally, Tischler reports that the affect of the transmission was minimal. The agency continued to be organized much as it had been before consumer control was a fact, and it offered services similar to those provided previously. The board assigned priority to services for the elderly and for children, with reallocations of personnel in keeping with these priorities. Community residents were included in greater numbers on the agency staff. An in-service training program was also set up to acquaint the staff with the life situation and particularly with the needs of the poor.

The functional changes that came about through the advent of community control involved modifications in the way much of the staff performed. Therefore, service delivery was clearly affected by the organizational shift. Tischler identifies four types of staff response during the transition period.

Some staff feared that the consumer would be entirely irrational and that caregivers would be turned on and destroyed by the anger and vindictiveness of community residents. From this viewpoint, turning control of the agency over to the consumer simply invited anarchy. These staff members felt that things were slipping out of their control; rumors about rape and theft in the parking lot proliferated, and there was much concern about the possibility that the staff would be assaulted. Anxiety among staff feeling this way was so intense that they were functionally "paralyzed" and incapable of meeting their responsibilities.

A second response pattern that resulted in a lessening of the quality of service was to deny that consumer control could ever be a reality. Some staff simply went along insisting to themselves and others that the status quo would remain essentially unshaken. They regarded efforts to institute consumer control to be an inconvenience imposed on them by a leadership that had failed to educate the community properly concerning the unshakeable realities in the mental health field. Such staff maintained that if the community were acquainted with these realities, it would have no interest in becoming involved in the management of mental health agencies. Staff members holding this view tended to become constricted in their functioning, and their lessened flexibility impaired their capacity to listen.

A third response pattern that compromised the quality of staff performance involved a complete surrender to community control. Staff members taking this position stood in awe of the consumer's expertise. They studied recent literature of the black movement carefully and discussed it with a reverence once reserved only for the towering figures in social work, psychiatry, and psychology. These staff members became dilletantes without a clear focus on their work with clients.

The most common response pattern found among staff of the agency described by Tischler might be characterized as an acceptance of the consumer as a collaborator combined with some sense of anxiety about how this collaboration would work out. The anxiety was associated with uncertainty about how a consumer controlled board might change existing service patterns, might alter established priorities, and the degree to which it might attempt to engage in the prescription of individual treatment patterns. For such staff members, consumer control was recognized as an opportunity for truly innovative programs that promised to be more effective than traditional ones, but the nagging concern remained that a board which reorders basic priorities might well remove many current staff from their jobs. Despite these concerns, the balance was toward a general positive reaction to consumer control among the staff members, and there was a willingness to base their judgments of the outcome of the venture on unfolding experience.

Tischler concludes his description of one agency's efforts to institute community control on a conservative note, despite its apparent success. He recognizes that the process of bringing about this type of agency reorganization is slow and that it is inevitably accompanied by considerable strain. Furthermore, he points out that no guarantees exist that service will be more responsive to society's needs or that society will make fewer demands on the agency when the consumer is included as a collaborator. He does argue, however, that the sharing of responsibility between service providers and consumers holds greater promise for those served and potentially greater rewards for those who are serving than do the more rigid traditional mental health care systems.

CONCLUSION

Traditional mental health agencies have been condemned as insensitive and unresponsive to the needs of large segments of our society. An obvious way of heightening agency sensitivity to the needs of the potential consumers is to invite consumer involvement or, in some instances actual control of the agency. Implementation of such programs, however, involves a variety of problems. The first concerns the confusion over how actually to define the community and how to locate it. Establishment of catchment areas of responsibility for specific community mental health centers actually compounds the problem instead of resolving it. Other problems in setting up effective community control involve the identification of representatives who can act for the community as a whole, the avoidance of special interest power groups within the community, and the overreliance on what may be an illusory expertise attributed to community members. Descriptions of agency programs in which efforts were made to incorporate community members on boards reflect considerable strain, seemingly wasted time, and much animosity between professionals and community members. The success of these programs demands considerable patience, the goodwill of both professionals and consumers, and the willingness of professionals to put up with many indignities.

Because within a given agency's area of responsibility, many different communities and social problems may exist, it is vital that the agency define for itself which community it will serve and which problems it can be realistically expected to address. Having established such an identity, it is probably only then feasible to invite consumer participation in a form appropriate to agency goals and staff needs.

References

Bredemeier, H. C. The socially handicapped and the agencies: a market analysis. In F. Riessman, J. Cohen, and A. Pearl (Eds.), *The mental health of the poor*. New York: Free Press, 1964. Pp. 98–109.

Duhl, L. Newark: Community or chaos. *Journal of Applied Behavioral Science,* 1969, *5,* 535–572.

Greer, S. *Social Organization.* New York: Random House, 1955.

Hersch, C. Social history, mental health, and community control. *American Psychologist,* 1972, *27,* 749–754.

Klein, D. C. *Community dynamics and mental health.* New York: Wiley, 1968.

Nisbet, R. A. *The Sociological Tradition.* New York: Basic Books, 1966.

Panzetta, A. F. *Community mental health: myth and reality.* Philadelphia: Lea & Febiger, 1971.

Reiff, R. "The wreck of the Lincoln lightship or "clinician, heal thyself." Unpublished manuscript. Albert Einstein College of Medicine, 1972.

Roman, M. Community control and the community mental health center: a view from the Lincoln bridge. Presented at NIMH staff meeting on Metropolitan

Topics—Dilemma of Community Control: University and Community Relations, Nov. 21, 1969, Washington, D. C.

Salber, E. J. Community participation in neighborhood health centers. *New England Journal of Medicine*, 1970, *283*, 515–518.

Smith, M. B., & Hobbs, N. The community and the community mental health center. *American Psychologist*, 1966, *21*, 499–509.

Tischler, G. L. The effects of consumer control on the delivery of services. *American Journal of Orthopsychiatry*, 1971, *41*, 501–505.

Toffler, A. *Future Shock*. New York: Random House, 1970.

Whitaker, L. Social reform and the comprehensive community mental health center: the model cities experiment. *American Journal of Public Health*, 1970, *60* 2003–2010.

15. *research in community psychology*

Community psychology is very much in its infancy. As such, a great many developing programs have been created by energetic professionals who hope that those programs will meet important human needs. The form of most programs is based on intuition, or the best hunches of well-intentioned workers. In the rush to develop service programs suited to meet pressing social needs, relatively little effort has been devoted to establishing firm empirical bases for what gets done and the way it gets done.

Several who are identified with the community psychology movement plead for serious attention to the research enterprise, particularly at this nascent stage of the field's development. As Cowen (1967, p. 443) states, ". . . the future shape of the mental health order can only be governed by empirics which are, as yet, unknown to us. This means that comprehensive and sophisticated research is a necessity of the highest priority if we are to aspire to sound and orderly progress in the decades to come." In essence he feels that the discouragement with the old mental health order that led to the development of community psychology was, to some extent, rooted in the fact that traditional approaches were based on a faith that professionals eventually came to feel was unjustified. Cowen hopes for a firmer foundation than simple faith for the community psychology movement. A somewhat similar point is made by Edgerton (1971, p. 89) who writes, "Our present opportunity is reminiscent of the situation confronting the long ago motorist on the midwestern plains who came to a sign which read; 'Choose your ruts, you'll be in them for the next 50 miles.' " Since community psychology may be in the position of forming ruts in which it will remain for the next 50 years, Edgerton regards it as vitally important that they be formed on the basis of the most valid data that can be collected at this time.

This support for research in the community mental health field is found among the spokesmen for large professional organizations as well as in the mandates set forth by the federal government, which funds a great deal of research in the mental health fields. Edgerton points out, for example, that the Community Mental Health Centers Act of 1963 as well as its amended form in 1965 stresses research and evaluation as one element of the services of a comprehensive mental health center. Furthermore, a small fraction of the monies made available by the federal government for the creation of comprehensive public health services can be used for research. The Joint Commission on Mental Illness and Health (1961) has recommended that $2\frac{1}{2}$ percent of the budget for patient services be allotted for research. Smith and Hobbs (1966) in their position paper representing the American Psychological Association call for setting aside 5 to 10 percent of the budget of every community mental health center for program evaluation and research. Some (Cowen, 1967) regard these percentages as niggardly and insufficient, considering the significance of the research enterprise. Nevertheless, the mandate for pursuing research and the means for doing it, at least on a small scale, is present. Thus it behooves the community psychologist to apply his research skills to foster a more orderly development of community psychology.

Despite the fact that the training of psychologists is steeped in a tradition of research, relatively few are prepared to engage in many types of research that are relevant to community psychology. As several writers have pointed out (Cohen, 1966; Miller, 1970; Roen, 1971), a most important research area for community psychology is the study of the social forces acting on man and the way in which these forces can aid or detract from his optimal development. Whereas psychologists have traditionally focused on laboratory studies of the individual and his internal processes, the type of research that will shed light on significant social forces requires a study of man in his natural habitat. Such studies involve methods and procedures that are relatively foreign to most psychologists. Procedures of this kind have been worked out in other fields, for example, the study of epidemiology in public health medicine. Other such approaches are only just being worked out within areas such as social psychology. Thus the researcher in community psychology will often find it necessary to adopt methods that are traditionally associated with other fields, or to participate in the development of new research methods to answer the kinds of questions that will make possible the advancement of his field. To be sure, some research, particularly that involving program evaluation, will be familiar to the traditionally trained psychologist without requiring a major retooling effort. In this chapter we describe various types of research approaches that are particularly relevant to community psychology.

EPIDEMIOLOGY

Epidemiology is a research approach that was developed in public health medicine and is concerned with understanding the spread of disease. Doull (1952) defines epidemiology as "the study and interpretation of the mass phenomena of health and disease." The unit of study in epidemiology is the population group rather than the single individual. Ideally its methodology involves the comparison of the incidence of a disease process in groups similar to each other with respect to all significant variables but one. Originally the approach was developed to understand and control the spread of epidemics, but its scope within medicine has been extended to include infectious diseases such as leprosy, syphillis, and tuberculosis, which do not ordinarily result in epidemics. To date noninfectious diseases such as accidents, and even measurable physiological attributes have been included in epidemiological studies.

The science of epidemiology draws its facts from the medical sciences and other sources such as sociology, demography and statistics, engineering, meteorology, and geography. The relationship between facts derived from these areas and previous knowledge of a subject should provide a basis for inferences concerning the likely cause of either a localized epidemic, or the basis for the incidence of some disorder. One such explanations are arrived at, one can hopefully take steps to prevent the further progress of disease processes. As previously mentioned, one of the classic examples of this use of epidemiology involves the work of Snow (MacMahon and Pugh, 1970) who was able to stem a cholera epidemic in mid-19th century London after finding that most of those coming down with the disease were being furnished their water by particular suppliers.

Prevention in that case simply involved removing the pump handles from the suspect wells.

An essential aspect of descriptive epidemiology is the measurement of disease frequency, since it permits comparison between populations and subgroups within populations (MacMahon and Pugh, 1970). The simplest disease frequency statement might read, "There are 500 cases of tuberculosis." This requires only a simple count of identified cases. Such a statement, however, is not very useful until it is qualified with respect to: (a) the population to which it refers, and (b) when these cases were identified. Thus a more useful statement would read, "On January 1, 1970, 500 cases of tuberculosis were identified in a given town." While this statement would be useful for planning health facilities in a particular town, it would still be of limited value if one were concerned with comparing one town to another to determine whether factors leading to the development of tuberculosis were stronger in one or the other. Frequencies may vary between two given locales simply because of the difference in population between them. New York City, for example, will very likely have more cases of most diseases than Butte, Montana because of the population differential, even if the factors leading to the disease are less prevalent in New York. To account for population differences, frequencies must be expressed in terms of *rates*.

The dictionary definition of a rate is a "quantity of a thing measured per unit of something else." In epidemiology the "thing measured" is the disease or trait under study and the "unit of something else" is the population from which the cases are drawn. The time when the cases are identified is, of course, a third essential fact in epidemiology. The frequency of tuberculosis on January 1, 1970 in a given city might be expressed as 500 cases per the two million inhabitants of the city. In actual practice, rapid comparison of rates is facilitated by stating them not in relation to total populations but with respect to some convenient unit of population size (usually some power of 10) such as 0.025 percent, 0.25 per thousand, or 250 per million. Such figures are arrived at by dividing the number of cases by the population figure and multiplying the result by the selected unit of size. Care must be taken to define both the numerator and the denominator of a rate in the same terms. Thus if the numerator refers to a specific age, sex, or racial group, the same must be true for the denominator.

Two indexes that are very commonly used to study the occurrence of disease or behavioral disorders in population groups are *incidence* and *prevalence*. Kramer (1957) defines incidence as "the number of new cases of a disease occurring within a specific period of time." It is necessary to define "new cases" as the first occurrence of a disease or disorder within a given individual's lifetime. The *incidence rate* is the ratio between the number of new cases, however defined, occurring within the specified interval and the total number in the population exposed to risk. Incidence rates may be specified with respect to many factors such as age, sex, marital status, geographic area, and socioeconomic status.

Prevalence is a measure of the number of cases of a disease or disorder present in a population group during a specified interval of time. That is, it includes incidence, since it is a combination of the number of cases that exist at the time the interval under study begins plus the number of new cases that develop during that interval. Thus it is crucial in quoting prevalence figures to specify the length of the interval under consideration. One can speak of the number of people who suffer a disorder during a given day, a given week, or during intervals as long as a month or a year. It is also necessary that the characteristics of those included as cases during such an interval be defined very carefully. The *prevalence rate* is the ratio between the number of cases found in a specified interval and the number of people in the appropriate population under study. As in the case of incidence rates, prevalence rates can be specified for particular age groups, sex categories, geographic areas, or socioeconomic groups. Although the incidence rate is regarded by Kramer (1957) as the fundamental epidemiological ratio, the prevalence rate is probably the one that is more easily determined, since it can be arrived at by simply-counting all cases of a disorder within a population group at some point in time.

It is well recognized within public health medicine that, assuming all individuals are equally subject to exposure to bacteria causing infectious diseases, the incidence of the disease is a function of the balance between the resistance of the population and the potency of the microorganisms causing the disease. Such a balance is referred to as the *force of morbidity*. In the case of a mental disorder, these rates would very likely depend on the balance between the resistance of the population to the disorder and those environmental forces—biological, cultural, psychological—that produce the stress which causes mental disorder. Prevalence, on the other hand, is a more complex concept. It is determined by both the force of morbidity and the interval between the onset and termination of a disorder. Thus prevalence rate is a function of both the incidence rate and the duration of the disorder.

Kramer (1957) illustrates this distinction through the use of three hypothetical examples in which incidence, duration, and prevalence vary. He conjures up three imaginary communities each having a stationary population of 100,000 which have been entirely free of mental disorder. Suddenly on January 1, 1940 in communities A and B, respectively, 1000 people, and in community C, 2000 people succumb to psychosis. Further simplifying, he assumes that they are all hospitalized immediately and that all suffer the same mental disorder. For each of the 10 following years Kramer also assumes that on every January 1, 1000 new cases of the same disorder appear in A and B and 2000 appear in C. Furthermore, he assumes that in each community a fixed number of individuals are released from the hospital at some specified rate as cured of their disorder, the interval between the date of hospitalization and the date of release representing the duration of the disorder. Table 1 taken from Kramer (1957, p. 828) depicts the prevalence of the hypothetical disorder in each community on January 1 of each year assuming that: (a) 100 people are cured annually in community A; (b) in community B 10 percent of each cohort of 1000 new cases of those who are still disturbed at the beginning of each year are cured during the following year; and (c) in each cohort of 2000 new cases in community C, 40 percent of those still disturbed at the beginning of each year are cured during the following year.

It can be seen that although the annual incidence of psychosis is identical in communities A and B, the prevalence rates on January 1 of each year begin to differ considerably after the first two years. By 1950, for example, in community A the prevalence rate becomes stationary at 5500 patients whereas the prevalence rate in community B increases steadily to 6859 cases by January 1, 1950. In community C, on the other

Table 1. Illustration of Ways Three Hypothetical Prevalence Situations Develop in Three Different Communities Under Various Assumptions of Incidence and Duration of Disease (from Kramer, 1967)

Community A. Assumptions: 1000 new cases annually, each of which occurs on January 1 of specified year; 100 patients annually are cured in each cohort of such new cases. The prevalence count will stabilize at 5500 cases on January 1, 1949.

Cohort of Year	Patients in Hospital on January 1 of Specified Year										
	1940	1941	1942	1943	1944	1945	1946	1947	1948	1949	1950
1940	1000	900	800	700	600	500	400	300	200	100	0
1941		1000	900	800	700	600	500	400	300	200	100
1942			1000	900	800	700	600	500	400	300	200
1943				1000	900	800	700	600	500	400	300
1944					1000	900	800	700	600	500	400
1945						1000	900	800	700	600	500
1946							1000	900	800	700	600
1947								1000	900	800	700
1948									1000	900	800
1949										1000	900
1950											1000
Total	1000	1900	2700	3400	4000	4500	4900	5200	5400	5500	5500

Community B. Assumptions: 1000 new cases annually, each of which occurs on January 1 of specified year; 10% of those ill at the beginning of each year are cured during that year. The prevalence count will stabilize at 10,000 cases on January 1, 2007.

Cohort of Year	Patients in Hospital on January 1 of Specified Year										
	1940	1941	1942	1943	1944	1945	1946	1947	1948	1949	1950
1940	1000	900	810	729	656	590	531	478	430	387	348
1941		1000	900	810	729	650	590	531	478	430	387
1942			1000	900	810	729	656	590	531	478	430
1943				1000	900	810	729	656	590	531	478
1944				1000	900	900	810	729	656	590	531
1945						1000	900	810	729	656	590
1946							1000	900	810	729	656
1947								1000	900	810	729
1948									1000	900	810
1949										1000	900
1950											1000
Total	1000	1900	2710	3439	4095	4685	5216	5694	6124	6511	6859

Community B. Assumptions: 1000 new cases annually, each of which occurs on January 1 of specified year; 40% of those ill at the beginning of each year are cured during that year. The prevalence count will stabilize at 5,000 cases on January 1, 1956.

Cohort of Year	Patients in Hospital on January 1 of Specified Year										
	1940	1941	1942	1943	1944	1945	1946	1947	1948	1949	1950
1940	2000	1200	720	432	259	155	93	56	34	20	12
1941		2000	1200	720	432	259	155	93	56	34	20
1942			2000	1200	720	432	259	155	93	56	34
1943				2000	1200	720	432	259	155	93	56
1944					2000	1200	720	432	259	155	93
1945						2000	1200	720	432	259	155
1946							2000	1200	720	432	259
1947								2000	1200	720	432
1948									2000	1200	720
1949										2000	1200
1950											2000
Total	2000	3200	3920	4352	4611	4766	4859	4915	4949	4969	4981

hand, where the incidence rate is 2000 per 100,000, double that of communities A and B, the prevalence figure reaches 4981 cases per 100,000 by 1950, the lowest in all three communities. This example clearly shows that although the prevalence of a disorder may differ among communities, one cannot infer that the community with the highest prevalence will also have the highest incidence. In this example the community having the highest incidence actually showed the lowest prevalence because prevalence is a function of both the incidence of the disorder and its duration.

To summarize, a higher prevalence rate in disease A than in disease B can be accounted for in a number of ways. First, the diseases can occur with equal incidence, but disease A can be of longer duration than disease B. Second, disease A may have a lower incidence but a disproportionately higher duration than disease B. Finally, disease A can have both a higher incidence and can be equal, slightly shorter, or of longer duration than disease B.

The purpose of epidemiological studies of mental disorders is to discover relationships that determine the factors leading to mental disorder. These associations are uncovered by determining the rate at which disorders develop in various population groups and in various subsegments of these populations, and the differential duration of the disorder in affected individuals. Data of this kind suggest possible etiological relationships that must then be more firmly established through detailed clinical or experimental studies.

Although Roen (1971) dates the beginnings of psychiatric epidemiology in 1949, a classic study was reported in 1939 by Faris and Dunham (1939) and two other studies appeared in the 1940s. The Faris and Dunham study was concerned with the differential rates of serious mental disorders in different areas of a large city (Chicago). A major finding of this study was that mental disorder rates are related to patient residence, with prevalence rates decreasing regularly as one moves from the center of the city to its periphery. Furthermore, specific types of disorder were found to be heavily concentrated in particular locations in the large urban area, a finding that led to the advancement of specific hypotheses concerning their etiology. For example, the heavy concentration of paranoid schizophrenia in the rooming house districts of the city suggested to Faris and Dunham that the disorder is caused by the social isolation and breakdown in communication patterns that characterize the living arrangement of the rooming house.

The two psychiatric epidemiology studies done in the 1940s were devoted primarily to assessing the magnitude of psychiatric disturbance in a given locale, but each analyzed its data with respect to variables such as sex, race, and age. The first to appear in print by Lemkau, Tietze, and Cooper (1941; 1942a; 1942b; 1942c) was a survey done in Baltimore, Maryland in 1936 of the files of existing institutions and agencies, revealing 3337 active cases. Beyond reporting prevalence figures for the area, these investigators reported that the mental deficiency rate was higher for males than for females and for negroes than for whites, and that neurotic traits, conduct disorders, and mental deficiency all appear to correlate inversely with family income.

The second psychiatric epidemiology study dating back to the early 1940s was done by Roth and Luton (1943) in Williamson County near Nashville, Tennessee. Its primary purpose was to assess the magnitude of the mental health problem in a representative rural county by identifying the prevalence of mental illness and mental adjustment. In addition, it was hoped that etiological factors, especially those peculiar to life in a rural area, might be uncovered. Case referrals were received from nurses, physicians, teachers, and the like, and a survey was done of an unbiased sample of the total population. The data were analyzed with respect to the distribution of cases by age and race.

In the early 1950s, the Leightons and co-workers (Leighton, Leighton, and Armstrong, 1964) began a long-range, more complex epidemiological study than had been seen up to that time in psychiatry. This was done in Stirling County, Nova Scotia, where in addition to attempting to establishing prevalence rates for various types of emotional disorder, and to determining how much professional psychiatric care would be required by the population, the study was used to test the hypothesis that more mental health problems would be found in a "disintegrated community" than in one manifesting greater integration. The integrative capacity of a given community was seen to depend on its ability to provide: " (a) perpetuation of itself through recruitment and indoctrination of new members; (b) subsistence; (c) protection against dangers; (d) promotion of harmony, and control of hostility; (e) division of labor; and (f) the functioning of leaders and followers" (Leighton, Leighton, and Armstrong, 1964, p. 168). Prevalence figures were compared between communities defined as disintegrated and others defined as integrated, and the Leightons report that more individuals from disintegrated communities were classified as "cases," a greater number of different kinds of symptoms were found among these individuals, and their impairment was greater than that of individuals coming from integrated communities. In fact, the integration level of the community in which the individual lived was found to be more strongly related to mental health than were factors such as sex, age, or occupational status.

Another epidemiological study of the 1950s that was done to test a particular hypothesis was conducted by Hollingshead and Redlich (1958). The hypothesis advanced by these authors was that mental illness in a given population was related to social class status. Furthermore, they were interested in the type of treatment received for mental illness as a function of class position. This study, carried out in New Haven, Connecticut, surveyed all of the local treatment agencies extracting detailed information from clinical psychiatric records. Prevalence figures were determined for psychiatric cases falling into various social classes. The findings of this study were in keeping with the investigators' hypotheses: the prevalence of psychiatric patients in the lower social classes was considerably higher than in the higher social classes. These relationships continue to hold up even when variables such as age, sex, race, religion, and marital status were controlled. Further analyses to determine whether types of mental illness distributed themselves differentially among the social classes revealed that neurotic disorders were more prevalent among the higher social classes while psychotic disorders were more prevalent in the lower social classes. Finally, Hollingshead and Redlich examined the relationship between social class and the types of treatment applied. Their findings were that psychotherapy, and particularly insight therapies, were applied disproportionately more frequently to neurotic patients of the higher social classes who were being treated by private practitioners than to members of the lower classes, who tended to be treated in state hospitals with organic therapies.

Perhaps the most elaborate of the psychiatric epidemiology studies that has been done to date was carried out in New York City and has come to be known as the Midtown Manhattan Study (Srole, Langner, Michael, Opler, and Rennie, 1962). The investigators in this study regarded their work as innovative among pscyhiatric epidemiological studies on two counts. First, in addition to being concerned with those area residents who were in treatment, and thereby were identified as psychiatric cases, they were also concerned with assessing the mental health status of those who were untreated. To achieve this, they interviewed 1660 resident adults representing a cross-sectional sample of the area population. Extensive home interviews were done with these subjects and, on the basis of the interview data, ratings were made of the mental health status of each individual. The second innovative feature of this study involved the investigators' attempt to relate their findings to a broader variety of demographic factors than was true of any previous epidemiological studies.

The basic prevalence findings in the Midtown study concerning the mental health status of the untreated group were that approximately 60 percent of the adults surveyed manifested subclinical symptomatology, that another 20 percent were found to be symptom free, and that the remaining 20 percent were rather seriously impaired. Since no similar studies had been done in other urban areas, it was not possible to compare these prevalence figures for midtown Manhattan with those of other urban areas.

When the untreated group was classified with respect to age and socioeconomic status, more impaired individuals were found among the older and lower socioeconomic groups than among the younger and higher economic groups. Conversely, fewer symptom free individuals were found among the older and lower socioeconomic groups than among the younger and higher socioeconomic groups. These findings replicate similar findings in a variety of studies in other locales.

Analysis with respect to other demographic variables indicated that no sex-related mental health differences could be detected in the Midtown sample, but that some differences were present with respect to religious origin (the faith in which the respondent's parents were reared). Along this dimension, the mental health picture among Jews in the sample was most favorable of all, with Protestants next, and Catholics manifesting the most mental health problems. Jews were found to be heavily concentrated in the subclinical, mild to moderate mental health category.

Another demographic variable that was carefully considered in the Midtown Manhattan study was the period of time each subject's family had been in the United States. Subjects were classified as generation I if they themselves were foreign born. American born children of immigrants were in Generation II. The grandchildren of immigrants were in generation III, and generation IV included all subjects who had four American born grandparents. It was hypothesized that generation IV subjects, coming from families that were clearly "at home" in American society, would manifest the fewest mental health problems whereas generation I subjects, who were uprooted from one society and transplanted to a new one to which they had to acculturate, would experience considerably more stress and would thereby suffer more mental health problems. Essentially it was expected that the mental health picture would be progressively more favorable as one moved from generation group I to IV. The findings with respect to this variable tended in the hypothesized direction with significant differences being found between the two extreme groups, generations I and IV. However, when controls for age and socioeconomic status were instituted, the original differences were practically eliminated entirely.

Rather than reject the hypothesis regarding the generation variable, the Midtown investigators probed more deeply into the data in search of still another mitigating variable that might account for the failure to find differences. They reasoned that there were essentially two types of immigrants among generation II subjects. One group had immigrant parents who arrived in this country during the period from 1901 to 1914, historically a turbulent time when the immigration flow was enormous and considerable political disorganization prevailed in the cities receiving immigrants. These conditions compounded adjustment problems for these immigrants. When free immigration was eliminated in the United States after the congressional acts of 1921 and 1924, a marked change took place in the makeup of the immigrant coming to this country. Among the pre-1921 immigrants (type O) the majority were poorly educated farm laborers, village dwellers, and predominantly men. During the post-1921 period, the new immigrants (type N) were more likely to be professionals, semiprofessionals, or white collar workers; and they did not enter into urban areas strained by the turmoil of rapid expansion. This was also true for generation I subjects who were themselves immigrants. It was hypothesized by the Midtown investigators that the adaptation problems for type N immigrants were far less acute than they were for type O immigrants. Indeed, a significantly higher percentage of generation I subjects whose backgrounds seemed to exemplify type O immigrants were rated as impaired in comparison to those of generation I whose backgrounds more closely resembled type N immigrants. These findings led the Midtown investigators to conclude that rejection of the hypothesis that the generation variable is significant for mental health ratings is unwarranted. What they did conclude was that transplanation from one cultural setting to another is not decisive per se, but that the degree of difference between the setting from which the immigrant comes and that to which he goes is decisive. Thus, if generation I had a majority of type O immigrants, high impairment rates would have been found in this group as was originally hypothesized.

The findings of the many complex analyses carried out in the Midtown study have led to several important conclusions and have suggested many hypotheses that should be put to test in more detailed studies. The first vitally important finding has to do with the large percentage of impaired subjects found among the untreated group. Of the approximately 20 percent of the Midtown sample regarded as seriously impaired, only 27 percent had ever been patients during their lifetime. The remaining 73 percent had never seen a psychotherapist, and of these, approximately 29 percent appeared quite ready to accept some sort of professional intervention in connection with their problems. What this points to is the very large potential among untreated individuals in the community for seeking the care of mental health professionals. Furthermore, this finding has important implications for researchers who, in the past, have characterized the mentally ill only on the basis of those individuals who were being treated, assuming that the untreated group was relatively few in number and that whatever their characteristics, they could not significantly affect generalizations drawn from a treated group. The Midtown findings indicate that the untreated are not few in number, and analyses of their demographic characteristics indicate that they are, indeed, different in many important ways from those impaired individuals who receive professional treatment.

The Midtown study found that although impairment rates increase with age, the rates of those among the impaired group who had been patients for an emotional problem tend to decrease with age. With respect to socioeconomic status it was revealed that although total patient rates decrease as one goes up the socioeconomic scale, impairment frequencies increase as one goes up the socioeconomic scale. What seems to be a contradiction here is clarified by the further finding that in the impaired group the ever-patient rates increase as one goes upward on the socioeconomic scale. This means that very few of the impaired individuals on the bottom of the socioeconomic scale become patients, whereas at the top of the scale a relatively small number of impaired cases contribute a large number of patients. It is also found that among the patient group one is more likely to see younger adults (in the age range of 20 to 39) from the upper or middle socioeconomic scales who are American born. The untreated group is more likely to contain older adults (ages 40 to 59) from the lower rungs of the socioeconomic scale and of foreign birth. These discrepancies between the two groups may in part be a function of a lack of awareness of professional resources for dealing with emotional problems. The Midtown investigators also attribute these discrepancies to a selection process initiated by professionals on the basis of assumptions about prognosis, treatability, or sociocultural congeniality.

The findings of the Midtown study have led its investigators to offer hypotheses regarding vulnerability to emotional disorder. One emphasizes the significance of socioeconomic status. The normal family unit is seen to operate in such a way as to smooth over potentially disruptive forces and to maintain a psychological and sociological balance that enhances its members' capacity to deal with unbalancing crises. The low socioeconomic status family has very likely experienced prolonged economic hardship which makes it difficult for the family unit to react smoothly when confronted by crises such as disability among the parents, unemployment, or death. Such a unit is seen to be "brittle and disintegrative." A wide range of wealth within a given community accentuates the deprivations of the low socioeconomic family and invariably affects a child's view of the adequacy of his parents, damages a father's sense of self-respect, and results in a great deal of frustration for the father which is converted into aggression against the wife and children. All of this adds to the problems besetting a family unit of this kind. Thus the Midtown investigators hypothesized that the finding that people growing up in families of low socioeconomic status have maximum vulnerability to mental disorder can be explained on the basis that they are handicapped with respect to their personality resources, their social skills, and the lack of an example of a cohesive family unit. Furthermore, they have been damaged by the combined effects of growing up in poverty and of suffering the stigma of the community that in many respects has rejected them.

The Midtown investigators hypothesized further that the same familial factors that create vulnerability in those at low socioeconomic levels can produce vulnerability in the socioeconomically advantaged. The combination of an inadequate personality, weak social skills, and a poor self-concept is seen to invariably predispose an individual, whatever his social origins, to emotional disorder when the pressures of unsettling events are encountered. Most significant, as a general class of such events, would be a necessity to change one's social role.

The immigrant is seen to be particularly vulnerable to emotional disorder because the very nature of being an immigrant involves a wrench from one type of role and cultural situation and the necessity to adapt to a drastically different setting. Here, however, the Midtown investigators hypothesized that the extent of the necessary change, as reflected in the degree of contrast between the native environment and that which is adopted, has an important bearing on vulnerability.

The Midtown study is discussed in some detail because it is a good example of a complex epidemiological study whose findings yield important information about the character of the community investigated, as well as hypotheses concerning the etiology of mental disturbance. It is precisely for this reason that epidemiological research is of great significance for the community psychology movement.

ECOLOGY

The term ecology refers to the scientific study of the interaction between the organism and its environment (Sells, 1969). Its concern is "the nature of the interaction of organisms and populations with the embedding environment, which supports, influences, and determines the limits of structure and function for the life that exists within it" (Sells, 1969, p. 15). Ecologic methods have been applied in biology, medicine, sociology, and more recently in psychology. Medical ecology emerged out of epidemiology when researchers became sensitive to the fact that disease processes could not be understood simply on the basis of the study of the bacterial agent causing disease. They recognized that in addition to the presence of this agent a variety of other environmental factors must pertain, if disease is to result (Gordon, 1952). Communicable disease came to be viewed as resulting from the reciprocal influence of an infectious agent, a host, and an intricately complex environment.

In the past, ecology has been a particular concern of biologists. Human ecology has involved the application of the concept to understanding certain aspects of human behavior, but it has been used principally by geographers and sociologists concerned with the way human population groups are distributed as a function of material resources, health, social, economic, and cultural patterns.

Emphasis on human ecology within psychology has been a recent development. Barker (1965), a social psychologist, points out that in operating from the traditional experimental viewpoint, the psychologist has exercised considerable control over the conditions under which data are received by the human subject, the interior conditions of the subject, and the output that the subject produces. In essence, the psychologist has injected himself into the phenomena he is attempting to understand by virtue of his role as an "operator." The advantage this role provides is that it allows the psychologist to focus intensively on segments of behavior and processes that are of particular interest to him. Research of this type is commonly carried out within the laboratory according to the experimental method and not uncommonly is seen to exclude the clinical methods.

Because psychological researchers have mainly been concerned with isolated fragments of the environment, Barker (1969) suggests it is not surprising that little psychological study has been done of the global environment and the force it exerts on behavior. In fact, in large measure researchers have looked on man's environment as "an unstructured, probabilistic, and largely passive arena within which man behaves according to the programming he carries about inside him" (Barker, 1969, p. 32). In essence Barker feels that, as a science, psychology has performed a circular self-validation concerning the environment. Prevailing research approaches have purposely fragmented the environment, studied it piecemeal, and after considerable experience in dealing with it this way has asserted that no order exists within the environment and the natural setting to be used as an element in the study of the organization of human behavior. For Barker this era began as soon as psychology established itself as a laboratory science in which the psychologist became a surrogate of the environment and the natural environment was ignored. Thus psychology has learned a great deal about man's behavior under certain artificial and highly controlled conditions, but it knows very little about his behavior in the natural environment where the interplay between internal and external factors is extraordinarily important.

Since the hallmark of community psychology is that it takes serious cognizance of the impact on man of his natural environment, the ecological approach supported by Barker is of fundamental importance. Barker stresses the interrelationship between psychological phenomena and the environment in which they occur. He points out that knowing about the theory of electrical generators does not allow one to explain the functioning of an internal combustion engine. Similarly, traditional psychological approaches cannot explain the functioning of taverns, school classes, or other settings found in man's natural life situation, and any theories about these settings are unable to account for the behavior of the people participating in them. Concepts and theories different from traditional ones must be used to characterize people and the settings that make up their real world. The distinction between the questions raised by poverty, technology, population, and those with which traditional psychological science has been dealing is very basic. Thus Barker calls for a radically new research approach.

Kelly (1966), a psychologist closely associated with the community psychology movement, has spoken forcefully for the necessity of assuming an ecological viewpoint toward mental health problems. He regards this viewpoint as being relevant in, at least, three separate contexts. One type of problem requires analysis within a community of the relationship between existing mental health services and other available services. From an ecological viewpoint any change in the operation of one service unit in a system will have an effect on the operation of all other units. For example, when one local mental health facility shows a dramatic increase in admissions, it is very likely balanced by a decrease in admissions to some other area facility, or by a change in social stress patterns which produces more patients. The second type of ecological problem involves the study of relationships between a setting's physical characteristics and individual behavior. Thus population density, or the upheavals of urban renewal programs may have profound effects on the lives of an area's residents. A third realm in which ecological approaches are relevant is the study of the relationship between individual behavior and the immediate social environment. Fundamental to this approach is the notion that individual behavior is related to the social situation in which it occurs, suggesting to Kelly the need to redefine the concept of pathology. For Kelly, behavior is:

"not viewed as sick or well but is defined as transactional—an outcome of reciprocal interaction between specific social situations and the individual. Adaptive behavior then can be expressed by any individual in a restricted number of social settings or in a variety of environments, and can vary from time to time as well as from place to place" (Kelly, 1966, p. 538).

A major problem in conducting ecological research on the human being in his natural environment and avoiding imposing limits on the stimuli that he experiences and the responses he can make, is deciding what units of behavior to observe. As Barker (1965) puts it, "but when an investigator does not impose his units on the stream of behavior, what are its units?" In attempting to deal with this issue, Barker and his co-workers started out by observing periods of behavior in specific settings. One such setting involved a child, Maud, in an interaction with her mother in a drugstore. During this interaction the child received 26 social inputs as depicted in Figure 1.

Of the 26 inputs received by Maud, she responded to only about one third. Other observations of human interaction studies by Barker and fellow researchers indicate that Maud was not particularly extreme in this respect. Still, such findings are disturbing to a traditionally schooled investigator. They may be likened to finding that only one half a colony of rats is willing to run a maze, or that a subject returns a questionnaire with only one half of the questions answered. On the other hand, despite the fact that Maud failed to respond to a large percentage of the inputs she was receiving, her behavior in the drugstore was actually appropriate to the setting. She had her ice cream cone and enjoyed it, she did not read the comics, she handled the Christmas cards only to a small degree, she sat on the stool, she was not given the soda that she requested, her coat was removed and later it was put back on, and she left the store in a gen-

---

Mother. "We'll all go to the drugstore."

Mother. "Not now; you're not having a comic now."

Mother. "Leave things [Christmas cards] alone."

Mother. "Come on now, get your coat off."

Mother. "Maud, come back and sit down."

Mother. Pushes Maud toward the stool.

Mother. "Now you sit here."

Mother. "What do you want, Maud?"

Mother. "Oh, you don't want a soda."

Mother. "No, you don't get a soda."

Mother. "What do you want?"

Mother. "You don't want a soda. Besides you wouldn't drink it if you had it."

Mother. "Do you want a coke?"

Mother. "Do you want an ice cream cone?"

Mother. "Do you want an ice cream cone?"

Clerk. "What flavor, Maud?"

Clerk. "Vanilla, that's the white one."

Clerk. "Don't eat Fred's cone."

Mother. "Come on. Get your coat on, Maud."

Mother. Refuses Maud's whispered request.

Fred. Snatches Maud's coat.

Clerk. "Hi, Maud," as she ruffles Maud's hair.

Mother. "Come on."

Mother. Pushes Maud toward her coat.

Fred. Asks Maud for gum (from gum-machine).

Mother. Urges children from store with words and motions.

Figure 1. Twenty six social inputs received by child in a drugstore situation (Barker, 1965).

erally agreeable fashion. If the entire episode is to be regarded as a test of Maud's drugstore behavior, it appears that she failed many of the specific items but still passed the test.

What this seems to point to is the fact that for understanding behavior in a particular setting there is probably little point in attempting to discriminate in detailed fashion the small inputs directed toward controlling behavior. Instead, behavior seems to be responsive to major environmental force units (Schoggen, 1963) defined as actions by an environmental agent toward a recognizable end state for a person, the unity of which derives from its constancy of direction with respect to the person on whom it bears. While this environmental force unit may involve a variety of discrete inputs, behavior seems responsive to the overall direction of the intact environmental force unit rather than to its separate components. Another way of stating it is that long segments of behavior relate more directly to global environmental forces than do short segments of behavior.

One of the problems in attempting to understand Maud's drugstore behavior on the basis of the 26 separate social inputs which she was receiving was that by breaking the environmental system into these units, the system as a whole was destroyed, and many of its separate parts came to be viewed as apparently ineffective inputs with respect to influencing behavior. Furthermore, the psychological impact of the environment on Maud included more than those inputs attributable to the people interacting with her in the drugstore. She was influenced not only by her mother and the clerk who was serving her, but also by other staff, other customers, equipment, the merchandise, the particular spacial and temporal arrangements, and by the rules of the drugstore as well. Barker asserts that a variety of studies besides his own indicate that it is the total impact of situations that influences behavior more than the people who are involved in the "mutual causal relations between the environment and behavior." Thus situations such as drugstores, streets and sidewalks, mealtimes, and arithmetic lessons have different effects on behavior even when they involve the same people.

This type of insight has led ecological researchers to study individuals in specific behavioral settings. One approach to conducting this kind of research involves identifying some dimension along which behavioral settings vary although they may be similar in most other respects, and then to examine behavior in the two different settings. Barker and Gump (1964) have been interested in school settings of varying size. Their observations led them to believe that a significant property of settings that has important behavioral consequences is the number of human components within them. They note, for example, that a sandlot baseball game in which there are four to a side imposes vastly different requirements on the players than a game having nine players on a side. Who the players are is immaterial. Once one engages in a game in which there are four on a team he enjoys certain privileges, such as batting more frequently, and suffers certain special burdens, such as covering a wider area of the field.

Barker and Gump (1964) have done extensive comparisons of a variety of student behaviors in large and small high schools. Total enrollment in the schools studied ranged from 35 to 2287. In this research the first task was to arrive at an estimate of the total number of parts contained by a given school. In attempting to partition an entity such as a school, the first thing that comes to mind are its various classes. However, these are not the only places in the school inhabited by students. Many interactions take place in the hall, in assemblies, in administrative offices, in the shower room, and the like. The ecological units that represent the parts of a school setting having significance for directing human behavior have been termed *behavior settings* by Barker and Gump. Viewed as "organized assemblies of behavior episodes, physical objects, spaces, and durations," behavior settings are seen to have marked coercive power over individual behavior. For example, students do not ordinarily dance in the chemistry laboratory, nor do they conduct chemistry experiments at a prom.

Barker and Gump point out that many earlier studies have helped to provide an understanding of behavior settings. One resulting part of the theory of behavior settings holds that "a setting is a homeostatic system with controls that maintain the setting intact and operating at a stable functional level under widely varying conditions" (Barker and Gump, 1964, p. 19). The forces making for stability within a setting originate in a variety of sources. Some arise from the setting itself; in the classroom, there is a time schedule, a set of rules, and the physical arrangement of the room. Other controls derive from the relationship of the setting to the exterior situation. The entire school, for example, runs according to a fixed schedule and a set of regulations that imposes requirements on individual classes. Still other controls derive from those individuals who inhabit the setting and from other factors internal to the setting itself; examples of such interior controls are the textbooks used in a class, and the students' level of maturity.

A second part of the theory of behavior settings holds that the behavior engaged in within the setting must conform to a set of constraints imposed on it by the rules and characteristics of the particular setting. In this sense the form of the setting may be compared to a chair, and behavior may be compared to the person who would sit in the chair. To a great extent, the individual must assume a form that is compatible with that provided by the chair he is sitting in.

A third part of the theory holds that behavior settings, to maintain themselves in operation, have an ideally optimal number of internal ele-

ments. For example, a baseball game requires approximately 20 participants, 18 players and 2 officials. Within limits, the setting can continue to
maintain itself with fewer internal elements but to the degree that it does
so, certain consequences follow for the individuals providing the behavioral input. Two of these are that: (1) the strength of the forces acting
on the participants increases; and (2) the range and direction of the
forces that act on participants increases.

The final aspect of the theory of behavior settings is that the setting
provides the opportunity for its inhabitants to derive many satisfactions
and to satisfy many personal motives. Furthermore, the different inhabitants of the same setting may have different needs that are met within it.
Thus the boy who pitches in a baseball game satisfies one set of social-
physical needs, his mother watching in the bleachers receives a different
set of satisfactions, and his coach is satisfied in still other ways. Related
to this aspect, is the inhabitant's obligation, while he is achieving satisfactions, also help maintain the setting so that it will continue to be possible
later for him to achieve satisfactions within it. When a threat to the maintenance of the stability of the setting is perceived to be strong enough to
threaten its occupants with a loss of the source of satisfactions, the force
to maintain the setting grows.

On the basis of the theory regarding behavior settings and a previously
worked out system for identifying them, Barker and Gump determined
the variety of behavior settings available to students in the schools that
they studied. Surprisingly, a comparison of the largest school with four
small schools revealed that although the large school had 20 times as
many students, it had only 5 times as many behavior settings and only
1.4 times as many varieties of settings. This suggests that the small school
is small only with respect to number of students but not necessarily with
repect to the number of its behaviorally significant parts.

The findings with respect to the extent of the differentiation of large
and small schools led Barker and Gump naturally to an interest in the degree to which students in such schools participated in school activities.
Comparisons of students in small and large schools reveal that, on the average, students in the small school engaged in approximately twice as
many extracurricular activities as students in the large schools. Furthermore, students of small schools were much more likely to hold positions
of responsibility within their behavior settings, and these positions were
occupied in more varieties of settings than was true for students of large
schools. Greater variation was found among students of large schools in
the number of settings in which they participated.

Barker and Gump also tried to assess the degree of satisfaction derived
by students from the activities they took part in as a function of their
school size. It was found that juniors from small schools as compared to

large schools felt they had achieved greater satisfactions from a growing sense of competence, a feeling of being challenged, a sense of doing something important, a feeling of being truly involved in group activities, and of achieving the values of their culture. Juniors in large schools were more likely to report that their satisfactions came through vicarious enjoyments, from being affiliated with large organizations, from learning about the people in the school and the affairs of the school, and from gaining points because they participate. Students in small schools also reported that they were more readily attracted and even pressured to taking part in nonclass behavior settings than were students in large schools. Their response to this indicated that they felt more involved and took on greater responsibility than did large school students.

Comparisons were also made of the community involvement of students of small and large high schools. It was found that community activities were more frequent for students who came from small schools and small towns than for those in large schools in urban areas. These differences were more prominent for boys than for girls but, in general, there seemed to be a harmony between the school and the community. Just as the small school provided more opportunity for the student to engage in responsible, important positions, so did the small community. Such opportunities were less frequent in the cities.

Studies were made by Barker and Gump of differences in school structure as a function of school size. It was found that about the same proportion of the behavior settings of schools of all sizes are devoted to the formal educational enterprise. However, fewer varieties of formal educational opportunities were found in small schools, and the number of different classes dealing with a particular subject was smaller in the small schools. Despite this, it was found that large school students participated in fewer varieties of classes than did small school students. Students specializing in music were studied in some detail with the finding that those in small schools acquired a broader experience within the subject than did those in large schools, although more large school students specialized in music.

Barker and Gump sum up their findings by urging that further research be done to determine the degree to which the relationships they found between school size and student behavior are inevitable. Hopefully, studies of this kind might begin to indicate the optimal school size for achieving certain desired goals. Good empirical answers to such questions would provide a basis for redesigning the structure of schools.

Another significant line of research carried out within the ecological framework was conducted by Kelly (1969) in keeping with some of his notions about adaptation as a function of the setting. Since Kelly's work is described in a previous chapter, it is summarized very briefly here. The major premise behind Kelly's research is that functional variations between environments produce differences in the development and control of norms within such settings, and also in the requirements for adaptation to those settings. Thus a given coping style may be adaptive in one setting and entirely maladaptive in another. To the extent that this notion is valid, Kelly believes it is important to specify the environmental conditions related to adapting and failing to adapt to various settings.

Kelly chose to compare the environments of two high schools varying with respect to student turnover rate. One of the schools he studied had an annual turnover rate of 42 percent whereas the turnover rate in the other was only 10 percent. The high turnover school was characterized as having a *fluid environment,* and the one with low turnover was considered to have a *constant environment.* It was hypothesized that living styles necessary for adaptation to each setting would differ. Specifically, Kelly predicted that in the fluid environment the social groupings would be relatively unstable and that there would be many bases for social stratification. Also, in the rapidly changing environment, it was expected that personal development would be highly valued. By contrast, in the constant environment the social status changes would be relatively rare, and the primary goal of the community member would be to make a place for himself within the status hierarchy rather than to develop. One's sense of worth in this setting would be determined more by the external regulating units of the society rather than by one's own internal standards.

A specific hypothesis that was tested in this study held that people who are high in exploratory behavior would cope more effectively in the fluid environment than in the constant environment. Conversely those low on exploratory behavior were expected to be regarded as the more effective copers in the constant environment.

Among Kelly's early findings is the fact that male high schoolers who are high in exploratory behavior are more likely to be regarded as deviant by the faculty of a constant environment school than are high exploratory males rated by faculty in a fluid school environment. In addition, subjective comparisons of schools having fluid and constant environments indicated that dress is more varied among students in a fluid environment; groupings of up to 12 students are more often found in the fluid environment than in the constant environment; and considerably more uniformity of dress exists in the constant environment than in the fluid one. Communication in the fluid school seems to follow two distinct patterns—either intense, dramatic gesturing and vocalization or no obvious communication at all. In the constant school only a single style of communication is observed—a generally "low level commentary." Observations in the fluid environment revealed a range of 30 to 110 entrances into the principal's office during a three-minute period by both students and teachers as compared to a range of only 1 to 15 entrances per three-minute period in a constant environment. In the hallways of the fluid environment, noise level tended to be higher than in the constant environment, and much conversation took place between group members, despite the presence of student and faculty monitors. Interviews with students revealed that newcomers to the constant environment were not welcomed whereas in the fluid setting a formal welcoming committee for newcomers was set up with varying membership.

Another example of an ecological approach to understanding behavior in the school setting is the subjective observational study of the kindergartner described by Sarason (1971). Sarason was interested in whether he could learn something of the culture of the school by observing kindergarten children. He approached the task simply by stationing himself in different parts of the school on random occasions to determine how frequently he would encounter a kindergartner in each location. Although Sarason was not systematic with respect either to the parts of the school studied or the recording of his observations, he did come away with some interesting impressions.

First, one place he never saw a kindergarten child was the lavatory, because in the school he studied, as is true in many schools, each kindergarten room had its own toilet facilities. A second impression was that the likelihood of seeing a pupil from the kindergarten decreased as distance from his room increased. Finally, the higher the pupil's grade the more likely he would be seen in different places in the school. The overall impression was that kindergartners are rarely allowed out of their classroom and they, therefore, see very little of their physical surroundings in the school.

These impressions prompted Sarason to question school personnel about why kindergartners seem so restricted in their range of contact with the diverse school parts. Responses to these questions implied, first, that this restriction is so deeply rooted in school tradition that it has been rarely reflected on. When reflection was provoked, respondents tended to indicate that kindergartners are different from older children in such a way that they require constant surveillance. Another aspect of this view was that the kindergarten is less a part of the school than it is a place to prepare the child for school. A further assumption underlying these practices was that the kindergarten youngster might be easily led astray by the older children.

While he acknowledges some merit in these views of the kindergarten pupil, Sarason also challenges them. He points out that the school culture's way of handling the kindergartner results in a self-fulfilling prophecy. The way the school experience is organized inevitably confirms the assumption that the child's movements must be restricted. If the opposite assumption were made (i.e., that the child should learn to get around on his own), the child's learning opportunities could undoubtedly be arranged so that he could quickly learn to get around the school building independently and without any obvious signs of fear. The reason for encouraging this exploratory behavior is, Sarason feels, that most children are curious about their surroundings and their fellow occupants of the school. This curiosity could be used to foster motivation for learning, and there is no compelling reason to delay its satisfaction. A strong argument in favor of Sarason's suggestion is that most children who are required to repeat the early school grades are characterized as "immature." Certainly the manner in which the kindergarten child is typically dealt with does little to foster the maturity necessary for later school success.

The types of studies that have been undertaken from an ecological viewpoint have very obvious relevance for community psychology. They promise to provide an understanding of settings that the community psychologist may want to alter or manipulate toward certain desired ends. The problem is that research in human ecology is truly in its infancy, and the methods that must be employed in this area are unfamiliar to the traditionally trained psychologist. Furthermore, as Barker (1969) argues, the necessary concepts and theories basic to an eco-behavioral science must be grounded on empirical data describing the way people live in their own natural settings. Barker makes several recommendations for facilitating the acquisition of these data.

First, Barker points out that the psychologist who would study phenomena in their natural state cannot induce the phenomena to occur. And since many of the phenomena in which he is interested will occur only infrequently, long periods of observation may be necessary to accumulate sufficient instances of these phenomena. This problem is actually similar to many that face other sciences. For example, those who would study earthquakes or bird migrations spend long periods simply waiting for the phenomena to occur. For such scientists the phenomenon's infrequent occurrence is not looked on as a negative feature but, instead, as an attribute that simply must be accepted. One way in which these scientists facilitate the study of a phenomenon is by accumulating as much observational data as possible about it and by making it generally available within some archive. Barker argues that to establish an eco-behavioral science, therefore, data archives must be set up. This would require the psychologist to learn a great deal about how to collect, preserve, and retrieve these data.

A second need Barker identifies as necessary for a developing eco-behavioral science is the establishment of field stations. Since the ecological scientist is not an input source into the phenomena that he studies, he cannot work in his own laboratory. He must do his business where the phenomena are to be found. Thus field stations, such as the Woods Holes and Mount Wilsons of other sciences, must be established and equipped. From his experience with such facilities, Barker specifies that the field station's location should be identifiable with respect to the characteristics of the larger context within which it is set, such as an inner-city ghetto, a rural community, or an industrial plant. Within the locale where they would work, investigators should apply no constraints of their own. Ideally, they must have access to a setting without actually interfering with the setting's function. This limits some of the studies that might be done and some of the techniques that might be applied. Kelly (1969) questions whether an observer can be entirely unobtrusive with respect to the phenomena he is observing in the natural setting. Certainly this issue will require considerable empirical study and, perhaps, the development of new methodological techniques.

A third important need for an eco-behavioral science identified by Barker is the development of new data analysis techniques for dealing with naturalistic phenomena. Traditionally trained psychologists are not equipped to deal with such phenomena. Their natural tendency is to apply statistical techniques, developed for use with laboratory problems, which have the effect of destroying the naturalistic phenomena being investigated. Barker feels that the data reduction methods used in quantitative botany, demography, geography, physiology, and economics may be more appropriate for the eco-behavioral scientist and should now be studied by psychologists.

GENERAL SYSTEMS THEORY

The general systems approach to studying organizational structures seems particularly relevant to community psychology because it is concerned with interrelationships between components within a particular system and the interrelationships of the system with related systems. von Bertalanffy (1968), a biologist, is generally credited with being the foremost spokesman for general systems theory, having developed it as a means of better understanding the functioning of living organisms. Roen (1971) points out that approaching mental health problems from the viewpoint of general systems theory seems particularly valuable because the mental health area is concerned with the general environmental context basic to community problems. The other advantage offered by general systems theory to community psychology is that the approach encourages thinking in terms of interdisciplinary relationships instead of holding to the inevitably narrow viewpoint of a single specialty.

Within general systems theory, various specialized approaches have been worked out to understand phenomena in specific social contexts. These include cybernetics, information theory, decision theory, and game theory. Cybernetics, regarded by von Bertalanffy as the foremost of the modern mechanistic systems sciences, is conceptually a relatively simple approach. Minimally, the cybernetic system requires a receptor that accepts stimuli or information, a "center" that in some way reacts to the message received, and an "effector" that reacts to the stimulus and makes a response. In addition, in the cybernetics system a feedback mechanism monitors responses to the receptor and shapes subsequent action of the system to obtain a desired result. In this way the system is not simply a passive receiver of information and a mechanistic reactor. It can regulate itself to some degree and thereby alter the nature of its interaction with stimuli. The heating thermostat is a simple example of a cybernetic system. The thermometer in the thermostat is the receptor and the output is the heat produced by the heating system. Room temperature resulting from the operation of the heating system is fed back to the receptor, and the subsequent system activation depends on the thermostat setting. von Bertalanffy points out that the cybernetics model is, however, a closed model with respect to exchanging information with the environment. It is self-regulating but can only receive information from the environment, unlike living systems whose component parts are continually destroyed and replaced in a process that we know as growth, development, and differentiation. Thus he views cybernetics as a special case of systems theory.

Information theory, decision theory, and game theory are less special cases of systems theory than cybernetics. Information theory is somewhat related to cybernetics but stresses the notion that information is a measureable quantity playing a basic role in the constant change taking place in interacting systems. Decision theory is concerned with the analysis of rational choices made within human organizations. Game theory is related to decision theory but uses mathematics to analyze the competition that takes place on a rational level between two or more antagonists who are striving for maximum gain and minimal loss.

Hutcheson and Krause (1969) have discussed the application of systems analysis to the mental health field. They point out its advantages as a rational aid to planning mental health services as well as its practical limitations. For these authors the systems approach is looked on as a rational, well ordered way of examining all of the angles of a complex problem and arriving at an optimal solution given the constraints under which one must operate.

Hutcheson and Krause describe the systems analysis approach as having several interrelated goals. These goals include: (a) deciding on the objectives of the program that is to be subjected to systems analysis; (b) designating the boundaries of the system to be studied and the subsystems that make it up; (c) determining how the system changes and the factors that cause that change; (d) building a model, either mathematical or graphic, taking into account all system elements; (e) manipulating the model to test the effect of theoretical changes; (f) selecting the most desirable outcome, given the general system objectives, and creating a program designed to reach this goal; and (g) considering time and cost variables as part of the design of the model to minimize costs and wasted time so that an optimally practical and efficient program will result.

Obviously systems analysis is most readily carried out in areas where the relevant variables are easily defined. Unfortunately, this is not true of the mental health service field. Usually it is possible to arrive at some broadly defined program objectives that most agree on. However, defining the boundaries of a system and analyzing it into subsystems, the necessary second step in system analysis, may be very difficult to carry out. For this reason, Hutcheson and Krause recommend that initial efforts to apply systems analysis focus on relatively limited problem areas. The most significant limitation to place on research in this area would, for these authors, be that of geography and topography. Applying system analysis techniques to the population of a small island, for example, having a relatively homogeneous population reduces the number of variables encountered and limits the magnitude of the boundary-drawing problem. Even in this instance, however, Hutcheson and Krause warn against limiting the analysis to the mental health service sphere, or to exclusive study of relationships between mental health or health and welfare subsystems. This is because many other variables such as unemployment rates are often found to be closely related to the overall mental health picture. Thus, all factors that have significant effects on the mental health of a given area must be taken into consideration. Another advantage of limiting systems analysis to a circumscribed region at the outset is that intervention which may be suggested by the outcome of the analysis is more easily instituted in the relatively simple society of the isolated small town than in large, socially complex regions.

Attempts to implement systems analysis techniques in the mental health field are understandably rare despite their seemingly high relevance for community psychology. Undoubtedly, considerably more effort will have to be devoted to the basic problem of defining the subunits of relevant social systems before the application of systems analysis will be feasible. In many respects this problem is similar to the one faced by the ecologist who must detect the relevant units of behavior in the natural environment as a first step in understanding the interplay of environmental forces.

EVALUATIVE RESEARCH

It would seem altogether reasonable that any new procedure, whether medical or psychological, should be evaluated objectively before it becomes widely used. Perhaps surprisingly, this has rarely been true. Carstairs (1967, p. 46) points out:

"One thing is quite clear: objective *evaluations of the effectiveness of new procedures have seldom, if ever, preceeded their gaining currency in psychiatric practice. But evaluation of some sort has taken place: many other practitioners have learned about the innovations and have judged them worthy of imitation. . . . The agents of persuasion were, I suggest, example, assertion, and dramatic illustration."*

Carstairs also points out that professional evaluators, with formal training in relevant research areas, inevitably regard the evaluation task in a different, more objective light than does the innovator who creates the program and attempts to evaluate it himself.

MacMahon, Pugh, and Hutchison (1969) distinguish between two types of evaluatory studies. The first called *evaluation of accomplishment* is a test of the hypothesis that a particular practice or procedure, if carried out successfully, has measurable beneficial effects. Although this type of evaluation would seem at face value to be most desirable, it is not particularly common. The most important reason why such studies are few in number is that establishing true cause and effect relationships is difficult. The second type of evaluation, described by MacMahon et al., is called *evaluation of technique.* In these studies, researchers are not attempting to establish cause and effect relationships but rather to determine whether a given technique is carried out according to some standard for how it should be done. These studies are quite common.

Logically, studies evaluating accomplishment should precede evaluations of technique, since if a technique fails to produce beneficial results, there is little point in establishing that it has been followed reliably. Once the value of the technique is established, however, continued studies evaluating the application of the technique have an important place. MacMahon et al. are careful to point out that "community acceptance" is no substitute for objective evaluations of accomplishment. They state:

"Before leaving the subject of categories of evaluation and their purposes, there is one concept which should be mentioned, if only to be dismissed. This is the idea that programs gaining 'community acceptance' are, ipso facto, beneficial. That this reasoning is a nonsequitur should be evident. It is demonstrated currently by the acceptance of well-advertised

nostrums, and historically by waves of enthusiasm that have been generated by a variety of medical cults" (MacMahon, Pugh, and Hutchison, 1969, p. 53).

Research evaluating the effectiveness of treatment and training programs is quite familiar to many psychologists. Thus the major retooling effort that is necessary for the psychologist to engage in epidemiological, ecological, and systems analysis approaches would not be required in this realm. Nonetheless, research of this kind is not easily implemented, and the community psychologist with a heavy investment in program development is not always the best person to carry out program evaluation. Cowen (1967, p. 442) has spoken cogently of this problem.

"To place the matter in a slightly different perspective, the professional, if he's to be effective, must believe in what he is doing and must be invested in his everyday activities. His role, understandably, does not conform to a stereotype of detached objectivity that we have for the scientist. To the extent that he serves simultaneously the roles of participator and the evaluator of a given set of events, he must be regarded as a biased observer for whom certain outcomes, whether consciously or otherwise, may be inimical and unacceptable. Though the observations of the participating professional may represent one admissible source of data, and, indeed, may constitute an especially fertile basis for generating hypotheses, to the extent that they are utilized as the prime vehicle for assessing the effectiveness of methods, we expose ourselves to systematic error that will obstruct progress."

Glidewell (1969) points to another significant problem in carrying out evaluative research in community psychology. Since the basic question in evaluative studies has to do with whether or not an intervention has produced the desired outcome, untreated control groups are generally necessary. The problem with using control groups is that one is required to withhold service from some research subjects as a means of assessing it. If the service is an old, accepted one, albeit untested, such a methodological practice may be looked on as unfair to those needing it and, even further, may be regarded as ethically questionable. Similar problems are encountered even with respect to new and relatively untried services. The practitioner is simply expected to do his best to help all who need it, and outsiders are hard put to understand a procedure that purposely withholds service.

Herzog (1958) outlines a number of other issues that complicate the process of carrying out evaluative research. Although the fundamental question of evaluative research can be stated fairly simply, that is, have a given group of individuals been helped by a particular program?, a closer examination reveals that this is really an extraordinarily complex issue. As Herzog (1958, p. 203) indicates: "This key question, however, is a very unstable compound. Under examination it breaks down into a cluster of questions: which ones have been helped? how much? how stable is the help? was it really the treatment or something else that helped? who says so? how do we know it is true?" Questions of this sort can be raised about the efforts of a single practitioner. If measures of the work of many practitioners or many different agencies are to be combined, several new questions can be added. Did each individual or agency try to help in the same way? Were the problems they were working with comparable in the beginning? Did they work with people who were comparable with respect to their capacity to change? Were observed changes comparable in degree, or stability?

Herzog asserts that experts generally agree that a satisfactory evaluation must deal with four types of issues. First, the purpose of the evaluation must be made clear. Second, concerning the efforts that are to be evaluated, the desired changes, and the means by which these changes are to be brought about must be indicated. Third, with respect to the methods for assessing change, the measures that are used must be reliable and valid, the points at which measurements are taken must be specified, the sample studied must be shown to be representative of the group one is concerned with, and any changes found must be demonstrably due to the treatment that was applied. Finally, any changes found must be demonstrated, and any unexpected consequences should be elaborated. Of course, each of these issues are interrelated, and few studies deal equally well with all of them.

Herzog distinguished three types of evaluative research. The first, *ultimate evaluation,* is generally desired by most people. This approach is concerned with the degree to which a treatment program or a service helps those it serves. Unfortunately, generally such a question is too broadly drawn to be answered in a single study. To speak of the effectiveness of psychotherapy may be as fruitless as attempting to evaluate in general the effectiveness of surgery. The second approach, *pre-evaluative research,* is the type that must be carried out to answer questions needing answers before satisfactory evaluative studies can be done. Pre-evaluative research involves issues such as what changes are to be produced, in whom, by what means, by whom, and the like. This approach can lead to the reformulation of mental health practices as well as to changing ideas concerning what might be desired from ultimate evaluations. For example, as the result of pre-evaluative research we may stop asking whether psychotherapy is effective and start asking how effective a particular approach is with particular kinds of patients in producing particular types of changes. Finally, the third approach to evaluation is *short-term evalua-*

tion, research that can be carried out within a few years. It can be useful in dealing with problems in the here and now and can be applied short of extensive pre-evaluative research. It cannot, however, provide the long-term answers that people most desire. Such answers must await extensive pre-evaluative research.

Herzog offers certain admonishments with respect to undertaking evaluative research. First, she suggests that one not embark on evaluative research if the purpose it is to serve can be accomplished in some other way, since research of this kind is expensive, time consuming, and difficult to carry out. Herzog warns against relying on agency records as the exclusive source of data in an evaluative study, since these records often lack data essential to the proper conduct of the study. Furthermore, they are seldom comparably explicit and detailed. Herzog recommends also that a great deal of time and effort not be spent in being precise about one feature of a research program, out of all proportion with other features. For example, little is gained in being extraordinarily precise about the reliability of measures, if the criteria used are relatively ambiguous.

Herzog points out that certain factors are essential to good evaluative research. These include bringing the researcher into the project early enough and thoroughly enough to do a proper job, having "intellectually hospitable" researchers and practitioners on the team, and having researchers who appreciate the potential rewards of evaluative research and coordinated efforts.

Certainly another significant set of problems in the conduct of evaluative research relates to the generally long-term nature of such an enterprise. To determine whether a program has had a significant effect often requires continued study long after the program has been instituted or completed. This requires keeping in touch with a significant portion of the subject population over very long periods of time. Among certain social groups and in groups residing in certain locales this requirement is difficult to achieve.

All of the problems associated with evaluative research contribute to its high cost which, in itself, becomes a problem. Many funding sources, as well as the general public, are much more willing to provide funds for service programs, even untried ones, than to put large sums of money into evaluative research. Service programs can often be "sold" on the basis of the faith and the enthusiasm of its developers, and they offer the hope that some good will be done for needy individuals. The researcher, on the other hand, is often less convincing in his enthusiasm for the research enterprise and, at best, can only produce documentation of the effectiveness of a program whose worth may have already been accepted on faith. At worst, the researcher can shatter the illusions of service providers and those who badly want to see them succeed. Thus funding for evaluative research must be provided by individuals or agencies taking a coldly rational viewpoint concerning the whole community psychology enterprise. Since large amounts of money are more likely to be provided for enterprises that seem exciting and of immediate benefit to needy individuals than to research enterprises that are very lengthy, complicated, and potentially deflating, the acquisition of funds for evaluative research remains a serious problem.

Since examples of evaluate research studies have been liberally reviewed throughout the preceding chapters of this book, none will be considered in this section in detail. A variety of community psychology programs have been subjected to more or less systematic evaluation. These include Rioch's program for training mental health counselors (Golann, Breiter, and Magoon, 1966; Magoon, and Golann, 1966), and the effects of a student volunteer program in a hospital setting (Holzberg, Gewirtz, and Ebner, 1964; Holzberg, and Knapp, 1965), all described in Chapter 3. Several studies evaluating the effects of a "token economy" on chronically disturbed mental patients (Atthowe and Krasner, 1968; Ayllon, 1963; Ayllon, and Azrin, 1965; Isaacs, Thomas, and Goldiamond, 1960) as well as other types of hospital programs (Fairweather, Sanders, Cressler, and Maynard, 1960; Samuels and Henderson, 1971; Sanders, Smith, and Weinman, 1967) are described in Chapter 4. In Chapter 5 are discussed evaluations of several programs for stimulating infants and preschool children (Gray, and Klaus, 1970; Irwin, 1960; Karnes, Teska, Hodgins and Badger, 1970; Klaus and Gray, 1968; Rheingold, 1956; Skeels, and Dye, 1939). The effects of primary preventive efforts in the school system are considered in many evaluative studies described in Chapter 6 (Leton, 1957; Levitt, 1955; Minuchin, Biber, Shapiro, and Zimiles, 1969; Muss, 1960; Ojemann, Levitt, Lyle, and Whiteside, 1955; Thomas, Becker, and Armstrong, 1968) while in Chapter 7 are examined several secondary preventive program evaluations (Cowen, Izzo, Miles, Telschow, Trost, and Zax, 1963; Cowen, Zax, Izzo, and Trost, 1966; Gildea, Glidewell, Kantor, 1967). Chapter 8 describes the evaluation of several preventive programs conducted on college campuses (Kysar, 1966; Sinnett, and Niedenthal, 1968; Sinnett, Wiesner, and Frieser, 1967; Spielberger, & Weitz, 1964; Webster, and Harris, 1958; Wolff, 1969). Finally, evaluations of programs based in the greater community are presented in Chapter 9 (McCord, McCord, and Zola, 1959; Powers, and Witmer, 1951; Sarason, 1968; Sarason, and Ganzer, 1969; Schwitzgabel and Kolb, 1964).

CONCLUSION

Community psychology, as a new approach to dealing with behavioral problems, must have its procedures and techniques established on sound empirical bases and its program shaped by realistic needs. In bringing this about, research will be fundamental. This research can be devoted to locating parts of the community that have the greatest need for service; can be essential in establishing which social forces are detrimental to good mental health; can be used to help create optimally efficient service delivery programs; and can be used to test the effectiveness of established service or training programs.

Characteristically, it has been easier to generate enthusiasm for the development of service programs that promise to improve the lot of suffering individuals than for the development of research programs. A further barrier to the establishment of the type of research programs needed in community psychology is that the traditionally trained psychologist is not well prepared for many of the relevant approaches. Furthermore, research in naturalistic settings, such as is required in the ecological approach, and system analysis techniques are only now being developed. Thus the community psychologist who would like to apply these approaches is virtually compelled to participate in developing basic research methods before he can do so.

Evaluative research is the approach relevant to community psychology for which the traditionally trained psychologist is best prepared. However, even research of this kind is not easily implemented because of the considerable time and money it requires as well as the many methodological difficulties involved in carrying it out.

Despite the many realistic handicaps to engaging in research, it is absolutely essential that community psychology take up the research quest very seriously. This is particularly true because, as a relatively new approach to dealing with behavior disorder, community psychology is competing with an order that has been established over a period of years. To supplant an already well-established way of looking at problems and dealing with them requires a monumental effort. In some respects, this enterprise can be likened to building sand castles on the seashore. As long as the castle builder is present and willing to invest a great deal of energy into repairing breaches in the wall made by the incoming tide, he can preserve the semblance of the castle. Once his enthusiasm flags, or he leaves the scene, it is simply a matter of time before all signs of his previous presence are washed away. Community psychology faces that danger. Only a solid empirical base for its programs and techniques, and good evidence of their effective outcome can lead to the building of permanent walls resistant to the tides of tradition.

References

Atthowe, J. M., Jr., & Krasner, L. Preliminary report on the application of contingent reinforcement procedures (token economy) on a "chronic" psychiatric ward. *Journal of Abnormal Psychology*, 1968, *37*, 37–43.

Ayllon, T. Intensive treatment of psychotic behavior by stimulus satiation and food reinforcement. *Behavior Research and Therapy*, 1963, *1*, 53–61.

Ayllon, T., & Azrin, N. H. The measurement and reinforcement of behavior of psychotics. *Journal of the Experimental Analysis of Behavior*, 1965, *8*, 357–384.

Barker, R. G. Explorations in ecological psychology. *American Psychologist*, 1965, *20*, 1–14.

Barker, R. G. Wanted: An eco-behavioral science. In E. P. Willems, & H. L. Raush (Eds.), *Naturalistic viewpoints in psychological research*. New York: Holt, Rinehart & Winston, 1969. Pp. 31–43.

Barker, R. G., & Gump, P. *Big school, small school*. Stanford: Stanford University Press, 1964.

Carstairs, G. M. Problems of Evaluative Research. In R. H. Williams, & L. D. Ozarin (Eds.), *Community mental health: an international perspective*. San Francisco: Jossey-Bass, 1968. Pp. 44–62.

Cohen, L. D. Strategies and logistics in mental health research. In L. S. Anderson, C. C. Bennett, S. Cooper, L. Hassol, D. C. Klein, & G. Rosenblum, *Community psychology: a report of the Boston conference on the education of psychologists for community mental health*. Boston: Boston University, 1966. Pp. 65–79.

Cowen, E. L. Emergent approaches to mental health problems: An overview and directions for future work. In E. L. Cowen, E. A. Gardner, & M. Zax (Eds.), *Emergent approaches to mental health problems*. New York: Appleton-Century-Crofts, 1967. Pp. 389–455.

Cowen, E. L., Izzo, L. D., Miles, H., Tels chow, E. F., Trost, M. A., & Zax, M. A mental health program in the school setting: description and evaluation. *Journal of Psychology*, 1963, *56*, 307–356.

Cowen, E. L., Zax, M., Izzo, L. D., & Trost, M. A. The prevention of emotional disorders in the school setting: a further investigation. *Journal of Consulting Psychology*, 1966, *30*, 381–387.

Doull, J. A. The bacteriological era (1876–1920). In F. H. Top (Ed.), *The history of American epidemiology*. St. Louis: The C. V. Mosby Co., 1952. Pp. 74–113.

Edgerton, J. W. Evaluation in community mental health. In G. Rosenblum (Ed.), *Issues in community psychology and preventive mental health*. New York: Behavioral Publications, Inc., 1971. Pp. 89–107.

Fairweather, G. W., Sanders, D. H., Cressler, D., & Maynard, H. *Community life for the mentally ill*. Chicago: Aldine Publishing Co., 1969.

Faris, R. E. L., & Dunham, H. W. *Mental disorders in urban areas.* Chicago: University of Chicago Press, 1939.

Gildea, M. C.-L., Glidewell, J. C., & Kantor, M. B. The St. Louis mental health project: history and evaluation. In E. L. Cowen, E. A. Gardner, & M. Zax (Eds.), *Emergent approaches to mental health problems.* New York: Appleton-Century-Crofts, 1967. Pp. 290–308.

Glidewell, J. C. Research problems in community psychology. In A. J. Bindman, & A. D. Spiegel (Eds.), *Perspectives in community mental health.* Chicago: Aldine Publishing Co., 1969. Pp. 669–682.

Golann, S. E., Brieter, D. E., & Magoon, T. M. A filmed interview applied to the evaluation of mental health counselors. *Psychotherapy,* 1966, *3,* 21–24.

Gordon, J. E. The twentieth century—yesterday, today and tomorrow— (1920–   ). In F. H. Top (Ed.), *The history of American epidemiology.* St Louis: The C. V. Mosby Co., 1952. Pp. 114–167.

Gray, S. W., & Klaus, R. A. The early training project: A seventh year report. *Child Development,* 1970, *41,* 909–924.

Herzog, E. How much are they helped? Some notes on evaluative research. *Children,* 1958, *5,* 203–209.

Hollingshead, A. B., & Redlich, F. C. *Social class and mental illness.* New York: Wiley, 1958.

Holzberg, J. D., Gewirtz, H., & Ebner, E. Changes in moral judgment and self-acceptance in college students as a function of companionship with hospitalized mental patients. *Journal of Consulting Psychology,* 1964, *28,* 299–303.

Holzberg, J. D., & Knapp, R. H. The social interaction of college students and chronically ill mental patients. *American Journal of Orthopsychiatry,* 1965, *35,* 487–492.

Hutcheson, B. R., & Krause, E. A. Systems analysis and mental health services. *Community Mental Health Journal,* 1969, *5,* 29–45.

Irwin, O. C. Effect of systematic reading of stories. *The Journal of Speech and Hearing Research,* 1960, *3,* 187–190.

Isaacs, W., Thomas, J., & Goldiamond, I. Applications of operant conditioning to reinstate verbal behavior in psychotics. *Journal of Speech and Hearing Disorders,* 1960, *25,* 8–12.

Joint Commission on Mental Illness and Health. *Action for mental health.* New York: Science Editions, 1961.

Karnes, M. B., Teska, J. A., Hodgins, A. S., & Badger, I. D. Educational intervention at home by mothers of disadvantaged infants. *Child Development,* 1970, *41,* 925–935.

Kelly, J. G. Ecological constraints on mental health services. *American Psychologist,* 1966, *33,* 535–439.

Kelly, J. G. Naturalistic observations in contrasting social environments. In E. P. Willems, and H. L. Raush, *Naturalistic Viewpoints in Psychological Research.* New York: Holt, Rinehart & Winston, 1969. Pp. 183–199.

Klaus, R. A., & Gray, S. W. The early training project for disadvantaged children: A report after five years. *Monographs of the Society for Research in Child Development*, 1968, *33*, 1–66.

Kramer, M. A discussion of the concepts of incidence and prevalence as related to epidemiologic studies of mental disorder. *American Journal of Public Health*, 1957, *47*, 826–840.

Kysar, J. E. Preventive psychiatry on the college campus. *Community Mental Health Journal*, 1966, *2*, 27–34.

Leighton, D. C., Leighton, A. H., & Armstrong, R. A. Community psychiatry in a rural area: A social psychiatric approach. In L. Bellak (Ed.), *Handbook of community psychiatry*. New York: Grune & Stratton, 1964. Pp. 166–176.

Lemkau, P., Tietze, C., & Cooper, M. Mental hygiene problems in an urban district. *Mental Hygiene*, 1941, *25*, 624–646.

Lemkau, P., Tietze, C., & Cooper, M. Mental hygiene problems in an urban district. Second paper. *Mental Hygiene*, 1942, *26*, 100–119. (a)

Lemkau, P., Tietze, C., & Cooper, M. Mental hygiene problems in an urban district. Third paper. *Mental Hygiene*, 1942, *26*, 275–288. (b)

Lemkau, P., Tietze, C., & Cooper, M. Mental hygiene problems in an urban district. Fourth paper. *Mental Hygiene*, 1942, *27*, 279–295. (c)

Leton, D. A. An evaluation of group methods in mental hygiene. *Mental Hygiene*, 1957, *41*, 525–533.

Levitt, E. E. The effect of a "casual" teacher training program in authoritarianism and responsibility in grade school children. *Psychological Reports*, 1955, *1*, 449–458.

MacMahon, B., & Pugh, T. F. *Epidemiology: principles and methods.* Boston: Little, Brown, 1970.

MacMahon, B., Pugh, T. F., & Hutchison, G. B. Principles in the Evaluation of Community Mental Health Programs. In H. C. Schulberg, A. Sheldon, & F. Baker, *Program evaluation in the health fields.* New York: Behavioral Publications, 1969. Pp. 51–58.

Magoon, T. M., & Golann, S. Nontraditionally trained women as mental health counselors/psychotherapists. *Personnel and Guidance Journal*, 1966, *44*, 788–793.

McCord, W., McCord, J., & Zola, I. K. *Origins of Crime: A new evaluation of the Cambridge-Somerville youth Study.* New York: Columbia University Press, 1959.

Miller, K. S. Research training in community mental health. In I. Iscoe, & C. D. Spielberger (Eds.), *Community psychology: perspectives in training and research.* New York: Appleton-Century-Crofts, 1970. Pp. 215–224.

Minuchin, P., Biber, B., Shapiro, E., & Zimiles, H. *The psychological impact of the school experience.* New York: Basic Books, 1969.

Muss, R. E. The effects of a one- and two-year causal learning program. *Journal of Personality*, 1960, *28*, 479–491.

Ojemann, R. H., Levitt, E. E., Lyle, W. H., & Whiteside, M. F. The effects of a "causal" teacher-training program and certain curricular changes on grade school children. *Journal of Experimental Education,* 1955, *24,* 95–114.

Powers, E., & Witmer, H. *An Experiment in the prevention of delinquency.* New York: Columbia University Press, 1951.

Rheingold, H. L. The modification of social responsiveness in institutional babies. *Monographs of the Society for Research in Child Development,* 1956, *21,* (2) (whole).

Roen, S. R. Evaluative research and community mental health. In A. E. Bergin, & S. L. Garfield (Eds.), *Handbook of psychotherapy and behavior change: an empirical analysis.* New York: Wiley, 1971. Pp. 776–811.

Roth, W. F., & Luton, F. B. The mental health program in Tennessee. *American Journal of Psychiatry,* 1943, *99,* 662–675.

Samuels, J. S., & Henderson, J. D. A Community-based operant learning environment III: Some outcome data. In R. D. Rubin, H. Fensterheim, A. A. Lazarus, & C. H. Franks (Eds.), *Advances in behavior therapy.* New York: Academic Press, 1971. Pp. 263–271.

Sanders, R., Smith, R., & Weinman, B. *Chronic psychoses and recovery: an experiment in socio-environment therapy.* San Francisco: Jossey-Bass, 1967.

Sarason, I. G. Verbal learning, modeling and juvenile delinquency. *American Psychologist,* 1968, *23,* 254–266.

Sarason, I. G., & Ganzer, V. J. Social influence techniques in clinical and community psychology. In C. D. Spielberger (Ed.), *Current topics in clinical and community psychology.* New York: Academic Press, 1969. Pp. 1–66.

Sarason, S. B. *The culture of the school and the problem of change.* Boston: Allyn & Bacon, 1971.

Schoggen, P. Environmental forces in the everyday lives of children. In R. G. Barker (Ed.), *The stream of behavior.* New York: Appleton-Century-Crofts, 1963. Pp. 42–69.

Schwitzgebel, R. L., & Kolb, D. A. Inducing Behavior change in adolescent delinquents. *Behavior Research & Therapy,* 1964, *1,* 297–304.

Sells, S. B. Ecology and the science of psychology. In E. P. Willems, & H. L. Raush, *Naturalistic viewpoints in psychological research.* New York: Holt, Rinehart & Winston, 1969. Pp. 15–30.

Sinnett, E. R., & Niedenthal, L. The use of indigenous volunteers in a rehabilitation living unit for disturbed college students. *Community Mental Health Journal,* 1968, *4,* 232–244.

Sinnett, E. R., Wiesner, E. F., & Frieser, W. S. Dormitory half-way house. *Rehabilitation Record,* 1967, *8,* 34–37.

Skeels, H. M., & Dye, H. B. The study of the effects of differential stimulation on mentally retarded children. *Journal of Psycho-asthenics,* 1939, *44,* 114–136.

Smith, M. B., & Hobbs, N. The community and the community mental health center. *American Psychologist,* 1966, *21,* 499–509.

Spielberger, C., & Weitz, H. Improving the academic performance of anxious college freshmen: A group counseling approach to prevention of underachievement. *Psychological Bulletin Monographs,* (whole, no. 590), 1964, *78,* 20pp.

Srole, L., Langner, T. S., Michael, S. T., Opler, M. K., & Rennie, T. A. *Mental health in the Metropolis: the midtown Manhattan study.* New York: McGraw-Hill, 1962.

Thomas, D. R., Becker, W. C., & Armstrong, M. Production and elimination of disruptive classroom behavior by systematically varying teacher's behavior. *Journal of Applied Behavior Analysis,* 1968, *1,* 35–45.

von Bertalanffy, L. *Organismic psychology and systems theory.* Worcester, Mass.: Clark University Press, 1968.

Webster, T., & Harris, H. Modified group psychotherapy, an experiment in group psychodynamics for college freshmen. *Group Psychotherapy,* 1958, *11,* 283–298.

Wolff, T. Community mental health on campus: Evaluating group discussions led by dormitory advisers and graduate students. Unpublished doctoral dissertation, University of Rochester, 1969.

16. summary and prospects

The purpose of this chapter is to highlight the book's major points and to forecast the direction of future development in community psychology. Hopefully, a broad summary of what has gone before will provide a background against which a meaningful forecast can be attempted.

We first considered how community psychology is defined. Unfortunately, it was not possible to offer a concise definition on which all have agreed. It was pointed out that a number of terms have been bandied about in the past several years that include the modifier "community." Community psychiatry and community mental health are two of these terms. Social psychiatry is another that has been widely discussed and that seems to bear some similarity to community approaches. A wide range of definitions was found for each of these terms with a considerable overlap between them. Definitions of community psychology were less variable, but they, too, overlapped considerably with the other terms generally used in the community area. The seemingly best resolution concerning a current definition of community psychology is to extract the common denominator running through varying definitions and to couch it broadly enough to encompass most program approaches that are generally regarded as exemplifying community psychology efforts. From this viewpoint, *community psychology is an approach to human behavior problems that emphasizes contributions made to the development of these problems by environmental forces as well as the potential contributions to be made toward their alleviation by the use of these forces.* Such a definition is sufficiently abstract to embrace under the community psychology rubric the programs that attempt to deal with behavior problems traditionally regarded as being in the province of the mental health field as well as the problems with which the mental health field has only recently become concerned. It encompasses the study of individuals in natural social settings, active intervention to prevent future stress, and the creation of social settings to enhance the positive aspects of human behavior.

The history of community psychology has been rooted mainly in evolving conceptions of behavior disorder. Tracing these ideas over the centuries shows that man's earliest concern about disordered behavior focused on the very deviant and the very dramatic. This relatively narrow view pertained among most professionals up to the late 19th century. One of Freud's most significant contributions was his broadening of the scope of behavior disorder through his interest in psychoneurotics. Furthermore, the theories that he advanced for explaining the development of neurotic disorders paved the way for the recognition of still more subtle behavior disorders, the character neuroses, as legitimate concerns for the mental health professional.

This tendency to broaden the scope of the mental health field has persisted to the point where the mental health fields have become sensitive to a variety of relatively subtle behavioral problems such as the failure to utilize inherent potentials, and the failure to benefit from life's opportunities. As the concern of the mental health professional was extended, responsibility was undertaken for dealing with ever larger numbers of people. The major revolutions within the mental health field have seemed to come about not because of important theoretical advances, but because of periodic redefinitions of the field's scope. Such redefinitions prompted the advancement of new ideas, the development of new ways of looking at and attempting to understand behavior, and the development of new approaches for dealing with behavior problems. Community psychology is seen as the most recent revolution in the mental health field promulgated by a scope-broadening redefinition. *One might well question whether such scope-broadening has reached a maximum and whether the future might not see some retrenchment on the field's mandate.*

Why should the mental health professions be broadening their scope at this particular stage in time? The answer to this question relates to a multitude of factors that seem to have converged in recent years. Certainly one was the emergence in the 1950s of much questioning of the effectiveness of traditional mental health functions. Such expressions shook complacent professionals and caused them to examine more carefully what they were doing and how effectively it was working, with the result that many began casting around for new approaches. Another aspect of the discontent with traditional mental health functions was a growing dissatisfaction at inequities in the delivery of services associated with traditional practices. The disadvantaged, most seriously disturbed segment of our population seemed to be receiving the attention of the least qualified and fewest number of mental health professionals, whereas the advantaged, among whom serious disorders were relatively few in number, benefited from a heavy concentration of professional resources. Furthermore, large-scale surveys uncovered a staggeringly high latent need for mental health services in the general population, despite the fact that most professionals were already hard put to cope with those having manifest needs.

Certainly another impetus to the recent development of community psychology was the ominous finding concerning the manpower situation in the mental health field. While the lack of sufficient numbers of professionals to deal with current mental health problems was obvious, the hope could be cherished that somehow the gap between the need for services and the supply of those who could render services might be closed by additional training efforts. Careful studies of this problem, however, revealed that the reverse was likely. Not only would manpower needs in the mental health field not be overcome in the foreseeable future, but it was even more likely that the gap between need and supply would widen.

Concurrent with the recognition that existing services and delivery systems were failing to meet societal needs, doubts grew among psychologists about the ultimate utility of the conceptual model on which the mental health establishment has been based. Community psychologists came to decry the fact that the typical mental health practitioner uses a service approach deriving from the "medical model." The aspect of this model that creates the most serious difficulty for the community psychologist is the passivity it imposes on the professional, blocking his engagement with the external forces seen to be so important in the development of disorder. The typical pose of the medical model practitioner finds him waiting in an office for a "patient" to present himself with a fully developed problem that the practitioner must deal with within the confines of that office. This leaves little room for environmental manipulation, or active preventive efforts. Thus considerable questioning of the medical model has occurred; and particularly for the community psychologist, some aspects of the model have been rejected. On the other hand, public health medicine has developed an approach that is much more relevant to the type of effort that the community psychologist would like to expend. This allows one to reach out into the community, to take steps to manipulate the social structure in growth-enhancing ways, to attempt to uncover environmenal contributions to the etiology of various behavior disorders, and to bring about environmental changes that nullify their effect.

Amidst the pessimism concerning the worthwhileness of continuing to apply traditional approaches exclusively, and the uncertainty about ever having sufficient manpower to do such a job properly, the example of public health medicine has offered a ray of hope. Epidemiological studies have helped to isolate the causes of some physical diseases and have led to effective prevention. For many, this example of attempting to prevent the development of serious behavior disorder has seemed the only feasible approach. Fortunately, the 1940s provided some examples of ways in which one could apply preventive measures in the mental health field, and during the 1950s a body of theory began to emerge that had tied to it many suggestions for practical applications. Thus a tangible basis was established for programs aimed at primary, secondary, and tertiary prevention.

The questioning of the establishment that occurred in the 1950s and the searching for new models of service delivery led to many bold new programs in a variety of settings. Underlying these new programs was an increased emphasis on the power of community forces to cause, worsen, prevent or ameliorate human behavioral dysfunction. Some programs were directed toward problems in the traditional province of the mental health worker, psychosis, psychoneurosis, and character disorders. Others, preventively oriented, dealt with undiagnosed individuals who normally would not have come to the attention of a mental health professional. Although the latter programs were obviously innovative in that they represented entirely new ways of dealing with an entirely new kind of service recipient, the programs that sprang up to deal with traditional problems seemed in many cases the more audacious because they flew in the face of established traditions.

Some of these programs continued to emphasize traditional psychotherapy, but they challenged the notion that such techniques could be applied only by professionals. In effect, these innovative efforts sought to mobilize new segments of the community on behalf of those whose problems had formerly been primarily the concern of a professional elite. Housewives were trained over a two-year period to be psychotherapists. College students with virtually no training were enlisted to lead "therapy" groups consisting of seriously disturbed mental patients. Seriously disturbed youngsters of school age were treated in educationally oriented programs, in some instances, through the use of volunteer housewives with teacher training, and in others through specially trained educational personnel. In many cases such youngsters would normally have been excluded from the school system and would have been confined in a residential treatment setting. In many hospitals across the country college students were enlisted as companions to hospitalized mental patients in the hope that they could motivate the patient to leave the hospital. Community mental health centers adopted many innovative approaches such as the day hospital, the night hospital, foster home care, home treatment services, and aftercare services.

Interesting changes also began to appear within one of the most stodgy of the traditional mental health agencies, the mental hospital. Many began to view the hospital as a community and to examine the impact that the typical mental hospital has on the patient and his capacity to function when he reenters the broader community. Much concern was expressed over the discrepancy between the behaviors required for adaptation to life in a mental hospital and those necessary to adapt outside of the hospital. Frequently it seemed that in order to be a "good" patient one had to behave passively, without initiative, and to submit to a variety of indignities, all of which would mark one as disturbed in normal society. Hospital communities were, therefore, created or restructured to resemble more closely the community outside of the hospital. In such hospital communities, responsibility is given the patient, freedoms are available to him, and he is expected to take an active part in deciding the course of his own life within the institution. These innovative hospital communities assumed a variety of forms with one even stressing the necessity for groups of patients to learn to live together within the hospital and to be discharged *en masse* to take up a communal life outside of the institution as a means of minimizing discrepancies between hospital roles and real world roles. Philosophically most innovations in hospital programs are oriented toward enhancing the patient's capacity to live outside of the institution. *An important unsolved problem is how to deal with the patient's extra-institutional world to maximize his chances of thriving there.* Discharging the patient as one of a group of patients who have learned to live adaptively together amounts to creating a new institution that may be necessary for some but is a poor solution for many.

The community psychology model has not been confined to the institutions where mental health goals and methods were already evident. If positive environment forces could aid the social outcast to return to adequate functioning, such forces could similarly prevent the breakdown in functioning from occurring in the first place. On this assumption, psychologists have begun to develop programs that reach out to segments of the community where traditional curative or ameliorative approaches are inappropriate.

Preventively oriented programs have emerged in a variety of realms directed generally toward particular age groups or social classes. Clearly, a favorite target for prevention programs has been the very young. It is almost reflexive in thinking of preventing the development of a disturbance to concentrate on the young. Maladaptive behavior patterns among youngsters are not yet well entrenched, and the young are seen as malleable. Since they are undergoing rapid personality change, positive influences are thought to have a particularly high likelihood of having significant impact on the lives of youngsters, and for the young the formation of a foundation for future adaptation is considered to be particularly important. In addition, parents generally have a great stake in their child's development and future growth, and where work with parents around a child's incipient problems may seem desirable, cooperation is generally easily attained. It is for these reasons that many preventive programs begin with preschool children and, at times, even with infants. Generally these programs are directed toward children who seem to lack the stimulation in their normal environment necessary for preparing them to make the most out of the school experience that is to follow. Unfortunately, many such programs have been approached with more enthusiasm than thoughtfulness, and their effects have not been altogether encouraging. The danger in this is that discouragement over unimpressive results will turn program designers away from work with the very young, despite the compelling arguments that favor proceeding with it.

Just as the mental hospital has been a prime access point for employing the concepts of community psychology for the benefit of those who have already experienced psychosocial failure, the school has been the locale for many programs that seek to serve those who have not yet been severely harmed by environmental forces. The school setting has been a popular site for both primary and secondary prevention programs. Primary preventive programs have in some cases focused on the total school atmosphere with the aim of maximizing adequate psychological development. Other primary preventive efforts have concentrated on introducing into the school curriculum materials that would have widespread impact on the adjustment of all students exposed. A third primary preventive approach aims at altering teacher techniques. Generally, this approach is practiced by behavioristic psychologists wishing to sensitize the teacher to the role that she plays in perpetuating undesirable behavior, and to show her how, through her own responses, she can shape desirable behavior. Such efforts are generally directed toward the badly behaved youngster, but are seen to have primary preventive impact in that the improved classroom atmosphere attending their success benefits all students. In the same sense, secondary preventive programs inevitably have primary preventive impact.

Several widely known secondary preventive programs have been instituted in the schools. Always concerned with identifying a target group manifesting the early signs of a problem, these secondary preventive programs have focused either on the parents of problem children, teachers, the children themselves, or on some combination of the three. A few secondary preventive programs have extended over a period of years and have undergone many metamorphoses in keeping with specific experiences. These programs seem to have demonstrated rather clearly that behavior problems can be identified in their incipient stages, but the overall effectiveness of preventive efforts is less well established. This is partly because evaluations of this kind are difficult to do and partly because the interventive models had to be built from the ground up making a fair amount of testing and changing inevitable. As in the preschool area, the absence of definitive evidence of the long-range success of secondary preventive efforts should not discourage continued and energetic effort. The potential gain of program success far outweights the costs of program failures experienced in the process of working out a worthwhile model. *In this area the most significant need is for the arduous process of program creation, implementation, and evaluation until well-tested models become available for widespread use.*

Another important arena for the establishment of preventive programs is the college community. The significance of this setting for prevention derives partly from the fact that it brings together young people at a point in life when their futures are being shaped in important ways. For many, too, entrance into college represents one of life's significant crisis points. Many college students will be living away from home for the first time, will be threatened by the need to establish an entirely new set of friends having diverse backgrounds, and also of having to prove themselves academically in a more select group of scholars than they have ever before encountered. Furthermore, the college experience is a final preparation for becoming an adult and settling on a life's work. In addition to these compelling arguments for the necessity of establishing preventive programs in the college setting, another advantage of working in those settings is that many program designers are themselves members of college faculties. Thus, presumably, they are on familiar turf in a community of which they are themselves a part.

Despite the significant arguments favoring creating preventive programs on college campuses, and despite the fact that a vast number of modern universities have accepted responsibility for seeing to it that a student's emotional state is conducive to benefiting from the educational opportunities before him, relatively few preventive program models have emerged in the college area. Doubtless, this seeming paradox is related to the fact that the community psychologist, as a member of the university community, may suffer some unique problems in acting as a change agent in a system of which he is a part. Precisely because he is a part of the community, any effort he expends toward changing it, especially in areas for which other community members have primary responsibility, may provoke unusual resentment and resistance.

Some data on the impact of small programs in college settings have shown that limited interventions have positive effects but fail to reach many students whose need for service may be as great or greater than that of program participants. Wide-scale programs have provided interesting models of new forms of service delivery but have been difficult to implement. No doubt, the advantages offered by the college campus as a community laboratory are too attractive to lie fallow for the indefinite future. Very likely more extensive efforts will be expended in college community programs in the future. *The most significant challenge for workers in the college community will be the need to discover ways to make that setting a truly growth-enhancing environment which, in many respects, is altogether in keeping with the goals of the educational enterprise.*

The choice by program innovators to focus on the forces operating in specific community settings, such as schools or colleges, has been more of a practical decision than a theoretical necessity. Prevention programs in the community at large have posed special implementation problems. Most community programs have been created within the specific agencies that bring together large numbers of the target population. Reaching out toward the wider community requires finding a locus that allows contact with those to whom service is to be brought. Nonetheless, what can be looked on as prevention programs in the larger community have a relatively long history. A number of these programs grew up during times of social upheaval and often were promulgated by other than mental health professionals. The Salvation Army for example was the product of a religious group concerned with rehabilitating the poor. The 19th- and early 20th-century settlement house movement was directed by idealists who were attempting to grapple with serious social problems created by the industrial revolution and great waves of immigration. Programs for controlling and treating juvenile delinquency were instituted in the 1930s in Chicago and in the Boston area by people who were deeply concerned with crime as a social problem but who themselves were not trained mental health workers.

Recent efforts in the greater community, as were many very early community programs, have been directed at the problems of shifting population groups. In the contemporary context this includes the adaptation of the newcomer to this country (Puerto Ricans), the comfortable assimilation of the rural black to the large urban area in which he is resettling, the proliferating delinquency problems of America's cities, and a concern with helping the economically and educationally disadvantaged to achieve meaningful life careers.

In many respects these programs seem more remote from the traditional mental health enterprise than any that have been discussed up to now. Their emphasis has been almost entirely on education, assistance in coping with practical everyday problems, and the provision of good identification models. Intrapsychic forces have been virtually ignored. These programs, too, have brought the mental health professional into an arena with which he is least familiar, the traditional stamping ground of the politician, the police, the social worker, the clergy, and the courts. It is still too soon to judge the long-range impact of such programs. What does seem clear, however is that the mental professional engaging in broad community programs has been significantly reshaped by his experience. *In this reshaping process a number of difficult issues have yet to be solved by those attempting to create programs in the greater community. Some of these include the question of how to gain the acceptance of those to be served, establishing a locus for providing services, resolving the question of the role political action is to play in such programs, facing the question of what assets and liabilities the professional possesses for engaging in the political struggle, and what role he should assume in such an enterprise.*

While the arguments favoring the development of community psychology with its revitalized efforts to combat mental disorder and its exciting prospects for preventing the development of emotional disturbances are persuasive, the field is nevertheless confronted by many problematic issues, and by criticisms from a variety of source. Objections to the development of community psychology arise both in society at large and within the mental health professions themselves. Criticisms from outside of the mental health professions tend to come from those who recoil at the projected high cost of wide-scale preventive programs, who express deep concern that preventive programs invade an individual's personal privacy, and who are distressed at the lack of an immediate payoff in community programs. In addition, such critics probably also harbor an unconscious need for society to be populated by "winners", and "losers." On careful reflection, many of these concerns seem less serious than they appear at first blush. On the other hand, society's need for winners and losers in life touches on some very basic human values that are not readily altered. The winners and losers theme is based on the idea that every man has an equal opportunity and that the well intentioned and hard working will succeed whereas those who fail are somehow lacking in the proper sentiments or motivation. According to this view the successful man can take comfort in an obvious sign of his inner goodness and can complacently look down on those failing to achieve his measure of accomplishment. In many important ways, community psychology calls this theme into question, attributes the success of many to their having started out with advantages, and denies both the inherent goodness of those who succeed as well as the inherent badness of those who fail. *Still the attitudes are there and how does the community psychologist go about altering them?*

Among mental health professionals opposition to community psychology is expressed in a questioning of the quality of treatment that community psychology approaches can provide for previously neglected social classes, and in disagreement with the theoretical viewpoint of community psychology on the etiology of behavior disorder. Less explicitly stated is a feeling of threat to a well-established professional role. It may well be that this concern over having to give up a well practiced mode of operating is the most serious threat felt by professionals and, being a very difficult thing to talk about overtly, it prompts objections couched in other terms. In truth, the community psychology movement is critical of traditional services as well as traditional modes of service delivery, and the proposed new programs do require drastic revision in the mental health worker's professional way of life. That revision requires giving up on much that has been traditional in the professional's early training, and undertaking retraining at a time when he has established considerable status and has invested considerable ego in a role that is still honored by a large segment of society. Although traditionally trained practitioners need not be left without clients to treat and can choose to continue their old functions unimpeded, the very existence of community psychology and the dissatisfaction and turmoil out of which it has grown inevitably imposes discomforting doubt and a threat of loss of status on the traditional mental health worker. *How, then, to temper the threat posed by community psychology to the traditional worker is a significant problem.*

Along with the opposition faced by community psychology from several quarters, one of the serious issues that must be dealt with in the field is the question of how professionals are to be trained for the new roles that must be assumed. Community psychology brings the professional into many arenas where he has not operated previously, in contact with many types of people he has never had experience with, where he is expected to perform many functions that are quite new to him. What form of training will best prepare him for those experiences? To date there has been relatively little agreement concerning a blueprint for training. The only point on which most trainers agree is that rigid training models should not be instituted, but that a variety of different approaches must be attempted since the field is in a formative stage. To some extent this idea sounds like an attempt to create virtue out of a chaotic and terribly ambiguous situation. On the other hand, it is a fact that no one can yet predict the many directions that community psychology may take and the many skills that may be required of its practioners. In such a case, flexibility in training is probably the only feasible course. It is already apparent, however, that community psychology is a sprawling field that can move into a variety of social institutions, each having its own unique framework and its own special problems. That being so, it is unlikely that any training program can hope to produce a generalist prepared to operate in any community setting. Thus it is expected that future community psychology training programs will train specialists to function in schools, mental hospitals, neighborhood service centers, university communities, and the like. Much as we may prefer a community psychologist who is a "universal man," the field probably has already outgrown such a practitioner model. The need to create training programs in an applied field that is itself not well formed is a formidable task confronting the community psychologist. *How can he make his best educated guesses about the shape programs of this kind should take even in their nascent stages and what must he do to test his hunches?*

Another issue confronting the community psychologist concerns the role of the nonprofessional in community programs. Clearly, one of any community's most important resources for coping with adverse circumstances and for improving the lot of the suffering is its own strongest members. Thus the so-called "nonprofessional" has been enlisted in many community programs to provide needed manpower, to serve as adequate models, and to serve as a bridge between the middle class professional and a community he is trying to help but which he does not completely understand, with which he may have difficulty communicating, and by which he is not completely trusted.

As is true with a number of other innovations introduced by community psychology, the logical argument for using nonprofessionals is compelling, but actually implementing a program involving nonprofessionals is fraught with a variety of practical problems. Developing techniques for selecting and training workers is the first of those problems. A review of programs involving nonprofessionals reveals that no widespread model for dealing with these issues has been developed. Another problem has to do with how the nonprofessional is to be used in a specific program, what type of service he is to render. Again, actual cases indicate that nonprofessionals are used in a variety of ways. Some are restricted to relatively menial and routine functions, while others are front-line workers. Frequently, nonprofessionals become pawns in a struggle between professionals, agency administrators, and fund-granting agencies. Another problem in the use of nonprofessionals involves the necessity of developing satisfactory working relationships between professionals who are threatened by the nonprofessionals' presence but who must still supervise them and accept them as colleagues. Yet another entire class of problems relates to the indigenous nonprofessional's need to abandon an old lifestyle when he becomes a human service worker. This new life-style, while having many advantages, inevitably isolates him from the community in which he has been living. Furthermore, in the new life-style he becomes aware of a status hierarchy in his service agency in which he finds himself on the bottom with the professional at the top. This often prompts a new conflict and the expenditure of considerable energy toward organizing, and struggling with the professional for status. Each of these problems drains energy that could be used in carrying out the nonprofessional's primary function as a service worker.

Another major class of problems for the community psychologist involves the question of what is the optimal role of the community in a given program. Ideally, the community served should play a central role in identifying the needs to be met, and the means by which a program deals with them. This would insure that important segments of the community would not be neglected, as they have been in the past, and that an agency's services would be relevant to the community's needs. Unfortunately, communities are difficult to define, their representatives are difficult to locate, their spokesmen are no freer from vested interests than any other individuals, and their simmering resentments about society's long neglect of them often boil over in ways that are destructive of the very agencies that are now struggling honestly to be of some use to them.

In the final analysis, many of the problems of community psychology can only be answered by carefully studying the operation of social forces and the means by which communities can change to effect their members more positively. An extensive investment in research is essential to progress in the field. Badly needed is basic research in epidemiology and ecology to provide the understanding of the community necessary to identify the most appropriate program targets, and to help define program forms. For most psychologists, engaging in this research will require a new kind of training and even participation in the development of new research approaches. In addition, there is a very serious need for extensive evaluative research. Such research is absolutely necessary for the refinement of training and service programs and for determining which programs merit the investment of energy and time and which should be discarded.

Forecasting the future of community psychology is extraordinarily difficult. The field is still quite new, it lacks a tightness of definition, its scope is uncertain, and it is developing in many different directions at the same time. Separate movements within community psychology are proceeding in response to felt social needs rather than on the basis of sound theoretical knowledge. No base of previous experience exists on which to build, and in a very real sense the field is lifting itself by its own bootstraps. Given this amorphous, changeable state, only the foolhardy would attempt to predict what is likely to happen next. Having acknowledged the futility of the venture, we can with impunity attempt to predict what future trends seem likely.

Perhaps the safest prediction that we can make is that the future will find less proliferation of programs than has occurred in the past. Caught up in the venturesome spirit encouraged by community psychology, program designers have been quite daring in the types of programs that they have created. Old taboos have been violated, old standards have been ignored, and programs have been created in parts of the community that have never before seen the presence of mental health professionals. By now, so much new ground has been broken that it is difficult to conceive of a program that will seem innovative. On the other hand, experience with novel programs has raised a number of important implementation issues that must be worked out.

Thus, while in the future there should be a development of fewer unprecedented types of programs, much community psychology literature should be devoted to problems arising in the carrying out of innovative programs. For example, further experience with the use of nonprofessionals and continued efforts to enlist community agencies will build a body of experience leading to the development of principles that are useful in guiding these efforts. No doubt, rigorous efforts will be made to evaluate various aspects of community programs as well as their overall effectiveness, and such results should also contribute to the development of principles that will assist those who would develop programs based on established models. In general, therefore, we predict that daring innovation will be less common in the near future, and that a period of consolidation will set in that will allow for the creation of programs based on something more than enthusiasm and intuition.

Associated with the conservatism that is forecast, some amount of retrenchment in community psychology's scope seems likely. It is entirely likely that program evaluations will at times be so discouraging as to prompt an abandonment of certain efforts. In some instances this may be an unfortunate result whereas in others it may be entirely appropriate. Community approaches cannot be expected to succeed in all of the diverse areas to which they have been applied. It is also conceivable that members of other professions will alter their functions in such a way as to obviate the necessity for the intervention of the community psychologist. For example, professional educators might change their techniques in such a way as to deal more effectively with many of the problems that mental health professionals have been attempting to treat in their programs. It is also possible that politicians, courts, and law enforcement agencies might change their approaches in ways that will make the mental health professional's efforts unnecessary.

Another likely occurrence is the institutionalization of new classes of mental health personnel. These are likely to occur at all levels of training to serve a variety of functions. Where not too many years ago the field of psychology was insisting that the full-fledged practitioner must have a doctorate, subdoctoral people are now playing and will continue to play an ever more significant role in community psychology. Workers with less than doctoral training will very likely serve in growing numbers in the front lines as direct service givers while doctoral level personnel will be program designers and supervisors. Already many state mental hygiene systems have provided positions for subdoctoral mental health workers; community mental health centers are hiring them to provide a variety of services; and governmental agencies are establishing career ladders for them. As this movement develops further it seems likely that training programs for predoctoral workers will begin to take forms showing less variety than has been true of many of these programs up to now. Development of tangible models will result in less novelty and diversity than has existed in the past.

Research in community psychology is likely to be concentrated in the area of evaluation. This is because the majority of those who become involved in community psychology at this stage are likely to be concerned with creating services to meet pressing human needs. If their interests exceed the bounds of providing service, they will very likely focus on the evaluation of their own service programs. The near future is not likely to see much concentrated effort on the basic research characterized by the epidemiological and ecological approaches described in a previous chapter, since such research promises no immediate service payoff. Basic research may await the time when community psychology attracts large numbers of workers from areas other than clinical psychology, such as social psychology, developmental psychology, and sociology. These professionals are less likely than the clinical psychologist to be heavily invested in service programs and are more readily drawn toward basic research problems. Thus far even the interdisciplinary training programs in community psychology have probably done less than is desirable to attract other than clinical psychologists. Hopefully, that state will change in the near future. But it is unlikely that it will change quickly enough to produce much basic research in a relatively short period of time, particularly when one considers the obstacles that exist to performing such research.

Having made a number of risky prognostications, we conclude with one more that probably entails greater certainty than any predictions made up to now. Despite all of the forces ranged against its establishment as a significant mode within the mental health sphere, community psychology has established a foothold that is likely to be permanent. It is fueled by an idea that seems "right" to many individuals but that had been badly neglected by psychologists for a surprisingly long time. At this particular time its development is also greatly encouraged by exceedingly important social needs that simply are not adequately met by traditional practices. Thus whatever form it takes in the future, community psychology is here to stay, and it is inevitable that future psychologists will be shaped in many important ways by its presence.

Name Index

Subject Index